Asia Past and Present

Asia Past and Present

A Brief History

Peter P. Wan

and

Thomas D. Reins

WILEY Blackwell

Registered Office

John Wiley & Sons, Inc., 111 River Street, Hoboken, NJ 07030, USA

Editorial Office

111 River Street, Hoboken, NJ 07030, USA

For details of our global editorial offices, customer services, and more information about Wiley products visit us at www.wiley.com.

Wiley also publishes its books in a variety of electronic formats and by print-on-demand. Some content that appears in standard print versions of this book may not be available in other formats.

Library of Congress Cataloging-in-Publication Data

Names: Reins, Thomas D. (Thomas David), author. | Wan, Peter P., author.
Title: Asia past and present: a brief history / Thomas D Reins, Peter P Wan.
Description: Hoboken, NJ: Wiley-Blackwell, 2020. | Includes index.
Identifiers: LCCN 2020020767 (print) | LCCN 2020020768 (ebook) | ISBN 9781118955185 (paperback) | ISBN 9781118955192 (paperback) | ISBN 9781118955208 (adobe pdf) | ISBN 9781118955215 (epub)
Subjects: LCSH: Asia–History. | Asia–Civilization. | Asia–Politics and government.
Classification: LCC DS33 .R39 2020 (print) | LCC DS33 (ebook) | DDC 950–dc23
LC record available at https://lccn.loc.gov/2020020767
LC ebook record available at https://lccn.loc.gov/2020020768

Cover Design: Wiley
Cover Images: The Forbidden City, Beijing © DuKai photographer/Getty Images, Red Fort Lal Qila with Indian flag. Delhi, India © f9photos/Getty Images

Set in 9.5/12.5pt STIXTwoText by SPi Global, Pondicherry, India

To my father and mother Hsin Wan and Ruth Rugg Wan, who set an example of common decency, and
   To my wife Laura L. Wan and to my late daughter Amy Q. Wan

   Peter P. Wan

To my father Harry Reins, who provided a challenging model of hard work and tenacity based on his daily life which I wisely attempted to follow, though with a few lapses, and
   To my wife Susan A. Reins and to my daughter Christine Reins-Jarin

   Thomas D. Reins

Contents

About the Authors

Peter P. Wan, PhD, Harvard University, 1997
Dr. Wan has taught at East China Normal University, Shanghai; at California State University, Fullerton and Los Angeles campuses; and at Fullerton College.

He has been awarded fellowships at the Harvard-Yenching Institute and the Fulbright Visiting Scholars Program.

Thomas D. Reins, PhD, Claremont Graduate School, 1981
Dr. Reins has lived and studied in several Asian locations, including Japan, the Philippines, Thailand, Taiwan, as well as a number of places in mainland China. He has taught at several institutions of higher education, including California State University, Fullerton and Los Angeles campuses; University of California, Riverside; Fullerton College; and currently Chapman University. His Asian history courses include Modern Asia, Modern China, Modern Japan, Modern Southeast Asia, Asian History and Film, and the Vietnam Wars.

His research focus is the opium trade in nineteenth- and early twentieth-century China, India, and globally.

Acknowledgments

Peter P. Wan

To my professors at Harvard University: Akira Iriye, Stephan Thernstrom, and the late Sacvan Bercovitch. Given my educational background, I would never have been able to complete my doctorate without their detailed and sustained guidance.

To William Cai, who provided indispensable research assistance.

Thomas D. Reins

To my Asian history professors, who guided me through the broad array of Asian cultures. My understanding of South Asia was greatly enhanced by decades of discussion with my colleague, the late Professor Seymour Scheinberg, whose study of and travels to India and the Himalayan nations gave me firsthand insights into the region; and to the late Alan Greenberger, whose classes on Indian history and culture provided an exciting and stimulating intellectual background for a lengthy and complex culture. Michael Onorato's Southeast Asian classes during those Vietnam War years presented insightful and thorough lectures on colonialism, its demise, and modernization issues that followed. My East Asian academic mentors are numerous. For Japan, I am indebted to Kinji Yada for his informative lectures and decades of discussion about Japan and life and culture beyond Asia; to Peter Duus, whose Tokugawa and Meiji seminar opened my eyes to the intricate and turbulent relationship between economic and political modernization; and to Gordon Berger, whose Taisho and Showa seminar afforded me a nuanced look into the impact of democracy, the depression, world war, and recovery in Japan. My training in Chinese history began with Linda Pomeranz's class in Modern China; in Taiwan, I had the opportunity to hear the lectures of Hsu Cho-yun on Zhou Dynasty socioeconomic change; the late Lloyd Eastman grounded me in nineteenth-century China in his materials seminar that included essential monographs and weekly discussions of them; Jerry Dennerline's class on premodern China afforded me a look at the tradition I needed to appreciate in order to understand the problems of the nation's modernization. And finally I owe a debt of gratitude to Arthur Rosenbaum, whose classes and reading seminars better prepared me for my research, and who as my dissertation advisor provided sage advice, which came quickly with each chapter I submitted to him.

I would also like to recognize three other mentors in my learning process. To Nelson Woodard, whose classes and seminar on American Foreign Policy were all models of meticulous academic preparation and delivery. David Pivar's seminar on Historical Thinking made me think, probably for the first time seriously, about historical thinking. And to Bob Leonard, who serves as a model of the patient teacher who persistently guides and motivates the plodding student.

The chapters of the text that I wrote—those beyond China, Japan, and Korea—benefitted from the careful reading and valuable commentary of Professor Jackson Putnam. His constant encouragement pushed me forward year by year. I appreciate as well the comments of Professor Laichen Sun, who kindly read and commented on some of the early iterations of my Southeast Asia writings. To both I extend my appreciation, though I alone am responsible for the final written product.

We also wish to thank two anonymous reviewers for their comments and suggestions regarding the organization and content of the manuscript. They helped us to add, subtract, or merge materials and to clarify numerous descriptions of people, places, and ideas. We furthermore need to acknowledge our appreciation for the work of Mr. Patrick Davison and Mr. Bo Kent, Internet wizards, for the electronic expertise they provided to an older, electronically clumsy generation.

Introduction

Asia Past and Present aims to provide the reader with a basic understanding of the long course of history formed by Asia's inhabitants, both indigenous and foreign. This will involve identifying and explaining the broad contours of cultures that emerged in Asia, geographically from Afghanistan, Pakistan, and Central Asia in the west to Japan and Papua New Guinea in the east, and chronologically from prehistory to the early twenty-first century. It will necessarily include a discussion of the interactions among Asian cultural elements and the subsequent development of two core cultures—Indian and Chinese—that became foundational models for the rest of Asia. It will also examine the cultural exchanges within the Asian realm and between the Asian and non-Asian worlds.

Such interactions indicate Asian history can be divided into three broad categories of cultural development. The formation of core cultures marks the first stage, which stretches from the earliest history to roughly 1200 CE. In Asia, India and China provide these core cultures, classical models of civilization that other peoples of Asia adopted and modified to meet their particular political, social, economic, intellectual, and religious needs. Most importantly, Indian and Chinese concepts of kingship, ideas of religious worship, and methods of writing dominate the cultural landscape of Asia. Generally, South and Southeast Asia embraced Indian ideas and institutions, while Vietnam, Korea, and Japan drew upon Chinese traditional practices. To give one example, the Thai monarchy best reflects Indian political principles, whereas the behavior of Vietnamese emperors clearly demonstrates the considerable influence of Chinese ways.

Notwithstanding the enormous cultural weight of India and China on the rest of Asia, each culture selected those aspects of the core models and adapted those parts to its particular, local needs. Thus Japan adapted the Chinese political concepts of mandate of heaven and dynastic cycle, which produced a succession of dynasties in the Middle Kingdom over the millennia, by retaining just one imperial family in the land of the rising sun. Similarly, the caste system, so crucial to daily life in India, had little impact on Southeast Asian societies otherwise well-disposed to thought and behavior from the Hindustan cultural core. Moreover, below the literate elite, the circumstances of the common people further dulled the edge of cultural borrowing. Local geography, vernacular languages, religious traditions, and economic practices transformed the original cultural borrowing somewhat, even as the broader contours of culture increasingly resembled the foreign model.

The impact of successful Muslim Middle Eastern, nomadic tribal Eurasian, and Christian European incursions into traditional agricultural Asian civilizations marks the second stage of Asian history. These new arrivals began with the Afghan Muslim conquest of India in 1206, continued with the Mongol invasions of China and much of the rest of Asia in the thirteenth century, and culminated in the European invasions throughout the continent after 1498. As a result, both

Asia Past and Present: A Brief History, First Edition. Peter P. Wan and Thomas D. Reins.
© 2021 John Wiley & Sons, Inc. Published 2021 by John Wiley & Sons, Inc.

the core cultures of India and China, as well as those of their cultural pupils in Asia, underwent significant transformations. Though the teachings of the core cultures remained preeminent down to the nineteenth century, two new religions—Islam and Christianity—began to compete for the allegiance of the people. New secular ideas—in the worlds of science, politics, and economics—increasingly caused substantial modifications of Asian thought and behavior.

The most obvious impact occurred in religious beliefs. Indonesia, today the largest Muslim country in the world, embraced Islam. However, it did so only after Afghan Delhi sultans took control of India, the heartland of core wisdom to Southeast Asians. Indonesians had long been aware of Islam through Arab traders, but until that faith came from India, Islam remained little more than a curiosity. The Philippines also underwent fundamental change, again religiously, as the Spanish brought and successfully transferred Catholicism to an Asian setting. Linguistically as well, major changes resulted from non-Asian sources. Several centuries ago, the Vietnamese adopted the Latin script—due to the influence of French Catholic priests—to replace Chinese characters. More recently, several other Asian nations have replaced Indian- or Arabic-based scripts with the Roman alphabet. The largest numbers of English-speaking people in a single country reside in Asia: in India. Furthermore, radical ideas contained in the European Renaissance, Reformation, scientific revolution, Enlightenment, agricultural revolution, capitalist business practices, and industrial revolutionary production began to upset traditional Asian verities. So too did the emergence in the nineteenth century of the idea of nationalism and the establishment of the "new imperialism." However, not until the shocking impact of the industrial revolution sometime in the first half of the nineteenth century did Asia's elite begin to reexamine their cultural heritages.

Thus, as the nineteenth century unfolded, so too did the third stage of Asian history, illustrated by attempts of various Asian cultures to restore a balance of wealth and power now so clearly dominated by the industrial nations of Europe, America, and Japan. Up to this time, the presence of foreigners in Asia had produced considerable cultural adjustments, but the essence of one's culture had not been ultimately seriously threatened. The Mongol and Manchu conquests of China failed to dislodge Confucian ways; indeed, the Confucian model was substantially utilized by the frontier nomads to govern agricultural China. Likewise, Hindu India absorbed first the Muslim Delhi sultans, then the Muslim Mughal emperors, and finally the Christian British. Initially, at least, the invaders did most of the adjusting to traditional Indian practices. Not until the full impact of the industrial revolution became apparent in the nineteenth century did Asia's cultural leadership seriously reassess traditional ways. Most all such leaders wondered why time-honored ideas and institutions had failed to keep the foreigner at bay, or if not at bay, why the intruder now had both the desire and ability to impose radically new ways of organizing and governing Asian societies.

Reassessment of established "habits of the heart" produced three broad conclusions among Asia's leadership before World War I. Some argued for a return to traditional ways of life, the departure from which had made their civilizations susceptible to invasion, occupation, and probably transformation. Others contended that adherence to tradition, far from being the solution to the foreign threat, had made their civilizations weak and thus incapable of defending itself. Only by doing away with custom and by embracing the ways of the invader could the necessary wealth and power be generated to dislodge the foreign presence. Somewhere between the world wars, a third conclusion came to dominate elite Asian thinking. Since neither an all-embracing reliance on tradition nor a complete abandonment of it seemed practicable, utilizing the best of both—foreign and native ideas and practices—appeared to be the best means to the several immediate and more distant ends. Once substantive change became legitimate, the next issue became identifying which parts of tradition justified retention and which disposal. At the same time, recognizing which elements from the outside world to adopt and which to disregard needed to be worked out. This turned out to be no simple task, and much of Asia still grapples with the implications of such choosing.

Although by World War I nearly all of Asia's elite could agree upon the necessity for independence, the principal means by which to accomplish this task became the topic of heated debate. Out of the discussions and disagreements emerged three usually conflicting approaches. Many advocated legally working within the imperial/colonial system and utilizing the system to ultimately destroy it, others favored nonviolent resistance to the system by undermining it where possible, and some preferred to resist the system through organized violence. Once independence succeeded, then new political and economic arrangements had to be set up.

Before the Great War, capitalism and democracy—broadly defined—seemed the destined, if difficult, paths to economic and political success. The industrial nations did not offer cookie-cutter guidelines to modernization, the differences among them often being significant. Both Japan and Germany, for example, could at best be considered nations "transitioning" to democratic practice, and both of their economies had modernized with considerable state intervention. Intellectuals across Asia realized this, and indeed many had witnessed it firsthand as students or political exiles in Japan. So long as modernizing prescriptions could be carried on in a flexible framework, particular cultures could pick and choose those aspects of modernization required for success as well as the means by which to internalize them to their nations. By this time, loyalty to one's nation-state had surpassed one's loyalty to its culture. Nationalism, not culturalism, would serve as the chief instrument of liberation and modernization.

World War I upset that default assumption in several ways. First, the 1917 Bolshevik Revolution in Russia produced a rival communist model of development. Second, the tenuous unity of the imperial powers, particularly regarding Asia, had splintered during the war. Not only did that conflict pit one imperial camp—the Germans and the Central Powers—against another, the Allies headed by Great Britain. But fissures developed in the Allied camp. Ally Japan's attempted expansion into China—the Twenty-One Demands of 1915—produced immediate British and American opposition. But even as Japan became democratic in 1919, it had long been harboring and now openly championed a specific Asian model of modernization. And finally, the Great War ushered in waves of pessimism and clouds of doubt as to the effectiveness of not only capitalism and democracy but also Western civilization itself.

The interwar years between 1919 and 1937, when World War II began with Japan's formal invasion of China, deepened the gloomy outlook. The Treaty of Versailles ending the Great War satisfied almost no one; radical Nazi, Fascist, and Communist movements sprouted up globally; new thought emerging in psychology, physics, philosophy, and the humanities seemed to produce not a comfort caused by greater understanding, but an anxiety rooted in intellectual confusion. The economic depression of the 1930s appeared to seal the fate of capitalism and democracy, as most industrial nations showed signs of heading for some form of state-controlled societies. That is to say, some form of authoritarianism seemed the likely future. It might not be the outright totalitarianism of the Soviet Union or Nazi Germany or the dictatorships of Fascist Italy and Spain, and militarist Japan. But neither would it be the liberal politics and economics of nineteenth-century Europe and America.

At the same time, global conflict strengthened independence movements. World War I resulted in the European colonial powers withdrawing much of their colonial military and bureaucracy away from the colonies to deal with adversaries threatening the homeland. This allowed anticolonial organizations to expand in a less restrictive environment. World War II eventually resulted in nearly every colonial regime in Asia being removed, initially by Japan and ultimately by the United States and its allies. While Japan dismantled Western colonial regimes, it instituted its own Greater East Asia Co-Prosperity Sphere. As the war raged on, two developments transpired to insure the end to colonial rule in the near future. First, combatants on both sides attempted to enlist indigenous organizations and individuals to join their fight, and with war's end, most everyone in Asia had access to weaponry. The second was America's determination to terminate colonial rule globally. Moreover, Britain's July 1945 general election brought to power the Labour Party, which had promised to begin the decolonization process.

Imminent independence forced Asia's leadership—whether traditionalist, reformist, or revolutionary—to put together a comprehensive platform for self-rule. Most still questioned the efficacy of the capitalist and democratic models of development. Consider some of the more important leaders who did emerge before, during, and after World War II: Mohandas Gandhi, Ho Chi Minh, Achmed Sukarno, and Mao Zedong—none of them stood tall for capitalism and democracy. And even of those who did accept some variation of capitalism and/or democracy—now redeemed somewhat by victory in World War II—they did so with less than roaring enthusiasm: Yoshida Shigeru in occupied Japan, Jawaharlal Nehru in India, Chiang Kai-shek in Taiwan, Filipino presidents with the exception of Ramon Magsaysay, South Korean presidents, and Singapore presidents. Colonial Hong Kong and Macao remained such until the 1990s. Even in the early twenty-first century, several nations have not yet begun or have taken only baby steps toward participatory government—North Korea, Vietnam, and Burma/Myanmar, for example.

Capitalism and democracy slowly emerged in the wake of World War II. The Cold War (1945–1991) between the United States and the Soviet Union energized America's efforts in Asia to provide counter-models to communist regimes in North Korea and mainland China as well as to insurgency movements in much of decolonizing Asia. In the process, Washington often put anti-communism ahead of democratic development. These efforts, chiefly in Japan, the Philippines, South Korea, Taiwan, Thailand, and South Vietnam, involved the infusion of much-needed capital, advanced technology, American markets, and political support—with military assistance, if necessary. Although political support and other aid depended to some extent on local efforts to broaden political participation and enhance economic opportunity, most often American support depended on an Asian ruler being less politically ruthless and more economically effective than the likely alternative. Transitions to democracy and markets, though important to Washington, remained secondary to the clash between "East" and "West."

The struggle between the United States and its allies and the Soviet Union and its allies concentrated on winning in three principle arenas: first, military; second, the decolonizing world; and, third, economic growth. Even though military supremacy remained primary, the Cold War setting would be played out between the West's surrogates and the East's surrogates, thus hopefully minimizing the likelihood of a direct military confrontation between the United States and Soviet Russia. This contest as well would not be the brief sprint that World War II turned out to be for America. Instead it would be a marathon, seen as such in the 1940s and into the 1980s. As such, it became a test of wills that alone was a leading index of which system, communist or capitalist, would win the hearts and minds of the decolonizing and developing world, including all of Asia. Just as significant as the will to prevail was the ability of one (broadly defined) system or the other to meet the needs of Asia's newly freed nations and people.

Well into the 1960s, Soviet Stalinist or Chinese Maoist forms of communism appeared to feature all the earmarks of front-running models, while elsewhere highly statist (India) and/or authoritarian (South Korea and Taiwan) regimes seemed to provide the other prototypes for modernization. America's withdrawal from Vietnam and at first blush from Asia in the mid-1970s, the Soviet invasion of Afghanistan along with the Iranian occupation of the American Embassy in Teheran in the late 1970s, America's slumping economy, its Vietnam syndrome, and what President Jimmy Carter called its "malaise" made it all but certain that Washington's influence globally, and undoubtedly in Asia, would gradually decline. On the surface, at least, competitive politics and markets appeared headed for the endangered species list, Japan being the only likely exception. Those nations not already communist or that had been on friendly terms with the United States beat hasty paths to Beijing and Moscow to acknowledge the expected victorious powers in that part of the world.

Below the surface, however, seismic changes long underway began to ascend. Japan and the "little dragons" of Taiwan, South Korea, Hong Kong, and Singapore had become wealthy through more open market practices, and they had also transitioned to more democratic political arrangements. More than a decade before the Berlin Wall fell in November 1989, Deng Xiaoping's China began to dismantle the Maoist economic nightmare and usher in some prosperity while gradually transitioning from totalitarian rule to a "soft authoritarian" control. Meanwhile, politics began transitioning from "soft authoritarianism" in Taiwan and South Korea to full-fledged democracy. In March 1985, the new Soviet leader Mikhail Gorbachev launched a reform movement to rescue a collapsing Soviet system. Labeled *glasnost* (liberalization) and *perestroika* (reconstruction), these programs gave Vietnam, a client state of the Soviet Union, the opportunity to institute in 1986 its own necessary reforms. Dubbed *doi moi*, it set up a market-oriented economy and commenced a less harsh political regime.

The formal collapse of the Soviet Union in 1991 did not, as Francis Fukuyama has interestingly argued, bring about the "end of history," by which he meant the global prevalence of some form of liberal politics and market economics. The war on terror provides ample evidence that a significant part of the world resists such a harmonious scenario. Moreover, two major Asian powers, China and Russia, still cling to what appears to be not-so-soft authoritarian political practices. And numerous Maoist and other insurgent or separatist movements can be found throughout the continent. Perhaps in the more distant future, Fukuyama's world of liberal ideas and institutions will prevail in Asia. But the larger issue will likely be not whether liberalism and modernization will triumph, but how some variation of the two will be adapted to each Asian culture.

This search for and adaptation of a new order did not begin in the twentieth century, nor did the processes occur quickly or without turmoil. In 1783 the United States became formally independent, but freedom from British rule merely began a new stage of development. What kind of country would emerge? America's first constitution, the Articles of Confederation, spoke loudly for small government and agrarian economics, but less than a decade later the Founding Fathers met at Philadelphia to craft a new constitution. The final product gave birth to a stronger central government, whose first leaders favored a more commercial economy. The War of 1812, the "Second War for Independence," convinced America's elite that a native industrial infrastructure needed to be built to augment the agricultural base in order for the country to be truly independent of Europe. All the while, the ugly issue of slavery continually forced Americans to raise the question of what kind of nation the people wanted. Even the Civil War failed to fully address that question. The problems involved in becoming modern affected the early industrializing nations of Europe and Japan. To expect the nations of Asia to avoid turmoil is to ignore historical experience.

The people of Asia will ultimately ask and answer the question of what kind of country they desire. The answer to this question will not likely emerge until the basic needs of the citizenry are met. How will the professed traditions of the past and perceived needs of the present combine with modern techniques and standards to produce a livable future? There will be toil and trouble along the road, and it remains uncertain that liberal core beliefs will prevail. But if they do, they will be liberal beliefs with distinctly Asian characteristics, reflecting the goals and principles of each particular Asian but increasingly global culture.

Part 1

Asian and Non-Asian Cultures Interact to circa 1850 CE

Introduction to Part 1

Asian and Non-Asian Cultures Interact to circa 1850 CE

Human development on the Asian continent passed through four distinct stages of historical and cultural development by the mid-nineteenth century of the Common Era (CE): Paleolithic, Neolithic, Pastoral Nomadic, and Civilized. Paleolithic humans departed their African origins for other parts of the world, arriving in Asia as early as 60,000 years ago. They brought with them ways of doing things, and those ways we collectively refer to as culture—people speaking, earning a living, making war, explaining the world, organizing the group, and so forth. As Paleolithic peoples spread across Asia, different kinds of culture appeared, reflecting diverse territories, distinctive climates, and language variations, circumstances that undoubtedly influenced group customs and values. Thus, as the Neolithic culture began to appear roughly 10,000 years ago, Asia boasted a wide range of cultural practices, though these peoples remained chiefly hunters and gatherers. The transition from Paleolithic existence to Neolithic farming occurred gradually and unevenly in Asia. Neolithic farmers experienced a much more abundant existence than their Paleolithic hunting and gathering predecessors. But as farm populations grew as a result of better diets and as the farmland lost its fertility due to soil exhaustion, villages had to move to virgin territory, and over the course of millennia eventually growers wore out the supply of arable land in Asia. These movements of farmers eventually led to the emergence of both Pastoral Nomadic and Civilized ways of life.

Pastoral Nomadic life likely evolved as the territory Paleolithic hunters and gatherers once depended on for livelihood steadily became cropland and villages for farmers. Not only did much of the plant and animal life get displaced as farmers cleared woodland for fields, but these cultivators also staked exclusive claim to surrounding terrain. Thus denied a means of livelihood, Paleolithic people were pushed to increasingly marginal territory. They became pastoral nomads by taking their hunting and gathering skills, as well as their awareness of land cultivation and animal domestication, to begin a new livelihood in what became known as the Eurasian steppe. This chiefly involved the herding of animals, though some agriculture frequently supplemented the skin, meat, and milk products of the herds. These pastoral nomads lived in tribes, which frequently came into conflict with one another, and once civilized life emerged, these tribes traded and warred with civilizations south of the steppe. Known by many names in different languages, the city dwellers typically called these pastoral nomads "barbarians."

Civilized life likely began in Asia along the Indus River in what is today Pakistan sometime between 3000 and 2500 BCE. Several centuries later, approximately 2000 BCE, city life in China commenced near the Yellow River in today's Henan Province. In both cases, dry climates probably pushed Neolithic farmers to the edge of subsistence, requiring them either to go the way of pastoral

Asia Past and Present: A Brief History, First Edition. Peter P. Wan and Thomas D. Reins.
© 2021 John Wiley & Sons, Inc. Published 2021 by John Wiley & Sons, Inc.

nomads or to find a means of adapting farming to hostile geography. The introduction of irrigation allowed farmers to settle along rivers. In normal times rivers provided water for fields, and when flooding occurred it resulted in the depositing of new topsoil on croplands. This in turn minimized the need for villagers to relocate in search of fertile land, as flooding constantly re-fertilized the farmers' fields. Reliable supplies of water and productive soil generated such large food surpluses that non-farming occupations could be supported. Instead of just one basic occupation found in Paleolithic times—hunting and gathering; just one occupation in Neolithic times—farming; and just one occupation in Pastoral Nomadic settings—herding, Civilized societies could boast a wide variety of specialized livelihoods.

In a Civilized culture, the city directs the activities in urban and surrounding rural areas, both of whose efforts by and large merge to serve a common purpose. Initially, at least, farmers realized the need for city services. These ranged from irrigation construction and maintenance to community security to market arrangements to artisan manufacturing as well as less tangible things such as religious advice. For these and other goods and services, farmers paid taxes to a governing administration. So too did most city inhabitants for the same fundamental reasons. Government promised to maintain essential services and to oversee the interaction of people performing different, often complementary, but frequently conflicting occupations. Farmers provided the necessary food for the city, which supplied the water. Over time, however, some occupations brought greater economic, psychic, and political rewards than others. City residents such as rulers (eventually usually monarchs), bureaucrats, priests, and merchants along with a rural elite (successful farmers, eventually usually a nobility) came to dominate the vast majority of the Civilized community, namely, the average farmer. Some of these cultivators continued to own their land or perhaps own some acreage and rent some; others only rented land; while still others lost their land and became day laborers or, worse, serfs or slaves.

Civilization in India and China produced three key accomplishments for Asia by approximately 1200 CE. First, both produced enduring, adaptable patterns of government practice and social custom, different as those patterns might have been. Politically, India ordinarily experienced regional governments while native central rule remained elusive, whereas China typically created effective central dynastic government, though periods of barbarian invasions and/or regionalism regularly occurred. What India lacked in political unity it made up for with religious cohesion, as Hinduism emerged in conjunction with the caste system to provide meaning and order for the ordinary person. In China, secular Confucianism and Legalism together with indigenous popular religions and Buddhism from India combined to make available understandable guides to daily behavior. Second, by the beginning of the Common Era, both Hinduism and Confucianism succeeded in the longer run by synthesizing competing systems of thought. Thus in Hinduism can be found strands of Buddhism and Jainism, while in Confucianism can be seen elements of Legalism, Daoism, and Buddhism. Third, Indian and Chinese civilizations provided political and cultural models for most of the rest of Asia.

India supplied Southeast Asia, except Vietnam and the Philippines, with a prototype of monarchy, written scripts, religions, economic practices, and other cultural traditions from which the region could pick and choose. Then these chosen Indian ideas and institutions underwent changes as they were adapted to local cultures and customs. The same process of cultural transmission transpired in Central Asia, although by the eighth century CE Islamic expansion, first Arab and eventually Turkish and Persian, began to eclipse Indian influence there. China had the same kind of cultural influence in Japan, Korea, and Vietnam. Chinese ideas and institutions—monarchy, writing, philosophy, religion, and assorted social practices—made their way to Confucian East Asia to be adopted and adapted.

Between roughly 1200 and 1850, Asia witnessed the dawning of three major jolts: the arrival of Islamic, Mongol, and Western military and cultural challenges. India began to be ruled by various peoples of Islamic background after 1206; the Mongols launched their assault on Eurasia in the thirteenth century; and by the early sixteenth century, the Europeans began to arrive. While the Mongol impact tended to be transitory, the Muslims and Europeans produced more lasting consequences in Asia. Today's Central Asia, Pakistan, Bangladesh, Indonesia, and Malaysia are Muslim majority nations, while substantial numbers of Muslims inhabit most remaining Asian nations. The Philippines is today Catholic majority, Vietnam has a large Catholic population, and South Korea claims a considerable Protestant population. Most other Asian nations have large and often growing Christian—Catholic and Protestant—communities. European spoken languages and Islamic- and European-derived writing systems can be seen everywhere in Asia. English dominates the intellectual and mercantile communities, while the languages of non-Asian colonial overlords retain regional significance. Non-Asian political, technological, educational, artistic, gastronomic, and assorted popular cultural influences continue to impact the Asian world.

Most of the seeds of these contemporary foreign influences on Asia got planted centuries ago, and for different reasons and at different times in India and China, the major generators of Asian cultural norms. In the early thirteenth century Afghans under the banner of Islam invaded, defeated, and ruled a politically weak India. With their Persian and Arab allies, these Delhi sultans and later the Mughal emperors created a climate that produced the emergence of a large native Indian Muslim population. And much of Southeast Asia, an ongoing consumer of Indian cultural thought and behavior, soon began to appropriate India's newest cultural item: Islam. While most would agree that India absorbed Islam and preserved the essence of its traditional ways, the same cannot be said of Indonesia and Malaysia. In both nations the vestiges of Indian culture continue, but the dominant influence in both is today clearly Islamic.

When the Chinese threw out the Mongol invaders in 1368, a crisis of cultural confidence remained as the Ming Dynasty turned inward, the early considerable voyages of Admiral Zheng He to Southeast Asia, India, East Africa, and the Arabian Peninsula in the early fifteenth century notwithstanding. The government initially handled the arrival of the West in the early sixteenth century chiefly through the tribute system, a highly ritualized process of tightly controlled Chinese–foreign interaction known to Westerners as the Guangzhou or Canton System. Until the early nineteenth century, the Chinese found little in the West worthy of embracing, the chief exceptions being Galilean astronomy and new crops from the Americas. The West, by contrast, desired many Chinese products—silk and tea, for example—paid for principally by the gold and silver from the Spanish empire in the Americas. However, major changes in European scientific thought and economic and political practice propelled the West past China and the rest of Asia in terms of wealth and power. By the beginning of the nineteenth century, many Western nations had well-established colonial regimes across the Asian continent. However, what had been largely commercial enterprises—East Indian companies chartered by European rulers—had often grown to become de facto government administrations with bureaucrats, armies, and educators in place to orchestrate an array of political, economic, social, and religious interactions with local leaders and subjects. Informal economic empire would soon become formal political empire directed by the industrial nations of the world.

The means by which Europeans came to dominate not only most of Asia but also most of the globe forced Asia's elite to question their cultural traditions. Eventually these elites and ultimately the common people opted to modify much of their cultural past and adopt much of the current Western cultural present. Defending the nation began to trump protecting the culture.

People in Asia, as well as people in the West and elsewhere, are still grappling with the problems associated with becoming and then being modern.

1

Cultures and the Development of Core Asian Civilizations

...social development is the bundle of technological, subsistence, organizational, and cultural accomplishments through which people feed, clothe, house, and reproduce themselves, explain the world around them, resolve disputes within their communities, extend their power at the expense of other communities, and defend themselves against others' attempts to extend power.[1]

What Is Asia?

This book will explore Asia chiefly from historical, social, and economic angles. Historically it will attempt to put into context the long course of events generated by numerous social and economic entities, ranging organizationally from tribes to nation-states and chronologically from Paleolithic times to the early twenty-first century. This will involve a good deal of political history, the container within which domestic and international activities can most easily be examined. Because there is no physically discrete Asia but instead a Eurasian landmass, and since "the division between Europe and Asia is entirely arbitrary," we will focus on terrain, including India, Afghanistan, and Central Asia eastward and Japan and New Guinea westward. The northern frontier will include Mongolia and the Russian Far East and extend southward to Indonesia. These territorial frontiers contain the civilizations that have most influenced what most scholars consider to be Asia.[2] Clearly the expansion of Islam and Western nations into Asia also greatly contributed to Asia's development, but India's and China's thought and institutions still constitute the cultural foundations, albeit reinforced by non-Asian sources, upon which contemporary Asian nations build their societies.

---

1 Ian Morris, *The Measure of Civilization: How Social Development Decides the Fate of Nations* (Princeton: Princeton University Press, 2013), p. 5.
2 Martin W. Lewis and Karen E. Wigen, *The Myth of Continents: A Critique of Metageography* (Berkeley: University of California Press, 1997), p. 3. The Association for Asian Studies, for instance, generally follows this geographical range.

Asia Past and Present: A Brief History, First Edition. Peter P. Wan and Thomas D. Reins.
© 2021 John Wiley & Sons, Inc. Published 2021 by John Wiley & Sons, Inc.

ASIA

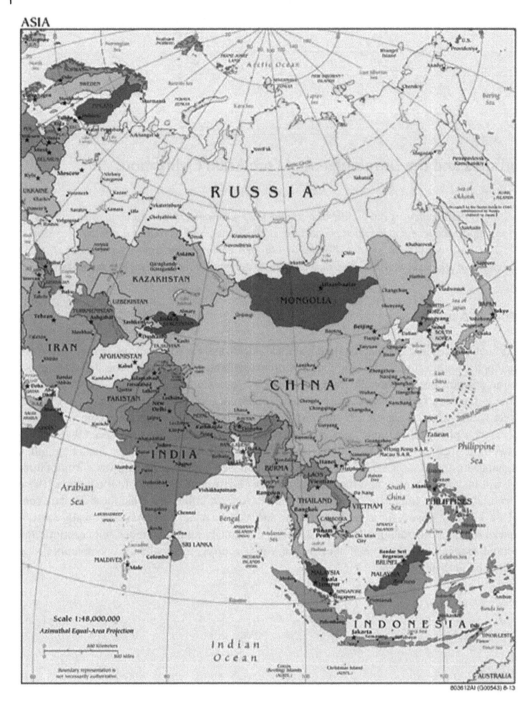

Asia in the early twenty-first century. *Source:* From https://www.cia.gov/library/publications/the-world-factbook/graphics/ref_maps/political/jpg/asia.jpg. Central Intelligence Agency. Public Domain.

What Is Culture?

The word culture suggests several possible subjects. It can refer to microorganisms in a Petri dish, to people with good "taste" who enjoy haute cuisine and classical music, to the literate elite (high culture) as opposed to the "great unwashed" (i.e., the masses), or to modern nations compared to the developing world. In this study of Asia through the centuries, culture indicates human culture, which includes the innumerable ideas and practices the people of the continent have created over the millennia to meet their needs, both real and apparent. Thus culture encompasses—but is not limited to—such things as religious rituals, political institutions, economic arrangements, marriage customs, artistic creations, linguistic conventions, eating habits, and so forth.

Cultures evolve, interact with other cultures or remain isolated, expand or disappear. Since culture includes all behavior, different societies emerged, reflecting diverse approaches to social relationships in communities of shared values. Societies have ranged in size from small bands of several dozen to tribes, clans, or lineages of several hundreds or thousands; to villages of quite a few hundred to many thousands; to cities of more than a few thousand to several million; to regions of tens of millions; to nations of scores to hundreds of millions; or to entities such as "the West," "Confucian Civilization," "the Islamic World," and "Hindustan," each with at least hundreds of millions of inhabitants. Of course, differences will exist even among members of any culture, but one culture's common beliefs, behaviors, and organizational techniques typically distinguish it as a separate society and set it off from others.

Societies have also reflected, as they do at present, a range of geographical and climatological settings. Thus, landlocked communities of the past did not likely engage in seafaring activities, while today's natural-resource-poor nations need to rely on other assets in order to survive or prosper. Consequently, peoples across Asia (and around the world) created somewhat varied or even radically heterodox measures to cope with different physical circumstances. The practices of some cultures produced successful material results, such as peace and prosperity, while the ways of life in other cultures brought about psychological and spiritual comfort, while at the same time still other cultures achieved both material and emotional success, even as others failed in both material and psychological respects.

Cultural Categories

Social scientists have classified human social development into four broad groupings, or ways of life, based on the principal means by which people organized and exploited their surroundings: Paleolithic, Neolithic, Pastoral Nomadic, and Civilized, the last of which can be divided into numerous categories and subcategories. As these ways of life are not mutually exclusive, some or all of them have been practiced at the same time in Asia (and around the globe). However, such drastically different customs typically produced conflict among diverse lifestyles when in close proximity. Thus, as farmers occupied gatherers' former hunting grounds after approximately 10,000 BCE, Neolithic and Paleolithic communities clashed; later, Neolithic farmers resisted but gradually came under the domination of Civilized urban elites beginning around 4000 BCE in Mesopotamia and Egypt, by roughly 3000 BCE in India, and just after 2000 BCE in China. And traditional civilizations based on agricultural productivity began colliding with civilizations based on industrial output after roughly 1800 CE. Although hunting communities, farming societies beyond the reach of civilization, and traditional agricultural civilizations declined in numbers, wealth, and/or power, they typically remained as vestigial ways of life transitioning to oblivion or "modernization." But the Paleolithic and Neolithic periods account for the majority of time that human beings have existed; Pastoral Nomadic and Civilized ways represent relatively new human arrangements.

Timeline: Cultures and the Development of Core Asian Civilizations	
4.5 billion years ago	Earth formed
64 million years ago	Dinosaurs become extinct
2.5 million–10,000 BCE	Paleolithic or Old Stone Age; hominid and human hunting and gathering develop
200,000 BCE	Human beings emerge in Africa
50,000 years ago	Humans arrive in South Asia
10,000 BCE	Neolithic or New Stone Age; agriculture begins
4000 BCE	Civilization begins in Mesopotamia and Egypt
3300 BCE	Indus Valley civilization begins
3000–2000 BCE	Bronze Age begins in various Eurasian locations
2000 BCE	Civilization begins in the North China Plain
1000 BCE	Iron Age commences in various Eurasian locations
Third century BCE	Chinese cultural and political influence evident in Vietnam
First century BCE	Indian cultural influence evident in most of Southeast Asia and much of Central Asia

Paleolithic Culture

Paleolithic or Old Stone Age culture employed two principal instruments that the earliest humans used to survive: crude stone tools and weapons, as well as hunting and food gathering. Paleolithic people foraged for wild plants that provided not only nutrition but also materials for clothing, tools, weapons, and artistic activities. Pottery shards have been unearthed throughout Asia, and in 2009 Chinese and Israeli archaeologists unearthed pieces of earthenware in southern China that were estimated to be 18,000 years old. At that point humans had begun the process of devising the ways and means of improving their standard of living. They learned by trial and error which products of the earth were edible or poisonous, possessed medical or manufacturing uses, or had recreational, religious, or other applications.

But such primitive people produced insufficient wealth to afford specialists who could focus on advancing secular and spiritual knowledge in any timely or reliable fashion. Nonetheless, part-time "experts" approximating artisans, shamans, and community leaders took up such roles on an ad hoc basis. Understanding of the natural and social worlds in which they operated remained primal, with most phenomena explained in supernatural terms and with little or no comprehension of why things happened. Such Paleolithic peoples inhabited most parts of today's Asia, and they created countless numbers of different Paleolithic cultures.

Neolithic Culture

Neolithic or New Stone Age life appeared around 10,000 years ago and revolved around sedentary farming instead of wandering foraging. The appearance of advanced tools and weapons along with an agricultural economy marks this new stage of human development. Some argue that farming began once foragers became more familiar with plant life. Others claim that climate forced foragers to farm as either the Ice Age or droughts relocated humans to regions more favorable to agriculture. Still others claim that population pressure required foragers to turn to farming, which was known but not practiced until hunting and gathering failed to feed the growing size of drifting bands of gatherers. In any case, farming increasingly became seen as the chief means of feeding people. Humans began to control nature by domesticating crops and animals rather than purely collecting or killing what nature made available, and these innovative endeavors had likely evolved over the centuries, much as economic and military utensils had improved, by ongoing trial and error. Very early in the Neolithic period, crops such as rice, millet, sugarcane, and hemp had become dependable sources of good nutrition and household materials.

Full-time farming resulted in positive and negative consequences. On the positive side, sedentary village life allowed cultivators to create permanent residences (most likely thatched huts), which gave meaningful protection against inclement weather and dangerous animals. During less hectic times of the agricultural season, villagers created and repaired tools and weapons and fabricated primitive textiles. They also frequently improved these products over time. Gourds, baskets, and eventually pottery allowed villagers to accumulate and stockpile crops and water as well as store tools, weapons, and clothing. More permanent residences permitted elderly villagers to survive longer, since they no longer needed to keep up with hunting bands or be left to the elements as in Paleolithic times. These survivors, no longer around-the-clock tillers, had time to pass on their experiences to younger villagers as well as to reflect on their surroundings. Thus apparently began the part-time shaman, offering advice and counsel to villagers, particularly instruction on fertility and how to achieve it for field and female. Other elders made recommendations concerning such issues as sanitation, childbirth, social relations, and so forth. Since little contact existed among distant villages, local knowledge tended to be viewed as universal knowledge.

On the negative side, village life immediately presented serious challenges. What crops were safe and could be produced in sufficient amounts to feed the village? Only trial and error, which is to say malnutrition or starvation if miscalculations were made, ultimately permitted farmers to select the most nontoxic and bountiful crops. How to deal with sanitation? Instead of a Paleolithic band of several dozen people constantly on the move and rarely concerned about human or other waste, villagers usually numbered in the hundreds, lived in close proximity to one another, and generated volumes of garbage. The rubbish in turn produced flies, rats, and other vermin capable of quickly spreading disease. Farming also meant dealing with nature in its many manifestations, especially drought, flood, locusts, frost, and heat, any one of which might spell crop failure and consequently famine. Thus, although lack of sanitation and episodic low food production resulted in early death, generally a high birth rate (once farmers worked out safe crops to plant) meant a larger village population. The slash-and-burn type of farming commonly practiced—whereby farmers cleared the land of trees and other vegetation, burned it, and then planted crops in the ash—eventually exhausted the soil and required farmers to search for more fertile land.

Evidence for Neolithic life in Asia indicates farming communities existed across the continent. In the Indian world, confirmation of village life can be found in nearly every region of Pakistan, India, Afghanistan, Kashmir, and elsewhere between 8000 and 2000 BCE. The most notable sites are Mehrgarh in today's western Pakistan and Shorapur Doab in southern India, both of which indicate plant and animal domestication. Chinese Neolithic locations date from about 7500 BCE, Hemudu along the lower Yangze River and Yangshao and Longshan near the Yellow River being the most prominent. The Ban Chiang site in northern Thailand, one of several Neolithic locations in that country, dates back to roughly 4500 BCE. Evidence from stone tools suggests that Neolithic culture came to the Philippines from Indonesia sometime after 3000 BCE. Phung Nguyen culture along the lower reaches of the Red River in northern Vietnam dates from 2000 BCE. Across much of Japan, Jomon or cord pottery culture began as early as 7500 years ago, while more recent and more sophisticated Yayoi culture materialized about 250 BCE and lasted nearly a half millennium. Farming did not arrive in Siberia until around 3000 BCE.

The larger Asian farming population and decreasing crop production due to soil exhaustion forced villagers to seek new lands. As more and more villages with greater and greater numbers of people moved across arable lands in Asia, those most productive lands became scarcer and scarcer. Since only 3 percent of the earth's land is arable and the remaining 97% is composed of forest, desert, or tundra, farmers eventually created an unsustainable standard of living. As Asia's arable land became insufficient to continue farming life as it had been traditionally lived, Neolithic ways began to be eclipsed by two new ways of life: Pastoral Nomadic and Civilized.

Pastoral Nomadic Culture

Nomadic herding of animals as a livelihood for a small part of humanity likely began not long after the advent of farming. However, the mature pastoral nomadic existence that developed to the north of civilization in Asia—across the Eurasian steppe—resulted from two basic causes: (1) the vanishing of hunting territory, which occurred because growers in Neolithic and Civilized settings consumed lands favorable to foraging; and (2) the domestication of the horse and camel about 2000 BCE, which made possible mobility across the steppe grasslands. Not only did hunters and gatherers get pushed off their lands by farmers, thus requiring these foragers to find another occupation; but planters also forced many of their fellow planters to the margins of agricultural subsistence, compelling many of them to take up a fresh line of work. In both cases, that new livelihood often involved herding on lands with only minimal access to water.

In Asia, pastoral nomadism is associated with the Eurasian steppe, grassy grazing land north of China and India that stretches east from the Ural Mountains to the Pacific Ocean. This includes most of today's Central Asia, southern Siberia, and Mongolia, where bands of a hundred or so kinfolk migrated via horse, camel, or wagon, leading the herd to the most likely locations offering water and fodder. Typically they herded sheep, goats, yaks, and cattle for the products they turned out, such as milk and its products, as well as meat for food, hides for clothing and yurts, and animal waste for fuel. These nomads characteristically came from Turkish, Mongolian, Manchu, Uighur, Hun, or Xiongnu backgrounds by the beginning of the Common Era. By that time, the Indo-Europeans from the steppe had migrated into India, Iran, or Europe. These nomads remained significant political and economic influences in Asia into the twentieth century.

Life on the steppe consisted of constant battles. The most common clash pitted nomad against nature. The sky provided the most essential product, rainwater, without which animals and humans perished. The rain also made possible the feed that sustained animals and herders. This meant migration as either water or fodder became insufficient in a particular area. Heat, cold, and wind also habitually challenged human and animal existence. As bands moved around the steppe in search of shelter or provisions necessary for survival, they encountered other bands in search of the same, often resulting in violent clashes. Quite often as well, fighting among band members added to the list of brutality that bands characteristically suffered. And eventually, pastoral nomads and civilized cultures collided. Although the two different ways of life regularly interacted to their mutual benefit, usually involving trade, they also often clashed.

These struggles had many causes, including famine on the steppe or instability in civilized settings. Most civilizations employed terms of scorn to characterize their nomadic neighbors, the most common one being "barbarian." Typically civilizations kept the nomads at bay, but occasionally nomads conquered and sometimes ruled their civilized neighbors. Life of the pastoral nomad changed very little from the introduction of the horse down to the twentieth century. The last emperor of the last dynasty in China was a Manchu, originally a pastoral nomadic/semi-agrarian people from Manchuria, and their Manchu Qing Dynasty survived until 1912.

Civilized Culture

No one knows for sure where or when civilization began, but most historians would today agree that it did not originate in Asia east of Afghanistan. As it stands at present, city life probably began in either Mesopotamia or Egypt sometime just after 4000 BCE. Perhaps further archaeological research will one day unearth evidence of earlier urban life elsewhere, conceivably in India, China, or another Asian location. Based on current scholarship, evidence of civilization in India can be traced back to roughly 3000 BCE and in China to about 2000 BCE, and there are other possible but as yet unverifiable sites that may have developed civilized ways even earlier. But it is fairly clear that it began as a result of farmers being pushed to the margins of land where rainfall became unreliable. A lack of water produced a search for it, and all four early civilizations—Mesopotamia, Egypt, India, and China—emerged along rivers flowing through terrain with minimal annual rainfall. Irrigation solved the water problem, at least temporarily.

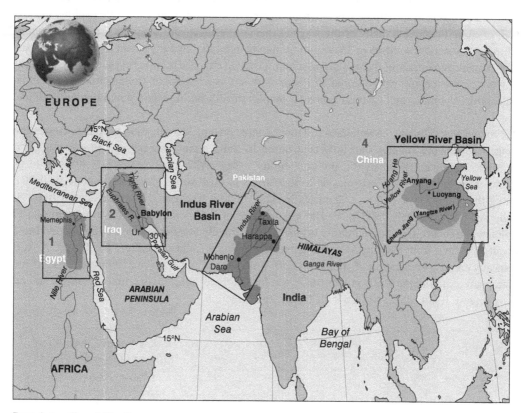

Four river valley civilizations.

What is civilization? Typically civilization includes a cluster of characteristics. It is urban; has rudimentary bureaucratic government that operates with the aid of writing; and can impose and collect taxes, provide for the community's defense, and dictate the community's common agenda. Whatever the program, it would be carried out by a society divided by specialization, the most significant cause of inequality. At the top of the hierarchy would be the political leader, usually a monarch of some kind, who would be assisted by bureaucratic advisors and be given leadership legitimacy by a priesthood. Below these elites, urbanites of every description provided all sorts of goods and services. Merchants, artisans, engineers, police, clerks, laborers, shamans, and other occupations emerged to meet the demands principally of their urban neighbors. Urbanites also serviced the needs and wants of the rural population, whose surplus agricultural output supported the city dwellers.

The farmers produced enough food surpluses to support the urban population chiefly because engineers made available an abundance of water via irrigation works. Not only did rivers provide water, enabling farming to occur in an arid or semi-arid environment, but also these natural waterways regularly flooded, depositing fresh topsoil on farmland, thereby swelling the agricultural output. Moreover, the constant reinvigoration of the fields by routine flooding eliminated the farmer's need to find new fertile fields. In the beginning, at least, civilized life seemed to generate win-win situations. True, not everyone was relatively equal as in Paleolithic, Neolithic, or Pastoral Nomadic times, but during early Civilized times everyone's standard of living had vastly increased. And as established civilizations developed and new civilizations emerged, ways of life within an urban culture produced a diversity of occupations and outlooks. The differences between civilizations also substantially diverged, producing distinctively remarkable uniqueness that resulted in some civilizations being more complex, prosperous, inventive, and enduring, while others either did less well or came to emulate many of the ways of their more successful neighbors. By the advent of Chinese civilization, some 25 to 35 million human beings inhabited the earth, most living in Asia. Only a small percentage of the world's population lived in civilized cultures at that time. Gradually, however, most people would come to reside within the compass of Civilized societies, while Paleolithic, Neolithic, and Pastoral Nomadic peoples steadily became part of marginal ways of life.

Ancient Indian Civilization   Academics still do not agree on which civilization in Asia possesses the longest continuous history. Certainly civilization in India began long before China's, but did it continue unbroken down to the present? Indus Valley civilization, sometimes referred to as Harappan civilization and at times as Indus-Saraswati civilization, originated about 3000 BCE along the Indus River and its tributaries in what is now Pakistan and northwestern India. It collapsed approximately 1500 BCE. Did the essence of that collapsed civilization continue to animate the subsequent Aryan culture of uncivilized, tribally organized people who entered India about that time from Central Asia and came to dominate India thereafter? Or did the Aryans basically create a civilization of their own with little or no input from the Harappan past? If the Harappan past fundamentally guides the Aryan future, then Indian civilization is continuous and thus longest. If not, China warrants the longevity distinction.

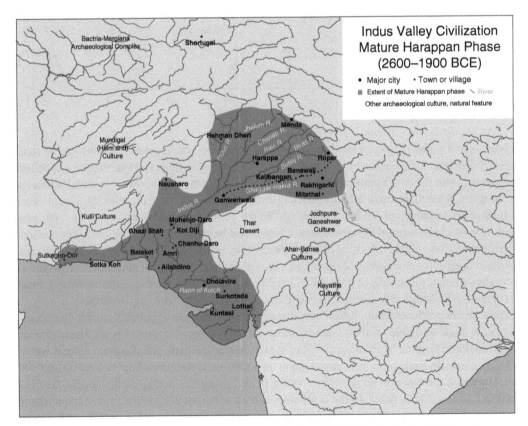

Indus Valley civilization, 2600–1900 BCE. *Source:* McIntosh, Jane. (2008). *The Ancient Indus Valley: New Perspectives.*

Evidence for civilization in ancient India, first hit upon in the mid-nineteenth century, comes chiefly from archaeological excavations conducted in 1921 and 1922. These digs revealed two major cities whose origins date back to the third millennium BCE. Harappa, apparently the model for most other Indus Valley cities, was unearthed along the Ravi River, a tributary of the Indus in northern Pakistan. Mohenjo Daro, the second major site uncovered, was found along the Indus in southern Pakistan. Subsequent excavations have brought to light another 1500 sites, two-thirds of which are along the now-desiccated Saraswati River, and the oldest of which is Kalibangan, located in northwestern India. Given Indus Valley civilization's proximity to the older Mesopotamian culture, the question of originality arises, since contact between the two existed. Here, too, whether Indus Valley civilization emerged on its own or owed its creation to outside influence will not likely be settled until the Harappan script is deciphered.

What do we know about India's earliest city life? The Indus River, which originates in the Himalayan Mountains, provided reliable access to water for both animal (humans, dogs, cats, cattle, and eventually horses and camels) and plant life (wheat, melons, peas, barley, rice, and other fruits and vegetables). The Indus and its tributaries also supplied dependable flooding that deposited fertile topsoil on nearby cropland. Consequently a plentiful quantity of food made it possible for the rural majority of farmers to support an urban minority of non-farming occupations. This symbiotic relationship resulted in a community of differing occupations bound together by an attitude of shared interests and values.

The cities, which appear to have been well planned, were divided into two distinct parts: an elevated citadel for the city's defense and refuge, and the lower city itself, which was organized along a grid pattern. Spacious homes made of brick contained drainage systems, verandas, living/bedrooms, and work areas, thus providing a fair amount of domestic comfort for many inhabitants. High-quality roads within each city made transportation and travel in the roughly five- to six-square-mile city relatively easy, while the Indus facilitated contact among the various city-states (which stretched more than a thousand miles along the river) as well as with the wider world, the gateway to which was the Arabian Sea, into which the Indus flows.

Unearthed artifacts such as pottery, seals, and tools (as well as the absence of some remains) offer clues to some of the thinking and behavior of these early Indians. The lack of remains signifying the presence of palaces strongly argues against the existence of a strong, awe-inspiring ruler, either in any particular city or among clusters of city-states that emerged in the ancient civilizations of Mesopotamia, Egypt, and China.

According to one scholar of India, "Trade seals with signs from the Harappan writing system have been found not only in the major cities of the Indus-Saraswati civilization but also overseas or overland at Ur in Babylon (South Iraq), at Ebla in North Syria and at numerous ports in the ancient Persian Gulf."[3] Apparently merchants and mercantile activities constituted important parts of the social order in these cities. Moreover, the Indus Valley writing system, seals, and pottery make a strong statement of orthographic and religious continuity. By 2000 BCE along the river corridor, it appears that Indus Valley civilization had reached its point of greatest development.

How did Harappan civilization collapse? Several theories, none of which are mutually exclusive, attempt to explain the disappearance of the numerous city-states for nearly 3500 years. One speculation asserts that prolonged drought, evidenced by the drying up of the Saraswati River, compelled Indus Valley residents to migrate east in search of a more farmer-friendly environment. Another theory stresses the likelihood of massive flooding either caused by unusually large amounts of Himalayan snowmelt or due to a tsunami from the sea. Given the nearness of the city-states to the Indus or its tributaries, such scenarios could have spelled doom for urban occupants. As well, a massive earthquake in this earthquake-prone area could have destroyed the region.

---

3 D. R. SarDesai, *India: The Definitive History* (Boulder, CO: Westview Press, 2008), p. 23.

Furthermore, the Aryan invaders from Central Asia had the potential of overrunning these hundreds of city-states. And finally, any combination of these catastrophes, not all simultaneously but over time, could have eroded and then destroyed the framework of Indus Valley civilization.

Ancient Chinese Civilization As in the other ancient civilizations of Mesopotamia, Egypt, and the Indus Valley, the initial stages of civilization in China originated in a dry region with easily worked soil near a large river. The Yellow River and its tributaries supplied both sufficient water for irrigation and regular annual flooding that deposited new topsoil on existing fields, an agricultural combination that generated the abundant harvests capable of supporting a large non-farming population. Exactly how and where Chinese civilization began is unclear, but social scientists generally agree that just after 2000 BCE a complex culture capable of constructing public buildings, crafting writing, using bronze, mobilizing manpower, and domesticating horses for chariot warfare and other tasks appeared in the vicinity of the Yellow River. As in the case of India, questions arise about whether Chinese civilization started on its own or if it owed its creation or at least much of its development to outside influences. Thus, the chariot and its similarity to those in other parts of Eurasia seem to indicate external contact. There is also dispute as to whether China's first historical dynasty, the Shang (ca. 1650–1050 BCE), in fact was preceded by an earlier dynasty. Growing evidence indicates the likelihood of an earlier dynasty the Chinese call the Xia.

Whatever future research authenticates, current evidence reveals the existence of a Shang Dynasty by at least the seventeenth century BCE, probably headquartered in today's Henan Province but extending across a good part of the North China Plain. An emperor or king, whose functions appear to have been both political and religious, presided over a central government. This ruler likely had to share power with a rural landowning elite but nevertheless could mobilize manpower and materials for numerous projects. Some of the larger undertakings included the building of palaces, city walls, and burial facilities for rulers, as well as the deployment of a host of talent that would organize laborers and artisans to construct the facilities. Priestly advisors or diviners or shamans provided the ruler with insight about the supernatural, chiefly by interpreting cracks on oracle bones. Since the ruler was linked to the supreme deity, he needed to know what to do or refrain from doing. Upsetting god might well result in one's government itself being upset.

The Shang Dynasty established the initial foundation for the ideal of central government in China that survives in amended form down to the twenty-first century. This central government model did not always operate successfully, failing to some extent between dynasties for greater or lesser periods of time. Unsuccessful central government rule occurred during times when dynasties were headed by weak rulers or when China's neighbors, usually nomadic ones to the north, invaded and temporarily took control. The principle of central direction orchestrated by rulers connected to divinity typically remained a Chinese political and intellectual ideal. By contrast, India seldom experienced central government rule by Indians. With the exception of two dynasties, the Mauryan (321–185 BCE) and the Gupta (320–540 CE), India either remained fragmented, governed by regional monarchs and lesser rulers—think of splintered Europe after the fall of the Roman Empire—or was ruled by foreigners until independence from Britain in 1947.

The Ongoing Influence of India and China in Asia

Yet whether Chinese central government or Indian regional rule, both centers of culture eventually provided guidance for those territories surrounding them. Indian culture remained the chief influence in Central Asia until the arrival of Islam in the eighth century CE and in most of

Southeast Asia at least until the arrival of the Europeans. Chinese ideas and institutions served as both a broad outline and frequently a detailed agenda for civilization in Vietnam, Korea, and Japan. From the concept of monarchy to writing systems and educational arrangements, religious attitudes and philosophical outlook, and secular observances and popular culture, India and China served as repositories of culture that adjacent peoples drew upon and modified to suit their particular needs. And by the eighteenth century, China began to influence those territories in Southeast Asia that initially embraced Indian practices. Chinese migrants made their way there in search of employment as least as far back as the Ming Dynasty (1368–1644) and carried with them cultural baggage from the homeland. They brought with them a distinctly Chinese way of looking at the world that competes with Indian practices even today.

Suggested Readings and Viewings

Thomas J. Barfield, *The Nomadic Alternative* (Englewood Cliffs, NJ: Prentice Hall, 1993).

Jean-Pierre Bocqute-Appel and Ofer Bar-Yosef, eds., *The Neolithic Demographic Transition and Its Consequences* (New York: Springer, 2008).

K. C. Chang, *The Archaeology of Ancient China*, 4th ed. (New Haven, CT: Yale University Press, 1986).

Joseph Hutchinson, *Farming and Food Supply: The Interdependence of Countryside and Town* (New York: Cambridge University Press, 2009).

Christopher Isett and Stephen Miller, *The Social History of Agriculture: From the Origins to the Current Crisis* (Lanham, MD: Rowman & Littlefield, 2017).

Jonathan Kenoyer, *Ancient Cities of the Indus Valley Civilization* (New York: Oxford University Press, 1998).

Nayanjot Lahiri, ed., *The Decline and Fall of the Indus Civilization* (New Delhi: Ravi Dayal Publisher, 2000).

Mongol (2007), dir. by Sergei Bodrov.

J. R. McNeill and William H. McNeill, *The Human Web: A Bird's Eye View of World History* (New York: W. W. Norton, 2003).

Dougald J. W. O'Reilly, *Early Civilizations of Southeast Asia* (New York: Rowman and Littlefield, 2007).

Himanshu Prabha Ray, *Sanghol and the Archaeology of Punjab* (New Delhi: Aryan Books International, 2010).

Robert Redfield, *The Primitive World and Its Transformations* (Ithaca, NY: Cornell University Press, 1953), especially chap. 1.

Robert Scarre, ed., *The Human Past: World Prehistory & the Development of Human Societies*, 4th ed. (New York: Thames and Hudson, 2018).

2

The Land and the People of Ancient China to 221 BCE:
Xia, Shang, and Zhou Dynasties

In order to understand a person, you must know his background. The same is true of nations. In order to understand a nation and interact with it successfully, you must know its history.

Introduction to the Study of Chinese History

China has attracted the attention of the West for many centuries. Its vast territory, large population, and long history are impossible to ignore. The Italian merchant-adventurer Marco Polo (ca. 1254–1324) purportedly visited China and returned home to tell his story. He was among the first to stir the West's imagination about the wealth and power of that distant civilization.

Until very recently, only a handful of Western missionaries, merchants, and scholars have taken a serious interest in China. But times have changed. Globalization has shrunk the world, and China's rapid rise has made it a major player in world affairs. Consequently, the study of Chinese history has taken on a new relevancy, urgency, and intensity. It has become an essential part of any person's education.

China is unique in that it has the oldest continuing civilization in today's world. The ancient civilizations of Egypt, Mesopotamia, and the Indian Subcontinent all had their day of glory, but then each was superseded by other civilizations long before modern times. The Chinese civilization, however, has gone through repeated cycles of rise and fall and rise yet again. It resembles the legendary phoenix that would burn and rise again from its own ashes.

The study of China's history is made easier by its rich store of historical information. The Chinese have had a deep reverence for history throughout the ages. They see history as a guide to current action, and believe that the lessons of history can point an individual or a nation in the right direction to avoid repeating past mistakes and move smoothly forward into the future. Thanks to this tradition, China has preserved more comprehensive records of its past than any other civilization.

China's historical records come in a great variety of shapes and forms. The Chinese made written records of their activities on oracle bones, bronze vessels, bamboo strips, silk fabrics, and paper. Their earliest inscriptions on oracle bones date back to 1200 BCE, and their oldest surviving books were written before 500 BCE. Bureaucrats at all levels of government and scribes of powerful clans were consumed with a passion for record keeping. They left behind mountains of records covering population numbers, taxes and revenues, good and bad harvests, floods and droughts and famines, trade, war and peace, diplomatic negotiations, and earthquakes and eclipses. Individuals kept personal accounts, diaries, and collections of poetry and essays. It is not uncommon for an average

Asia Past and Present: A Brief History, First Edition. Peter P. Wan and Thomas D. Reins.
© 2021 John Wiley & Sons, Inc. Published 2021 by John Wiley & Sons, Inc.

Timeline: Ancient China	
1500th century BCE–100th century BCE	Old Stone Age: "Beijing Ape Man" unearthed at Zhoukou Dian 700,000 years ago; hunters and gatherers
100th century BCE–24th century BCE	New Stone Age: Banpo Village ca. 6000 years ago; farmers
ca. 2300–2100 BCE	Three ancient kings: Legendary Sage-Kings Yao, Shun, and Yu
ca. 2000 BCE	Bronze Age: Bronze used to make weapons and ceremonial items
ca. 2000–1600 BCE	Xia Dynasty: No direct evidence but likely China's first dynasty
ca. 1600–1100 BCE	Peak of China's Bronze Age; first direct evidence for civilization in China unearthed at Anyang, Henan Province
1046–221 BCE	Shang Dynasty overthrown by Zhou Dynasty, the first recorded dynastic change; China ruled by "Son of Heaven," whose mandate provides future dynasties political legitimacy
1122–770 BCE	Western Zhou Dynasty: Feudal political order presided over by the Zhou monarchs at Xian capital; introduction of iron upsets ancient political and social order; frontier barbarians force the Zhou rulers to move capital east to Luoyang
770–221 BCE	Eastern Zhou Dynasty: The emergence of numerous political states that challenge both the dynasty and each other, producing ongoing political chaos and intellectual resourcefulness; eventually the State of Qin will end the Warring States period by unifying China in 221 BCE; the Hundred Schools of Thought will deliver basic political and intellectual tools to create China's bureaucratic model of government that lasts until 1912 CE

Chinese family to be able to trace its family tree back many centuries. Private and government-sponsored discussions had their records as well. Therefore, we have detailed accounts of intense polemics at the highest levels of government on the benefits of government intervention in the marketplace, as well as philosophical debates on the merits of Buddhism and individual autonomy. Historians, poets, and novelists drew epical portraits of their times. Secular and religious art and literature provide in-depth portrayals of the lives and psyches of China's people, covering the whole spectrum of humanity from royalty to ordinary people.

Archaeological sites are numerous in China. The remains of imperial palaces and burial sites, temples, villages, private collections of artifacts, and so on serve to round out the modern historian's knowledge of China's past. As China's modernization moves ahead at a dizzy pace, archaeologists are unearthing artifacts that were buried for millennia. Paradoxically, while more and more of China's past is coming to light, so is more and more of it being destroyed. The discovery of the Qin terra-cotta armies is an example of the former, and the building of the Three Gorges Dam on the Yangtze River is an example of the latter.

Today, China has the world's largest population of over 1.4 billion. In other words, one person out of every five living on the face of the earth is Chinese. Its territory is among the largest in the world, being a close fourth after Russia, Canada, and the United States. Its GDP ranks a distant second to that of the United States. It is one of the five permanent members of the Security Council of the United Nations. The role it plays in world affairs is steadily on the increase.

The Land and the People in Paleolithic and Neolithic Times

China has had a relatively stable core population of Han Chinese throughout its history, and they continue to make up well over 90 percent of the entire modern Chinese population. China is also a multiethnic country composed of over 50 ethnic groups. Ancient Han Chinese believed for a long time that their country was at the center of the world, and called it the "Central Country." They also believed that their land was the only civilized land, and so they called all the people living beyond their borders "barbarians."

Early Han Chinese lived along the Yellow River. It had a loess soil that was highly fertile, a warm climate, and ample rainfall in ancient times. This richly endowed natural environment easily sustained plant, animal, and human life. But the rich silt in the rivers would frequently clog the riverbeds and cause serious floods. That is why the river is known not only as the "Cradle of Chinese Civilization" but also as "China's Sorrow."

Archaeologists unearthed the remains of China's earliest humanlike beings at Zhoukoudian near modern Beijing. Known popularly as the "Beijing Ape Man" (*Homo erectus pekinensis*), they stood erect, used fire, and made crude stone tools. They acquired their food by hunting, fishing, and gathering. In one cave were found the skeletal remains of over 40 individuals of both sexes and all ages, over 100,000 items of crude stone tools, and layer upon layer of ashes. They date back to 700,000 years ago and belong to the Old Stone Age.

Archaeologists also found a human habitat at Banpo Village in the Yellow River Valley near modern Xian. Carbon dated to 6000 years ago, it had an estimated population of 400 to 600 people. Their dwellings were built in half-pits covered with steep thatched roofs, they grew millet as their main food crop, and they kept sheep, goats, pigs, and dogs. They used stone tools and stone weapons. They were a people who had made the transition from the Old Stone Age to the New Stone Age and from hunting and gathering to agriculture and animal husbandry. They probably lived in a matriarchal society.

The dawning of Chinese civilization took place between the "Beijing Ape Man" and the Banpo people over a period of thousands of years. Artifacts of this period are rare, and those with symbols on them are not only rare but also difficult to decipher. Consequently, the picture they present is very murky.

Fortunately, these primitive ancestors of the Chinese were storytellers. Their stories were passed on by word of mouth from generation to generation, and later put down in writing by scholars. We call these stories myths. Myths are distorted reflections of the real-life experiences of our primitive ancestors and their attempts at making sense of it all. Their knowledge and understanding of things were scrappy and incoherent, and they used their imagination to fill in the gaps. They created gods, godlike men and women, and part-human and part-beast or -bird figures who control everything in their universe. However inadequate, these myths provided people with a semblance of order in an otherwise chaotic, dangerous, and incomprehensible environment that threatened their very existence.

Savvy historians can extrapolate a wealth of information from these myths, and shed light on China's murky prehistoric past. The central figures of the myths are called "culture heroes"; they are characters who represent entire developmental stages of human culture.

Chinese mythology has a "creation myth" just like other civilizations. In it, Pan Gu is the creator of heaven and earth. When he dies, his breath becomes wind, his voice becomes thunder, his left eye becomes the sun, his right eye becomes the moon, his limbs become mountain ranges, his blood becomes creeks and rivers, and his muscles become farm land. Nuwa Shi stands out as a female. She takes yellow clay to make the first humans in her own image, and then gives them male and female identities. Other "culture heroes" teach the people to hunt, fish, and domesticate wild animals; build treehouses; or make fires and cook food. Shennong Shi is the superhero. He enjoys the lofty title of "Immortal Patron of Agriculture" for introducing farming to hunting and gathering people, and teaching them to make farm tools and clay pots.

Dynasties and the "Dynastic Cycle." Traditionally, the Chinese structured their chronology by dynasty. A dynasty is a period of time when a sequence of members from the same family rule. The Chinese also employ the term "dynastic cycle," which means the repeating pattern of the rise and fall of one dynasty after another. Since history never repeats itself in exactly the same way, the dynastic cycle should be seen as a pattern with variations.

These terms may be less than scientifically accurate. But as tools, they are useful in structuring a narrative and in tracking time, events, regimes, and significant changes.

In traditional historiography, the mythical "culture heroes" are followed by the "Three Kings" of Yao, Shun, and Yu. They are allegedly elected king by their clan for their outstanding character and achievements. But Yu, who is elected king on his merit of saving his people from a great flood, passes his throne to his son Qi instead of giving it up to an elected successor. The Yu-to-Qi succession is from father to son. It ends the system of electing leaders, and launches the system of hereditary dynasties. Henceforth, birth, not merit, determines who is to rule. Qi's Xia Dynasty is China's first dynasty in traditional historiography. However, some modern historians are willing to use it only as a working hypothesis until solid physical evidence is found.

China in the Bronze Age: The Xia, Shang, and Western Zhou Dynasties

There were two major Stone Age cultures along the Yellow River: the Yangshao and Longshan cultures. They later merged, and their settlements developed into towns and cities surrounded by thick walls. The people of late Longshan cities produced fine pottery and bronzes, and cut characters into animal bones for divination purposes (oracle-bone characters). It was these people who ushered Chinese civilization into the Bronze Age.

The people of the pre-historic Xia Dynasty continued to use stone or wood to make knives, fishhooks, and spearheads, but they also began to use crude bronze and to build primitive irrigation projects. These are indications that they were in a stage of transition from the largely agrarian New Stone Age to an increasingly stratified civilized Bronze Age. Their family structure was also evolving. Patriarchy gradually replaced matriarchy while monogamy replaced polygamy. The nuclear family with a male head of household was becoming the basic unit of society as the status of women began to decline.

The Shang Dynasty (ca. 17th–11th centuries BCE) left us with a wealth of knowledge based on solid physical evidence. A significant historical discovery was made in 1899 when a Chinese scholar, walking into a traditional Chinese drugstore, noticed that the clerks were grinding up some flat pieces of bone to sell as medicine. Remarkably, he observed that the bones were inscribed with an archaic form of pictographic writing. These bones were known as "dragon bones" or "oracle bones." Their source was traced to modern Anyang, and scientific excavations followed. Now known as the "Shang Ruins," the site is the remains of a walled city that was the capital of the Shang Dynasty for its last three centuries. Buried underground are the graves of its last 12 kings, as well as palaces, ancestral temples, clan settlements, sacrificial pits, markets, and craft workshops. It has also produced huge collections of "oracle bones."

Shang civilization has three distinguishing features: bronze metallurgy, writing on oracle bones, and the emergence of clearly definable social classes. Bronze appeared in China around the twenty-first century BCE, likely introduced from Central Asia. The Shang people became superb Bronze craftsmen, and the beauty and sophistication of Shang bronzes have never been surpassed in quality. Shang bronze symbolizes Shang civilization, and lends its name to an entire age—the Bronze Age. But bronze did not contribute directly to the increase of Shang's agricultural productivity, for its use was generally limited to making weapons and ceremonial vessels, because of its rarity and prohibitive cost. The Shang king was both the supreme secular ruler and the high priest. His power tended to be absolute. He relied on a state machine and a strong army to maintain his rule. He had the capacity to field an army of 3000 to 5000 strong.

Shang society divided people into social classes: the king, the aristocrats, the government officials, the warriors, and the multitudes of peasants and slaves. The divide between the upper and lower classes was sharp and wide. The Shang people developed a rudimentary calendar based on the movements of the sun, the moon, and the stars. They had the concepts of day, month, and year. A year was divided into 12 months, and a month into 30 days. They also made the first recorded observation of an eclipse.

These ancient people lived in constant fear of the terrifying forces that surrounded them—thunder and lightning, flood and drought, frigid winters and scorching summers, disease and plagues, giant snakes and wild beasts, and war with neighboring tribes. They saw ghosts and spirits in everything. They believed in "afterlife" and buried articles of value and everyday use with their deceased owners. Their wide range of deities included "Heaven," their early leaders and ancestors, as well as forces of nature. They believed that the gods controlled the forces of nature, the fertility of the land, the growth of crops, and the fate of humans. They also believed that the gods were persuadable. Accordingly, they diligently staged elaborate religious ceremonies to pray to their gods to court their favor. Archaeologists have found at a single site the remains of 300 to 400 men and women who were killed in a sacrificial ritual. The Shang people were notorious for using human sacrifice and out-of-control drinking.

The diviner of a tribe was the mediator between humans and the gods and spirits. He frequently communicated with the gods in a divination ritual: He would take questions from people of importance, cut the words into a flat bone, heat up the bone over a fire till it cracked and produced a pattern of lines, and then he or the king would "read" and interpret the cracks. The "oracle bones" are usually turtle shells or cattle collarbones. They contain mostly questions that relate to the weather and crops, war and peace, the health of the king and the childbirth of his wives, even someone's toothache. They only occasionally contain answers, interpretations, or the outcome of a prediction. They also contain the names of virtually all the Shang rulers and the dates of many eclipses. The pictographic writing on oracle bones and bronzes shows that the Shang people had already developed a sophisticated writing system. The Shang characters have such a striking resemblance to modern Chinese characters that an educated modern Chinese person can take a fair shot at the meaning of some of them.

Many concepts that existed in Shang thinking would evolve to dominate Chinese thinking in the future. For example, they believed in a deity called "Heaven" or the "Deity Above," and that he had installed the Shang king and given him the "Mandate of Heaven" to rule; hence, the title of the "Son of Heaven" for the ruler of the land. This linking of the ruler to Heaven would give astronomy a special place in traditional Chinese thinking. And since the ancestors of major tribes were often elevated to the status of gods and worshiped, "ancestor worship" was prevalent in traditional Chinese culture as well.

Traditional accounts of late Shang portray a series of ignorant, incompetent, and cruel kings. They launched wars they could not win, and instigated rebellions they could not suppress. As the dynasty became drained of its vitality, conditions were ripe for one dynasty to fall and another to rise.

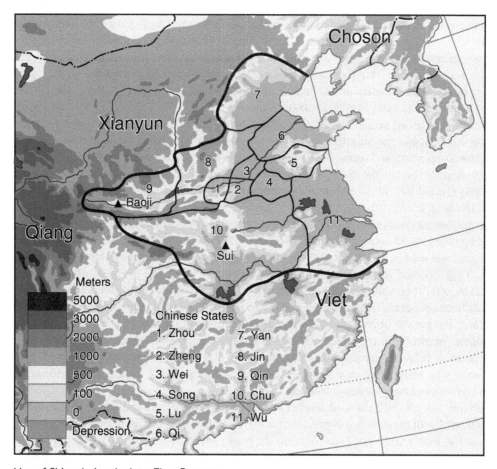

Map of China during the later Zhou Dynasty.

The rising star was the Zhou clan. It was originally a small clan located in backward regions along the Wei River west of the Shang domain, but it gradually grew in strength and size. Its king saw an opportunity in the weakness of the Shang, and successfully led his army in the capture of the Shang capital. He founded the Zhou Dynasty (1046 BCE–221 BCE), and set up his capital near modern-day Xian. He declared himself the "Son of Heaven," and justified his seizure of power on the grounds that Heaven had stripped the Shang king of the "Mandate of Heaven" for his wickedness, and bestowed it on him for his virtue. Future rulers of all stripes and colors down to the twentieth century would all make a similar claim.

Early Zhou Dynasty is characterized by its full-fledged feudal system. The "Son of Heaven" headed a clan-centered, hierarchically structured government and society. He was the supreme ruler of the state, the supreme commander of the army, the chief priest, and the owner of all the lands and populations within his territory. He staked out the best lands to be his own domain, and exercised direct control over it. He granted lands to his family and loyal followers, making them aristocrats. The aristocrats had their own domains and enjoyed considerable autonomy therein, but they were required to pledge their loyalty to the king, and funnel taxes, labor service, and troops to him. The cultivators of the land worked on land that belonged to the king and lords, paid their taxes in kind, and did labor and military service.

The Zhou king built an elaborate centralized system of government to govern his vast and complex kingdom. He laid down detailed rules for the ranking of the nobility and government officials, primogeniture, farming, criminal law, army composition and discipline, and social rituals and etiquette. Improved farming technology contributed to increased crop yield and population growth. Commerce, especially barter trade, also increased.

The Zhou people were more enlightened than their Shang predecessors. Belief in ghosts and witchcraft had lost some of its sway. Human sacrifice had become less common. Schools were set up for the education of the children of the elite. The content of education included morality, rituals and etiquette, and practical skills. It was during this time that some of China's most important classical works were written, and they would become a major source of Confucianism.

A natural tension existed between the agricultural Han Chinese and their nomadic neighbors. When the ethnic Chinese were strong and united, they would forcibly push back the nomadic tribes, and bring their grasslands under agricultural cultivation. And when the nomadic tribes were strong, they would launch looting and killing raids on the sedentary Han Chinese (a term typically used to indicate ethnic Chinese people, who constitute more than 90% of today's Chinese population). This would be a recurring pattern over the millennia. In general, the sedentary lifestyle of the farmers made them poor soldiers, while the rough-and-tumble lifestyle of the nomadic tribes made them much better warriors.

China Enters the Iron Age: The Eastern Zhou Dynasty, 770–221 BCE

A non-Han nomadic tribe captured and sacked the Zhou capital and killed its king. The succeeding Zhou king relocated his capital from near modern Xian eastward to Luoyang. This move marks a divide between the Western and Eastern Zhou Dynasties. As well, the use of iron appeared in China in the eighth century BCE. It was far superior to bronze for making tools and weapons, and it was readily available and inexpensive. Farmers began to make affordable iron tools, such as plowshares, hoes, shovels, and picks that were hard, strong, and good at holding a point or blade. And when they harnessed a powerful ox to an iron plow, they could open up virgin land, dig deep pits and furrows, and create waterways for irrigation and drainage. It was an agricultural revolution. As a result, agricultural production reached new heights and population growth followed. Iron also made agriculture more practical in the more difficult terrain of central and southern China, while more regular rainfall reduced the necessity of elaborate irrigation systems of the North China Plain.

> The **relocation of a capital** would happen during many dynasties. It was usually prompted by one of two factors. One was to escape raids and encroachment by nomadic tribes, which usually came from the north and the west. The second was to move to a region of greater natural resources, greater wealth, or a larger population, which was often to the east and the south. In either case, the new capitals would be to the east or south of the old one. Hence, in chronological order, Western and Eastern Zhou, Western and Eastern Han, and Northern and Southern Song.

The agricultural revolution provided surplus food and goods, which were traded on the market. Lively trading created a demand for a larger volume of currency, so iron coins were added to copper coins to meet the demand. The flow of goods from one region to another increased the wealth of all parties involved and improved their standards of living. Small, closed, and self-sufficient communities began to reach out and interact with others. These factors generated a commercial revolution.

The dramatic increase and spread of wealth across the land upset the old balance of power. The "Sons of Heaven" of the late Zhou Dynasty watched haplessly as power slipped from their hands. They would never be able to reestablish the kind of centralized authority enjoyed by their predecessors. As their power declined, their vassals (aristocrats and local lords) asserted ever-greater regional autonomy. Soon the vassals were only paying lip service to the "Son of Heaven," who now ruled only in name. The feudal system was in a state of disintegration.

The regional powers, now free of the restraints placed on them by the Zhou king, began invading each other's territories. But they were sitting on volcanoes of their own, for their subordinates were also scheming to topple them. Consequently, this was a time marked by extreme examples of intrigue and violence within and between the powerful regional warlords. Out of a hodgepodge of big and small warlords fighting for control of land, population, and hegemony, seven hegemons emerged standing tall and strong. They headed regional states, not city-states, where they built centralized monarchies. These emerging hegemons were called the "Seven Overlords of the Warring States," who launched the Warring States Period, ca. 500–221 BCE.

Chinese who lived in times of declining central authority have never had anything good to say about their times, and historians have traditionally considered them bad times. But history has shown that, while they have their terrible downsides, the absence of a stifling central authority can also create an environment that induces great outbursts of energy and creativity. Late Zhou is a case in point.

The Golden Age of Classical Chinese Philosophy: Confucianism,

> Confucius believed that humans are good by nature, and "the love of humanity" constitutes the core of Confucianism.
> Legalists believed that "humans are evil by nature, and goodness is artificial." —Xun Zi
> Daoism taught, "Heaven and earth are unfeeling; they treat all things with indifference. The sage is unfeeling; he treats the multitudes of common people with indifference." —Lao Zi

Daoism, and Legalism

The profound changes introduced by the use of iron destroyed the old order, and created a new reality that was chaotic and brutally competitive. People felt an urgency to find answers to the life-and-death questions of how to survive in this new environment. This very practical need fueled the "Golden Age of Classical Chinese Philosophy." It is described as a time when "a hundred flowers bloomed and a hundred schools of thought contended." Men motivated by all kinds of purposes stepped forward with all kinds of answers. They were not nerdy men living in ivory towers. Most of them were hard-nosed realists. They combined philosophy, statecraft, and common sense, often combined with great literary skill, to provide real answers to the real challenges of the day. This was the time when China's three main schools of classical philosophy took shape.

Kong Zi and Confucianism

Kong Zi founded the Confucian school of philosophy, which is a comprehensive ideological system that embraces his thinking on virtue, politics, history, historiography, aesthetics, and education.

He created a sociopolitical vision that was based on an idealized "Golden Age" of the Western Zhou period, and his lifelong ambition was to restore the stability and harmony of that distant and idealized past.

Confucius. *Source:* DEA PICTURE LIBRARY/Getty Images.

Kong Zi (aka Confucius, 551–479 BCE) was born in the State of Lu, just downriver from the "Cradle of Chinese Civilization." He learned to read and write as a child, but suffered from poverty because his father died when he was very young. As an adult, he played music at funerals, which was considered a very demeaning vocation at the time. Later, he became a petty official whose duty was to maintain social order and pursue thieves and robbers.

But he had great talent and ambition. He studied the Zhou classics and developed a vision of an ideal society. He traveled from state to state, seeking the ear of men in power to promote his vision. Advocating the rule of virtue and benevolent governance was a hard sell in a land ravaged by war. No one took him seriously, although some regarded him as a sage.

Disillusioned with politics by age 68, he remained unshaken in his idealism. He rededicated the remaining years of his life to education. He became a private teacher, taking students regardless of their social status. He tutored them in the "six arts": morality and rituals, music and poetry, archery, horsemanship, reading and writing, and mathematics. He allegedly had 3000 students over the years, 70 of whom became prominent.

At the core of his philosophy is the concept of "benevolence," which he defines as "the love of humanity," which is supported by the concepts of "hierarchy" and "reciprocity." His ideal family is headed by a father who has the responsibility of caring for his family, while other family members have the duty of showing filial respect to him, and caring for one another. His ideal state is modeled on an expanded family. The ruler is the head of the state, just as the father is the head of the family. He has the duty of practicing benevolent governance, and has the right to demand loyalty from his subjects, who have the duty of being loyal and obedient to him and living in harmony with one another. In this arrangement, one must obey one's superior, but in turn, one has the right to expect guidance and protection from him. Both the family and the state structures are hierarchic, and people in them relate to one another in unequal but reciprocal ways.

According to Confucius, a ruler who is virtuous and competent receives the "Mandate of Heaven" to rule. However, the mandate is conditional and transient: A ruler enjoys this privilege only as long as he provides benevolent governance. Should he fail, the multitudes of common people would suffer, and Heaven would hear their cries, snatch the mandate from him, and bestow it on a deserving successor.

Confucius believed that the "Golden Age" of Western Zhou embodied this kind of virtue, harmony, and stability. And he believed that the only way to restore it was to reestablish a social hierarchy in which each person has a designated place, stays in that place, and dutifully plays his or her designated role. Follow this prescription and all may live happily ever after; violate this principle and society loses its equilibrium and plunges into chaos.

Confucius believed that people are good by nature. However, it takes education to bring out that innate goodness. He divided people into the "superior person" and the "inferior person." The two categories are defined by virtue, not by birth or wealth. Consequently, he put a premium on education, and advocated the principle that "education knows no class distinction." Up to his time, education was the exclusive realm occupied by the elite, but he threw wide open the doors of education to the commoners. Later generations honored him as the "Model Teacher of All Time."

His aesthetic thinking required a unity of goodness and beauty (i.e., the integration of literary refinement and political morality). This placed the heavy burden of moral and political functions on art and literature. It caused later rulers to require works of art and literature to be morally and politically "correct."

Confucius focused his attention on people—their relationships to one another and to society. He had little to say about economics or science and technology. And in a time when most people were profoundly influenced by their beliefs in the supernatural, he conspicuously advised them, "Respect the ghosts and gods, but keep at a distance."

Meng Zi (aka Mencius, 372–289 BCE) was a Confucian sage, second only to Confucius. He emphasized a man's duty to his family, his clan, and his country. He was sidelined by conservatives in later times because of his radical idea that the multitude of common people is more precious than the ruler and state, and a popular uprising against a despotic government (*Qi Yi*, or bringing up righteousness) is justified.

Lao Zi and Daoism

Lao Zi (571?–471 BCE), the founder of Daoism, was a contemporary of Kong Zi, and his teachings were collected in the book *Lao Zi* (aka *Dao De Jing*). His focus was on the role of "Dao"—Chinese for "the way." To him, Dao is not a volitional being with a will to intervene in human affairs, but rather a cosmic force, or a set of universal truths or natural laws. He is quoted as saying, "Man is submissive to the Earth, the Earth is observant of Heaven, Heaven is in compliance with Dao, and Dao conforms to nature." His ultimate goal was to achieve harmony between humans and nature and among humans themselves. While Confucius endeavored to create an ideal society through social activism, Lao Zi believed in letting all things take their natural course with minimal human intervention. His core concepts are the "void" (nothingness), "non-action" (to do nothing), and the dialectic (unity of opposites). He used parables to illustrate his abstract ideas. He said, "Nothing is the mother of all things." To illustrate his point, he pointed out that the use of a house is the empty spaces (a void) between the solid walls, just as the use of a wheel is the hole (a void) that holds the axle of the cart. He believed in non-action, asserting, "Dao does nothing, and accomplishes all things." Sow the seed, let nature take its course, and the plant will grow on its own. Whatever one's goal, be it to grow a plant, fight a battle, rule a country, or survive adverse circumstances, the best approach is to let things take their natural course.

In his ideal state, the ruler is content to control a small territory with a small population, and govern by non-action (or laissez-faire). He would discourage education in order to prevent ambition; cuts off commerce and travel to hold back greed and cunning; and keep his subjects bodily strong but mentally ignorant, so they can toil in the fields and live a simple and peaceful life. Thus, the ruler would have no need for active intervention; he can reign by doing nothing.

Lao Zi had a keen sense of how the principle of the unity of opposites applies to all things: light and darkness, male and female, good and evil, high and low, fortune and misfortune. Each exists in relation to its opposite, each is inseparable from its opposite, and each may evolve into its opposite. His idea of the unity of yin and yang, a primitive form of dialectic, lives on as a core concept in modern Chinese thinking.

Legalism: Xun Zi and Han Fei Zi

Xun Zi (313–238 BCE) was a political thinker and writer. He started out as a disciple of Confucius, but parted ways with his mentor over the fundamental issue of whether humans are good or evil by nature. He argues bluntly that "humans are evil by nature; goodness is artificial." On that premise, he established the school of Legalism. His disciple Han Fei Zi (280?–233 BCE) synthesized the teachings of various Legalists to provide a practical blueprint for a Legalist state.

The Legalist goal is to build a "rich country, strong army." But they have no illusions about achieving their goal by promoting personal virtue as is urged by the Confucians, or by doing nothing as is advised by the Daoists. On the contrary, they believe in ruthless activism. Han Fei Zi states that human nature is selfish, so people instinctively "rush toward what benefits them, and flee from what harms them." Therefore, the ruler should make laws that provide rich rewards to those who contribute to his goals, and impose harsh punishment on those who don't; and he should apply those laws equally to all persons, regardless of whether they are aristocrats or commoners, or rich or poor. Thus, the king can enhance his power and achieve his goals. It is noteworthy that the laws are promulgated by the ruler to strengthen his powers, not to limit them.

The overlords of the Warring States were ambitious empire builders. They lived in a constant state of war, and their main goal was to acquire the wealth necessary to build up their armies to win wars. It's not hard to imagine how they contemptuously brushed aside mushy Confucianism and Daoism, and jumped to embrace Legalism as a practical guide to action. They would pursue its goal of "rich country, strong army" and follow its prescript of making harsh laws and vigorously enforcing them.

Suggested Readings and Viewings

Kwang-chih Chang [Zhang Guangzhi], *The Formation of Chinese Civilization: An Archaeological Perspective* (New Haven, CT: Yale University Press, 2002).

Xingcan Chen, *The Archaeology of China: From the Late Paleolithic to the Early Bronze Age* (Cambridge: Cambridge University Press, 2012).

Confucius (2010), dir. by Hu Mei.

Cho-yun Hsu [Xu Zhuoyun], *Ancient China in Transition: An Analysis of Social Mobility*, 722–222 BC (Stanford, CA: Stanford University Press, 1965).

Feng Li, Early China: *A Social and Cultural History* (Cambridge: Cambridge University Press, 2013).

Benjamin Schwartz, *The World of Thought in Ancient China* (Cambridge, MA: Harvard University Press, 1985).

3

China's First Empire: The Qin and Han Dynasties, 221 BCE–220 CE

When the sage rules the state, he does not count on people doing good of themselves, but employs such measures that will keep them from doing any evil.[1]

Historians sometimes join the Qin and Han Dynasties in a continuum, calling it "China's First Empire." There is good reason for doing so: The Qin Dynasty initiated an unprecedented form of centralized bureaucratic government, but was unable to sustain it. The successor Han Dynasty improved on the Qin prototype, making it not only powerful but also sustainable. All succeeding dynasties in the next 20 centuries would adopt the amalgam of the Qin and Han models of imperial government.

The Founding of China's First Empire: The Qin Dynasty (221–207 BCE)

The State of Qin produced one of the "Seven Overlords" fighting for hegemony during the Warring States period but it was weak, backward, and geographically on the fringe of "China Proper." Its king, however, made it a viable contender after he employed Legalist Shang Yang as his advisor and imposed draconian reforms. His descendant, the future Qin Shihuang, continued to carry out bold and drastic Legalist reforms with the assistance of his prime minister Li Si (284–208 BCE) until he had turned Qin into a model of "rich country, strong army." In 10 years of continuous wars, he defeated the other six overlords and unified all of China Proper for the first time in China's history.

Shang Yang (390–338 BCE) was a Legalist who believed that it is agriculture and war that make a nation rich and strong. As advisor to the king of Qin, he carried out reforms to achieve that goal. He rewarded peasants with exemption from labor service for increasing their crop yields and bringing new lands under cultivation, and he abolished aristocrats' inherited privileges and ranked men according to their contribution in war. These reforms naturally incurred the hatred of the old-guard aristocrats. When the old king died, they had Shang Yang executed by quartering: His limbs and neck were tied to five horses, and drawn until his body was torn to pieces.

---

1 Han Feizi, the Legalist school's chief theoretician, provided that advice to prospective rulers of China, as quoted in William Theodore de Bary, comp., *Sources of Chinese Tradition*, vol. 1 (New York: Columbia University Press, 1960), p. 127.

Asia Past and Present: A Brief History, First Edition. Peter P. Wan and Thomas D. Reins.
© 2021 John Wiley & Sons, Inc. Published 2021 by John Wiley & Sons, Inc.

Timeline: Qin and Han Dynasties and the Era of Division, 221 BCE–581 CE	
221–207 BCE	Qin Dynasty.
390–338 BCE	Shang Yang: Legalist prime minister to the king of Qin before unification under Qin Shihuang
284–208 BCE	Li Si: Legalist prime minister under Qin Shihuang
259–210 BCE	Ying Zheng, who becomes Qin Shihuang in 221 BCE as he unifies China, constructs the Great Wall, and gives China its name from the name of the State of Qin
207 BCE–220 CE	Han Dynasty: embraces the Qin administrative system but tempers its tyrannical methods by adopting Confucian moral principles, creates the imperial examination system for bureaucratic civil service applicants, and gives the Chinese people their name, Han Ren, or Han people (i.e., Chinese people)
256–195 BCE	Commoner Liu Bang becomes Han Gaozu, the founding emperor of the Western or Former Han Dynasty at Chang'an/Xian
179–104 BCE	Thinker Dong Zhongshu revises classical Confucianism to enhance the status of the emperor; Confucianism becomes the official ideology of dynastic China
156–87 BCE	Liu Che (aka Han Wudi, or the Martial Emperor) launches successive wars against China's neighboring nomadic tribes
145–86 BCE	Sima Qian, founder of China's traditional historiography and author of *Records of the Grand Historian*
81 BCE	Salt and Iron Debates discuss the role of government in the economy
9–23 CE	Xi Dynasty under reformer Wang Mang briefly supplants Han Dynasty
25–220	Eastern or Later Han Dynasty rules from Luoyang
220–581	Period of Disunity begins after the fall of the Han Dynasty
220–265	Three Kingdoms period
265–317	Western Jin
265–420	Eastern Jin
317–581	Northern and Southern Dynasties
581–589	Reunification of China under the Sui Dynasty

As the supreme ruler of the country, he created a brand-new title for himself—Qin Shi Huangdi, which means "The First Emperor of the Qin Dynasty." The implication of the title was that his descendants would rule from generation to generation until eternity. He also created an unprecedented form of government: It centralized all power in the hands of one man—the emperor. Earlier, the Zhou "Son of Heaven" had direct control only of his own domain, while local lords enjoyed autonomy within their domains. But Qin Shihuang set up a centralized government bureaucracy that reached from the imperial court down to the county level, staffed it with officials he appointed and dismissed at his pleasure, and made laws that they enforced across the land. For the first time in its history, China had one ruler who exercised personal, direct, and total control over the entire population and territory. He had ended feudalism in its classical sense. The totalitarian bureaucratic state of empire was in; the semiautonomous feudal state was out.

秦始皇

Qin Shi Huangdi (259–210 BCE). *Source:* Album / Alamy Stock Photo.

A wealthy and influential merchant class emerged from the agricultural and commercial revolutions of the Warring States period, and they began entering politics. Lu Buwei (?–235 BCE) was one of them, and he was deeply involved in Qin politics. When the Qin king died, Lu became regent to the 13-year-old boy king. The able and ambitious boy king grew up in Lu's shadow, and felt disgraced. He banished Lu as soon as he was officially crowned at age 20. Lu, out of fear, committed suicide in exile.

The Qin Empire had started out as a mishmash of seven formerly independent states that each had its own set of standards. But the emperor needed uniformity to ensure the smooth operation of his state machine across the extent of the empire. So he made laws to establish nationwide standards for everything. His laws established standards for the measurement of length, weight, and volume. He imposed a single monetary system and a single style of character writing. He ordered the building of a network of roads that radiated outward from the capital to all corners of the empire, and conformed to one single standard of width. This enabled him to ride in his carriage on his numerous inspection tours to all parts of the country, to send his mounted messengers to deliver his orders to anyone anywhere, and to dispatch his troops to crush any rebellion.

Chinese history was plagued by perennial conflict between the Han Chinese and their non-Han neighbors. The Han Chinese were an agricultural people. They had the propensity of expanding into neighboring territories, but as a sedentary people they were also vulnerable to sudden attack. Their non-Han neighbors, on the other hand, were nomadic tribal people who were capable of launching lightning-fast raids either to defend their territories or to loot and kill. The Xiongnu, who roamed the steppes of Mongolia and Russia to the north of China, were the most feared of the nomadic tribes. To put an end to this threat, Qin Shihuang dispatched a force of 300,000 troops to drive them farther north.

To keep the nomads out, he ordered the building of the Great Wall. It was a project of unprecedented scale. But his absolute power enabled him to muster the human and material resources of the entire nation to drive toward that single goal. The completed Great Wall ran across China's northern frontier, providing vital protection for the Han farming populations against nomadic attack. It would be renovated and extended in future dynasties.

Qin Shihuang was a bold and ruthless reformer and innovator. Confucianism required its followers to advise a ruler on the principles of benevolence and status quo, even if speaking out put their lives at stake. Qin Shihuang was certainly guilty of violating those principles, so the Confucian scholars bravely criticized him, thereby incurring his wrath and getting themselves executed. The emperor was adamant on having uniformity in thinking, just as he required uniformity in everything else. So he outlawed Confucianism, and confiscated their texts and burned them. He also rounded up over 460 Confucian scholars who stubbornly clung to their principles, and buried them alive. Henceforth, students of the land would be permitted to study only such practical subjects as farming, medicine, divination, and the official history of Qin, and to do so only under the tutorage of government officials.

Qin Shihuang had created precedents for two strains in China's political tradition. One, educated people imbued with Confucianism would see it as their inescapable duty to speak out on issues concerning the well-being of their country and people, even at the risk of their lives and fortunes. And, two, the rulers would resort to banning and burning books and persecuting dissidents in an attempt to control people's thinking. This dual tradition repeatedly asserted itself down to modern times.

Li Bing and the Dujiang Dikes. Li Bing and his son were put in charge of building an irrigation network to water the farmlands of the Chengdu Plain in 256 BCE. The project included drilling a tunnel through a mountain range to channel water from the Min River on its western slope to the farmlands on its eastern plains. How could they manage such a gigantic project without modern machinery?

Li Bing's peasant workers began by digging a cave into the side of the mountain with hand tools, piling firewood in it, and starting a fire to produce an intense heat. When the temperature of the surrounding rock reached its peak, they would throw cold water on the burning hot rock. The sudden drop in surface temperature would cause the rock to crack and collapse. Again with hand tools, they would smash and remove the cracked rocks. By repeating the process, they eventually reached the other side of the mountain range, leaving behind them a long tunnel.

The Dujiang irrigation system has been watering the Chengdu Plain for the past 2000 years, and it continues to do so.

Legalism was not all about war and persecution. Its goal was "rich country, strong army." But Qin Shihuang's numerous wars, huge construction projects, and extravagant lifestyle consumed enormous amounts of human and material resources. To furnish his coffers, his government mercilessly pushed for increased production as well as increased tax and labor service.

The burden fell especially heavily on the backs of the peasantry. When the burden became unbearable, the peasants rose in armed rebellion. The outbreak of peasant revolt in the declining stages of a dynasty would become a recurring event throughout Chinese history. It is a sure sign of the pending downfall of a dynasty. Qin Shihuang died in 210 BCE on one of his many inspection tours of his empire. Court intrigues and assassinations followed in a power struggle. His second son became emperor but was killed by one of his courtiers only two years into his reign. That was the end of the Qin Dynasty. Qin Shihuang had created the title *Shihuang* for himself, implying that his descendants would reign till eternity. In fact, his dynasty lasted for only 13 years. But the government structure of a centralized bureaucratic empire he invented served as a model for dynastic China for the next 20 centuries.

Qin Shihuang had two additional gargantuan civil engineering projects: the construction of the Eh Fang Palace and his massive mausoleum (the site of the terra-cotta army). He intended his mausoleum to be a place where he would dwell and continue his rule after death. But it was burned, ransacked, and forgotten by history soon after his death. Then in 1974, a peasant digging in the fields discovered signs of it by accident. It is still only partially excavated, but the portion that is unearthed is enough to inspire awe with its thousands of lifelike terra-cotta warriors and horses, numerous weapons, many bronze war chariots, and finely crafted luxury goods. The excavation has touched only a small portion of the massive mausoleum, leaving the rest for a later date when funding and technology can ensure better preservation.

The Chinese are deeply ambivalent about Qin Shihuang: They admire him for the unparalleled ability he showed in unifying the country and making it rich and strong, but they abhor the brutal means he used to achieve his ends.

Scholars have struggled with the question of why China was able to create such a sophisticated, powerful, and stable government so very early in its history. One tentative answer is that it was simply a matter of necessity. For China faced two existential challenges throughout its history: (1) an unruly Yellow River, and (2) perennial conflicts with its nomadic neighbors. Both challenges called for a centralized government capable of bringing together all human and material resources to deal with those life-and-death challenges. They argue that, had China not had such a form of government, it would not have survived.

The Han Dynasty (206 BCE–220 CE): The Consolidation of China's System of Empire

One can seize the throne on horseback, but can one govern on horseback too?
—Lu Jia

The collapse of the Qin Empire left a power vacuum. Various interest groups jumped into a frenzied struggle to seize the throne. Liu Bang emerged from the scramble on top, and founded the Han Dynasty. The Qin–Han succession would become a pattern: The founder of the earlier of the two dynasties proved to be an exceptionally competent man who employed the most ruthless and cunning means to defeat his rivals, unify the country, and reestablish order. His dynasty then collapsed after his death, the incompetence of his successor son, and infighting among civilian and military officials. The Qin dynasty lasted 15 years. The founder of the next dynasty – the Han, whose name now identifies ethnic Chinese – took advantage of the accomplishments of the earlier regime, adopted a more measured approach to governance, and succeeded in building a stable dynasty that lasted more than four centuries.

Emperor Liu Bang (aka Han Gaozu, 256–195 BCE) is considered one of the most able, though not one of the finer, emperors in Chinese history. He started life as a village hoodlum and petty government official, and rose to the top by means of vision, cunning, brutality, and sheer brazenness. He employed men who were humble by birth like himself and had fought with him in founding his dynasty, but then got rid of them when he became suspicious of their loyalty. His dynasty was one of China's longest-lasting and became the model for imperial government down to the early twentieth century.

Liu Bang had shown a disdain for Confucianism during the war years when he was fighting to seize the throne. But when he was firmly seated on the throne, his advisor cautioned him that he could seize power on horseback (by the use of force), but could not govern a nation in the same manner. In other words, the Legalists' naked reliance on greed and fear was an inadequate ideology to sustain a great empire. Liu Bang and his immediate successors took to heart the lesson of the quick demise of the Qin Dynasty, and developed an eclectic state philosophy that merged Confucianism, Legalism, and Daoism.

Confucianism appealed to any sitting emperor, because of its vision of a ruler of absolute power positioned at the pinnacle of a hierarchically structured government, commanding a bureaucracy staffed with loyal and educated officials, shepherding a population of loyal subjects dutifully going about their business as scholars, bureaucrats, soldiers, peasants, artisans, and merchants in obedience to him and in harmony with one another. Daoism provided the philosophical underpinning for statecraft. And Legalism remained essential with its practical blueprint for promoting a supreme ruler and building a bureaucracy by which the ruler can make strict laws and enforce them ruthlessly. The Legalist means are harsh, but they work, and their amorality can be balanced by Confucian compassion and Daoist restraint.

For the next 20 centuries, Chinese rulers would all embrace a variable, eclectic mix of Confucianism, Daoism, and Legalism. Although they may emphasize different elements of this mix, they would always discreetly call it Confucianism, for the brand name of Legalism had become taboo because of its blood-stained association with Qin rule.

Emperor Liu Bang put his emphasis on Daoist restraint, for he understood that what the nation most needed after decades of Qin tyranny and war was a time for the people to recuperate and for the economy to recover. He wisely kept his government small and frugal, refrained from undertaking self-aggrandizing construction projects, and avoided war with his neighbors. This emphasis on restraint enabled him to reduce taxes and labor service, which in turn gave the peasants a chance to live and toil peacefully on the land, and produce the wealth necessary to sustain a great empire. He set an example of government restraint and magnanimity. His successors in the early Han Dynasty followed his example. Together, they laid and institutionalized China's political and intellectual foundations for the next two millennia.

As well, Emperor Liu Bang surrounded himself with men who had risen from the lower levels of society like himself and had contributed to the founding of his dynasty. But he soon suspected them of plotting against him, and cautiously removed them one by one from power. At the same time, he granted to members of his royal family the title of "prince" and private domains, hoping to consolidate his position through family support.

The Martial Emperor Han Wudi (Liu Che, 156–87 BCE) ascended to the throne when China was back on its feet—strong, prosperous, and stable. And he had a matching ambition: He envisioned himself as a highly active emperor ruling over a highly centralized empire of unprecedented wealth and power. He abandoned the earlier emphasis on restraint and frugality and redirect the nation toward greatness.

He needed a new state ideology to support his ambitious goals, and a prominent scholar of Confucianism, Dong Zhongshu (179–104 BCE), served up a new version of Confucianism. His theory of the "Grand Unity" claims that Heaven, the emperor, and humans form a hierarchic unity: Heaven is above the emperor, and the emperor is above all men. From this he extrapolates a fundamental rule for social behavior: The emperor dominates over his ministers, the father dominates over his sons, and the husband dominates over his wife. And his theory of "telepathy between Heaven and man" further claims that Heaven uses omens to inform the emperor of his evaluation of the latter's performance. The Martial Emperor liked this new brew of philosophy and religion, made it the official state ideology, and relegated all other philosophies to a lower tier without banning them.

Dong's theory of the Grand Unity established the supremacy of the Martial Emperor; his theory of telepathy gave Heaven an active role in human affairs, and encouraged the emperor to engage obsessively in elaborate rituals to ingratiate himself to Heaven; and the designation of Confucianism as the supreme ideology of the state ended the free competition of ideas on a level playing field, stifling Chinese thinking through the ages.

The Martial Emperor used his newly elevated status to demand uniformity in thinking. Few men who crossed him would survive. He also founded a state-run university to train students in his version of Confucianism, and selected students who excelled to fill government posts. This institutional innovation led eventually to the creation of a system of imperial examinations for the selection of men for the civil service. Men selected through this process are known as scholar-officials.

Sima Qian (ca. 145–86 BCE) was the greatest historian in Chinese history, yet the exact dates of his birth and death are lost to history. He was the Martial Emperor's court historian and chief of the Imperial Secretariat. But when he dared to disagree with the emperor over an issue, the emperor condemned him to castration. Three years later, he was restored to his former official positions, but he had to live out his life in disgrace. Secretly, he focused his energies on writing China's greatest historical work—*Records of the Grand Historian*. This 130-volume work covers Chinese history from its mythological origins to the Han Empire of his day. It presents the past in biographies of men and women ranging from emperors to commoners, from great generals to merchants, craftsmen, and bandits, and from great scholars to outstanding entertainers. The biographies read like literature for their vivid character portrayal. Best of all, he makes every effort to use primary sources. He was so successful that later emperors would sponsor the writing of the histories of their own dynasties on the same model.

Sima Qian. *Source:* Paul Fearn / Alamy Stock Photo.

At the time of the Han Dynasty's founding, Emperor Liu Bang had granted the title of "prince" and private domains to men of the royal family. These expedient steps were taken from a position of weakness to gain their much-needed support. But now that the Martial Emperor was in a position of strength, the princes' autonomy had become an obstacle to his absolute rule. So he made laws to end their hereditary privileges: He reduced the size of their domains, stripped them of autonomy, and put government officials in charge of their jurisdiction. Simultaneously, he subjected government officials to the oversight of inspectors, and established a standing army under his direct control. The Martial Emperor, in a position of strength, had returned to the Qin model of absolute centralized power.

The nomadic Xiongnu tribes continued to pose a grave threat to China, despite Qin Shihuang's earlier military victories over them. The Martial Emperor was determined to put an end to the threat once and for all. During his half-century reign, he launched over a dozen wars and mobilized as many as 2 million troops against them. He adopted a new strategy of taking the fight to the Xiongnu in the boundless steppes and wiping them out. To do this, he sent envoys into Central Asia on the far side of the Xiongnu to persuade local tribes to enter trade relations and military alliances with China. In the first century CE, his troops successfully drove the Xiongnu tribes from China's northern frontiers. One theory is that the fleeing Xiongnu became the Huns who later terrorized Europe.

The wars to defeat the Xiongnu led to the opening of the Silk Road. This was not a single road, but rather a sprawling network of routes that originated at the Han capital Chang'an, reached westward into modern Xinjiang Province, and continued to connect with Central Asia, India, North Africa, and Europe. It soon became a main artery across Eurasia, facilitating the exchange of commodities, people, and ideas. Much of the contact was indirect, with Persian merchants serving as the major intermediary. China's main export was silk. To wear Chinese silk became a status symbol at the Roman court, and moralists there became alarmed at the way silk dresses revealed a woman's curves. China's main imports were horses, furs, aromatic spices, and jade from Central Asia; and iron, glass, and precious metals from Rome. Eventually China's know-how in making paper, printing with movable type, and manufacturing gunpowder was soon introduced to Central

Asia and on to the West. The religions of Buddhism, Islam, and Christianity traveled eastward to China on this road as well.

The Martial Emperor also established government monopolies to control the manufacture and trading of salt and iron, thereby greatly expanding the role of government in the economic realm. In early Han, salt and iron were traded freely on the market, and taxed by the government. The merchants in the business became immensely wealthy. The Martial Emperor, in the meantime, was constantly running out of funds for his extended wars. So he set up government agencies that monopolized the trade, appointed experienced merchants to manage them, and funneled the profits into his war chest. He also set up a state agency to "buy high and sell low" in the marketplace in an effort to regulate market prices. These measures brought new revenues to his coffers, and had some effect at restraining big landowners and big merchants from manipulating the market to rip off the common people. But the system evolved to make very high officials and very big merchants ever richer at the expense of people at the middle and bottom of society. This accumulation of wealth at the higher end of society eventually reduced government revenues to the point where they could no longer sustain the Martial Emperor's wars.

The new policy had an unintended consequence. Earlier, merchants and their descendants were explicitly banned from holding government office, but this new policy gave them a place in government. Later, high government officials would often double as big merchants and use government power to skew the market in their favor. Government intervention in the economy was something unprecedented, and it was intensely controversial both then and later.

By the beginning of the first millennium, the Han regime had entered a state of total decline. Liu Xiu, a member of the royal family, seized the throne and relocated the capital to Luoyang, east of Chang'an and farther down the Yellow River. This move marked the divide between the Western and Eastern Han Dynasties. (A brief Xin Dynasty separated the two Han administrations.) Eastern Han suffered a perennial problem of endless infighting at the highest echelons of power among the various centers of power: the emperor, the empress's family, the eunuch cliques, and the scholar-officials' cliques. Government was corrupt and incompetent.

True to the pattern of outbreaks of peasant rebellions in the final stage of a dynastic cycle, the Yellow Turban Peasant Rebellion erupted in 184 CE and lasted two decades. Its leader used a religion, the "Path of Peace," to mobilize and organize its followers. He made the bogus claim that Lao Zi was its founder, and called it the Daoist religion. (*Note*: This should not be confused with the philosophy of Daoism.) As desperate peasants flooded its ranks, the rebellion spread like wildfire across China's heartland. After capturing a place, they would kill local officials, and loot and burn in general.

The peasant rebellion posed such a serious threat to the establishment that the various power centers had to put their differences aside and join forces to fight their common enemy. They successfully squashed the rebellion. But in the course of fighting the peasant rebellion, the Han regime was weakened and collapsed in 220 CE. Regional warlords staked out their individual domains and fought one another even as nomadic tribes took advantage of Han weakness to invade China Proper. Thus, China entered its longest period of disunity.

The Qin and Han Dynasties, along with the preceding Xia, Shang, and Zhou Dynasties, shaped the broad contours of Chinese civilization. Their fundamental characteristics have survived to this day. The English words "China" and "Chinese" are derived from the Chinese word "Qin." China's overwhelming ethnic-majority population is called the Han people, a word derived from the Han Dynasty.

Disunity and the "Melting Pot" (220-581)

The fall of the Han Dynasty ushered in a period of disunity that lasted for three and a half centuries. The fact that China's disunity lasted for so long is an indication that the people of this vast area still didn't share adequately in a common culture and economy. But by the time of the reunification by the Sui and Tang Dynasties after the period of disunity, the general population in "China Proper" had been mixed and kneaded into one people who shared all the essential characteristics of modern Han Chinese.

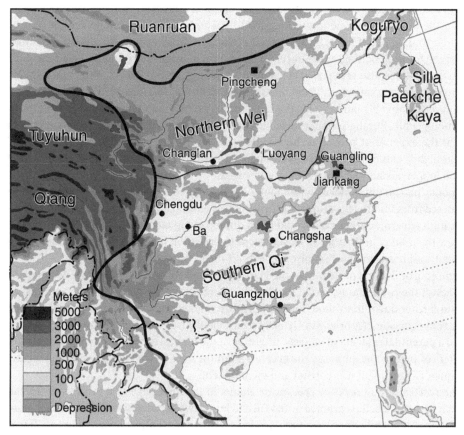

Map of Northern Wei and Southern Qi (ca. 4th-6th centuries).

The main dynasties of the period of disunity were the Three Kingdoms (220–265), the Jin Dynasty (265–420), and the Northern and Southern Dynasties (420–581). The Three Kingdoms occurred at a time when three warlords divided up China Proper. The Jin Dynasty defeated the three kingdoms and reestablished its capital at Luoyang on the Yellow River. But the nomadic tribes had, in the meantime, taken over control of much of China Proper along the borders, and they soon advanced and captured the whole of North China. The Jin Dynasty was forced to relocate its capital from Luoyang to Jinling (modern Nanjing) on the Yangtze River in 317.

This ushered in the Northern and Southern States period, when northern nomadic states faced off with the Southern Han Chinese state across the Yangtze River. While the nomadic tribes took over what used to be Han Chinese territories in North China, Northern Han Chinese fled across the Yangtze River to settle in South China, and drove the local inhabitants into the mountainous regions. This was a huge population shift for the nomadic tribes, the Northern Chinese, and the Southern Chinese.

Northern Wei nomadic tribes founded 16 regimes to rule North China in a merry-go-round for one and a half centuries. Eventually, one of the 16 non-Han regimes, Northern Wei (386–557), unified North China and ruled for another one and a half centuries. It was a nomadic Xianbei dynasty, but its early emperors believed that they could survive only if they abandoned their nomadic ways of life and adopted the Han Chinese ways of life. Their emperor relocated his capital to Luoyang (493) and began adopting Chinese ways on a grand scale. He encouraged, coaxed, and coerced his people into giving up their animal husbandry and roaming lifestyle, and adopt the Han Chinese agricultural way of life. He made them intermarry with Han Chinese, and give up their language and family names in favor of the Han language and names. He also adopted the Han Chinese form of centralized bureaucratic government, its system of tax collection, and its ideology of Confucianism. As a result, a centralized state took shape, their nomadic economy evolved into an agricultural economy, their aristocrats became landed feudal lords, and science and culture flourished. His efforts at Sinicization were so thorough that, by the time of the Sui and Tang Dynasties, the Xianbei people had totally merged with the Han population and disappeared as a distinct ethnic group.

Meanwhile, the great amount of manpower, capital, and know-how the Han population brought with them to South China combined with the vast natural resources of South China to create a flourishing economy. China's economic center shifted from the North to the country's Central and South. It would not be long before the Lower Yangtze Valley would be China's granary, and its commerce and culture would thrive as well.

China became a huge "melting pot" during the four centuries of disunity. All the racial and ethnic groups were thrown in the pot to stew together. They were stirred, mixed, and blended mercilessly into a single stew. The lines of race and ethnicity were blurred in the long years of war and peace, migration and intermarriage, and learning to live and work in close proximity whether they liked it or not. This big heterogeneous mix eventually coalesced into a single multiethnic people that had all the essential characteristics of the modern Han Chinese population. Influence went both ways, but the main thrust was in the direction of the Sinicization of the non-Han peoples.

Chinese have traditionally subscribed to the idea that unity under a strong, centralized government is a good thing, and disunity is bad. But this dictum does not always apply. Take the Han Dynasty, for example. The Martial Emperor had a very strong, centralized, and stable government that controlled a vast territory, a huge population, vital portions of the economy, and even people's thinking, but it produced no outstanding intellectual figures. (Sima Qian wrote his great work, *Historical Record*, in secret.) On the other hand, during the periods of disunity of the Warring States and the Northern and Southern Dynasties, there was a galaxy of intellectual talents. It seems evident that a strong despotic government stifles intellectual creativity, while the removal of the heavy hand of government releases creative energies.

Two outstanding works, one on agriculture and the other on geography, were written during the sixth century. Jia Sixie's *Vital Technologies That Benefit the Common People* is a systematic summery of the Han people's methods of growing grains, fruit trees, and forests; raising domestic animals, fowl, and fish; processing and preserving foods; and utilizing feral plants. Li Daoyuan's *On the Waterways* describes over a thousand rivers in China's network of waterways; it also reports on the towns, cities, and produce along the rivers, and the local customs, legends, and histories. It is of great literary merit as well.

The decline and fall of dynasties throughout the ages have much in common. A manageable list of contributing factors might look something like this:

1) An emperor's personal flaws were often the biggest problem. Since his primary qualification for becoming emperor was birth and not merit, his personal traits—such as his ignorance and arrogance, his extravagant lifestyles and costly construction projects, and worst of all his unnecessary wars—would often inflict irreparable damage to the dynasty. And since there were no institutional checks and balances on his power, or only inadequate ones, his destructive behavior would generally continue until his demise.

2) The existence of multiple centers of power was always a threat to the survival of a regime. These challengers usually came from the queen's family, powerful bureaucrats at the imperial court, frontier generals, and eunuch cliques. The increase of power of these factions would reduce the emperor to a figurehead and induce paralysis at the highest levels of power. Discordance, palace intrigues, wars, famines, peasant rebellions, and nomadic invasions would follow.

3) The polarization of wealth and poverty always intensified as dynasties aged. The rich and powerful social groups would gradually acquire tax exemption status, reducing the size of the taxable land and population, and shifting the tax burden onto the small landholders and peasants. Excessive taxation, backed by inescapable harsh repression, would increase social tensions and shake the foundations of imperial rule.

4) The peasantry would be driven to rise in armed rebellion when the burden of taxes and labor service became unbearable, or when natural disaster (such as drought, flood, and locusts) struck. Most would soon be wiped out by government forces, but not before they had shaken the foundations of the old, dysfunctional regime. Peasant rebellions never managed to create a distinctly new and sustainable regime. A few would succeed in founding a new dynasty, and such emperors would always outdo their traditional counterparts in their brazen tyranny and brutality.

5) The struggle between the agricultural Han Chinese and their nomadic non-Han neighbors was an ongoing problem in Chinese history. When a Han Chinese regime was strong, it would expand and encroach on nomadic territories; and when the non-Han nomads grew in strength, they would raid and invade Han Chinese territories. These struggles did damage to both parties in the long run.

Suggested Readings and Viewings

The Emperor and the Assassin (1998), dir. by Chen Kaige.

Grant Hardy and Anne Behnke Kinney, *The Establishment of the Han Empire and Imperial China* (Westport, CT: Greenwood Press, 2005).

Diana Lary, *Chinese Migrations: The Movement of People, Goods, and Ideas over Four Millennia* (Boulder, CO: Rowman and Littlefield, 2012).

Mark Edward Lewis, *China between Empires: The Northern and Southern Dynasties* (Cambridge: Cambridge University Press, 2008).

Qian Sima, *Records of the First Emperor* (New York: Oxford University Press, 2009).

Yingshi Yu, *Trade and Expansion in Han China: A Study in the Structure of Sino-Barbarian Economic Relations* (Cambridge, MA: Harvard University Press, 1967).

4

The Golden Age of Imperial China: The Sui and Tang Dynasties, 581–960

The emperor is a ship, and the common people are the water. The water can lift the ship, and it can capsize it.

—Li Shimin

The Sui (581–618) and Tang (618–907) Dynasties repeated the earlier Qin and Han pattern of a short dynasty paving the road for a long and stable dynasty to follow. They are sometimes seen as a continuum constituting China's Second Empire. Together, the two dynasties reigned a little over three centuries. The Tang, building on the Sui foundation, became the crowning glory of China's imperial rule.

Timeline: Sui and Tang Dynasties, and Five Dynasties and Ten Kingdoms, 581–960	
581–618	Sui Dynasty reunifies China, constructs the Grand Canal
618–907	Tang Dynasty produces the Golden Age of Imperial China
599–649	Li Shimin, posthumously Tang Taizong, second emperor of China; generally considered the best emperor in Chinese history
Early Tang China	*Great Book of Tang Law*, a comprehensive collection of Tang laws that influences the future legal systems of China and nearby Confucian countries
602–664	Buddhist monk Xuan Zang visits India and brings back Buddhist scriptures and information about the region
624–705	Wu Zetian (Wu Zhao) becomes the one and only Chinese empress
755–763	Non-Han General An Lushan leads rebellion that signals the end of the Tang Golden Age
8th–9th centuries	Golden Age of Classical Chinese Poetry, exemplified in the works of Li Bai (701–762), Du Fu (712–770), and Bai Juyi
878–884	Huang Chao Peasant Rebellion, indicating the impending fall of the Tang
907–960	Disorder: Five Dynasties and Ten Kingdoms

Asia Past and Present: A Brief History, First Edition. Peter P. Wan and Thomas D. Reins.
© 2021 John Wiley & Sons, Inc. Published 2021 by John Wiley & Sons, Inc.

The Sui Dynasty (581–618): Reunification

Emperor Sui Wendi (Yang Jian, 541–604) founded the Sui Dynasty, and he has the distinction of being the principal unifier of China after four centuries of disunity. He was able to achieve this daunting task because the divide between the Han and non-Han racial and ethnic groups were blurred after four centuries of mixing and remixing in the "melting pot." The core population he reigned over was the emerging Han Chinese of today. His multicultural personal background was also of tremendous help to him in dealing with the multicultural reality of his empire. He was Han Chinese by birth, but he once served as a high official in the non-Han Xianbei court, took a Xianbei name, and married the daughter of a Xianbei aristocratic family for his queen. He resumed his Han Chinese name after he became emperor, and required all Han Chinese to do the same.

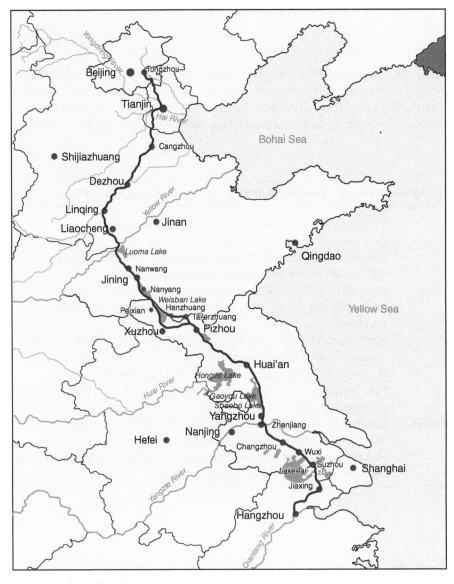

Map of the Grand Canal.

He adopted an eclectic state ideology to match the complex situation he faced. He used Confucianism to extol the power of the emperor and strengthen the cohesion of the population; used Legalism to uphold the law and impose harsh penalties on both government officials and commoners who broke it; and promoted Buddhism, which was already deeply rooted in both the North and the South. He introduced reforms to create a highly efficient centralized government bureaucracy, realigning it more closely with the Qin–Han model of imperial rule.

His son emperor Sui Yangdi (Yang Guang, 569–618) was the second and last emperor of the Sui Dynasty. He was a man of great talent and ability, but his own arrogance, vanity, and recklessness combined to undermine his rule. In addition, his Sui government faced a major economic challenge—a challenge, however, that resulted in the creation of one of China's greatest accomplishments. The country's economic center had been shifting from the Yellow River to the Lower Yangtze River during the preceding Period of Disunity. This created a disconnect between demand and supply: The emperor needed an unending supply of taxes, food, and manpower in the North, where he had his national government and major garrisons, but the sources of most of those supplies resided in central and southern China. Founding emperor Sui Wendi launched the colossal project of building the Grand Canal to connect the north and the south, and his son Sui Yangdi completed it. Eventually, the Grand Canal would be extended to link China's two major river systems (the Yellow and Yangtze Rivers) and China's four major cities (Luoyang, Yangzhou, Hangzhou, and Dadu/modern Beijing).

Sui Yangdi had many other important accomplishments. He supervised the design and construction of the new capital city of Luoyang to replace Chang'an. He took a personal interest in education, and the royal library in Luoyang was the largest in Chinese history. He constructed a national network of royal highways, expanded China's territories, went on a half-year inspection tour to the northwestern frontiers to enhance the prestige of his empire, and reopened the Silk Road for trade.

But his extraordinary achievements came at a price. He had ascended to the throne by stealing the title of "crown prince" from his older brother, and then killing his father. He turned his father's practical canal project into an extravaganza to flaunt his wealth and power. He launched three unnecessary and unsuccessful wars against Goguryeo (an ancient state on the Korean Peninsula). To sustain his wars and construction projects, he had to increase taxes and draft millions upon millions of peasants to serve as soldiers and laborers. To further add to the burden of the people, he lived a lifestyle of extreme extravagance, built elaborate palaces, and traveled in extraordinary grandeur. Quite naturally, the burden he placed on the backs of the peasantry generated peasant revolts and rebellions.

He was so full of himself that he would execute high officials and their entire families for speaking disparagingly of him. His despotic behavior caused widespread fear and hatred. Eventually, the commander of his palace guard captured and strangled him to death in a mutiny.

The Tang Dynasty (618–907): The "Golden Age" of Imperial China

Chaos followed the murder of the Sui emperor. A frontier general of the Sui Dynasty, Li Yuan (566–635), seized the throne and founded the Tang Dynasty. But one of his younger sons, Li Shimin (posthumously titled Tang Taizong, 599–649), soon staged a bloody coup d'état, killing the crown prince and forcing his father to abdicate and pass the throne on to him. He justified his conduct by claiming that the crown prince was plotting to kill him and he was only reacting to the threat.

Emperor Tang Taizong had the nickname "Green-Eyed Lad," which is an unmistakable indication of his Xianbei heritage. And that is not surprising, since the ruling families of both the Sui and Tang Dynasties were racially mixed for many generations.

Chinese historians proudly refer to Early Tang as the "Golden Age" of imperial China. The founding of the Tang regime came at the perfect juncture of history, for the nation was ready for great things. The newly reunified country would soon boast of a population of 90 million (in 755) and a territory of 12.50 million square kilometers (in 669). It would be the most powerful and longest-lasting imperial dynasty in Chinese history.

Emperor Tang Taizong had a proven record of being an outstanding military commander and civil administrator from the days when he was helping his father in the fight to seize the throne. He had also taken to heart the historical lesson of how Sui Yangdi's despotism had cost him his life and his empire. So, despite his exceptional ability, he modestly sought council and encouraged advice and criticism. He declared upon his coronation that he would adopt policies to ban extravagance, tighten expenditures, reduce taxes and labor service, and select frugal and law-abiding officials, in order to allow the common people to recuperate and enjoy an abundance of food and clothing. Many historians honor Emperor Tang Taizong as the "model emperor" of imperial China, mainly for his capacity to accept criticism and advice, and his achievements during the 22 years of his reign.

Tang's Capital Chang'an and the Silk Road

The Tang capital Chang'an (modern Xian) had been the capital of many dynasties, and now Emperor Tang Taizong would personally oversee its redesign on a grand master plan. Designed to impress, the capital was massive, orderly, and magnificent. It was seven times as large as ancient Rome or Constantinople. Surrounded by towering thick walls, it was laid out on a grid and divided into separate zones. The palace was located to the north of the city; to its immediate south were the government buildings; farther south were the residential and commercial zones. The city was shut down at night as soldiers patrolled the streets and enforced curfew. A million residents lived within the city, and another million lived in its suburbs. It was the world's largest metropolis and a hub of international commercial and cultural exchanges.

It was the starting point of the Silk Road, which was first established in the Han Dynasty and was by now a well-traveled thoroughfare that connected China with Central Asia, India, and Europe. People, goods, and ideas flowed along the road in both directions in great volume. Among Chang'an's foreign residents were 30,000 foreign merchants, envoys, students, and monks, who were Persians, Arabs, Jews, and Indians. They brought all the major religions of the world here, including Buddhism, Zoroastrianism, Islam, Judaism, and early Christianity, and established their own houses of worship. Foreign merchants had separate sections where they lived, did business, and worshiped their gods in their own temples. Life in Chang'an was cosmopolitan, sophisticated, worldly, and upbeat.

Government and Law

The Tang Dynasty did not leave good government to the uncertainties of an emperor's personality and moral choices; rather, it put in place institutional structures and procedures to ensure good government. Emperor Tang Taizong borrowed from the Sui model to develop a highly structured national government bureaucracy. It was centralized, balanced, and efficient. It functioned in compliance with a clear division of duties and strict procedures.

First, he enhanced the power of the emperor by eliminating the powerful position of prime minister and dividing his powers among three specialized secretariats, each with a minister and deputy ministers. Each secretariat had its defined duties: (1) to draft laws and orders in the name of the emperor; (2) to review and approve them after the ministers had discussed them and reached unanimous agreement, and the emperor had signed them; and (3) to oversee their implementation. All major issues were required to be discussed and approved in an open joint session of the three secretariats. An order missing any one of the three-step procedure was considered legally incomplete.

The secretariat responsible for implementation had one minister and six deputy ministers responsible for the six government departments in charge of such matters as government personnel (the officials), census and revenue (tax collection), law enforcement, war, and land, water, and engineering. There was also a supervision board and a supreme court. This government structure enhanced the emperor's power by removing the prime minister, but it also checked and balanced his power by creating the other government agencies and procedures.

The 30-volume *Great Book of Tang Law* was an expanded version of the laws promulgated by Emperor Tang Taizong. It aimed for simplicity and leniency, in contrast to the earlier harsh and cumbersome Sui laws. A milestone in the history of Chinese legislation, it was also the model for successive Chinese dynasties, and was instrumental in shaping the legal systems of Korea, Japan, and Vietnam.

Land and Tax Reform

Tang's prosperity and stability owed much to its land and tax systems. Early Tang had a law for the "Equal Distribution of Land." It gave a peasant family "user's rights" to a grant of land based on the number of people in the family, while upholding the principle that the emperor holds ultimate title to all lands. A portion of the peasant's land grant was designated to growing food grain, and it had to be returned to the state when the individual died. Another portion was for growing mulberry trees, elm trees, or flax; this land could be passed on in the family, or sold in the event of a death in the family. Aristocrats would receive large land grants that were inheritable and tax-exempt. Lower-level officials received land grants that would pay for their salary and office expenses.

The government required a peasant family to pay taxes and provide labor service in proportion to the land grant it received. It could demand 20 days of labor service per year without paying. If it needed more, it must reduce taxes in proportion; but it may not, under any circumstance, demand more than 30 days of labor service per year. Later, a new law allowed a peasant family to pay cash in lieu of labor service. This allowed a peasant to remain on the land continuously in order to keep in pace with the rhythmic cycle of agricultural production. Early Tang law taxed the person, but it was later changed to taxing the land. A tax law based on the person required the government to exert itself to tie the peasant to the land. A tax law based on the land gave the peasant more freedom to relocate to find virgin land to till, which would benefit both him and the government.

To make the land and tax laws work, the government had to have full and accurate information on the population and the land. So it undertook the compilation of a "household registry (census)" and a "land registry." With this information in hand, the government knew whether an aristocratic family was holding more land than allowed by law, and whether a peasant family was misreporting able-bodied adults as children or old people in order to avoid paying taxes in full.

To collect, organize, and keep current so much information was a daunting task. The fact that the Tang government bureaucracy was able to accomplish the task demonstrates its ability to organize a huge staff of highly skilled and disciplined men to work over a period of many years to achieve a goal. Succeeding dynasties and other Asian governments would try to duplicate the system with varying degrees of success.

These land and tax laws were well suited to the realities of Early Tang. Long years of war had shrunk the population, leaving large tracts of farm land unclaimed and uncultivated. This gave the emperor a free hand to distribute these abandoned lands to his supporters and landless peasants. But as time passed, conditions changed, and the system fell apart. Powerful families took possession of estates of ever-increasing size, and passed them on within the family. This left the government with an ever-shrinking reserve of land to distribute to an ever-increasing peasant population. Consequently, the government had to give up the system.

Confucianism and the System of Imperial Examinations for the Civil Service

The System of Imperial Examinations for the Civil Service was introduced in the Han, strengthened in the Sui, and fully developed in the Tang. The Tang government, eager to reestablish Confucianism as the state ideology after it had been losing ground to Buddhism during the Northern and Southern Dynasties, founded state-run universities to teach Confucian courses, and strengthened the Imperial Examination System. The exams tested the candidates on their knowledge of Confucian classics and their ability to apply its principles to solve contemporaneous issues. Successful candidates would be reviewed by the ministry of officeholders and appointed to government office according to their ability. These candidates had been trained in the basic skills of reading and writing and the Confucian and Legalist schools of statecraft, and indoctrinated to be loyal to the emperor. It was a meritocratic system: Its measure of a man's qualification for office was his merit, not his birth. It ensured that the emperor would have the best and brightest men in his service. And since a blue bloodline alone would no longer qualify a man for high office, it broke the monopoly on government office by aristocratic families and opened up opportunities to the common man.

Now a direct link connected the mastery of Confucian scholarship and the holding of government office, which also meant access to personal wealth and power. Henceforth, young scholars would flock to state and private academies to study Confucianism with the express purpose of passing the exams and acquiring an appointment to government office. This was a uniquely Chinese route to upward mobility.

In theory, the imperial examination system was open to all men—rich and poor, high and low in birth. In practical terms, it was generally true that only upper-class families could afford to provide their children with an education that would take a decade or two to complete. But there were always the lucky few, who, coming from lowly families, had the talent and opportunity to rise in legendary fashion to the very top. Poor talent could often draw on the wealth of his extended family or of the prosperous local landowners or merchants to pursue an academic and bureaucratic career.

In general, the examination system herded talented and ambitious young men into the bureaucracy in the service of the emperor, and the bulk of the candidates thus recruited would make competent bureaucrats loyal to the emperor. But it had an unintended consequence: A man could fail in the imperial examinations, turn his resentment against the establishment, and join the opposition or even join a rebel force. There would be more than a few such cases.

The "Golden Age" of Classical Chinese Poetry

Early Tang emperors were men full of confidence, which allowed them to view cultural diversity with tolerance. They did not persecute men for what they said or wrote, as did Qin Shihuang in his "literary inquisitions." Instead, they patronized the arts and encouraged exchanges between Tang China and its neighbors. This social-political environment ushered in the "Golden Age" of Chinese classical poetry, and produced some of China's all-time great poets. Even to this day, ordinary Chinese in their everyday life read and quote their favorite Tang poets.

Imperial examinations required the candidates to write poetry. The belief was that their poetry, as well as their handwriting, not only demonstrated their scholarship but also revealed their personal character. This made poetry writing a required course in one's education. Soon every educated man could write poetry. And poetry soon took on a wide range of social functions as well: One would write a poem to mark a special occasion (such as a birthday, wedding, or funeral), to communicate with a friend, to seek the audience of an official, to praise the emperor or the gods and spirits, or as a personal pastime. In some cases, an emperor who was a poet himself would influence social taste by raising the social status of literary men.

China's three all-time best-loved poets appeared in the Tang Dynasty.

Li Bai (701–762) was inspired by Daoism. His poems are free in spirit and dazzlingly colorful and flamboyant. They display a strong sense of individual autonomy expressed in a romantic style that is rich in imagery and imagination. He socialized with people of outstanding talent and status, but never rose in social status because of his idiosyncrasies. He refused to conform to norms of social behavior and indulged in long and heavy bouts of drinking. He is known as the "Poet Immortal."

Du Fu (712–770), unlike the free-spirited Li Bai, was imbued in the Confucian teachings of loyalty to the emperor and compassion for the common people. That made him self-effacing. Most of his poems came at a time when Tang China was falling from the "Golden Age" and into a stage of decline and disintegration. The tensions between his lofty Confucian idealism and the abysmal reality before his eyes define the somber and heavy tone of his poetry. His poems conform impeccably to the strictest formal requirements of classical poetry. His great poetry never brought him worldly gain, and he spent his whole life as a petty government official. He is known as the "Poet Sage."

Bai Juyi (772–846) was an exceptionally successful scholar-official. Some of his poems, like Du Fu's, express a deep sympathy for the plight of the common people. But his most memorable works are two romantic ballads: one about the unfulfilled love of an emperor, and the other about the quiet despair of a scholar-official in exile. He is famed for writing in a colloquial style that is so simple and plain that even an uneducated old woman can appreciate them.

Buddhism

The Tang government practiced religious tolerance. While both Buddhism and Daoism were popular, the royal family increasingly moved from patronizing Buddhism to favoring Daoism, as did the royal family in the early Han Dynasty. Buddhism originated in India and entered China by way of the Silk Road toward the end of the Han Dynasty. The decline of the Han Dynasty discredited Confucianism and created a "belief vacuum," which was fertile soil for Buddhism to take root in. Buddhist teachings that all people are equal, all people can enter Heaven, and all people should love one another had a strong appeal to people who lived precariously in a war-ravaged land. Its belief in reincarnation gave hope to the hopeless. Its cosmology, abstract thinking, and emphasis on spirituality provided welcome relief to Han Chinese from their dry and rigid earth-bound Confucianism. Its rich store of art, literature, and architecture also facilitated its spread. Later, the Kingdom of Northern Wei promoted it vigorously with the express purpose of using it as a tool to shape a national identity distinct from the Confucian culture of the Han Chinese.

This Indian religion propelled China's sculptural art into maturity. At Yungang and Longmen, huge Buddhist statues and temples are carved into the sides of sheer mountains or into the inside walls of grottoes. They represent the highest levels of cultural achievement in ancient Chinese sculptural art and continue to inspire awe in us today.

Dunhuang was located at a crossroad along the Silk Road in the middle of the Gobi Desert that bustled with commercial and cultural activity. Buddhism entered China through this gateway, and spread across the country. In the early twentieth century, a monk accidentally discovered a treasure trove of ancient artifacts in the grottoes at the foot of a local mountain. It was mainly Buddhist manuscripts, ancient books and documents, and exquisite frescoes and sculptures in Chinese and many other languages. It also included writings of popular entertainment, such as poetry, music, and drama. The richness and significance of the deposit have given birth to a new academic discipline—Dunhuang Studies.

Buddhism coexisted with Daoism, and became a broad-based and deeply rooted religion across the country in Tang China. Its followers came from all walks of life—from royalty to commoners, and from peasants to merchants. Buddhist monasteries mushroomed across the country.

In Early Tang, the royal family had a passion for translating Buddhist texts from their original Sanskrit to Chinese. Xuan Zang (602–664), a Buddhist monk, made the arduous round-trip pilgrimage from Chang'an to India, where he studied Buddhism and returned with 567 Buddhist scriptures. The emperor ordered the formation of a "translation bureau" where Xuan Zang and his followers devoted their lives to translating the scriptures. This might be said to be the beginning of China's long tradition of translating foreign-language works into Chinese. His account of his pilgrimage is a complete and systematic account of the history, geography, natural conditions, and local practices of the vast regions that cover today's Xinjiang, Central Asia, Iran, and India. It is a major source of information about the region of that period.

Buddhist monasteries enjoyed royal patronage and exemption from tax and labor service. Men and women entered monastery life in droves, abandoning normal, productive ways of life. This abnormal way of life was unsustainable. Since the government could not reach the monasteries with its taxing arm, it shifted more of the tax burden onto the remainder of the peasantry. This increased tensions across the country—between the government and the peasants, and between the government and the Buddhist establishment. As tensions heightened, Buddhist monasteries and teachings came under harsh scrutiny and attack. Its foreign origin was a favorite target. The emperor cracked down on Buddhism in 845. He destroyed 4600 Buddhist monasteries, confiscated millions of acres of tax-exempt land, and forced 260,000 monks and nuns to return to secular life and productive work. Buddhist influence went into sharp decline.

Fundamentally, this was a power struggle between church and state over control of human and material resources. The fact that the emperor himself was an ardent Daoist devotee could reasonably be suspected of contributing to the harshness of his crackdown. (It is noteworthy that China's religious institutions, unlike their European counterparts, never outranked its political institutions; the emperor and his government were never subservient to the abbots and monasteries.) Buddhist metaphysical philosophy and religious practices would gradually become Sinicized and merge into Chinese culture as an organic part of it. The Neo-Confucianism of the Song Dynasty would be strongly influenced by Buddhist philosophy.

The Tang Dynasty produced China's one and only female ruler of the empire. Wu Zetian (Wu Zhao, 624–705) was the widowed concubine of Emperor Tang Taizong, wife of his son, and empress dowager of his grandson. She first held the reins of power from behind the throne for over 20 years, then openly seized the throne, took the title of emperor, founded her own dynasty, and ruled for another 15 years. In total, she was China's de facto ruler for over 35 years.

She ruled with an iron fist. Her administration crushed opposition by employing spies, merciless and unscrupulous officials, and torture. She stamped out rebellion with troops. She also used favoritism to foster personal loyalty. She expanded the examination system to rope in a new crop of scholar-officials who were beholden only to her, and used them to replace men who had served in previous regimes. Her long reign was stable and prosperous: there were no peasant rebellions. When she was 82, her prime minister mounted a coup that forced her to return the throne to her son and go into retirement. Confined to her quarters in the rear of the palace, she died later the same year.

Historians have attacked her for her non-aristocratic origin, her scheming and cruelty, and her licentious lifestyle. But the most serious accusation was that, as a woman, she dared to usurp the throne, which was the exclusive domain of males. But no amount of mudslinging can deny her success as a ruler.

The Shift of China's Economic Center from the Yellow to the Yangtze River Valley

Over time, wealth and power corrupted the rulers of the Tang Dynasty. They became complacent, extravagant, and indulgent. Scholar-officials in high office and eunuchs close to the royal family formed cliques, and focused their energies on grabbing power and fortunes. The Tang royal court, like the Roman court, began relying on nomadic generals and their troops to defend their borders. One royal court favorite was An Lushan (703–757), a frontier general of non-Han origin. He turned against the court and marched his troops on the capital Chang'an. His troops looted and burned the world's richest city to the ground. Although he was eventually defeated, the eight-year An Lushan Rebellion (755–763) marked the end of Tang's Golden Age.

The government's power and the nation's economy plummeted. Peasant rebellions broke out and swept across the land. Huang Chao (820–884) led the most devastating of them. His rebellion adopted guerrilla warfare, marauding across the country, and wreaking havoc wherever they showed up. They ransacked Guangzhou and killed some 200,000 Arab and Persian merchants who had come to the port to trade. Then they captured the capital city of Chang'an without even laying siege to it, and went on a spree of looting and slaughter, leaving it in ruins again. Now Huang Chao proclaimed himself emperor of a new dynasty, but as is always the case, the rebel army became fractured by internal strife and was crushed by government troops. Huang Chao committed suicide. It is noteworthy that Huang Chao's rebellion championed the idea of "leveling the rich and the poor," which was a big draw to the peasants.

Granted, both rebellions had failed, but just as the Roman Empire was shaken but not toppled by Spartacus' slave rebellion, the Tang Empire was left standing, though on very shaky legs. A string of weak and dissolute emperors soon brought about its total collapse.

Following Tang's fall, China again entered a period of disunion. Large areas of the North came under the rule of non-Han nomadic tribes. This period is known as the period of the "Five Dynasties [in the North] and Ten States [in the South]." Notably, this period of disunity lasted only half a century. In the future, China would continue to go through cycles of unity and disunity, but periods of disunity would become increasingly shorter, indicating a more thorough merging of the various ethnic, racial, and geographical groups throughout the land.

Suggested Readings and Viewings

Charles Benn, *China's Golden Age: Everyday Life in the Tang Dynasty* (New York: Oxford University Press, 2004).

Peter K. Bol, *"This Culture of Ours": Intellectual Transitions in Tang and Sung [Song] China* (Stanford, CA: Stanford University Press, 1994).

Jacques Gernet and Franciscus Verellen, *Buddhism in Chinese Society: An Economic History from the Fifth to the Tenth Centuries* (New York: Columbia University Press, 1998).

Peter Harris, ed., *Three Hundred Tang Poems* (New York: Everyman's Library, 2009).

Bret Hinsch, *Women in Imperial China* (Boulder, CO: Rowman and Littlefield, 2016).

House of Flying Daggers (2004), dir. by Zhang Yimou.

Victor Cunrui Xiong, *Emperor Yang of the Sui Dynasty: His Life, Times, and Legacy* (Albany: State University of New York Press, 2006).

5

The Peaking of Traditional Chinese Civilization: The Song and Yuan Dynasties, 960–1368

Within the empire the security of the state is a cause for some anxiety, and on our borders there is the constant threat of the barbarians. Day by day the resources of the nation become more depleted and exhausted, while the moral tone and habits of life among the people daily deteriorate.[1]

The Song and Yuan Dynasties project the boldest of contrasts. The Song Empire was run by scholar-officials, and it was the least oppressive of all major dynasties. It enjoyed unprecedented economic wealth and cultural sophistication. When we think of traditional China, the picture that is likely to come to mind is that of Song China. But it existed under the constant threat of its numerous nomadic neighbors, and it was eventually conquered by the unstoppable Mongol cavalries. The Mongol conquerors founded the Yuan Dynasty, which was a barbaric alien regime dominated by nomadic warlords.

The Song Dynasty (960–1279): The Epitome of Traditional Chinese Civilization

The government of the Song Dynasty was the least oppressive of all major Chinese dynasties, and it was relatively clean and enlightened. It experienced an agricultural revolution, a commercial revolution, an upsurge in manufacturing and technological inventions, rapid growth in overseas trade, and a renaissance of Confucianism. Its thriving culture is as important to Chinese history as the Renaissance is to European history.

But the Song Dynasty was also a diminished empire. It was the smallest in territorial size of all the major dynasties, hemmed in and bullied by several powerful non-Han states throughout its reign. And the regime suffered from perennial problems of an impoverished government and a weak military.

---

1 Wang An-Shih [Wang Anshi], "Memorial to the Emperor Jen-tsung [Renzong]," quoted in William Theodore de Bary, comp., *Sources of Chinese Tradition*, vol. 1 (New York: Columbia University Press, 1960), p. 414.

Asia Past and Present: A Brief History, First Edition. Peter P. Wan and Thomas D. Reins.
© 2021 John Wiley & Sons, Inc. Published 2021 by John Wiley & Sons, Inc.

Timeline: Song and Yuan Dynasties, 960–1368	
960–1279	Song Dynasty: The epitome of traditional China
1023	Song China is the world's first country to use paper currency
1041–1048	The invention of movable-type printing by Bi Sheng (?–1051)
1069–1085	Reforms of Prime Minister Wang Anshi (1021–1086) attempt to use big government to arrest the decline of the dynasty; he failed
1085–1145	Zhang Zeduan, Song court painter, wins lasting fame for his masterpiece *A Stroll along the River in Spring*
1127	Song capital Kaifeng seized by nomadic State of Jin, ending the Northern Song Dynasty; Song court moves to Hangzhou, creating the Southern Song Dynasty
12th century	Completion of shift of China's economic center from the North (along the Yellow River) to the South (along the Lower Yangze River)
1130–1200	Zhu Xi creates what becomes Neo-Confucianism, which will be the dominant interpretation of Confucianism among educated Chinese
1245?–1330	Huang Daopo: Innovator of technology for cotton growing and processing, leading to a cotton revolution
By 1279	Completion of the Four Great Inventions: compass, gunpowder, paper, and movable-type printing
1279–1368	Yuan Dynasty: China under Mongol rule
1190–1244	Yelu Chucai: Yuan statesman who advises Mongol Emperor Genghis Khan to adopt Han Chinese ways; has limited success
1279–	Cotton revolution stimulates growth of market economy along the Yangze River
1274 and 1281	Two Mongol attempted invasions of Japan; both fail
1280	Chinese mathematician Guo Shoujing (1231–1316) makes a calendar that specifies a tropical year of 365.2425 days, the same as the Gregorian calendar
1313	Wang Zhen (1271–1368) publishes *Book on Farming*, which has 22 volumes and 306 illustrations

The Song Dynasty's founder Zhao Kuangying was the commander of his king's palace guard when a military coup d'état put him on the throne. This personal experience made him deeply distrustful of military generals, and motivated him to take extraordinary precautions to keep them on a short leash.

Zhao Kuangying (927–976) was the founding emperor of the Song Dynasty. Although he was a soldier, he had very subtle ways of enhancing his power. One night after feasting, he brought together his closest buddies who had helped him seize the throne and now commanded his palace guard. He complained to them that he was unable to sleep soundly at night. When asked why, he said that it was great to be emperor, but knowing so many men coveted the throne kept him awake at night. The generals got the message, and submitted their resignations the next morning. True to his word, he married his sister and daughters to them or their sons, and assigned them to positions of frontier generals far away from his capital.

Here's another example. Early in his reign, the emperor held court with his ministers in front of him sitting in chairs. But one day that changed. When one of the ministers referred to a written document when making a report, the emperor asked him to hand him the document. As the minister rose and stepped forward to deliver the document to the emperor, a servant quietly walked up and removed the chair. Henceforth, Song courtiers would stand in the emperor's presence.

Potential threats to his power came from three sources: the military generals, the old aristocratic families, and non-Han nomadic states on China's borders. To deal with the threat coming from the military, he put military generals under the control of civilian officials, and then kept the civilian officials under his personal control. To prevent the generals from cultivating personal loyalty in their troops, he constantly switched the generals around to command different troops. He also restricted local governors' access to troops and financial resources.

He reinvigorated Confucianism and the imperial examination system for the civil service. He set up academies, expanded the scope of the imperial examination system, filled government positions mainly with successful examination candidates, and paid them handsome salaries. The old aristocratic families, complacent from generations of privilege, were unfit for the stiff competition in the examination system; and a fresh crop of officials beholden to the emperor personally soon replaced the old guard in the government bureaucracy.

While enhancing the powers of the civil government, he downgraded the status of the civil officials staffing it. High officials during the Tang Dynasty sat face-to-face with the emperor in chairs as they discussed matters of state. In the Song Dynasty, they were required to stand before him. By the Ming Dynasty, ministers must kneel before the emperor, and by the Qing Dynasty, they must kneel and cast their eyes down to the floor or run the risk of losing their heads.

The above measures weakened the potential challenges coming from the military, the old aristocratic families, and even the new crop of civil officials. They enabled early Song to run an efficient government staffed with scholar-officials, firmly secure control over China Proper, and reduce taxes. The resulting social stability led to a surge in population growth and an outburst of economic energy.

Agriculture thrived in South China. The natural conditions there were ideal for growing crops: higher temperatures, greater rainfall, rich soil, and vast networks of rivers. The government also made unprecedented efforts to encourage agricultural growth. Government and private individuals used the newly improved methods of printing to compile, print, and circulate instructional manuals for agricultural. The focus was on "intensive cultivation," that is, to increase unit output by making greater investments of manpower and equipment. Farmers acquired new strains of crops, improved plowshares, and created more efficient mechanical irrigation devices. Rice was a staple food crop in the South. A superior strain of rice introduced from Vietnam thrived. Per-unit yield kept rising while new lands were brought under cultivation. A big jump in rice harvests gave a big boost to the entire economy.

Manufacturing reached amazing heights. The rich wore silk and the poor wore flax before the cotton revolution occurred, and the production of silk was the pillar of the textile industry. The government owned and operated silk textile plants that had hundreds of looms and thousands of workers. The best of them would have sophisticated machinery powered by water.

Song iron plants had learned to use wood bellows to pump pressured air into a coal-burning furnace to produce the intense heat required to make an iron of superior quality. This new technology encouraged people to build more and more iron mines, smelting furnaces, and casting plants.

The production of porcelain was another major industry. It was used to make both household utensils and artistic objects, and it was an important export commodity. State and private porcelain kilns dotted the landscape across the country. The southeast city of Jingdezhen became famous for being China's "porcelain capital," and continues to hold that title today.

Zhang Zeduan (1085–1145) was a Song court painter, renowned for his paintings of cities, streets, bridges, and boats. His masterpiece, *A Stroll along the River in Spring*, is a scroll that measures 5.28 meters long, and depicts the city and suburbs of the Song capital Kaifeng in the spring. It has 684 persons, 96 animals, 122 rooms and buildings, 174 trees, 25 boats, 15 carts and wagons, and 8 sedans (these numbers vary by source). It is a detailed account of the great variety of commercial and recreational activities of the time. It set a precedent for later dynasties to commission artists to paint similar scrolls, often in exaggerated fashion to extol the peaceful and affluent life of the dynasty.

Paper was in great demand as a result of a flourishing printing and publishing industry backed by a highly developed paper-making technology and the invention of movable-type printing. Artisans set up workshops to produce directly for the market; private cottage industries were numerous.

The need to transport products to the market stimulated the shipping industry. The government ran many shipyards with an annual output of thousands of ships.

A commercial revolution was underway. Markets had already taken shape around the capital city back in the Tang Dynasty, but now they were popping up everywhere around large, medium, and even smaller cities and towns. The Song capital Kaifeng was a booming commercial center where a variety of markets attracted grains from the South, cattle and sheep from the North and the West, seafood from the coastal East, and silk, paper, books, and tea from the South. It also imported fans from Japan, writing ink from Korea, and spices from India. China had trade relations with over 50 countries in Europe, the Middle East, Southeast Asia, and Africa. It also attracted European Jewish immigrants, who mingled with the Han and Hui Chinese (Chinese Muslims) and gradually integrated into their larger populations.

At the time, traders in rice, tea, and salt were the most common. Merchants in precious metals and cotton fabrics were the richest. Restaurants, hotels, and inns were everywhere. Merchants had their guilds, which often had their own restaurants where the merchants met to socialize, exchange information, examine goods, and make deals. There were often performers of song and dance, call girls, and prostitutes in these places.

The commercial revolution expanded the volume of trade, which in turn created demand for a larger supply of currency. In early Song, the main form of currency was copper and iron coins, supplemented by silver ingots. By late Song, the supply of copper coins was falling dangerously behind demand. A group of big merchants sought and obtained government authorization to issue paper currency (1023). Song China became the world's first country to use paper money, and it had the world's largest volume of goods and currency in circulation. (Sweden was the first European country to issue paper money in 1661.) The government soon saw the benefits of having an exclusive right to issue paper currency, and established a monopoly to do so. But its insatiable appetite led to issuing paper money recklessly without any kind of backup reserve, causing runaway devaluation and inflation.

The Song government was in favor of overseas trade. The Silk Road overland to the west was disrupted by non-Han nomadic tribes and states, so the Song government focused on vigorously developing a sea route of the Silk Road. It started at the port city of Quanzhou in southeast China, and followed a winding course to reach Southeast Asia, India, Persia, and the Arab countries, as well as Korea and Japan. Quanzhou was the largest port city in China or anywhere else in the world in its heyday. China's major exports were silks, porcelain, tea, and metals, while its major imports were spices, medicines, furs, horses, glassware, ivory, coral, and precious stones. Eager to prevent the outflow of Chinese cash currency, the government ordered merchants to make payment for imports with silks and porcelains.

As foreign trade expanded, the government set up special agencies to tax and regulate it. Taxes collected on imports and exports became an important source of government revenue.

All major Chinese dynasties follow a similar pattern: They thrive under the first few emperors; then enter a period of stagnation and decline; then they make an effort to rejuvenate through reforms; and when the reforms fail, they head for final decline and fall. The Song Dynasty was no exception. It had adopted a policy of bloating the civil bureaucracy in an effort to maintain social stability. But the upkeep of such a big government was a serious drain on its resources, and it imposed a heavy burden on the peasants, artisans, and merchants. While it contributed to short-term stability, it created the long-term problem of polarizing society, the tensions from which would destabilize society.

To halt the decline of the dynasty, the emperor appointed Prime Minister Wang Anshi (1021–1086) to make institutional reforms in government (1069–1085). Wang devised an elaborate system of reforms with the traditional goal of "rich country, strong army." One measure was to resurvey the land to compile a new land registry, and to recalculate taxes based on the new land registry. This would enable the government to make one's taxes commensurate to one's land holdings. This was fairer tax law, and it put more money into the government's depleted coffers. But it hit big landowners who were accustomed to evading taxes with new taxes. Another measure of his gave the government power to regulate market prices. This reined in speculation, but hurt big merchants who were used to fleecing the buyers by manipulating market prices.

On the whole, his measures achieved to a moderate degree the goal of "rich country, strong army," but they hurt the interests of big landowners and big merchants, who fought back furiously. They used every excuse to attack him, going as far as to blame him for the occurrence of a severe drought.

Wang Anshi's Reforms, 1069–1085

1) Government low-interest loans to peasants
2) Government regulation of market prices
3) Government resurvey of all lands, and recalculation of land taxes to ascertain that title, amount owned, and taxes paid were all true and in compliance with the law
4) Government takeover of the construction and maintenance of waterworks, charging the beneficiary for the cost
5) Conversion of labor service into cash payment, in order to free peasants from disruptive labor service
6) The "Baojia System": a collective-responsibility system that organizes households into units of 10, 50, 500, and so on, making member households collectively responsible for paying taxes, community security, and forming a militia. This system extends government power all the way down to the level of the household.
7) Government appointment of generals to train and command troops; this changed the earlier practice of separating commanders from the troops they commanded.

The reforms also had major flaws: Their implementation was extremely complicated, which opened the door for rampant corruption and general waste and inefficiency. When the emperor who sponsored his reforms died, he was left totally without support and protection. What the reforms had achieved in 16 years of unremitting effort was wiped out in a single year. The great reformer died the next year in despair and anguish. And the Song regime never did solve its chronic problems of an impoverished government and a weak military.

The nomads of the State of Jin invaded the Song, and captured and looted its capital Kaifeng (1127). When they returned to their grasslands a year later, they took in tow the Song emperor and his queen, concubines, sons, and ministers. One of the emperor's sons managed to escape and become the next emperor. He relocated the Song capital to Hangzhou, south of the Yangtze River, far away from the reach of the Jin cavalry. This relocation of the Song capital marks the divide between Northern Song and Southern Song.

Southern Song thrived despite its greatly reduced size, for the relocation of the Song capital was followed by an exodus of panicking Han Chinese people from the North to the South. Population, capital, and know-how flowed from the more developed North to the less developed South. Hangzhou replaced Kaifeng as the nation's political, economic, and cultural center. It became the world's largest city with a huge concentration of wealth and population (1.24 million). To match their wealth, cultural sophistication, and natural beauty, Hangzhou and Suzhou were known as "Heaven on Earth." The shift of China's economic center from the North to the South, begun during the post-Han Period of Disunity and furthered during the Tang Dynasty, was now complete.

Chinese philosophical thinking experienced a second blossoming during the Song Dynasty. Out of it came Neo-Confucianism represented by Zhu Xi (1130–1200). He kept the Confucian core of benevolence, hierarchy, and reciprocity, removed Dong Zhongshu's supernatural rantings, and added elements of Indian Buddhist metaphysics. His landmark contribution was to give classical Confucianism an elaborate systemic structure with rigid detail.

Zhu Xi. *Source: CHU HSI (1130–1200)*. Chinese philosopher. Paper album leaf by unknown artist.

Zhu's social structure is made up of four classes under the emperor: scholar-officials, peasants, artisans, and merchants in descending order. A person's station in life, however, is mobile: One can move up the social hierarchy, with the imperial examination system providing the major channel for social mobility. He relegates women to the confines of the domestic sphere: to bear and rear children and do the household chores, totally subordinate and inferior to men. Divorce and remarriage become taboo. The cruel practice of foot-binding spreads from the upper classes to the lower classes, becoming a nationwide scourge. He requires children to obey their elders in every way. Specific and detailed rules are laid out on how a child should behave with regard to dress, speech, conduct, reading, writing, and food and drink. To act strictly in accordance to one's station in life is made a moral imperative.

The purpose of **foot-binding** was to keep a girl's feet small. The practice began with upper-class families, and spread throughout all classes of society. It lasted for a thousand years, from the Song Dynasty to the Republic of China. When it was banned in the early twentieth century, an estimated 100% of upper-class Han Chinese females and 50% of all Han Chinese females had bound feet.

A girl with natural feet was commonly considered unacceptable as a wife or daughter-in-law. Therefore, parents felt obliged to put their pre-puberty daughters through this inhumane torture. They usually hired a foot-binding practitioner who would break the girl's toes and arches, tuck the broken toes under the broken arches, and wrap the broken foot in layers of cotton bandages. The bandages would stay on for years, preventing the foot from growing normally. The procedure caused extreme pain and left the girl handicapped for life.

An aesthetic explanation for this cruel practice was that walking on delicate little feet enhanced a girl's beauty and sexual appeal. A practical explanation was that it physically prevented a female from leaving the house and neglecting her domestic duties.

The nomadic Mongol and Manchu conquerors of China did not have this tradition. The Manchu Qing Empress Dowager Cixi tried to ban it without success. The Republic of China officially banned it with limited success. The Communist regime finally banned it entirely after 1949.

Zhu's rigid social structure is unnatural and inhumane. To defend his grotesque system, he screams out, "Promote Heaven's principles; wipe out human desire." His interpretation of Confucian classics would be adopted as standard answers in imperial examinations. Neo-Confucianism would be official orthodoxy for the remainder of imperial China.

Science and technology reached new heights in Song China. Substantive improvements were made to China's "Four Great Inventions": the compass, gunpowder, paper making, and movable-type printing. These inventions were used for spreading information, navigating oceangoing ships, and conducting warfare. They had a far-reaching impact on the advance of Chinese civilization, and their introduction into Europe accelerated the West's entry into the Modern Age.

Emperors throughout the Song Dynasty stuck to the principle of keeping the military weak that was laid down by its founding emperor. While this policy indeed reduced the threat to the throne from the military, it left China vulnerable to the military threats from the non-Han nomadic states on its borders. The emperors of late Song adopted a strategy of forming alliances with one nomadic state to fend off another, or a strategy of "appeasement" (i.e., giving precious gifts of silver, silk, tea, and copper cash in the hope of pacifying the aggressors). These strategies worked in the short run, but did nothing to make up for Song's military deficiency. When the unstoppable Mongol cavalry came galloping out of the steppes, the Song Dynasty fell and the Mongol Yuan Dynasty began its century-long rule over China.

The Yuan Dynasty (1271–1368): China under Mongol Rule

For close to four out of the next six centuries, Han Chinese would be under non-Han rule: The Yuan Dynasty was Mongol, the Qing Dynasty was Manchu, and only the Ming Dynasty that came between was Han Chinese. Historically China's troubles with non-Han neighbors go back to at least 770 BCE, when the Zhou Dynasty moved its capital east to Luoyang, away from invading barbarians. The Han Dynasty also suffered the same humiliation, also relocating its capital eastward away from marauders. The Han Dynasty collapsed in large measure because it failed to deal with the northern frontier, and for the next 350 years China experienced invasions from the north. The reunification of the country by the Sui and Tang Dynasties required a strong military, but renegade generals became a domestic problem. To rein in the military meant sacrificing some of the nation's ability to keep the northern frontier peoples in check. Accordingly, when the Song Dynasty came to power it never took control of the numerous frontier tribes. Eventually the Song retreated south and one of those tribes, the Mongols, swept the Song away.

The "Four Great Inventions"

1) *The compass.* Chinese had known that iron magnets had the quality of pointing the north-south orientation as far back as the Warring States period (476–221 BCE). They made magnetized iron spoons and needles to use as compasses. The Song troops used compasses to determine direction at night and in heavy fog. Later, oceangoing ships adopted it. Arab merchants who often traveled on Chinese ships introduced it to Europe, thereby helping Europeans in their global exploration.

2) *Gunpowder.* Ancient Daoist alchemists, in their pursuit of a drug that would bring eternal life, had discovered that applying heat to a mixture of nitrate, sulfur, and charcoal would produce an explosion. The mixture was soon widely used to make fireworks. By late Tang, however, this mixture was used as gunpowder: Attached to the head-end of an arrow, it was projected into the enemy camp to start a fire. It became widely employed in warfare in early Song. Further advances were made in its weaponization in the Song and Yuan Dynasties. A sophisticated formula for manufacturing gunpowder was recorded in an encyclopedic military book, *Wujing Zongyao*, in 1044. A tubular "fire cannon" was invented in 1259: It had a length of bamboo as the gun barrel, which was filled with gunpowder and projectiles. When lit, the gunpowder would explode, hurtling the projectiles at the enemy. Iron and copper tubes replaced the fragile bamboo barrels in the Yuan and Ming Dynasties (thirteenth to fourteenth centuries). It became the main weapon of the army in the Qing Dynasty.

3) *3–4. Paper-making technology and movable-type printing.* China had a long tradition of inscribing characters on flat bones, bronzeware, woodblocks, and stone slabs and pillars. Later, characters were written on strips of wood, bamboo, or silk. Cai Lun (61–121), a eunuch in the Han Dynasty, invented the technology of making paper from plant fiber (105). Henceforth, Chinese would write on paper with a writing brush and ink. In Tang, people began woodblock printing: cutting the characters of texts into woodblocks and printing them off on paper. Commoner Bi Sheng (?–1051) is credited with the invention of movable-type printing in the Song Dynasty (1041). In this new method, one single character is cut into one single clay cube, and the clay cube is then hardened through baking. Since each tiny cube bears only one single character, the printer can use the same piece of type in different arrangements to print different texts. Going from woodblock printing to movable-type printing was a big step forward. To print texts with movable types on paper greatly facilitated the dissemination of knowledge. Government documents, agricultural manuals,

religious texts, and financial records could now be kept and transmitted with much greater ease, precision, and reliability. Unfortunately, Bi Sheng's movable-type printing was not widely adopted in China. (Metal movable-type printing was invented in Korea in the early thirteenth century. Mechanical movable-type printing was introduced to Europe in 1439 by German blacksmith, goldsmith, printer, and publisher Johannes Gutenberg [1398–1468].)

The Mongol Empire began with Genghis Khan (1162–1227), who united the various nomadic tribes on the Mongol steppes in 1206 and then launched out on his wars of global conquest. At its height, his empire straddled Eurasia, including today's Mongolia, Iran, Russia, Poland, and Hungary. His grandson Kublai Khan (1216–1294) conquered China and Korea, and founded the Mongol Yuan Dynasty. He located his capital at Dadu (modern Beijing), close to his grassland home base in Mongolia. Yuan rule had some brilliant successes. The mere fact that it was part of a vast empire sprawling across the entirety of the Eurasian landmass enabled it to accomplish much that was unthinkable in other times.

Kublai Khan's first challenge was how his tiny minority of Mongols would rule over a huge multiethnic population across such a large territory. His answer was a strategy of "divide and rule." He divided the populations in China into four classes according to their ethnicity, and plugged them into an ethnically defined hierarchic structure. They were unequal as defined by law. The Mongols were perched at the top of the totem pole; the Muslims in the Mongol Empire ranked second to the top; the Han Chinese of North China made up the third class, which also included Khitans, Jurchens, and Koreans; and the Han Chinese of South China were assigned to the bottom of the pyramid as punishment for their long and stubborn resistance to Mongol conquest. The first two categories made up only 3% of the households in the empire, and the remaining two made up 97%.

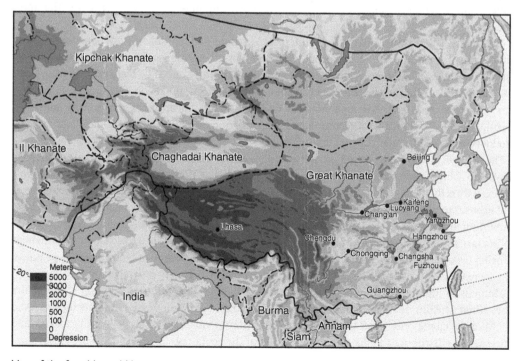

Map of the four Mongol khanates.

Traditionally, the Mongols were organized into tribal units that included the military command, the civil government, and the civilian population. When they won a war, the commander would divide up the spoils of war among the tribal leaders, and reward them with grants of land; and the tribal leaders would then distribute the war booty among their followers. The nomadic victors naturally used the seized land as grazing land for raising their livestock. Since the early wars were generally fought between nomadic peoples, the change of hands of the land had no significant economic impact; the grazing land remained grazing land. But when the Mongols conquered China, the tradition had devastating consequences, for the land the Mongols seized was farmland, and the new masters readily converted it into pastureland. This had a twofold consequence. The Han Chinese farmers who lost their land lost their livelihood, and became a roaming population; the settled population of North China dropped by two-thirds. This also hurt the Mongol government: It lost its potential agricultural tax revenues, and the roaming landless Han Chinese peasants were a tinderbox ready to explode anytime into peasant rebellion.

Yelu Chucai (1190–1244) was an advisor and prime minister to Genghis Khan. He came from an aristocratic ethnic Khitan family, but also had a thorough knowledge of Han Chinese practices. And he pointed out to the Khan that the Mongols' long-term interests depended on modifying their traditional nomadic ways and adopting the Chinese agricultural way of life. He urged the Khan to establish a civil government, make laws to ensure the civil government's control over the land, keep Han farmers on the land, and collect agricultural taxes. The Khan was persuaded, but old habits were hard to break. The nomadic tradition of making land grants and then turning farmland into grazing land was never entirely abandoned. However, the government did make laws to encourage farming, and to protect farmland and farmers, and it issued detailed and informative agricultural manuals.

Wang Zhen (1271–1368), a Yuan government official, published his *Book on Farming*, which consists of 22 volumes and contains 306 illustrations (1313). It is an encyclopedic work that describes China's agricultural practices and equipment up to his day. Its sections on new techniques and mechanical devices for growing cotton and making cotton cloth are the most fascinating.

The Mongols had always taken a keen interest in artisans and manufacture. Whenever they captured a city, they would round up the artisans and carry them off as prisoners. Artisans enjoyed certain privileges: They were given stipends and issued rations, and they were exempt from taxes and labor service. But they were also deprived of personal freedom: The law required their sons to carry on their trade and their daughters to do embroidery. Government-run artisan industries became highly developed under centralized government control and support. Their war artisans produced excellent tubular copper cannon, and their civil artisans produced exquisite carpets.

The Mongol government played an active role in economic activities. It freely used its coercive powers to achieve economic benefits for itself at the expense of the normal functioning of economic forces. It directly managed monopolies of gold, silver, copper, iron, and salt. It sold monopoly rights and licenses to merchants to trade in everything from tea, liquor, farm tools, bamboo, and timber to aluminum and zinc. It also sold licenses to Muslims to act as government agents —tax farming— to collect taxes. This system had a serious built-in flaw: Since the agents paid a fixed fee for the privilege of being tax collectors, they would stop at nothing to extract the last drop of blood from the peasants. The increased tax burden on the peasants would eventually force them into rebellion.

Mongols in high places often had the dual role of high government official and big merchant. They hired Muslim financial agents to manage their trading and money-lending businesses. And the Muslim agents often used their privileged position to violate normal business practices, and cause serious disruptions to the normal operation of the economy.

The cotton revolution that took place in the Yuan Dynasty brought about profound changes in China's economy. The cotton plant is native to India; it was first introduced into China in its southern frontier regions, then gradually spread across the country. It found the two essential elements it needed to thrive along the Lower Yangtze River: a favorable natural environment and an abundance of manpower. The Lower Yangtze had been a rice-growing region, but since cotton yielded better returns, it soon overtook rice to become the main crop. The growing of cotton, along with the manufacture and trading of cotton textiles, became the major source of income for many farming families there. This changed the nature of agriculture in the Yangtze Delta: Commercial agriculture was replacing subsistence agriculture, and thriving.

Huang Daopo (1245?–1330) was a catalyst of the cotton revolution. She was a native of Songjiang (near modern Shanghai). Fleeing from domestic abuse, she snuck aboard an ocean-going ship as a stowaway, and arrived at Hainan Island off the South China coast. There she lived among the native Li people, and learned the techniques of cotton spinning and weaving. When she returned to her native home, cotton growing was already quite widespread, but spinning and weaving technology still lagged behind. She taught the local women what she had learned from the Li people, and improved or invented new machinery for spinning and weaving. Her technology launched the textile industry in her hometown, and made it a center of the cotton textile industry for centuries.

Another big boost was made to the industry when the water-powered spinning wheel with dozens of spindles appeared during the Yuan Dynasty, four centuries earlier than it did in England.

Trade thrived under Mongol rule. Their far-flung empire and its well-developed road system facilitated trade over vast territories. The Silk Road by land was restored and expanded. The Silk Road by sea was expanded to reach from China's eastern coast to the Persian Gulf, Africa, and on to the Baltic Sea. China's exports were silk, tea, and porcelain. Imports included gold, copper, spices, jewelry, and ivory.

The government expanded the role of paper currency to meet the demand of the ever-growing volume of trade. The paper money was first put on a silk standard, and later on a silver standard. But the government was unable to restrain its appetite for printing ever more paper money without valuable reserves to back it up. In late Yuan, paper money became worthless, and inflation spun out of control.

The Yuan capital Dadu was much farther north than earlier Chinese capitals, while the country's economic center had completed its shift to the South. Much of the government's revenue came in the form of rice, silk, and cotton cloth, which were all produced in the South and had to be shipped north by sea. This practice continued even after the Grand Canal was restored and extended to Dadu.

The Yuan government adopted a policy of religious tolerance to bring the many races, nations, and cultures under one big tent. The Mongols themselves embraced Shamanism and Lamaism (a Tibetan branch of Buddhism). As they advanced westward, the religions of occupied regions were backfilled into China. In their capital Dadu, many religions coexisted and thrived, including Islam, Christianity, and Judaism. There were large numbers of Muslims from Central Asia, Catholics from Europe, and 30,000 Protestant Christians. The Yuan emperors exchanged letters with the pope of the Roman Catholic Church and the king of France, and met with their emissaries.

Muslim scientists were at the forefront of science and technology. Their influence reverberated both westward into Europe and eastward into China. Jamā al-Din (?–1290) was a Persian astronomer and calendar maker in Kublai Khan's court, and brought the best of Arab astronomy to China. He developed the Muslim calendar and erected seven Arab astronomical instruments in Dadu. Guo Shoujing (1231–1316) was a Chinese mathematician, astronomer, and calendar maker who also served at the imperial court. He made a calendar in 1280 that specified that one tropical year contained 365.2425 days. This measurement is only off by 26 seconds, the same as that of the Gregorian calendar, which was issued three centuries later and is still in use today. Guo's achievement clearly benefitted from Jamā al-Din's accomplishments.

The Yuan government made a few gestures at restoring the status of Confucianism and the imperial examination system. But they were sporadic and halfhearted, just like its attempts at reforming the land system. As a result, large numbers of educated Han Chinese scholars were left outside the system with a social status somewhere between beggars and whores. As outcasts of the establishment, some of them turned their talents to literary endeavor. They developed a new poetic genre, the Qu, which is a highly sophisticated form of poetic drama that combines a plebeian Han Chinese vocabulary with a heavy dose of non-Han musical influences. Its versatility made it a popular vehicle for the expression of the emotions of the common people, which often gave away a rebellious spirit against the social evils of the day. It was antiestablishment and subversive to Mongol rule. The poetic genres of Yuan Qu, along with Tang Shi and Song Ci, are among China's most cherished literary heritages.

Other educated Han Chinese rejected by the Mongol establishment easily gravitated to rebel forces toward the end of the Yuan Dynasty. Late Yuan government was corrupt and incompetent to the extreme. Riddled with factional strife and palace intrigue, it had eight emperors in a span of 25 years. Taxes and labor service soared. A rash of rebellions broke out across the country. A major rallying center for rebellions was a secret society—the White Lotus Sect and its military arm known as the Red Turbans. Battered from all sides, the Yuan Mongol regime collapsed. The Yuan Empire lasted less than a hundred years, making it one of the shortest of China's major dynasties. Its short lifespan was partly due to the fact that the empire was held together by military force with little internal cohesion—it had no common ethnicity, no common culture, and no common economy. It was forged by the sword, and when the sword became blunt and rusted, the empire collapsed and shattered. The numerous territories that were once one single empire returned to their pre-Mongol state of being many nations and many governments. Although the Mongols conquered China and Korea, their attempts at other Asian conquests (including Japan, Vietnam, Java, and Burma) all ended in abysmal failure.

Suggested Readings and Viewings

Jacques Gernet, *Daily Life in China on the Eve of the Mongol Invasion, 1250–1276* (Stanford, CA: Stanford University Press, 1962).

Mark Halperin, *Out of the Cloister: Literati Perspectives on Buddhism in Sung [Song] China, 960–1279* (Cambridge, MA: Harvard University Press, 2006).

Dieter Kuhn, *The Age of Confucian Rule: The Song Transformation of China* (Cambridge, MA: Harvard University Press, 2011).

Mongol (2008), dir. by Sergei Bodrov.

Morris Rossabi, *Khubilai Khan: His Life and Times* (Berkeley: University of California Press, 1988).

Yoshinobu Shiba, *Commerce and Society in Sung [Song] China* (Ann Arbor: University of Michigan Center for Chinese Studies, 1969).

Cong Ellen Zhang, *Transformative Journeys: Travel and Culture in Song China* (Honolulu: University of Hawaii Press, 2010).

Zhu Ruixin et al., *The Social History of Middle-Period China: The Song, Liao, Western Xia and Jin Dynasties* (Cambridge: Cambridge University Press, 2017).

6

The Decline of Imperial China: The Ming and Early Qing Dynasties, 1368–1840

To restore order in chaotic times, I have no choice but to use harsh measures.
—Zhu Yuanzhang, founding emperor of the Ming Dynasty

The Ming and Qing Dynasties were China's last two dynasties, each lasting nearly three centuries. At their peak, China surpassed all other nations in the world in terms of wealth, population, territory, and science and technology. But despite the power and magnificence they exhibited, their extreme despotism and conservatism stifled the vigor and creativity that had distinguished Chinese culture during the Tang and Song Dynasties.

The Ming Dynasty (1368–1644): Powerful, Majestic, Conservative, and Brutal

Zhu Yuanzhang (1328–1398) was the founder of the Ming Dynasty. He marched his peasant rebel army under the slogan of "Expel the Mongols—Restore Han China," captured the Mongol-Yuan capital of Dadu (1368), and relocated China's capital to Nanjing. He designated his grandson to inherit his throne, but another son of his seized the throne. The new Emperor Yongle (1360–1424) relocated the capital back to Dadu and renamed it Beijing. Beijing was China's capital for the next six centuries; the Imperial Palace and the Great Wall as they stand today are renovations of Ming structures.

Zhu Yuanzhang (1328–1398) had the humblest of origins among all major Chinese emperors. He was orphaned in his mid-teens when his home province was devastated by flood, and his family was wiped out by the plague. Homeless and starving, he took refuge in a small Buddhist monastery. But he soon went drifting again, for the temple had no way of feeding its monks, since it could not collect land rent when there was no harvest. At 25, he joined a major peasant rebel force, the Red Turban Army; married the daughter of his commander; and rose through the ranks to the very top. His wife, who would be the future Empress Ma, was of great help to him on his road to taking the throne. But while he was extremely brutal and paranoid, she was magnanimous. When she became terminally ill, she refused treatment by the physicians her husband had summoned to the palace, for she knew that, if she died after taking their medicine, he would execute them on suspicion of having poisoned her.

Asia Past and Present: A Brief History, First Edition. Peter P. Wan and Thomas D. Reins.
© 2021 John Wiley & Sons, Inc. Published 2021 by John Wiley & Sons, Inc.

Zhu Yuanzhang faced the formidable task of reestablishing Chinese values and institutions after a century of nomadic Mongol rule. Following the ancient maxim that "chaotic times call for harsh measures," he was personally more despotic than his predecessors, and built a government more centralized than those in earlier dynasties. He promulgated a four-volume criminal code that provided punishment of extraordinary harshness, showing no mercy to either government officials or the common people. With such brutal means, he strengthened China's traditional system of monarchism, set standards for government operations, and defined criteria for an individual's behavior in society.

He stripped his ministers of their independent powers, successfully removing the checks and balances that were put in place during the Tang Dynasty to restrain the powers of the emperor. His control of the government was direct and tight: He could personally make all important decisions, totally free of outside restraints. He employed caning in the royal court as an open punishment for high officials. Other forms of harsh punishment included cutting off fingers, hands, tendons, or kneecaps; castration; public execution by a thousand cuts; skinning alive; and so on. He personally controlled secret agencies that had their own spies and informants who kept close watch on government officials, scholars, celebrities, and the ordinary people. They had the power to make secret arrests, confine suspects in their own jails, use torture in interrogation, and carry out executions.

Timeline: Ming and Early Qing Dynasties, 1368–1842	
1368–1644	Ming Dynasty returns China to Han Chinese rule, builds the Forbidden City, and rebuilds the Great Wall
1328–1398	Zhu Yuanzhang, founder of the Ming Dynasty, notorious for being brutal and paranoid; restructures Ming government on Mongol model
1370–1373	Policy of "seclusion"; so-called "Japanese pirate problem"
Early Ming	Commercial revolution follows cotton revolution to create commercialized, market-oriented, and currency-based economy. Much of China is now a money society
1380	Prime Minister Hu Weiyong (?–1380) is framed and executed; over 30,000 people are put to death for guilt by association; new waves of "literary inquisitions"
1405–1433	Admiral Zheng He (1371–1433) makes seven voyages in 28 years, reaching the eastern coast of Africa and the Arabian Peninsula
1472–1529	Wang Shouren's philosophy of the "Doctrine of the Heart" emphasizes the autonomy of the individual, challenging Confucianism
1644	Fall of the Ming Dynasty: peasant rebel leader Li Zicheng (1606–1645) enters Beijing with his troops; Ming emperor hangs himself; the Manchu army routs the rebel forces, enters Beijing, and founds the Manchu Qing Dynasty
1644–1911	Manchu Qing Dynasty rules China
1661	National hero Zheng Chenggong (1624–1662) takes Taiwan from the Dutch and fights a doomed battle with Qing forces to save the Ming Dynasty
1681–1796	Qing Golden Age under three competent emperors: Kangxi, Yongzheng, and Qianlong

17th century	Corn, potato, sweet potato, and peanuts are introduced into China by Westerners, providing abundant nutrition and allowing for great population increase
1724	Emperor Yongzheng's crackdown on the Catholic Church
1772–1781	Compilation of the *Complete Collection of the Chinese Classics*
1760–1842	Qing government creates the Guangzhou System to channel all foreign trade through the southern port of Guangzhou
18th century	Cao Xueqin (1715–1764) writes *Dream of the Red Chamber*, the pinnacle of Chinese fiction
1793	Macartney Mission to discuss Sino-British trade
1795–1804	White Lotus Rebellion
1820–	Opium problem creates diplomatic and currency problems
1839–1842	Opium or First Anglo-Chinese War

His paranoia and massive executions were notorious. Even those who had fought with him to put him on the throne could not escape his suspicion and persecution. In order to remove anyone who might challenge him or his descendants, he would frame high civil officials and military commanders and put them to death. The fate of his earlier Prime Minister Hu Weiyong (?–1380) is a vivid illustration of his paranoia and brutality. When he became suspicious that Hu was gathering too much power in his hands, he charged him with plotting treason, promptly executed him, and abolished the position of prime minister. He went on to order the execution of Hu's relatives, students, and subordinates, as well as many ministers and generals. This case lasted 12 years, and it compromised over 30,000 people who were put to death. It is a typical example of China's age-old practice of "guilt by association." There has been no official position of prime minister in China's dynasties since. The degree of brutality that Zhu employed to strengthen his absolute power was unknown in earlier Han Chinese history, and was likely influenced by the century-long Mongol rule.

People from high-ranking officials down to the grassroots lived in constant fear of their lives. His ruthless measures, however, did result in a solid monarchy and a highly centralized and powerful government that would withstand the test of time. Throughout the Ming Dynasty, the regime was never seriously challenged by power centers beyond the throne, such as the families of the queen or empress dowager, cliques among the court officials or eunuchs, or insubordinate frontier generals.

Zhu Yuanzhang personifies a paranoid and brutal despot in the Chinese consciousness. But he was also unsurpassed in his unrelenting diligence, great talent, and bold vision in matters of government and warfare. He vigorously built schools and promoted education, and revived a robust imperial examination system. Candidates were tested not only on their knowledge of the Confucian classics, but also on their ability to apply those principles to resolve contemporary issues. Those who passed written examinations would further undergo tests of archery, horsemanship, math, and knowledge of the law.

His government again took up the arduous task of compiling registries of households and land ownership. This system was initiated in the Tang Dynasty and carried on in following dynasties to varying degrees. The registries contained detailed information on land and population, which served as the basis for determining taxes, labor service, and draft quotas. Households were organized into the "Baojia System," a collective-responsibility system wherein all households in a village were collectively responsible for collecting taxes, providing labor service, drafting soldiers, enforcing the law, and monitoring each individual's behavior. An individual, a family, or a neighborhood that got on the wrong side of the law would bring penalties to the entire village.

Zhu Yuanzhang reinvigorated China's agriculture, which had been crippled by a century of Mongol misrule and war. His government rewarded peasants with tax exemptions and farm animals for reclaiming abandoned farmland and dredging rivers. It relocated millions of people to settle in regions that had suffered radical population loss because of war, flood, and plague.

A commercial revolution was in full swing in Ming China, following the cotton revolution in the Yuan Dynasty. It began in the textile industry in the Lower Yangtze Valley, which was a rice-growing region and known as China's granary during the Tang and Song Dynasties. The cotton revolution offered incentives to peasants to switch from growing rice to more profitable labor like growing cotton, raising mulberry trees and silkworms, and manufacturing cotton and silk fabrics. Cotton and silk textile industries created fabulous prosperity that centered in Suzhou. Rice growing was sidelined and gradually shifted upriver, turning the middle reaches of the Yangtze River into China's new granary. Such regional economic specialization and division of labor finally turned the Lower Yangtze Valley from a rice exporter to a rice importer.

But the producers of these cottage industries could realize economic benefits only by selling their goods and buying what they didn't produce in the marketplace. To conduct those transactions, they needed currency. Hence, a commercialized, market-oriented, and currency-based economy gradually took shape to replace the earlier self-sufficient and self-contained agricultural economy. Silver was soon the main form of currency, and the government converted taxes, labor service, and the salaries of government officials into silver as well. Much of China was now a money society.

Zhu Yuanzhang passed his throne on to his grandson, but a son of his seized the throne, and is known as Emperor Yongle (1360–1424). One of his most memorable undertakings was the dispatch of Admiral Zheng He on seven overseas voyages along the maritime Silk Road over a 28-year period. His fleet visited today's Southeast Asian countries (Vietnam, Indonesia, Malaysia, the Philippines, and Thailand), the South Asian subcontinent (India, Sri Lanka, and Pakistan), the Middle East (Iran and Saudi Arabia), and the eastern coast of Africa (Madagascar, Somalia, and Kenya). He offered expensive gifts to local rulers and extolled the wealth, power, and benevolence of China and the Chinese emperor. He also did a little trading and went after a band of Chinese pirates along the way. He made friends on these voyages, and brought back precious and exotic gifts from local rulers to the Chinese emperor. One eye-popping gift was a giraffe from Africa!

> On his first voyage, Zheng He had a magnificent nine-mast flagship that measured 151 meters in length and 61 meters in width with a carrying capacity of 800 tons. He had a fleet of 240 oceangoing vessels carrying roughly 27,800 people. The ships were of diverse design and function: to carry passengers, to carry cargo, and to fight in combat. They were armed with the most advanced cannon in the world.

It would be no exaggeration to call Zheng He's voyages "China's Age of Discovery." Unfortunately, they were discontinued when Emperor Yongle died in 1424, and Zheng himself died in 1433. The next emperor not only terminated the voyages abruptly but also ordered the destruction of the voyage diaries, the data collected on the voyages, and even the docks where the ships were built. He also re-imposed a harsh policy of "seclusion" that closed the Chinese coast to all foreign contact: Foreigners were banned from entering China, Chinese subjects were banned from leaving the

Statue of Zheng He. *Source:* WGBH Educational Foundation.

country, and those who did leave were banned from reentering. Official trade with foreign countries was choked to a dribble. Private business contact with foreigners was absolutely forbidden. The "seclusion" policy held firm through the Ming and Qing Dynasties for six centuries. China's outreach to the world withered on the vine. And except for occasional eruptions of violence, China slumbered in isolation within its borders.

Why?
The reasons why Admiral Zheng He's expeditions were terminated pose a fascinating question. So what were the reasons behind the about-face of policy?   1) Emperor Yongle, the initiator and backer of the expeditions, died in 1424, and Zheng He died in India in 1433 while on his seventh voyage.   2) The founding emperor Zhu Yuanzhang had issued "seclusion" orders and kept reinforcing them throughout his reign. So Zheng He's explorations could be an aberration from the tradition.   3) Emperor Yongle's purpose for sending Zheng He on his voyages was to extol the greatness of the Chinese emperor and extend the tribute-trade system. Normal trade was of minor interest, and territorial conquest was never a goal. Since the expeditions brought no

tangible benefits, and were not even self-sustaining, they were indefensible against charges of being costly vainglory. (In contrast, the Western expeditions were driven mainly by the desire to reach new markets and colonize new territories. They survived and flourished on the profits, loot, lands, and slaves they acquired.)

4) Zheng He had long been a target at the imperial court. His forefathers were Muslim Arabs who had served for generations in high office in the Mongol Yuan government. When Mongol rule was overthrown, he was captured as a boy of 10, castrated, and sent to work in the household of the future Emperor Yongle. He became a close confidant to his master, helped him in his struggle to seize the throne, and was appointed Admiral of the Ming Fleet. His personal faith in Buddhism and his knowledge of Muslim faith and culture gave him a great advantage in carrying out his diplomatic missions in the lands of Buddhism and Islam. But his opponents claimed that he was unfit to command the emperor's fleet because he was a eunuch and a Muslim.

5) Why did the succeeding emperor go so far as to try to wipe out all traces of a 28-year endeavor? Overseas trade was encouraged in the Song Dynasty and enormously expanded in the Yuan Dynasty. So why couldn't the Ming do the same? Scholars have tried to answer the question.

First of all, the Ming Dynasty capital Beijing was located in the north, far from the southeastern coast. Therefore, its top priority had to be defending its borders against the looming threats coming from the Mongols and Manchus on its northern frontiers.

Second, the Ming emperors could reasonably be concerned that a thriving overseas trade would make the distant southern provinces too powerful to control. And as Western powers such as Portugal and Spain were already colonizing parts of the Indian subcontinent and Southeast Asia, opening the door to foreign trade could also mean opening the door to the wolves.

Clearly, clamping down on overseas trade hurt China's economic development, but it was not a kneejerk reaction.

Zheng He's epochal voyages of discovery soon faded into oblivion. Meanwhile, the Europeans were going through their "Age of Discovery" (fifteenth to seventeenth centuries). They were pushing ahead with their overseas exploration, even as they went through the Enlightenment, nation-state building, the commercial revolution, the industrial revolution, and global colonial conquests. And they would change the course of human history.

Ironically, the "seclusion" policy came at a time when China's domestic economy was becoming increasingly commercialized, and private capital was building up huge reserves that sought new markets. Domestic economic forces demanded overseas trade. The profits to be had from foreign trade were irresistible. So despite government policy to smother it, smuggling and piracy thrived, while legal overseas trade dwindled to a trickle. What became known as the "Japanese pirates" were actually bands of Chinese and Japanese merchants and pirates, often based in Japan, conducting illegal trade, raiding ships, and looting Chinese coastal towns and villages. It remained a challenge to the government throughout the Ming Dynasty.

Zheng Chenggong (1624–1662) is an interesting case study of the true nature of the so-called "Japanese pirates." His father was a Han Chinese who was the head of a huge group of pirates and maritime merchants. He had a home in Japan, and one of his wives was a Japanese woman who was the mother of Zheng Chenggong. The Ming government seduced him to return to China by granting him a high position in the Ming navy. While commanding Ming troops, he continued to conduct trade with Japan. He brought his son back to China to receive a Chinese education, and the son grew up to manage much of his father's military and mercantile enterprise. When the Manchus were in the course of conquering China, the father went over to the Manchus. The son broke with his father and became a major resistance leader. He established his base along the coast and on the offshore islands, and conducted maritime trade and piracy. The largest island off the coast was Taiwan, which had been under Dutch control for nearly three decades. Zheng sent his troops to retake it by force, and governed it in the name of the Ming Dynasty. He also tried to extend his control to Southeast Asia through the local Chinese population, but was unsuccessful. The Manchus managed to capture Taiwan in 1683, thereby removing the last anti-Manchu stronghold and bringing all of China under Manchu rule.

The Ming government faced another challenge of a philosophical nature. Wang Shouren (1472–1529), who was a scholar-official and army general of high standing, put forth the "Doctrine of the Heart," despite the government's harsh enforcement of Zhu Xi's ultraconservative Neo-Confucianism. His theory claimed that both Heaven's principles and human's good conscience exist in an individual's heart, that truth can be found through introspection, and that "knowing is acting, and acting is knowing." His philosophy substituted an individual's personal beliefs in Confucian classics as the basis for ultimate truth. It was a liberating force that restored an individual's autonomy and freed an individual from the shackles of Confucianism's classics and its hierarchy. Obviously, it was a frontal attack on Zhu Xi's demand to "promote Heaven's principles; wipe out human desire," and was viewed as out-and-out heresy. But it had a flip side. Carrying individualism to absurd extremes, many of Wang's followers indulged in unchecked flights of fantasy and empty talk, and lost their anchor in reality. Scholars would pride themselves on not reading and not discussing real issues, and officials would brag about their ignorance of matters of state.

Ming China reached great heights of achievement. It was the world's largest country in terms of territory and population, and also the world's richest country. It had the world's most advanced science and technology. But all that power and splendor was a swan song. In late Ming, the malignant growth of political corruption, high-level infighting, eunuchs' interference in state affairs, and the employment of secret agents were out of control. Against this background of rot and decay, two major forces rose to bring down the dynasty. One was a storm of peasant rebellions, and the other was the non-Han Manchu invasion.

Li Zicheng (1606–1645) was the leader of the strongest peasant rebel army. He started life as a shepherd boy, then worked at a government post house. When wanted for multiple murders, he fled and joined the army, where he was promoted, but was again involved in murders. He incited a mutiny, joined a rebel army (1629), and worked his way up to becoming the commander of the largest rebel army of half a million strong. He engaged government troops in hit-and-run warfare, never bothering to establish a permanent base. His marauding troops left behind large swaths of devastation as they swept through the country, and they eventually took the Ming capital Beijing

(1644); the cornered Ming emperor hanged himself. Li declared himself emperor, as his rebel troops indulged in looting luxurious homes, and raping and killing freely. The rebel army's fighting capacity melted away, as discipline broke down and infighting broke out.

While China was in turmoil, the Manchus on China's northeastern frontier were getting ready to launch an invasion. Ming General Wu Sangui went over to the Manchus and joined their fight against the rebels. When they breached the defenses of rebel-held Beijing, Li Zicheng fled and continued to fight and run till he was presumed dead. How he died is one of the more intriguing enigmas in Chinese history. The Ming regime had collapsed, and the rebellion was crushed. The invading Manchus took over the country, and Han Chinese fell under Manchu rule for the next three centuries, just as they had earlier been under Mongol rule for one century.

Why Not?

Ming China more or less coincided with the Europe that was emerging from the Middle Ages and entering the Modern Age. But China never took the step forward. China was large and prosperous. It had a large and thriving domestic market, advanced science and technology, a huge reserve of capital, and a vigorous merchant class, so why didn't modern capitalism develop there? Scholars cite a range of reasons, but they all boil down to the absolute power of the emperor and his government.

Emperors always viewed large concentrations of wealth as prey or threat. With absolute power and unrestrained by law, they could arbitrarily prevent the formation of great concentrations of wealth, or exploit or destroy it.

1) State monopolies had existed since the Han Dynasty. These supersized economic entities used ultra-economic measures to take control of upper-stream resources, such as rice, salt, iron, copper, gold, and silver. The imperial nation's wealth was actually the private property of the emperor and a few high officials. They had many ways of confiscating large concentrations of private wealth on false charges or demanding big merchants to donate to state projects and supply the government with funds for war. The cards were stacked against the merchants without government ties.

2) The state ideology of Confucianism ranked merchants at the very bottom of society. The ultimate goal of a rich merchant was, rather than encouraging his sons to be more successful in his business, to instead give his sons a good education in the hope that someday they would pass the imperial examinations and enter the establishment as government officials. China's merchant class could never develop into a revolutionary force as its Western counterparts did.

3) The abolition of primogeniture was a uniquely Chinese way to prevent wealth concentration and weaken potential threats to the throne. By demanding the equal division of an inheritance among the sons, the fortunes of a potential rival were scattered and the threat was defused.

Ming merchant Shen Wansan (1296–1376) was a good example of how vulnerable a wealthy merchant was, as he was exposed to the emperor's arbitrary powers and unprotected by the law. Shen had accumulated his legendary wealth by doing overseas trade and expanding his landholdings. He was said to have made large gifts of gold and silver to Emperor Zhu Yuanzhang, and paid for one-third of the cost of building the city wall of the capital Nanjing. But the paranoid and envious emperor saw him as a threat. He exiled Shen to the frontier and let him die there. Still unsatisfied, he later found excuses to imprison and execute major members of Shen's extended family, thus bringing an end to the family commercial empire.

China under Sinicized Manchu Rule: The Early Qing Dynasty (1644–1839)

The Manchu Qing Dynasty compiled the Complete Collection of Chinese Classics, and in the course of it brought about the demise of Chinese classics.

—Wu Han, modern Chinese historian

The Manchu (the early Nüzhen) were a seminomadic people who lived along the rivers and valleys of Manchuria in northeastern China Proper. As the tribes grew in population and strength, they coalesced under one ruler and readied themselves to invade China Proper. They saw their opportunity when the Ming capital fell to Li Zicheng's rebel army and the Ming emperor hanged himself. They launched their invasion, defeated the rebel army, captured Beijing, and declared that the Ming Dynasty had run its course and that Heaven had passed the "Mandate of Heaven" to the Manchu. They founded the Manchu Qing Dynasty.

The Manchu, like the Mongols, were a non-Han people. But unlike the nomadic Mongols, they engaged in both stock raising and farming, and they were highly Sinicized. Structuring their government on the Ming model, the Manchu emperors ruled China in a Confucian way, as any Han Chinese emperor did. But they outdid the Ming by being more autocratic and conservative. The Manchu constitute only 2 percent of China's population. To make up for this numerical disadvantage, they employed extreme brutality. In the early stages of their war of conquest, they carried out extended campaigns of slaughter, arson, and rape to any tenacious resistance, leaving cities and countryside desolate. Their slaughter at Yangzhou and Jiading are notorious examples. Large regions of China were left with drastically reduced populations, and the Qing government later had to relocate people from one province to another to reclaim abandoned farmland and repopulate cities.

To break the Chinese people's sense of national identity, the Manchu conquerors ordered that every Han Chinese man must uniformly adopt the Manchu hairstyle—clean-shaven front crown and long ponytail braid on the back of the head. The saying was: If you keep your hair, you lose your head. The new rulers of China made a vigorous and sustained effort to exert mind control to force the Chinese into total submission. A major literary project the regime undertook was the compilation of the *Complete Collection of the Chinese Classics* (1772–1781). Officials throughout the country were ordered to collect and submit to Beijing copies of every book for review and consideration for inclusion in the *Collection*. The completed *Collection* contained over 3500 categories in about 80,000 volumes. It took 13 years for over 360 high official-scholars and more than 3800 scribes to complete the compilation. It was officially extolled as a great project for preserving Chinese cultural heritage, but it turned out to be the opposite. For in the process of collecting and compiling, books amounting to 150,000 copies of 13,600 volumes as well as over 10 million files of archives of the Ming Dynasty were censured and burned. Intended burning, deletion, distortion, and falsification of books and historical documents made the *Collection* defective. That is why Chinese historians have lamented the compilation of the *Complete Collection of the Chinese Classics* as an act of destroying Chinese culture.

The Qing regime was notorious for its waves of "literary inquisitions," that is, witch-hunts for oblique or fabricated attacks on Manchu rule expressed in the writings of poetry, literature, or history. Victims were routinely imprisoned, exiled, or executed, and their families and relatives often suffered the same punishment through "guilt by association." Literary inquisitions had a chilling effect on the scholar-official class and stifled free and creative thinking in a way that affected generation after generation of educated people. However, once the Manchu were firmly in control, they brought Han Chinese into the regime as junior partners to acquire broader support. This might partially explain how a tiny minority could rule over a vast empire for almost three centuries.

When the Qing Dynasty was first established, China was suffering from the aftermath of wars, rebellions, and dynastic change. The people were desperate for a peaceful environment where they could make their livelihood. Three successive emperors of the early Qing Dynasty (Kangxi, Yongzheng, and Qianlong) are credited for taking successful steps to revitalize the exhausted population and economy. Some historians see the entire period of their reigns (1661–1796) as a "Golden Age of peace and abundance." Others refer to this period as the High Qing.

At the time, China had vast amounts of abandoned farmland. It was either land that once belonged to the royal families of the Ming who were now toppled, or that belonged to cultivators who had died in wars and massacres. The early Qing emperors offered rewards of cash and farm animals to peasants who relocated to the abandoned farmland, took up farming, and raised large families. They also encouraged the adoption of new food crops and new farming techniques. Peasants began to grow high-yield food crops such as corn, potato, and sweet potato, which were recently introduced from South America and could grow in poor soil. In the South, peasants adopted "double cropping," sowing and reaping rice twice a year on the same piece of land. The government helped by constructing irrigation and flood-control projects, broadened the tax base by stripping large numbers of government officials and landed gentry of their tax exemption, and loosened the laws that tied peasants to the land. Emperor Yongzheng went as far as to lift the Exclusion Act to allow foreign trade with Southeast Asia.

Qianlong Emperor. *Source:* Láng Shìníng.

These measures improved agriculture and contributed to social stability. Back on the land, uprooted peasants were now able to make a living for themselves. Food supply became more plentiful. Tensions between the Han Chinese subjects and their Manchu masters gradually receded into the background. Also, they increased the government's revenues. This was a period of peace, stability, and economic growth. China's population more than doubled in the first two centuries of Qing rule, reaching 100 million, and was adequately fed by increased agricultural output. Under Manchu rule, China was the world's largest, richest, and most populous country as the Qianlong Emperor's reign neared its conclusion.

Some of the best reform policies were highly effective in early Qing but had negative impacts in late Qing. The population increase turned into a population explosion, and created grim problems. Per capita farmland dropped by half, food grain prices shot up by five times, and per capita food consumption dropped. When natural disasters struck, widespread famine followed, which in turn evoked massive resistance to paying rents and taxes. Starving and desperate peasants began to flee from famine-stricken areas and raid private and government granaries. Part of them joined secret religious societies, among which the strongest was the White Lotus Society. As a secret folk sect allegedly founded in 1133, it was integrated with other religious sects (one of them rooted in Persia) and continued to grow through the Yuan, Ming, and Qing Dynasties. Its leaders claimed to have superhuman powers to communicate with the spiritual world, perform miracles, heal the sick, and forecast the future. It was the most complex, mystical, and rigidly hierarchical religious sect in China's history. Over the centuries, it had attracted followers struggling at the bottom of society, such as destitute peasants, bankrupted artisans, and even bandits and thieves. When times were bad, it empowered the powerless against the government. When suppressed, it would conversely gain strength. Now it erupted into the White Lotus Society Rebellion (1795–1804). It was one of the largest peasant rebellions during the Qing Dynasty, sweeping across Central China and lasting nearly a decade. The government eventually managed to put it down, but the heavy toll of lives and high cost in fortune left the Qing government exhausted and impoverished.

Ever-increasing successful candidates in the expanded imperial examination system made the government enlarge the size of its bureaucracy to position them, but only a portion of them could be accommodated. Those left out of the establishment were likely to turn against it as critics or rebel advisors. The handwriting on the wall loomed. Seemingly doomed by the age-old dynastic cycle, the Qing Dynasty had entered its declining phase. It would be reasonable to expect that the fall of the Qing Dynasty would be followed by the rise of another dynasty. But that didn't happen, for a powerful alien force was ready to jump into the fray. The new intruders were not the traditional "barbarians" sweeping southward from the boundless steppes, but "ocean barbarians" on ships armed with firearms approaching China's seashore from out of nowhere. They would prove immune to Sinicization, and they would push Chinese history in entirely new directions.

The arrival of the West, particularly the appearance of the British, created major challenges. London wanted greater access to the China market, which remained limited under the Guangzhou System. When the West first arrived in China, both Europe and China conducted trade on a mercantilist monopoly-to-monopoly basis. By the late eighteenth century, Europe's—particularly Britain's—economic guidelines began to favor a more laissez-faire approach. Ultimately that resulted in merchants on both sides who were legally excluded from trade successfully evading the strict monopoly-to-monopoly guidelines. Moreover, one of the items of trade—opium—began to drain silver from China to pay for the drug. That made the purchase of silver with copper coins increasingly expensive. Ultimately it led to the Opium War, China's defeat, and the erosion of many fundamental Chinese ideas and institutions.

China's four greatest novels were produced in the Ming–Qing period, and continue to be part of everyday life in contemporary China. What sets them apart is (1) the authors portray a vast cast of characters in detail on a broad canvas; (2) they were exquisitely written in a classical-vernacular vocabulary that any Chinese with a rudimentary education can understand and pass on orally; (3) they all defy traditional orthodoxy to some degree; and (4) they are inexhaustible resources tapped by Chinese literature, drama, film, art, and traditional operas.

1) *The Water Margin* by Shi Nai'an (1296–1372) is about the legendary exploits of 108 hero-outlaws in the Song Dynasty. The men and women characters run the gamut of society: everyday fishermen, innkeepers, petty civil and military officials, petty thugs, thieves and bandits, and rich and powerful landowners. They share one common experience—they are all forced to join the outlaw community by government corruption and oppression. The novel advocates a loyal code of brotherhood in rebellion against the government.

2) *Romance of the Three Kingdoms* by Luo Guanzhong (1330?–1400?) is a historical novel based on the figures and events in the period after the fall of the Han Dynasty. The characters of various hues, moving through intricate plots, demonstrate ancient wisdom in state-craft and military strategy. The novel has been viewed as a textbook of politics, diplomacy, and military art; and those historical figures have become household names. It cast a spell on the Chinese national consciousness. It is also very popular in Japan and Korea. Two of its characters stand out in bold relief. One is Cao Cao (155–220), a central figure in the novel who continues to ignite intense debate even today on whether he is a "good guy" or "bad guy" in accordance with his achievements as well as the treacherous and ruthless means he employed to achieve his ends. The Chinese hesitate to love him, but nevertheless can't help admiring him. The other is Guan Yu, a general of military prowess and personal loyalty who is widely revered as a folk god.

3) *Westward Journey* by Wu Cheng'en (1501–1582) is a hilariously humorous fantasy tale. Its central character Tang Sen is very loosely based on Buddhist monk Xuan Zang (602–664) in the Tang Dynasty and his 16-year pilgrimage from China to India. He has three disciple-assistants: the Monkey King, the Pig, and the River Monster; and his mount is the Dragon Prince in the form of a white horse. The pages are populated with good and evil humans, immortals and gods, as well as wild beasts, demons, monsters, and witches living in strange and distant lands. They throw obstacles one by one in their way, but eventually, the pilgrims overcome them all, acquire Buddhist scriptures, and return to the Tang capital.

   The novelist drew heavily on Chinese mythology, religions, and Taoist and Buddhist stories. What meets the eye immediately are hair-raising adventures and side-splitting humor created by the most uninhibited imagination. It clearly extols human goodness and radiates with optimism that evil can never prevail over good. Monkey King, who is unafraid of evil and embodies goodness, wit, and courage, amuses readers with his mischievousness and human frailties. He is a universal favorite.

4) *Dream of the Red Mansion* is the pinnacle of classical Chinese fiction. It is believed to be an autobiography. Its author Cao Xueqin (1715–1764) was born into the family of a wealthy and powerful Manchu official, but in the end, he died alone in destitution and despair after his family was destroyed in imperial purges. Most of what happens in the novel takes place behind the high walls of the family compound with its magnificent mansions, spacious courtyards, and manicured gardens, where the masters and their big families live in luxury, surrounded by servants, maids, and slave-girls in large numbers. However, the author

cleverly makes it a panoramic miniature of the colorful life from top to the very bottom in the outside world.

The novel is an encyclopedia of all aspects of Chinese society and life in the mid-eighteenth century as the Qing Dynasty went from prosperity to decline. It has given birth to a brand-new academic discipline—Red-ology.

Suggested Readings and Viewings

Timothy Brook, *The Troubled Empire: China in the Yuan and Ming Dynasties* (Cambridge, MA: Harvard University Press, 2013).

Crouching Tiger, Hidden Dragon (2001), dir. by Ang Lee.

John W. Dardess, *Ming China, 1368–1644: A Concise History of a Resilient Empire* (Boulder, CO: Rowman and Littlefield, 2011).

Mark C. Elliott, *The Manchu Way: The Eight Banners and Ethnic Identity in Late Imperial China* (Stanford, CA: Stanford University Press, 2001).

Mark C. Elliott, *Emperor Qianlong: Son of Heaven, Man of the World* (Upper Saddle River, NJ: Longman, 2009).

Louise Levanthes, *When China Ruled the Seas: The Treasure Fleet of the Dragon Throne, 1405–1433* (New York: Oxford University Press, 1997).

Peter C. Perdue, *China Marches West: The Qing Conquest of Central Eurasia* (Cambridge, MA: Harvard University Press, 2010).

Richard J. Smith, *The Qing Dynasty and Traditional Chinese Culture* (Boulder, CO: Rowman and Littlefield, 2015).

Jonathan D. Spence, *Emperor of China: Self-Portrait of Kang Hsi* (New York: Knopf, 1974).

7

Premodern Japan and Korea

Premodern Japan

The Imperial Court is the forbidden precinct. Happily, the line descended from Amaterasu has possessed hereditary authority for the countless generations. Accordingly, even though a military general [the Tokugawa Shogun] has grasped the power and directs government and letters within the four seas, this is nevertheless for the reason that he has been commanded to oversee all state affairs on behalf of the Imperial Court, and his serving of the Imperial Court diligently, without the slightest negligence, is in accordance with the great propriety obtaining between lord and subject.[1]

—Yamago Sogo, explaining why the Shogun rules

Ancient Japan: The Land and the People (to the Seventh Century)

Japan is an island country consisting of four main islands and many smaller islands. Its four home islands stretch from Hokkaido in the far north to Kyushu near the equator, placing most of the country in the temperate zone. Its main island Honshu has a mountain range stretching down its middle and reaching out to the coasts. On its eastern coast are two major plains: the Yamato Plain where Kyoto is located, and the Kanto Plain where Tokyo (Edo) is located. Most of its farmland is scattered along the coast on tiny plains. The soil is generally poor, and only 17% of its land area is under cultivation, but the warm and moist maritime climate allows crops to thrive. The scattered and isolated distribution of its arable land delayed the unification of the country for a long time.

Japan is often thought of as "small," but its territory is actually larger than Great Britain, although smaller than either France or California. It is also often thought of as "isolated," but it actually is separated from the Asian continent by no more than 120 miles at its closest point to Korea. This was a considerable distance by the standards of ancient times, and posed a formidable barrier to the ambitions of its stronger neighbors. But it was not an insurmountable obstacle to the Japanese, who were determined to borrow from the more advanced cultures of their neighbors. Stone Age cultures were widely scattered across the islands of Japan by 40,000 BCE, and the Jomon culture was one of them. These typically constituted hunting, gathering, and fishing people who lived in sunken pit shelters. They were likely the Ainu people, whose physical appearance was more like Caucasians than modern Japanese.

---

1 Quoted in Conrad Totman, *Early Modern Japan* (Berkeley: University of California Press, 1993), p. 170.

Asia Past and Present: A Brief History, First Edition. Peter P. Wan and Thomas D. Reins.
© 2021 John Wiley & Sons, Inc. Published 2021 by John Wiley & Sons, Inc.

Premodern Japan to circa 1868

ca. 40,000 BCE	Old Stone Age: Hunting and gathering
ca. 14,000–300 BCE	Jomon period begins transition from hunting and gathering to agriculture; the people are likely the Ainu, who have Caucasian features
300 BCE–300 CE	Yayoi people arrive from Korea and conquer the Ainu, bring new advanced methods of agriculture, and utilize bronze and iron. They are seen as the ancestors of the modern Japanese people
4th–7th centuries	Yamato period: Great Kings rule the tribes on the Yamato Plain
538	Korean King Seong of Baekje introduces Buddhism to Japan
604	Prince Shotoku (574–622) promulgates the Seventeen-Article Charter to officially adopt Confucianism and Buddhism; sends first mission to Tang Dynasty China
646	Taika Reform of Emperor Kotoku (596–654) introduces institutional reforms to transform Japan into a centralized state under the emperor, based on the Chinese model
7th century	Traditional Japanese state is formed on the Yamato Plain, the title "emperor" replaces "king," and gradually the government and culture of the Yamato people spread across Japan
710–794	Nara period reflects Japanese borrowing from China, including the capital Nara, which was based on China's then-capital Chang'an
754	Chinese Buddhist monk Jianzhen (Gajin) arrives in Japan
794–1185	Heian period finds the emperor's role in government usurped by the Fujiwara family, which marries into the imperial family and controls it
839	Last envoy to Tang China
ca. 1010	Fujiwara court life told in the novel *The Tale of Genji*
12th–16th centuries	Age of the Shoguns: Emperors reign, Shoguns rule
1185–1333	Kamakura Shogunate, where the Shogun rules over a feudal political and social order, although the Hojo family does marry into the Shogunate after 1203 and controls it
1274, 1281	Mongol invasions turned back by *kamikaze*, or "divine wind"
1336–1573	Ashikaga Shogunate troubled by the emergence of northern and southern imperial courts and the arrival of the Europeans, and with them the beginning of Nanban Trade
14th century	During the Ashikaga period, the peasant foot soldier begins to displace the elite mounted samurai
1467–1603	Warring States period when Oda Nobunaga, Toyotomi Hideyoshi, and Tokugawa Ieyasu struggle to unify Japan
1603–1868	Tokugawa Shogunate unifies Japan, creates a centralized feudal society, closes the country to foreign contact, and lays the foundation for modernization from its capital at Edo (today's Tokyo)
1853–1854	Americans end the seclusion of Japan and sign a treaty with the Shogunate, which begins a rebellion against the Tokugawa
1868	The Meiji Restoration ends the Tokugawa rule and the feudal system, and launches a rapid, successful modernization program

By 300 BCE, the Yayoi people had migrated from the Korean Peninsula to the Japanese islands and conquered the Jomon people. They would become the ancestors of the modern Japanese people. They were like the Koreans in that they had originated in Siberia and Manchuria and migrated to Korea; but unlike the Koreans, they had kept going until they landed in Japan. They spoke an Altaic language related to Korean, but not to Chinese. The Yayoi culture emerged on the Japanese islands with amazing suddenness. They brought with them an advanced New Stone Age agriculture, and employed bronze and iron. These technologies had originated in China, spread to Korea, and now settled in Japan. They built huge earthen mounds over the tombs of their prominent men, which was a typical Korean practice. They were still essentially the same as the Koreans, but had absorbed some of the indigenous Ainu population through intermarriage, and driven the rest northward. In modern times, the Ainu people have lived a relatively primitive way of life on reservations on the northernmost island of Hokkaido, and are suffering from a shrinking population.

The Age of the Kings and Emperors (Seventh–Twelfth Centuries)

The Japanese have a "creation myth" just like other civilizations. In their mythology, the Japanese people (the Yamato people) are descended from the Sun Goddess Amaterasu and her brother-husband. Traditional Japanese historiography claims that Emperor Jimmu founded the State of Japan in 660 BCE. Verifiable history puts the appearance of the first Japanese state on the Yamato Plain at the seventh century BCE. The earliest reliable information on early Japanese life is found in post–Han Dynasty Chinese sources. They describe Japan as an agricultural society made up of clans that are in transition from matriarchal to patriarchal society; the clans control territories and are headed by a man or woman who combines the functions of chieftain and high priest, and the Yamato clan dominates the various other clans.

The indigenous religion of Japan is Shinto, the "Way of the Gods." It celebrates the *kamis*, who are nature spirits who dwell in unique natural objects, such as a magnificent mountain, a gnarled tree, or a clear creek. Shinto has simple rituals, a cheerful spirit, exuberant holidays, and an emphasis on cleanliness. It has no sacred scripts, doctrinal demands, or theoretical elaborations. Its simplicity may explain its staying power.

The Yamato clan gradually developed a Yamato State on the Chinese model replete with a ruler called the "great king," a royal court, and a centralized administrative structure, but it had no permanent capital. The "great king" was a military overlord who dominated over the regional lords, and held land and granaries throughout the country. He allowed those clans that yielded to his authority to maintain local autonomy, appointed their chiefs to serve as officials at his court, and placed their gods in a pantheon of gods with the Yamato Sun Goddess at its pinnacle. He ruled over a hierarchic sociopolitical structure that included regional lords, peasants, craftsmen, and slaves. A warrior class dominated the commoners. Over time, the Yamato kings extended their rule over the entire land, and the "Yamato" name came to stand for all of Japan.

Chinese culture and Buddhism reached Japan via Korea in the fifth and sixth centuries. Prince Shotoku (574–622) promoted cultural exchange with China. He sent regular missions to China composed of students, Buddhist monks, merchants, and government officials to study and learn, and they returned to inform the Japanese of Chinese culture. He officially embraced Chinese culture with the promulgation of the Seventeen-Article Constitution of 604, whose purpose was to establish a Chinese-style government to strengthen the position of the "great king," and he urged conversion to Buddhism. Later, the Taika Reforms in 646, introduced by Emperor Kotoku, created institutional reforms to transform Japan based on the Chinese political model. Significantly, he changed his title from "great king" to "emperor," and rewarded his supporters with titles and positions in a government bureaucracy. The Japanese built their first real city, Nara, on the model of Tang China's capital Chang'an in 710. Japanese emperors would rule from their capitals at Nara and nearby Heian for the next 600 years.

The Nara period was a time of wholesale cultural borrowing from China. The emperor even tried to adopt China's "equal fields system," but abandoned the attempt when he found it to be too complex to maintain. Instead, he decided it would be easier to set tax quotas for the provinces, and delegate the power of tax collection to provincial officials. In the actual execution of the system, however, greedy officials at each level would collect more than the set quota and pocket the difference. This put the cultivators at the mercy of the grasping officials. The system was made worse when the emperor granted the imperial family, aristocrats, and monasteries exemption from taxes and government jurisdiction. Local lords saw a loophole in the exemptions. They would formally sign the ownership of their land over to a privileged individual in the royal court, and then nominally pay a small rent for the right to use the same piece of land, and thus be exempted from taxes and government control. Small cultivators followed suit; they gave up title of ownership to tax-exempt local lords and powerful institutions, thus freeing themselves from the arbitrary control of local government. But the system had unintended consequences: (1) It created a class of absentee landowners, who would hire local "stewards" to manage their lands; and (2) this new arrangement reduced large numbers of free peasants to serfdom.

Large landholders were essentially tax-exempt under this system. Powerful men at the royal court became titleholders of lands they did not honestly own, manage, or cultivate, but they benefitted from it by collecting small but steady payments in rent. The peasants, who were the original owners and cultivators of the land, were now tenants or serfs—but even they were glad to be beyond the reach of the government officials. The ultimate loser was the emperor and government, for they had lost control of a good portion of their tax base.

This intricate system of land ownership and taxation is a good example of the unique multilayered structures of Japanese society: The titleholder of the land was neither the true owner nor the cultivator, and the true owner and cultivator wasn't the titleholder.

The emperor also decided that the Chinese system of a recruited army was too expensive and inefficient. So he organized locally recruited mounted warriors, whose function was to collect taxes and maintain local law and order. These were men of means, for only they could afford to undergo the long years of training and purchase their horses, armor, and weapons. They soon became an elite class of professional warriors or *bushi*, also called *samurai* from the Japanese verb *saburai*, "to serve." These warriors served their higher, liege lord and ultimately, in theory, the emperor. Local government officials, stewards, and an occasional aristocrat would follow the emperor's example and hire their own samurai. A strong personal bond existed between a local lord and his samurai, for the lord gave his samurai land or a salary, and a samurai in return pledged his loyalty to the lord.

The samurai developed a code of conduct, called *bushido* or the "way of the warrior." It is an amalgam of traditional Japanese warrior ethic, Chinese Confucianism, and Zen Buddhism. It emphasizes discipline, austerity, loyalty, and self-sacrifice. The cherry blossom came to symbolize the samurai, for a parallel was seen between the cherry blossom in its vitality and fiery burst of color in springtime and the brief and violent life of a samurai. A true samurai accepted a valiant life and an early death as the honorable norm.

The aristocratic Fujiwara family lent their name to an exquisite and sophisticated Fujiwara culture that dominated Japan's high society in the Heian period. Fujiwara Michinaga (966–1028) dominated the royal court for 30 years, as the father of four empresses, the grandfather of three emperors, and the uncle of two emperors. He was wealthy and powerful, and he was learned in history, poetry, literature, music, and Buddhism. These qualities made him the embodiment of Fujiwara culture, in which birth, rank, and breeding were everything, and the focus was on the pleasures of leisure and beauty.

The Tale of Genji (ca. 1010) is a long novel about life in Heian Japan. It is variously called the world's first modern novel, the first psychological novel, or a historical novel. Its author, Murasaki Shikibu, was born to a minor noble Fujiwara family, and her father served in the imperial court as a scholar-official. Recognizing her talents, her erudite father decided to teach her classical Chinese literature and poetry and kanji, all of which were traditionally reserved for the education of men. She grew up to become a lady-in-waiting to Empress Shoshi, and had a front seat to observe Fujiwara's culture up-close.

The novel's central character, Genji, is a handsome imperial officer, and the plot follows him on his many romantic ventures. A love child of his later becomes emperor, and appoints him to high office. But when his beloved lady companion, also named Murasaki, dies, he contemplates the fleeting and illusory nature of life.

While the novel centers on Genji's life, it also reaches out to paint a broad canvas of the society surrounding him, which makes the novel a rich tapestry of the times.

The royal family relocated to Heian (modern Kyoto) after residing in Nara for less than a hundred years. The move coincided with the decline and fall of China's Tang Dynasty, and Japan stopped sending missions to China to learn Chinese ways. Japan had arrived at a turning point: It would end its wholesale borrowing from China, and launch out on its own. But the preceding period of cultural borrowing would prove invaluable to its future development.

The aristocratic Fujiwara family ruled Japan during the Heian period. They gained control over the throne without any violent and abrupt coup d'état, but by marrying their daughters to the emperors generation after generation. This often made a Fujiwara the grandfather and regent of a very young emperor. Thus, the Fujiwara aristocrats would rule, while the emperor would continue to reign, but his time and energy would all be consumed by purely ceremonial functions. To escape manipulation by the Fujiwara family, he might abdicate the throne to his son, take Buddhist vows, and try to influence events from behind the scenes. This system was called "cloistered politics." By the eleventh century, the emperor had joined other aristocratic families as a contender for wealth and power. Layer piled upon layer, Japan's political structure had become just as convoluted as its land and tax systems.

The "Age of the Shogun" (Twelfth–Sixteenth Centuries)

The Heian government had become dysfunctional by the twelfth century as the great aristocratic families and local lords fought fiercely for power. Minamoto Yoritomo emerged victoriously out of the ensuing civil wars. He was recognized as the overlord of all samurai because of his military prowess, and the emperor bestowed on him the title of *shogun*, meaning "barbarian-subduing-generalissimo" or "general-in-chief." He set up a *bakufu* (literally a "tent government," i.e., military government) at Kamakura, and from there he ruled the entire country. He ruled over a semicentralized feudal society: He had the power to confirm the hereditary land rights of a *daimyo*, "great name" or great lord. The daimyo enjoyed autonomy within his own domains or *han*, but swore his loyalty to the shogun, and paid taxes and provided military service to him. Nominally, the emperor had granted the shogun his title, and appointed him to rule as the emperor's deputy. In fact, the emperor had been reduced to a figurehead, conducting endless ceremonial functions in Heian, away from the power center at Kamakura. Thus began the "Age of the Shogun."

The emperor reigned, the shogun ruled, and the local lords enjoyed autonomy in their own domains. This basic government structure would dominate Japan, with some exceptions, until the Meiji Restoration in the mid-nineteenth century. It was an extremely intricate system that the Joei law code of 1232 attempted to clarify and explain. But the Hojo Regency during the late thirteenth and much of the fourteenth centuries complicated political relationships across Japan. Just as the Fujiwara family co-opted imperial power during the Heian period, so too a power behind the shogun soon emerged. The Minamoto Shogun's family soon lost power to the Hojo family, who became the real power during the Minamoto Shogunate. Hojo daughters married into the Minamoto family and pushed the shogun's family aside to join the emperor as a figurehead. Another layer of complexity was added to the already bewilderingly complex power structure.

The tradition of aristocratic cultural refinement of the Heian era was preserved in the Kamakura era of shoguns. The samurai class adopted the Zen sect of Buddhism with its emphasis on restraint and austerity, and the samurai's Zen culture would replace the aristocratic culture of refinement over time. Japanese Zen gardens and minimalist ink paintings are good expressions of the Zen aesthetic.

Kublai Khan, the Mongol conqueror of China and Korea, made two attempts in the 1270s and 1280s to invade Japan from Korea. He managed to land some Mongol troops on Japanese soil at one point, but they were beaten back by the Japanese samurai, and the typhoons sank all his ships and drowned all his men. Many Japanese believed that "divine intervention" had taken place—that the gods had sent the *kamikaze* or "divine wind" to destroy their enemy and save Japan.

The Hojo-dominated Shogunate had stopped the Mongol invasions, but it was a hollow victory for him because the long period of preparedness against the attacks was costly, and the victory offered no war booty and no land with which he could reward his samurai for their services. Samurai discontent spread, and the Hojo family lost control. Chaotic fighting broke out among the shogun's family, the imperial family, the local lords, and bands of samurai.

Ashikaga Takauji (1305–1358) came out on top and founded the Ashikaga *bakufu*. But the reach of his government was limited, for the local lords and bands of samurai had retained their control at the local level, and engaged one another in endless warfare. This was the chaotic and violent Warring States or Sengoku period (1467–1600). It was a time of unending military conflict, chronic social disorder, and dark political intrigue. For a century and a half, the Japanese landscape would be a battlefield dominated by the elite class of armor-wearing, sword-wielding, and arrow-shooting samurai warriors galloping on horseback.

A "Foot Soldier Revolution" that began in the fourteenth century soon changed the face of warfare. First, the heavy spear was introduced into combat. It could penetrate the armor of a charging samurai on horseback. Second, local lords began recruiting massive numbers of peasants, and training them quickly and easily into spear-bearing foot soldiers. After the Europeans introduced firearms to Japan in the sixteenth century, these peasant foot soldiers were further armed with muskets. The massive formations of spear- and musket-bearing foot soldiers became the bulk of a fighting force that could effectively contend with any band of samurai warriors. Warfare reached new heights in scale and brutality. The samurai kept losing ground until they reached the verge of extinction as a class of elite warriors; they would, however, survive as a class with a fundamentally different function.

Earlier, local lords had built moderately fortified castles that were sufficient to fend off attacks by mounted samurai with bows and arrows. But these castles would burn and collapse under attack by firearms. Rising to the challenge, local lords built larger and stronger castles to fend off attack by muskets and cannon. They also turned these new castles into the seat of their governments, from which they would gather their troops and administer their domains. These expanded castles soon grew into "castle towns" by attracting ordinary people and merchants.

A strong local lord would go to war with the vision of bringing all of Japan under his control. The successful unifier was Overlord Oda Nobunaga (1534–1584). He conquered the country with his massive peasant armies bearing spears and muskets. He then built strong castles at strategic locations to serve as military and administrative centers. He standardized currency, eliminated customs barriers, and opened up Nagasaki to foreign trade. When he was murdered, his general and successor Toyotomi Hideyoshi (1536–1598) continued the drive for unification. Hideyoshi undertook a national survey to compile registries of land, population, and towns and villages. It was of profound significance, for information in the registries became the basis for measures to collect land taxes, impose drafts, and tie peasants to the land. His creation of a powerful and centralized state would serve as a solid foundation for the great period of peace and prosperity and dramatic social change under the Tokugawa.

When Hideyoshi died, Tokugawa Ieyasu (1543–1616) became regent to his infant son, but he seized the reins of power and became shogun instead. He relocated his *bakufu* from Kamakura down the road to Edo (modern Tokyo), and further strengthened and centralized the government bureaucracy. His restructured government worked so well that he was able to complete Japan's unification, end the slaughter and destruction of endless civil wars, and create two and a half centuries of peace, stability, and economic growth. His Tokugawa Shogunate was the last and greatest of the shogunates.

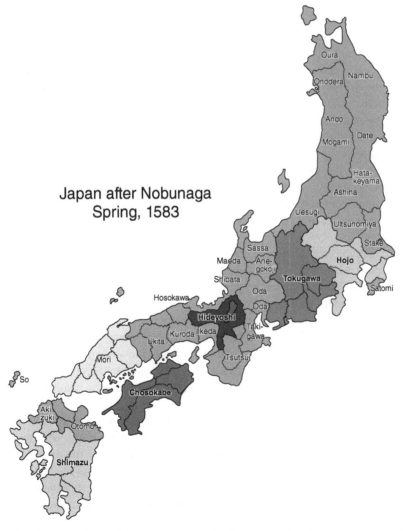

Map of Japan during and after Oda Nobunaga's reign. *Source:* From https://www.samurai-archives.com/image/1583.gif. Reproduced with permission of C.E. West and F.W. Seal.

The Tokugawa shoguns adopted many measures to consolidate their power. One measure was the Alternate Residence System. The shoguns required the local lords to spend alternate years in residence in Edo, to leave their favorite wives and sons behind as hostages when they returned to their domains, and to spend lavishly on maintaining elaborate residences both in the capital and at home. This system gave the shogun the institutional apparatus to hit two birds with one stone: It enabled him to exercise physical control over the person of the local lords even as he emptied their coffers. The shoguns also frequently called on the local lords to "make loans" to the government to support such public projects as waterworks, and it was understood that these "loans" would never be paid back. The shoguns quickly built up their strength and filled up their coffers at the expense of the local lords. It wasn't long before the local lords found themselves still in possession of their domains, but no longer enjoying autonomy. The Tokugawa shoguns had created a centralized feudal state.

Although Tokugawa Ieyasu came from peasant stock, he enforced a policy of freezing class lines and creating a system that was nearly a caste system. The royal family was set apart and above all other classes. The rest of society was divided into four classes: the samurai, the peasants, the artisans, and the merchants, in descending order. This Japanese social structure was a modification of the Chinese model, in which the Japanese samurai warrior class replaced the Chinese scholar-official class.

The Tokugawa shoguns had little use for the military prowess of the samurai warriors in a unified country where peace reigned. But they did face a new demand for a large number of civil administrators to run their elaborate government bureaucracy. Under these new circumstances, the samurai class of sword-wielding warriors morphed into a class of pen-pushing bureaucrats. But to make the transition, they had to go through the crucible of studying the Confucian classics, for it would teach them the essential skills of a bureaucrat—reading and writing—and instill in them a strong sense of loyalty to the emperor (and, by extension, to the shogun).

The warrior-turned-bureaucrat samurai were given the privilege of being the only men permitted to staff the state bureaucracy as civil officials. But the privilege came at a price: They were required to reside in the castle-towns and give up their right to own land in exchange for a fixed stipend. They were also banned from switching masters, which had been a common cause of social instability. Thus, the once-proud class of warriors was turned into a class of salaried administrators sitting in government offices.

Peasants were confined to living on the land and cultivating crops in the countryside. They were banned from owning weapons. Merchants were officially relegated to the bottom of society as the fourth class. A near-frozen caste-like system was now in place.

The Tokugawa policies produced the unintended consequence of a commercial revolution. First, they created a stable and peaceful environment that was inductive to economic and population growth. Second, the local lords had to sell the harvests from their land in order to acquire cash to purchase goods and services they needed in the capital and their castle-towns, and this created a sharp increase in the demand for trade and cash. Osaka became the commercial center of Japan, especially of its rice trade. The commercialization of Japan's economy turned the country into a money society.

The lords and samurai were inept at managing money, and the lowly merchants were soon the money managers of their social superiors. When inflation hit, however, the samurai with their fixed stipends became impoverished, and were often reduced to being debtors to the merchants who were managing their money. The officially high status of the samurai class and the officially low status of the merchant class were no longer reflective of reality. In fact, the reverse was true: Merchants had become a wealthy and influential class, while the samurai's status was badly diminished. In most cases, a town's economy was controlled by big merchant families who enjoyed special privileges granted to them by the government.

The Tokugawa government's main source of revenue came from tax farming, and it levied these taxes on a village as an entity, rather than on the individual land owners or cultivators. The government had a hands-off policy as long as a village paid its taxes. This autonomy allowed the villages to manage their own business, and agricultural production surged. A vigorous economy promoted the division of labor. "Big houses" in a village would go into the manufacture of silk and sake, or operate pawn shops. "Head men" from the "big houses" would develop leadership qualities. The villages in Tokugawa Japan grew into solid social entities.

Japan's traditional merchants enjoyed many privileges under Tokugawa rule. They had great vested interests in the existing order, and therefore had no incentive to be agents of change. As traditional Japan moved toward modernization, the traditional merchant class would fade into obscurity. This trait distinguishes the traditional Japanese merchant from its counterpart in Europe and America, where the merchant class was a driving force for change and revolution.

Tokugawa stability was not stagnation. Rather, it was a time when Japan created a sophisticated national government staffed with educated and disciplined samurai, developed a prosperous money economy, cultivated a strong and productive agricultural population, and wove a strong social fabric. Tokugawa Japan was creating the building blocks of a modern Japan. In Japan's drive toward modernization, the samurai-turned-administrators would quickly assume leadership roles in civil government, the military, and business; the village "headmen" would become grassroots leaders of a modern Japanese state; and the villages would provide the initial capital for its early industrialization.

Premodern Korea

Ancient Korea: The Land and the People

The Korean Peninsula is about 600 miles long and 125–200 miles wide. It borders with China and Russia to the north, and its southernmost shore is less than 120 miles from Japan across the ocean. A massive mountain range runs along its eastern coastline, leaving most of its plains and valleys to the west and south. Only 14% of its territory is fit for cultivation.

The ancestors of modern-day Koreans were migrants from Siberia and Manchuria who settled on the Korean Peninsula. Ethnically, the Koreans and the Japanese share a common origin with the indigenous people of Siberia and Manchuria. Linguistically, they both speak an Altaic language, which is unrelated to Han Chinese. Early Koreans were a tribal people who relied on fishing, hunting, and gathering for subsistence. As agriculture grew, they built villages and towns. Chinese know-how, from early crop growing and animal husbandry to later metallurgy, flowed from China to Korea, and enabled Korean civilization to advance at a much faster pace than what was normal for other civilizations. This cultural influence was then relayed to Japan. The Koreans also adopted the Chinese writing system (Han Chinese characters), Confucianism, and China's centralized bureaucratic structure of government. Korea is part of the cultural sphere of Confucianism, along with China, Japan, and Vietnam.

Archaeological discoveries suggest that humanlike beings inhabited the Korean Peninsula as far back as 700,000 BCE, they entered the Stone Age around 500,000 BCE, local bronze production began around the eighth century BCE, and local iron production began around the third century BCE.

Timeline: Premodern Korea to 1897	
700,000 BCE	Humanlike beings appear on the Korean Peninsula
10,000 BCE	Paleolithic hunters and gatherers of the Old Stone Age
1500 BCE	Agricultural villages appear; rice cultivation introduced from China 1200–900 BCE
800 BCE	Bronze Age begins
ca. 4th century BCE	GoJoseon Dynasty established; centralized kingdom
3rd century BCE	Iron Age begins
200–100 BCE	Jin State emerges in southern Korean Peninsula
194–198 BCE	Wiman Joseon Dynasty founded by defeated rebel Han Chinese general at Pyongyang
109–108 BCE	China's Han Wudi, the Martial Emperor, unseats Wiman Joseon Dynasty and sets up Four Chinese Commanderies

57 BCE–668 CE	Three Kingdoms
	    37 BCE–668 CE: Goguryeo
	    57 BCE–935 CE: Silla
	    18 BCE–660 CE: Baekje

698–926	Northern and Southern Dynasties
	    668–935: Unified Silla
	    698–926: Unified Balhae

892–936	Later Three Kingdoms: Silla, Later Baekje, and Later Goguryeo
918–1392	Unified Goryeo, from where the English word "Korea" comes
1234	Metal, moveable-type printing press invented
1270–1350s	Mongol conquest
1392–1897	Unified Yi Joseon Dynasty
1402	Paper currency in circulation
1424	Compilation of *History of Koryo* completed
1446	Hangeul, the Korean phonetic spelling system, adopted
1592, 1598	Toyotomi Hideyoshi attempts to conquer Korea but is defeated by Korean Admiral Yi Sun-sin's "turtle boats"
1627, 1636	Manchu Qing China invades Korea and turns it into a tributary state
1880s–1890s	China and Japan work to keep Russia out of Korea
1894–1895	Japan defeats China in the First Sino-Japanese War, ending Korea's tributary and protectorate status
1897	Yi Joseon Dynasty collapses; Korean Empire created

The earliest forms of agricultural society on the Korean Peninsula had emerged by 1500 BCE. Villages surfaced and grew into societies led by chieftains. In southern Korea, they engaged in intensive agriculture in dry and paddy fields, and grew a multitude of crops, such as millet, red bean, soybean, and rice. As was the case in other civilizations, bronze was only used to make weapons and ceremonial items, but not farm tools. Most of the population lived in rectangular pit-houses, but walled cities were already appearing. Dolmen burial sites became increasingly elaborate and numerous. (A dolmen is a single-chamber megalithic tomb for the burial of important persons. Over 40% of the world's dolmens are found on the Korean Peninsula.)

Korean mythology has it that the first Korean state, often called the GoJoseon Dynasty, was founded in 2333 BCE by the son of the Divine Creator and a female bear in human form. Modern historians generally agree that the GoJoseon Dynasty became a centralized kingdom before the fourth century BCE. (*Note*: In Korean, "Joseon" means "Land of the Morning Calm," and "go" means "ancient." To combine "Go" and "Joseon" distinguishes this ancient Joseon dynasty from the Yi Joseon Dynasty of the fourteenth century.)

Traditional Korea

A defeated rebel general of China's Han Empire fled to Korea and founded the Wiman Joseon Dynasty (194–108 BCE). It was a Sinicized state whose capital was at Pyongyang (today's capital of North Korea) and whose territory straddled the northern part of the Korean Peninsula and part of Manchuria (in modern China's northeast) and Mongolia. The Han Martial Emperor's troops unseated it and established four Chinese military commanderies in 109–108 BCE; two of these, the Xuantu and Lelang Commanderies, were in existence for another four centuries before they were overrun by indigenous Korean forces in 302 and 313 CE, respectively. The existence of these Chinese military colonies in Korea for a total of five centuries left its mark on Korean culture. A parallel can be drawn between these outposts and those of the ancient Romans in the lands of the Gaulish and Germanic peoples.

The Chinese-controlled territories in the northern regions coexisted with three Korean kingdoms to the south: Silla (57 BCE–935 CE), Goguryeo (37 BCE–668 CE), and Baekje (318 BCE–660 CE). When China's Han Empire fell in the early third century, the three Korean kingdoms fought one another for dominance. The Silla Kingdom strengthened its hand by forming an alliance with China's Tang Empire, defeated its rivals, and then expelled the Chinese forces. It achieved the unification of most of the Korean Peninsula (676), accepted the status of vassal state to China's Tang Empire, and embraced a policy of wholesale borrowing from China. It sent frequent and large missions to China, who brought Chinese ways back to Korea. It built a centralized bureaucratic government, adopted Confucianism as its state ideology, and used Han Chinese as its official language. It adopted a land policy that nationalized all land ownership, and then distributed it to government officials and peasants. This policy granted large concentrations of land to high government officials, and tied the peasants to the land, subjecting them to the burden of taxes and labor service. Although the Silla borrowed extensively from China, it nevertheless was successful in resisting Chinese political control and defending its cultural identity. The Silla Dynasty imported Buddhism, and began building temples and shrines, casting huge bells in bronze and iron, and carving stone Buddhas. Korean monks traveled to China to study Buddhism, and their missionaries crossed the ocean to make Japanese Buddhist converts. Korea was a bridge in the transfer of Chinese civilization to Japan.

The Silla Dynasty was wiped out in a palace coup and replaced by the Goryeo Dynasty (918–1368). (The English word "Korea" is derived from "Goryeo.") The Goryeo Dynasty moved its capital south to a location near modern Seoul, the capital of today's South Korea. It built an elaborate capital, set up a centralized government bureaucracy, and installed an imperial examination system, all on Chinese models. But the Korean examination system was much more aristocratic than the Chinese original: High office was reserved for high-ranking aristocratic families. Korea produced the world's first document printed by a metal movable-type printing press (1234). They later used the metal movable-type printing press to reproduce their libraries that had been destroyed by the Mongols. Although the Chinese had invented the technique of movable-type printing in the mid-eleventh century, it had failed to put it to wide use. The Koreans were the first to use this technology with the added innovation of metal type to print large numbers of books.

The Goryeo Dynasty tottered after the palace guard carried out a massacre of its royal court. Military strongman General Choe Chung-han assumed the role of de facto ruler of Korea, but allowed the Goryeo king to continue to reign in name.

Northern Asia was experiencing radical shifts in the balance of power during the period of 800–1400. The nomadic tribes of the Chi-tans, Nüzhens, and Mongols were getting more powerful as they whittled away at the territories of China's Song Empire. Eventually, the Mongols conquered the Song Empire and founded the Mongol Yuan Empire in China. They also conquered Korea and ruled it with an iron fist (1270–1350s), and they drained Korean resources to back their doomed invasions of Japan. However, they left Korean rulers in place as figureheads. This dual structure of government was nothing new. Korean strongman Choe Chung-han had ruled while he allowed the king to reign; in Japan, the shogun ruled and the emperor reigned for eight centuries. And the Japanese would rule Korea while a Korean king reigned during Japan's colonial rule of Korea between 1910 and 1945.

When the Mongol Empire fell, the Goryeo Dynasty was too weak to stand on its own legs. Korean General Yi Seonggye took over in a largely bloodless coup, and founded the Yi Joseon Dynasty with its capital at Hanyang (modern Seoul). As Korea's last and longest dynasty, spanning five centuries, it left Korea with a substantial legacy.

First of all, the Yi Joseon Dynasty (1392–1897) established effective control over all of the Korean Peninsula, banning the private ownership of armies that could challenge its power. It formed close ties with China's Ming Empire and continued a policy of borrowing from China. It revived reverence for books and book learning to overcome the consequences of the barbaric rule of the Mongols. It internalized Zhu Xi's Neo-Confucianism so deeply into Korean culture and society that it continues to shape Korea's social structure, moral values, etiquette, folk customs, and politics to this day. The Yi Joseon Dynasty introduced fundamental changes. Earlier, the Silla Dynasty had a system of land ownership that gave huge landholdings to a handful of highly placed aristocrats and various levels of officialdom, creating a new and much larger landholding aristocracy of civil and military officials. The new class system placed the royal family at the top of a hierarchic system of four classes: an expanded aristocracy of land- and officeholders, the middle class of government employees, the commoners who were mostly various kinds of professionals, and the "lowborn." The lowborn consisted of slaves and serfs, reputedly making up one-third of the population; they were owned privately or by the government. (The Joseon government ordered the freeing of government-owned slaves in 1801 and abolished the class system in 1894.)

Traditional Korean culture reached its peak in the Yi Joseon Dynasty. Scholarship and technology flourished. The royal court presided over the creation of a new Korean writing system in 1443. Known as Hangul, it was a phonetic alphabet system that freed the Korean language from the much more rigid and difficult Chinese system of characters. Substantial economic growth took place between 1600 and 1800. As agriculture grew, a surplus became available for trading, which stimulated the growth of the merchant class. Wealthy merchants began buying their way into the elite classes, just as their counterparts did in China and Japan. Trade with the Japanese, the Manchus, the Chinese, and even the Arabs grew. Pyongnam became an important international trading port. But the merchants' eagerness for foreign trade was at odds with the regime's desire to keep out foreign influence. Heightened activity in smuggling and piracy, often based in Japan and threatening sea lanes, became an increasing scourge. Similar developments were taking place in Ming China at the same time.

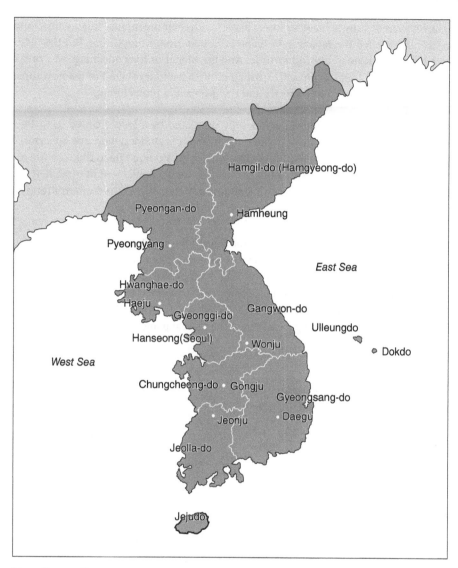

Map of Joseo**n Korea.**

Despite its successes, Korea's economic growth was slow and difficult. Its mountainous terrain and bitterly cold winters limited agricultural productivity. Chronic infighting among domestic factions and repeated foreign invasions were destructive as well. With a relatively weak economy and a divided body politic, Korea was ill-prepared to face the challenges of the nineteenth century.

Foreign Invasions of Korea

Korea's geopolitical location has subjected it to repeated invasions by its larger and stronger neighbors: the Chinese, the Japanese, the Mongols, the Manchus, and later the Western powers. It has responded by putting up heroic and sometimes successful resistance. Sui China launched a series of attacks against it (598–), which, successfully rebuffed by the Koreans, contributed to the Sui's quick demise. Japanese warlord Toyotomi Hideyoshi led two invasions of Korea (1592 and 1598, respectively). The Koreans destroyed his navy in sea battles with their ingenious "turtle ships," and eventually successfully repelled the Japanese invasion with help from Ming China. But the fighting had taken a huge toll on Korean life and fortune. And the Manchus took advantage of Korea's weakness to invade (1627 and 1636), eventually turning it into a tributary state. For the next three centuries, the Manchus ruled over China directly and saw Korea as a protectorate.

The **turtle ship** is a large warship whose deck is fully protected by a shield called a "turtle shell." The shield, perhaps of iron, can deflect cannon fire, and it is studded with iron spikes to deter enemies from boarding. It has a metal prow, mounted with a dragon head that can fire a cannon, emit poisonous smoke, or release a smokescreen to hide its movement in combat. It is powered by rowers underdeck. It can ram and sink almost any ship. It was used intermittently from the fifteenth to the nineteenth centuries.

By the late nineteenth century, Tsarist Russia built the Trans-Siberian Railway that took Moscow eastward to the Pacific Ocean. This presented a threat to numerous nations, including China, Korea, Great Britain, and particularly Japan. Should Russia take control of Korea, it would place Moscow less than 200 miles from Japan. Eventually Japan went to war with China in 1894 in order to replace Beijing as the protector of Korea, and with Russia in 1904 to keep Moscow out of Korea. The Hermit Kingdom became an unwilling pawn in another "great game" in Asia.

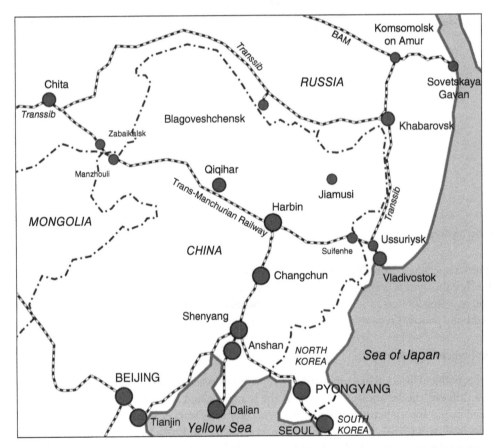

Map of the Trans-Manchurian Railroad. *BAM*: Baikal–Amur Mainline. *Transsib*: Trans-Siberian Railway.
Source: Wikimedia User Vmenkov, https://commons.wikimedia.org/wiki/File:Chinese_Eastern_Railway-en.svg.

Suggested Readings and Viewings

John B. Duncan, *The Origins of the Choson Dynasty* (Seattle: University of Washington Press, 2000).

Peter Duus, *Feudalism in Japan*, 3rd ed. (New York: McGraw-Hill, 1993).

Wayne Farris, *Population, Disease, and Land in Early Japan, 645–900* (Cambridge, MA: Harvard University Press, 1985).

Wayne Farris, *Sacred Texts and Buried Treasures: Issues in the Historical Archaeology of Early Japan* (Honolulu: University of Hawaii Press, 1998).

John W. Hall, *Government and Local Power in Japan, 500–1700* (Princeton, NJ: Princeton University Press, 1966).

Peter Lee, ed., *Sourcebook of Korean Civilization*, vol. 1 (New York: Columbia University Press, 1993).

Li Narangoa and Robert Cribb, *Historical Atlas of Northeast Asia, 1590–2010: Korea, Manchuria, Mongolia, and Eastern Siberia* (New York: Columbia University Press, 2014).

Ran (1985), dir. by Akira Kurosawa.

Conrad Schirokauer, David Lurie, and Suzanne Gay, *A Brief History of Japanese Civilization*, 4th ed. (Boston: Wadsworth, 2013).

Michael J. Seth, *A Concise History of Korea*; 2nd ed. (New York: Rowman and Littlefield, 2016).

Conrad Totman, *Early Modern Japan* (Berkeley: University of California Press, 1993).

8

The Formation of Indian Civilization: 1200 BCE–185 BCE

The fools who delight in this sacrificial ritual as the highest spiritual good go again and again through the cycle of old age and death.

—Mundaka Upanishad

Aryan Conquest

The Aryan invasion of India in the vicinity of 1500 BCE likely represented the straw that broke the camel's back for Indus Valley civilization. Political deterioration and natural disasters eroded the foundations of those hundreds of municipalities, as evidenced by the "decline in the use of writing and trading seals."[1] The fragile condition of the city-states made the task of conquest that much easier for the tribal invaders from Central Asia. They likely came to India in search of pastures and decided to stay. For the next several centuries, the Aryans settled down to become farmers and gradually moved east across the current north India, where numerous rivers and greater monsoon rainfall made agriculture a more sustainable way of life. As the Aryans marched into India and afterward journeyed east, they brought with them Sanskrit, the language in which originally oral traditions and eventually classical writings got transmitted. They also brought legends about their past that, in conjunction with an uncertain number and assortment of Indus Valley social practices, became the underpinnings for Indian civilization.

The advent of literacy in post-Harappan India cannot be precisely established, but by the end of the Vedic period (ca. 1200–600 BCE) or shortly thereafter, scholars began to physically record the Aryan oral traditions, which stretched back to pre-Indian days. Apparently tribal priests memorized sacred poems and passed them on, theoretically unedited, from generation to generation. According to a leading scholar of India, "The hymns composed by their priests in their new home were carefully handed down by word of mouth, and in the early first millennium B.C. were collected and arranged. They were still not committed to writing, but by now they were looked upon as so sacred that even minor alterations in their text were not permitted."[2] These priests, it has been argued, resisted the writing down of the revered accounts of the past lest their exclusive role as guardians and interpreters of the chronicles be undermined. No doubt the poor quality of writing materials, for example the use of palm leaves, made memorization a more reliable method of

---

1 D. R. SarDesai, *India: The Definitive History* (Boulder, CO: Westview Press, 2008), p. 26. For a critique of the Aryan Invasion Theory, see pp. 44–48.

2 A. L. Basham, *The Wonder That Was India* (New York: Grove Press, 1954), p. 30.

Asia Past and Present: A Brief History, First Edition. Peter P. Wan and Thomas D. Reins.
© 2021 John Wiley & Sons, Inc. Published 2021 by John Wiley & Sons, Inc.

transmitting sanctified ideas. Whether edited or in original form, a body of classical literature emerged in India, and by approximately the middle of the first millennium BCE this collection of holy work included the essence of what would become Hindu, Jain, and Buddhist teachings.

Timeline: India, 1500–185 BCE	
1500 BCE	Aryans conquer Indus Valley civilization
1500–1200 BCE	*Rigveda* created
1100 BCE	Iron Age begins
1000 BCE	Aryans move east across northern India
800–400 BCE	*Upanishads* composed
6th century BCE	Jainism founded by Mahavira
5th century BCE	Siddhartha Gautama creates Buddhism
5th century BCE–3rd century CE	*Mahabharata* compiled
5th century–1st century BCE	Poet Valmiki composes *Ramayana* in that period
326 BCE	Alexander the Great invades northern India
324–298 BCE	King Chandragupta Maurya of Magadha forms Mauryan Empire but soon abdicates to become a Jain
322–185 BCE	Mauryan Empire creates centralized government
298–269 BCE	Bindasura inherits Mauryan throne and expands the empire to the Deccan
269–232 BCE	Ashoka unifies much of India, converts to Buddhism, and spreads its message across India via numerous Pillar Edicts
185 BCE	Mauryan Empire collapses; India fragments into numerous states and regions; Hinduism and caste provide cultural cohesion

Vedic Period

The word Veda literally means knowledge, but usually it is used to denote the basic sacred oral traditions (later books) of Brahmanism, the original name of the religion the Aryans brought. The ideas and practices of Brahmanism transformed into what would be known as Hinduism. As there is scanty archaeological evidence for the Vedic period, these Vedas provide the best information available to evaluate the course of Indian history down to the middle of the second millennium BCE. The *Rigveda*, the earliest, most authoritative sacred source, provides glimpses into the Aryans' thinking about their origins, social order, and development. During this period as well, the social hierarchy of the Aryans underwent an important change.

Originally the social pecking order likely found warriors in the top position given the chronic clashes among pastoral nomads and the consequent need for military expertise and leadership. For instance, the warrior ruler Indra from the mythological Aryan past became a god. Such Aryan warrior-kings were followed in the social order by priests and tribespeople, with non-Aryans absorbed along the way occupying the bottom stratum. Many of the early Aryan gods exhibit a more bellicose appearance, strongly suggesting a pre-Indian Aryan leadership more concerned with the group's immediate survival now than individual salvation later. Nonetheless, by the time the Aryans settled down along the Indus and other nearby rivers, a more permanent Aryan social organization had emerged to form the foundation for future Indian social and religious practices.

In that new order, the priestly class replaced the warriors at the top of the social setting. According to one Indian specialist, the priests "not only managed to usurp the first position by claiming that they alone could bestow divinity on the king (which was by now essential to kingship) but they also gave religious sanction"[3] to social arrangements. Religions increasingly became countrywide (if not exactly uniform) organizations, with leaders, explanations, and guidelines the average person could understand and observe. The *Kshatriya*—kings, princes, and warriors—on the other hand, typically presided over a patchwork of political domains. Rulers in the Indian historical context refer to a host of regional and local authorities, since rarely did the country possess a centralized political structure with a single governing monarch. Much like the Christian church in Europe during the Middle Ages, what eventually emerged as Hinduism (as sectarian as it became) represented the only India-wide institution; political leaders of local or regional stature clearly represented only a secondary level of legitimacy. The *Vaishya* characteristically included significant but nonetheless merely third-tier members of society: landlords who oversaw the agricultural economy and the lives of the vast peasantry, and merchants, bankers, and other urbanites who facilitated the exchange of goods, services, and additional economic activities. These top three classes are considered twice-born and thus eligible to proceed along the path to salvation.

The vast majority of the population was considered once-born, of lesser social standing and thus ineligible (along with females of any class or caste) to follow the path to spiritual salvation in this individual incarnation. *Sudras* belonged to occupations—largely farming and rural artisanship—that typically provided goods and services for those of twice-born backgrounds. The outcastes comprise people deemed beyond caste membership because of their foul occupations considered polluting—such as dealing with human waste or dead animals—a result of immoral behavior in a previous incarnation. They are commonly known as untouchables, or *Dalits* ("broken people"), and were referred to as *Harijan* or "children of God" by Mohandas Gandhi; today Dalits are known officially by the Indian government as members of "Scheduled Castes."

The reform of Brahmanism and the emergence of two additional religions begin by roughly 700 BCE. By then, significant social and economic changes in India had begun. They were occasioned by the introduction of iron, which facilitated the movement of the Aryans from the drier Indus River region eastward across northern India to areas with greater rainfall but also more difficult lands to clear and plow. The result was greater and more predictable harvests and thus

The Aryan Social Hierarchy

Varna/Class/Color	Occupations	Religious Standing
Brahman	Priests and religious officials	Twice-born (*dvija*)
Kshatriya	Rulers and warriors	Twice-born (*dvija*)
Vaishya	Landowners, merchants, and bankers	Twice-born (*dvija*)
Sudra/non-Aryan	Cultivators, artisans, and servants of the above	Once-born
Untouchable/Dalit	Nastiest	Beyond the pale

Source: U.S. Library of Congress, Country Studies, *India, A Country Study*, "Caste and Class," available online at countrystudies.us.

---

3 Romila Thapar, *A History of India*, vol. 1 (Baltimore: Penguin Books, 1966), p. 39.

greater wealth production and a more complex social order. Such changes often called into question many traditional ideas and institutions. As Aryan society became more settled and secure, it seems, people's focus began to expand beyond concerns about sheer physical survival—always important—to concerns of a nonmaterial, especially religious, nature. This people's quest for grander life outcomes, a result of successful—if imperfect—social and economic developments, produced a "revolution of rising expectations." Religion became the vehicle for achieving those expectations.

Religion

Toward the end of the Vedic period, a flurry of intellectual activity of chiefly a religious nature produced speculation about individual existence, the meaning of life, and the possibility of an afterlife. Clearly the practices of the Brahman priests, stressing as they did the need for proper sacrifice to receive desired earthly rewards, failed to satisfy fully the emotional needs of people in a society undergoing radical transformations. Both the Vedas and later the *Brahmanas*—texts dealing with physical sacrifice and ritual as well as some commentary on the Vedas—gave the priests great psychological leverage over the population. The sacrifices offered by priests promised worldly benefits such as wealth, health, and success in this world and in the next world a heavenly way of life. Yet fears arose that all of the priestly ritual action, *karma*, might not be sufficient for an eternal heavenly existence: "The conclusion was slowly reached that the phenomenal world, brought forth and maintained by ritual speech and action, might in the end be a trap in which man no less than the rest of nature was caught up in continuing cycles of creation and destruction."[4] In other words, how does one face the prospect of transmigration of the soul, or reincarnation?

As the Aryans moved east across north India, they encountered yet more indigenous peoples who needed to be absorbed. Greater agricultural activity, the introduction of iron sometime after 1000 BCE resulting in more efficient farming, and the cultivation of the more lucrative rice crop all fueled trade activity and stimulated the development of crafts. As more complex social arrangements emerged and urban centers sprang up, the older sacrifice-based Brahman religion shaped for simpler times and circumstances seemed incapable of explaining satisfactorily the changing complex world to the inhabitants of the emerging Indian civilization. A protest movement within the Brahman religious framework, exemplified by the Upanishadic writings, along with two new religions—Jainism and Buddhism—appeared to provide advanced guides to life in a now more complicated but less comprehensible world.

The Vedas

Veda	Function
Rigveda	Hymns recited by the priest
Yajurveda	Formulas recited by the priest
Samaveda	Formulas chanted by the priest
Atharvaveda	A collection of stories, hymns, predictions and so forth

Source: S. W. Jamison and M. Witzel, *Vedic Hinduism* (1992), p. 6, available online at people.fas.harvard.edu.

---

4 Thomas J. Hopkins, *The Hindu Religious Tradition* (Encino, CA: Dickinson Publishing, 1971), p. 34.

The progression to a different or perhaps more complete religious understanding could be seen in the *Aranyakas* or "forest books," a probable reference to hermits of the forest speculating about man and his place in the cosmos. Just as the earlier *Brahmanas* took small steps to clarify the Vedas and begin to connect man with the hereafter, so too the *Aranyakas* attempted to advance a fuller explanation of the Vedas and in the process enable highly knowledgeable people to comprehend the secret or inner significance of the physical rituals involved in the sacrifices. In the forest, away from the interference of daily life in the community, one could apply thought, reason, and speculation—different angles of vision—to interpret the Vedas and the sacrifices therein and thus perhaps understand oneself. This brought the individual, without benefit of priest, one step closer to understanding a person's relationship to god. This the *Upanishads* accomplished. Upanishadic writings, most composed sometime between 800 and 400 BCE, explained how the individual could achieve permanent salvation. *Upanishad*, meaning sit next to or near, indicates the close relationship between student and teacher or guru, who in Socratic fashion sought to illuminate the ancient sacred texts and thus enable people to adjust their lives to the natural order of the universe. The *Upanishads*, known today as the Vedanta or the end of the Vedas, include at least 108 treatises. These writings "mark the high point of a line of evolution of thought from the time of the Rig Veda through the *Brahmanas* and *Aranyakas,* from a pantheistic faith centered on nature gods to an all-encompassing cosmic reality with the agnostic notion of identification of the individual soul with its cosmic counterpart."[5]

Eventually the word for individual, *atman*, came to represent the essence or soul of the person; and ultimately the word *brahman*, originally meaning the strength of the ritual chants in sacrifices, came to represent *Brahman*, the creator of the universe. *Karma* came to signify not just individual action but mindful behavior, which could be either good or bad. Until the stockpile of good behavior made it possible for the soul or *atman* to reunite with *Brahman*—a condition known as *moksha* or liberation (from the body)—the soul would transmigrate (*samsara*) from body to body, or even from body to another species, depending on one's behavior in life. Thus, by the late Vedic period, the role of the priest in Brahmanism somewhat lessened as the physical sacrifice became less significant to one's salvation and as one's conduct took on greater consequence. Keeping in mind that religions customarily change over time, Brahmanism will evolve, modifying some of its doctrines and practices. It will also embrace essential elements of the emerging Jain and Buddhist religions, as well as accommodate in the distant future non-Indian religious ideas contained in Islam and Christianity.

Jainism

The protest against Brahmanism's disproportionate emphasis on ritual and sacrifice produced dissent within the religion, chiefly in locations where Aryans dominated, and that discontent is best illustrated in the Upanishadic writings. The reformist urge also generated two new religions as well—Jainism and Buddhism—both of which originated in territories where non-Aryans resided in large numbers. Nonetheless both Jains and Buddhists accepted two key concepts crucial to Brahmanism, *karma* and *samsara*. The chief disagreements with Brahmanism, later Hinduism, had to do with how one broke the cycle of birth and death and rebirth.

No one knows when Jainism began, and one tradition holds that the religion has no beginning and no end. Legend has it that Rishabhdeva founded the religion. He was the first *tirthankara*

---

5 SarDesai, *India*, pp. 38–39.

(literally, "one who fords" [a body of water, that is, life's sorrows, especially *samsara*]), or one who has achieved enlightenment via asceticism. He later became the first ruler of India, taught the people how to farm, and eventually became an ascetic in search of salvation. Historically speaking, Jain ideas can be traced back to Parshvanatha, the 23rd *tirthankara* living in the ninth century BCE, who began life as a prince but later abandoned his position in society and searched for (and achieved) enlightenment. Parshvanatha is associated with the Nirgrantha ("free from ties") naked mendicants whose four principles (discussed further in this chapter) form the foundation of Jainism. This story gets repeated in the life of Mahavira (great hero) Vardhamana, Jainism's most famous teacher and practically speaking the founder of Jainism (from *Jina*, to conquer [the temptations of life]). Mahavira, born about 600 BCE of King Siddartha and Queen Trishala of the Republic of Vaishli in what is today the State of Bihar, relinquished his princely position as he approached 30. He then wandered for a dozen years, begging and meditating, in search of truth. This he accomplished, according to belief, at age 42, and for the next three decades passed on his wisdom in sermons (in the Ardhamagadhi dialect) and teachings. He died in 527 BCE, the 24th (and last) *tirthankara*.

The Jain code of belief, based on the Nirgrantha code and Mahavira's accompaniments, resides in five core principles: (1) nonviolence/*ahimsa*, (2) truthfulness/*satya*, (3) honesty/*asteya*, (4) chastity/*bramacharya*, and (5) non-possession/*aparigraha*. For monks and nuns, these guidelines must be followed strictly. For laypeople, they are instructed to be observed as best as possible. At the nucleus of the Jain core of beliefs is *ahimsa*, which forbids both physical and psychological violence against other living things. Realistically speaking, humans commit violence inadvertently in the process of living. Therefore one needs to minimize the brutality, which Jains evaluate on a scale of value for living entities based on the number of the five senses they possess. Thus, for example, humans have five senses, as do most animals; creatures with four include flies and bees; those with three comprise ants and lice; two-sense beings consist of worms and similar things; and the basic elements (of earth, fire, air, and water) plus vegetables have but one sense. Since harming those entities with many senses produces more damage, Jains characteristically practice vegetarianism. Nor can a person speak the truth, the second cardinal principle, unless one has overcome vices such as anger, greed, fear, ego, and so forth. Honesty, the third standard, requires one to refrain from actual theft as well as any immoral or underhanded method by which you obtain another's property. The fourth tenet, chastity, includes thought and deed, and applies strictly to the clergy (celibacy) and less exactingly to laypeople. Non-possession, the fifth principle, holds that the craving for possessions leads to improper behavior in order to gain those desired possessions. These possessions include material things such as a home or wealth; relationships such as family, friends, or (in the case of monks) disciples as well; and feelings such as anything your mind or senses might conjure up.

As with the Upanishadic writers and Buddhists, the Jains believed in *karma*, which is to say, they judged people to be in control of their spiritual destiny. Only by conquering (*jina*) one's baser thoughts and actions can one's soul achieve liberation from the cycle of birth, death, and rebirth (*samsara*), and only ascetics and men could possibly achieve this release. Women and those males not strictly ascetic would need to be reborn, at which point the possibility of this release or liberation (*moksha*) could occur. After the death of Mahavira, his disciples started to compile his teachings, a task completed in the fifth century CE at a Jain council, which endorsed 45 texts as the religious canon. The religion gained a following when Chandragupta Maurya, the first emperor of the Mauryan Empire (321–185 BCE), became a Jain, renounced the throne, and became a monk.

Today there only 5 million Jains in India and fewer still in the Indian diaspora, likely owing to the austere lifestyle the religion requires of its acolytes.

Buddhism

Buddhism also arose as a religious dissent against the ritualism of Brahmanism. Born Gautama Siddhartha but also known as Sakyamuni (sage of the Sakyas) and the Buddha (Enlightened One), this son of Chief Suddhodana of the Sakyas and Mahamaya came into the world circa 583 BCE in Lumbini, Nepal, just north of the Indian border. A contemporary of Mahavira, Gautama grew up in a privileged environment, married, and had a son, but upon departing his sheltered setting became aware of suffering and its numerous causes. Approaching the age of 30, Gautama abandoned his family, determined to discover the cure for suffering. After examining and rejecting several schools of thought and religious practices, including the life of an ascetic, he realized that a new approach to life—a middle path—needed to be devised. He concluded that the extreme ritualism of Brahmanism, the dense theology of the Upanishads, and the severe asceticism of Jainism failed to bring about solutions to the problem of suffering. Thereupon, tradition states, he sat down under the "Bodhi Tree" (in Bihar) and meditated for 49 days. These seven weeks of contemplation culminated in the achievement of enlightenment and consequently he came to be known as the Buddha, or Enlightened One. Shortly afterward he traveled to Varanasi to give his *First Sermon on the Doctrine of Righteousness*, and for the remainder of his years the Buddha trekked across India, lecturing, proselytizing the people, and mentoring monks.

Buddhism opened its spiritual arms to all, regardless of class, caste (as it was then emerging), gender, or other conditions in life. As in the case of the Upanishadic reformers and the Jain ascetics, the Buddha offered both an explanation of life's experiences and an individual route to salvation. His "Middle Path" revolved around two sets of ideas, which he labeled the Four Noble Truths and the Eightfold Path. The Four Noble Truths state that (1) all of one's existence is suffering; (2) suffering is caused by desire, which in turn leads to rebirth, a form of suffering; (3) as one eliminates desire, one also removes pain; and (4) the end of desire ends rebirth and thus suffering as one achieves Nirvana by following the Eightfold or Right/Correct Path. This "how to be a good person" guide includes right understanding, right thought, right speech, right action, right livelihood, right effort, right mindfulness, and right concentration. There is no soul (*atman*) either to get reborn or to unite with the universal soul (*Brahman*). Instead, karmic action produced either Nirvana or "rebirth." But the Buddha "said that individuals, like everything else, are constantly in flux; life is an ever-flowing stream of events. Rebirth is not transmigration [of the soul] but 'continuity in life series, in which process karma serves as a causal connection.'"[6]

The development of Buddhism after the founder's death in 483 BCE resulted in the emergence of one of the world's major religions. Initially, disagreements among monks and Buddhist councils resulted in many sects, but the ascendency of Ashoka (r. 273–232 BCE) of the Mauryan Dynasty and his conversion to Buddhism resulted in its growing popularity as well as the appearance of two chief Buddhist schools of thought into which the various sects fell: Hinayana or Theravada (using Pali and Magadhi dialects) and Mahayana (using Sanskrit). The Hinayana, also known as the Lesser Vehicle, maintained that individuals achieved Nirvana by their own efforts and moreover that no

---

6 SarDesai, *India*, p. 55.

person stood above others. Mahayana, or "Greater Vehicle," Buddhists dubbed their Theravada (meaning "Elders") opponents Hinayana, or lesser and therefore inferior. Mahayana followers believed that those who had achieved extraordinary enlightenment, and therefore were more equal than others spiritually, had the ability to remain behind as *bodhisattvas* to aid others in the quest for Nirvana. When Theravada Buddhists refer to *bodhisattvas*, they typically mean just people well along the path to enlightenment.

By the beginning of the Common Era, Buddhism contended with Jainism and a surging Hinduism, the latter a synthesis of Upanishadic, Jain, Buddhist, as well as older Brahman ideas and practices. By that time Buddhism had spread to most of the rest of Asia, largely Theravada to Central and Southeast Asia, and principally Mahayana to China, Japan, Korea, and Vietnam.

Republics and Monarchies, 600–321 BCE

As the Vedic period concluded, the political makeup of India over the centuries began to take shape. Typically that makeup did not include an imperial central government as the norm but rather an India composed of larger and smaller kingdoms, rarely unified under Indian control. Down to the Mauryan Empire, one of those imperial exceptions, that framework consisted of larger and smaller political entities, the former republics and the latter monarchies. Republics typically originated from a tribe or confederation of tribes where assemblies composed of representatives of the tribe(s) gathered, chose a *raja* to preside over the meeting, and then proceeded to discuss issues and arrive at courses of action to deal with the concerns. Some argue that these republics represented a secular Aryan dissent against the existing Aryan political power structures, just as the Upanishads, Jainism, and Buddhism characterized a religious rebellion against Brahmanism. Across north India where Indian civilization existed at the time, these republics were apt to be found in the foothills, while monarchies tended to be located along the plains. Kingdoms likely appeared as the territory of tribal units or confederations expanded to the point that assemblies became impractical. Moreover, monarchs utilized the power of the priests to become hereditary and divine. According to one historian of India, the priests "depicted the king as an exceptional person in communicating with the gods, even if only through the priests. The priests too were not ordinary mortals, since they were in effect the transmitters of divinity. Thus the throne and the priesthood worked hand in hand."[7]

For several hundred years, successful kingdoms gobbled up failed states or ones that proved too small to resist their neighbors' aggressions. The so-called 16 republics and monarchs (*mahajanapadas*) of 600–400 BCE ultimately gave way first to the Magadha "Empire" (624–424 BCE), which controlled roughly today's northeastern India, and then to the Nanda "Empire" (424–321 BCE), which governed a good part of northern India. Although neither "empire" ever controlled even half of the Indian subcontinent, both are viewed as models for empire building, prototypes for the leaders of the succeeding Mauryan Empire. Had Nanda rulers pushed further west, two powerful armies would certainly have clashed, one Greek and one Indian. As it turned out, Alexander the Great ended his India campaign (327–326 BCE) in the Punjab region of the northwest. As Alexander departed India and the Nanda Dynasty collapsed, a truly imperial political institution arose to take control of most of the Indian subcontinent.

---

[7] Thapar, *A History of India*, p. 54.

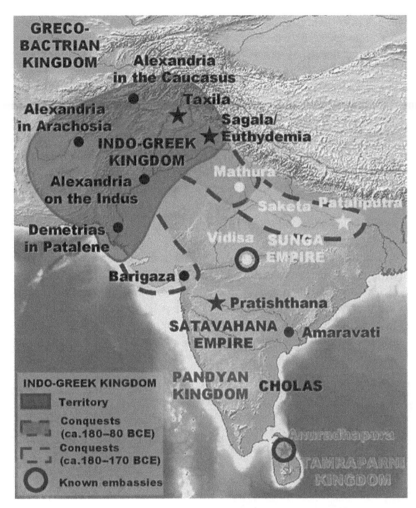

India, ca. 350–150 BCE. *Source:* https://upload.wikimedia.org/wikipedia/commons/thumb/f/fa/Indo-GreekMapColor.jpg/500px-Indo-GreekMapColor.jpg.

Mauryan Empire (321–185 BCE)

The unification of northern India and later most of the rest of the subcontinent by Chandragupta Maurya and his successors created more standardized practices at home, and abroad created the ability for all of India to confront Alexander's successor general, Seleucus Nikator. But it was Alexander's conquest of India's northwest (today's northwestern India, Pakistan, and much of Afghanistan) that gave rise to discontent in those conquered territories, in conjunction with dissatisfaction with Nanda rule, that largely led to the creation of the Mauryan Empire. Although little is known about its founder, Chandragupta Maurya likely came from humble beginnings in roughly the same India–Nepal frontier region as the Buddha. As with many other empire founders from Cyrus the Great in Persia to Qin Shi Huangdi in China, he probably possessed management skills that, along with with the dissatisfactions with existing rulers and institutions, combined to fashion a leader capable of mobilizing people for common purposes. The first three Mauryan emperors established, expanded, and consolidated the realm, beginning with creator Chandragupta Maurya (r. 321–292 BCE); his heir Bindusara

(r. 292–272 BCE), who extended political control to the Deccan in central India; and subsequently Ashoka the Great (r. 272–232 BCE), who presided over a regime that controlled all but the southern tip of the subcontinent. After Ashoka, however, the dynasty soon became a feeble shadow of its former stature as the government lost control of the provinces and proved incapable of keeping Greek raiders out of the northwest.

A good deal of what is known about the Mauryan Empire comes from three basic sources. One is the Greeks who traveled to India, especially Megasthenes, who served as the Seleucid emissary to the Mauryan court. A second is the *Arthashastra*, a political tract written by Chanakya under the pseudonym Kautilya in 322 BCE, though the work did not likely appear in final form until after the collapse of the dynasty. Chanakya tutored the young Chandragupta Maurya, and it is fair to say he influenced the politics of the time. But he and his thinking also continue to have an impact on Indian politicians. Jawaharlal Nehru, the first prime minister of India after independence from Great Britain in 1947, commented on this political classic:

> There was hardly anything Chanakya would have refrained from doing to achieve his purpose; he was unscrupulous enough; yet he was also wise enough to know that this very purpose may be defeated by means unsuited to the end. Long before Clausewitz, he is reported to have said that war is only a continuance of state policy by other means. But he adds, war must always serve the larger ends of policy and not become an end in itself; the statesman's objective must always be the betterment of the state as a result of war.[8]

Ashoka (r. 272–232 BCE), as depicted in the motion picture *Asoka*. *Source:* Dinodia Photos/Getty Images.

---

8 Jawaharlal Nehru, *The Discovery of India* (New York: Anchor Books, 1960), p. 80.

Certainly Ashoka the warrior fits the characterization of "unscrupulous" since his battle for Kalinga in 260 BCE cost a quarter million casualties. As the story goes, his victory produced a scene so horrific that he converted to Buddhism and promoted *ahimsa*. In any case, his expansion into central and southern India extended the influence of Buddhism to those locations as well. At home in the capital (Pataliputra, today's Patna, capital of Bihar) as well as along the roads across the empire, the third rich source of insights into Mauryan times can be found in Ashoka's erected pillars and positioned rocks with inscriptions containing the ruler's political and religious convictions. The Seventh Pillar Edict illustrates the emperor's desire to impose uniform values throughout the empire. "In the past kings sought to make the people progress in Righteousness, but they did not progress.... And I asked myself how I might uplift them through progress in Righteousness.... Thus I decided to have them instructed in Righteousness, and to issue ordinances of Righteousness, so that by hearing them, the people might conform."[9]

The Fourth Pillar Edict stresses the need for righteous government: "My governors are placed in charge of hundreds of thousands of people. Under my authority they have the power to judge and to punish, that they calmly and fearlessly carry out their duties, and that they may bring welfare and happiness to the people of the province and be of help to them."[10] His paternal responsibility for his subjects can be clearly seen in the Sixth Rock Edict: "I am not satisfied simply with hard work or carrying out the affairs of state, for I consider my work to be the welfare of the whole world.... There is no better deed than to work for the welfare of the whole world, and all my efforts are made that I may clear my debt to all beings."[11]

Pillar Edict.

---

[9] Wm. Theodore De Bary, ed., *Sources of Indian Tradition*, vol. 1 (New York: Columbia University Press, 1958), p. 149.
10 De Bary, *Sources of Indian Tradition*, 1:147.
11 De Bary, *Sources of Indian Tradition*, 1:146.

The Mauryan Empire for the first time brought to most of the Indian subcontinent a political integration, however fleeting, that served as the ideal for future rulers. Mauryan unification also brought about the development of a cultural assimilation that allowed for diversity of local practices within a broad, increasingly Hindu framework. Even as Buddhism spread, so too did other non-Vedic religious traditions, as well as reformed Brahmanism—Hinduism—which probably remained the religious doctrine of choice. The Mauryans as well presided over a vast urban growth requiring greater standardization of law (as seen in the Pillar and Rock Edicts) and of weights and measures, as well as a common script. Moreover the monarch, his advisors, and the central bureaucracy began to take on paternalistic functions that were once the exclusive preserve of Brahman priests. The central government also started to supervise tasks once overseen by regional or local elites, mobilizing manpower for projects such as the clearing of land for farming and the digging of irrigation ditches for the cleared land. Thus when the last of the Mauryan rulers, Brihadrath, had his throne usurped, a host of disaffected priests and politicians took the opportunity to reassert their preeminence. As in Europe after the fall of Rome, the objective of a restored Roman empire remained an elusive ideal, as it would in India. With the exception of the similarly transitory Gupta Empire (320–550 CE), India's political future consisted of regional and local kingdoms or considerably centralized government under foreign rule until 1947.

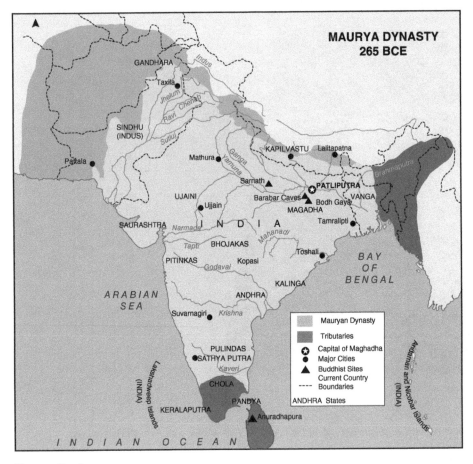

Mauryan Empire.

Hinduism and the caste system operated during most of the Common Era to provide cultural unity. Hinduism represented a synthesis of the old Brahmanism with its stress on priests and sacrifices in conjunction with the reform ideas contained in the *Upanishads* and their stress on behavior as keys to salvation. Hinduism also drew from Jain ideas such as nonviolence and a minimally materialistic lifestyle as well as Buddhist thought and behavioral paths to Nirvana. The caste system provided specific guides to one's daily life that complemented religious teachings. The emerging Hinduism and the evolving caste system will be discussed in Chapter 9.

Suggested Readings and Viewings

Asoka (2001), dir. by Santosh Sivan.

A. L. Basham, *The Origins and Development of Classical Hinduism* (New York: Oxford University Press, 1991).

Wm. Theodore De Bary, ed., *Sources of Indian Tradition*, vol. 1 (New York: Columbia University Press, 1958).

Robert Decaroli, *Haunting the Buddha: Indian Popular Religions and the Formation of Buddhism* (New York: Oxford University Press, 2004).

Paul Dundas, *The Jains* (London: Routledge, 2002).

Gavin D. Flood, *An Introduction to Hinduism* (Cambridge: Cambridge University Press, 1996).

Patrick Olivelle, trans., *The Law Code of Manu* (New York: Oxford University Press, 2004).

Asko Parpola, *The Roots of Hinduism: The Early Aryans and Indus Civilization* (New York: Oxford University Press, 2015).

Ram Sharan Sharma, *India's Ancient Past* (New York: Oxford University Press, 2005).

9

The Hindu Synthesis at Home: 185 BCE–1200 CE

Those persons who, meditating on Me without any thought of another god, worship Me—to them, who constantly apply themselves [to that worship], I bring attainment [of what they do not have] and preservation [of what they have attained].

—Bhagavad Gita[1]

The Emergence of India's Cultural and Geographical Contours

As the Mauryan Empire collapsed, three distinct characteristics of the future India took shape. Politically, regionalism instead of centralized government became the norm. Culturally, Hinduism bound together with the caste system successfully captured the hearts of the vast majority of Indians, though Jainism and Buddhism, and eventually Islam, Sikhism, and Christianity, all demonstrated continued numerical and cultural influence. Geographically, the Indian subcontinent comprised three broad regions: the north Indian plain, across which the major rivers flow and where Indo-European languages predominate into the twenty-first century; the Deccan Plateau of central India demarcated by mountain ranges, the Vindhya to the north and the eastern and western Ghats; and south India, where Dravidian languages still hold sway even as Indo-European Hindi expands there via modern communications. And within those geographical and linguistic blocs, still further subdivisions based on yet more confined partitions of language and geography exist. In north India, for instance, both Bengal and Punjab are culturally distinct regions where local dialects and different religions set them off from both central and southern India, as well as from the rest of northern India. Much the same kinds of divisions can be seen in India as a whole.

Timeline: Hindu Synthesis at Home, 185 BCE–1200 CE	
170 BCE	Bactrians expand into northwest India
ca. 170 BCE	Sumati Bhargava composes the *Laws of Manu*, a code of behavior for Hindus
100 BCE	The *Bhagavad Gita* is written
ca. 27 BCE–375 CE	Kushan Empire controls much of northwestern and central India
ca. 150 CE	The *Kama Sutra* is written
275–897	Pallava Dynasty controls much of southern India

---

1 William Theodore de Bary, ed., *Sources of Indian Tradition*, vol. 1 (New York: Columbia University Press, 1958), p. 289.

Asia Past and Present: A Brief History, First Edition. Peter P. Wan and Thomas D. Reins.
© 2021 John Wiley & Sons, Inc. Published 2021 by John Wiley & Sons, Inc.

320–550 CE	Gupta Empire, the cultural Golden Age of Indian civilization, controls all of northern India and parts of the eastern coastline
5th century CE	Indians develop the concept of "full" zero
ca. 500–600	Indians develop what are called Hindu-Arabic numerals that Persians and Arabs later transmit to the West
712	Islam arrives in northern India
753–1190	Chola Empire in central and southern India
	Indian culture spreads to Southeast Asia before but mainly during Chola Empire and later times
1206	Beginning of the Muslim Delhi Sultanate (1206–1526)

What held such a vast expanse of difficult geography and cultural diversity together over the centuries? In the face of domestic factionalism and frequent foreign incursions, an integrative ideology—Hinduism entwined with the caste system—put a premium on assimilating various and sundry peoples in ways understandable and acceptable to the vast majority. In the words of one scholar, such a concept is a "system of collectively held normative and reputedly factual ideas and beliefs and attitudes advocating and/or justifying a particular pattern of political and/or economic relationships, arrangements, and conduct, which its proponents seek to promote, realize, pursue or maintain."[2] The "proponents" consisted of the social elites, from monarch and priest to caste overseer, village chief, and family head.

Still, religion can be a human construction without necessarily being simply the product of scheming elites bent on manipulating the masses. We can see religion—both the outdoor public behavior of going to church, temple, or mosque, and the private individual understanding of the cosmos and the person's place in it—as a "sacred canopy." This "canopy" covers an assortment of sanctified symbols and meanings under which the individual can operate. Religion gives a person reasons for occurrences in the outside world that would otherwise be beyond comprehension. In this framework, both elites and masses are served by faith in religious explanations, the former getting, among other things, a more orderly society, and the latter a guide to this world and (getting to) the next. Thus a person's relationship to the neighboring social and physical environments can be better understood and accepted through the sacred symbols and meanings associated with Hinduism and the caste system.

Nor does this necessarily indicate that the social elites had no faith but merely a cynical craving for a triumphant reign over tranquil peasants who meekly accept their lot in life. Although some private secular atheism or agnosticism or simply cynicism undoubtedly existed across cultures and time, true religious conviction likely remained the norm for the vast majority of both privileged and commoner down to the advent of the industrial revolution. The fact that religion can be and was utilized to maintain a social equilibrium, the status quo, hardly invalidates religion as a bona fide phenomenon; indeed, it seems to point to the people's embrace of religion and the elites' recognition of that embrace.

Religion not only defined the larger part of Indian culture but also indicated the territorial extent of India, which expanded and contracted depending on the power of the various cultures on India's frontiers. The exact geographical territory that can be labeled India—or Hindustan, or Aryavart (where Aryans lived), or Bharatvarsha—has changed over the centuries. Certainly it includes the

---

2 Malcolm Hamilton, "The Elements of the Concept of Ideology," *Political Studies* 35 (1987): 38.

Indian subcontinent by the Common Era and down to independence in 1947. But before the expansion of Islam, it generally referred to those locations where Brahmanism, Buddhism, Jainism, and eventually Hinduism were practiced. Less defined by strict political territorial lines, India included areas where Indian culture—particularly lands where its religions, languages, and political institutions—prevailed.

Regionalism and Foreign Invaders: Northern India and Central Asia, 185 BCE–1200 CE

The collapse of the Mauryan Empire in 185 BCE produced a succession of domestic and foreign regional rulers until the transitory Gupta Empire in 320–550 CE. But even the Guptas at their height failed to control major segments of the South Asian subcontinent. Indeed, until the conquest by the Delhi sultans in 1206, Indian politics remained fragmented even as Indian culture, particularly religion, provided the cohesive bond that held the diverse populace considerably together.

The native Sunga Empire, founded by Pushyamitra Sunga, the military commander of the last Mauryan emperor, controlled most of northern India for several decades, but foreign incursions gradually eroded both its territory and ultimately its control. The Sunga Dynasty collapsed about 75 BCE. During and after its administration, over much of the north and especially the northwest, it suffered invasions from Bactrians, Parthians, and Scythians, mainly due to barbarian migrations on the Eurasian steppe that pushed peoples on the frontier into India proper. Qin Shi Huangdi, the unifier of China in 221 BCE, constructed the Great Wall and pushed west many of the nomadic tribes, some of which would later impact India.

Bactrians (aka Indo-Scythians) dominated much of what is today Central Asia, Afghanistan, and Pakistan. A steppe people, the Bactrians came under the influence of the Persians, later of the Greeks during and after Alexander's campaigns in Asia, and finally of the Indians. Their influence stretched from Greece, with which they allied, to China, with which they traded. By the time the Bactrians were overthrown in the first century CE by the Kushan steppe people, the Bactrians living in greater India had been integrated into Hindu society. They are early relatives of the Pashtuns/Pushtuns, Uzbeks, and Tajiks.

Another foreign people, the Parthians of Persian background, occupied parts of northwestern India. They likely originated somewhere along the northern frontier of Persia, and by the time of Cyrus the Great in the sixth century BCE they came under the control of his Achaemenid Dynasty, later under the Greek Seleucid Dynasty, and finally under the Arsaced Dynasty, after the leader Arsaces, probably a native of Bactria. The Parthians threw off Greek control, came to control Persia, and formed an empire that controlled the Silk Road and stretched from the eastern Mediterranean to parts of northwestern India. In 224 CE Ardasir, a vassal of the Parthians, successfully revolted and formed the Sassanian Empire (224–651), the last pre-Islamic Persian government. Though Parthian incursions into India never extended as far east as the Indus River, they did result in constant conflict between regional Indian rulers and yet another foreign adversary after the fall of the Mauryan Empire.

The Scythian Empire at its height extended from contemporary Eastern Europe to China's northwestern province of Xinjiang and controlled greater or lesser territory from before Alexander's time to the fifth century CE. Scythian tribes migrating into India became known as Indo-Scythians or Sakas/Shakas. They controlled much of today's Afghanistan (the southern part of which is often still referred to as Sakastan), Pakistan, and parts of northwestern as well as pieces of central India.

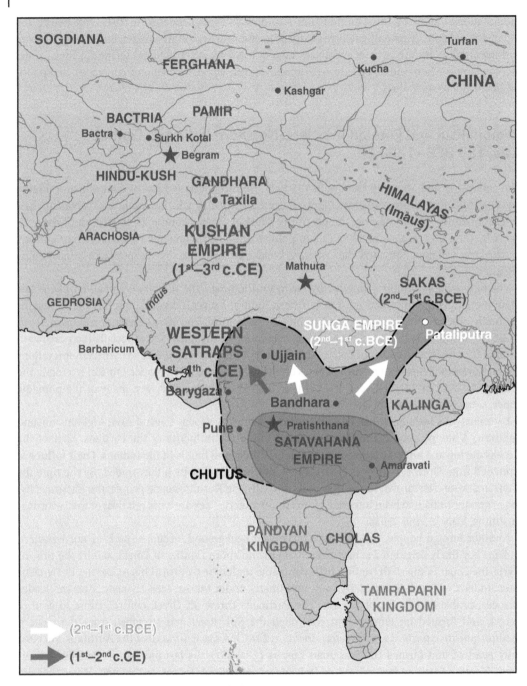

India after the Mauryan Empire, 184 BCE–200 CE.

They established an ongoing land contact between India and China. Many consider them to be the ancestors of India's Jatts and Rajputs.

The Kushanas, descendants of the central/inner Asian nomads the Chinese called Yue Zhi, had been pushed west away from the eastern steppe, just ahead of the Xiongnu or Huns. China under Qin Shi Huangdi had unified China in the late third century BCE. The Qin Dynasty cobbled together the

Great Wall from the walls of formerly independent states in northern China to keep barbarians out of the Middle Kingdom. It then gave chase to various and sundry nomads on China's frontier and frequently did battle with them. The successor Han Dynasty (206 BCE–220 CE) advanced an equally aggressive inner Asian policy to keep the barbarians in check, often shoving nomadic peoples farther west. The Yue Zhi first settled just north of India and later proceeded to invade Hindustan during the first century CE. They set up headquarters near modern Peshawar in today's Pakistan, and defeated the Sakas and other foreign rulers in northern India as they expanded east. As Kushanas they settled down, embraced Buddhism, and especially under Kanishka (r. 78–101 CE) promoted its expansion into Central Asia and China. Even though the Kushanas were not themselves Sakas, Kanishka designated his regime the Saka era, and it is still referred to today in India as such.

Indian Politics, Religion, and Commerce: Domestic Developments and Their Influences Abroad

From the fall of the Mauryan Empire until the rise of the Delhi Sultanate in 1206 CE, Indian society experienced several setbacks but also generated a number of achievements. The chief goal of Indian political leaders—a central government—remained unfulfilled. Defense of India did not fare well, as foreign intruders regularly attacked and often controlled significant parts of northern India. At the same time a wide array of cultural activities—in literature, mathematics, and religion—flourished. Commercially, as well, domestic and foreign trade thrived. During that time Indian culture spread to nearly every corner of Asia. Buddhism flourished in South, Central, Southeast, and East Asia; Hinduism, though less popular abroad, also won converts. The Indian model of centralized monarchy, though largely a failure at home, nonetheless became attractive to rulers in cultures surrounding India. Systems of Indian-derived writing emerged, chiefly in Southeast Asia. Even the martial arts obtained inspiration from India. Legend has it that Indian monk Bodhidharma introduced *gong fu*–style fighting (and *Chan/Zen/Dhyana* meditation practices) to China's Shao Lin Temple in the early sixth century.

Shao Lin monks, Shao Lin Buddhist Temple, Henan Province, China. *Source:* Wikimedia Commons, CC BY-SA 3.0, https://commons.wikimedia.org/wiki/File:Shi_DeRu_and_Shi_DeYang.jpg.

One of the last native attempts to unify India politically, before foreign consolidation began in the thirteenth century (and lasted until 1947), occurred under the Gupta Empire. At home the Guptas presided over what scholars refer to as the Golden Age of India (320–550 CE), when Hinduism synthesized earlier Brahman, Jain, and Buddhist religious ideas and practices; when the caste system reached maturity; and when Indian civilization reached its premodern pinnacle, as exemplified in such areas as poetry, drama, mathematics, and philosophy. Understandably, it also coincided with the spread of Indian cultural ways to Southeast Asia. A good deal of what we know about India during the Gupta and later regional monarchs comes from Chinese Buddhist travelers Faxian (ca. 337–422 CE) and Xuanzang (ca. 602–664 CE). These pilgrims trekked to India, to the Buddha's homeland, to locate original Buddhist scriptures to take back to China, where the religion had gained legions of followers since the appearance of the first Chinese Buddhist in 65 CE. They recorded as well their impressions of Indian society as it operated during their lengthy visits.

The Gupta Empire originated in the historic Magadha region of northeastern India where the Mauryan and other political regimes located their capitals, usually at Pataliputra. It began the process of unifying India in 320 CE under its first monarch, Chandra Gupta (r. 320–335), who used a political marriage to the long-powerful Licchavi family to form a strong alliance for expansion across northern India. The second, and many say the best, of the Gupta monarchs, Samudra Gupta (r. 335–375 CE), expanded into parts of central and southern India, forcing local rulers to pay tribute and eventually to acknowledge his sovereignty. Chandra Gupta II (r. 376–415 CE), grandson of the dynasty's founder, subdued the heretofore independent Sakas in the northwest. Thus, by the onset of the fifth century, the Guptas had convincingly extended control over most of the northern half of India and along the east coast into the Deccan and points south. Indian culture also began to attract local elites in much of Southeast Asia. But it was also a time when the Huns from Central Asia began a protracted assault on northern India, requiring the Guptas to deploy money and soldiers to meet the threat there. This allowed those local rulers who had submitted to Gupta supremacy to forgo tribute payments and even to renounce subservience to Gupta authority.

Two of those vassal Gupta territories, Maukhari and Sthanvisvarsa in north-central India, emerged under Harsha or Harshavardhana (r. 606–647) in the early seventh century. Just as the early Gupta military and administrative successes resulted in large part from a political marriage, so too did the Vardhan Dynasty, founded by Harsha's father, Prabhakar Vardhan. Harsha's sister had married the king of Maukhari and, together with Prabhakar's State of Sthanvisvara, Harsha assembled a force to take control of northern India for a brief period, but he never had the capability to move south to unify the subcontinent. Indeed, even Harsha's "dynasty" in the north collapsed upon his death, having left no heirs (nor apparently the political institutions) to continue his political agenda. Still, during his lengthy rule Harsha presided over a religiously tolerant and culturally creative society. Born a Hindu, he favored Buddhism, perhaps a result of the Chinese Buddhist pilgrim Xuanzang's influence at court. But by then Buddhism's influence in India was on the decline as Hinduism's theology absorbed and modified many of the features of Jainism (see the Four Stages of Life in the "Hindu Synthesis and Non-Hindu Religions" section, this chapter) and Buddhism, with the Hindus declaring the Buddha to be an incarnation of the Hindu god Vishnu. Harsha also strengthened ties to China, sending a diplomatic delegation to the Middle Kingdom after Xuanzang's return to his homeland.

The Pala Dynasty (7501–120) of Bengal, so named because all of the kings' names ended with "-pala," expanded from its base into most of the territories once controlled by Harsha in northern, central, and southeastern India. This Buddhist but religiously tolerant dynasty helped to spread the religion to Nepal, Bhutan, Tibet, Myanmar, Malaysia, and Indonesia. It also established a Buddhist center of learning, Nandala, to which scholars from South and Southeast Asia traveled

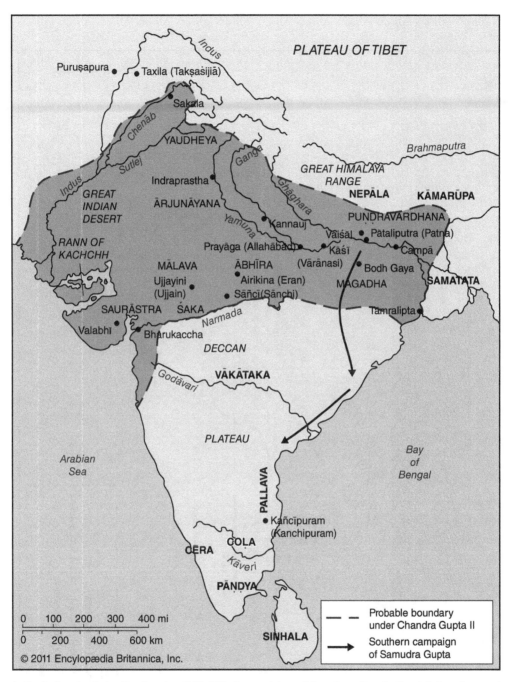

India during the Gupta Empire, circa 240–590. *Source:* Adapted from http://media-2.web.britannica.com/
eb-media/03/1603-050-E28C4592.jpg.

for religious study. It represented the last major dynastic supporter of Buddhism in India as
Hinduism began to replace it. By the time of Muslim occupation, Buddhism had become a highly
monastic faith providing only tenuous contact with the common people. With the demise of the
Pala rulers, northern India fragmented into numerous domestic and foreign minor monarchies
and remained politically splintered until the thirteenth century.

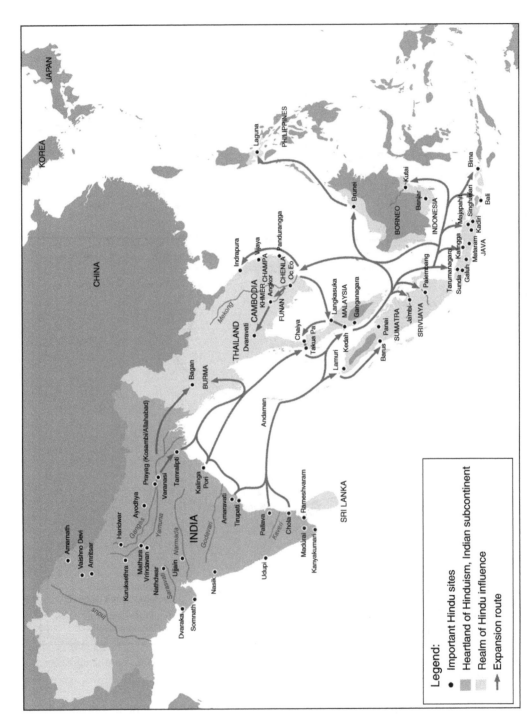

India's cultural connection with Southeast Asia before circa 1200 CE. *Source:* ©John Wiley & Sons, Inc.

Legend:
- • Important Hindu sites
- Heartland of Hinduism, Indian subcontinent
- Realm of Hindu influence
- → Expansion route

Central and Southern India and Ceylon, circa 300–1200

The control of the Deccan and parts of southern India fell into the hands of the Satvahana (or Andhra) Empire (ca. 230 BCE–220 CE), whose rulers established a modicum of order and kept the foreign invaders at bay. In south India, several Tamil dynasties governed into the fourteenth century. Tamil, a Dravidian language spoken by most people in southern India and part of Sri Lanka, can also refer to the people in southern India and indicates south India itself. The Tamil Pandyan Dynasty had roots that extended back to at least the fourth century BCE and contended for control of the south with rival kingdoms, particularly Chola, Chera, and Pallava. The territorial limits of the various Tamil kingdoms "were defined by immemorial tradition and well recognized, although the frontiers of the kingdoms varied continuously and enormously from time to time."[3] Geography and trade allowed central and southern India to consider ideas from and to do business with the north, as mountains and the Deccan Plateau minimized the spillover of political turmoil from native and foreign contestants for power there.

Hindu Synthesis and Non-Hindu Religions

As India fragmented politically, it came together culturally. Hinduism and the caste system in tandem articulated a worldview for both elite and commoner that provided more than sufficient cohesion as successive foreign military, religious, and commercial incursions challenged India's ideas and institutions. By the time that Islamic (after 1200 CE) and then European (after 1500 CE) occupations brought about substantive additions and adjustments to Indian society, Hindu cultural foundations had been firmly established. The Hinduism that emerged contained the essence of its predecessors, ritualistic Brahmanism of the Vedic period, the metaphysical speculations of the Upanishadic writers, and in non-Hindu religions the key Jain tenets of nonviolence and asceticism, as well as the "middle path" or moderate practices of Buddhism. Although many Indians would come to embrace Islam, Sikhism, and Christianity in the future, the preponderance of the population, the bulk of the social practices, and the fundamental nature of the institutions remain inextricably linked to the Hindu tradition.

Although Hinduism, like all major religions, included numerous sects, denominations, and schools of thought, it also contained—again, as in other important religious traditions—common sacred texts, beliefs, and practices that animate and unite believers. Hindu law or *Dharma* (virtue or duty) derives from two sources: *Sruti*, or things revealed, heard; and *Smriti*, or things remembered. The *Sruti*, the most authoritative sources of Hinduism, comprised the Vedas (knowledge): *Rigveda, Samaveda, Yajurveda*, and *Atharvaveda*; as well as the *Brahmanas*, the *Aranyakas*, and the *Upanishads*. This literature essentially became the preserve of Brahman priests and their students, those religiously eligible to study the texts. Such eligibility fell to only the twice-born (born again, or reborn) who were occupants of the upper three *varnas* in the caste system, which effectively eliminated most servants, peasants, and people of meaner occupations. These sources were divinely revealed to the priests who transmitted them from generation to generation, at first orally and eventually via text.

The *Smriti* consist of the wisdom and practices of sages and moral exemplars. Examples of such religious insight can be found in three sources: the Epics, the *Mahabhrata* and the *Ramayana*; the

---

3 Vincent A. Smith, *The Oxford History of India*, 3rd ed. (Oxford: Oxford University Press, 1958), p. 220.

Puranas, or "Ancient Stories"; and the *Dharmasastra* (religious and legal duty). Both of the Epics began as secular stories that eventually achieved religious status. The *Mahabharata*, likely begun before the Common Era, attained its final form around the second century CE and contains two sections that greatly affected the future of Hinduism. One is the *Bhagavad Gita* (or *Song of the Lord*, Mohandas Gandhi's "bible") and the other is *Harivamsa*, both of which discuss Lord Krishna, seen as an avatar of Vishnu, the supreme god in one Hindu tradition. Krishna will play a prominent role in the Bhakti devotional movement, which emerges by the eighth century. The *Puranas* describe the creation and evolution of the universe, as well as the genealogies and lives of the numerous influential gods, learned spiritual thinkers, and sagacious political leaders. The 18 accepted authentic *Puranas* sought to promote devotion to the gods, especially Krishna, as well as adherence to one's *dharma*, as dictated by one's caste membership. The *Puranas* especially attempted to appeal to women and people of lower castes. In orthodox Brahmanism, once-born or female individuals had not been qualified for salvation since they were ineligible for the Four Stages of Life (discussed further in this section). In orthodox practice one needed to go through the Four Stages of Life, which were the only accepted routes to *moksha*, the end of reincarnation. *Dharmasastra*, most particularly the *Manusmriti* or *Laws of Manu*, contain manmade laws and codes of conduct for individuals, castes, and nations that better enabled the people, the priesthood, and political leaders to adhere to the divinely instituted commandments found in the Vedas.

Beginning around the early sixth century CE, the Bhakti or devotional movement in Hinduism sprang from the messages contained in the *Puranas*. These messages focused primarily on the ability of anyone to achieve salvation if the individual offered proper devotion to the all-wise and powerful God. This deity regularly descended to earth, took on numerous appearances, and in various incarnations provided examples of proper behavior for the people to emulate.

One's devotion involved

> emulating Him, walking in His footsteps, taking refuge under Him, abandoning the sense of oneself as the agent, having faith in His grace and compassion rather than in one's own capacity, confessing one's shortcomings and praying to Him, adoring Him, repeating His name, wearing emblems to identify oneself as belonging to Him, singing or writing of Him, worshiping Him in an image at one's home or in a temple, communing with fellow worshipers, seeing His immanence in all beings and therefore venerating all humanity—all these are ways of practicing devotion to Him and thereby realizing Him.[4]

Such devotion to God required no special status, no literacy, and no analytical mind. Consequently the average peasant or outcaste could hope to get off the cycle of birth and death and rebirth via sincere devotion. Indeed, "advocates of devotion insisted that without it all austerities, rituals, virtues, learning, or any other aspect of spiritual endeavor would be meaningless and ineffective. It was devotion that gave one real status, not birth. Among devotees there was no caste, no distinction of high or low, except that those who lacked devotion were considered the lowest."[5]

The Bhakti movement expanded popular participation in an evolving Hinduism that had heretofore not opened up the practical possibility of salvation to the vast majority of Indians. Both the Four Stages of Life and the Four Ends of Man, which outlined the Hindu paths to salvation, effectively left out all but those of twice-born background (Brahmin, Kshatriya, and Vaishya), rejecting the preponderance of the population. The Four Stages of Life are: student, householder, retired,

---

4 de Bary, *Sources of Indian Tradition*, 1:324.
5 de Bary, *Sources of Indian Tradition*, 1:326.

and ascetic. A young boy entered the first stage at an elementary school age and was introduced to the Vedas and the various rituals of the religion. In substance, this initiation via a detailed ceremony (*samskara*) resembles the Confirmation rite in Christianity and the Bar Mitzvah rite in Judaism, indicating the youth has reached the age of reason and understands the significance of his religious heritage as well as his religious responsibilities. This Brahmanic commencement has been described thus:

> The initiation was restricted to the first three castes. The age at which it was undergone depended on the caste, being eight in the case of the *brahman*, eleven for a *ksatriya* and twelve for a *vaisya*. It was the most important sacrament, called upanayana or "second birth," and opened the way to ritual instruction which was indispensable for a child if he was to become a *ghrhastha* [householder, the second stage of life] eventually. This, then was the beginning of an entirely new life and was considered a most solemn occasion.[6]

Females did not undergo such initiation but "acquired religious merit from their husbands."[7] By the young man's late teens another rite of passage occurs, the transition to the householder or second stage of life. This entails getting married, producing children, and securing an occupation that can support not only wife and children but also others in the broader family at those stages of their lives when no income was possible. The third stage begins when one's son has become capable of taking on the responsibilities of supporting family members, thus allowing the father to proceed to the retirement stage. In this setting one begins to divest himself of household responsibilities and to disengage from social relationships, thereby preparing for the fourth stage, that of an ascetic or *sannyasin* (abandonment).

The ascetic cut all ties to the past, including family and caste, "declaring his renunciation of the world." Such a life involved a minimum of material things and a maximum of spiritual resolve:

> Wearing only sandals, loincloth, and an ochre-colored upper garment, and taking with him only a staff, water jug, and a begging bowl, he should from this point on live alone and not seek the company of others. His life should be characterized by restraint of speech (observance of silence), restraint of action (noninjury to any other creature), and restraint of mind (performance of breath control, meditation, and other yogic practices); by these he would gradually purify himself, attain desirelessness (*vairagya*), and active knowledge of self and Brahman that would bring final release.[8]

Thus the ascetic wandered, pondering the meaning of life and searching for freedom from *samsara* or the cycle of birth and death and rebirth. That release or *moksha* signified that one had achieved the fourth end of man. The Four Ends of Man are: *Dharma*, law, duty, or virtue; *Artha*, material gain; *Kama*, pleasure; and *Moksha*, release.

Dharma has been characterized as "the moral law which sustains the world, human society, and the individual." According to one Hindu religious text (*Taittiriya Aranyaka*), "Dharma is the foundation of the whole universe. In this world people go unto a person who is best versed in dharma for guidance. By means of dharma one drives away evil. Upon dharma everything is founded.

---

6 Jeannine Auboyer, *Daily Life in Ancient India from 200 BC to 700 AD* (New York: Macmillan, 1965), p. 167.
7 Hopkins, *The Hindu Religious Tradition*, p. 78.
8 Hopkins, *The Hindu Religious Tradition*, p. 83.

Therefore dharma is called the highest good."[9] *Artha* focuses on man's place in society, particularly the relationship between the individuals and the government but more broadly with individuals and material gain. This end of man has inspired a good deal of political literature over the centuries. The *Artha Sastra*, for example, observes: "Only if a king is himself energetically active, do his officers follow him energetically. If he is sluggish, they too remain sluggish. And, besides, they eat up his works (vitiate his efforts). He is thereby easily overpowered by his enemies. Therefore, he should ever dedicate himself energetically to activity."[10] *Kama*, or pleasure properly regulated, has been viewed by Hindus as a necessary part of "a well-rounded personality." The most-quoted piece of writing dealing with pleasure is the *Kama Sutra*, which contains advice on all aspects of making a pleasurable life, including sexual enjoyment. The spectrum of gratification was wide, given this admonition: "He should arrange excursions in parties for attending festivals, salons for enjoying literature and art, drinking parties, excursions to parks, and group games."[11] The fourth and final end of man is *moksha*, the deliverance from the pains of the physical world achieved by unifying one's soul (*atman*) with god (*Brahman*). This unification occurred when one came to realize, given the individual's experiences in the first three stages of life and the placing of these occurrences in perspective during the fourth stage, that one does the right thing because it is the proper thing to do, not for any earthly or heavenly rewards.

The caste system represents the product of evolutionary development, and at every step it bonded with Brahmanism and Hinduism. Early distinctions among people in India can be found in the Vedic period (to ca. 600 BCE), when the population was divided into occupations by *varna* or color: *Brahmans*, *Kshatriyas*, *Vaishyas*, and *Sudras*. There also evolved a fifth group, *pancama*, people referred to variously as outcastes, untouchables, or Scheduled Castes. This theoretically neat classification, apparently of light-skinned Aryan creation as they encountered the dark-skinned Dravidians after 1500 BCE, experienced realistic problems on two major fronts. First, in the early centuries of the social sorting, each *varna* contained few occupations, but as Indian society became more complex by the end of the Vedic period, so too did the number of occupations. Into which *varna* did the new occupations fall? And, second, the issue of color itself was complicated by the fact that color alone could not always identify one's class. There were darker Brahmans and lighter Sudras, which cried out for further explanation, as did the fact that individuals from lower *varnas* often behaved more righteously than their supposed Brahman superiors. These and other anomalies of the *varna* system were explained, to some extent, by the emerging *jati* system, not mentioned in the Vedas but widely practiced by the Common Era.

Jati or "birth" are subcategories within each *varna* and best represent the term "caste," a word of Portuguese origin. An increasingly strict set of guidelines defined a person's *jati*:

> Relations within classes and social groups in later [post-Vedic] Hinduism were governed by rules of endogamy (marriage was only legitimate within the group), commensality (food was only to be received from and eaten in the presence of members of the same or a higher group), and craft-exclusiveness (each man was to live by the trade or profession of his own group, and not take up that of another).[12]

---

9 de Bary, *Sources of Indian Tradition*, 1:206, 1:215–216.
10 de Bary, *Sources of Indian Tradition*, 1:241–242.
11 de Bary, *Sources of Indian Tradition*, 1:253, 1:256.
12 A. L. Basham, *The Wonder That Was India* (New York: Grove Press, 1954), p. 147.

It seems that during the Vedic period, although *varna* determined one's occupation in society, one could change *varna* by changing occupation. By the time of the *Upanishads*, social mobility became less flexible. While stricter or looser adherence to caste rules and practices varied over the centuries, a person's standing in society ever more derived chiefly from one's *jati*, of which there are more than 3000 at the turn of the twenty-first century. And it would be *jati* that held India together after 1200 during centuries of Islamic and Christian rule. A. L. Basham's conclusion about the cohesive qualities of *jati* deserves some reflection.

> The organization of the castes, independent of the government, and with social ostracism as its most severe sanction, was a powerful factor in the survival of Hinduism. The Hindu, living under an alien political order imposed from above, retained his cultural individuality largely through his caste, which received most of the loyalty elsewhere felt towards king, nation and city.[13]

Conclusions

By 1200, the Indian political tradition that had evolved seemed to indicate a marked inability to produce a strong central government for any length of time over any significant portion of the Indian subcontinent. Whether the result of domestic disputes brought on by geography, language, religion, and institutional flaws, or the consequence of chronic foreign invasions from Central Asia, or a product of all of those difficulties, India typically operated governmentally within a fragmented condition. Although the imperial ideal remained alive in the exploits of Ashoka, the Gupta monarchs, and Harsha as well as in the epics *Mahabharata* and *Ramayana*, it remained only an ideal, one that eluded India until independence from Britain in 1947.

Yet even as the subcontinent failed to cohere politically, its cultural unity seemed to grow stronger. As Hinduism evolved to embrace the principal concepts of Buddhism and Jainism, it also expanded to allow meaningful participation for the entire population. The Four Stages of Life and the Four Ends of Man, the traditional paths to salvation for the twice-born, continued to be the desired corridor to *moksha*. These phases and purposes in life allowed the individual to lead a relatively normal, even quite full, secular life and yet, once the material desires of man had been legitimately pursued, the individual could then turn to more spiritual quests via ascetic routines. And when the Bhakti movement emerged to enable even the once-born, through devotional practices, to reach *moksha* without taking the more classical route of the twice-born, Hinduism insured popular participation by the preponderance of the population. By the seventh or eighth century, even a beggar could be considered an ascetic, essentially putting one on that launching pad to *moksha*. All disciples now had the power to achieve salvation by following certain behavioral practices, an optimistic situation making Hinduism powerfully attractive to nearly everyone. This religious cohesion, which never officially included the caste system, enabled Indian culture to survive first the Islamic and later the European challenges. As we shall see in Chapter 10, Indian culture also became attractive to the elites beyond the Indian frontiers, particularly in Southeast Asia, and without political pressure from the subcontinent.

---

13 Basham, *The Wonder That Was India*, p. 151.

Suggested Readings and Viewings

Daud Ali, *Courtly Culture and Political Life in Early Medieval India* (Cambridge: Cambridge University Press, 2004).

A. L. Basham, ed., *A Cultural History of India*, 2015 ed. (Oxford: Oxford University Press, 2015).

Peter Berger, *The Sacred Canopy: Elements of a Sociological Theory of Religion* (New York: Knopf Doubleday, 1990).

Abraham Eraly, *The First Spring: The Golden Age of India* (New York: Penguin, 2011).

Murugar Gunasingam, *Tamils in Sri Lanka: A Comprehensive History* (Sydney: MV Publication, 2014).

Jayant Lele, *Tradition and Modernity in Bhakti Movements* (Leiden: Brill, 1981).

Radhakumud Mookerji, *The Gupta Empire* (New Delhi: Motilal Banarsidass, 2007).

Kim Plofker, *Mathematics in India* (Princeton, NJ: Princeton University Press, 2009).

Sheldon Pollock, ed., *Literary Cultures in History: Reconstructions from South Asia* (Berkeley: University of California Press, 2003).

Shyam Saran, ed., *Cultural and Civilizational Links between India and Southeast Asia: Historical and Contemporary Dimensions* (New York: Palgrave Macmillan, 2018).

Tansen Sen, *Buddhism, Diplomacy, and Trade: The Realignment of Sino-Indian Relations, 600–1400* (Honolulu: University of Hawaii Press, 2003).

Michael Wood, writer and presenter, *The Story of India*, 6 episodes (London: BBC, 2007), see episodes 2–4.

10

The Indianization of South, Central, Southeast, and East Asia: 185 BCE–1200 CE

The various elites in Southeast Asia could have chosen the Chinese model, for China was also a trading partner, but did not do so. Why not? As the peoples of northern Vietnam later found out, China was an expansionist nation as the Indian principalities were not; an adoption of Chinese-style imperial bureaucracy would have meant a burdensome and humiliating submission to the Middle Kingdom, and the lessening of their own powers. With China, it was all or nothing. In contrast, the Hindu religion and its trappings offered the benefits of royal ideology tailor-made for nascent Southeast Asian kings, with no political strings attached.[1]

Indian Culture beyond India

The cultural attraction of India can be seen throughout the Eurasian world. Trade routes and Indian traders spread aspects of their homeland to regions nearby Hindustan as well as to more distant locations. They took Buddhist beliefs and other features of Indian society westward to Greece, Mesopotamia, Egypt, Persia, and even Rome. Closer to home, Indian culture often made deep and in most cases enduring impressions on Ceylon, Central Asia, Southeast Asia, China, Tibet, and East Asia. While the cultural impact varied with location, numerous Indian ideas and institutions took deep root in Ceylon/Sri Lanka and most of Southeast Asia, while Buddhism became India's chief cultural export to China and East Asia. Those influences are numerous and quite visible today. To the west and north of India, the early and heartfelt embrace of Indian thought and behavior—particularly Buddhism, its worldview, and its accompanying architecture, art, literature, food practices, roles for women, and so forth—would sharply contrast with the Islamic outlook that arrived with Arab expansion into the region surrounding India.

One highly regarded scholar has defined Indianization as a phenomenon that "must be understood essentially as the expansion of an organized culture that was founded upon the Indian conception of royalty, was characterized by Hinduist or Buddhist cults, the mythology of the *Puranas*, and the observance of the *Dharmasastras*, and expressed itself in the Sanskrit language."[2] That is to say, non-Indians in contact with the Indian subcontinent who embraced the Indian

---

1 From *Angkor and the Khmer Civilization* by Michael D Coe and Damian Evans, © 2003 Michael D. Coe. Reprinted by kind permission of Thames & Hudson Ltd, London.
2 G. Coedes, *The Indianized States of Southeast Asia,* ed. Walter F. Vella (Honolulu: University of Hawaii Press, 1964), pp. 15–16. *Dharmasastras* are Sanskrit Hindu texts dealing with *dharma,* Hindu law. The *Puranas* are poems—such as the *Mahabharata* or *Ramayana*—or other literature compiled largely in the Common Era that offer praise to the various Hindu deities.

Asia Past and Present: A Brief History, First Edition. Peter P. Wan and Thomas D. Reins.
© 2021 John Wiley & Sons, Inc. Published 2021 by John Wiley & Sons, Inc.

concept of monarchy, the Indian system of writing, and the religious and social practices associated with Hinduism and Buddhism could be said to have been Indianized. Naturally, any such embrace has to be seen in the context of local customs and practices that assimilate into the broader Indian model of society. Strictly speaking, only Sri Lanka and the Himalayan nations would fit this Indianization classification. There, monarchy, religion, writings, and sometimes aspects of the caste system all generally reflected the Indian ideas that inspired them. Southeast Asian societies also replicate extensive Indian influence, though without the caste system component. Further away from India culturally speaking would be East Asia, which devotedly embraced Buddhism but gave it decidedly Chinese, Japanese, Korean, or Vietnamese characteristics and largely ignored additional Indian cultural features. But to the west and north of India, where Buddhism and other Indian traditions had made serious inroads in Persia, Afghanistan, and Central Asia, the arrival of Islam in the seventh century soon reversed a millennium of deep Indian cultural influence.

Timeline: Indian Cultural Influence beyond India, 184 BCE to Fourteenth Century CE	
3rd century BCE	Indian Emperor Ashoka embraces Buddhism and sends missionaries across India and beyond, to Persia, Afghanistan, Central Asia, and the Silk Road
1st century CE	Buddhism arrives in China via Indian merchants on Silk Road; also arrives in Burma via merchants and eventually reaches all of Asia
2nd century	Buddhism comes to Vietnam via China
3rd century	Indian Buddhist monastery at Nalanda in today's Bihar serves as an intellectual center for students across Asia
4th century	Buddhism arrives in Cambodia and Korea
	Buddhist statuary complex begun on Silk Road in Dunhuang, Gansu Province in China
	Buddhist monk Faxian travels to India (late 4th and early 5th centuries)
	Hinduism arrives in the Kingdom of Champa in today's central Vietnam
5th century	Indian merchants carry Indian culture from the eastern Mediterranean to the western Pacific
6th century	Legend has it that Indian Buddhist monk Bodhidharma brings two gifts to China's Shao Lin Temple: (1) Dhyana/Chan/Zen meditative Buddhism and (2) Indian martial arts techniques
	Buddhist statuary complex erected in Bamiyan, Afghanistan (destroyed by Taliban in 2001)
	Buddhism arrives in Japan
7th century	Srivijaya Empire: A Buddhist monarchy on the Indonesian island of Sumatra until the 13th century
8th century	Buddhism arrives in Tibet
9th century	Borobudur Buddhist temple complex in Java, Indonesia
10th century	Hindu Chams start to convert to Islam
11th century	By 1000 CE, Indian models of kingship, writing systems, and religions become the basis of high culture in most of Southeast Asia
12th century	Angkor Wat temple complex (originally Hindu but later Buddhist) built in Cambodia
13th century	Buddhism comes to Mongolia via Tibet; Islam begins to supplant Hinduism and Buddhism in Indonesia and Malaya

India in Ceylon/Sri Lanka and the Himalayan Kingdoms

Ceylon has been known by many names and is today usually referred to as Sri Lanka. The island is located off the southeast corner of India, from which it derived much of its population and many of its customs. As early as the fifth century BCE, more light-skinned Indo-Aryan Indians from the north arrived, the ancestors of today's Sinhalese who are normally Buddhist. A century or so later the more dark-skinned Dravidian people from the south reached the island, becoming the descendants of today's Tamils who are typically Hindus. Both groups brought with them ideas and practices that took root with local characteristics. The much less harsh and rigid caste system and thinking associated with an emerging Hinduism became a part of the island's social order. Indian writing and literature, the concept of monarchy, and other cultural habits from the mainland also continued to arrive. Linguistically Sanskrit became the language of the Tamil Hindus on Ceylon, while the majority Buddhist Sinhalese utilized the language of Buddhism, Pali.

From the time of Emperor Ashoka, who linked Buddhist religion and politics, the Sinhalese who typically ruled Ceylon continued the practice. In the first millennium CE, Buddhism on the subcontinent began to decline due to its growing monasticism and consequent separation from the lives of the people. At the same time, Hinduism won the people's support as the Bhakti movement brought the average person an optimistic outlook on his or her spiritual future. But on Ceylon, Hinduism remained a minority religion while Buddhism flourished. Thus ongoing struggles between Sinhalese and Tamils and between those of high caste and lower caste became permanent features of social life in Ceylon. Nonetheless, at the top of the political structure on the island sat a Sinhalese monarch, theoretically absolute but practically assumed to be bound to universal laws, namely *dharma*. As well, Sinhalese rulers had to consider that with Buddhism declining on the mainland and Hinduism on the ascendancy there, Indian rulers—especially in kingdoms in south India—might interfere to support the Tamil minority on Ceylon. And indeed, from the third century BCE until the Delhi Sultanate was established in 1206 CE, Hindu monarchs from the mainland frequently invaded Ceylon and often ruled for periods of time. By that time, conflict between Ceylonese Sinhalese and Tamils as well as invasions from the mainland gradually created an ethnic division of the island. The Tamils tended to occupy northern parts of the island, and the Sinhalese the central and south. Nonetheless, Sri Lanka had become Indianized and remains so today.

To India's north, the Himalayan Kingdom of Nepal became the birthplace of the Buddha, so in theory there is no cultural transfer of Buddhism from India to Nepal. Nonetheless, though he was born in Lumbini—Buddhism's Mecca—the location of the Buddha's enlightenment (Bodh Gaya), first sermon (Sarnath), and death (Kushinagar) all took place in India. Moreover, even though today Nepal is officially a Hindu country, it has been an importer of various forms of Indian culture. Bhutan indirectly received Indian influence with the importation of Buddhism in the seventh century CE from neighboring Tibet. For the first century of Buddhist development in Bhutan, Tibet influenced religious thinking. After the arrival of Indian monk Padmasambhava, also known as Guru Rimpoche, Tibet had to compete with Indian influence. As in Tibet, where the original religion of Bon gave way to Buddhism, so too in Bhutan. And in both countries, Buddhism served as a unifying force in territories divided by numerous local monarchies and imposing mountains.

India in Persia, Afghanistan, and Central and Inner Asia

Indian culture—particularly Buddhism—initially succeeded in attracting people to the subcontinent's west and north. Of all the locations to which Indian culture migrated, Persia, Afghanistan, and Central Asia represent the lands where Indian cultural influence had the least staying power. Buddhism and other Indian cultural imports had, in pre-Islamic times, provided considerable

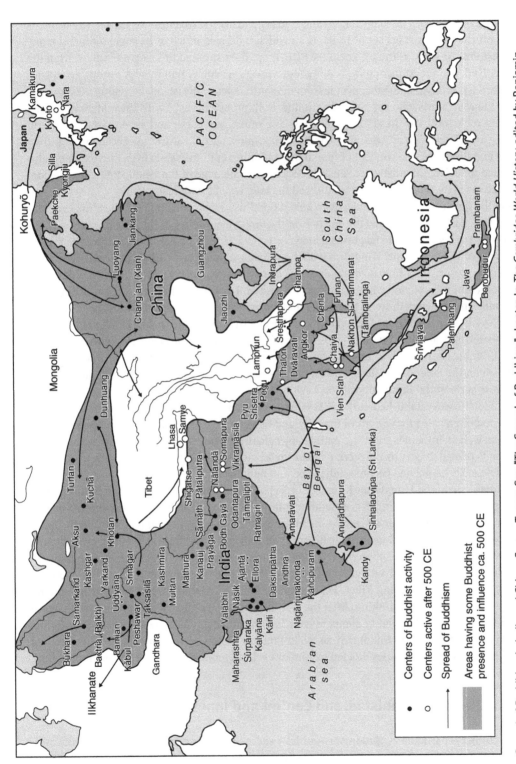

Spread of Buddhism in India and China. *Source:* Tansen Sen, "The Spread of Buddhism" chapter. In *The Cambridge World History,* edited by Benjamin Z. Kedar and Merry E. Wiesner-Hanks, vol. 5, pp. 447–480. Cambridge: Cambridge University Press, 2015. doi:10.1017/CBO9780511667480.018. Reproduced with permission of Cambridge University Press.

social attractions, principally in religion, politics, and the arts. By the eighth century, Islam had begun to erode Indian culture. As the Delhi Sultanate began to rule India in 1206, Islamic ideas and institutions had eclipsed Indian cultural influence in Persia, Afghanistan, and Central Asia. How did that influence develop, and why did it weaken and all but disappear? In answering those questions, the reader also needs to ponder why Buddhism failed to hold the loyalty of believers in India, where the religion had become increasingly irrelevant before the Muslims arrived.

Buddhism began to develop and expand at roughly the same time as Persia, about 500 BCE. As Persian dynasties expanded and contracted geographically, the Persian Empire could extend from Greece in the west to parts of today's Pakistan and northwestern India and even to the Chinese frontier in the east. Frequently, Persia included today's Afghanistan and Central Asia as well. Indian influence in all of those regions can be seen in the remains of Buddhist monasteries, art, rock carvings, and sculptures.

In what is currently Persia/Iran, the decline of Buddhist and more broadly Indian practices began when the Sassanian Dynasty made Zoroastrianism the official religion in 224 CE. Persecution of Buddhists and destruction of Buddhist temples followed, though Buddhist groups continued to conduct religious services until the arrival of the Arabs in the seventh century. The religion all but disappeared thereafter. The Bamiyan Valley in central Afghanistan was home to a sizable Buddhist community extending back centuries. Bamiyan was on the Silk Road, a major route taken by Buddhist monks as they spread the message eastward to China and westward as far as Mesopotamia. Chinese monks Faxian in the fifth century and Xuanzang in the seventh century spoke of flourishing Buddhist activities there. They wrote of numerous monasteries and magnificent Buddhist statues located there. The two largest of these statues (one 180 feet high, the other 120 feet, probably carved in the fifth century CE) were destroyed in March 2001 by the Taliban. Buddhism in most of Afghanistan had been displaced by Islam by the eighth century. Much the same religious story took place in Central Asia. Major Buddhist centers appeared along the Silk Road, such as Kashgar, Hotan, and Dunhuang. Moreover, key Buddhist sites located on connector roads to the Silk Road, such as Karakorum in Mongolia and Lhasa in Tibet, have survived to the present.

India in Southeast Asia

Southeast Asia owes a great deal of its current cultural substance to India and China. The common term "Indochina" reflects the influence of both core Asian cultures to the region. A substantial part of mainland Southeast Asia's population came from China and brought with them their local languages. The Burman and Pyu arrived from China, as did the Tai people of Thailand, the Lao of Laos, the Hmong of Laos and other Southeast Asian locations, the Vietnamese, and the Khmer of Cambodia. Most of the people of insular Southeast Asia are of Austronesian background in today's Philippines, Indonesia, and Malaysia. India and China also provided written and spoken languages, arts and architecture, political and social thought and institutions, as well as river systems, to list only the most obvious contributions. Until the arrival of the Europeans in the sixteenth century and their recruitment of ethnic Chinese in large numbers for labor, however, India provided the preponderance of outside cultural impact.

These kinds of influences began in a significant way around the third century BCE, as Ashoka unified India and Qin Shi Huangdi unified China. These two highly sophisticated societies had great appeal to the elites in Southeast Asia, themselves seeking to develop more unified political and stable social foundations. On the eve of the Mongol invasions in the thirteenth century CE, Indianized kingdoms had emerged in most of Southeast Asia, while Vietnam progressively became

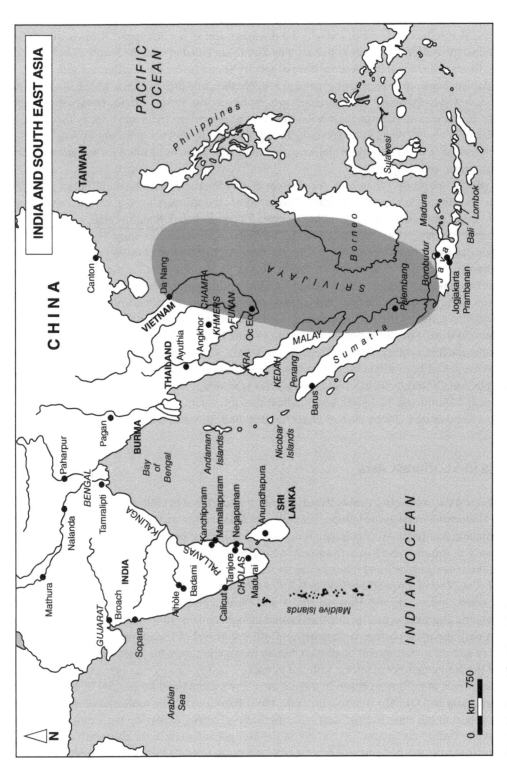

Map of India and Southeast Asia.

Confucian Chinese in outlook. The Philippine Islands remained largely outside the Indo-Chinese cultural melding, though trade and other cultural contacts existed with island and mainland Southeast Asia and even China. In Southeast Asia, Indianization typically meant:

- The rich and complex Hindu religion, its mythology and cosmology, and its ritual; in particular, the cults of the gods Shiva and Vishnu, with whom local kings could identify
- The Sanskrit language, the vehicle of Hinduism and one sect of Buddhism, and the source of many loanwords in early Khmer
- The Indic (*Brahmi*) writing system, with stone inscriptions and palm-leaf books
- The Hindu temple complex and an architectural tradition of brick and/or stone based upon Gupta prototypes
- Statuary representing gods, kings, and the Buddha
- Cremation burial, at least of the upper stratum of society
- Rectilinear town and city plans
- Artificial water systems, including rectangular reservoirs (the *srah* and *baray* of Classic Khmer culture) as well as canals
- Wheel-made pottery, which supplemented but did not supplant the local paddle-and-anvil ceramic tradition.[3]

From India came Buddhism, Hinduism, and (after the thirteenth century) Islam. Sanskrit became the official system of writing in most of Southeast Asia, although Pali, the formal language of Buddhism, was also adopted across the region. Political thinking and institutional administrations reflected the Indian ideal of the good and wise ruler. The king was viewed as a model of integrity who followed the law or *dharma* and was typically considered a *devaraja* or divine ruler in either Hindu-style or Buddhist-influenced monarchies. Architecture imitated Indian religious and political ideas of spirituality and majesty, while art, dance, and music emulated Indian notions of high culture. The adoption of things Indian took place in a setting free from coercion. Though Indians engaged in vigorous trade with most of Southeast Asia before 1200, very few permanently migrated there, and no colonization occurred (although the south Indian Kingdom of Chola attempted to conquer the Srivijaya Empire in today's Indonesia, as it had in Sri Lanka in the eleventh century). And, as we shall see, Islam became prominent in Southeast Asia only after its arrival, not from Arabia but from India under Muslim rulers after 1206.

During the first millennium CE, numerous Southeast Asian kingdoms emerged. They engaged in trade with each other and the outside world, fought wars with each other and the outside world, and experimented with foreign ideas and institutions they believed would make life more understandable and stable. The Pyu city-states and the Kingdom of Pagan in Burma set the stage for the Pagan Empire in the eleventh century. The Kingdom of Funan occupied southern Vietnam, Cambodia, Thailand, and much of the Malay Peninsula from the first to the sixth centuries CE, while Chenla ruled in what is today's Thailand, Cambodia, and southern Vietnam from the sixth to eighth centuries. Champa ruled central Vietnam from the seventh century, though its hold on Vietnamese territory declined and completely disappeared by the nineteenth century. Insular Southeast Asia produced several kingdoms and empires before the thirteenth century in what is today Indonesia: The Srivijaya Empire on the island of Sumatra flourished from the seventh to thirteenth centuries. All of these kingdoms had one thing in common—they enthusiastically adopted Indian practices, including Hinduism and Buddhism, Sanskrit and Pali writing, and the Indian model of kingship. Indeed, one monarch in the Kingdom of Borobudur in eighth-century

---

3 Coe, *Angkor and Its Khmer Civilization*, p. 63.

Java took the name King Vishnu, thus producing a cultural hat trick: an Indian-style monarchy, in a Buddhist kingdom, with a monarch named after a Hindu god.

These and other early kingdoms in Southeast Asia did not anticipate future permanent geographical frontiers, but they did establish more sophisticated organizational tools and reasonable explanations that justified a monarch's rule. While the organizational tools, with local features, will remain fairly constant into the twentieth century, explanations will undergo fundamental changes. The arrival of Islam in Indonesia and Malaya will replace Buddhist and/or Hindu descriptions of the roles of government, religion, and royal subjects. The new monarchs will be sultans, shahs, and emirs whose legitimacy will now come from the Quran and interpretations of it. The coming of the Europeans in the sixteenth century will further culturally jolt all of Southeast Asia. They will introduce new religions, languages, political concepts, and intellectual developments, especially in the world of science. Europe's colonization of Southeast Asia will result in the massive migration of ethnic Chinese, further complicating already troubled ethnic relationships. In that setting, frontiers of the region's emerging nation-states will be drawn by Europeans.

India in China and East Asia

China and its East Asian Confucian associates in Japan, Korea, and Vietnam also had access to the cultural exports of India. But they already possessed a system of writing, a secular Confucian outlook on social life, and sophisticated—if sometimes flawed—political organizations. They also

White Horse Temple, Luoyang, Henan Province, China. Author Thomas Reins in foreground.

practiced native religions: Daoism and local religions in China, Shinto in Japan, indigenous religions such as Dao Mau mother goddess worship in Vietnam, and various forms of shamanism in Korea. Both political and religious institutions in East Asia had their shortcomings. Nonetheless Confucianism ultimately retained elite and popular allegiance, thus removing the likelihood of an Indian substitution. But Buddhism became the overwhelming religious choice of East Asians, even as their traditional religions continued to retain ongoing acceptance. Different religions in most non-Abrahamic faiths tend not to be mutually exclusive but instead complementary.

Buddhism likely first came to China during the middle of the Han Dynasty, probably during the first century CE. It was certainly there by 68 CE, when the White Horse Temple was established in the Han Dynasty capital of Luoyang. Buddhism probably made its way east from India across the Silk Road to northern China, though some argue that it arrived via a maritime route to southern China. During the third century BCE, as Ashoka promoted the spread of Buddhism to Central Asia, the early Chinese Han Dynasty expanded into its northern and western border territories to better observe and manage the various ethnic tribes on the frontier. This brought the Indians and Chinese together in Central Asia. Indian merchants and Buddhist monks transmitted Buddhist writings and practices, and the Chinese gradually embraced the Mahayana form of Buddhism. Indian monks such as Kumarajiva arrived in the late fourth century CE, and began teaching eager Chinese students and translating many of the Buddhist scriptures. Bodhidharma reached China, legend has it, in the late fifth or early sixth century and became famous for teaching his meditation techniques associated with Chan/Zen Buddhism. He also launched a tradition of martial arts at the Shao Lin Temple, combining meditative physical inaction with self-defense physical movement.

Bodhidharma by Tsukioka Yoshitoshi (1887). *Source:* The Picture Art Collection / Alamy Stock Photo.

With the fall of the Han Dynasty in 220 CE, China became divided over the next 350 years. Confucianism, which had just been made the official ideology of China under the Han emperors, lost a good deal of its appeal. As in the case of the fall of Rome where Christianity had been blamed for the government's collapse after having been made the official religion, much the same thinking occurred in China. Indeed, many of China's elite considered Buddhism to be a possible replacement for Confucianism, while much of the peasant population became attracted to the new religion in the chaotic times. When many of the rulers of the numerous Chinese states that emerged after 220 adopted Buddhism, they often made it the official religion. Thus, even after China reunified in the late sixth century under Confucianism, Buddhism continued to grow in popularity.

Buddhism became widespread geographically and demographically by the time China reunified in the late sixth century for a number of reasons. For many people opposed to Confucianism, Buddhism served as a counterweight—a sort of opposition party. To many Confucians, Buddhism's popularity indicated the need to absorb its core ideas, and in the process secular Confucianism could claim to possess a religious component. Indeed this thinking eventually produced neo-Confucianism, a combination of Confucianism, Buddhism, and Daoism. So attractive was the religion to the Chinese that numerous magnificent Buddhist statues carved during the Tang Dynasty can be found in caves and grottoes in western and northern China: the Giant Buddha in Leshan, Sichuan; the Longmen Grottoes near Luoyang, Henan; the Dunhuang Caves in Gansu; and the Yungang Grottoes near Datong, Shanxi.

As well, several of China's Buddhist monks traveled to India to study the original scriptures in the religion's cultural setting. Faxian (337–422) left Chang'an in 399 on the Silk Road, stopping in Dunhuang, passing through Central Asia, and visiting Buddhist monasteries in different cultural settings along the way before arriving in India. While there, he sought Buddhist texts unavailable in China at the time and relics of the Buddha that he could acquire and take back to his homeland. He traveled a maritime route back home, visiting Sri Lanka and passing through the Strait of Malacca before returning to China, likely in 414. The chief historical consequence of Faxian's travels was *A Record of the Buddhist Kingdoms*, which provided China with a picture of political and social as well as religious practices in Central and South Asia.

Some two centuries after Faxian's return, Xuanzang (602–664) departed for India in the late 620s and returned in 645. He too left Chang'an and traveled west, though he stopped at many different locations in Central Asia than Faxian before arriving in India. Whereas Faxian's trip began as a religious pilgrimage, Xuanzang's missions were both religious and diplomatic, though he never had official instructions from any Tang Dynasty emperor. His geographical explorations covered most of the Indian subcontinent, while Faxian had toured chiefly in north India. Xuanzang's *Records of the Western Regions Visited during the Great Tang Dynasty* provides a fuller picture of Central Asia and India, particularly of Indian politics and its then-ruler Harsha, whom he portrays as virtuous and friendly to Buddhism. He describes various aspects of society, and much of what is known about caste in India comes from his written accounts of that institution. Upon his homecoming in 645, the emperor recognized Xuanzang's religious and diplomatic understanding of the outside world and gave him a government appointment.

Mathematician, astronomer, and Buddhist monk Yixing/Seng Yixing or Zhang Sui (635–713) departed for India a generation after Xuanzang's return. Leaving Chang'an in 671, he went to Yangzhou from where he took a maritime route to India, stopping off in the Srivijaya Kingdom located on the island of Sumatra in today's Indonesia. He then proceeded to Malaya and finally arrived in northeastern India. Yixing's chief objective was to compare Chinese and Indian Buddhist practices and how they corresponded to original religious traditions. His conclusions about how the likely cultural differences between India and China produced somewhat different religious practices can be found in *The Record of Buddhism as Practiced in India Sent Home from the Southern Seas*. Yixing's *Memoirs of Eminent Monks Who Visited India and Neighboring Regions in Search of the Law during the Great Tang Dynasty* describes the Chinese monks who traveled to India during the seventh century. Upon his maritime return to China in 695, he spent most of his remaining years in study with Indian Buddhist monks residing in Chang'an.

From China, Buddhist ideas made their way to Korea, Japan, and Vietnam. Thought and behavior coming from China always had great appeal in East Asia, just as Indian thought and behavior had similar allure in Southeast Asia. Chinese monks introduced Buddhism to Korea in the fourth century, and thereafter Korean monks traveled to China to learn more about the religion. By the time Korea was unified under the Silla Dynasty, Buddhism gradually gained popular favor and eventually government support, which it retained until the fourteenth century. The Koreans likely introduced Buddhism to Japan in the sixth century and received the patronage of Prince Shotoku, who embraced numerous ideas and institutions from the Asian mainland. Further evidence of Japanese interest in Buddhism can be seen in the monk Ennin, also known as Mibu and Jikaku Daishi, who traveled to Tang China hoping to get a better idea of Buddhist, particularly the Tiantai/Tendai school, practices. His diaries record numerous customs and events from 838 to 847 and indicate that he achieved that better understanding of not only Buddhism but also Chinese customs and practices. This included a Chinese government crackdown on Buddhist institutions in the mid-840s. In the case of Vietnam, Indian influence came more directly. Of course, Champa in central Vietnam was heavily influenced by India, but in the northern part of Vietnam where the Vietnamese then resided, Buddhism arrived with numerous Buddhist monks around the first century CE. Apparently the missionary mandate issued by Ashoka had been kept alive. As well, living under Chinese control until the tenth century, the Vietnamese absorbed Chinese notions of Buddhist practices.

Conclusions

An extensive Indian cultural influence began to spread across Asia by the second century BCE. In Ceylon/Sri Lanka and much of Southeast Asia, foundational ideas and institutions got established there and most remain down to the present. Buddhism spread to Persia, Afghanistan, and Central Asia with great promise, but it was supplanted by Islam after the eighth century. China came to realize that Asia was home to a cultural coequal with the arrival of Buddhism, which gradually became the chief religion of the Middle Kingdom. By the Tang Dynasty, religious concepts in Buddhism became a crucial part of an evolving secular Confucian doctrine resulting in Neo-Confucianism. Zen, one of the many Buddhist sects, also contributed a new approach to meditation and contributed to the birth of a Chinese cultural phenomenon. Indian Buddhist monk Bodhidharma came to the Shao Lin Temple and among other things taught physical exercises to the Chinese monks that eventually became *gong fu*. In conjunction with the indigenous martial art Taiji Quan was born a martial arts legend that in modern times resulted in numerous martial arts movies and heroic Chinese cultural symbols such as Bruce Lee and Jackie Chan. From China to the rest of East Asia, Buddhism became an integral part of cultural life in Korea, Japan, and Vietnam.

India's cultural contributions to the rest of Asia had mixed though generally beneficial and commonly enduring consequences. In "greater" India—Sri Lanka and the Himalayan states—as well as in Tibet, the triumph of Buddhism down to today remains unmistakable. Additionally the importance of Indian political ideals, intellectual foundations, and social practices (including caste intermittently) is obvious. But India's early cultural influence in cultures to its west and north did not survive the test of time. What began as the enthusiastic embrace of many Indian ideas and institutions—particularly Buddhism—in Persia, Afghanistan, and Central Asia by the eighth century became a passionate rejection. Islam displaced most of the Indian cultural offerings. Indian culture fared much better in Southeast Asia, where Indian notions of monarchy, writing systems, religions, and social practices flourished, though mediated by local customs and conditions. East Asia typically ignored Indian concepts and practices with the clear exception of Buddhism. But even the success of Buddhism in East Asia occurred as Chinese, Japanese, Korean, and Vietnamese cultures gave the foreign religion a home-grown makeover best illustrated in the dissimilar styles in art and architecture.

Thus, the extent of Indianization in Asia varied by location. It became most thorough in Sri Lanka, the Himalayan kingdoms, and Tibet. Southeast Asia today also reflects to a considerable extent—though with local modifications—the cultural exports of India. East Asia embraced and made indigenous Buddhist practices but disregarded most other Indian ideas and institutions. The most thorough rejection of India's methods for ordering a society can be seen in territories to its west and north, which came to embrace Islam and its political and social institutions. And by the thirteenth century, when the Delhi sultans inaugurated a half-millennium of Muslim rule in India, both India and Southeast Asia began to absorb Arab and Persian ideas and institutions.

Suggested Readings and Viewings

Michael Aung-Thwin, *The Mists of Ramanna* (Honolulu: University of Hawaii Press, 2005).

Stephen C. Berkwitz, *South Asian Buddhism: A Survey* (New York: Taylor and Francis, 2009).

Robert L. *Brown, The Dvaravati Wheels of the Law and the Indianization of Southeast Asia* (Leiden: E. J. Brill, 1996).

G. Coedes, *The Indianized States of Southeast Asia*, ed. Walter F. Vella (Honolulu: University of Hawaii Press, 1964).

Johan Elverskog, *Buddhism and Islam on the Silk Road* (Philadelphia: University of Pennsylvania Press, 2013).

In the Footsteps of Marco Polo (2012), dir. by Emir Lewis.

James Legge, *A Record of Buddhist Kingdoms: Being an Account by the Chinese Monk Fa Hsian [Faxian] of His Travels in India and Ceylon (A.D. 399–414)* (reprint; New York: Dover, 1965).

Xinru Liu, *Ancient China and Ancient India: Trade and Religious Exchanges, AD 1–600* (New York: Oxford University Press, 1988).

B. N. Puri, *Buddhism in Central Asia* (New Delhi: Motilal Banarsidass, 1987).

Edwin O. *Reischauer, trans., Ennin's Travels to Tang China* (New York: Ronald Press, 1955).

D. R. SarDesai, *Southeast Asia: Past and Present*, 5th ed. (Boulder, CO: Westview Press, 2003).

Lynda Norene Shaffer, *Maritime Southeast Asia to 1500* (Armonk, NY: M. E. Sharpe, 1996).

Susan Whitfeld, *The Silk Route: Trade, Travel, War and Faith* (London: British Museum, 2004).

Sally Hovey Wriggins, *Xuanzang: A Buddhist Pilgrim on the Silk Road* (Boulder, CO: Westview Press, 1996).

11

India under Islamic Rule: The Delhi Sultanate and Mughal Empire, 1206–1707

He who resists the Prophet after the right way has been made clear to him, we will cause him to suffer the fate he has earned. We shall cause him to burn in Hell.
—Fakhr ud-din al-Razi, on the eve of Delhi Sultanate rule

Introduction

When the Afghans took control of India under the Delhi Sultanate in 1206, nearly all Muslims in that country were foreigners: Afghans, Persians, Arabs, and so forth. By 1526, when India had slightly more than 100 million inhabitants, nearly all Muslims in India were native born. Not only did an increasing segment of the Indian population convert to Islam, but Afghan Delhi sultans and their Persian advisors soon realized that to govern a civilization the size of India successfully, they would need to exercise a bit more religious and cultural toleration toward the subject population. This included, among other things, the eventual granting of *dhimmi* status to non-Muslim Indians. Gone, for the most part, were the early days of sultanate rule when Hindu temple destruction and heavy taxation were commonplace occurrences. Thus, fourteenth-century Moroccan Muslim traveler Ibn Battuta noted that Hindus had sufficient freedom under the Delhi sultans to go on religious pilgrimages. When the Mughals deposed the last of the sultans in 1526, they continued a moderate policy toward the Hindus, best exemplified during the rule of the sympathetic Akbar, which continued nonetheless under less sensitive Mughal emperors. By the time British rule began to supplant Mughal authority in the eighteenth century, in other words, an institutionalized practice of religious toleration and cultural interdependence became the norm. Not until the late nineteenth century, with the advent of nationalism, did significant differences between Hindu and Muslim resurface.

Islamic Expansion into India: The Background

The Turko-Mongol conquests of India challenged the foundations of traditional Hindu ideas and institutions. Unlike earlier foreign invasions, which were numerous and chronic, these Muslim incursions pitted two apparently mutually exclusive approaches to life in a zero-sum battle where only one approach could prevail. Such had been largely the case as Islam spread beyond its place of origin on the Arabian Peninsula, first into the eastern Mediterranean, then across North Africa and

Asia Past and Present: A Brief History, First Edition. Peter P. Wan and Thomas D. Reins.
© 2021 John Wiley & Sons, Inc. Published 2021 by John Wiley & Sons, Inc.

into Spain, as well as through Persia, Central Asia, and across the Eurasian steppe into "Chinese Turkestan" (China's Xinjiang Province). Perhaps India, too, would experience the same outcome.

Although in theory the *dhimmi* or non-Muslim peoples under Muslim rule could freely follow their faiths, in practice Islamic government meant only small percentages of the conquered peoples continued to do so. Places where Islam came by conquest typically did not bode well for the local religions. Christianity and Judaism in the Muslim-controlled Mediterranean suffered prejudice and marginalization, Zoroastrianism in Persia all but vanished, while numerous smaller local religions became extinct as Islam absorbed the subjugated native populations. Indeed, even non-Arab converts to Islam, the *mawali*, lived second-class lives under Arab regimes. Places where Islam arrived by commerce, such as Southeast Asia and Sub-Saharan Africa, resulted in voluntary acceptance by the local inhabitants.

The religious situation in India played out differently. Although Muslims arrived as conquerors and had every intention of banishing Hinduism and Buddhism, India today remains a Hindu nation. What happened to make India different? Earlier conquerors of India, whether the Greeks, pre-Islamic Persians, Huns, or others, neither dominated the greater part of the Indian subcontinent, nor did they remain in power for lengthy enough periods to institutionalize their cultural practices. Nor did they arrive with a messianic urge to transform completely the essence of Indian society. By contrast, the Delhi sultans ruled for more than three centuries and the Mughal emperors for another two centuries before the British began to govern through them. Eventually, these Muslim leaders largely controlled or substantially managed—directly or indirectly—a majority of the subcontinent; and, at least initially, these leaders sought to eradicate the native religions and thus transform the Indian worldview. Ultimately they succeeded in adding yet another religion to the Indian melting pot, but failed to uproot Indian fundamentals: the primacy of Hinduism, the centrality of the caste system, the Indian concept of monarchy, the classical and vernacular Indian languages, or the heroic Indian models of behavior. To understand why India absorbed Islam, some background on the origins and development of Islam is required.

Islam, or submission to the will of God, began on the Arabian Peninsula in the seventh century. According to tradition, a middle-aged businessman named Muhammad (570–632) encountered an angel while he was praying on the outskirts of Mecca. Revelations from God in the first and later angelic encounters became the contents of the Quran (Koran), the various parts of which got transmitted orally and in writing until reaching its final, united appearance in 651. The Quran is Islam's sacred book, which provided a code of proper behavior for each Muslim, or one who submits. Most particularly, the Five Pillars of Islam furnish a guide that unites the Muslim community, or *umma*, cutting across tribal, ethnic, and other identities. First, all Muslims must acknowledge the existence of only one God, Allah; they must pray five times a day facing Mecca; they must also offer alms to the poor; they are required to fast from sunrise to sunset during the holy month of Ramadan; and finally, during one's life each Muslim should, if possible, make a pilgrimage (the *hajj*) to Mecca. Supplementing the Quran is the Hadith, a nonprophetic compilation of writings about the prophet's proverbs and activities, which serves as a guide to understanding correct conduct for the individual. The final guide to appropriate behavior is based on traditional practices of the Muslim community over time, which together with the Quran and Hadith make up Shari'a or Islamic law. Although the Ulema and later other Muslim clerics provided direction for the community, the individual ultimately acted as the chief interpreter of correct Islamic conduct.

Muslims believe that Muhammad represents God's final prophet (*khatam al-anbiya*), the last and most perfect in a long line that included those of the Jewish Old Testament (such as Moses) and the Christian New Testament (Jesus). As Muhammad began proselytizing the people of Mecca and winning converts to his new religion, he encountered a good deal of opposition. Since he opposed the multiplicity of gods worshipped at the Black Stone Shrine (the Ka'ba/Kaaba) in Mecca, merchants feared worshippers of those other gods might forgo pilgrimage to Mecca and thus reduce the city's income. He also fought traditional practices such as tribal warfare, alcohol consumption, infanticide, gambling, and other wicked activities, thus generating antagonisms from many Meccan residents. In 622 he migrated north to Medina (the *hegira*, which begins the Muslim calendar) to add to and regroup his forces, returning to and capturing Mecca in 630 and rededicating the Black Stone Shrine to Allah. When Muhammad died two years later, most of the tribes of the Arabian Peninsula had acknowledged his leadership.

Even as Islam expanded beyond the Arabian Peninsula after Muhammad's death, two major problems of Arab leadership emerged as well. One involved the legitimate successor of Muhammad. Of course no one could claim to be religious heir, since Muhammad was the last prophet. But the secular successor, or caliph (*khalifah*), supervised the implementation of Allah's plan as transmitted by Muhammad. Caliphs thus assumed the duties of overseer and protector of the Muslim faithful everywhere. When Muhammad's father-in-law, Abu Bakr, was selected caliph instead of Ali, Muhammad's son-in-law, a political and religious split occurred in the new religion. The Sunni Muslims acknowledged the legitimacy of Abu Bakr and subsequent caliphs, while Shi'a Muslims claimed Muhammad wanted his son-in-law to succeed him and thus Ali represented the authentic Islamic leadership. From the seventh century to today, Sunni Muslims have been the substantial majority in Islam.

The second problem was dynastic and involved which family would control the Caliphate. The first five caliphs, or the Al-Rashidun or "Rightly Guided," did in fact hold the Muslim community together, but none was able to create a dynasty. Although Ali (the last of the "Rightly Guided" rulers) and his son Hasan eventually served as caliphs, Hasan after a brief reign handed over the Caliphate to Muawiyah, who created the Umayyad Dynasty in 661. By that time, Arab-Islamic expansion extended across much of North Africa, as well as into the eastern Mediterranean, Persian-controlled Mesopotamia, and Persia itself. Successful expansion made a compelling case (to both Arabs and non-Arabs) for Mohammad being Allah's instrument on Earth.

The Sunni Umayyad Dynasty (661–750) emerged from the struggle between Sunni and Shi'a Islamic factions to lead the Muslim community. During their rule, the Arab-Islamic empire spread west across North Africa, then into Spain, and eventually entered France, where the Muslim warriors were stopped by Charles Martel at Tours in 732. To the east, Umayyad forces marched to the Indus River in India, into Central Asia, and eventually reached the Chinese frontier, defeating the Chinese in the Battle of Talas (in today's Kyrgyzstan) in 751. A year earlier, the Umayyad Caliphate had collapsed owing to internal fighting. Abu-al-Abbas rallied both Sunni and Shi'a forces against the Umayyad leadership and established the Abbasid Dynasty (750–1258), a Sunni reign broadly accepted by Muslims because it also had a link to Muhammad's family. But while the Abbasids religiously, socially, and economically integrated non-Arab peoples in newly conquered territories into an Arab-Islamic community, it failed, as did the previous Umayyad rulers and future caliphs, to establish a stable, centralized political administration.

Both Arab and non-Arab challenges to the Caliphate after the tenth century resulted in the creation of local or regional Muslim monarchs (usually titled "Sultan," meaning power or authority) in Europe, Africa, and Eurasia. These monarchs typically had only a nominal political connection to the Caliphate, which became merely the titular head of the Islamic world. The final blow to Abbasid rule came in 1258, when the Mongols, led by Genghis Khan's grandson Hulagu Khan, sacked Baghdad. Into this turmoil came first the Seljuk and then the Ottoman Turks who had migrated from Central Asia, worked for Abbasid rulers, converted to Sunni Islam, and ultimately took control of much of the Abbasid Empire.

Arab contact with India and the rest of Asia preceded Islam. Arab merchants had been trading in a vast commercial network involving East Africa, Persia, India, Sri Lanka, Southeast Asia, and southern China. Even after the Arabs had become Muslim, their small communities in India had little religious impact on India. Only after the Arab conquest of Sind (a province of today's Pakistan) in retaliation for the capture of shipwrecked Arab traders by a local Indian ruler did the issue of Indian religion surface. In theory, only Jews and Christians as "people of the book" (the Bible) warranted Muslim toleration, but the Arab conqueror of Sind (in 712) applied much the same principle to Hindus, Buddhists, and practitioners of other religions by labeling Indians *dhimmi*, or those being cared for, the price of which was the *jizya* or head tax and/or the *kharaj* or land tax imposed on people in conquered territories. But the application of *dhimmi* status to Indians typically occurred after conquest and plunder, and usually was applied capriciously by Muslim invaders.

Muslim raids into India continued, but not until the Turko-Afghan ruler Mahmud of Ghazni (reigned 997–1030 from his capital of Ghazni in Afghanistan) did military campaigns into India result in significant Muslim territorial conquests. He conquered most of what is today Pakistan and governed it directly, while his occupation of other parts of India resulted in indirect rule through Hindu vassals. Another Turko-Afghan group led by Muhammad of Ghur (also in Afghanistan) in 1175 attacked the territories once controlled by Mahmud of Ghazni, and then expanded Muslim-controlled territories as far east as Bengal. In 1193 the city of Nalanda, Buddhism's cultural center for more than a millennium, was sacked. Thousands of students and teachers fled, and its priceless library was virtually destroyed. All of these attacks on India produced death and destruction, the chief victim being followers of Buddhism. Although all Indian religions initially endured Muslim assaults, Buddhism nearly vanished as it was quite concentrated in monasteries and urban centers and thus more easily identified and uprooted. Most Buddhist survivors escaped to Nepal and Tibet.

India under Muslim Rule, 1206–1707	
632	The Prophet Muhammad dies
632–750	Arab armies conquer territories stretching from Spain to the Indian and Chinese frontiers, spreading Islam in the process
751	Battle of Talas (in today's Kyrgyzstan)—at that time a dividing line between Confucian and Buddhist cultural influence in Central Asia—halts Arab expansion eastward
750–1258	Collapse of Arab Abbasid Caliphate in 1258 in the wake of the Mongol destruction of Baghdad; Turkish and Mongol Muslims displace Arabs for leadership of the Muslim world
11th–13th centuries	Turkish and Mongol Muslims raid India with increasing frequency
1206–1526	The Afghan Delhi Sultanate, divided into four dynasties, takes control of India
13th–14th centuries	Ongoing Mongol raids into India
1398	Muslim Turko-Mongol leader Tamerlane invades India and captures and briefly occupies Delhi
16th century	Arrival of Europeans in India and the rest of Asia

1526	Mughals from Uzbekistan in Central Asia oust the Delhi sultans
1556–1605	Reign of Mughal Emperor Akbar
1600	English East India Company chartered by Queen Elizabeth I
1632	Mughal Emperor Shah Jahan commissions the building of the Taj Mahal
1707	Death of Aurangzeb in 1707 practically speaking ends Mughal control of India, which Britain governs through titular Mughal emperors
1858	Mughal Empire deposed by British

The Delhi Sultanate, 1206–1526

The Delhi sultans, who ruled India for more than three centuries, originated in Afghanistan, organized themselves tribally there, and had a Turko-Afghan ethnic background. These sultans, most of whom died by violence while in office, came from several families that formed dynasties: the Mamluk Slave Kings (1206–1290), Khaljis (1290–1320), Tughluqs (1320–1414), Sayyids (1414–1451), and Lodis (1451–1526). Once northern India came under their control and their capital was established at Delhi in north-central India, the new rulers needed to adjust their thinking about their newly won territory. Tribal organization and persecution of native religions could not hope to bring about any kind of permanent political control in this *Dar-ul-Islam*, or land of submission.

Although the Mamluk sultans always experienced palace intrigues, they established important domestic and foreign policies that enabled them as well as future Delhi sultans to maintain political control. Abroad, these new rulers carefully acknowledged the ultimate supremacy of the Baghdad caliph and their own subordinate status. As well, the Mongols raided India—even as far as Delhi—but never were capable of occupying territory for any length of time owing to the sultanate's military vigor and diplomatic shrewdness. At home, the sultans parceled out territory or revenue to Turkish military leaders, allowed local Indian elites to govern with sultanate permission, and pursued a policy of religious tolerance so long as the local elites did not resist Delhi's authority. And progressively the combination of Persian imperial techniques and traditional Hindu courtly practices allowed these Turko-Afghan tribal leaders to create the institutions of bureaucratic empire. For example, Balban (r. 1246–1266) "never hesitated to stamp out any opposition in the environs of his court by calling for his elephants, and he used the glittering façade of Persian ritual and royal pomp to overawe his populace.... Prostrating and toe kissing were both insisted upon by this slave who became sultan."[1]

Balban's grandsons could not hold the dynasty together, and it was overthrown by Jalal-ud-din Firuz Khalji. The Khalji Dynasty, though brief, accomplished several key objectives. It continued to repel Mongol attacks. It began to consolidate Delhi's power in much of northern India by removing the feudal status of Indian, Turkish, and Afghan vassals and replacing them with centrally appointed officials. And the Khaljis began to extend the sultan's authority into the Deccan, where central Indian rulers gradually fell under Delhi's sway. Ghazi Malik, a general on the Indian frontier, overthrew the last Khalji ruler and became the founder of the third dynasty of Delhi sultans, the Tughluqs, governing as Ghiyas-ud-din-Tughluq Shah. For nearly a century the Tughluqs faced constant political challenges at court and in the provinces, not to mention a period of major famine (1335–1342), economic problems resulting from the debasement of the

---

1 Stanley Wolpert, *A New History of India*, 6th ed. (New York: Oxford University Press, 2000), p. 110.

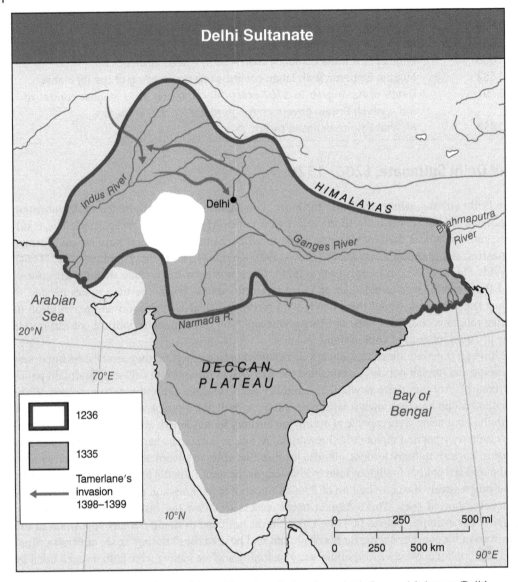

Delhi Sultanate

Delhi Sultanate, 1206–1526. Source: Adapted from http://educationpoint.in/images/gk_images/Delhi_Sultanate.gif.

currency (government-issued copper equal to silver), as well as ongoing frontier skirmishes with the Mongols. Nonetheless, the Tughluqs consolidated control over much of central and southern India by ending Hindu monarchs' vassal status there and establishing central government authority, at least until the reign of Firuz (1351–1388).

The death of Firuz and the appearance of several weak successors, combined with the invasion of India and the plunder of Delhi in 1398 by Tamerlane, brought an end to the Tughluqs and ushered in the fourth dynasty of Delhi sultans, the Sayyids, whose first ruler was Khizr Khan. All four Sayyid rulers, it appears, presided over the ever-weakening sultanate, whose control over the outlying provinces deteriorated and signified the end of Turkish control. The Afghan Lodi clan administered the final 75 years of the Delhi Sultanate. Buhlul Lodi, a capable official in the Punjab, was invited to take control of the sultanate and reverse its declining fortunes. But he and his descendants proved to be no more successful than the final Tughluq sultans. As the central government in Delhi began to collapse during the concluding century of sultanate rule, provincial and regional kingdoms emerged to take charge of political affairs across the subcontinent. Ultimately, Ibrahim (1517–1526) became the final Delhi sultan, who was pushed aside by an empire builder, Babur. As one historian describes the transition:

> The king of Kabul, Babur (1483–1530), the "Tiger," descended from Timus the Barlas Turk on his father's side and Ghengiz Khan the great Mongol on his mother's. Kaulat Khan, the governor of Lahore, had invited Babur to "save" him from Ibrahim, and the Tiger ... readily accepted the invitation. He came to India, however, not as an ally of the Viceroy of the Punjab, but as founder of the greatest Muslim dynasty in Indian history, as the first *Padishah* ("emperor") of the Mughals.[2]

The collapse of the Delhi Sultanate overshadowed three major occurrences that would profoundly shape India's future. One involved the growth of the Indian-born Muslim population, which over the centuries had converted to Islam to get out from under the stigma of low caste status, to become eligible to hold office in Muslim administrations, to avoid the non-Muslim taxes, or out of religious conviction switched to a religion whose doctrine appeared more suitable. The second was the emergence in the sixteenth century of the Sikh religion, which attempted to harmonize the central truths in both Hinduism and Islam. And, thirdly, the arrival of the Europeans foreshadowed the creation of new Asian empires and colonies, the construction and administration of which paved the way for the introduction of new religions, novel intellectual methods, fresh political possibilities, as well as the emergence of nationalism, independence movements, and revolutionary social changes.

The Mughal Empire, 1526–1858

Mughal rulers, like many foreign conquerors of India, came from the Central Asian frontier, in this case from Uzbekistan. Their founders included ancestors of various frontier backgrounds, including Mongol, a word the British Anglicized to become Mughal. Not all of the emperors possessed the drive, determination, cleverness, and luck to suggest that the empire would succeed in holding together a subcontinent typically politically fragmented. Earlier Indian and foreign sovereigns experienced dynastic infighting, which usually resulted in a failure to impose central government control in the provinces, which in turn complicated efforts to protect the frontier. Indian governments thus often found themselves fighting on three fronts: within the imperial headquarters, in the provinces, and on the borders. The Mughals by contrast had fewer problems at the center, as best evidenced by the highly successful—if sometimes violent—transfers of power among the early emperors. And even when challenged by outsiders, as when the Afghan Pashtun leader Sher Shah Sur attempted to oust Babur's inept son Humayun, the Mughals had the double luck of Sher Shah's timely death in 1545 as well as the benefit of his reorganization and consolidation of the imperial bureaucracy.

What territory Babur conquered and what political and economic guidelines Sher Shah systematized, the third Mughal ruler, Akbar (Jalaluddin Muhammad Akbar, r. 1556–1605),

---

2 Wolpert, *A New History of India*, p. 121.

combined with his own governing itinerary into an administration that made him the most successful of Mughal monarchs. After both Hindu and Afghan challenges to his rule failed, and as he achieved his majority in the early 1560s, Akbar proceeded to launch his own political agenda. For more than two decades he focused on subduing domestic opponents and applying his court's jurisdiction, the latter nonetheless allowing the Ulema to judge Islamic law and Brahmans or the village councils (*panchayats*) to interpret Hindu law (the *Dharmashastras*) in cases involving only Hindus. Still, even though all decisions could be appealed to the emperor, Akbar went out of his way to minimize legal issues to prevent them from swelling into religious or cultural conflict.

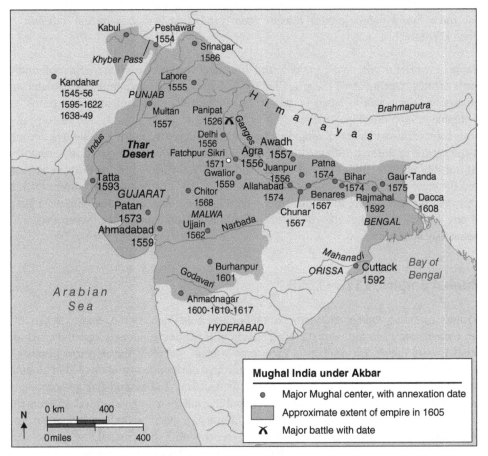

Mughal Empire (1526–1858) at the time of Akbar (r. 1556–1605). Source: Adapted from http://websupport1.citytech.cuny.edu/Faculty/pcatapano/Modern_World/MW_Maps/Map20.3vonSivers.jpg.

This first required winning over the majority Hindu population (roughly 75%), but it also involved working out the government's own position on both Sunni and Shi'a Islam, since neighboring Persia was a Shi'a state. Furthermore, though born a Sunni Muslim, Akbar's childhood guardian in Persia (Bairam Khan) was a Shi'a. Ultimately, Akbar practiced religious tolerance (*sulah-I kul*) toward not only Hinduism but also the newly formed Sikh religion and the recently arrived Christianity. He married two Rajput Hindu princesses who were not required to renounce their faith, marriages that strengthened his standing in the eyes of Hindus and also gave him important Hindu political and military collaborators. Akbar also did away with two taxes that Hindus despised: the *jizya* or non-Muslim head tax (re-imposed by Emperor Aurangzeb in 1679) and the pilgrim tax one paid to visit a Hindu shrine (reinstated by the British). And Akbar finalized a gradually developing Muslim policy (going back to at least the beginning of the Delhi Sultanate) of appointing Hindus to positions in the government and military. Two problems minimized the number of Hindu officials in government. One was the general Hindu hostility to a foreign conqueror and the stigma of traitor the Hindu official would acquire. As the Mughals became viewed progressively more as an Indian government, more Hindus entered imperial service. The second problem, closely tied to the first, involved the official Persian language used at court. Again, as the Mughals became more "native," greater numbers of non-Muslim Indians began to learn Persian and thus become eligible for office.

Indeed, Akbar's concern with religious toleration led him to create his own version of a universal religion, the *Din-i-Ilahi* or Divine Faith, which chiefly combined mystical Sufi Islam with devotional Bhakti Hinduism but also included elements of Christianity, Zoroastrianism, Jainism, and Sikhism. Indeed, historically Indian rulers have always had to deal with local popular religious practices (as did rulers across the globe), and so did the spokesmen for the more universal outlooks of Hinduism and Islam. Akbar also held religious conferences at which representatives of various religions and even atheists got together and discussed theological issues. His desire for universal cooperation and national harmony had lasting impact. India's first prime minister, Jawaharlal Nehru, said of Akbar:

> Round himself Akbar collected a brilliant group of men, devoted to him and his ideals.... His court became a meeting place for men of all faiths and all who had some new idea or new invention. His toleration of views and his encouragement of all kinds of beliefs and opinions went so far as to anger some of the more orthodox Muslims. He even tried to start a new synthetic faith to suit everybody. It was in his reign that the cultural amalgamation of Hindu and Moslem in north India took a long step forward.... The Moghul dynasty became firmly established as India's own.[3]

Although his universal religion died with him, and even though subsequent emperors failed to support his religiously tolerant policies, increasingly Muslims and Hindus came to accept one another.

Perhaps the chief cause of Akbar's success had to do with his approach to governing, which in substance became increasingly Indian while retaining the style of Muslim rulers in Persia. "The elegant decadence of Mughal dress, décor, manners, and morals all reflected Persian court life and custom. Mughal culture was, however, more than an import; by Akbar's era it had acquired something of a 'national' patina."[4] Akbar eventually governed through local elites who paid tribute and governed what often amounted to feudal fiefs, so long as these elites or "vassals" made the tribute payments. As well, in addition to the elimination of the *jizya* and the pilgrimage tax, Akbar also cancelled the tax on cows while he generally respected the local customs. His court often supported non-Muslim people of merit and organizations of distinction. Since most of these "vassals" were Hindu, Akbar won their respect or at least their neutrality. In any case, his policies certainly improved the relationship between the alien governors and the native governed.

---

3 Jawaharlal Nehru, *The Discovery of India* (Garden City, NY: Anchor Books, c. 1946, 1960), pp. 163–164.
4 Wolpert, *A New History of India*, p. 133.

Akbar (1542–1605). Source: Dinodia Photos / Alamy Stock Photo.

While such cultural and religious freethinking appealed to Hindus, it began to produce both religious and lay Islamic opposition within India. For instance, the historian Al-Badaoni (1540–1615) took issue with the emperor's ecumenical attitude toward non-Muslim religions.

Everything that pleased him [Akbar], he picked and chose from anyone except a Moslem, and anything that was against his disposition, and ran counter his wishes he thought fit to reject and cast aside. From childhood to manhood, and from manhood to his declining years the Emperor had combined in himself various phases from various religions and opposite sectarian beliefs.... Thus a faith of a materialistic character became painted on the mirror of his mind and the storehouse of his imagination, and from the general impression form, like an engraving upon a stone, that there are wise men of asceticism, and recipients of revelation and workers of miracles among all nations and that the Truth is an inhabitant of every place: and that consequently how could it be right or consider it as confined to one religion or creed, and that, one which had only recently made its appearance [Sikhism] and had not as yet endure a thousand years! And why assert one thing and deny another, and claim pre-eminence for that which is not essentially pre-eminent?[5]

5 J. Kelley Sowards, *Makers of World History*, vol. 2 (New York: St. Martin's Press, 1992), p. 9.

Ultimately this reaction, combined with later emperors' antagonism to Akbar's policies, diluted but did not extinguish the Indian subjects' broad acceptance of people's differences. As one Punjabi resident recalls of his early twentieth-century life, "As a child and an adolescent, I got in tune with the spirit of the town, and a spirit it certainly had. It possessed a self-contained unity of life in which the people worked at their hereditary crafts and professions, and lived in their *biradaris* [lineages in villages], friendly and tolerant of each other." And though differences existed that produced social friction, rarely did this discord result in "any tumult on the surface."[6]

It was in this environment of relative toleration that a new religion, Sikhism, began to thrive. Tradition proclaims that Guru Nanak of Hindu background founded Sikhism in 1469 to bridge the ongoing religious divide between Hindus and Muslims during the Delhi Sultanate. Testimony to this belief can be seen in the Sikh "bible," the flowing *Guru Granth Sahib*. It contains poems and hymns from both Guru Nanak and his successors as well as from non-Sikh religious traditions. "Sikh" means follower, student, or disciple in the Punjabi dialect, and it originated in Talwandi, in what was then India's northwestern state of Punjab (divided between India and Pakistan after 1947). Today the vast majority of the world's 30 million Sikhs live in the Indian portion of the Punjab. The basic tenets of Sikhism, the world's fifth-largest organized religion, derive from Guru Nanak and his first nine successors and thereafter from the *Guru Granth Sahib*, a collection of the original 10 gurus' writings and sayings.

Sikhism is a monotheistic, revealed religion. Legend has it that Nanak encountered God, who offered him the "Liquid of Immortality," which Nanak drank. God commanded Nanak—now filled with divine inspiration—to preach God's word. Indeed, whatever Guru Nanak spoke had the authority of God since he spoke only what God inspired him to say.

As Nanak declares,

> I was a minstrel (*dhadi*) without an occupation, but God gave me an occupation. He ordered me to sing His praises. He called the *dhadi* to His abode of Truth, and gave him the robe of "true praise and adoration." The true nectar of the Name had been sent as food. They are happy who taste it to the full in accordance with the Guru's instructions. The *dhadi* openly proclaims the glory of the Word. By adoring the Truth, Nanak has found the Perfect One.[7]

Nanak accentuated the equality of humans in the eyes of God, thus challenging Hindu attitudes about caste and the position of women in Indian society as well as the concept that life was nothing but an illusion. Early Sikhism opposed emphasis on religious ritual, a crucial part of everyday Hinduism. On the other hand, the relationship between Muslim rulers and the Sikhs at first tended to be cordial, with Akbar actually meeting with the third guru, Amar Das. But the year after Akbar's death in 1605, the succeeding Mughal Emperor Jahangir had the fifth guru, Arjan, executed; 70 years later, the ninth guru suffered the same fate. Thereafter Sikhism began to militarize to protect its followers. In 1699, the tenth guru, Gobind Singh, formalized the militarization with the creation of the *Khalsa*, the community of initiated Sikhs. Subsequently the "living" guru was the Guru Granth Sahib, while practical leadership of the community was the head of the *Khalsa*, the first one being Banda Singh Bahadur. Down to today, the Sikhs have had stormy relations with the Mughals, the British, and ultimately the independent Indian government after 1947.

---

6 Prakash Tandon, *Punjabi Century, 1847–1947* (Berkeley: University of California Press, 1968), p. 103.
7 J. S. Grewal, *The Sikhs of the Punjab*, vol. II.3 in *The New Cambridge History of India* (Cambridge: Cambridge University Press, 1990), p. 39.

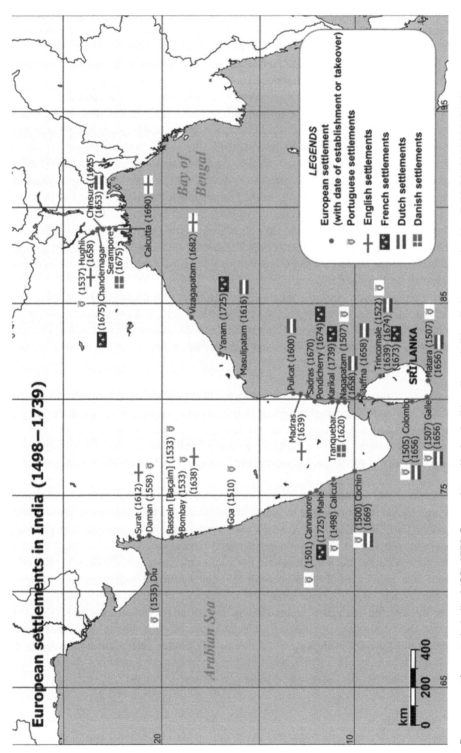

European settlements in India, 1498–1739. Source: https://upload.wikimedia.org/wikipedia/commons/archive/3/32/20100302204913%21European_settlements_in_India_1501-1739.png.

Akbar's death commenced a decline of imperial power. The court eventually proved incapable of keeping the Europeans, and ultimately the British, from co-opting the Mughal position as the final political authority in increasingly larger parts of the Indian subcontinent. Jahangir (r. 1605–1627) had intrigued against Akbar during his father's last years. This produced a struggle for succession to the throne after Akbar's death, which Jahangir won by military might and diplomatic finesse. He allowed most former rivals to keep their government positions, and some even received promotions. But this promising start, which also involved a dubious continuation of Akbar's religious toleration, soon waned. His wife Nur Jahan, the widow of a Persian nobleman, began to marginalize her new husband's power and to appoint Persians to high positions in the Mughal bureaucracy.

This directly led to doing away with Akbar's policy of balancing Indian and Persian influence at court, which was no longer headquartered at Delhi but now relocated to Agra. Jahangir consoled himself with wine, women, and song while both he and his wife spent profligately. Shah Jahan (1627–1658) succeeded his father and continued to spend lavishly, his most notable expenditure being for construction of the Taj Mahal. More expensive, however, were the economic and political costs of a waning monarchy. Weakness at Agra encouraged rulers in the Deccan and in southern India to resist the Mughal court, which launched expeditions south to maintain the emperor's authority. Aurangzeb (r. 1658–1707) had to fight his way to power. As his father proved too ill to rule and his older brother Dara Shukoh attempted to seize royal powers, Aurangzeb confronted and defeated his brother in battle, deposed his father in July 1658 (he died in 1666), and assumed the throne officially in 1659.

Aurangzeb's military and administrative abilities (as well as his ruthlessness) suggested a reversal of declining fortunes for the empire. But numerous and considerable opponents dominated Aurangzeb's managerial agenda. He angered Hindus by appointing an enforcer of Islamic law, banned Hindu religious fairs, forbade the construction of new Hindu temples and the repair of existing ones, and restored the *jizya* tax on non-Muslims. He also upset many Hindus with a 1664 ban on suttee/suti, the practice of widows immolating themselves along with their dearly departed husbands. As well, Aurangzeb upset much of the population with crackdowns on prostitution, gambling, and drinking. And although he eliminated internal tariffs since they were not allowed by Islamic law, this hardly compensated for other onerous policies, and the ending of the internal taxes left the free-spending court with less income.

Although Aurangzeb succeeded in extending the court's authority to the eastern parts of Bengal, and in the northwest by establishing a friendly relationship with people on the Afghan frontier, he had to deal with ongoing deteriorating relations with domestic insurgents. The Sikhs had long resisted Mughal authority once the religiously tolerant Akbar died. And though costly military campaigns against the Sikhs proved successful in restoring a peaceful relationship in the short run, that rapport did not survive Aurangzeb's reign. In the Deccan, Aurangzeb inherited a continuing feud the court had with the Marathas, whose leader Shivaji Bhonsle (1627–1680) formally created the Maratha Confederacy in 1674, proclaiming himself king and claiming to be the reincarnation of the Hindu God Shiva. Aurangzeb finally subdued Maratha (roughly today's Maharashtra) in 1687, yet when the emperor died in 1707 Maratha resistance continued in the form of guerrilla warfare. The Marathas remained a thorn in the side of the moribund Mughals until the British defeated them in 1818. By then the British had co-opted the Mughals, governed through them, and were in the process of further unifying a subcontinent seemingly politically disconnected though culturally fairly cohesive. In 1858 the British formally ended what remained of Mughal rule in India.

Suggested Readings and Viewings

Muzaffar Alam, *The Languages of Political Islam, India 1200–1800* (Chicago: University of Chicago Press, 2004).

Pierre Du Jarric, *Akbar and the Jesuits: An Account of the Jesuit Missions to the Court of Akbar* (London: Routledge, 1926, 2004).

Abraham Eraly, *The Mughal World: Life in India's Last Golden Age* (New York: Penguin, 2007).

J.S. Grewal, *The Sikhs of the Punjab* (Cambridge: Cambridge University Press, 1998).

Irfan Habib, *An Atlas of the Mughal Empire* (New Delhi: Oxford University Press, 1982).

Peter Jackson, *The Delhi Sultanate: A Political and Military History* (Cambridge: Cambridge University Press, 1999).

John Keay, *The Honourable Company: A History of the English East India Company* (London: HarperCollins, 1991).

Bernard Lewis, *Islam: The Religion and the People* (Philadelphia: Wharton School Publishing, 2008).

Rekha Pande, *Succession in the Delhi Sultanate* (New Delhi: Commonwealth Publishers, 1990).

John F. Richards, *The Mughal Empire* (Cambridge: Cambridge University Press, 1996).

Michael Wood, writer and presenter, "The Meeting of Two Oceans," in *The Story of India* (London: BBC, 2007), episode 5.

12

On the Indian and Chinese Northern Frontiers: Asian Empires and Kingdoms on the Central and Inner Asian Steppe, circa 1100–1850

There is no doubt that the Mongol rulers interested themselves in [Lamaism] for the purpose of creating a national unity that would consolidate the Mongols and at the same time differentiate themselves from the Chinese. They wanted to make the Mongols a permanent ruling class, with a code of its own sanctioned by an organized religion.[1]

Introduction

The Delhi Sultanate and the Mughal Empire illustrate, as do imperial regimes across the globe and through time, that empires expand and contract geographically, rise and fall politically, and thrive and deteriorate culturally. As well, no empire or region is an island but instead appears connected with larger cultural, economic, or geographical regions (such as the Pacific, South Asia, or the Eurasian steppe), and beyond those—increasingly after 1500—to global networks and organizations. This chapter will explore the rise and extension of the Mongol, Manchu, and Russian Empires to the north of China and India, as well as these empires' expansion into territories south such as China and India.

Little remains today of two empires. The Mongols reverted to nomadic life by the fifteenth century, were absorbed by the Manchu Qing Dynasty of China, fell under Tsarist Russian and then Soviet Russian rule for most of the twentieth century, and recently became democratic by 1990 as the Soviet Union began to come apart. The Manchus all but disappeared as an identifiable ethnic group when their Qing Dynasty collapsed in 1912. The Republic of China pensioned off the Manchu elite and absorbed Manchuria, allowing millions of ethnic Chinese to migrate there to acquire land or obtain factory jobs in Japanese-created industries begun there. Ultimately, the People's Republic of China absorbed Manchuria, and the "last emperor" died a gardener in Beijing in 1966 as the Cultural Revolution commenced.

While the influences of Mongol activities little affect the twenty-first century, Manchu actions on China's frontier produced issues that are unresolved to this day. The Qing Dynasty laid claim to frontier territory only lightly inhabited by ethnic Chinese,[2] chiefly in Taiwan, Tibet, and Xinjiang (Chinese Turkestan). Taiwan resisted absorption by the People's Republic, while the other frontier territories contained ethnic and religious minorities that denounced Beijing's treatment of them.

---

1 Owen Lattimore, *Inner Asian Frontiers of China* (Boston: Beacon Press, 1940, 1951), pp. 80–81.
2 Ethnic Chinese are typically referred to as Han Chinese, as opposed to Manchus, Mongols, Tibetans, Turks, and other ethnic groups. The term "Han" has been used in this exclusive sense since the Ming Dynasty.

Asia Past and Present: A Brief History, First Edition. Peter P. Wan and Thomas D. Reins.
© 2021 John Wiley & Sons, Inc. Published 2021 by John Wiley & Sons, Inc.

Russia under the tsars, the Soviets, and now post-Communist regimes still controls a vast swath of land running east from the Ural Mountains—mainly Siberia—to the Pacific coast. As well, Russian influence in Central Asia remains substantial.

The Mongol Empire

The Mongols created the largest contiguous empire in world history, reaching its height during the thirteenth century, a period that was bookended by the reigns of Genghis Khan and Kublai Khan. Still, the Russian Empire reached considerable mass, and the later Spanish and British Empires possessed—in scattered locations—more territory and people and continued longer. The Mongol domain extended from the Pacific Ocean (today's Russia, China, Korea, and parts of Southeast Asia) in the east to Central and Eastern Europe and pieces of the Middle East to the west. Of the major Eurasian civilizations, only India under the Delhi Sultanate succeeded in preventing a Mongol subjugation.

Empires on the Indian and Chinese Northern Frontiers, 1100–1850	
ca. 1165	Temujin (later Genghis Khan) is born
12th–13th centuries	Jurchen/Nüzhen tribe, earliest identifiable Manchus, creates the Jin Dynasty (1115–1234), which was destroyed by the Mongols
1206–1368	All (Great) Mongol State created
1227	Genghis Khan dies
1237	Mongols invade Russia
1279–1368	Mongols rule China as the Yuan Dynasty
1264–1294	Reign of Kublai Khan: promotes Lamaism as unifying force but continues to embrace traditional religious practices as well as tolerate other religions
16th century	Russian forces defeat several declining khanates, and Cossacks begin conquest of Siberia
1644–1912	Manchu tribes on the northeastern frontier of China defeat Ming Dynasty in 1644 and rule with the dynastic name Qing
1661–1722	Kangxi Emperor's reign
1689	Treaty of Nerchinsk establishes border between Russia and China
1727	Treaty of Kiakhta sets border between Russia and Mongolia (then controlled by Manchu Qing China)
1736–1796/1799	Qianlong Emperor's reign; he abdicates in 1796 but continues to rule until his death in 1799; during the intervening years his son, the Jiaqing Emperor, officially reigned
1839–1842	First Opium War, ended by the Treaty of Nanjing

The empire emerged as Temujin (1165–1227) united what had been fiercely independent Mongol tribes into a single organization (the *Khamag Mongol Ulus* or All Mongol State) by 1206. By then the various tribes bestowed the title of Chinggis Khan/Genghis Khan, "Resolute Ruler," on him.

He then "reorganized the social structure by dissolving old tribal lines and regrouping them into an army based on a decimal system (units of 10, 100, and 1000) ... and as well instilled a strong sense of discipline into the army."[3] Soon thereafter Chinggis Khan captured most of northern China, then controlled by the Tangut Xixia Dynasty in the northwest and the Manchu Jin Dynasty in the northeast. Before Temujin died, Mongol forces had attacked and occupied a good deal of Central Asia, much of which was then under the control of the Persians. Responding to the massacre of a Mongol caravan in today's Uzbekistan, Temujin launched a campaign against the Persian shah, who died while fleeing from Mongol forces. Temujin then (and in future similar victorious campaigns) legitimized his conquests there by proclaiming he was God's retribution for evildoers. "O people know that you have committed great sins, and that the great ones among you have committed these sins. If you ask me what proof I have for these words, I say it is because I am the punishment of God. If you had not committed great sins, God would not have sent a punishment like me upon you."[4]

Chinggis Khan (1162–1227).

Shortly before his death, Chinggis Khan divided the empire into several khanates—Chagatai, Golden Horde, Il-Khanate, and China of the Yuan Dynasty. He hoped that a common religious faith would help unite the various clans and their different shamanistic practices. Although he was

---

3 Timothy May, "The Mongol Empire in World History," *World History Connected* 5, no. 2 (May 2008): 1.
4 May, "The Mongol Empire," 2.

a believer in shamanism and the sky god *Tengri* ("the Eternal Blue Sky"), and although his clan *Borjigin* or Clan of the Grey Wolf influenced his religious outlook, Chinggis Khan and his successors increasingly drew from many religious traditions: ancestor worship, Daoism, Christianity, Islam, and Buddhism. In the end, however, it was Tibetan Buddhism (Lamaism) that emerged as the choice of Mongols. It was likely Kublai Khan (1215–1294), impressed by Tibetan monk Phags-pa (1235–1280), who tipped the balance in favor of Lamaism. Nonetheless, the Mongols continued to follow a policy of religious toleration.

In the short term, the practice of a common religion helped to make the Mongols more cohesive, but in the longer term religion proved insufficient to keep the growing empire united. Nor did the ongoing problem of Mongol political succession get resolved through religion. Chinggis Khan named his son Ogedei as primary successor or Great Khan. He hoped no succession crisis would emerge, and the hope seemed realistic as Tolui, his fourth son, swore to be faithful to his brother, saying, "If he forgets something, I shall be there to remind him; if he falls asleep, I shall wake him. I shall be like the whip of his horse. In long campaigns as in sudden scrimmage, I shall fight at his side."[5] The Chagatai Khanate, initially headed by Chinggis Khan's second son Chagatai, controlled most of current Central Asia and extended into Chinese Turkestan. However, it constantly faced leadership and succession problems at home and commonly experienced conflict with other khanates. By the seventeenth century, the territories had been frequently subdivided among Chagatai's descendants; gradually they became Turkish, and eventually Islamic law (*sharia*) replaced Mongol law (*yasa*).

Other khanates suffered much the same fate. The Golden Horde Khanate had occupied much of Eastern Europe, most of Russia, and Kazakhstan, but by the fifteenth century it collapsed as a meaningful political entity. The chief causes of decline were internal squabbling and external clashes. By then, it too had become essentially Turkish and Muslim. The Il-Khanate or "subordinate" khanate included Persia, Mesopotamia, parts of today's southern Russia, and pieces of the eastern Mediterranean. Conqueror of those territories and first ruler of the Il-Khanate, Hulegu (likely a Buddhist, with a traditional Mongol *Tengri* amalgam) owed much of his success to the support of Shiite Muslims and Nestorian Christians who suffered under the Sunni Muslim rulers of the Abbasid Caliphate headquartered in Baghdad. But soon after his conquest of Baghdad in 1258, Hulegu incurred the wrath of the Muslim ruler of the Golden Horde, Berke; and when his brother the Great Khan Mongke died in 1259, he returned to Mongolia to support his brother Kublai against his other brother Ariq Boke for the Great Khan leadership position. During his absence, the Mamluk Turkish Sultanate in Cairo and the Ottoman Turks in Anatolia (today's Turkey) halted the Mongol push into the eastern Mediterranean. By the time of Kublai Khan's death in 1294, the last of the Il-Khanate rulers to favor Buddhism passed from the scene, and the following year Ghazan, a Sunni Muslim, took control of what became an Islamic state. Thereafter the question of religion revolved around a Sunni–Shia struggle for power. Indeed, in Western Asia, Islamic culture absorbed the Mongol invasions.

Ogedei headed the entire Mongol Empire and directly oversaw activities in East Asia. He consolidated power in northern China and along its northern frontier by pacifying what remained of Tangut Xixia resistance in the late 1220s and crushing the Jin opposition to Mongol rule in 1234. By the time of Ogedei's death in 1241, he and his generals had conquered Persia, Armenia, Georgia, a good part of Russia, as well as Hungary and Poland. And before Kublai/Qubilai Khan

---

5 Rene Grousset, *Conqueror of the World: The Life of Chingis-khan* (New York: Viking, 1966), p. 215.

Great Khans	
Name	**Reign or Regency**
Chinggis Khan	1206–1227
Tolui (regent; son of Chinggis Khan)	1227–1229
Ogedei (son of Chinggis Khan)	1229–1241
Toregene Khatun (regent; wife of Ogedei; mother of Guyuk)	1241–1246
Guyuk (son of Ogedei)	1246–1248
Mongke/Mengku Khan (cousin of Ogedei)	1251–1259
Kublai Khan and Ariq Boke fight for Great Khan position	1260–1264
Kublai Khan* (brother of Mongke, Hulegu, and Ariq Boke)	1264–1294

* Later Mongol rulers assumed a Chinese reign title during the Yuan Dynasty (1279–1368). The last great Mongol ruler, Timur or Tamerlane, died in 1405. His empire consisted of Chagatai's territories in parts of Central Asia and Chinese Turkestan as well as Persia and Mesopotamia.

took power in 1260 (officially in 1264), parts of today's Turkey and the cultural capital of Islam, Baghdad, had fallen to Mongol warriors. Kublai Khan conquered the Southern Song dynasty in 1279 and established the Mongol Yuan dynasty, attempted twice (1274 and 1281) but failed to defeat Japan (due to bad weather, the *kamikaze* or "divine wind"), and attacked but fell short of conquering Southeast Asian territories due to ferocious resistance there, particularly by the Vietnamese and Burmese.

The death of Kublai Khan in 1294 began a downward spiral of Mongol power due mainly to the weakness of his successors in China, which threw out the Mongols in 1368, and to an ongoing inability of the various khanates to create any kind of cohesion. This resulted considerably from the western parts of the empire becoming culturally Turkish and religiously Islamic, while most of the eastern parts tended to be Confucian and Buddhist. It was also a consequence of size; just as the early Arab conquests produced territories too large and diverse to directly govern, so too with the Mongols. Conquest requires one set of abilities, while governing requires still other talents. By the fourteenth century, the Mongols could no longer draw on leaders with a flair for governing.

Although the creation of the Mongol Empire represented a spectacular military accomplishment, its brief ascendancy nonetheless provided a number of consequences often overlooked amid the excitement surrounding the conquests. Mongol rule, chiefly under Kublai Khan, provided a relatively open environment for intellectual and religious activities. Numerous khans patronized people of various religious backgrounds, including Daoism, Christianity, Islam, and Buddhism. They made use of Confucian scholars, Italian merchants, and Persian astronomers as well as allowing for the relatively free exchange of ideas, technology, peoples, and merchandise to travel across the comparatively safe Silk Road from China to Europe. This *Pax Mongolica* enabled Marco Polo, John of Plano Carpini, and William of Rubruck plus countless other travelers to visit locations under Mongol control with a fair assurance of security of person and property.

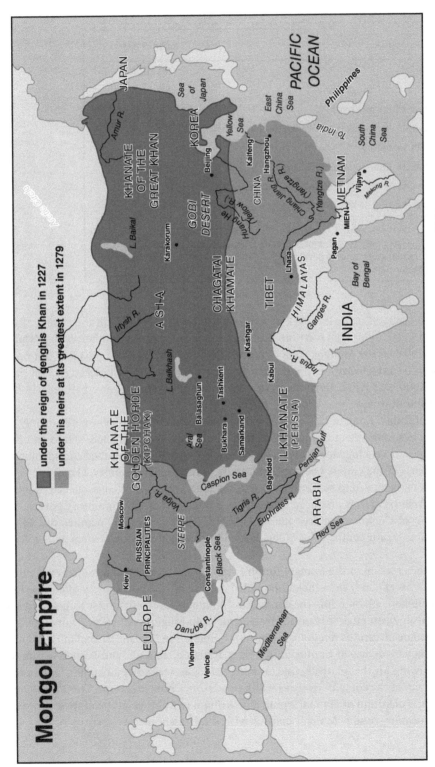

The Mongol Empire, 1294. *Source*: Adapted from http:/bhoffert.faculty.noctrl.edu/hst261/Map.MongolEmpire.1294.png.

The Manchu Empire

The Manchus originated in what is today northeastern China and what the outside world has typically referred to as Manchuria. The Jurchen/Nüzhen tribe represents the earliest identifiable Manchus. They can be traced back to the twelfth century as the creators of the Jin Dynasty (1115–1234). Located on China's northern frontier, the Jurchen competed with the existing ethnic-Chinese Song Dynasty (906–1279) for the Mandate of Heaven. When the Mongols conquered China and created the Yuan Dynasty in 1279, the Manchus were absorbed, and the fall of the Mongols to the ethnic-Chinese Ming Dynasty (1368–1644) allowed the Manchus to recover some control over Manchuria. The Manchus, though tribally organized, had developed a more sedentary existence involving an agricultural way of life. This made indirect Ming administration of Manchu territories less complicated. By the seventeenth century, a host of problems—fiscal mismanagement, a silver crisis, high taxes, bad weather, and famine—led to unrest and ultimately to spreading rebellion that the Ming failed to handle effectively.

Numerous Ming difficulties set the stage for the Manchu subjugation under the Qing Dynasty (1644–1912). The Manchu Empire began in Manchuria, a Chinese frontier region; it then engulfed China proper, absorbed Mongolia (inner and outer), defeated Ming loyalists on Taiwan, and "marched west." There it made what are now the western parts of China—Yunnan, Tibet, Qinghai, and Xinjiang Provinces—more culturally Chinese by both greater Beijing management in those regions and further ethnic Chinese migration there. As the Manchus largely adopted Chinese governing practices, Manchu expansion eventually chiefly meant Chinese expansion, and with the fall of the Manchus in 1912 ethnic Han Chinese politicians and intellectuals assumed that China had inherited Manchu conquests.

Exactly what constituted geographical China over the centuries? From the period of Qin unification in 221 BCE to today, the Chinese borders have expanded and contracted according to the strength and weakness of China and its neighbors. From a Chinese point of view, there has been an enduring "preoccupation with bringing together 'all under heaven'—interpreted minimally as the territories of the traditional Chinese heartland (the 'lesser empire') and maximally including all the lands claimed by the Han and Tang dynasties at their furthest extent (the 'greater empire')."[6] During the Han and Tang Dynasties, China's reach did extend into Central Asia and what is now Mongolia, but its authority in Tibet and today's southwest China (most of Yunnan and Guizhou Provinces) was more tenuous, and its link with Taiwan nearly nonexistent. China's relations with frontier territories varied with time and territory.

There was no unified "tribute system," an attempted Chinese-centered uniform hierarchical relationship between the Chinese Middle Kingdom and the outside world. Instead, different functional ceremonial and diplomatic practices were designed for the numerous foreign entities: for nomads to the north, for Korea and Japan, for Southeast Asian states, and later for the Europeans. Territories surrounding China usually paid tribute to China when it was strong, while China often acknowledged equality or even superiority in other states in times of weakness. By early Manchu Qing times, the dynasty could boast the respect of most all foreigners, which is to say that most surrounding territories deferred to China. All the while, ethnic Chinese males paid tribute to the Manchu conquerors by shaving their heads and wearing the Manchu queue. These humiliating practices were accepted given the alternative. A common adage of the time was "Lose your hair

6 Mark C. Elliott, *Emperor Qianlong: Son of Heaven, Man of the World* (New York: Longman, 2009), p. 86.

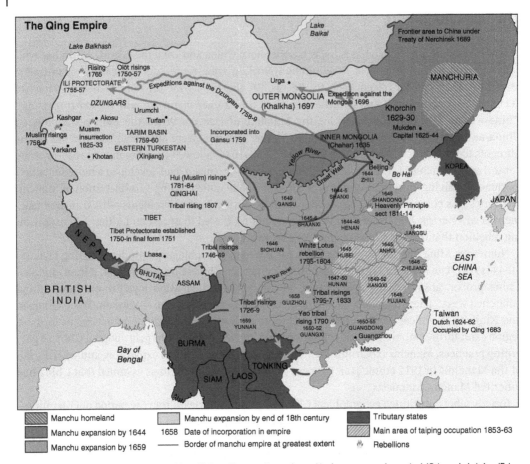

Origin and expansion of Manchu Qing China. *Source:* From http://rubens.anu.edu.au/raid2/no_dgb/pics/5/large/aah_ch_map_qing.jpg. Reproduced with permission of Cambridge University Press.

and keep your head, or keep your hair and lose your head."[7] It was from this position of strength that the Manchus proceeded to govern China and to incorporate Taiwan, the southwest, the northwest, and parts of Mongolia into "the greater empire."

Qing Dynasty expansion into its frontier territories in the seventeenth and eighteenth centuries has been compared to the colonialism of the industrial nations of Europe, America, and Japan in the nineteenth century. Once the decision to expand Chinese influence in frontier territories was made, the Qing government—like the industrial powers a century or so later—had to devise means of administrating the newly occupied regions, which involved creating working arrangements with the local elites, financing the military and administrative costs, and attempting to impose mutually acceptable behavioral guidelines of interaction. The creation of such guidelines assumed that the local cultural practices needed to be respected, but it also presupposed the stronger power would establish the substantive parts of any understanding between the mother country and the dependency. Was Qing China colonizing its frontier territories the way the industrial nations later set up colonies in Africa and Asia?

---

7 David G. Atwill and Yurong Y. Atwell, eds., *Sources in Chinese History: Diverse Perspectives from 1644 to the Present* (Upper Saddle River, NJ: Prentice Hall, 2010), p. 5.

Before the Qing Dynasty, Taiwan had only the most meager of ties to China and its culture. Aboriginal Austronesian people inhabited the island until the arrival of the Dutch and the Spanish in the seventeenth century. As Ming Dynasty loyalist Zheng Chenggong (Koxinga) expelled the Dutch, perhaps 100,000 ethnic Chinese crossed the Taiwan Strait from the mainland to escape the Manchus, who ultimately captured Taiwan in 1683 and made it a prefecture of adjacent Fujian Province. Thereafter, population pressure on the mainland forced peoples to migrate to frontier locations with access to land. This is a classic cause for colonization, and by the time Taiwan became a province in 1887, due to fear of Japanese encroachment, more than 2 million ethnic Chinese populated the island. China's defeat in the First Sino-Japanese War (1894–1895) resulted in Taiwan becoming a Japanese colony until 1945, at which point it was returned to a China then in the midst of a civil war. It remains disputed territory, Taiwanese not wishing mainland Chinese rule, Beijing wanting it returned to mainland control.

On the southwestern frontier, the Kingdom of Nanzhao emerged in the eighth century, caught between the larger Tibetan and Chinese Empires. Working with and later against China, Nanzhao survived until the early tenth century, when it was replaced by the Kingdom of Dali, which the invading Mongols defeated. In 1274 the Dali realm and surrounding terrain became Yunnan Province under Mongol Yuan rule. Subsequent ethnic Chinese migration (military and civilian) there resulted in the predominantly Tai population selectively borrowing aspects of Chinese culture. By the Qing Dynasty, the local elites still exercised some freedom of action within the Chinese bureaucratic setup. In the early twenty-first century, Yunnan's population is roughly 60% ethnic Chinese. In neighboring Guizhou, which became a province in 1413, the Ming Dynasty and later the Qing persistently faced rebellions by minority peoples, chief among them the Nasu Yi, requiring the dispatch of several hundred thousand troops to pacify and occupy the territory. Guizhou being one of the three feudatories of the early Qing to revolt, the Kangxi Emperor employed force to defeat rebel Wu Sangui, established a preponderance of power there, and accelerated the ethnic Chinese migration into the sparsely populated territory.

Tibet was an empire that competed with Tang Dynasty China (from the seventh to tenth centuries), but the Mongol ascendency found both countries swallowed up by a more aggressive imperial power. When Beijing became the headquarters of the Mongol Empire under Kublai Khan, China inherited (according to the Chinese) authority over Tibet (Tibetans, of course, disagree). The defeat of the Mongol Yuan Dynasty at the hands of the new Ming Dynasty did not change Tibet's status as a part of China, a situation that continued with the overthrow of the Ming by the Manchu Qing. The Manchus oversaw relations with frontier peoples—such as the Mongols, Russians, and Tibetans—through an agency of their creation, the Lifan Yuan, a sort of foreign office that dealt with dependencies or vassal states. The Kangxi, Yongzheng, and Qianlong emperors all intervened in an ongoing Tibetan civil war that had drawn in the Mongols. Two imperial officials (*amban/zhuzha dachen*) and a military occupying force remained in Tibet thereafter to oversee Tibetan government operations, now symbolically and to some extent practically run by the Dalai Lama. This remained the case throughout the Qing period and the Republican era (1912–1949). Tighter Communist rule since 1949 has produced resistance in Tibet even as greater ethnic Chinese migration (military and civilian) there has begun to affect the local culture, especially in Lhasa, the capital.

China's Xinjiang Province has gone by many names, the most common of which are Chinese Turkestan, East Turkestan (as opposed to West Turkestan, the parts of Central Asia controlled by Russia in the nineteenth century), and Uyghurstan. From Beijing's point of view, Xinjiang has been inhabited by a number of peoples—Sai (Sak), Rouzhi (Yueh Zhi), Wusun (Usun), Qiang, Xiongnu (Huns), and Han Chinese—since the early Han Dynasty. As China's Information Office of the State Council put it in 2003:

In 101 B.C., the Han Empire began to station garrison troops to open up wasteland for cultivation of farm crops in Luntai (Bugur), Quli and some other places. Later, it sent troops to all other parts of Xinjiang for the same purpose. All the garrison reclamation points became early settlements for the Han people after they entered Xinjiang. Since the Western Region Frontier Command was established in 60 B.C., the inflow of the Han people to Xinjiang, including officials, soldiers and merchants, has never stopped.[8]

While strictly speaking accurate, the fuller picture reveals that until the establishment of the People's Republic in 1949, the ethnic Han Chinese residents remained slight, while the Turkish Uighur inhabitants accounted for roughly 75% of the province's population. In the early twenty-first century, the Turkish-speaking Uighurs still represent the largest ethnic group (but not a majority of the province's population). This is a situation likely to end as nearly as many Han Chinese live there and continue to migrate there, although ongoing ethnic insurgencies make future political control of the region tentative.

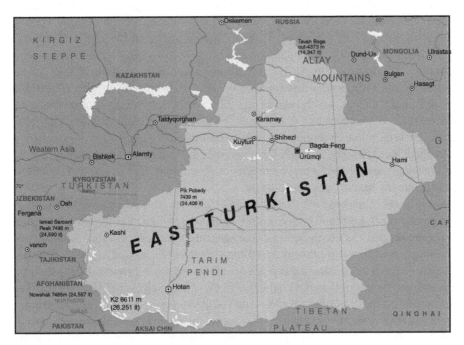

Current Uighur map of East Turkistan now controlled by China.

During the Qing period, as in earlier times, territories to the north and west of China required constant oversight, regular political and economic manipulation, and occasional military intervention to better sustain or advance China's interests. The Mongols presented an ongoing threat to China's Tibetan frontier, where Dzungars (Oirats, a western Mongol tribe) interfered in Tibetan affairs, and to China's northwestern frontier, where they also invaded and occupied parts of Xinjiang. The Kangxi Emperor launched a military expedition in 1696 to defeat the Dzungar leader,

---

8 People's Republic of China, Information Office of the State Council, "History and Development of Xinjiang," May 2003, http://news.xinhuanet.com/zhengfu/2003 - 06_916306.htm.

Galdan, but it would take additional Chinese campaigns launched by the Qianlong Emperor in the 1750s to put an end to Dzungar resistance.

Qianlong Emperor's Assessment of His Military Campaigns on China's Frontiers, 1792
The ten instances of military merit include the two pacifications of the Dzungars, the quelling of the Muslim tribes, the two annihilations of the Jinchuan [rebels], the restoring of peace to Taiwan, and the subjugation of Burma and Vietnam; adding the recent capitulations of the Gurkhas makes ten in all. Why is there any need to include those three trivial rebellions in the inner provinces?
From "The Record of the Ten Perfects," as quoted in Mark C. Elliott, *Emperor Qianlong: Son of Heaven, Man of the World* (Upper Saddle River, NJ: Longman, 2009), p. 89.

As the Dzungar problem ended in 1757, a religious upheaval between rival Muslim denominations broke out in Xinjiang, requiring further Qing military campaigns in the region. To further stabilize the region and to better assure the Manchu territorial claim, the Qianlong Emperor launched what amounted to a Han colonization program to settle sparsely populated terrain. The military conquests and colonization program enlarged the Qing Empire, but it was "not done in the name of the 'nation.' It was done to extol his [Qianlong's] fame, to demonstrate that the business of the Qing dynastic house and its servants was also Heaven's business."[9] By the end of the eighteenth century, the Qing government had both incorporated Xinjiang into the Chinese administrative system and checked Tsarist Russian expansion in the eastern parts of Central Asia.

Mongolia after the collapse of the Mongol Yuan Dynasty in China characteristically reverted to tribalism and pastoral nomadism, though occasionally tribal leaders emerged to unify a number of tribes. Aside from Timur, who provided the Indians, Persians, Ottoman Turks, and Russians constant challenges, the most troublesome Mongol rulers from a Chinese point of view were Dayan Khan, Altan Khan, and Galdan Khan. From roughly 1500 to 1700, these three as well as other khans alarmed Ming and Qing Dynasty officials with their constant interference in Tibetan affairs and their regular incursions into Chinese territory. Dayan Khan nearly overran Beijing in 1517; Altan Khan nearly succeeded taking Beijing in 1550; and Galdan Khan, after conquering much of Central Asia, turned east to resist Manchu expansion into Mongolia during the early Qing period, but ultimately fell to the Kangxi Emperor's forces in 1697. Galdan represented the last Mongol threat to China, which under the Manchus now finally controlled its northern frontier.

As the eighteenth century unfolded, China and Russia replaced the Mongols and Turks as the major powers in Central and Inner Asia. Into the twentieth century, Beijing and Moscow (to be joined by the British) struggled to maximize their Asian empires.

Siberia

Meaningful Russian contact with Asia dates back to the Mongol Golden Horde, which overran most of Russia and Eastern Europe in the mid-thirteenth century. Although officially in existence until 1783, the Golden Horde had become Islamic, suffered the effects of the Black Death in the

---

9 Elliott, *Emperor Qianlong*, p. 99.

fourteenth century, and eventually began fragmenting into smaller khanates in the fifteenth century. Russian territorial growth, which had chiefly occurred in Europe before the seventeenth century, began persistent expansion into Asia during the Romanov Dynasty (1613–1917). Russia utilized most of the same techniques the Chinese employed to colonize their frontiers. This involved the introduction of imperial cultural practices, expectations, and organizations while accepting many of the local cultural customs. Gradually this synthesis of cultures integrated the Siberian population into the Russian fold. Thus Cossacks and other Russians moved east—to serve the tsar by extending the empire and by collecting tribute from the local people; to obtain land and freedom; to promote commercial activities, especially the fur trade; or to suffer exile. The Russian population began the transmission of ideas and institutions even as, from the east, China was also transmitting its thinking and organizations northward and westward. The two empires increasingly demarcated where each of the cultures would operate through a series of treaties.

By the 1640s Russia reached the Amur River, which today divides Russia and China. Beijing considered a peaceful relationship with its new European neighbor crucial, as the Manchu Qing government under the Kangxi Emperor was just amalgamating its control of China and managing its several frontiers. Thus the Russians did not appear on the list of China's tribute-bearing nations, and diplomatically Beijing dealt with Moscow on the basis of equality. Moscow did not have sufficient military presence in Asia to do battle with the Chinese in the late seventeenth century and had a Siberian frontier that took precedence over challenging China in Mongolia or much of Central Asia.

Accordingly, the two empires negotiated the Treaty of Nerchinsk, signed in September 1689, which established the Sino-Russian border at the Argun and Amur Rivers. It also allowed for a freer Chinese trade relationship with Russia than the Chinese allowed with other foreign

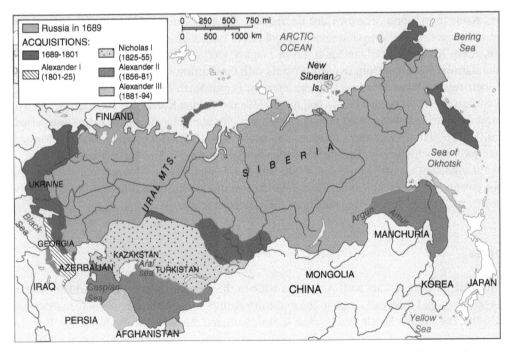

Map of Tsarist Russian Siberia. *Source:* Adapted from https://www.britannica.com/topic/history-of-Central-Asia/The-modern-period-the-age-of-decadence#ref59856.

countries. A generation later the Treaty of Kiakhta in 1727 set the border between Russia and Mongolia (now fully under Manchu control), extended trade between the two nations, and permitted the Russians to establish a religious mission in Beijing. Russia's Siberian colonization continued into the nineteenth century, and its relationship with China remained relatively harmonious (if guarded) until the industrial revolution began to upset established affiliations. The British defeated a weakened, declining Manchu Qing Dynasty in 1842, while Japan emerged as a major power as its successful modernization program after 1868 enabled Tokyo to confront Russian expansion in Siberia and Korea.

Suggested Readings and Viewings

Tonio Andrade, *How Taiwan Became Chinese: Dutch, Spanish, and Han Colonization in the Seventeenth Century* (New York: Columbia University Press, 2007).

Thomas Barfield, *The Perilous Frontier: Nomadic Empires and China* (Cambridge: Blackwell, 1989).

Ruth W. Dunnell, *Chinggis Khan: World Conqueror* (Upper Saddle River, NJ: Longman, 2010).

Mark C. Elliott, *The Manchu Way: The Eight Banners and Ethnic Identity in Late Imperial China* (Stanford, CA: Stanford University Press, 2001).

C. Patterson Giersch, *Asian Borderlands: The Transformation of Qing China's Yunnan Frontier* (Cambridge, MA: Harvard University Press, 2006).

John E. Herman, *Amid the Clouds and Mist: China's Colonization of Guizhou, 1200–1700* (Cambridge, MA: Harvard University Press, 2007).

Michael Khordarkovsky, *Russia's Steppe Frontier: The Making of a Colonial Empire, 1500–1800* (Bloomington: Indiana University Press, 2002).

Mongol (2007), dir. by. Sergey Bodrov.

Peter Perdue, *China Marches West: The Qing Conquest of Central Eurasia* (Cambridge, MA: Harvard University Press, 2005).

Morris Rossabi, *Kubilai Khan: His Life and Times*. (Berkeley: University of California Press, 1988).

S. Frederick Starr, *Lost Enlightenment: Central Asia's Golden Age from the Arab Conquest to Tamerlane* (Princeton, NJ: Princeton University Press, 2013).

13

On the Indian and Chinese Southern Frontiers: Asian Empires and Kingdoms in Southeast Asia, circa 1100–1850

There is no doubt that the culture of India had a profound effect on the cultures of Southeast Asia and that Indian ideals, art, and religion left an indelible mark on the region. However, the idea of a process of Indianization has begun to change. Scholars now place more emphasis on the role of native cultures in the rise of political complexity in Southeast Asia.[1]

At the beginning of the fourteenth century, Sanskrit culture was in full decline; the last Sanskrit inscriptions date from 1253 in Champa, from around 1330 in Cambodia, from 1378 in Sumatra. In Menam and Mekong basins, what remained of Hinduism and Mahayana Buddhism gave way to the orthodoxy of Singhalese Buddhism.. . . The Indian period in the history of Father India was beginning to close following the decrease in cultural exchanges with India proper that resulted from the Muslim invasions that took place there.[2]

Development of Kingdoms in Southeast Asia

While territorial lines of demarcation began to emerge in regions north of India and China, so too the southern frontiers of those two core Asian cultures began to show signs of consolidating into emerging nations. The more recent arrival of Islam also indicated the creation of new religious contours in a region largely dominated by Buddhist, Hindu, and local faiths. These patterns of national and cultural development occurred both before the arrival of the Europeans as well as under their colonial administrations, particularly on the mainland of Southeast Asia. Although the Europeans rapidly and significantly altered religious practices in parts of Southeast Asia, not until the nineteenth century did their arrival fundamentally challenge traditional ways of life there. As well, Chinese migration to Southeast Asia began to influence culture in that region. Nonetheless, Indian cultural patterns—Theravada Buddhism, Indian writing scripts, and Indian-style monarchies—had already undergone centuries of local adaptations across Southeast Asia. Islamic, Christian European, and ethnic Chinese thought and behavior would similarly experience transformations in the Southeast Asian environment.

In the future, local, Indian, Islamic, European, and Chinese cultures mixed to produce evolving Southeast Asian traditions.

---

1 Dougald J.W. O'Reilly, *Early Civilization of Southeast Asia* (Lanham, MD: AltaMira Press, 2007), p. 187.
2 G. Coedes, *The Indianized States of Southeast Asia*, ed. Walter F. Vella (Honolulu: University of Hawaii Press, 1968), p. 218.

Asia Past and Present: A Brief History, First Edition. Peter P. Wan and Thomas D. Reins.
© 2021 John Wiley & Sons, Inc. Published 2021 by John Wiley & Sons, Inc.

Emergence of Kingdoms and Arrival of Europeans in Southeast Asia	
1000 BCE–1 CE	Civilization surrounded by agricultural communities emerges on mainland and island Southeast Asia; bronze and iron appear
207 BCE	Chinese general takes control over today's northern Vietnam and establishes the State of Nam Viet
207 BCE–939 CE	China rules Nam Viet in northern Vietnam; Vietnamese embrace Chinese culture but rebel against Chinese rule
1st–6th centuries CE	Kingdom of Funan covers peninsular Malaysia, Thailand, Cambodia, and southern Vietnam and is socially a mixture of uncertain local Austronesian-speaking peoples who embrace a Hindu cultural framework
1st century BCE–9th century CE	State of Pyu occupies the central inland parts of today's Burma/Myanmar
2nd–18th centuries	Kingdom of Champa occupies central Vietnam and practices Hindu cultural conventions
7th–8th centuries	Kingdom of Chenla occupies parts of today's Laos, Thailand, Cambodia, and Vietnam and follows Hindu and local traditions
7th–13th centuries	The seafaring and commercial Srivijaya Empire embraces Mahayana Buddhism and operates from its capital on the Indonesian island of Sumatra
8th–10th centuries	Nanzhao Kingdom formed by Tai tribes centered in today's Yunnan Province in China and spread into mainland Southeast Asia
9th–15th centuries	Khmer Empire at one point encompasses most of mainland Southeast Asia; a successor state to Funan and Chenla, it embraces both Hindu and Buddhist cultural practices
9th–11th centuries	Ethnic Mons create the Mon (Hanthawaddy) Kingdom, occupy southern and eastern Burma, and adopt Theravada Buddhism
9th–14th centuries	Ethnic Burmans create Pagan monarchy in northern Burma, begin to unify Burma by the 11th century, and eventually become the largest and leading ethnic group
969–1850s	Vietnam becomes independent from China but politically fragmented as it moves into central and southern Vietnam
1287	Sukhothai, a part of the Pagan Empire, forms a Tai kingdom with the collapse of Pagan
13th–16th centuries	Majapahit Empire, headquartered on the island of Java, began as a Hindu kingdom that controlled at one time much of today's Indonesia as well as parts of Malaysia and the Philippines; Indian merchants brought Islam to Indonesia as the Delhi Sultanate took power in India
14th–18th centuries	Ayutthaya embraces the commingling of Hindu and Buddhist traditions as in neighboring Khmer Empire, both religions enhancing power of the monarch
16th century	Europeans begin to arrive in Southeast Asia
1521–1898	Spaniard Ferdinand Magellan lands in the Philippines, is killed by the locals, but begins the process of Spanish colonization
1782	Beginning of the current Chakri Dynasty in Thailand centered in Bangkok
1824–1826	First Anglo-Burmese War results in Britain obtaining the first of many parts of Burma

Cambodia/Kampuchea

Cambodia's origins can be traced at least back to the State of Funan, which controlled much of mainland Southeast Asia from the first to sixth centuries CE. Although there are doubts as to whether the Funanese were people of Khmer ethnicity, there is little doubt that the Khmers who succeeded Funan authorities drew much of their culture from their political predecessor.

Information about Funan comes mainly from Chinese, Cham (pre-Vietnamese in Vietnam), and archaeological records. The name Funan itself comes from Chinese records. The two best examples are *Funan Zhuan* (*Chronicle of Funan*), written by emissaries from the State of Wu (Kang Tai and Zhu Ying) during the Three Kingdoms period (220–280 CE), and *Nanzhou Yiwu Zhi* (*Rarities in the Southern Territories*), written by Wan Zhen, also from the State of Wu. During the third century Funan's greatest monarch, Fan Shiman, ruled over a culture that combined Indian and local practices. Sanskrit was the language of court, and the people practiced chiefly Hinduism, Buddhism (Mahayana Buddhism to the thirteenth century, and Theravada thereafter), and local religions. Funan was largely an agricultural society whose capital was located in the Mekong Delta in today's southern Vietnam. But archaeological evidence also indicates that Funan engaged in a great deal of long-distance trade, mainly with China and India, and artifacts from as far away as Rome have been unearthed.

The State of Chenla, likely a vassal state of Funan, gradually absorbed its overlord and governed roughly the same mainland Southeast Asian territory from 550 to 802. Shortly thereafter, the state divided into Northern/Upper (Chenla of the Land) and Southern/Lower (Chenla of the Seas). During the split, Javanese Indonesian rivals for commercial supremacy in the region defeated Southern Chenla in the 790s, producing a Khmer unity under Jayavarman II. He expelled the Indonesians and also decided to move the capital from the Mekong Delta to western Cambodia. Khmer monarchs used the god-king (*Devaraja*) cult from India to bolster their legitimacy, as best illustrated in Jayavarman II's creation of a temple structure at the top of his capital, Mount Mahendra; a later and larger version of this structure was constructed at Angkor Wat in the twelfth century. Thus began the Khmer/Angkor Empire (802–1431).

For more than six centuries, the centralized monarchy of the Khmer Empire probably governed much as pre-Islamic monarchs in various parts of India. Although royal authority predominated around the capital, the outlying provinces likely were vassal states with unstable connections to central power. A road system linked the various parts of the realm to Angkor. By the twelfth century, the empire acquired territories in Myanmar/Burma and Champa in central Vietnam. Economically, the empire depended upon agriculture, which in turn depended upon an extensive and well-maintained irrigation system that drew water from Tonle Sap Lake, which in turn required dams and dikes to prevent flooding. Religiously, Hinduism and Buddhism in conjunction with local spiritual practices provided cohesive glue holding together disparate interests and peoples throughout the empire. Angkor Wat (at first a Hindu temple, then a Buddhist one), built by Suryavarman II (r. 1113–1150), illustrates the connection between royal authority and religion as well as the Indian influence.

> Angkor reflected the world structure according to the Hindu cosmology. The capital was surrounded by a wall and a moat, just as the universe was believed to be encircled by rock and ocean. Exactly at the middle point of the capital city stood the pyramidal temple, representing the sacred mountain [Mount Meru], with the *linga* [phallic symbol] at the center.

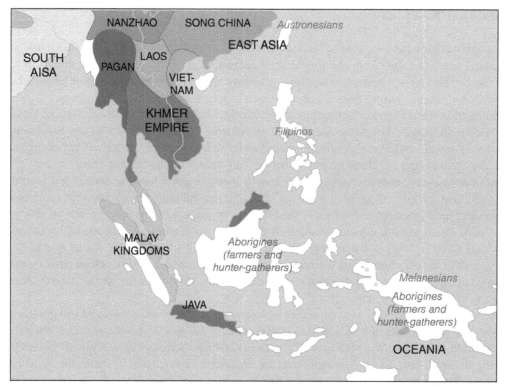

Principal kingdoms of Southeast Asia, circa 1215. *Source:* From https://www.timemaps.com/history/south-east-asia-1215ad/. Reproduced with permisison of TimeMaps Ltd.

The edifice was a symbol of the union between king and God, establishing harmony between the microcosms' of the human world and the macrocosmos of the divine world.[3]

The decline of Khmer power began with the reign of Jayavarman II (1181–1219) owing to excessive building projects, chiefly roads and religious shrines, the latter housing some 300,000 priests. Unsuccessful wars with Champa and the expanding Thais also proved costly, while the emergence of an egalitarian Theravada Buddhism eroded the support for divine right kingship. The Thai capture of Angkor in 1431 officially ended the empire. Three years later the Khmer government set up headquarters at its new capital, Phnom Penh. Recent research indicates that Angkor's collapse had environmental causes as well. Lengthy periods of drought followed by monsoon rains resulted in flooding. Extreme amounts of water in turn dumped mud into the canals, which clogged the irrigation system that sustained agriculture. Although reviving the old Angkor capital remained a Khmer goal, and while its fame attracted the Japanese who created settlements there in the seventeenth century, Angkor was abandoned sometime in that century and was not "rediscovered" until 1861 by Henri Mouhot. Only two years later, Cambodia came under French colonial rule.

---

3 D.R. SarDesai, *Southeast Asia: Past and Present*, 5th ed. (Boulder, CO: Westview Press, 2003), p. 29.

Siam/Thailand

The rise of the Thais/Tais begins with the Tai states of Nanzhao and Dali in contemporary China's Yunnan Province, but Tai-speaking people also inhabited much of mainland Southeast Asia. The Mongol defeat of Dali in 1253 accelerated an ongoing Tai migration south, a move made easier due to the Mongol defeat of the Pagan Kingdom (in Burma/Myanmar) in 1287 and the declining power of the Khmer Empire. This set the stage for the creation of the Ayutthaya Kingdom (1351–1767), whose capital city was named after Ayodhya, Rama's capital city as described in the Indian epic and religious guide *Ramayana*. Nation building under the direction of a number of highly competent monarchs laid the foundation for modern Thailand. "Some of their accomplishments, notably in language, script, and religion, have remained an integral part of Thai culture to this date, while their impact on administration and law persisted almost to the end of the nineteenth century, giving Thailand a more stable base than any other state in Southeast Asia."[4] This firm governmental foundation likely protected Thailand from colonization by a European power and gave the Thais more control in picking and choosing foreign ideas and institutions.

Burma/Myanmar

As in Cambodia and Thailand, the cultural influence of India in Myanmar can be observed in religion (Hinduism and especially Buddhism), political ideas and institutions (legally, the *Code of Manu*; politically, the concept of monarchy), and culture (Sanskrit in general, the classics *Ramayana* and *Mahabharata*, and festivals). As well, Myanmar's history revolved around the entry of successive waves of ethnic groups, which added to the country's cultural heritage. Of the more than 100 officially recognized ethnicities today, three provide the underpinnings for modern Myanmar: the Mons, the Pyus, and the Burmans/Bamars—the latter representing more than two-thirds of the current population. The Mons likely arrived from China via Thailand sometime after 1500 BCE and soon absorbed many Indian cultural practices, particularly Theravada Buddhism, which along with other Indian cultural ways they transmitted to subsequent ethnic arrivals.

Despite the early Mon presence in Myanmar, there is little evidence for a Mon kingdom before the ninth century CE. Several Mon kingdoms existed across Myanmar down to the eighteenth century, simultaneous with other ethnic kingdoms throughout the country. The Pyu people, who likely came from southwest China, established the first royal dynasty, occupying central and northern Myanmar and lasting from about 100 CE to 840, when they were overthrown by the Mons. Shortly thereafter began the rise of Pagan/Bagan, headed by Burmans who came from northwest China, probably Gansu Province. The Pagan Kingdom (849–1287) defeated rival monarchies under King Anawartha/Aniruddha (r. 1044–1077), but in vanquishing the Mons they absorbed many Mon ways, such as embracing Theravada Buddhism and allowing the Pagan court to be dominated by Mon scholars. Pagan collapsed as the Mongols from the outside and the Shan minority from northeast Myanmar strangled the dynasty. Thereafter, several kingdoms—especially the Ava, the Shan, the Rakhine (Arakanese), and the Taungoo—governed a divided Myanmar as the Europeans arrived in Asia, and by the mid-nineteenth century Great Britain, after a series of Anglo-Burmese Wars, colonized the country.

---

4 SarDesai, *Southeast Asia*, p. 53.

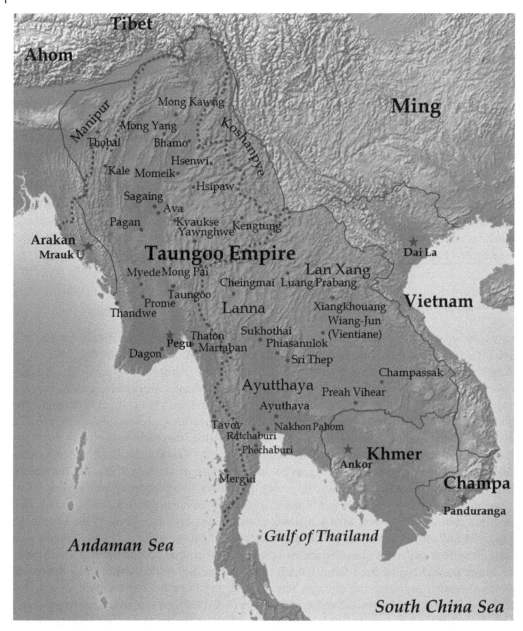

Taungoo Empire, 1531–1752. *Source:* Illustration by Soewinhan, https://commons.wikimedia.org/wiki/File:Map_of_Taungoo_Empire_(1580).png.

Indonesia

Indonesia, formerly known as the Spice Islands, the Moluccas, the East Indies, or the Dutch East Indies, is the largest Muslim country in the world. Like most of the rest of Southeast Asia, it derived many of its cultural fundamentals from India, including Islam, which was embraced only after India under Muslim rule transmitted it. Given its geographical setting, Indonesia served as a vital link in the trade between East Asia, East Africa, the Middle East, and often eventually Europe; it also became a major transit site for goods on the way to China from India, to India from China, and between various Southeast Asian destinations. Before the arrival of the Europeans, the Indonesian cultural and often political influence extended to today's Malaysia, Brunei, and much of the southern Philippines. The modern Indonesians likely are primarily the descendants of the aboriginal people in the archipelago, who either migrated there out of Africa or perhaps evolved there independent of African migrants.

Before the embrace of Islam in the thirteenth century, Indonesia reflected the mixture of local and Indian culture, politically in the concept of monarchy and religiously in Hinduism (without the caste system) and Buddhism. The Srivijaya Kingdom founded in the seventh century represents the earliest centralized government to emerge, headquartered in eastern Sumatra and controlling Sumatra, western Java, and more than half of the Malay Peninsula. Its power came substantially from the wealth generated by trade, but it also became a cultural hub attracting Buddhist monks and scholars from across Asia. The Chinese monk Yi Jing (Zhang Wenming) traveled there in the late seventh century on his way to Nalanda (in India), like Srivijaya a Buddhist cultural hub.

Several other kingdoms also appeared, notably the Mataram Kingdom (eighth to eleventh centuries) in central and east Java, which was absorbed by the Sailendra Kingdom (eighth to tenth

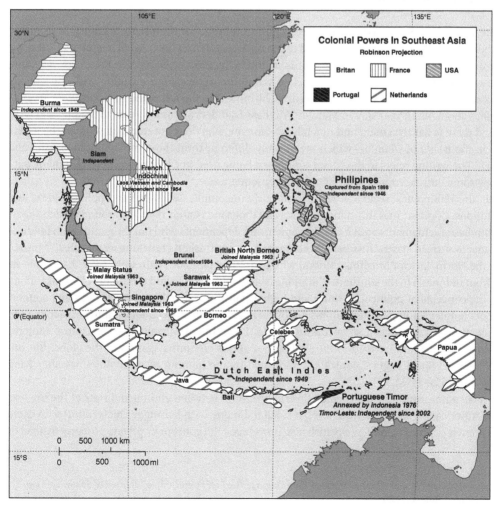

Southeast Asia, 1500–1800.

centuries), also headquartered in central Java but controlling far-flung maritime ports; the Sunda Kingdom (seventh to sixteenth centuries) in west and central Java; the Kediri Kingdom (eleventh to thirteenth centuries) in east Java; and the Singhasari Kingdom (thirteenth century) in central and east Java. Clearly there existed a great deal of overlap, in both time and territory, among these "kingdoms," and many of them failed to expand beyond Java or even control the entire island.

By contrast, the Majapahit Kingdom (1293–1527) extended beyond Indonesia to include the Malay Peninsula, southern Thailand, and parts of the Philippines. Much of its strength derived from commercial activities, and its longevity was due to a succession of capable monarchs, especially during the fourteenth century. This last major Hindu kingdom in Southeast Asia fell to the sultan of Demak (Raden Pateh, related to Majapahit royalty) in 1527, and thereafter Indonesia remained fragmented politically until the sixteenth century. By then the Dutch East India Company began an informal colonial system, and after 1800 the Dutch government formalized its control over the Netherlands East Indies. Indonesia remained a Dutch colony until independence in December 1949.

Philippines and Guam

Whereas the rest of Southeast Asia obtained significant influence from India or China (or from one another), the Philippine Islands remained relatively isolated from their Asian neighbors. Although their more distant location from the mainland and being positioned outside the major maritime trade routes minimized contact, nonetheless some important communication with the outside world took place. In 1604 Jesuit priest Pedro Chirino wrote the following in *Relacion de las Islas Filipinas* about his 12-year stay in Manila: "All these islanders are much given to reading and writing and there is hardly a man, and much less a woman, who does not read and write in the letters used in the island of Manila—which are entirely different from those of China, Japon [sic] and India."[5] The writing refers to the Cham script then being used in Champa in central Vietnam, suggesting some outside contact with important consequences.

Still, the Philippines' seclusion resulted in fairly uncomplicated social and political ideas and institutions. Communities throughout the several thousand islands revolved around the *barangay*, kinship-based settlements with a chief, freemen, and dependents who ran the gamut from landless peasants to serfs to slaves. Just before the Spanish arrived, Islam (Muslims were called "Moros," after the North African Muslims [Moors] who controlled parts of Spain until 1492) had made its way from Indonesia to the southern Philippine island of Mindanao and eventually elsewhere along with the concepts of political territory and higher political leadership, such as rajas and sultans. Lack of complex Philippine institutions doubtless made the Spanish conquest much easier and the introduction of Catholicism so successful. In 1521 Ferdinand Magellan, a Portuguese explorer operating out of Spain, arrived in the Philippines on his circumnavigation of the globe. But not until 1565 did Spain begin colonization, indicated by the naming of the Philippines after King Philip II (r. 1556–1598).

Spanish administration consisted of close cooperation between church and state at the top—as in the Americas—and, at the local level, it ruled indirectly with *barangay* chiefs (*datu*) who came to be known as *principales*. The Spanish also introduced the concept of private property instead of

---

5 As quoted in Geoff Wade, "On the Possible Cham Origin of the Philippine Scripts," *Journal of Southeast Asian Studies* 24, no. 1 (March 1993): 44.

the traditional communal property. International trade expanded as the Manila galleons brought gold and silver from Acapulco to be used for the purchase of Chinese goods. Increased trade opportunities brought Chinese migrants to Manila, and soon they became more numerous than the Spaniards. Society became more complex, with most roles clearly defined. The Spaniards ran the government and the church, the *principales* became the rural elite, the peasants did the farming, and the Chinese emerged as the urban middle-class entrepreneurs. Anti-Chinese campaigns alarmed the Chinese, who nonetheless have remained a crucial part of the Philippine economy down to the present.

Spain's reputation in the Philippines suffered during the Seven Years' War (1754–1763), in which it allied with the French against the British, who attacked and captured the capital, Manila. Meanwhile, as the Chinese supported the British, the Moros took advantage of Spain's problems to rebel, as did several Filipino opponents of Spanish rule, particularly Diego Silang. The Treaty of Paris (1763), which ended the Seven Years' War, returned captured Philippine territory to Spain, which then began a program of economic development focusing on export crops including tobacco, indigo, tea, silk, opium, and hemp. But the gold and silver supplies from the new world that sustained the Spanish Empire began to dry up even as independence movements in its colonies got underway. By the early nineteenth century, Spain could not keep its global empire intact, and it was only a matter of time before Filipino independence activities, in conjunction with the Spanish-American War (1898), would end Spain's control of the Philippines.

Magellan also visited Guam in the Mariana island chain in 1521, and for the next 150 years the native Chamorros experienced a mixture of harsh Spanish military rule and conciliatory Catholic Church activities. Guam became a port stop for the Manila galleons en route from Mexico to the Philippines, and the Spanish military wanted to prevent the local people from interfering with maritime commerce. The church not only instructed the Chamorros in Christianity but also taught them agricultural techniques, particularly the sowing of corn. The ongoing conflicts between Chamorros and Spaniards reduced the native population, which today is a hybrid of locals and foreign stock, largely Spaniards and Filipinos. Guam remained a Spanish territory until 1898, when it was transferred to the United States as a result of the Spanish-American War.

Vietnam

The modern nation of Vietnam can trace its beginnings to several early cultural traditions. The original migrants, likely from Indonesia, arrived in Paleolithic times and occupied territory along the Red River in northern Vietnam, and by Neolithic times numerous migratory groups had passed through or settled in Vietnam. Dong Son Bronze Age culture (800–300 BCE) developed in this area. These groups—with Tibetan, Mon, Tai, and Khmer backgrounds—constitute a small segment of the current Vietnamese inhabitants, and they most likely became highlanders who were gradually pushed out of the Red River valley by the arriving Yue/Yueh or Viet from southeastern China. These new China arrivals were lowlanders who became historically at odds with mountain peoples. These Yue/Viet escapees from turmoil in central and southern China began moving into northern Vietnam in the fourth century BCE. They make up the larger part (roughly 85%) of the contemporary Vietnamese population and were those most responsible for the adoption of Chinese cultural practices. The Chams represent the third important group. They were probably the people of Sa Huynh culture and later a culture in a state the Chinese called Lin Yi. The Chams created the State of Champa in 192 CE in what is now central Vietnam. Cambodia (the states of Funan, then Chenla, and later Angkor/Khmer) controlled the southern part of contemporary Vietnam.

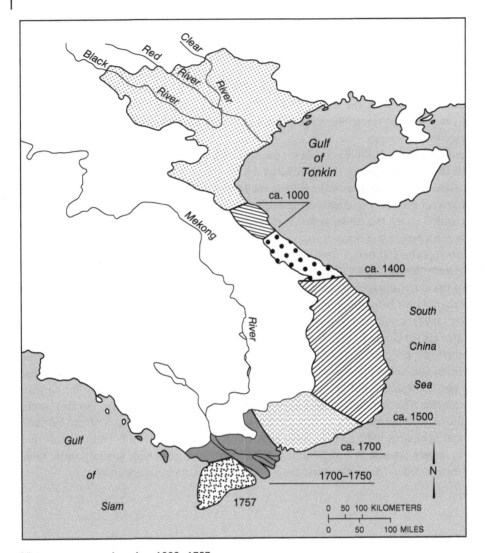

Vietnamese expansion, circa 1000–1757.

Until the tenth century CE, today's Vietnam served as a cultural and military battleground. The principal contestants in this struggle were the tribal highlanders, the Yue/Viet people, the Chams, the Khmers from Cambodia, and the Chinese. The Hung Dynasty controlled the original Vietnamese state, which legend holds extended back to 2879 BCE. Its last king was deposed in 258 BCE, replaced by King An Duong and the brief Au Lac Dynasty (257–207 BCE), which likely represents the first ethnic Vietnamese/Yue/Viet-dominated government. Au Lac authority fell to the invading Chinese under General Zhao Tuo (Trieu Da in Vietnamese; thus, Trieu Dynasty) under the new Qin Dynasty (221–208 BCE) in China, now unified under Qin Shi Huangdi. But Zhao resisted Qin rule and set up his own state of Nam Viet (southern Viet/Yue), even as the Qin Dynasty fell to the Han Dynasty (208 BCE–220 CE). Chinese Emperor Han Wudi crushed Nam Viet and annexed what is now the northern part of Vietnam into the Chinese imperial system in 111 BCE.

Though the Vietnamese embraced much of Chinese culture, including the concepts of monarchy, Confucianism, and the civil service exam system, as well as a great deal of popular culture such as Chinese New Year (Tet), they resisted Chinese political control. This was manifested in numerous rebellions over the centuries, the most celebrated of which remains the uprising of the Trung sisters in 39–43 CE. As the Chinese Tang Dynasty collapsed in the early tenth century, along with a millennium of developing a Vietnamese culture distinct from China, the Vietnamese proved ready to throw off the foreign yoke. This officially occurred in 939, demonstrated by the revival of the Nam Viet name. As one historian explains the impact of a millennium of Chinese rule:

> the more they [Vietnamese] absorbed of the skills, customs, ideas of the Chinese, the smaller grew the likelihood of their ever becoming part of the Chinese people. In fact, it was during the centuries of intensive efforts to turn them into Chinese that the Vietnamese came into their own as a separate people, with political and cultural aspects of their own.[6]

While the Vietnamese resisted China, they also attempted to push south into Champa, which itself pushed south into Mekong Delta territory then under various Cambodian regimes. By the fourth century, Champa had absorbed a great deal of Indian culture. This is best illustrated in the name of its capital city (near today's Danang), Indrapura or City of Indra. Hinduism and Buddhism also dominated the religious life of Champa, indicated by their numerous temples throughout the realm. Champa also had maritime contact with India and picked up additional Indian culture as it pressed on Funan, an Indianized Cambodian state. But eventually Champa's conflicts with its neighbors took a heavy toll, particularly after the eleventh century. The State of Champa came to an end in 1471 with a decisive military defeat by Vietnam, now called Dai Viet ("Great Viet"). But it was only the final reversal after centuries of invasions by the Vietnamese, the Khmers, the Han Chinese, and later the Chinese under Mongol rule. By that time the Chams had converted to Islam, and most of the survivors migrated to a much smaller Cambodia, as the Mekong Delta fell to the Vietnamese and the Angkor/Khmer Empire was defeated by the Thais. Only 40,000 Chams remain in Vietnam today.

The fall of the Chinese Tang Dynasty in 906 and the subsequent half-century of political disorder gave the Vietnamese another opportunity to break China's hold on the country, which they did in 939. Dai Viet (1010–1527) emerged after the short-lived Ngo and Dinh Dynasties began the task of building an independent Vietnam. Both the Ly Dynasty (1010–1225) and the Tran Dynasty (1225–1400) produced strong and able rulers who adopted a Chinese-style imperial administration, staffed by scholars who passed civil service examinations based on Confucian classics and commentaries on the classics. The Vietnamese elite became imbued with (or at least thoroughly familiar with) Confucian principles. But domestic political troubles brought foreign difficulties. In 1407, the Chinese Ming Dynasty under the Yongle Emperor invaded Vietnam, then in the midst of a civil conflict over dynastic succession. The incursion produced Vietnamese resistance, led chiefly by Le Loi whose Lam Son rebellion defeated a massive Chinese army, which lost several hundred thousand soldiers in the conflict.

Down to 1885, Vietnam remained wary of the Chinese but nonetheless acknowledged a tributary relationship with Beijing, in part from a practical need to keep the Chinese happy and in part from the belief that being a tributary state would bring Vietnam protection from other potential adversaries, particularly the Thais.

---

6 Joseph Buttinger, *Vietnam: A Political History* (New York: Praeger, 1968), as quoted in D.R. SarDesai, *Vietnam: Past and Present*, 4th ed. (Boulder, CO: Westview Press, 2005), p. 17.

Le Loi on Sino-Vietnamese Relations

Our great country is a country where prosperity
Abounds. Where civilization reigns supreme.
Its mountains, its rivers, its frontiers are its own;
Its customs are distinct, in North and South
Trieu, Dinh, Ly and Tran
Created our Nation
Whilst Han, Tang, Song and Yuan
Ruled over Theirs.
Over the Centuries,
We have been sometimes strong, and sometimes weak,
But never yet have we been lacking in heroes
Of that let our history be the proof.

As quoted in SarDesai, *Vietnam*, p. 25.

With the Chinese driven out, the following year Le Loi established the Later Le Dynasty, which on paper lasted from 1428 to 1788. In fact a number of competing dynasties emerged over the next three centuries, reflecting the disunited state of Vietnamese politics that continued well into the twentieth century. As Vietnam spread south, it expanded faster than any central government proved capable of efficiently administering. Essentially the Le Dynasty served to provide legitimacy to two families: the Trinhs, who came to power in Tongking in northern Vietnam, and the Nguyen family, who governed for the Le Dynasty in the south. An ongoing battle between the two families was ended in 1673 when both agreed to the Chinese-sponsored cease-fire, which divided the country in half at roughly the 17th parallel (the dividing line also set by the Geneva Conference in 1954). A century later, both the Trinh and Nguyen regimes were deposed, the result of the Tayson Rebellion (1778–1802). Three brothers from the village of Tayson instigated rebellion and adopted the Nguyen surname, suggesting they had connection to the Nguyen family ruling in the south, and attempted to seize power. They failed, and the Mandate of Heaven passed to a legitimate heir of the genuine Nguyen family, thus creating Vietnam's last dynasty, the Nguyen (1802–1945).

By then, the French had been in Vietnam for two centuries. French missionaries had succeeded in converting nearly one million Vietnamese to Catholicism by the mid-seventeenth century and had convinced the Vietnamese elite to Romanize the language in order to facilitate the spread of literacy. As the new Nguyen Dynasty consolidated its position, it began an anti-Christian movement under Emperor Minh Mang (r. 1820–1841) and his successors. China's disastrous encounter with the British in the Opium War (1839–1842) gave the Vietnamese good reason to worry about French political intentions. Christianity also concerned Vietnam's leaders. The religion had inspired a Chinese civil service candidate—convinced that he was the brother of Jesus Christ—to launch the Taiping Rebellion (1850–1864), which resulted in the deaths of perhaps 40 million people. Could such religious turmoil make its way to Vietnam? Growing Vietnamese resistance to the French presence and to Napoleon III's mounting desire to create an empire generated ongoing friction between the two nations. But French colonization was well underway and would succeed in the short term until World War II. The industrial revolution made possible a new kind of imperialism.

Suggested Readings and Videos

Michael D. Coe, *Angkor and the Khmer Civilization* (New York: Thames and Hudson, 2003).

G. Coedes, *The Making of Southeast Asia*, trans. H. M. Wright (Berkeley: University of California Press, 1969).

C. Patterson Giersch, *Asian Borderlands: The Transformation of Qing China's Yunnan Frontier* (Cambridge, MA: Harvard University Press, 2006).

D.G.E. Hall, *Atlas of South-East Asia* (New York: St. Martin's Press, 1964).

D.G.E. Hall, *A History of South-East Asia*, 4th ed. (London: Macmillan, 1981).

Kenneth R. Hall, *A History of Early Southeast Asia: Maritime Trade and Societal Development, 100–1500* (Lanham, MD: Rowman and Littlefield, 2011).

Jewels in the Jungle: Angkor Wat (London: BBC, 2013).

Victor B. Lieberman, *Strange Parallels: Southeast Asia in Global Context, c. 800–1830*, 2 vols. (Cambridge: Cambridge University Press, 2003, 2009).

Dougald J.W. O'Reilly, *Early Civilizations of Southeast Asia* (Lanham, MD: AltaMira Press, 2007).

Lynda N. Shaffer, *Maritime Southeast Asia* (Armonk, NY: M. E. Sharpe, 1996).

Laichen Sun and Geoff Wade, eds., *Southeast Asia in the 15th Century: The Ming Factor* (Singapore: Singapore University Press, 2009).

Nicholas Tarling, ed., *From Early Times to c. 1500, vol. 1, part 1 of The Cambridge History of Southeast Asia* (Cambridge: Cambridge University Press, c. 1992, 1999).

Wang Gungwu, *The Chinese Overseas: From Earthbound China to the Quest for Autonomy* (Cambridge, MA: Harvard University Press, 2000).

14

European Empires in Asia: The Foundations for Revolutionary Transformation, circa 1500–1850

I was to be always at the [Kangxi] Emperor's side, so that I might make in his presence the necessary observations for determining the state of the heavens.

—Ferdinand Verbiest

Introduction

Although Europeans had made their way to Asia since imperial Roman times, their numbers were few and their impact was marginal until Marco Polo's travels there in the late thirteenth century. Even then, Europe remained poor and underdeveloped with little to offer the major civilizations of Asia, while people poor and rich in the Mediterranean and Atlantic world dreamed of or consumed the products of the East. Marco Polo's descriptions of his Asian journeys only heightened Europe's awareness and curiosity about that East. That region of the world made significant contributions to the "ascent of man." India provided the concept of zero, Arabic numbers, the ruler, the weighing scale, and the domestication of cotton. China contributed silk, tea, porcelain, paper, printing, gunpowder, the compass, and many lesser items in common use today. Southeast Asian spices helped to preserve food and to "spice up" the flavor of many otherwise bland foods.

> **Marco Polo (1254–1324)** is widely known as an Italian merchant and traveler from Venice. He allegedly spent 17 years in China, and *The Travels of Marco Polo* is allegedly based on his oral account of his adventures. The book claims that he went to the Mongol Yuan Dynasty's capital of Dadu by way of the Silk Road in 1271, paid homage to the emperor, and was appointed the magistrate of Yangzhou, a bustling commercial hub at the confluence of the Yangze River and the Grand Canal. He gives vivid descriptions of Chinese cities, ways of life, and unique practices. The book played a major role in exciting the imagination of early modern Europeans about China. Debates about the authenticity of the book have never stopped.

As late as the eighteenth-century Enlightenment in the West, Asia continued to stimulate European thinkers. Much of this stimulation came from Jesuits who had resided in and then commented on the ways of the East, and from merchants and sailors who also brought back impressions of their travels to various parts of Asia. Enlightenment philosophers like Voltaire, Montesquieu, Benjamin Franklin, Thomas Jefferson, and others associated Confucian Chinese scholar-officials with enlightened governing. The Chinese civil service, composed of such

Asia Past and Present: A Brief History, First Edition. Peter P. Wan and Thomas D. Reins.
© 2021 John Wiley & Sons, Inc. Published 2021 by John Wiley & Sons, Inc.

enlightened scholar-officials, later became a model for civil service reform in England and America. Akbar, a pious Muslim emperor of the Mughal Dynasty, ruled during the time of Elizabeth I in England. He also became a model for enlightened rule among Western intellectuals. Part of Akbar's popularity had to do with his attempt to bring about religious toleration in a Hindu India under the rule of a Muslim dynasty. In short, until the end of the eighteenth century, the cultural and commercial exchanges between Europe and Asia were decidedly one-sided. Sometime before 1800, however, these exchanges began to shift: Asia started accepting more from the West, as Western thinking about Asia now began to portray the onetime cultural font of wisdom as benighted and backward.

The Revolutionary West in Asia

When Vasco da Gama sailed around the Cape of Good Hope and entered the Indian Ocean in 1498, his voyage began a process of change that deeply affected both Europe and Asia as well as the rest of the world. Nation-states in Western Europe typically began to expand and develop via the sea, whereas the empires of Eastern Europe favored expansion by land. Nation-states typically focused on commerce as the principal source of non-agricultural economic growth, whereas the empires viewed land as the economic base. Coming out of the "Dark Ages," Europe was still searching for an acceptable mode of life to replace the Roman imperial ways and the savagery of the barbarian invasions that followed Rome's collapse and plagued the continent for at least half a millennium (roughly 500–1000 CE). Would the "Holy Roman Empire," created in 800 CE to replace the now-defunct original Roman Empire, emerge as the model of development for Europe once the barbarian invasions subsided around 1000 CE? Or would nation-states and city-states perform that function?

We can now look back with perfect hindsight and see that the Holy Roman Empire had little chance of succeeding. But when we realize that the Holy Roman Empire did not go out of existence until Napoleon ended it in 1806, and that the nations of Germany and Italy did not emerge until 1870–1871, it is perhaps best to see the empire versus nation-state struggle as very real and the outcome of this struggle quite uncertain. What likely tipped the balance toward nation-state supremacy were the consequences of capture of Constantinople in 1453 and its continued march into Europe. The loss of Constantinople to Christianity also meant the loss of Asian trade. Historically Asian goods made their way over the land Silk Road or the maritime Silk Road, eventually arriving at Constantinople. There, the Italians would pick up the goods and transport them to northern Europe.

To reconnect with the Asian sources of goods and perhaps to ally with Asians against the expanding Turks, European nation-states launched overseas expeditions to find another route to Asia. Remember, the Chinese Admiral Zheng He was at first encouraged and ultimately discouraged by China from engaging in maritime activities in the early fifteenth century. In contrast, although the Italian Christopher Columbus could not get sufficient economic support at home, he still had other options in late fifteenth-century Europe. He eventually made use of the available options and went to Spain. No overarching European imperial bureaucracy stood in his way.

Since the nation-states (particularly Portugal, Spain, Holland, France, and England) came to dominate the European trade with Asia, it would be the ideas and institutions of these nations that most affected not only Asia but the entire world. Europe plugged into the Asian trade directly and tied the Americas, Asia, the Middle East, coastal Africa, and themselves into an early global commercial network. This set of connections exchanged tangible commercial merchandise, to be sure, but it also transmitted ideas. Along with ships, crews, and businessmen eventually came missionaries, educators, and soldiers. The items of trade that traditionally made their way to Europe from Asia—silk, tea, spices, and porcelain—now continued but in much increased quantity and at a much lower cost. The Americas also added enormous amounts of bullion—gold and silver—to the global commercial exchange, making it possible for bullion-poor Europe to purchase more goods from Asia. Since Asians bought little from the Europeans, the West would have, without the added bullion, been involved in a much less robust commercial exchange. New American crops—especially peanuts, corn, and potatoes—produced increased nutritional and demographic results in the "old world." In the realm of thought, the revolutionary ideas percolating in the nation-states gradually ended up in Asia and steadily gained adherents there.

New thinking about the legitimacy of commerce and economic growth, about farming and manufacturing methods, about the role of religion and church–state relations, about understanding the natural world, about the nature of government and the common person—all of these topics and more led to the transformation of Europe, making it the cutting edge of change after 1500. Eventually serious discussion of these same topics by Asia's elite slowly began to erode major aspects of traditional Asian civilizations. Europe's overwhelming wealth and power after 1700, generated by the industrial revolution—which initially made imperialism so successful—caused many of Asia's leadership to call into question their customary cultural arrangements, which failed to protect their nations. By World War I nationalism had swept across Asia, leading many to conclude that the modernization that would change their culture would nonetheless be the means to save their nation.

Revolutionary Western Civilization

By the time the European explorations began in the late fifteenth century, nations in the western part of the continent had already experienced a number of significant developments. Stronger and wealthier kings, less fearful of the Christian church in Rome, exhibited more tolerance of secular ideas and behavior. The kings' wealth, made possible by the end of barbarian invasions, the subsequent growth of urban centers, and the growing acceptance of business as a legitimate profession, set the stage for the Renaissance commencing in the fourteenth century. The Renaissance outlook stressed optimism and man's ability to better understand and thus improve his material condition without sacrificing basic spiritual aspirations; individualism championed each person's uniqueness without abandoning family, village, church, or community; secularism focused on the here-and-now without rejecting the quest for a spiritual eternity; and humanism spoke of creating a society in which all could pursue and perhaps achieve one's earthly potential. Although the Renaissance was confined largely to a small group of urbanites and while the new ideas took place within a Christian context, a significant step toward what can be termed modernization had been taken.

As the search for a suitable society continued, the Western European outward thrust began. The fall of Constantinople to the Turks in 1453 created two problems, the possible solutions to which encouraged overseas exploration. This collapse cut off the Chinese and Asian trade, which heretofore passed through what now became a hostile Istanbul. Accordingly, Europeans began the search for another route to Asia. As well, the Turkish conquest of what was the Eastern Roman or Byzantine Empire foreshadowed, in the eyes of Christian Europe, an Islamic Turkish onslaught into Europe, which indeed occurred. Not until 1683, at Vienna, did the Ottoman Turkish threat subside. In the search for allies against the Turks, one proposed solution was an alliance with the Chinese, known not to be Muslim. And of course the economic benefits of a Chinese connection appealed to merchants and kings. Meanwhile, the possibility of converting Chinese and others "over there" fascinated the Church. In any case, by the sixteenth century, European explorers, adventurers, missionaries, and merchants had traveled to most of the populated regions on Earth, made contact with most of the major civilizations, conquered and governed some of them, and established trading routes across the globe. Material and intellectual exchanges in the first century or so of contact likely affected Europe as much as Asia. By the early nineteenth century, it became more of a one-way transfer, from by then a much more materially advanced Western Europe to an Asia less able to defend itself.

The Protestant Reformation beginning in 1517 shattered a relatively uniform Christian theology and undermined the Church's ability to impose its worldview on European society. Ever since the fall of Rome, the Church had been not only the religious wellspring but also the intellectual reservoir of Europe, especially after public government and learning collapsed with the Roman Empire. As kings emerged after the barbarian invasions ended around 1000 CE, monarchs began to compete with the Church (and each other) for political supremacy, economic assets, and intellectual talent. But until Martin Luther challenged Church practices, Rome had been able to threaten kings and lesser mortals with religious sanctions that would likely cause political or spiritual trouble. By 1517, Luther got the support of German princes, and his survival led to the creation of other Protestant faiths. The consequences that followed set the stage for an intellectual revolution, for if Luther and other religious leaders could successfully challenge Rome's religious authority, so too could intellectuals question Rome's ability to speak authoritatively on more mundane issues.

The scientific revolution, essentially beginning in the sixteenth century, got underway when someone asked how one can know that the Church knows what is true. No longer could the Church rely on *ex cathedra* (from the cathedral, or "because we said so") statements when declaring something to be true or false. Even assuming the Church did not purposely deceive, the question remained: How did one establish the validity of a Church claim? Scientists like Frances Bacon (1561–1626) argued that by applying the proper technique of inquiry, the inductive method, one could draw conclusions about phenomena experienced by the senses. This upset received wisdom, particularly Church thinking, which asserted (as had Plato) that the material world was inferior to the spiritual, and that in any case the feeble senses served as highly unreliable guides to knowledge. How could fallible senses possibly understand a material world that was constantly changing? The scientists answered, "Create an instrument to compensate," such as a telescope.

Thus astronomers from Nicolaus Copernicus to Isaac Newton, taking issue with earlier Church-approved accounts of the heavens, put forth increasingly better explanations of how the universe operates, encountering only minor Church impediments along the way. Newton believed God created a universe that operated according to natural law, and all inquiring minds needed to do was search for those laws—in physics, chemistry, biology, and so forth.

Depending upon where scientists operated, orthodox explanation could be investigated and, if warranted, overturned without much fear of Church or state. Perhaps Europe was not an ideal intellectual environment compared to the freedom found in many twenty-first-century nations, but it proved good enough for revolutionary advancements in thinking. Asian leaders gradually began to take account of new Western ideas, such as Galilean astronomy, which the Kangxi Emperor studied under a Jesuit priest, Ferdinand Verbiest.

Kangxi Emperor (1654–1722). *Source:* The Picture Art Collection/Alamy Stock Photo.

The Kangxi Emperor on Scientific Method

After the Treaty of Nerchinsk had been signed with the Russians, I ordered the Jesuits Thomas Gerbillon, and Bouvet to study Manchu also, and to compose treatises in that language on Western arithmetic and the geometry of Euclid. In the early 1690's I often worked several hours a day with them. With Verbeist I had examined each stage of the forging of cannon, and made him build a water fountain that operated in conjunction with an organ, and erect a windmill in the court; with the new group—who were later joined by Brocard and Jartoux, and worked in the Yang-hsin [Yang'xin] Palace under the general direction of my eldest son Yin-t'l [Yin'ti]—I worked on clocks and mechanics. Pereira taught me to play the tune "Pu-yan-chou" on the harpsichord and the structure of the eight-note scale. Pedrini taught my sons musical theory, and Gherardina painted portraits at the Court. I also learned to calculate the weight and volume of spheres, cubes, and cones, and to measure distances and the angle of river banks. On inspection tours, I later used these Western methods to show my officials how to make more accurate calculations when planning their river works.

Source: Kangxi Emperor, as quoted in Jonathan Spence, *Emperor of China: Self-Portrait of K'ang-hsi* [Kangxi] (New York: Vintage Books, 1974), pp. 72–73.

The Enlightenment, a social scientific revolution (or perhaps the Renaissance on steroids), dominated eighteenth-century European and American thinking. It produced intellectuals who believed that natural laws existed in the social as well as the physical world. These intellectuals or *philosophes* in this so-called Age of Reason realized that society had flaws, even serious defects, which with the application of reason could be reduced or removed. But for reason to reach its fullest potential, superstition needed to be marginalized. Since many *philosophes* believed that organized religion perpetrated superstition, the role of churches needed to be seriously diminished or even eliminated. In the place of organized religion the *philosophes* offered Deism, or the natural religion, whose chief doctrine (according to Thomas Paine and Thomas Jefferson, among others) centered on one's mind being one's church. Natural law in economics came to be seen not as the state-guided mercantilism then current, but as *laissez-faire*, the idea that a government's role in the economic sphere should be minimal. The individual, argued Adam Smith in his *Wealth of Nations*, would be best served by the market as opposed to the prevailing mercantilist wisdom, which claimed only government direction could produce a wealthy and powerful nation. In politics, natural law required constitutional government whose chief task was the protection of the individual's life, liberty, and property.

Political revolution in Europe also changed how increasing parts of the world viewed government's role in the life of the people and the nation. By the sixteenth and seventeenth centuries, kings in Europe grew stronger, to the point that they could claim, and the church would acknowledge, monarchs had a divine and absolute right to rule. But as absolutism became more widely accepted, challenges to it got underway. The Dutch Republic beginning in 1648 produced an alternative to absolutism politically and a model for religious toleration as well. But the best example of anti-absolutism can be seen in the English Glorious or Bloodless Revolution of 1688–1689. In that upheaval, absolutist ruler James II was overthrown and replaced by a constitutional monarch (his daughter Mary II). The social theorist John Locke, the godfather of modern democracy, directly challenged the religious and secular supporters of absolutism. He explained the relationship between government and citizen as a social contract. In this relationship, the government had responsibilities, chief among them being the protection of citizens' lives, liberties, and properties, but it could fulfill those duties only within an acceptable set of guidelines as set forth in a constitution. If the government failed to meet its responsibilities or met them by using unconstitutional means, then the people had the right to void the contract between people and ruler and set up a new government.

These were the very same ideas that Thomas Jefferson put forth in the Declaration of Independence to justify the American colonial rebellion against Great Britain in 1776. Thirteen years later the French Revolution broke out, overthrowing absolutist monarchy there in the name of liberty, equality, and fraternity. A century later, on the eve of World War I, Britain, America, and France—with all their domestic problems during that century—constituted three of the five most wealthy and powerful nations on Earth. And of the other two—Japan and Germany—Japan was on the winning side in World War I, and it began in 1919 a parliamentary democracy.

The economic changes experienced by much of Europe after 1300 produced very substantial consequences as well. The commercial revolution that helped end the Middle Ages and usher in the Renaissance, along with the economic benefits the overseas explorations created, improved the acceptability of business as a profession. The overseas ventures also resulted in the creation of joint stock companies, very similar to a modern corporation, which enabled private enterprise to get involved in the global trade. Although the early Spanish and Portuguese monarchies funded the original expeditions, their resources would likely not have been capable, over the longer term, of funding as many as they desired to launch. Not only did private capital get pooled in these companies, but they would form the backbone of most European colonial enterprises. The various East India Companies not only had national monopolies to do business in most of Asia, but they also ended up serving as official or semi-official governing agencies there. The British East India

Company, for example, de facto ruled India until 1858. Indeed, governments encouraged economic development, supporting mercantilist practices that would promote self-sufficiency, which in turn would more likely amass gold and silver for the nation; and they supported the acquisition of colonies, whose raw materials and markets would serve the mother country.

As well, changes in farming, manufacturing, and commercial practices turned the economic structures of Western European nations upside down. Before the Renaissance, economic activity was viewed as a necessary evil by the Church and nobility, but kings soon tapped non-agricultural sources of wealth. The elites who oversaw premodern economies dominated by priest and lord typically sought economic stability, not growth; mercantilism directed by kings changed that mindset, which opted for expansion. Economic activity in medieval thinking spoke of working for the benefit of society; mercantilism managed by monarchs declared that states should be the chief beneficiary of people's labor. Premodern labor characteristically involved cooperative activity, whether on the farm, in the manufacturing realm, or in the commercial sector. The new *laissez-faire* economics stressed competition. In agriculture, inefficient open-field farming practices, which included the customs of keeping fallow land and having farmers plant the same crops, gave way to the more resourceful enclosure. This involved the consolidation and enclosing of farmers' lands, the planting of all land (using certain crops, such as legumes, and rotating them from field to field to ensure the ongoing fertility of the soil), and allowing each farmer to choose which crops to plant. In manufacturing, the traditional monopoly guild system, which produced products according to each guild's notion of social benefit, gave way to the cottage industry (or domestic industry or putting-out system), which generated goods and services based more on the demands of the market. Similarly in commerce, the guild—and eventually even mercantilism—gradually gave way to free-trade ideas and practices, which resisted excessive government interference in the economy. As in politics, so too in economics: monarchs gradually lost substantial power to the people.

The industrial revolution began in England in the late seventeenth century, developed slowly in its place of birth during the eighteenth century, and gradually spread to some of continental Europe, the Americas, and Japan by the end of the nineteenth century, and eventually to most of the rest of the world in the twentieth century. It began in England for a number of reasons and would develop elsewhere under somewhat or even radically different circumstances, the most important reason being the perceived need for non-industrial nations to catch up with Britain as quickly as possible. The industrial revolution involved the use of new, nonhuman power in production. Old nonhuman power included such things as wind, water, and animals; steam provided the new source of power. Steam engines and later electricity and nuclear energy provided reliable and relatively cheap power that enabled machinery to mass-produce materials. That is to say, production focused on the masses that now possessed, because of enclosure, cheaper food and thus some disposable income to purchase mass-produced items. This gave private inventors and investors the incentive to build the factories that could more likely sell its products. Cheap food also made available cheap labor (in most locations), since low food prices allowed for low wages and thus a lower cost of production. Britain also had a great transportation and communication system—roads, canals, and rivers at home, and markets in the numerous colonies—which enabled manufacturers to get their products to markets inexpensively. Large quantities of accessible fuel—coal—also reduced the final cost of a product. And the industrial revolution—beginning as it did as the English Revolution, when John Locke argued for government that would protect life, liberty, and property—gave assurance to investors that their assets likely would not fall victim to a capricious government.

Since other countries would have had to wait for such favorable circumstances to emerge, and since that likely would take an unacceptably long time, governments in Europe, America, and Japan in the nineteenth century and elsewhere in the twentieth century opted for some (slight or considerable) national public efforts to support rapid industrialization. Depending on the nation, this could involve the government accumulation of capital necessary for factory building, the establishment of government subsidies to build transportation systems, the establishment of government tariffs to protect infant industries from foreign competition, or even government management of the factories, transportation systems, banks, or other institutions deemed essential to successful industrial development. And though industrialization produced enormous environmental and human problems, by the end of the nineteenth century, few would deny that industry also produced increased national wealth and power, and an increased standard of living as had never been produced before.

Revolutionary Western Civilization Moves East

All of these ideas and many of the institutions that took half a millennium to develop in Europe made their way to the rest of the world, and under extreme pressure many of the traditional practices in locations beyond Western Europe were called into question. In order to catch up, the new modernizers in Asia (and most everywhere else) had to cram into a century or less time the requirements of modernization that Europe had addressed over half a millennium. Traditional cultures came under attack by the mid-nineteenth century in part because Europeans (and eventually Americans and Japanese) moved beyond chiefly doing business in Asia to controlling politics and manipulating customary practices there. A century or more of empire building by the industrial nations, of nationalist resistance by those colonized, and of empire collapse ensued.

The "old imperialism," by which imperial powers largely focused on creating trading ports and conducted business via informal institutions while leaving local social routines free to operate, gave way to the "new imperialism." This updated version, underway by at least the 1870s, seemed to require the imperial powers to have formal political control over the entire geographical territory—that is, to establish colonies—where a perceived common culture prevailed. It told other imperial nations to keep their hands off, and it intensified a process long underway to bring the local cultures more into line with the cultural practices of the colonial overlord. The principal cause of this new imperialism was fear. Fear by the dominant imperial power, Britain, that its leading global position would be challenged by newly emerging industrial powers such as Germany, the United States, France, and Japan. Fear by the emerging industrial powers that their rivals would outperform them in generating wealth and power. And since much of a nation's wealth and power got calculated based in large part on possession of colonial territory and strategic locations, a nation's fear of insufficient holdings dominated foreign policy thinking.

Between 1850 and 1870, Britain still controlled a good part of the world, directly or indirectly. In addition to colonial holdings, for example, Britain also dictated how foreigners did business with Qing Dynasty China after having defeated the Chinese in the Opium War (1839–1842). To take another illustration, the British Navy enforced the United States' Monroe Doctrine (1823), opposing the recolonization of the Americas after most of Latin America became independent from Spain. The United States did not have the naval capability and indeed seemed a nation on the road to disunity. No Germany or Italy existed before 1870, and Japan remained divided into dozens of local domains isolated from the outside world. And up to this point, informal political institutions such as East India companies seemed sufficient to protect the home country's interests.

By 1870, Britain faced three major competitors: the United States, Japan, and Germany. The American Civil War had ended, and the United States launched a potent industrial revolution likely to make it a global power in short order. The Meiji Restoration of 1868 took an anti-foreign nation fragmented by civil war and launched Japan on a path to modernization in just a generation. And most of the more than three dozen German-speaking states formed into the new German state in 1871, which soon became a major imperial power. The opening of the Suez Canal in 1869 provided a much shorter route to the jewel in the crown of the British Empire, India. British insecurity over future international arrangements led to a scramble for territory among the industrial nations: for coaling stations, to lock in raw materials or to discover new ones, to create military outposts, and as locations to dump surplus manufactured goods, surplus population, and surplus capital. Before the end of the nineteenth century, almost all of Africa, Asia, and the Pacific islands had been conquered, and those territories not officially spoken for—such as China and Siam—nonetheless experienced what has been termed semicolonial status. What made the new imperialism possible?

Clearly the industrial revolution created most of the means that made the conquest and administration of far-flung territories feasible. The weapons of war—such as steamships capable of going up and down rivers or between ports in almost any weather, armed with artillery, and containing combat forces—put the industrial nations at an advantage. So did the telegraph and later undersea cables, providing communications advantages. Increasingly modern medicine, such as quinine, enabled imperial personnel to deal with tropical diseases more effectively. So too did the emerging nationalism in the industrial world, as recent and imperfect as it was. The colonies, by contrast, typically were divided by languages, religions, ethnicities, tribes, regions, and other traditional outlooks. The invading industrial nations never faced a united adversary in the nineteenth century. By World War I, that was no longer the case.

Furthermore, several significant ideas propelled the industrial nations' expansionist programs. Social Darwinism applied the biological ideas of Darwin to domestic and international relations. In the international realm, it spoke of the world being a jungle inhabited by nations struggling to survive, and in this life-and-death struggle only the fittest survived. There was no morality involved, just doing what was necessary to survive. Military thinking, particularly the ideas of Alfred Thayer Mahan, argued that great nations had great navies, and in the late nineteenth century, these navies moved on steam and were manufactured with steel. The steam came from coal, thus requiring coaling stations; but a nation took not only needed locations for refueling but all possible sites, thus denying as well as possible one's competitors. Economically, John Hobson's book *Imperialism* argued that capitalism needed safe places to dump surplus capital in order to survive, adding one more reason for grabbing territory. Perhaps the Social Darwinists, Mahan, and Hobson were correct in their assessments; perhaps not. Why take a chance? As the philosopher Hannah Arendt explained it:

> The only grandeur of imperialism lies in the nation's losing battle against it. The tragedy of this half-hearted opposition was not that many national representatives could be bought by the new imperialist businessmen; worse than corruption was the fact that the incorruptible were convinced that imperialism was the only way to conduct world politics. Since maritime stations and access to raw materials were really necessary for all nations, they came to believe that annexation and expansion worked for the salvation of the nation. They were the first to fail to understand the fundamental difference between the old foundation of trade and maritime stations for the sake of trade and the new policy of expansion.[1]

As well, writers like Rudyard Kipling maintained that imperialism, properly administered, would produce positive results. In his poem "White Man's Burden," Kipling claimed that it was the duty

---

1 Hannah Arendt and Peter Baehr, *The Portable Hannah Arendt* (New York: Penguin Classics, 2003), p. 112.

of industrial nations to uplift those cultures that had fallen behind the times. He and some others may have genuinely believed this, but many used it as an excuse for expansion.

Most of the consequences of the "new imperialism" developed slowly, but the immediate outcome was armed resistance. The first of these larger conflicts occurred in India with the Sepoy Mutiny of 1857–1858. Another took place in the Philippines, officially between 1899 and 1902 but practically speaking lasting more than a decade. At this point, indigenous elites then attempted to determine the causes of and solutions to the problem of colonization. Three broad themes emerged. One school of thought argued that failure to abide by traditional ways made the country open to invasion. Return to tradition, the thinking went, and the foreign problem would be solved. Another group declared that adherence to traditions made the country weak. Dump the tradition and embrace what made the imperial powers strong, and victory would follow. Since neither of these approaches seemed promising, eventually a third approach surfaced: Take the best of both. But that begged a number of questions, the two most important and least easy to answer being: What was the best of one's tradition? And what was the best of the foreign ideas and institutions?

As colonial elites grappled with these questions and led resistance movements against the imperial powers, nationalism within the colonies began to take root. Nationalism emerged as national identity began to take on greater importance among people than the differences in language, religion, ethnicity, race, class, tribe, region, or other traditional ties. Such distinctions under the umbrella of a common culture held people together only tenuously before the nineteenth century. What had been simply anti-foreignism in the past now became a demand for political self-determination for the nation. For if the consequence in a struggle to protect one's culture from change was a heroic defeat, then the fate of one's culture ended up in the hands of the foreigner. By World War I, the larger part of the indigenous elite concluded that it would be better to adjust the culture to meet the danger.

One pertinent example of the surging popularity of nationalism in the colonized world can be found in the writings of Indian thinker Aurobindo Ghose (1872–1950), who had studied in England for more than a decade. His ideas about national self-reliance and independence and how to achieve them (mass mobilization and passive resistance) greatly influenced Mohandas Gandhi. Chief among these ideas was the foreign concept of nationalism.

> There is a creed in India today which calls itself Nationalism, a creed which has come to you from Bengal. This is a creed which many of you have accepted when you called yourselves Nationalists. Have you realized, have you yet realized what that means? Have you realized what it is that you have taken in hand? Or is it that you have merely accepted it in the pride of a superior intellectual conviction? You call yourselves Nationalists. What is Nationalism? Nationalism is not a mere political program; Nationalism is a religion that has come from God; Nationalism is a creed which you shall have to live. Let no man dare to call himself a Nationalist if he does so merely with a sort of intellectual pride, thinking that is more patriotic, thinking that he is something higher than those who do not call themselves by that name. If you are going to be a nationalist, if you are going to assent to this religion of Nationalism, you must do it in the religious spirit. You must remember that you are the instruments of God.[2]

The anticolonial movements in Asia during the nineteenth and twentieth centuries differed in terms of leadership, organization, ideology, and post-independence objectives. They were guided

---

2 William Theodore de Bary, ed., *Sources of Indian Tradition*, vol. 2 (New York: Columbia University Press, 1958), pp. 176–177.

in part by the colonial adversary they faced, by their leaders' independence agendas, and by developments in the industrial world as well. That is to say, considerable disagreement among anticolonial activists existed from rookie efforts through veteran attempts to dislodge colonial overlords. Some favored nonviolence, others armed struggle. Some endorsed a capitalist and democratic postindependence future, others a fascist or communist agenda, and still others a return to more traditional ways.

Matteo Ricci and Xu Guangqi. *Source:* Athanasius Kircher.

Whatever differences among the various independence and modernizing movements, all of them eventually drew upon the growing feeling of nationalism, a sentiment that successful political organizations used to mobilize elite and commoner. And much of that nationalism contains vital traditional cultural attitudes and practices. Even the Philippines, a majority Catholic country, is a Catholic country with Philippine cultural characteristics. Both individuals and nations have, as a rule, been selective in what of their culture they keep and what of the outside world they accept. Perhaps Xu Guangqi, a Ming Dynasty official, best represents the limits of cross-cultural exchanges, even in the twenty-first century.

Xu Guangqi (or **Paul Hsu [Xu]**, 1562–1633) was a Confucian scholar-official in the Ming court, holding positions of Deputy Prime Minister of the Cabinet and the Minister of Rites (Minister of Culture, Education, and Foreign Affairs). He studied Western science and technology while working with the Italian Jesuit Matteo Ricci in translating several classic Western texts into Chinese, as well as several Chinese Confucian texts into Latin. Xu excelled in mathematics, astronomy, and agricultural technology. He translated Euclid's *Elements* and other works into Chinese, which makes him China's first translator of European works. He was baptized a Roman Catholic in 1603. As the first Chinese individual in whom Chinese and Western learning met, he became a strong proponent for introducing Western learning into China.

But Xu Guangqi is an exception. In general, the Chinese might be interested in Western science and technology, but resistant to Western political, social, and religious doctrines. This is a pattern that continues into modern times. Hence, the introduction of modern Western values into China has been slow and beset with difficulty, be it Christianity, democracy, communism, or human rights.

Paul Xu and other Asian intellectuals interested in Western ideas and institutions were exceptions to their time and cultures. By the end of the nineteenth century such attitudes were still in the minority, but that rapidly changed by World War I. Western concepts and practices would thereafter be selectively adopted, then adapted, to produce modernization with various Asian characteristics.

The remainder of this book will focus on the various Asian paths to the future.

Suggested Readings and Viewings

Michael Barone, *Our First Revolution: The Remarkable British Upheaval That Inspired America's Founding Fathers* (New York: Three Rivers Press, 2007).

Civilization: The West and the Rest (2012), with Niall Ferguson; 2 DVD disks.

Robert B. Ekelund, Jr., and Robert B. Tollison, *Politicized Economies: Monarchy*, Monopoly and *Mercantilism* (College Station: Texas A&M University Press, 1997).

Gertrude Himmelfarb, *The Roads to Modernity: The British, French, and American Enlightenments* (New York: Vintage Books, 2004).

Margaret C. Jacob, *The Scientific Revolution: A Brief History with Documents* (Boston: Bedford/St. Martin's, 2010).

Kenneth Pomeranz, *The Great Divergence: China, Europe, and the Making of the Modern World Economy* (Princeton, NJ: Princeton University Press, 1993).

Kenneth Pomeranz and Steven Topik, *The World That Trade Created: Society, Culture, and the World Economy*, 2nd ed. (Armonk, NY: M.E. Sharpe, 2006).

Joseph A. Schumpeter, *Capitalism, Socialism, and Democracy* (New York: Harper, 1950).

Jonathan D. Spence, *The Memory Palace of Matteo Ricci* (New York: Penguin, 1985).

Jonathan Spence, *To Change China: Western Advisers in China, 1620–1960* (Boston: Little, Brown, 1969).

Peter N. Stearns, *The Industrial Revolution in World History* (Boulder, CO: Westview Press, 2007).

Part 2

The Age of Transformations: Nationalism and Modernization in the Era of Global Wars and the Search for New Social Arrangements, circa 1800 to Present

Introduction to Part 2

The Age of Transformations: Nationalism and Modernization in the Era of Global Wars and the Search for New Social Arrangements, circa 1800 to Present

Asia between 1200 and 1800 witnessed numerous substantial and tumultuous shocks to its cultural centers. Already as the nineteenth century unfolded, most of the continent had fallen under the direct control or considerable influence of invaders, Asian or otherwise. The Manchus controlled China and the Spanish the Philippines, while other European nations imposed informal but widespread economic, political, and social practices on the remainder of the continent. And although the British by the early nineteenth century had rendered impotent the Mughal emperors in India, the cultural impact of six centuries of Muslim rule there could be seen in terms of religion, both Islam and Sikhism; the arts, particularly Mughal poetry; and architecture, such as the Taj Mahal. And yet, for all the cultural accretions both Asians and non-Asians produced in territories they inhabited, occupied, or ruled, the basics of Chinese, Indian, and most other Asian societies remained alive, animating still the daily lives of the people, though in conjunction with some foreign practices. It was not until the early 1800s that the effects of the industrial revolution, chiefly wealth and power, began to challenge the existing Asian ideas and institutions in ways that forced the upholders of their cultural traditions to reexamine established beliefs.

The foremost major alarm came with Britain's defeat of China in the First Opium War (1839–1842), but numerous other military defeats over the nineteenth century culminating in the Boxer Rebellion (1899–1900) added to an ongoing and profound sense of peril. Asian civilizations had been overrun by superior armed forces over the millennia, but the British victory resulted in China having to alter, and then abandon, its time-honored (most of the time) tribute system of foreign relations. Eventually, the Confucian educational curriculum, which served as the foundation for the civil service examinations, which in turn produced the empire's officials, eventually expanded to include Western "techniques." Although the civil service exams continued to test candidates on their knowledge of Confucius, parallel though unofficial educational institutions sprang up to add calculus, chemistry, and other "techniques" to a more functional program of study. When the examination system was eliminated in 1905, a modern curriculum and public schooling stood prepared to educate a small but growing percentage of the population.

In Hindustan, the Sepoy Mutiny (1857–1858) likewise signaled recognition that the core of Indian civilization, by this time including Islamic components, had come under attack from the British. As in the case of China, India's elite began to question whether traditional practices would suffice to manage successfully a foreign occupation—indeed, whether the Indian way of life itself

Asia Past and Present: A Brief History, First Edition. Peter P. Wan and Thomas D. Reins.
© 2021 John Wiley & Sons, Inc. Published 2021 by John Wiley & Sons, Inc.

could survive. Russia's growing presence in Central and Inner Asia similarly began to upset local traditional norms, as did the colonization of Southeast Asia by industrial nations from the West.

The "new imperialism," principally formal political control, as opposed to the "old imperialism" of chiefly informal economic arrangements, appeared bent on transforming, instead of merely accessing, the societies that the invaders encountered. Whereas heretofore such alien thoughts and techniques could be and usually were adapted to traditional patterns of civilization or outright rejected, after 1800 Asia's elite came to realize what the old elite of Europe had recognized: namely, that the wealth and power created by industrialization also created new elites and new patterns of life.

The "new imperialism" resulted from the newly emerging nations that posed a threat to British hegemony, which emerged after Napoleon's defeat in 1814–1815. Between 1865 and 1871, the United States, Japan, and Germany unified under modernizing governments that seemed certain to challenge British supremacy. At the very least, Britain would have to take into consideration the outlook of the United States as far as the Western hemisphere was concerned, of Japan as far as Asia was concerned, and of Germany as far as Europe was concerned. Moreover, the 1869 opening of the Suez Canal made it a strategic location on Britain's transportation connection to India. Faced with impending and serious global competition, Britain first bought shares in the Canal and eventually occupied Egypt. London then unleashed a campaign of colonization that formalized relationships with existing colonies and scrambled to acquire those territories not yet spoken for. Much of the rest of Europe as well as the United States and Japan joined in the chase. Two factors facilitated the physical control of older colonies and newer territories by the imperial powers. One was clearly the industrial revolution, which produced the tools of empire, particularly weapons and communications systems. Increasing national unity—early nationalism—provided another instrument. The imperial nations had these tools and the colonized did not. Additional ideas contributed rationales for conquest. Social Darwinism, for example, spoke of the international arena as a jungle in which nations struggle for survival, while "white man's burden" professed the uplifting benefits of being colonized.

Successful colonization, however, generated an intensified reaction to foreign incursions. Much of Asia's elite eventually concluded that only modern techniques could effectively weaken or dislodge alien aggression. By the turn of the twentieth century, they began to abandon or downplay defense of culture—often seen as the cause of a country's weakness—for the protection of the nation, thus initiating the nationalist movements that could be found everywhere in Asia by the end of World War I. Mass mobilization became closely tied to nationalist strategies of liberation. Western ideas of government, economics, and society fortified nationalist movements. Indeed, by the 1920s nationalists needed to answer two basic questions: (1) Would independence best be gained by violence or nonviolence? And (2) would the newly independent nations be more capitalist and democratic or socialist (whether democratic, Fascist, Nazi, or Communist) and have some variety of authoritarian or highly centralized rule?

World War I called the values of the West into question, and the depression made capitalism look less attractive. Indeed, as the Communist Revolution in Russia unfolded, it increasingly seemed more suited to newly developing nations as both possessed little of a modernizing infrastructure. And the Soviets also touted their "anti-imperialist" stance, a claim that appeared legitimate to many as the newly incorporated non-Russian Soviet Socialist Republics reputedly had equal standing with the Russian Soviet Republic. Indeed, as World War II approached, command economies and authoritarian rule in the Soviet Union, Nazi Germany, Fascist Italy, and militarist Japan appeared to be the most likely path to the future for industrial and modernizing nations alike. The Hitler–Stalin Pact of 1939 further strengthened the belief that perhaps totalitarian rule would push democracies into the dustbin of history.

World War II helped to redeem the West at home and in the eyes of those abroad. It began with the Japanese attack on China in 1937, spread to Europe after Soviet and German invasions of Poland in 1939, and became global with Japan's bombing of Pearl Harbor and the occupation of Europe's and America's Asian colonial territories in 1941. The conflict fatally undermined imperial control in Asia, and by 1950 the vast majority of colonial holdings there had become independent. Not only had the democratic West (along with totalitarian and nondemocratic governments) defeated the Fascists, Nazis, and militarists, but the war also undermined colonial regimes in all of Asia. Many new nations emerged with little or no opposition from the former overlords, as was the case of Japanese (for obvious reasons), American, and British colonies. The French and Dutch resisted giving up their holdings, and wars of independence ensued. But trouble also faced territories where domestic rivalries existed, as in the Philippines, Malaya, Korea, India, Vietnam, and Burma. China, never a formal colony, also descended into civil war.

Complicating independence and nation building after the war was the Cold War (1945–1991), which pitted the United States and its allies against the Soviet Union and its followers. Thus civil war, cold war, and economic development all happened simultaneously in much of Asia. The ensuing turmoil often drew the United States and Soviet Union into domestic developments as economic, political, and military advisors. The Cold War clearly represented a contest to see which system—American or Soviet—provided a better path to the future across the globe, but chiefly among the developing nations, and more particularly the nations in Asia.

Although the Cold War in Asia greatly influenced nations' paths to modernization, it did not determine the particular paths ultimately taken. At a more basic national or cultural level, local factors and practical considerations ultimately decided how Asia would proceed to the future. Between and within the broad framework of capitalism and democracy on one hand and some form of socialism and dictatorship on the other, all sorts of modernization efforts surfaced in Asia. The more open societies, supported and encouraged by the United States, tended to prosper. Thus, Japan, South Korea, Taiwan, Hong Kong, Thailand, Singapore, Malaysia, and even the Philippines and Indonesia established modern infrastructures, varying degrees of economic growth, and freer societies by the end of the Cold War. While each experienced some reversals and all needed time to work out problems associated with nation building, most of them became models of development.

The more closed societies, most supported by the Soviet Union or China after the Communist victory in 1949, experienced much worse standards of living along with little or no political freedom. Thus North Korea, Vietnam, Laos, Kampuchea, Mongolia, the Central Asian Soviet Republics, and the People's Republic of China established many modern institutions. But those nations often failed to provide their people basic human rights and usually few of the consumer goods and services associated with modern life. Between the two poles of modernization stood India, Pakistan, and Burma. India, the largest democracy in the world (corruption and all), forged a path of neutrality in foreign affairs and social democratic economics then popular in England. Only after the Cold War's conclusion did New Delhi's political leadership launch a more market-based economy and begin to fuel robust development. Pakistan careened through the Cold War politically and economically, and remains on the verge of failed-state status. Similarly, Burma suffered the "Burmese Path to Socialism" and assorted military rulers, though it did manage to keep free of most Cold War intrigues. Not until 2012 did the military there begin to take baby steps toward more popular participation in government.

Even before the "death" or at least terminal status of communism, Communist and other authoritarian leaders in Asia took note of which kinds of societies prospered and which kinds didn't. How to navigate to prosperity without giving up political control became the trick for the more closed regimes. More open and prosperous societies had to deal with the results of material success and individual freedom, which often produced such problems as pollution, questionable business ethics, political corruption (though open societies can more easily take their leaders to task), drugs, unemployment, and the changing system of values associated with freedom to choose (often wrongly). For many in Asia, soft authoritarianism—as seen in today's Singapore—seemed to be a comfortable middle path between dictatorship and democracy.

But as the Cold War recedes into history and material prosperity comes within reach, four major issues need attention. One is globalization, involving the peaceful and least detrimental integration of national economies, which can produce the potential for troubles associated with trade. Another is terrorism, manifestations of which have occurred in nearly every country on numerous occasions. The terrorists are typically, but not exclusively, members of Islamic movements throughout Asia, and they are found in both majority Muslim as well as non-Muslim countries. As with most insurrectionary movements, they tend to prosper in failed states like Afghanistan or regions where religious conflict has been chronic as in the southern Philippines, in Sri Lanka, or in parts of India. Perhaps terrorism represents the last stand against modernization, perhaps the use of religion to gain political power for other purposes, but it will remain a threat to stability and economic growth that all countries of Asia need to address, as will numerous separatist movements across the continent. A third issue, nuclear weapons proliferation, has the potential to destabilize the entire region, affecting economic growth or leading to military conflicts. Environmental problems represent the fourth major difficulty facing modernizing nations in Asia. Of course, these represent only the most serious issues, and the list of additional problems is long.

At home, as rising expectations increasingly become accepted realities in Asia, the problems of growing prosperity will gradually replace the search for minimal standards of living. Abroad, the rise of India and China combined with the relative decline in American influence in Asia will likely produce the more uncertain aspects of Asia's future. Its economic developments have to a large extent been made possible by the comparatively free flow of goods and services, made possible until recently by the American military. Can or will Washington maintain the conditions necessary for such an ongoing free flow, or will more restrictive rules of economic engagement emerge? Often perceived political necessity trumps economic advantage. In any case, the new market arrangements, whether relatively free or restrictively mercantilist, will likely be the default economic agenda for most Asian regimes. The long-term political and social measures, on the other hand, remain works in progress and have the potential to produce instability at home and war abroad.

15

Foreign Incursions, Domestic Challenges, and Late Qing Dynastic Decline: China's Long Road to Modernization, 1840–1911

By hsin-min *[xinmin or new citizen], I do not mean to suggest a distinction between a new person and the one who makes him new. Instead, I mean for each of our people to renovate himself.*[1]

—Liang Qichao

Introduction

By the middle of the nineteenth century, Western nations were rapidly becoming modern industrial societies, but China remained fundamentally agricultural and largely closed to the outside world. China would have to suffer several crushing military defeats before some of its enlightened leaders would reluctantly concede that ancient Chinese civilization no longer stood head and shoulders above other nations, that Western civilization was superior, at least in its guns, cannon, and steam-powered ships. China needed to catch up.

For over 150 years, enlightened Chinese would seek to remake China based on Western models: the capitalist-democratic model of England and the United States, the militarist model of Germany and Japan, or the communist model of Soviet Russia. Over time these foreign countries would be seen as friend and foe, models to emulate and aggressors to fend off, and idols of adulation and targets of hatred. China's own highly sophisticated and deeply rooted civilization would also be viewed as both an asset and "historical baggage." The ongoing story of China's long struggle for modernization remains the substance of modern Chinese history.

The beginning of the story surfaces with the First Opium War.

First and Second Opium Wars Reduce Imperial China to a Semi-Colony

Great Britain, as the first industrial and rapidly modernizing power, sought to access more of China's vast markets to sell its products and acquire raw materials. It sent three delegations to China in the late eighteenth century. Their purpose was to establish a broader trade relationship with China. The existing trade process, a monopoly-to-monopoly relationship, reflected the mercantilist outlook that both the Western nations and China deemed suitable in 1700, but less than a century later the two sides were too far apart to find common commercial ground. Britain's demand for "free trade" was

---

1 As quoted in Philip C. Huang, *Liang Ch'i-ch'ao [Liang Qichao] and Modern Chinese Liberalism* (Seattle: University of Washington Press, 1972), p. 65.

Asia Past and Present: A Brief History, First Edition. Peter P. Wan and Thomas D. Reins.
© 2021 John Wiley & Sons, Inc. Published 2021 by John Wiley & Sons, Inc.

incompatible with China's traditional "tribute system" and the relative seclusion that ensued. When the 1793 Macartney Mission arrived, the Qing Emperor Qianlong gave it some gifts to demonstrate China's wealth, sophistication, and power. But he brushed aside Britain's request for wider trade relations, saying China had no need for commercial interaction with the West.

At the time, China had an essentially self-sufficient agricultural economy. The Chinese market produced little demand for imports from Europe, whereas European markets had a huge appetite for such Chinese goods as tea, silk, and porcelain. The Chinese government's official policies further discouraged imports. As a result, British merchants were purchasing much more than they were selling in their trade with China. As the eighteenth century ended, so too did the once-reliable gold and silver from the Americas that had funded much of Europe's purchases from China. This resulted in an ongoing unfavorable balance of trade, thus requiring European nations to find some other source of bullion to buy Chinese products.

Timeline of Late Qing Dynasty China, 1839–1911	
1839	Special Commissioner Lin Zexu (1785–1850) arrives in Guangzhou to enforce the ban on opium trade; hardest hit are British and American opium traders
1839–1842	First Anglo-Chinese Opium War; China defeated
1842	Anglo-Chinese Treaty of Nanjing, the first in a series of "unequal treaties" with Europeans, Americans, and Japanese; emergence of "treaty ports"
1851–1864	Taiping Peasant Rebellion, China's largest, longest, and deadliest (perhaps 40 million dead) uprising, shakes the Manchu Qing regime to its foundation; Zeng Guofan (1811–1872) organizes local militia to defeat Taipings; control of the military begins to shift from Manchu court in Beijing to local Han Chinese elites
1856–1860	Events leading to the Second Opium or Anglo-French War, and the Treaty of Tianjin in 1858 and the Convention of Beijing in 1860, all of which opened up China to much greater foreign penetration
1860s–1890s	Zeng Guofan leads Self-Strengthening Movement to modernize China by employing the concept of using "Chinese principles, Western means" while fighting the Taiping Rebellion
1828–1912	Rong Hong (aka Yung Wing), first Chinese student to graduate from an American college (Yale, 1854), the "pioneer of pioneers" to promote U.S.–China relations
1870	Tianjin Incident involved rioting and atrocities against Catholic Church activities in China; like issues surrounding the Boxer Rebellion some three decades later
1894–1895	First Sino-Japanese War over control of Korea; China loses war, pays reparations, and cedes Taiwan to Japan
1898	Imperial Hundred Days of Reform launched by Guangxu Emperor (1871–1908; r. 1875–1908) scholars Kang Youwei, Liang Qichao, and Tan Sitong; crushed by Dowager Empress Cixi, who had been and would remain power behind the throne
1899–1900	America's Open Door policy sought to keep foreign "spheres of influence" open to all foreign nations
1899–1901	Boxer Rebellion was a peasant uprising directed largely against foreigners; crushed in Beijing by a coalition of eight foreign armies; Boxer Protocol of 1900 opens China further to foreigners, and China pays indemnity
1900–1908	Cixi approves major reforms: political, educational, opium; she dies in 1908
1911	Chinese Republican Revolution ends dynastic government

Britain soon turned the tables on China by finding a new product to sell to the Chinese—opium. The British East India Company grew opium in India, London's colony, and sold it in China and across Asia. Opium revenues soon reversed the unfavorable balance of trade for Britain, providing the necessary gold and silver to buy Chinese goods. Indeed, the Chinese demand for opium became so enormous that America and other countries got involved in the opium trade. The consequences for China were largely negative. While many Chinese (and British and Americans) took opium for medical reasons—to relieve pain, or treat but not cure tuberculosis—most opium users everywhere likely were engaging in "ceremonial chemistry," that is, getting high to minimize a host of life's troubles. Whether the physical pain was excruciating or the psychological agony unbearable, the drug cost money, and it most negatively affected the poor. The result of addiction spread across the populace: peasants, artisans, soldiers, and government officials. Worse yet, the great demand created a black market in the drug, producing massive corruption at all levels of officialdom. The Guangzhou or Canton System all but collapsed as drug dealers plied their trade everywhere demand existed, which eventually became most everywhere.

By the late 1830s the Qing Dynasty was forced to crack down on the trade because of the outflow of silver, which produced higher taxes. It took more copper coins, the currency of most of the Chinese people, to purchase the silver that was needed to pay taxes. Since economic troubles tended to foreshadow political adversity, the Qing court began an anti-opium movement at home. The emperor sent Special Commissioner Lin Zexu (1785–1850) to Guangzhou in 1839 to reinforce its ban on opium and the opium trade. Lin warned both the Chinese and foreigners before he acted, but his warnings went unheeded. When he acted, he did so decisively. He executed Chinese opium dealers, confiscated a six-month supply of opium that belonged to foreign merchants, and burned it all in public. The British and the Americans were the hardest hit.

The British government had learned from its diplomatic missions to China that, despite its imposing appearance, China was like a broken ship, adrift and sinking. So London took this burning of East India Company opium as a pretext to make war on China. The British war goal was not limited to the question of the opium trade. Economically, it needed to open up the Chinese market to British goods, including but not limited to opium. Diplomatically, it wanted to end China's tribute system and substitute a British approach to international diplomacy.

Commissioner Lin Zexu.

Britain started the war by attacking China's coastal cities and easily won the military conflict in what became known as the First Opium War (1839–1842). It had the advantage of rifles, cannon, steam-powered ships, and sophisticated tactics and training. The military campaigns were supported by an industrial base and the world's best navy. A defeated China signed the Anglo-Chinese Treaty of Nanjing in 1842 on a British warship. The treaty was the first in a series of "unequal treaties" China signed, typically after being defeated by one Western power or another or by Japan.

China signed the Treaty of Nanjing in 1842 with a gun held to its head. In it, China agreed to pay heavy reparations in silver dollars to Britain for its losses in the war and the earlier confiscation and destruction of opium; to open up "treaty ports" where it could station its consuls and where its nationals could enjoy free trade with anyone, de facto ending the "tribute system," the policy of relative seclusion, and the Guangzhou or Canton System; to hold negotiations with Britain to set a fixed tariff; and to cede Hong Kong to Britain. The treaty also provided for extraterritoriality, a sort of diplomatic immunity for all British subjects in China. Opium was not mentioned in the treaty, but in fact it became a legal commodity and henceforth the opium trade thrived. By the end of the nineteenth century, China had become the largest producer of opium in the world.

America and France followed to demand most of the British privileges. America added a "most-favored nation" clause to its treaty, which would automatically extend to America any privilege China might give to another foreign power. All other foreign powers then followed America's example to demand similar concessions. The most-favored nation clause would serve to unite the foreign powers in China with a common interest at China's expense. The issues surrounding what became the Second Opium War illustrate this point well.

As the British attempted in 1856 to open the port of Guangzhou, promised by the Chinese in the Treaty of Nanjing, Guangzhou-area Qing officials captured the *Arrow*, a cargo ship under British registry. A series of confrontations occurred between British and Chinese forces as a spring 1857 parliamentary election was pending and as the Sepoy Mutiny was erupting in British India. The British found an ally to chastise the Chinese when a French missionary was killed in Guangxi Province. Thus, London and Paris joined to punish the Qing rulers for these hostile acts, thus commencing the Second Opium or Anglo-French War, officially between 1858 and 1860. The Chinese suffered yet another military defeat, Beijing was occupied, and the Imperial Gardens ("Garden of Gardens") was sacked and burned. Chinese vandals and Boxer rebels would later complete the destruction of this national treasure.

The victors demanded new concessions in the treaties connected with the conflict. These included more reparations, more treaty ports, the legalization of the opium trade, the right to preach Christianity anywhere in China, and the right to station diplomats in the capital, Beijing. China's main import in the war's wake was opium, and its main exports were tea and silk. A flood of foreign merchants, missionaries, medical doctors, educators, diplomats, and troops poured into China. While Britain and France were encroaching on China's territory from the south and the east, Russia—involved in the treaty-making process—was gobbling up large chunks of Chinese territory in the far northeast (much of today's Siberia).

Various unequal treaties interlocked to become a "system of unequal treaties." It totally shattered what remained of the tribute system and Chinese control over foreigners residing in the Middle Kingdom. The once powerful and arrogant empire was now down on its knees. It had been reduced to the status of a semi-colony. The national government remained in name, but it had lost its territorial integrity and administrative independence.

The Western incursions shook traditional China to its foundations. Overbearing Western governments undermined the authority of the Manchu-ruled Chinese government. Christianity cast doubt on

Confucianism, as did the scientific knowledge that enabled the industrial revolution to create wealthy and powerful Britain and other modernizing nations. Cheaper and better foreign-manufactured goods destroyed China's self-sufficient agricultural economy, while foreign nationals behaved lawlessly in China since they were beyond the reach of China's courts and laws because of extraterritoriality. China's stable, albeit seemingly contented society found itself in the worst of all historical situations: major domestic disorder with the raging Taiping Rebellion and implacable foreign aggression.

The Chinese population had nearly tripled since 1750 and was seething because of economic dislocation and national humiliation. Outbreaks of mob violence against Christian missionaries and their Chinese converts occurred increasingly frequently as greater numbers of foreigners had traveled beyond the coastal cities to the country's vast interior. As foreign Christians erected churches in Chinese communities and converted Chinese to Christianity, the local gentry were often found stoking the flames of mob hysteria from behind the scenes. China's Confucian elite hated the foreigners for undermining their traditional authority as leaders of their communities. Responding to such violence against their countrymen, Western governments both brought in gunboats and troops and put pressure on the Chinese government to crack down on Chinese perpetrators. The Qing government, fearing Western military retaliation, would punish local officials for losing control of the situation, and order action against the troublemakers.

The 1870 Tianjin Incident or Massacre, the Chinese killing of foreign missionaries and Chinese converts, offers a case in point. After the riot was quelled and order restored, the Chinese and French governments entered protracted negotiations. China agreed to the French demands to execute or exile the rabblerousers, and to remove from office and exile two magistrates who had failed to keep the mob in check. The Chinese government also agreed to pay a large reparation, and to send a high-level delegation to Paris to make formal apologies. France did not pursue the case, since it had more pressing matters at home, namely the Franco-Prussian War of 1870–1871. But the incidents have broader repercussions. The loss of Western lives and property convinced the Western powers that the Chinese government could not be trusted to protect their nationals and their investments. The Qing government and much of the Chinese population became more convinced than ever that the Westerners constituted a bunch of bullies riding roughshod over the Chinese. The mutual hatred and distrust would find strong expression in the eruption of the Boxer Rebellion and the foreign intervention that ensued in 1900.

The Tianjin Incident

In the summer of 1870, sensational rumors were in rampant circulation in Tianjin, claiming that the local Catholic orphanage was taking in Chinese infants to gouge out their eyes and rip out their hearts to use in making medicines. The rumors originated in the Catholic practice of taking sick and abandoned infants into their orphanages and providing them with care; they went as far as accepting fatally ill infants in order to perform deathbed baptism for them. On a sultry sunny day, a crowd of locals gathered in front of the Catholic cathedral making angry accusations, while the French priests and nuns, along with their Chinese converts, tried to explain. Tempers flared and tensions reached a breaking point. The crowd morphed into a rioting mob. They surrounded the cathedral, throwing bricks and getting into fistfights. The French consul arrived and engaged the Chinese officials. But the situation got out of control when he drew his sword and fired his gun, killing a Chinese official's assistant. Three hours of rioting followed. The rioters killed the French consul and his assistant, and dumped their bodies into the river. They took the French nuns, stripped them naked, raped them, and then mutilated their bodies. The Chinese converts were not spared either. The total death toll was roughly 20 Westerners and 60 Chinese converts. Also destroyed were three Catholic churches, the French Consulate, and four Protestant churches run by British and American missionaries.

Rebellion and Reform

China's defeat in the First Opium War indicated that the Manchu Qing Dynasty had entered its final stage of decline and fall. A coalition of mighty and chaotic forces was engulfing China. Foreign powers were expanding their privileges in China, enlightened men were attempting to introduce modernization reforms to the old political system, and violent peasant uprisings called into question not only the dynasty but Confucian dynastic government itself. The Qing regime proved itself incapable of rejuvenation, notwithstanding a bold if unsuccessful Tongzhi Restoration reform program of the 1860s and 1870s. Likewise, the Self-Strengthening Movement to modernize the economy and the military after 1860 proved a failure when Japan crushed China in the First Sino-Japanese War of 1894–1895. At the same time, after Empress Dowager Cixi de facto took control of the Qing government in 1862, she kept it until her death in 1908. The nation's policy choices reflected to a large extent an alien Manchu leader's attempt to walk a tightrope between, on the one hand, Han Chinese willingness to cooperate with the dynasty (as nationalism became a growing concern for the Manchus, would Han Chinese be more interested in saving traditional culture or in protecting the nation?), and, on the other hand, foreign governments' willingness to accept China's attempts to comply with the treaties China signed. Foreign nations desired a compliant Qing foreign policy, since any new dynasty or revolutionary movement that came to power might well renounce the treaties, as the Taiping government promised to do in the 1850s and the Communist government in fact did in the 1950s.

The Taiping Rebellion, 1850–1864

The Taiping Rebellion exploded from the bottom of society, swept across half of China, and lasted 14 deadly and destructive years. The rebellion produced bizarre and unprecedented consequences that could be seen across the domestic scene well into the twentieth century. And while China never succumbed to complete colonization, foreign encroachment added to the domestic turmoil.

Hong Xiuquan, the Taiping leader, rallied millions of destitute men and women into his ranks. They were mainly peasants, artisans, and transport workers who had lost their livelihoods. Once mobilized, these rebels formed a fluid, loosely organized mass that marauded across South China, sweeping aside Qing government forces and leaving behind vast areas of depleted life and property. Originating in Guangxi Province in the southwest in late 1850, the Taipings entered what became their chosen capital Nanjing in 1853, formally establishing the Heavenly Kingdom of Great Peace or *Taiping Tianguo* in the southern half of China, which they controlled.

Hong inspired the Taiping rebels with a peculiar mix of traditional Chinese peasant utopianism and fragments of the Christian Old Testament. It comprised such concepts as monotheism, common ownership of property, and equality among all people. That included equality between the sexes and among nations. When he launched his rebellion, Hong ordered his followers to sell their property and to pool the proceeds into public coffers. While his troops were crisscrossing South China in unending combat, they looted government storehouses, dispossessed the rich, and shared the loot. After settling in at Nanjing, Hong issued a document for the distribution of land to the peasants. Although it remained a paper project that was never implemented, it did indicate the direction of his thinking.

Hong faced an agonizing dilemma in his relationship with the West. He initially announced that the Christian foreigners were his brethren in Christ. But slowly and reluctantly he came to realize that, although his ideology had spun off from Western Christianity, the Western powers never intended to recognize the legitimacy of his religion or his regime. The interests of the Western nations were tied to the system of unequal treaties with the Qing government; thus those treaties would survive only so long as the Qing government survived.

Hong Xiuquan. *Source:* FLHC 55/Alamy Stock Photo.

But even though the Manchu Qing government was dilapidated to the point of crumbling, it nonetheless found means to survive. The Manchu administration sought help from the "foreign devils" and from the ethnic Han Chinese. The Western powers openly sided with the Qing regime, helping it to arm, organize, and finance its troops, even to the point of engaging directly in the fighting. The British also actually collected foreign customs duties for the Qing rulers, even as the British and French were engaged in the Second Opium War against them.

Another marriage of convenience can be seen in the Qing decision to utilize Han Chinese militia to defeat the Taipings. Since Manchu armies proved utterly incapable of stopping the Taiping military, Beijing promoted the creation of local militia formed and led by local Han Chinese gentry. Although aliens, the Manchus upheld Confucianism and the traditional sociopolitical order, especially land ownership. The Taipings, though Han Chinese, challenged traditional Confucian ideology and economic arrangements. Here the Manchu rulers and Han Chinese elite had a commonality of interest—defeat of the Taipings. The Qing rulers wanted their dynasty to survive, and the Han Chinese elite wanted the traditional Confucian political and social order to survive. In the process, though, the Manchus legitimized the transfer of military power to their Han Chinese subjects, while the Han Confucian elite surrendered temporarily the law of avoidance principle that prohibited government officials from serving in their home provinces.

Zeng Guofan led the Han Chinese elite who formed numerous militias, and his protégé Li Hongzhang became his successor. Both were prominent scholar-officials serving in the Manchu government. According to Manchu procedures, Han Chinese were not allowed to command troops. But times had changed, and when no Manchu military leaders could stop the Taipings, out of desperation the Qing court invited Zeng to organize militia in 1852. Zeng's militia, the Xiang Army, came from Zeng's home province of Hunan, a region commonly referred to as Xiang. Zeng eventually retook the Taiping capital of Nanjing in 1864. In the meantime, Zeng sent Li Hongzhang to Li's home province of Anhui to form the Huai Army, named after the river in the area. These Han-led militia units remained loyal to the Manchus until just before the Revolution of 1911, which ended dynastic government.

Zeng's militia was clan-based and locally financed, and it relied on personal leadership rather than direct central government management. The troops, from top generals to foot soldiers, were all connected through family and clan ties, and they enjoyed broad-based backing from the Han Chinese population. With imperial court support and Western arms and logistical support, these militias provided the main fighting force to crush the Taiping Rebellion. Zeng's and Li's armies became models for other local militia, and after the collapse of the Taipings served as the chief military units in campaigns against several Muslim rebellions and in the Sino-French War of the 1880s; in the First Sino-Japanese War of 1894–1895; for the Beiyang Army, China's first modern military command; and ultimately for warlord regimes after World War I.

The Taiping movement had begun to lose momentum after settling down in its capital. The once mobile and aggressive fighting regime deteriorated into a static and flaccid bureaucratic force whose principal occupation became exploitation of the Heavenly King's subject people. The upper echelons became corrupt to the core. Its leaders plunged headlong into seizing personal wealth and power. They preoccupied themselves with infighting, killing one another in bloody feuds. Many veteran leaders fell victim to assassinations. One deserted, taking his troops with him. Such disarray at the top of the movement set the stage for Zeng Guofan's protracted siege and ensuing capture of the capital. Just before Zeng entered Nanjing, Heavenly King Hong Xiuquan committed suicide. The regime collapsed, and pockets of resistance were soon wiped out as well.

Zeng Guofan (1811–1872) has been described as the "last man in traditional Chinese history, and the first man in modern Chinese history." To many, he was the epitome of a Confucian scholar-official who combined scholarship, wisdom, and personal integrity with the abilities of a man of the world. Men as different as Jiang Jieshi (Chiang Kai-shek) and Mao Zedong have expressed deep admiration for him.

Zeng rose through the imperial examination system to be a scholar-official in the court in Beijing. But when the Taiping rebels were ravaging South China, he returned to his native province with the blessing of the Manchu court to build and command a militia. In the course of the prolonged fighting with the rebels, he came to realize the importance of modernization, and became the leader of the Self-Strengthening Movement. He was responsible for building China's first arsenal, first steamboat, and first publishing house for translating and publishing Western books, and for dispatching China's first government-sponsored students to study in the United States.

Zeng was one of the most powerful officials in the Qing government, but as a Han Chinese he could survive only so long as he could maintain the delicate balance among the Manchu court, the Han Chinese bureaucrats and generals, and the Western powers. He managed brilliantly for decades. But then the Manchu court appointed him to take charge of the negotiations with France over the Tianjin Incident, and when public opinion turned against the outcome of those negotiations, the court made him a scapegoat. When he died shortly thereafter, many Han Chinese considered him to be a despicable traitor.

The Taiping Rebellion reflected the desperation of the people at the bottom of society at a time of dramatic social disintegration. It failed, like other grassroots rebellions down the ages, but left in its wake changes that would prove irreversible. The non-Han Manchu regime had reached its final stage of decline. The Han Chinese elite were in position to take over control of the country, but would have to find a new way of governing. Foreign powers had insinuated themselves deeply into much of daily China. The country's foreign relations increasingly reflected a Western concept of how nations interacted. Domestically business, education, social practices, and political thinking progressively mirrored Western practices. China found itself at the gates of a new era, but few had much of an idea of what that new era would look like, much less how to get there.

The Self-Strengthening Movement (1860s–1890s) and the First Sino-Japanese War (1894–1895)

The Self-Strengthening Movement represented China's first institutional effort at modernization. Led by Zeng Guofan in its early years, its ambition was the age-old goal of "rich country, strong army." But the old maxim was recast to meet the demands of a world where industry, not agriculture, produced the desired wealth and power. That meant modernization, which was fraught with explosive cultural components, which in turn challenged most of China's traditional ideas and institutions. Chemistry and calculus would start to marginalize Confucius. A battle ensued between traditionalists and modernizers, and the court, which had embraced those Confucian ideas and institutions in order to govern China, now had to watch from the sidelines and attempt to balance different Han Chinese debates over paths to the future. Too much modernization would anger traditionalists; too little would check China's ability to keep the foreigners at bay. Either could prove fatal to the Manchus.

An intellectual compromise emerged, in the short run, to justify the modernizing Self-Strengthening Movement. Essential Confucian principles (*ti*) would provide the cultural foundation while Western techniques (*yong*), operating within the Confucian framework, would deliver practical uses to create a modern industrial capacity. China would "fight the aliens with their own means." But from the beginning, traditionalist Confucians argued that the techniques would alter the basic Confucian principles. The result of the Confucian debate insured that the Manchu court could not, like Meiji Japan at the time, commit to a full-throttled modernization program for fear of alienating a substantial number of either conservative or liberal Han Chinese.

Nonetheless China's Self-Strengthening Movement commenced. The program began in the arms industry when Zeng constructed an arsenal and a shipyard in Shanghai even as the Taiping Rebellion raged on. But he also came to understand that Western wealth and power did not rest on the armaments industry alone but required a much broader base consisting of a modern economy based on science and technology. So he branched out to the commercial industries of mining, steel, shipbuilding, railroads, the telephone and telegraph, and textiles. Both government and private investors held stock in these new enterprises. The government policy for running these joint public-private companies was "government supervision, merchant management" (*Guandu Shangban*). While government involvement in a nation's successful modernizing efforts was not all that unusual in nineteenth-century Japan, Germany, and even the United States during and after Abraham Lincoln's administration, these countries were more unified than China and none was run by an alien government as in China.

Nor did China possess the consensus, at least at the top of the political hierarchy, to make the hard choices that any modernizing country requires. Therefore the argument that business could benefit from government investments in infrastructure and in businesses mistakenly assumed public and private (or different government agencies or different businesses) were on the same modernization page or at least in the same book. Usually businesses were subjected to endless arbitrary government interference and exploitation. The China Merchant Steam Navigation Company is a case in point. Partly funded by the government, it enjoyed a monopoly on the shipment of tax rice. But it was also required to provide free transportation for government troops and to accept political appointees. In the end, the irreconcilable conflicts between the company's business requirements and the government's capricious demands kept the company constantly on the verge of bankruptcy.

The Self-Strengthening Movement also involved some reform in government. China established a Foreign Office in the central government to handle foreign affairs (often termed "barbarian affairs"). In addition to diplomatic activities, these affairs included Imperial Customs to collect import duties and a school to teach Western languages and translate Western books. The government also sent Chinese teenagers to the United States in the 1870s to receive a complete American education. The potential benefits of these reforms were minimized by both Manchu and Chinese officials. A good example of both the tangible and restricted impact of Western-educated Chinese in Self-Strengthening can be seen in the career of Yung Wing.

Rong Hong (aka Yung Wing, 1828–1912) has been called the "pioneer of pioneers" in building a bridge between America and China. He was born into an impoverished peasant family, enrolled into a missionary school, was brought to America by an American mission-ary-teacher, and became the first Chinese to graduate from an American college, Yale University, in 1854. He married an American lady, had two boys, and spent the rest of his life traveling between China and the United States to promote trade and educational exchange.

He joined Zeng Guofan's staff in 1863 and played an important role as Zeng launched his trailblazing projects to build a modern arsenal and to send Chinese students to study at American schools. He led the first group of Chinese students to America in 1872. The plan anticipated that these boys would return to China with a Western education to work with the Qing government in the diplomatic, military, and financial-economic areas.

Zeng and his successor Li Hongzhang came under intense pressure from conservatives to terminate the mission. The reasons were many. The cost to the Chinese government was high, the boys were enthusiastically embracing American ways and values, and clashes between the students and their conservative guardians were frequent. But the last straw was not the cultural tensions, but the American government's refusal to admit Chinese students into its military academies. Zeng and Li could not defend the high cost of the mission if the students could not receive a military education in America. The boys were recalled in 1881.

Rong Hong was a staunch supporter of reform and later revolution in China. He took a strong interest in the Taiping movement, and in his old age he actively supported Sun Yat-sen's republican revolution.

He lived out his life as a "marginal man." In America he faced strong racial discrimination, and in China he was shunned by high-level scholar-officials because he lacked a traditional Chinese education. He died in lonely poverty in America.

China's lopsided defeat in the First Sino-Japanese War of 1894–1895 brought an abrupt end to the Self-Strengthening Movement. The successful modernization movement in Meiji Japan had begun at roughly the same time as the Self-Strengthening Movement. Militarily speaking, the war clearly indicated that China's modernization efforts did not measure up.

The war originated in a struggle between China and Japan over how to keep Tsarist Russia out of Korea. China regarded Korea as a protectorate, while Japan viewed it as a security threat if Russia ever took control there, only a hundred or so miles from the Japanese homeland. Japan tended to back Korean reformers, China more traditionalist Koreans. Both Beijing and Tokyo had troops and advisors in Korea. Since China proved incapable of keeping aggressive Westerners out of China, Meiji leaders finally concluded that pushing the Chinese out of the peninsula gave Japan a stronger likelihood of keeping the Russians out. When domestic disturbances erupted in Korea in 1894, both China and Japan sent soldiers, but Japan seized the opportunity to launch a surprise attack on China's troops. A modernized Japan routed China's military and forced them out of Korea, and in naval engagements wiped out China's navy. The one-sided conflict lasted less than a year, and in the ensuing peace settlement, the Treaty of Shimonoseki, China agreed to give up its suzerain position in Korea, to cede Taiwan to Japan, and to pay an astronomical amount in reparations. The following year, Japan acquired most-favored-nation status, obtaining all the privileges that the Western power had in China. Tokyo now had a "sphere of influence" in Korea, Taiwan, and part of China's northeast, Manchuria.

The failure of the Self-Strengthening Movement became apparent to China's leadership, but what was to be done to stem the growing Western and Japanese assaults on China? Defeat and humiliation in the war and treaty settlement with Japan exposed to foreign powers how weak and vulnerable the country really was. Britain, France, and Russia took their cue from Japan and scrambled to obtain their own "spheres of influence." The United States was still preoccupied with consolidating its hold on its Philippine colony. Fearful that Europe and Japan would carve out spheres of influence in China, leaving nothing for America, Washington proposed an "Open Door" policy in 1899. It stipulated that every power in China grant equal commercial opportunity to all foreign powers in each sphere of influence. Since America had no sphere of influence, it would still have access to Chinese markets regardless of which nation controlled any part of China.

Although the foreign nations in China remained jointly competitive, each came to realize that no single foreign power was strong enough to take control of all of China. And because there would be many spheres of influence in tense coexistence, it would be in everyone's interest to accept America's Open Door proposal. A tentative alliance among the powers, it was concluded, had a much better chance of maximizing the various national interests in China, particularly when dealing with an imperial Chinese government in disarray and a leadership debating disparate courses of action the nation might take.

As the nineteenth century concluded, an alarm bell was sounding across China. The clarion call to "Save China" reverberated across the land. A new generation of thinkers, activists, and organizers emerged to meet the foreign challenge. The "Chinese values, Western means" of the Self-Strengthening Movement had failed and needed to be replaced by something more promising. China was awash in people with policies to save China: traditionalist Confucians, radical reforming Confucians, and revolutionary nationalists to name the most prominent. These likely future leaders had two principal models of development: the Anglo-American model of capitalism and democracy,

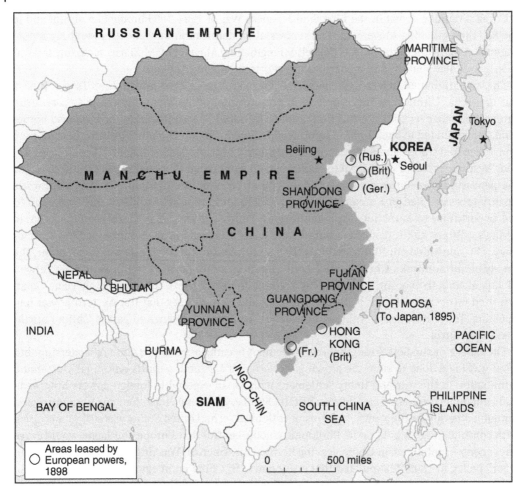

Domestic and foreign troubles in China, circa 1850–1914; names in Wade-Giles Romanization. *Source:* Adapted from Times Books.

and the authoritarian statist model of Germany and Japan. By the end of World War I, the totalitarian model of communism emerged in the Soviet Union after the Russian Revolution in 1917.

The process of China's modernization, heretofore underway with baby steps, moved more quickly toward more radical nostrums. The search for some consensus on a Chinese model of modernization, still ongoing, has been fraught with knotty issues and agonizing choices. As China entered the twentieth century, its leaders experimented with major reforms as the dynasty collapsed, attempted revolution with republican characteristics, and struggled with communism under several interpreters of the doctrine. It remains a work in progress. The first of these began in the wake of the First Sino-Japanese War.

The Imperial Hundred Days of Reform in 1898

A small group of scholars convinced the Emperor Guangxu (1871–1908; r. 1875–1908) to launch a major reform movement on June 11, 1898. It was put down on September 22 by Dowager Empress Cixi (1835–1908), the emperor's aunt and the power behind the throne. The Han Chinese group was led by Kang Youwei and included scholars Liang Qichao and Tan Sitong. Along with the emperor, the group put forth a plan to reorganize the country along the lines of Japan's successful Meiji Restoration in 1868 and the country's highly effective modernization program.

Kang Youwei (1858–1927) was an accomplished Confucian scholar with a smattering of knowledge of the West, and he advocated a new form of government. His inspiration came from Russian Tsar Peter the Great and the Japanese Meiji Restoration. Kang also argued forcefully for institutional reform, the creation of a constitutional monarchy to replace China's absolutist monarchy, and popular participation in political decision making. During the imperial examinations in 1885, Kang rallied 1300 exam takers to write an open letter to the emperor pleading for reform, another example of a long tradition of student protest. That specific letter never reached the emperor, but later letters did.

Persuaded by Kang's eloquence, Emperor Guangxu decided to adopt his proposals in 1898. The emperor issued a flurry of edicts ordering sweeping reforms. They included the elimination of the eight-legged essay from imperial exams, the establishment of Western-style schools, the writing of books and the translation of Western books, and the freedom to publish private newspapers and to form associations. The government was tasked to encourage the establishment of banks, railways, a postal service, and modern enterprise. Glaringly absent from the list of reforms was any mention of a constitution or a representative legislature. The Hundred Days of Reform lasted 103 days, put down by Dowager Empress Cixi. Kang and Liang found immediate asylum in foreign legations, but Tan was killed. The emperor ended up under house arrest until his death. Two years later, in the wake of the ill-fated Boxer Rebellion, Cixi launched even more radical reforms.

The reform movement from the top down proved short-lived, but its impact was significant. Unlike the Self-Strengthening Movement, which clung to traditional Chinese values and institutions, the Hundred Days of Reform aimed at institutional and systemic restructuring. Leading reformers had come to realize Western wealth and military might resulted from Western political, social, and economic systems that fostered national development. China could not expect to become rich and powerful unless it substantially modified its culture sufficiently to move beyond values based on an agricultural social order to one supportive of an industrial nation. If China's traditional culture could not protect the nation, then the imperial foreign presence would impose cultural adjustments to suit their needs. Better, most Chinese patriots argued, that China oversee whatever change was necessary than the foreigners. The pot of intellectual discourse was boiling. Printing houses turned out a flood of books and periodicals covering a wide range of subjects. These included writings on not only science and technology but also Western political and educational thinking. Hot topics of discussion even involved social practices such as opium smoking, women's foot-binding, and men's long braided hair.

The Boxer Rebellion and Foreign Intervention, 1900

Emperor Guangxu's efforts at reform by edict from the top failed, but rebellion from the bottom up was percolating. Now that the Chinese populace in general felt that the foreign powers wanted to dismember China, a general xenophobia burst forth. Chinese became increasingly fearful and hateful of foreigners or anything foreign. The Boxer Rebellion (officially from November 2, 1899, to September 7, 1901) reflected this sentiment.

The Boxer Rebellion represented a new round of grassroots upheaval. The Boxers got their name from the kind of traditional martial arts that they practiced, which included secret rituals and chanted incantations. They believed that such practices made them invulnerable to any attack by sword or gun. The movement had its roots in the White Lotus Sect, which was a secret peasant society that was active during the Yuan and Ming Dynasties. After the Manchu conquest of China, their goal was the overthrow of the alien Manchu Qing regime. But by the end of the nineteenth century, their hatred for the foreign powers exceeded their hatred of the Qing rulers. Their hatred of Christianity had extended to its missionaries, churches, and Chinese converts. They burned Western books and schools and even destroyed Western-style matches and pencils. Their attacks on Christian missionaries and churches simply continued a trend of violence extending back to the First Opium War.

The rebellion spread like wildfire across parts of northeast China, stretching from Shandong Province west and north to the outskirts of Beijing. As the Boxers neared the capital, the Empress Dowager Cixi made an opportunistic judgment. Believing that she could use the Boxers against the foreigners, she gave the Boxers permission to enter the capital city to lay siege to the foreign legations and ordered Chinese troops to join them. The Boxers adjusted their strategy accordingly. They abandoned their earlier dual goal of fighting both the "Manchu aliens" and the "ocean devils," and instead focused on the single goal of destroying the foreigners. The Beijing portion of the rebellion lasted from the spring through summer of 1900.

Under the siege, the foreign powers united to form an Eight-Power Expeditionary Force, which included warships, marines, and ground forces. It captured Beijing, lifted the two-month siege, rescued foreign diplomats and nationals, and proceeded to loot the city. The Empress Dowager fled her Forbidden City and paid the price of her Boxer escapade. Again defeated in war, China signed under extreme duress the Boxer Protocol in September 1901. The concessions included the same kinds of terms and reparations as earlier treaties and protocols, but now China had to swallow a new humiliation—the Protocol granted the foreign powers the right to station troops in Beijing indefinitely. There most remained until the onset of World War II in China in 1937.

The Boxer Rebellion turned out to be largely disastrous. Mobs, whipped into xenophobic hysteria, committed many atrocities. Some historical structures, including the surviving portions of the Imperial Garden, were destroyed by vandals. A few dilapidated walls and cracked pillars stand forlorn today in testimony to its onetime magnificence. The behavior of the Empress Dowager and her Boxer minions can be partially explained by their ignorance and by foreign provocation. But it also demonstrated the danger for rulers to play with the ignorant passions of mobs. Mao Zedong would do the same a half-century later, bringing policy failure to himself and catastrophe to the nation.

Yet the Boxer Rebellion may have produced some positive outcomes. It apparently convinced foreign powers that China was too large, too homogeneous, and too militant to colonize like India. As well, the American and British portions of the monetary indemnity contained in the Boxer Protocol were used by America and Great Britain to fund Chinese students studying in their respective countries. The rebellion also ended moderate attempts to preserve Confucian ideas and institutions in the world of Darwinian international relations. Henceforth Manchu and Han Chinese leadership opted for radical reform or revolution as the best means of protecting the Chinese nation.

Empress Dowager Cixi's Reforms and the End of Dynastic Government, 1900–1911

The leadership consensus for substantial change is best exemplified in the reforms of Cixi. The *Xinzheng* (new government or new administration or new policies), launched in 1901, included an array of institutional innovations or changes designed to protect the dynasty and the nation. So began a serious attempt at state building. Between 1901 and Cixi's death in 1908, government administrations at the central, provincial, and local levels were created that included assemblies at each level. Clearly the court and leading Han Chinese officials such as Li Hongzhang had concluded that China needed what Liang Qichao had been preaching from his Japanese exile: a new

(Chinese) citizen. Absolutist monarchies throughout the millennia ruled over subjects, not citizens. Citizens participated, in some fashion, in government. In Liang's mind, citizenship was an essential ingredient in state building. Among the many global governmental systems studied by reformers, the German and Japanese models of authoritarian constitutional government seemed most suitable for China. Of course, many political activists considered mere reform insufficient to China's needs, the prime example being revolutionary Sun Yat-sen.

Empress Dowager Cixi. *Source:* GL Archive/Alamy Stock Photo.

Educational reform began in 1901 with the creation of new, Western-style schools with modern curricula. Instead of the Confucian classics, innovative schools taught new subjects such as physics, chemistry, mathematics, and a new version of Chinese history that would, down the road, serve as a vehicle for nationalist and anti-imperialistic sentiments. The civil service examination, so much a part of China's elite educational past, was abolished in 1905. Henceforth government officials would be selected from new-school graduates. In addition to government promoting national and local educational goals, voluntary associations involved in education and other social undertakings also contributed both to the advancement of knowledge and to popular participation in community and government activities.

A serious attempt at social improvement also became one of Cixi's major reforms. The court launched an anti-opium movement in 1906 in the hope of eliminating the production, distribution, and consumption of the drug. China, then the world's largest producer of opium, would sacrifice the enormous domestic profits from the drug. The domestic opium operation enriched growers, distributors, and government officials, and largely financed China's military and other modernization projects. Perhaps then Britain, then the largest opium trader to China, would reciprocate and halt importation.[2] Much success could be seen in the early years, but the failure to mobilize the people in this effort, the death of the Empress Dowager, and then the collapse of the dynasty and the onset of warlordism ultimately doomed the project.

Li Hongzhang. *Source:* FLHC3/Alamy Stock Photo.

One of the most important of the post-Boxer modernization projects was the building of a capable military. Some of the Self-Strengthening activities in the late nineteenth century involved military modernization, and the person most associated with this effort was Yuan Shikai (1859–1916). Yuan joined the Huai Army, which was formed by Li Hongzhang to put down the Taiping Rebellion, and as a junior officer in one of its units he was sent to Korea in 1882. A palace struggle at the time was underway between Korean conservatives and liberals, and China supported the more conservative faction to counter Japan's support for the liberal bloc. By 1885 Yuan became Qing China's Imperial Resident in Korea and was there when the First Sino-Japanese War began. In 1895 Li charged Yuan

2 Thomas D. Reins, "Reform, Nationalism and Internationalism: The Opium Suppression Movement in China and the Anglo-American Influence, 1900–1908," *Modern Asian Studies* 25, no. 1 (1991): 114–124.

with training what became the Beiyang (Northern Ocean) Army and Navy, and Yuan concurrently held several important central government positions. As commander of military forces, Yuan sided with Cixi and against the Emperor Guangxu and put down the Hundred Days of Reform. As governor of Shandong Province where the Boxers originated, Yuan drove the rebels out of the province and did not allow his soldiers to engage the Eight-Power Expeditionary Force.

Upon the death of Li Hongzhang in 1901, Yuan became the most significant of Han Chinese leaders in the Manchu government. He would remain such until the death of Cixi in November 1908, when a three-year-old prince became Emperor Pu Yi. The young emperor's father, now the young boy-emperor's regent, detested Yuan for having betrayed the Hundred Days of Reform, a betrayal that resulted in the Emperor Guangxu being kept under house arrest until his death. Yuan was abruptly fired, but three years later the Manchu leadership called him back to service. The Qing court wanted Yuan to take control of the military he largely created, and its commanders whom he largely selected, in order to put down several provincial uprisings. Major reforms frequently produce unexpected and unwanted consequences. In less than a year, Yuan turned on the Manchus, setting the stage for the October 10, 1911, Republican Revolution and ending more than two millennia of imperial government. China continues to search for a replacement.

Selected Readings and Viewings

Marie-Claire Bergère, *Sun Yat-sen* (Stanford, CA: Stanford University Press, 2000).

Lloyd E. Eastman, *Throne and Mandarins: China's Search for a Policy during the Sino-French Controversy, 1880–1885* (Cambridge, MA: Harvard University Press, 1967).

Joseph W. Esherick, *The Origins of the Boxer Uprising* (Berkeley: University of California Press, 1988).

Stephen A. MacKinnon, *Power and Politics in Late Imperial China: Yuan Shikai in Beijing and Tianjin, 1901–1908* (Berkeley: University of California Press, 1981).

Joyce A. Madancy, *The Troublesome Legacy of Commissioner Lin: The Opium Trade and Opium Suppression in Fujian Province, 1820s to 1920s* (Cambridge, MA: Harvard University Press, 2004).

Once Upon a Time in China (1991), dir. by Tsui Hark.

S. C. M. Paine, *The Sino-Japanese War of 1894–1895: Perceptions, Power, and Primacy* (Cambridge: Cambridge University Press, 2005).

Edward J. M. Rhoads, *Stepping Forth into the World: The Chinese Educational Mission to the United States, 1872–1881* (Hong Kong: Hong Kong University Press, 2011).

Jonathan D. Spence, *God's Chinese Son: The Taiping Heavenly Kingdom of Hong Xiuquan* (New York: W. W. Norton, 1996).

Xiaobing Tang, *Global Space and the Nationalist Discourse of Modernity: The Historical Thinking of Liang Qichao* (Stanford, CA: Stanford University Press, 1996).

Mary C. Wright, *The Last Stand of Chinese Conservatism: The Tung-Chih [Tongzhi] Restoration, 1862–1874*, 3rd ed. (New York: Atheneum, 1969).

16

The Birth of Republicanism in China, 1911–1949

[W]e are being crushed by the economic strength of the Powers to a greater degree than if we were a full colony. China is not the colony of one nation but of all.... I think we ought to be called a "hypo-colony."

—Sun Yat-sen (Sun Zhongshan)[1]

The Republican Revolution (1911) and the Founding of the Republic of China (1912)

On October 10, 1911, the New Army's revolution-leaning soldiers and officers shocked the world with an armed uprising in Nanchang in central China. People in other parts of the country rallied to the call of the insurgents, and turned against the Manchu Qing monarchy. The overripe dynasty, weak and rotten to the core, fell without putting up a fight. Representatives from 17 provinces gathered in Nanjing to form a new Provisional Government in 1911. It represented a hodgepodge of political forces with no clear structure or leadership. But one man stood out: Sun Zhongshan (aka Dr. Sun Yat-sen, 1866–1925).

Dr. Sun Yat-sen/Sun Zhongshan (1866–1925). *Source:* Art Collection 2 / Alamy Stock Photo.

1 Quoted in David B. Gordon, *Sun Yatsen: Seeking a Newer China* (Boston: Prentice Hall, 2010), p. 44. Sun viewed China as a nation divided by clan, region, dialect, and other identities that made the country easy pickings for the industrial powers. National identity would be the foundation for China's revival.

Asia Past and Present: A Brief History, First Edition. Peter P. Wan and Thomas D. Reins.
© 2021 John Wiley & Sons, Inc. Published 2021 by John Wiley & Sons, Inc.

Timeline for Republican China, 1912–1949

1911	Wuchang Uprising deposes Qing Dynasty and China's dynastic system
1912	Sun Yat-sen/Sun Zhongshan elected First Provisional President of the Republic of China (ROC); he has no army, thus no power
1912	Pu Yi, the last Qing Dynasty emperor, abdicates; Yuan Shikai becomes president
1915	Japan imposes Twenty-One Demands on China; United States and Great Britain protest
1915	Yuan Shikai attempts to restore monarchy
1915	New Culture Movement begins
1916	Yuan Shikai dies; warlordism begins
1919	May 4th Movement symbolizes the emergence of Chinese nationalism
1919	Treaty of Versailles awards China's Qingdao/Tsingtao to Japan
1921–1922	Washington Conference: China gets Qingdao back; Anglo-Japanese Alliance of 1902 ends; naval disarmament deal means Japan will dominate the seas of East Asia
1921	Chinese Communist Party (CCP) founded in Shanghai
1923–1927	Soviet Russia brokers the First United Front between Guomindang (GMD) and CCP
1924	Whampoa Military Academy established
1925	Sun Yat-sen dies; National Revolutionary Army created
1926–1928	Northern Expedition launched under Jiang Jieshi/Chiang Kai-shek to destroy the warlords and unite China
1927	After the Northern Expedition takes Shanghai, Jiang turns on CCP
1929	China regains tariff autonomy
1929	Depression begins, and shortly thereafter the nascent German and Japanese democracies will collapse
1931–1933	Japan attacks and eventually colonizes Manchuria under the puppet emperor Pu Yi; League of Nations doesn't recognize Japan's move
1935–1945	Popular Front begins, with Stalin allowing national communist parties to downplay communism and emphasize nationalism
1936	Xian Incident: Jiang Jieshi held hostage by General Zhang Xueliang; CCP envoy Zhou Enlai works out the creation of the Second United Front (1937–1945) between GMD and CCP
1937	World War II begins when Japan attacks China (July 7, 1937); Rape of Nanjing begins that December
1939	Nazi–Soviet Pact completed; World War II begins
1940	Matsuoka–Henri wagreement allows Japanese military access to French Indochina
1941	Japan attacks Pearl Harbor; America declares war on Japan
1941–1945	America supports China with war matériel via India to Kunming
1943	America repeals Chinese Exclusion Act
1945–1949	End of the Second United Front; beginning of the GMD/CCP civil war
1945–1991	Cold War between Soviet Russia and the United States
1949	CCP under Mao Zedong/Mao Tse-tung defeats Jiang and GMD; Mao "leans to one side" and joins the Soviet camp, at least for a while

Born in China, Sun lived in the United States, and drew his support from largely Chinese students and intellectuals at home and overseas. (The term "intellectuals" in Chinese usage is loosely applied to those who have received a postsecondary education, including teachers and professors, doctors, engineers, journalist, lawyers, etc.). But he had a long history of conducting fundraising in America and instigating revolutionary propaganda and agitation among the lower ranks of the New Army, and in traditional secret peasant societies, bandit groups, and the floating populations. He had a well-established reputation as a strong advocate and supporter of republicanism and armed uprisings against the Qing government. His political philosophy can best be seen in the Three Principles of the People, consisting of Nationalism, Democracy, and the People's Livelihood (land reform). His call to revolution was "Expel the aliens (the Manchus and foreign powers); Restore Han China; Establish a republic; Equalize land ownership."

The delegates to the Provisional Government gathered in Nanjing and elected Sun "Provisional President" of the Provisional Government. But his choice, ironically, resulted as much from his weakness as from his strength. For the old pattern of power struggle had reasserted itself: a rash of power centers had emerged following the collapse of the Qing government, and under such circumstances, only a leader with a strong military base had any chance of taking control. The fact that Sun had no direct control of any armed forces, nor did he even have strong ties to any political forces inside China, made him unthreatening, and therefore an ideal compromise candidate. But it also destined him to the role of a transitional figure.

Yuan Shikai was a military strongman. He was the Qing government's prime minister, commander-in-chief of its military forces, and the founder of the New Army. Taking advantage of the power vacuum left in the wake of the collapse of the Qing regime, Yuan seized control of the military and the civil government in Beijing and demanded that Sun resign and support him as president. It was commonly believed that civil war would break out if Sun refused to accept Yuan's terms, and that in turn would give foreign powers an excuse for intervention. Sun capitulated and resigned; in return, Yuan declared his commitment to upholding the republic and was sworn in as President of the Republic, giving him the distinction of being China's first elected president. He set up a National Congress and used the army, took bribes, and sanctioned assassinations to suppress opposition. In the meantime, Sun organized the Nationalist Party (aka Guomindang [GMD] or Kuomintang [KMT]) to compete in Yuan's National Congress.

The outbreak of World War I complicated Yuan's tenure in office. China was divided over whether or not to join the war effort on the allied side. Japan was already involved on the allied side and had taken Germany's leasehold in Shandong, and Tokyo wanted to expand its influence in China. This was best exemplified in the 1915 Twenty-One Demands Japan made on China. With European nations chiefly concerned with the conflict at home and given Japan's major contributions to the allied war effort—neutralizing Germany in Asia and the Pacific, and moving manpower and war matériel from Asia and Africa to the Middle East and Europe—Tokyo assumed it could expand its influence in China without too much European opposition.

Japan's **Twenty-One Demands**, presented to China in early 1915, was a plan to turn China into a Japanese colonial protectorate. The document included confirmation of Japan's recent acquisition of Germany's sphere of influence in China, and the expansion of Japan's sphere of influence in Manchuria and Inner Mongolia. It demanded the right for Japan to appoint Japanese advisors to the Chinese central government, and control the Chinese police force. It would also bar China from giving additional coastal or island concessions to Western powers.

Yuan needed Japan's aid and support for his bid for the throne, so he succumbed to Japanese pressure and accepted certain portions of the treaty. Western powers acquiesced despite Japan's expansion in defiance of the Open Door Policy. The signing of Japan's Twenty-One Demands was seen by the Chinese as a national humiliation, and led to an unprecedented outburst of anti-Japanese sentiment.

Not satisfied with being president or that republicanism was feasible, Yuan proclaimed himself emperor in 1915. His attempt to turn back the hands of the clock backfired. Protests broke out across the country. Military commanders, provincial governors, assemblies, and public opinion leaders rushed to denounce him as a traitor to the cause of republicanism. Various provinces declared their independence, some going as far as to declare war on his regime. Yuan died a broken man in three months, launching more than two decades of warlordism. A century later China still searches for a consensus on just what constitutes the nation's acceptable form of government.

Yuan Shikai (1859–1916). *Source:* Hum Images / Alamy Stock Photo.

Warlordism (1916–1928)

Yuan's death left a power vacuum no one could fill. The government he had headed continued to claim to be the national government of all China, but real power was scattered in the hands of regional warlords. The age-old pattern of disunity after the fall of a dynasty had reasserted itself. China found itself in yet another period of warlordism: There was no single military strongman who could dominate a country bristling with many regional warlords supported by various foreign powers. Warlordism spelled disaster. Their governments were thoroughly corrupt, repressive, and ineffective. They engaged in endlessly shifting alliances and bloody battles. To satisfy their immediate need and greed, they levied taxes decades in advance.

Ironically, this decade of warlordism was also a time of economic growth, intellectual blossoming, and commercial expansion. Decentralized warlord governments were weak. The power of Western nations in China was also weaker than it had been, for they were preoccupied with their life-and-death struggle on the battlefields of Europe in World War I, and had no choice but to loosen their grip on China. Facing reduced Western competition, Chinese merchants and industrialists began building up their own enterprises. And with weak government control, an intellectual discourse known as the New Culture Movement exploded onto the Chinese scene in 1915. The hottest topics of discussion focused on Western ideas and their applicability to China. Modern art and literature thrived. And these activities usually took place in the "Concessions," those sections of a city dominated by foreign powers where there was more freedom of speech and publication. Such cities as Shanghai, Guangzhou, Hankou, and Tianjin were among the most active. This brief period of intellectual blossoming was reminiscent of the "Hundred Flowers" period in ancient China, a time that Chinese still think of with nostalgia today. New Culture thinking exploded onto the scene with the May 4th Movement.

The May 4th Movement (1919)

The victors of World War I held the Paris Peace Conference and signed the Treaty of Versailles in 1919. Although China attended the conference as a member of the victorious allies, they were not included in the big five—Great Britain, France, Italy, the United States, and Japan—who bore the preponderance of the war burden. In consequence, three of the other victors (the United States, Great Britain, and France) decided to turn over to a fourth victor, Japan, defeated Germany's pre-war sphere of influence in China, namely Qingdao/Tsingtao.

Philosopher Hu Shi (1891–1962).

When news of this outrageous injustice reached Beijing, it set off a firestorm of popular protests. Peking University students, as was their tradition, spearheaded the protests. They first gathered on campus, and then took to the streets. Street demonstrations spread like wildfire across the country as city after city responded in solidarity. They were especially intense at such major cities as Shanghai, Guangzhou, Nanjing, and Wuhan. As the movement gathered momentum, its ranks swelled to include not only students but also educated people in general and even industrial workers. Japan was the primary target, and a nationwide boycott was aimed at Japanese goods. Other foreign powers and the Chinese government were not spared either. Since the protest started in Beijing on May 4th, it became known as the May 4th Movement.

The May 4th Movement was a multifaceted undertaking. As a political movement, it targeted traditional Chinese ills, as well as the contemporary Chinese warlord governments and foreign powers in China. Culturally, it raised the daring and all-embracing slogan "Smash Confucianism!," called for science and democracy, and demonstrated a strong sense of modern nationalism and patriotism.

It crusaded for a New Culture that would belong to the common people. And in that spirit, it advocated the replacement of *wenyanwen* (an elitist classics style of writing) with *baihuawen* (a popular style of writing based on vernacular Chinese). It believed that *baihuawen* would make education more accessible to the common people. (The battle between Latin and English in Early Modern England represents a similar case.) The May 4th Movement found its voice in the journal *New Youth*. Chen Duxiu (1879–1942) was its editor, and Li Dazhao (1889–1927) contributed radical articles; both were Peking University professors and strongly influenced by the Russian Communist Revolution of 1917. With help from the Soviet Union Communist Party, they became leaders in the founding of the Chinese Communist Party (CCP) in Shanghai (1921). Not all May 4th protestors and their supporters were communists.

Lu Xun (1881–1936) is generally acknowledged as the most profound writer of modern Chinese literature. He studied medicine in Japan briefly, but quit when he became convinced that the Chinese were more in need of having their souls saved than their bodies treated, and that he had a better chance of doing it through literature.

In his novelette *A Madman's Diary*, he describes traditional Confucian Chinese society as a "feast where humans eat humans." The short story "Kong Yiji" portrays an unsuccessful Confucian scholar who has no way of making a living and no moral fortitude, and who dies and is totally forgotten. His novelette "The True Story of Ah Q" tells the story of a farmhand who lives and dies in subjection, ignorance, and prejudice. It is an unflinching critique of what the author sees as baseness in the Chinese character. His fictional writings embrace universal themes with a profound sense of despair.

Lu Xun's essays are openly political. With caustic satire, he pulls no punches in his attacks on warlord regimes and Jiang Jieshi's (Chiang Kai-shek's) government. Mysteriously, he never touches on the subject of Japanese aggression and atrocities. As well his relationship with the CCP was a difficult one. Although he was a leading figure in the left-wing literary movement, he never joined the CCP. His closest friends and associates would later all be purged by Mao.

May Fourth intellectuals laid the foundation for a broad agenda that would banish tradition, defeat the warlords, and oust the foreigners, the necessary preconditions for finding a consensus on how best to modernize China. Lu Xun, a leftist, wrote his renowned novelette *A Madman's Diary* as a criticism of traditional Chinese culture. He wrote in the vernacular *baihuawen*, not the classical *wenyanwen*. Hu Shi took his inspiration from Western liberalism and would evolve into a leading public intellectual. They were also professors in Peking. Mao Zedong (1893–1976) made his political debut in 1918 by forming a communist studies group in Hunan Province, his birthplace. Both the GMD and CCP claimed to be the guardian of the holy grail of the May 4th Movement, but neither would allow intellectual freedom when they came to power.

The Chinese Nationalist Party (GMD) and Chinese Communist Party (CCP)

Sun Zhongshan faced a China that was divided up by regional warlords. He concluded that he had to go the route of military conquest in order to achieve his goal of a reunified China with a republican form of government. But he controlled no military; warlords and foreign powers controlled all the armies, and they weren't sympathetic to his cause. He had few allies and was left forlorn to wander in a political wilderness.

But the Guangdong Military Government invited him to be their nominal leader in 1919, and then the Russian Communist Party sent a representative to offer its assistance. Russia had lost some of its clout in China after World War I. Its own Bolshevik communist revolution in 1917 removed the Tsarist government but also led to a four-year domestic struggle with Russian anticommunists. Both Bolshevik leader Vladimir Lenin and his ultimate successor Josef Stalin believed their emerging Soviet Union could reasonably expect to recreate a presence in China if it was smart enough to pick and support the future winner of the present chaotic scramble for power there. It placed its bet on Sun, his GMD, and the Guangdong Military Government. Responding to the Russian offer, Sun revised his "Three Principles of the People" to include three new policies in 1924: "Unite with Soviet Russia," "Unite with the Chinese Communists," and "Nurture the peasants and workers." He put Russian advisors on his staff, reorganized his Nationalist Party on the model of the Russian Communist Party, allowed CCP members to join the Nationalist Party as individuals, and established Huangpu Military Academy. This was the first GMD–CCP cooperation, officially known as the First GMD-CCP United Front (1924–1927). Sun's position improved, but he died in 1925.

Chiang Kai-shek/Jiang Jieshi/Jiang Zhongzheng (1887–1975). *Source:* colaimages / Alamy Stock Photo.

Jiang Jieshi succeeded Sun and consolidated his control over the GMD by virtue of his close relationship to Sun and his command of the GMD army; Jiang had been Sun's right-hand man and the commandant of Huangpu Military Academy. This enabled him to defeat the left wing of the GMD and eventually take full control of a reorganized GMD Party with 200,000 members, a party-controlled army of 10,000 strong, and the Huangpu Military Academy that had graduated several thousand officers. He then proceeded to begin the reunification of the country. In 1927, as the commander-in-chief of the newly organized National Revolutionary Army, Jiang set out from Guangzhou on the Northern Expedition and successfully captured Nanjing and Shanghai. By the time his forces arrived in Shanghai that year, he then turned on the CCP, his other significant political competition.

Jiang had worried about the growing strength of the CCP within his party. Taking advantage of the United Front, the CCP had acquired a legitimate arena in which to grow and gather strength. Jiang watched them and their Russian advisors with increasing suspicion. He became convinced that they were plotting to overthrow him, and he cautiously maneuvered to reduce their influence. After his capture of Shanghai on the Northern Expedition, he sprang a sudden coup d'état on them, killing large numbers of CCP members and their followers in a bloodbath. The first GMD–CCP joint venture had come to a bloody end. Because the CCP leadership continued to follow Stalin's advice to take the cities where the working class resided, the CCP was nearly completely eradicated. Not until the mid-1930s did that leadership change, henceforth focusing on peasants and their emerging nationalist ardor.

Jiang and the Republic of China: The Nanjing Decade (1928–1937)

Jiang continued his Northern Expedition until he captured Beijing (meaning "Northern Capital") in 1928, renaming it Beiping ("Northern Peace"). He reestablished the Republic of China (ROC) with Nanjing ("Southern Capital") as its capital. The GMD gave its name to the new Nationalist Government, and Jiang became its president. By now he had defeated most of the warlords in South China, and gained nominal submission of those in other parts of the country. Most of the foreign powers had recognized the ROC as the legitimate government representing all of China. Therefore, at least nominally, warlordism had come to an end, and Jiang became the head of a more unified China. He was now the new embodiment of Chinese nationalism. But his coup d'état against the CCP had led to a rupture between the two major political parties and launched a 10-year civil war.

Jiang was in power, but his hold on power was tenuous. The jurisdiction of his government did not reach beyond coastal China and the middle and lower reaches of the Yangtze River. His support came mainly from Chinese businesspeople in treaty ports, landowners in the countryside, and foreign powers. Many regions were still under de facto warlord control, local authority remained in the hands of powerful local landed families, and foreign powers still enjoyed many privileges they had wrested from the Qing government. Nonetheless, Jiang had a close working relationship with America and Britain given that all were fearful of an expansionist Japan. Gradually, China under Jiang would begin to gain back rights lost to the foreigners, the first in 1929 being tariff autonomy, which China had lost during the Taiping Rebellion.

The "peasant problem" has always been China's most pressing problem. Peasants made up over 90% of the population, their most urgent demand was for land, and Sun had advocated land reform to give land to the tillers of the land. But Jiang could not carry out land reform for fear of eroding the tenuous support he had among the landed gentry, the warlords, and the foreign powers. This left Jiang too weak to push Sun's revolutionary agenda any further. Without any kind of land reform, Sun's economic revolution was withering on Jiang's vine, and Jiang was painfully aware of it.

Jiang concluded that only a dictatorship could save China. For a state ideology, he adopted the Nazi principle of "one state, one leader, one party, and one military." He already controlled the GMD Party, so he appointed its members to all critical positions in the government to cement his control over the government. He hired German military advisors to reorganize and expand his army into a modernized fighting force of 300,000 strong. He used the secret Blue Shirts, obviously named after Hitler's Brown Shirts and Mussolini's Black Shirts, against underground communists and critics of his regime. He appointed Huangpu graduates to head the military and the secret services, counting on their personal loyalty to him. This restructuring gave him all the essentials of a dictatorship. For economic development, he turned to the Anglo-American model. He successfully built some railroads, some industrial plants, a modern banking system, and a modern educational system. He launched the New Life Movement in 1934 to modernize society with a few Western ideas and practices, such as personal hygiene, and a heavy dose of Confucianism.

However, his Nanjing regime was under two constant threats: The domestic threat came from Mao Zedong and his CCP, and the foreign threat came from Japan. Mao Zedong (1893–1976) was a minor player in the founding of the CCP, fled Shanghai after Jiang's bloody purge, and established a revolutionary base in the tough terrain of Jinggangshan in Jiangxi Province in southeastern China. He had a deep understanding of the Chinese peasantry and their age-old craving for land, and he would mobilize support for his regime with the promise of land reform. For the next three decades, he would manipulate the peasantry with various land reform policies to win their support, and it would always work.

Crowned with the title of "Generalissimo," Jiang launched five military campaigns to "Encircle and Annihilate" Mao's Communist base (the Jiangxi Soviet) in Jinggangshan, Jiangxi province. On the fifth try, with help from his Nazi German military advisors, he routed the Communists and eliminated their base. Mao and his followers in 1934 then fled along a zigzag course, the Long March, with the GMD troops in pursuit. Mao eventually managed to re-entrench himself at Yan'an on the bone-dry loess plateau of China's impoverished Northwest, where Jiang kept an encirclement around him.

The Long March (1934–1936). After military defeat, Mao was chased from his base in Jinggangshan, and began to flee on foot with Jiang's troops in pursuit. It was a difficult march, especially since they had to cross rushing rivers, snow-capped mountains, and vast stretches of marshy grassland. When they finally arrived at Yan'an over a year later, after covering 6000 miles, only 10 percent of the 10,000 people who set out on the march had survived. Although it was a desperate route, it turned out to be a crucible—for Mao was able to use it to forge the survivors into the core of the CCP and lay the foundations for his dominant position in the Party. As a tight-knit, battle-hardened, and highly disciplined group, CCP members would hold all top positions in the Party, the army, and the government for the next three decades. And Mao's propaganda machine would spare no efforts to memorialize the Long March as a brilliant strategic maneuver.

Jiang was not as lucky in dealing with Japanese aggression. Japan had gradually colonized Korea after its victory in the First Sino-Japanese War. It had also steadily replaced Russia in China's Manchuria after its victory in the Russo-Japanese War (1904–1905). When Jiang's Northern Expedition threatened its interests in China, Japan's Kwantung (Guandong) Army engineered a military coup; installed a puppet government in the State of Manchuria, which it renamed Manchukuo (1932–1945); and propped up Pu Yi, the last emperor of the Qing Dynasty, as its head of state. The Japanese army proceeded to expand into China Proper in the following years. Vehement anti-Japanese sentiment exploded, and mounting Chinese nationalism demanded immediate resistance to Japanese aggression. Faced with a domestic rebel force and a foreign invader, Jiang insisted on a strategy to "pacify domestic rebels first; then expel foreign aggressors." He sent his best troops to lay siege to the newly established Communist base around Yan'an. But when he went to the front to inspect his troops, his two frontline commanders staged a mutiny, held him hostage, and forced him to agree to form a new alliance between the Nationalists and Communists against Japan. Under house arrest, Jiang made an oral statement to that effect and was released. The "Xian Incident" in December 1936 produced the Second GMD-CCP United Front in the impending war against Japan, which began July 7, 1937.

Jiang and Mao were the leaders of the two sides in the alliance in this national struggle for survival against the Japanese invaders. Jiang was the recognized national leader and the commander-in-chief of China's main armed forces. Mao and the CCP had been reduced to a remnant force holding onto life in a tiny "revolutionary base" in the remote and dust-swept plateau of Northwest China following the Long March. But the Second United Front had turned them from an illegitimate rebel force into a legitimate junior partner in the war. Mao seized the opportunity. He furled the banner of communist revolution and raised the banner of nationalism. This greatly improved his appeal to a nation burning with nationalism and patriotism. Reinvigorated, he developed guerrilla forces and "anti-Japanese bases" behind Japanese lines.

The Second Sino-Japanese War (1937–1945) and World War II (1939–1945)

Japan had followed a path of gradual expansion in China, and China's resistance had been anything but forceful. Consequently, no large-scale war broke out. But things had now changed: Japan's occupation of China's Northeast (1931) and its advance into China Proper had set off a surging wave of anti-Japanese sentiment that created a National United Front against Japan. Now a small spark would have the potential of starting a major war. That spark came in the form of the Lugouqiao Incident (or the Marco Polo Bridge Incident). It was a skirmish between Japanese and Chinese troops in July 1937 just outside Peking (aka Beijing). The incident quickly flared into China's eight-year full-scale War of Resistance against Japanese aggression.

The Nanjing Massacre (aka the "Rape of Nanking"). When the Imperial Japanese Army captured Nanjing, its military command set the troops free for six weeks of killing, burning, looting, and raping.

There are no accurate figures on the event because most of the Japanese military records on the subject were deliberately destroyed shortly after its surrender. The Allies' International Military Tribunal of the Far East puts the estimated number of Chinese killed at over 200,000. The Chinese Nanjing Military Tribunal for War Crimes puts the figure at over 300,000. The victims were civilian men, women, and children, as well as captured and unarmed Chinese soldiers. Many of the victims were lined up and mowed down by machine gun, or buried alive in groups. The Japanese troops also went looting, raping, and burning across the city, often under the command of their officers. Arson destroyed one-third of the city.

Some Japanese officers turned the act of murder into a sport. The most horrifying case was a "killing contest" between two lieutenants, which was reported in the Japanese newspapers like a sporting event with regular updates. The International Military Tribunal of the Far East and the Nanjing Military Tribunal for War Crimes later tried several of the key perpetrators, found them guilty of the atrocities, and had them executed.

There is an international consensus that the incident was one of the most gruesome atrocities of World War II, as well as a war crime and a crime against humanity. However, the extent of the atrocities is a topic of heated debate. In Japan, public opinion varies widely. While there is little doubt the massacre did occur, some claim it was greatly exaggerated, and some extremists deny that the incident ever occurred. Such denials surface from time to time to poison Japan's relations with China and other Asian-Pacific nations, such as North and South Korea, Singapore, and the Philippines.

Jiang was the nationally recognized war leader, and his forces would bear the main burden of the war. He put up a heroic but losing fight. The Japanese Imperial Army captured China's capital, Nanjing, in December 1937. The "Great Massacre of Nanjing" that followed was one of the most savage war crimes of World War II. Jiang relocated his capital to Chongqing, which is an inland city far up the Yangtze River, tucked behind steep mountain barriers and under heavy cloud cover. Although he was safer there, he faced a bleak future, for he was far from his coastal power base, surrounded by hostile local warlords, and cut off from the outside world. China was initially essentially fighting alone. What little foreign aid Jiang received came from the Soviet Union, but it quickly dried up when World War II broke out in Europe in 1939. The United States was in the embrace of isolationism as it struggled with the Great Depression. But Jiang's position improved in 1941. For when Japan marched its troops into the French colony of Indochina (Vietnam, Cambodia, and Laos), poised to attack oil-and-rubber-rich Dutch East Indies (aka Indonesia), the United States responded by adopting a hard line: It demanded that Japan withdraw all its troops from China (excluding Manchuria). When Japan refused, America tightened the screws by imposing an oil and scrap iron embargo on it, and froze its assets in America. It then extended lend-lease assistance to China, and even allowed General Claire Chennault to organize the "Flying Tigers," an American volunteer air corps, to aid China in its war against Japan.

Since Japan was poor in natural resources and relied on America for oil and iron, the embargo would force the Japanese economy and war machine to grind to a standstill in a matter of months. Japan faced a tough choice: Either capitulate to America's demands and withdraw from China, or go to war with America. It made the fatal mistake of choosing the latter. It launched a sneak attack on America's naval base at Pearl Harbor in 1941, and America declared war on Japan. Germany and Italy honored their treaty obligation to Japan and declared war on America. The world became formally divided between the Allied Nations (the United States, Great Britain, France, the Soviet Union, and China) and the Axis Nations (Germany, Italy, and Japan). A full-blown global war would soon change numerous international and various domestic maps.

Japan's attack on America totally changed the fate of China. Jiang was now a part of a powerful global alliance after virtually fighting alone for four years. American President Franklin D. Roosevelt had a plan to give China a new role to play in and after the war: China would serve as a base from which America would eventually launch its invasion of the Japanese home islands during the war, and it would emerge from the war as a great power to replace Japan as a stabilizing force in East Asia. Roosevelt appointed General Joseph Stilwell as Supreme Commander of US troops in the China, Burma, and India Theater, and assigned him the mission of training and arming Chinese troops, and building a road from Burma into China's Yunnan Province. The "Yunnan-Burma Road" would be China's only connection to the outside world, and all American aid would enter China by this road.

Stilwell's partnership with Jiang was a difficult one. He was single-mindedly focused on the immediate mission of the military defeat of Japan. Jiang and Mao, on the other hand, were looking beyond the war against Japan, and preparing for what they saw as an inevitable civil war between them. In fact, Jiang dispatched some of his best troops to encircle Mao's "revolutionary base" in Yan'an. As for Mao, he had developed a devious strategy of secretly coordinating with the Japanese to avoid frontal confrontations that would inflict heavy losses on him, and extending his territorial control at the expense of Jiang. He also expanded his party network across the country and infiltrated the Nationalist Party and its armed forces. Stilwell saw what Jiang was doing, but failed to see what Mao was up to. Furious at Jiang and sympathetic to Mao, he persuaded President Roosevelt that America should divert a portion of US aid to Mao, and pressure Jiang to turn over the command of the Chinese troops to him (Stilwell). Jiang flatly rejected the proposals that came from President Roosevelt, and requested the recall of Stilwell from China. US–China relations reached an all-time low. But that did not trouble Roosevelt. As the tide of war in the Pacific Theater shifted in favor of America, China had lost its strategic importance as a springboard for the final assault on Japan. Instead of moving American and Chinese troops from western China to the east coast, Roosevelt's military opted for the quicker and less deadly island hopping to Tokyo. This minimized China's role in the conflict.

The Nationalist-Communist Civil War, 1945–1949

When Japan surrendered to the Allied Powers in August 1945, an unofficial Chinese civil war got underway. Troops under GMD control and those under CCP control rushed to retake Chinese territories from the Japanese. Old hostilities flared up again. Jiang and Mao had formed a half-hearted Second United Front in the face of Japan's invasion. Now that Japan was defeated, the cement that had held the alliance together was gone, and they faced the question of whether their alliance would survive in the form of a coalition government that would oversee the rebuilding of China, or whether the alliance would collapse and lead to another civil war.

The United States had not given up on the idea of a peaceful, prosperous, and democratic postwar China. US President Harry Truman tried to be a neutral mediator in building a coalition government, sending George Marshall, his senior general, to work out some accommodation that would thereby avert a renewal of civil war. Jiang and Mao humored him by paying lip service to the US goals, but each prepared feverishly for war. Talks over the building of a coalition government dragged on for years without producing tangible results. Then the world situation took a dramatic turn: The Cold War divided the world in two between 1945 and 1991: the Free World led by the United States, and the Communist Bloc led by the Soviet Union. All international issues were now seen through the prism of the Cold War. All major players would now have to take sides. Jiang joined the US-led bloc, and Mao joined the Soviet Union–led bloc. Civil war resumed in 1946.

When Japan conceded defeat, Mao's troops were in place in large areas in North and Northeast China to accept Japanese surrender. They were also well-placed to received support from the Soviet Union. Mao's strength soared. And he had a deep understanding of two fundamental truths about China. The first was that the Chinese people aspired to genuine national independence. The second was that the "peasant issue" was China's central issue: Only by satisfying the peasantry's hunger for land could anyone win majority support in China. So he launched the most radical forms of land reform.

Jiang Jieshi and Mao Zedong in Chongqing in 1945 at World War II's end. *Source:* Jack Wilkes/Getty Images.

Meanwhile, Jiang wasn't faring too well. His forces had sustained heavy losses fighting the Japanese. And in the many years he had taken a defensive posture behind the steep mountain ranges of Southwest China, his leadership circle had become eroded by corruption and cronyism. Granted, he was a staunch nationalist, but he had lost touch with his people in general. He relied too heavily on the strength of his resilient personality and his military forces. His power base was exclusively made up of the urban moneyed classes and the rural landlord class. Practically speaking he ignored the "peasant issue." The massive infusion of American aid with the outbreak of the civil war made his armed forces look impressively modern. But it was a giant with feet of clay. Mao's massive troops, powerful propaganda machine, omnipresent secret party cells, and radical land reform policy had succeeded in winning over popular support.

The collapse of Jiang's armed forces and government was rapid and total. He and his supporters fled to the island of Taiwan, where he reestablished the Republic of China, which still exists today. Meanwhile, on the Chinese mainland, a triumphant Mao announced the founding of the People's Republic of China (PRC). Both governments claimed to represent the whole of China, rejecting any suggestion that each was an independent and sovereign state.

Suggested Readings and Viewings

Marie-Claire Bergère, *Sun Yat-sen*, trans. Janet Lloyd (Stanford, CA: Stanford University Press, 2000).

Lloyd E. Eastman, *Abortive Revolution: China under Nationalist Rule, 1927–1937* (Cambridge, MA: Harvard University Press, 1990).

Lloyd E. Eastman, *Seeds of Destruction: Nationalist China in War and Revolution, 1937–1949* (Stanford, CA: Stanford University Press, 1984).

Chalmers Johnson, *Peasant Nationalism and Communist Power: The Emergence of Revolutionary China, 1937–1945* (Stanford, CA: Stanford University Press, 1963).

Lucian W. Pye, *Warlord Politics: Conflict and Coalition in the Politics of Modernization of Republican China* (New York: Praeger, 1971).

Raise the Red Lantern (1991), dir. by Zhang Yimou.

Vera Schwarcz, *The Chinese Enlightenment: Intellectuals and the Legacy of the May Fourth Movement of 1919* (Berkeley: University of California Press, 1990).

Patrick Fuliang Shan, *Yuan Shikai: A Reappraisal* (Vancouver: University of British Columbia Press, 2018).

Jay Taylor, *The Generalissimo: Chiang Kai-shek and the Struggle for Modern China* (Cambridge, MA: Harvard University Press, 2011).

17

The People's Republic of China, 1949–

China could again boast of its unification and independence. Traditionally, the founder of an empire would try to build a stable and prosperous state. But Mao was no traditional empire-builder. He was a visionary who was committed to "continuous revolution." He would strive not only to restore China's glorious past, but also to create a new communist heaven here on Earth.

Mao's 27 Years (1949–1976)

A triumphant Mao presided over a ceremony of marching columns of soldiers and civilians in Beijing's Tiananmen Square on October 1, 1949. He announced the founding of the People's Republic of China, and made the famous declaration "The Chinese people have stood up!" The strong sentiments of national pride and patriotism in his words resonated with the population in general. They aspired to a new beginning after two centuries of war, economic hardship, corrupt government, and humiliation by foreign powers. Mao's coffers overflowed with political capital, but he would squander it quickly.

Mao held unprecedented power in his hands. First, he projected a vision that won the support of a large portion of the population. They believed he was the fulfillment of their nationalistic and patriotic aspirations. Two, he had absolute control over the Chinese Communist Party (CCP) and the People's Liberation Army (PLA). They were a hierarchically organized and highly disciplined cadre of military commanders and civil administrators. The party had a membership of 4.5 million in 1949, and they were placed in leadership positions at all levels of government and the military, reaching all the way down to factories, stores, schools, urban neighborhood offices, and rural villagers' committees. When Mao issued an order, the Party machine would implement it throughout the country. His control of the country and the population was tighter than that of any previous Chinese regime, imperial or otherwise.

Mao published his essay *On The People's Democratic Dictatorship* just before the founding of the PRC. In it, he lays out a blueprint for the new republic. He promises land to the peasants, leadership roles to the working class, freedom to the intellectuals, and the opportunity for growth to the capitalist class. He also promises a government "of the people, for the people, and by the people" as described by Abraham Lincoln. He claims that the new regime will practice "democracy toward the people" and "dictatorship toward the enemy," but makes a significant omission: He evades the crucial question of how an individual or a social class is identified as "the people" or "the enemy."

Asia Past and Present: A Brief History, First Edition. Peter P. Wan and Thomas D. Reins.
© 2021 John Wiley & Sons, Inc. Published 2021 by John Wiley & Sons, Inc.

As it turned out, he would personally, without any institutional mandate or restraint, label anyone a "class enemy."

Once he was in power, he broke all his promises: He dispossessed the peasants and the capitalists, declared the educated class "bourgeois intellectuals" and crushed them, and even stripped the working class of their right to unionize.

Immediately after the founding of the new regime, Mao personally initiated the practice of having the entire nation honor him with the slogan "Long live Chairman Mao!" Significantly, this was a chant reserved exclusively for honoring the emperors in imperial China. This was the beginning of his shameless promotion of a "personality cult" centered on himself. But people were too naive to see it. Wielding absolute power, he became unstoppable in his blind pursuit of fanatical goals. They plunged the country into one disaster after another, and ended only when he died. He best illustrates how absolute power corrupts absolutely.

Mao had a skillful command of traditional Chinese statecraft, reinforced with Communist Russia's techniques of building a semi-modern totalitarian state machine. He had no match for his devious and brutal tactics. Over the decades Mao had developed what he called the "mass line" as a tool to implement his policies. He would always mobilize the masses of people to drive his agenda, whether it was to fight a war, spur economic growth, or destroy an opponent. Throughout the 27 years of the Mao era, he launched one mass campaign after another until the day of his death.

Mao Zedong (1893–1976). *Source:* INTERFOTO / Alamy Stock Photo.

The Korean War (1950–1953)

After World War II, the Korean Peninsula stood divided at the 38th Parallel. South Korea had a pro-American regime that was strongly anticommunist, nominally democratic, and militarily weak.

North Korea had a communist regime with a strong military. Its leader Kim Il-sung was eager to unify the entire peninsula under his regime. And he eventually persuaded Soviet Russian dictator Josef Stalin to give him the green light to launch an all-out invasion of South Korea in 1950. Kim's troops quickly overran South Korea, driving its forces in a rout all the way to the southernmost point of the Korean Peninsula. U.S. President Harry Truman got the United Nations to declare North Korea an aggressor nation, and since the Soviet Union was then boycotting the world body over its recognition of Chiang Kai-shek's Republic of China (ROC), Moscow could not veto the UN move. Truman organized a multinational UN force to drive out North Korea and restore South Korea. While many nations contributed troops to the UN Force, American troops made up the bulk of it, and American General Douglas MacArthur was its commander-in-chief. MacArthur's troops quickly checked the North Korean offensive, crossed the 38th Parallel, and continued to advance until they approached the Korea–China border. MacArthur openly spoke of attacking China with atomic bombs.

Mao's regime was less than a year old and not yet firmly established. But Stalin made him send Chinese troops across the border to salvage the North Korea regime. Mao dispatched China's regular troops in the name of "volunteers," and they tipped the balance of power immediately. The joint Chinese and North Korean troops pushed the UN troops back. After a brutal period of see-sawing, the fighting stalemated along the 38th Parallel, and the two sides signed a ceasefire agreement in 1953, an armistice that remains in force today. They were now positioned roughly where they were at the outbreak of war. During the war, the United States also sent its Seventh Fleet into the Taiwan Straits to defend the ROC from potential PRC invasion.

The Korean War was the first major military confrontation between the Free World and the Communist Bloc in the Cold War. It demonstrated that the Soviet Union had ambitions of global domination through "world revolution," and that the United States was determined to lead the Free World in a "holy war" against communist expansion. This bloody experience left a deep animosity between America and China that would continue to poison U.S.–China relations long after the fighting was over.

The Consolidation of One-Party Rule in a Communist Regime

The Korean War was an existential threat to Mao's regime. Mao felt an urgency to consolidate his home base. He launched the Campaign to Repress Counterrevolutionaries, which purged his regime of those who had served in the former regime. Tens of millions of people were arrested, sent to prisons and labor camps, or executed.

Mao now needed the support of the peasants more than ever, for they were the main source of the country's food supply and the manpower of his troops. So he adopted an exceptionally radical form of "land reform" to deal with the gravity of the threat (1950). He sent "land reform work teams," headed by CCP members, to the countryside to mobilize the peasants. They organized "struggle sessions" to encourage peasants who owned little or no land to vent their hatred at those who did own land. They not only allowed but encouraged physical abuse. Humiliations, beatings, killings, and suicides were commonplace. By the time the campaign was over, land ownership had changed hands. "Landlords" as a socioeconomic class were eradicated. Those individuals who survived, as well as their family members, became second-class citizens, subject to harsh discrimination for the duration of Mao's rule.

Mao's vision of a New China had no room for private businesses either. So he launched another campaign to strip private business owners of their independent ownership (1956). Not even tiny mom-and-pop stores were spared. The dispossessed private business owners were given token compensation, but lost control over their businesses. Mao had essentially wiped out big and small capitalists as a socioeconomic class of people.

The government launched a series of "Five-Year Plans" on the Soviet Russian model to promote economic development. The goal was to develop a planned economy under CCP control. This system would have the party/government bureaucracy set policies for China's rapid industrialization, giving priority to the heavy and military industries. Since these industries consumed huge quantities of resources, consumer industries were left to struggle on short supplies of raw materials. This created a severe shortage of consumer goods. To deal with the shortage, the government erected a rationing system of unprecedented scale and complexity. Almost everything was rationed: rice and wheat flour, meat, cooking oil, cloth and clothing, even matches, cigarettes, and toilet paper. Coupons became a basic necessity of every household. Mao now had complete control of both the rural and urban economies. He also established complete control over both the rural and urban population, for no individual could survive outside the system without the coupons.

But Mao's control would not be complete without mind control. He made Mao Zedong Thought, his version of Marxism-Leninism, the state ideology. But the thinking of China's educated class was anything but Marxist, since they came largely from business and land-owning families, and their education was either Confucian or Western. So he launched a campaign to brainwash China's intellectuals. (Note: In Chinese usage, the word "intellectual" is often loosely applied to a person who has received a secondary education or better: a school teacher, professor, scientist, engineer, doctor, author, etc.)

Educated people were put into study groups in their workplace (i.e., government agencies, schools, universities, factories, stores, etc.), where they were required to do self-criticism and accept criticism. Anyone who showed the slightest signs of resistance would be physically isolated from his colleagues, family, and friends to break his spirit. Then he would be dragged out to face a fired-up crowd who had been rehearsed to condemn every aspect of him. This could go on for days and weeks and even months. If his influence was nationwide, his criticism and self-criticism would be distributed over the national media to the point of saturation. The individual would have no place to hide. This collective pressure was such that it would break even the strongest of them. He would confess to the most outrageous charges of being a slavish worshipper of the West, a traitor to the country, a blood-sucking parasite, a criminal, and the scum of the earth. Then he would be allowed to be "reborn" in compliance to Mao's thinking. Nearly all educated people were reformed or silenced. The unrepentant were sent into exile.

But Mao's distrust of them lingered. And the waves of anti-Stalin criticism that swept across Eastern Europe and the Soviet Union after Stalin's death in 1953 seemed to confirm his suspicions. But how could he identify his hidden enemies? He devised a devious plot to ferret them out. He invited leading intellectuals to big and small meetings, and asked them to speak frankly about their suggestions and criticisms of the Party and the government in order to help them do a better job of governing. He claimed that he wanted to recreate an environment that matched the pre-Qin era when "a hundred flowers blossomed, and a hundred schools of thought contended." The intellectuals were still in a state of "once bitten, twice shy." But Mao's display eventually won them over. They took the bait. Persuaded that they were really free to speak their minds, they gushed out with criticism of his every mass campaign. What they saw as the crux of everything wrong was Mao's one-party dictatorship. Mao held back until he was satisfied that he had identified his hidden enemies, and sprang the trap. His crackdown is known as the Anti-Rightist Campaign (1957). Anyone who had criticized Mao or the CCP, no matter how mildly, was branded a "Rightist" (i.e., a person politically on the right of center). Most of these unlucky "intellectuals" were sent to factories and farms to do the most menial of manual work. Some were locked up in prison, confined to labor camps, or exiled to the harshest and remotest parts of the country. Under unbearable pressure, many went insane, committed suicide, and suffered divorces, while others wasted the best years of their lives rotting away. Their family members instantly became second-class citizens, losing their right to normal education and employment. The total number tarred with the brush of "Rightist" was around three million. The cream of China's educated people was destroyed. China's intellectuals were again silenced.

But the CCP was not monolithic. The views of the "Rightists" were also reflected within the CCP. So Mao launched another mass campaign to purge critics who were CCP members. Convinced that he had successfully crushed his critics both inside and outside his Party, he felt free to indulge his megalomaniac fantasies. His ostensible blueprint would lead the nation on a reckless course of self-destruction.

The "Great Leap Forward"

As a visionary, Mao had embraced an age-old peasant vision of an egalitarian utopia in which all people share all things equally. He also embraced the Legalists' goal of "rich country, strong army." And he envied the West for being much richer and stronger than China was. Still, though he had promoted land reform for decades, Mao was never a true believer of giving each peasant his own plot of land, which would make them small property owners. The distribution of land was a tactical move in a multistep maneuver to eventually abolish private ownership of land. Therefore, as the new regime stabilized, he launched campaign after campaign to force an ever-increasing degree of collectivization on the peasantry. First it was "mutual aid groups," where peasants kept their tiny plots of land, but helped one another when help was needed. Then in 1953 it was "agricultural cooperatives," where the peasants' private plots, farm tools, and farm animals were taken from them and invested in the coop. At this stage, a peasant's share of the coop's total harvest was determined not only by the amount of labor he put in, but also by the size of his investment. Two people who did the same amount of work could be rewarded differently if their investments were different. And this "inequality" didn't sit well with Mao. So in 1958 he decided to replace the cooperatives with the "people's communes" where all private property would be abolished, all work would be shared, and all rewards would be uniform. One's contribution of land, farm tools, and labor would no longer be taken into consideration. Mao saw this system as approaching his vision of an egalitarian society. As the policy was implemented, reports poured in about bumper harvests and happy commune members eating their fill at commune mess halls for free. He began to muse contentedly about what to do with the reported huge surpluses of crops.

Backyard furnace, Great Leap Forward. *Source:* JACQUET-FRANCILLON/Getty Images.

But Mao's daydreams became a dark nightmare in reality. The abolition of private property and the leveling of income totally deprived peasants of incentive to work hard and live frugally. First hunger appeared, and then starvation set in. But any Party official who tried to speak the truth about the devastation caused by the people's communes would be removed from his position. So officials continued to sing the praises of Mao and report ever-larger "bumper harvests" with absurd astronomical figures.

Although the reported figures were fabricated, they had real consequences. For agricultural taxes were based on agricultural output, so now the government would levy high taxes based on the reported high yields. The totalitarian government had the means to extract every last bushel of grain from the peasants. A nationwide famine set in between 1958 and 1961. People died like flies in the countryside. Urban residents faired marginally better thanks to a strict rationing system, but malnutrition was prevalent. An estimated total of 30–40 million people died of starvation. The "Great Famine" happened at a time when there were no wars and no natural disasters, yet it was officially called the "Three Years of Natural Disaster." Mao's handiwork turned his utopia into a dystopia, but he stubbornly refused to change course.

Mao had begun to be impatient with Russia's slow pace of economic development by the late 1950s. He insisted that China could advance in leaps and bounds in its drive for industrialization. Knowing nothing about modern science and industry, he had the simplistic view that the degree of a nation's industrialization was mainly a matter of its steel output. So he resorted to his tried-and-true method of launching mass campaigns: He would mobilize the whole nation to make steel. He initially set the target of surpassing Great Britain in 15 years, and catching up with America in 50 years. But the goals soon morphed into surpassing Britain in three to five years, and catching up with America soon thereafter. Everyone in the country began making steel: Factory workers and peasants, students and teachers, housewives and retirees—in a words, almost anyone who could lift a finger—was soon plunged into building crude furnaces, collecting scrap iron, and working around the clock to make steel. It was a ridiculous scene. Furnaces lit up the night sky in cities and in the countryside across the nation. Huge amounts of manpower, iron, and fuel were consumed to produce crude steel that was utterly useless. Meanwhile, the more efficient factories were forced to stand idle because of shortages of raw materials. Farm land was left unattended because the peasants were taken away to make steel. Hills and valleys were stripped bare of trees and bushes to provide fuel for the crude furnaces that pockmarked the landscape.

The composition of Mao's knowledge was an unbalanced mix. He came from a peasant family in an extremely isolated village. His formal education went only as far as attending a teachers' training college in the provincial capital. He was an avid reader, but the range of his reading was limited to the scanty holdings of the local libraries, and he had a natural distaste for math and science.

Mao was a master of traditional Chinese learning: He was thoroughly familiar with Chinese history, wrote classical Chinese poetry, and above all had an uncanny command of Chinese statecraft. His knowledge of Marxism was as limited as was his interest in it, and he knew nothing about modern European social democracy. A Chinese peasant mindset and an ambition to outdo China's First Emperor Qin Shihuang made him scornful of modern democracy. He clung to the age-old dream of Chinese peasants—an egalitarian utopia ruled over by an all-powerful emperor.

The mass campaigns to set up people's communes and make steel were together called the "Great Leap Forward." But they turned out to be a great leap backward. The economy was in shambles. Industrial and agricultural output plummeted. The entire nation was starving. Mao could not escape responsibility for leading his country into the abyss. He had no choice but to step aside at the Lushan Conference in 1959. He went into semi-retirement. This again was a tactical move on his part, and a face-saving gesture for the CCP. A new pragmatic troika took over the reins of state in 1962: President Liu Shaoqi, Premier Zhou Enlai, and General Secretary Deng Xiaoping. They faced the daunting task of reviving the economy. Frantically, they went about undoing what Mao had done. They redistributed the land to peasant households, dismantled all the ramshackle steel furnaces, allowed small businesses to operate, and gave educated people a wider margin of freedom. These policies worked remarkably well.

Mao's Cultural Revolution (1966–1976): A "Ten-Year Disaster"

Mao watched from the sidelines and plotted his return to power. He held a grudge against the troika that he believed had taken advantage of his setbacks to reduce him to a figurehead, and he believed their policies were capitalist and revisionist. He had an additional agenda that would be unknown to anyone for a decade or two: He wanted to hand over his power to members of his own family when he died. That was what Chinese emperors had done for two thousand years. It would also be what rulers throughout the Asian "Cultural Sphere of Confucianism" would do in the near future: Jiang Jieshi (Chiang Kai-shek) would be succeeded by his son Jiang Jingguo in Taiwan, Kim Il-sung by his son Kim Jong Il in North Korea, and Lee Kuan Yew by his son Lee Hsien Loong in Singapore.

Mao launched the "Cultural Revolution" to remove Liu, Zhou, and Deng from power at the outset of the campaign in 1966. Eventually he put his wife, Madame Mao or Jiang Qing, in power to carry on his vision of a perfect society. But this was no easy task. Liu, Zhou, and Deng were veteran leaders of the Chinese Revolution and firmly entrenched in the power structure. He would have to demolish the party and government structures before he could remove them from power. Never a man to back off from challenges, he was ready to sacrifice the party and government structures in his pursuit of the destruction of his enemies. This created a bizarre situation: Mao, the "great helmsman," destroying the very party and government apparatus that he had worked so long and hard to construct.

Mao had a great advantage: He symbolized the Chinese Revolution. Even his semi-retirement had not diminished his stature. Furthermore, his designated successor, Field Marshal Lin Biao, was whipping up a frenzy of his "personality cult." The masses began rhapsodizing him as the "Red, Red Sun" and the "People's Savior." The *Little Red Book* of his quotes became an amulet every person must carry at all times. Mao seized the political high ground by passing off his power grab as an effort to maintain the purity of the Chinese Revolution, and labeled his enemies "revisionists of Marxism" and "traitors of the Chinese Revolution." Cynically taking advantage of the idealism and naiveté of young people, he called on students at universities and secondary schools to spearhead his offensive. The students organized into "Red Guards," and plunged into what in their misguided minds was a revolutionary crusade. Factory workers in cities soon joined and organized "Worker Rebels Brigades." Some peasants also took part later. Mao had successfully let the genies out of the bottle.

Little Red Book. Source: Kevin Tichenor/
Shutterstock.com.

Mao button. *Source:* huzhiqiang/123RF.

The Red Guard's first step was a soft target—the intellectuals. They searched their homes, confiscated their belongings, burned their books, made them kneel on cement or under a blazing sun, and paraded them on the campus or through the streets with placards hanging around their necks. Their attacks quickly extended to other easy targets, such as former landlords, former capitalists, and "Rightists." All legal and humanitarian considerations were denounced and abandoned. Volcanic anarchism broke out.

Mao had tight control over the military and the secret services, but he made sure they didn't step in to stop the spread of terror. He had deliberately created the chaotic situation to break down the defenses of his targets, and expose them to roiled-up mobs. Party, government, and military officials at all levels now suffered the same fate as the intellectuals and former landlords and capitalists. They were paraded through the streets with placards hanging from their necks, kicked around, beaten up, and tortured. Head of state President Liu Shaoqi was denounced and humiliated in public, and soon died in agony and obscurity in a secret prison cell.

Mao's tactics ripped society apart. The schism began at the very top levels of power in Beijing, and reached down to all provinces, cities, factories, universities, and even families. Verbal denunciations among opposing factions soon escalated into fistfights; then became clashes involving the use of sticks, knives, and spears; and eventually graduated into regular war that involved the military armed with machineguns and armored vehicles. Violence and killing became rampant. The worst of human nature was released from all restraints of civilization.

The Red Guards soon deteriorated into warring bands of self-seekers. They had been corrupted by their unchecked power in an anarchist environment. And Mao had no further use for them either, for they had served his purpose of bringing down his political enemies. So he issued orders to put schools and the Red Guards under martial law. Then he sent them to live and work in the countryside and paramilitary farms in border provinces for "reeducation," where they were left to rot. In one masterful stroke, he had put the genie back into the bottle, while solving the problem of massive unemployment among the urban youth. This was the tragic end of the Red Guard Movement. A generation of young people had grown up bitter, uneducated, and disillusioned. Some of them who had connections might rise again, but the overwhelming majority would end their lives in obscurity at the bottom of society. Its negative impact on society would be felt for generations.

Mao began rebuilding the Party and government in 1969 under his two most trusted followers: his wife Madame Mao and Field Marshal Lin Biao. But he soon suspected Marshal Lin of involvement in a plot to subvert him. He acted swiftly to subdue him, but Lin refused to capitulate. Instead, he and his wife and son fled in a plane, and were all killed when their plane crashed in the deserts of Mongolia in 1971. Mao's wife headed the "Gang of Four" (i.e., Madame Mao and her three Leftist associates), which would oversee the rebuilt party and its revolutionary agenda. But Lin Biao's departure began the end of Mao. His advancing years and declining health, the Cultural Revolution's destruction of party structure, and Jiang Qing's lack of leadership combined to erode the capability of Mao's reconstructed party even before his death in 1976. As well, the Lin Biao Incident weakened Mao's ability to inspire confidence in the ailing "great leader." The myth of his infallibility began to unravel: Something must be terribly wrong, people began to muse timidly, if his handpicked successor has turned against him. Mao's physical and mental health deteriorated dramatically. He would go into uncontrollable fits of rage, suspicion, and self-pity. And yet, he would pull off a last feat before he died.

Comrade Jiang Qing and supporters during the Cultural Revolution. *Source:* Everett Collection Historical/ Alamy Stock Photo.

Lin Biao, Mao's close comrade in arms. *Source:* MARKA / Alamy Stock Photo.

When Stalin died in 1953, Mao began to see himself as the only man deserving of succeeding him as the leader of the world communist movement. But to Stalin's successor in the Soviet Union, Nikita Khrushchev, Mao was nothing but a country bumpkin. Mao countered by applying his favorite label "revisionist" to Khrushchev, and charging him of giving up the global communist revolution for fear of getting into a war with the United States. Personal rivalry entangled with ideological differences escalated into armed border clashes in 1969. Russia even explored the feasibility of attacking China with nuclear weapons.

Ever since the founding of the PRC, Mao had adopted a foreign policy of "leaning to one side"— the Soviet Union's side. And the Chinese propaganda machine had never tired of attacking America as China's "Number One Enemy." But Mao's rabid attacks on both the Soviet Union and the United States left him in total international isolation. And this was happening when he was losing control at home as well. He desperately needed a way out.

Enter U.S. President Richard Nixon. He had a clear perception of the world as multipolar instead of bipolar and the confidence that he could adopt a strategy of the "balance of power" to pry Mao's China out of the Communist Bloc. His critics derided him for daydreaming, but he would prove them wrong. In February 1972, he took the world by surprise when he showed up on China's Great Wall.

Nixon held talks with Mao in the Chinese leader's Beijing study. They needed each other. Mao needed Nixon's help to break out of his international isolation. Nixon needed Mao's help primarily to deescalate the nuclear arms race and secondarily further separate the Soviet and Chinese communists, and also get America out of the Vietnam War. So they made a deal. Mao agreed to make a clean break with Russia, and step down China's aid to North Vietnam. In return, Nixon promised to reject Russia's proposal to destroy China's nuclear facilities with a preemptive air strike, and the

United States would condone the PRC's takeover of China's seat in the UN Security Council. The 1972 Shanghai Communique that concluded their talks spoke of eventual diplomatic relations between Washington and Beijing; stated that no power should pursue "hegemony" in the Asia-Pacific region; and reaffirmed the One-China policy that Beijing, Taipei, and Washington had long upheld, though with somewhat different interpretations of just what that meant. In 1979, the United States ended its military alliance with Taiwan and shifted its diplomatic recognition from the ROC to the PRC. Washington continues to maintain strong political, economic, and military ties with Taiwan under the Taiwan Relations Act. When the United States extended diplomatic recognition to the PRC, China had finally broken out of its diplomatic isolation.

Mao died in September 1976. He had appointed Hua Guofeng (1921–2008) to succeed him as a transitional figure before Madame Mao would take over. But Hua lost no time to rally the support of the Old Guard and arrest the Gang of Four. Madame Mao ended up in prison where she committed suicide 15 years later. The curtain had fallen on Mao's "Cultural Revolution." The "ten years of disaster" had come to an end. The nation celebrated in wild jubilation. Mao's era had expired with the Great Helmsman.

Deng Xiaoping's Reforms (1978–1989)

China was in a mess. Most Chinese put the blame squarely at Mao's feet. They looked to having a new leader to take them in a different direction. Hua was a weak helmsman amid stormy power struggles and palace intrigues. Strongman Deng Xiaoping seized the reins of power with the backing of the Old Guard in the military and government bureaucracy. As the paramount leader of the country, he quickly steered China onto an irreversible course of reform.

Deng Xiaoping (1904–1997). *Source:* Sovfoto/UIG/Bridgeman Images.

Deng was a pragmatist. One of his oft-quoted sayings is: "A good cat is one that catches mice; it doesn't matter if its color is black or white." Another Deng maxim cautioned, "Wade across the river by feeling for stones on the riverbed." In these folksy adages, he was sending a serious message: He was ready to abandon purist Maoism and focus on economic development, and although he had no ready roadmap, he would have to learn through trial and error.

Deng replaced Mao's egalitarian peasant utopia with the promise to "Let the few get rich first." In 1978 he restated the nation's goal as the "four modernizations"—modern industry, modern agriculture, modern defense, and modern science and technology. Conspicuously absent from his vision of a modern China was democracy. That omission was quickly noted by dissident Wei Jingsheng, who used Democracy Wall to promote the Fifth Modernization, democracy. Wei spent more than a decade in and out of jail for his political temerity. All the same, Deng used the tried-and-true formula adopted by Japan, South Korea, Singapore, and Taiwan: capitalist economic modernization (the market) without democracy. Deng was quick to undo Mao's two decades of land reform and collectivization. Peasants received user's rights to small plots of land for their private use, and were allowed to sell their harvests on the market. He also gave them more personal freedom of movement. Traditionally, the "household registry system" tied peasants to their villages of birth; even during the "Great Famine," they were forcibly required to stay in their villages and starve. Deng's reforms allowed them to drift to the cities in large numbers. "Peasant laborers," as they were called, became a huge floating population. They constituted a new underclass of laborers, doing all the heaviest, dirtiest, and most dangerous work, while receiving the lowest wages. These migrants had no residency rights or labor rights. They had no medical or unemployment insurance system that would protect them from losing their livelihood in case of illness, work-related injuries, or unemployment. Their children couldn't enroll in local public schools.

These "internal immigrants," constituting perhaps a quarter billion people in 2018, were on the one hand a source of cheap labor that fueled China's economic miracle, and on the other hand a powder keg for social unrest. They were a double-edged sword. In Mao's days, state-owned enterprises (SOEs) made up the bulk of the nation's economy. But they suffered from the common failings of serious waste and inefficiency. SOEs couldn't survive without such privileges as large infusions of government investments, low-interest bank loans, priority access to raw materials, and low tax rates. And these privileges put a crushing burden on the government and the economy. Reform was essential. Deng's reforms kept the state in direct control over strategic industries through state-owned monopolies, but privatized many other large businesses or turned them over to government-appointed agents, and outright sold off small and midsized businesses to private citizens.

Deng's policy of limited privatization had an instant and powerful impact. Private businesses sprang up everywhere, and the whole country began to buzz with business activity. Deng's reform policies grew China's GDP at a miraculous annual average of roughly 10% over the next three decades. Its GDP surpassed that of Japan in 2010, to rank number 2 in the world, second only to the United States. The fast and steady increase of the GDP drove urbanization and fostered a middle class. Nearly half of its population was living in urban areas by 2014, and over half of them had graduated into the middle class by 2015. Nonetheless these numbers can be misleading. For by 2014, China's per capita GDP was only 10% that of the United States, 25% that of Japan, and 40% that of Taiwan, ranking it number 74 worldwide, somewhere between Russia and Turkmenistan. Put in another way, China's current degree of development is about that of the United States in the 1950s.

Deng had education reform high on his priority list. Schools had been virtually closed for ten years. He reopened schools and reinstalled national examinations for university admission. Diplomas were hot again. Students and scholars were allowed and even encouraged to study abroad.

Candidates for government positions were soon required to take civil service examinations. China's age-old tradition of upward mobility through book-learning and exam-taking was back.

Deng Xiaoping (1904–1997) was born to a big and powerful local land-owning family. He turned his back on his family, went to France on a work-study program at age 15, joined the CCP in France, studied in Soviet Russia, and returned to China where he joined Mao. In the following years of war and peace, he proved himself an outstanding military commander and civil administrator. But he was in Mao's bad book for his role in the troika that rolled back Mao's "People's Communes." Mao named him "China's number 2 capitalist-roader"; number 1 was Liu Shaoqi.

Back in power, Deng brilliantly launched China on a new path of reform. Unlike Mao, he admired the modern economies of the capitalist West, and would give priority to spurring economic growth. But like Mao, he believed in one-party rule, and tried desperately to rebuild and reinvigorate the Communist Party after the setback. He ruled with an iron fist and devious maneuvers. When social tension came to a head in the "June 4 Incident" of 1989 at Tiananmen Square, he ordered his troops to crush it with tanks and machineguns, which left him with a seriously tarnished reputation. He also did the very unusual thing of appointing not only his successor, but also the successor at one remove.

Deng had no way of sidestepping the thorny issue of a reevaluation of Mao. But his approach was circumspect, since he wanted to preserve Mao as the CCP's brand name. He negated Mao's Cultural Revolution with no hesitation, but let Mao off the hook for his many other grave misdeeds. This was only a tiny step toward a more objective reevaluation of Mao, but the decriminalization of the slightest criticism of Mao lifted the heavy lid on any discussion of Mao's record. People rushed toward that opening and pushed against its limits. They plunged into intense discussions on such sensitive topics as Mao's place in history, the role of the CCP, China's future, and universal values (such as democracy, humanism, freedom, justice, equality before the law, etc.). There was a touch of spring in the air for a while. But all the talk about freedom and democracy rubbed Deng the wrong way. He reiterated the absolute principle of maintaining the CCP's one-party rule. It cast a chill across the intellectual landscape.

Problems

All was not well with Deng's reforms. Although they brought about great economic progress, they also created staggering problems that Deng and his successors would have to deal with. He anointed two successors but eventually banished both for lacking in certitude in upholding his tenet of one-party rule. Then before his death, he did something unheard of: He appointed not only his immediate successor but also the successor to his successor, Jiang Zemin and Hu Jintao respectively.

Deng's reforms had turned China into the "world's factory," producing an economic miracle of high-speed development at an annual rate of around 10% over a period of three decades. But his model was unsustainable. For while it depended on exploiting China's great reserve of cheap labor to produce low-tech products for export, it consumed disproportionate amounts of natural resources, left the environment seriously polluted, did little to expand the domestic market, and ignored human rights.

Deng's policies of privatization and "letting the few get rich first" opened the door for those close to his ruling elite to get rich overnight. Party and government officials morphed into board chairmen, CEOs, general managers, and even tycoons. Straddling the public and private sectors, they shamelessly manipulated the public power and resources in their hands to enrich themselves. They became fabulously wealthy and powerful, and soon developed into a new class of wealth-and-power elites. A similar situation occurred in Japan during the Meiji Reformation.

China's distribution of wealth became alarmingly skewed: A recent report stated that the top 1% of the population owns one-third of its wealth, while the bottom 25% owns only 1%. Urban white-collar employees began enjoying the lifestyle of a consumer society, but the average wage-earners and peasant workers struggled to earn a living wage. And as businesses shed large numbers of their workers, the ranks of the unemployed swelled. Geographical distribution of the reform benefits was also skewed: They favored the coastal and urban regions while leaving inland and rural regions far behind. The social safety net was flimsy to nonexistent. A majority of families staggered under the crushing weight of the ever-rising costs of housing, education, and medical care.

The emergence of distinct interest groups created deep chasms in society. The common people had neither constitutionally guaranteed rights nor avenues of peaceful protest. So their pent-up frustration would occasionally erupt in violent outbursts of public protest. Their targets were generally the new elite who abused their power. Protests came from the depressed wages of factory workers and peasant workers whose wages had not kept up with the nation's economic growth. Even the non-political could see dangerous degradation of the environment. The protests grew in frequency and intensity during the first decade of Deng's reforms, indicating an increase of the Chinese loss of confidence in the Party and government.

All the forces that had emerged during Deng's reforms erupted into an explosive collision in the spring of 1989, culminating in the Tiananmen Square Massacre. The best and the brightest of the new crop of students, professors, and journalists had gotten a peek of the West, and it only served to whet their appetite for more of the freedom and material well-being that people in the West enjoyed. Even the state-run media were taken over by resolute demands for academic freedom, freedom of expression, free elections, and less restrictions on going overseas. Some brave voices began criticizing Mao and the CCP. Deng felt threatened, and he unleashed a counteroffensive. He flooded the media with harsh attacks on the educated class. Angry students had no legitimate forum to air their grievances, so they took to the streets in protest. Prominent intellectuals waded in by signing a letter of support. Even Deng's anointed successor, Zhao Ziyang, seemed to support the call for greater freedom.

What turned a popular protest movement into an existential threat to Deng and the Communist Party resulted from the death and non-Party memorial for Deng's first anointed successor, Hu Yaobang. Hu, like his successor Zhao Ziyang, had favored greater freedoms, a backing that likely gave rise to a major protest movement in 1987. Deng fired Hu, and when he died in April 1989, Beijing protestors used the occasion to memorialize Hu and thus criticize Deng. Protest momentum soon spread to the general population in Beijing and other cities. A limited protest that had originated on college campuses now swelled into a roaring torrent of mass protest. Its agenda had expanded denunciation of government corruption, unemployment, and inflation, and demands for clean and transparent government. The protesters set up camp in Tiananmen Square and surrounded themselves with barricades. Provocateurs and saboteurs sneaked in to create mischief. Some protest leaders called for bloodshed, or at least seemed to, when student leader Chai Ling indicated that it might take blood to reform the system.

Violence broke out. The normal functioning of the capital was so disrupted that Deng was unable to hold an official welcoming ceremony in Tiananmen Square for the visiting Soviet Russian head of state Mikhail Gorbachev. Deng sensed a real threat to his one-party rule and his signature reforms. He again ordered a crackdown—only this time it was a military crackdown. His troops marched into the city in combat formation, armed with machineguns and backed by tanks. Ultimately they fired indiscriminately into the clusters of protesters remaining in Tiananmen Square, the bystanders, and the surrounding buildings. They dispersed the protesters, and removed the barricades. This was the "Tiananmen Incident" of June 4, 1989, better known in America as the "Tiananmen Square Massacre." The number of casualties remains a tightly kept state secret to this day. The democracy activists were subjected to arrest, imprisonment, and torture. Some managed to flee to the West; among the most prominent were Chai Ling and her husband, as well as noted Chinese astrophysicist Fang Lizhi. A freezing chill settled across the intellectual landscape. Any talk about democracy or human rights became taboo. Deng succeeded in crushing the protest movement overnight in a bloodbath, but the date of June 4 became forever etched in the public's memory, and would be a rallying point for future political protest.

Liu Xiaobo, who was a participant of the June 4 Movement, went on to become a leading advocate of nonviolent struggle for constitutional government and human rights. He received the 2010 Nobel Peace Prize while in prison for coauthoring the "Charter 2008 Manifesto." The Charter, signed by over 300 Chinese intellectuals and activists, called for democracy and human rights. How the authorities respond to the public demand to exonerate dissidents like Liu Xiaobo and the victims of the June 4 Incident is a weathervane of the direction they wish to steer China. Liu died in 2017 and his wife, Liu Xia, remained under house arrest until July 10, 2018, when she was released and allowed to leave for Germany. Although officially free, she feared making a statement two days later on the first anniversary of her husband's death because her brother remained in China, an easy government target. Big Brother is alive and active.

Even Deng reforms whose ends typically received popular support often ended up being opposed because of the means employed. The One Child Policy is a case in point. The CCP put the "one-child-per-family policy" in place in the late 1970s. Although its vigorous and often brutal enforcement managed to bring down the birth rate, it also had an alarming unintended consequence: A low birth rate, combined with an increased life expectancy, produced an imbalance between working-age persons and retirees. It also aggravated a traditional Chinese preference for male offspring and female infanticide, creating a serious imbalance between males and females. The policy also produced a phenomenon that was unheard of in human history: A young couple in their twenties could end up caring for one child and four retired parents, and a large number of children would grow up with no brothers and sisters, no cousins, and no uncles and aunts. Surrounded by pampering adults, many of them would become "problem children." By the 2010s China began running into the problem of labor shortage, and in 2015 the CCP replaced its one-child policy with a "two-child policy."

China has been challenged by foreign control of Chinese territories and/or independence movements in Tibet, Xinjiang, Taiwan, and Hong Kong for decades. Great Britain acquired Hong Kong when China ceded it after its defeat in the First Opium War. It then acquired a hundred-year lease on the adjacent New Territory when it found that the ceded territory was too small to be self-sustaining. When the lease was about to expire in 1997, Britain had no choice but to return both Hong Kong and the New Territory to China. China regained sovereignty over Hong Kong after 155 years of British colonial rule. Portugal gained residency rights in nearby Macao during China's Ming Dynasty in 1553, formally transformed it into a Portuguese colony in 1887, and returned it to China in 1999. The PRC implemented a "one country, two systems" policy toward Hong Kong and Macao: Although legally integral parts of the PRC, they are granted the privilege of retaining their Western-style economic and political systems. The functioning of the hybrid system in Hong Kong has been stormy in recent years. There have been frequent outbreaks of violent demands for democracy and even independence.

Ethnic minorities constitute less than 10% of China's total population, but they make up the majority in over 40% of China's territory. Their greatest concentrations are in Tibet where they are Buddhist Tibetan and in Xinjiang where they are Muslim Uyghur. A Tibetan separatist rebellion erupted in 1956. Defeated, their spiritual leader Dalai Lama led them in flight to India, where they set up a government-in-exile. Inconclusive negotiations with the PRC central government for their repatriation have been going on intermittently for decades. The separatist movement in Xinjiang is known as the East Turkistan Independence Movement, which has ties to the global Islamic fundamentalist movement. It has carried out several acts of terror in recent years, and Beijing's response has been swift and harsh.

The Republic of China on the island of Taiwan was once the government of all of China. Defeated by Mao in civil war, it fled to the island of Taiwan where it reestablished itself in a standoff with the PRC on the mainland. Jiang Jieshi was succeeded by his son Jiang Jingguo (1910–1988), who continued to rule Taiwan under a one-party dictatorship and martial law until, in his later years, he astonishingly opened up the island to multiparty democratic politics and a free press. His reforms created the "Taiwan Miracle" of economic prosperity and democratic government. The changes he brought to the island have won him the admiration of Mainland Chinese people.

However, Taiwan faces two major challenges. First, its politics is deeply divided between Jiang's Nationalist Party, which draws its support mainly from a shrinking population that migrated from the Mainland to the island with the ROC government in 1949, and the Democratic Progressive Party, which is supported by the locally rooted population. The former embraces the principle of "One China," while the latter leans toward Taiwan's independence. Currently, the Beijing government emphasizes a policy of "peaceful unification" but has never abandoned the option of "reunification by use of force." PRC President Xi Jinping and ROC President Ma Yingjiu held talks in Singapore in 2015 in an unprecedented gesture of mutual recognition of each other as two parts of the same country. However, the Nationalist Party lost to the DPP in the 2016 election, which leaves the future of the relations between the two sides hanging in the balance.

View of Taipei. *Source:* CHEN MIN CHUN/Shutterstock.com.

China's future will be determined by the balance of power among several forces: An ultra-Leftist group of diehard Maoists continues to advocate a one-party dictatorship, a state-run economy, the abolition of private property, and tight ideological control. They are made up of the losers in Deng's reforms. They are a small but rowdy group that has little support either inside the party and government establishment or among the public. Next, the new wealth-and-power elite are the biggest winners in Deng's reforms. They have a big stake in having a strong one-party rule, a mixed economy dominated by state-owned corporations that they control, and a tightly controlled media. They are fighting tooth and nail to hold onto their power. Then there is the frightening voice from the hawks in the military. They argue for competing in a global arena where the jungle law prevails. They claim that the economy must be modernized with an emphasis on modernization of the military, and that China should unflinchingly confront the United States and other hostile nations. They sum up their thinking in a vivid phrase—"modernization under the saber."

At the other extreme of the political spectrum are the liberal intellectuals. They hold up the Scandinavian countries as a model, advocating constitutional social democracy and condemning violent social revolution. They are likely to be university professors, scholars, journalists, and better-educated party and government officials. The middle class and the private business class have still not found their own independent voice. They appear to still cower in front of the overwhelming power of the party and government and the new wealth-and-power elite.

The strongest voices of the above groups have one thing in common: They all come from the "princeling club," which is a term loosely applied to the sons and daughters of the top echelon of the veteran Communists. The current PRC President and CCP General Secretary Xi Jinping is one of them. His father was a powerful party and government official; and he became a Red Guard during the Cultural Revolution, eventually serving in the countryside to work like a peasant. Xi also studied briefly at an American university, and returned to work his way up the CCP hierarchy until he reached the pinnacle of power. At the 19th National CCP Congress in October 2017, Xi let it be known that he needed greater power to control the economy, where the One Belt, One Road project would give the central government, not the market, greater priority in the nation's economic development both at home and in China's priorities abroad. Not surprisingly, Xi not so subtly indicated at the Congress and subsequently that he wanted to be freed from the recent party custom of changing party (and national) leadership every decade. Xi will also likely depart from Deng's policies of greater market economics and avoidance of a major confrontation with the United States. Xi and Trump, two new leaders breaking with recent political practices and policies, will certainly give the world an interesting time in which to live.

China suffered for its backwardness for over a century. The rise of China offers great opportunities as well as crucial challenges to both its own people and the world. The major global powers would do well to review history at this critical juncture. The rise of a new nation always upsets the old balance of power, and threatens the old world order. The repositioning of nations can lead to war if the new powers press ahead with reckless determination, and the old powers hold onto their privileged status with arrogant inflexibility. But if handled with reason and restraint, it can lead to peace, prosperity, and stability. The former happened in the first half of the twentieth century, leading to two world wars. The latter happened to some degree in the second half of the twentieth century. China is a giant of a country, and it is bound to play an increasingly important role in international affairs. It will be in the interest of all humanity if all the major powers can work in cooperation to build a new world order that is more just and peaceful. Will that mean integrating China into an existing but evolving liberal world order, or will it involve dismantling the substance of that liberal world order with one more to the liking of Beijing hardliners? Are there other alternatives?

Suggested Readings and Viewings

Frank Dikotter, *The Cultural Revolution: A People's History, 1962–1976* (New York: Bloomsbury Press, 2016).

Frank Dikotter, *The Tragedy of Liberation: A History of the Chinese Revolution, 1945–1957* (New York: Bloomsbury Press, 2013).

David M. Lampton, *Following the Leader: Beijing China, from Deng Xiaoping to Xi Jinping* (Berkeley: University of California Press, 2014).

Andrew J. Nathan and Andrew Scobell, *China's Search for Security* (New York: Columbia University Press, 2012).

Minxin Pei, China's Crony Capitalism: *The Dynamics of Regime Decay* (Cambridge, MA: Harvard University Press, 2016).

Michael Pillsbury, *The Hundred-Year Marathon: China's Secret Strategy to Replace America as the Great Superpower* (New York: St. Martin's Griffin, 2016).

To Live (1994), dir. by Zhang Yimou.

Yang Jisheng, *Tombstone: The Great Chinese Famine, 1958–1962* (New York: Farrar, Straus and Giroux, 2008).

18

Japan's Rapid Modernization, 1868–1918

Knowledge shall be sought throughout the world so as to strengthen the foundations of imperial rule.

—Charter Oath[1]

Meiji Restoration, 1868–1873

The collapse of the Tokugawa Shogunate was quick and sudden. The samurai rulers of Choshu and Satsuma were minor lords who were geographically far from the center of power, and had a long history of feuding with the Tokugawa family. Now they shrewdly saw an opportunity in the weakness of the Tokugawa shogun, formed an anti-Tokugawa alliance, and launched a military assault on the tottering Tokugawa regime. What set them apart and above other local lords was the fact that they had experienced the Western bombardments, recognized the superior power of Western technology, and scored some success in building a modern military. To legitimize their rebellion, their call to rally their troops was "Revere the emperor, Expel the foreigners." They successfully destroyed the Tokugawa regime in 1868, declared that the 16-year-old Emperor Meiji (1852–1912) was restored to the full powers of emperor, and relocated the royal capital from Heian (renaming it Kyoto) to Edo (renaming it Tokyo). By issuing the Charter Oath in the emperor's name, they outlined their vision of a modernized Japan, and the road to take to attain it. It was a sketchy map laid out in broad and vague brushstrokes, but it contained landmark new ideas: It called for a legislative body and the rule of law, the freeing of people from a near-caste system, the acceptance of international law, and openness to foreign ideas. Historians refer to these fundamental changes in ideas and institutions as the Meiji Restoration of 1868.

The Meiji Restoration constituted a series of radical reforms that many Japanese, then and today, considered revolutionary. Originating in the southwestern domains or *Han*, it was a bundle of contradictions. Its rallying cry, "Revere the emperor, expel the barbarian," sought to bring down the shogun and restore power to the emperor. In fact, these southwestern domain leaders, or *Hanbatsu*, seized the reins of power themselves and set up the emperor as a figurehead who

---

1 Quoted in Kyusaku Tsunoda, William Theodore de Bary, and Donald Keene, eds., *Sources of Japanese Tradition*, vol. 2 (New York: Columbia University Press, 1958), p. 137. Advisors to the young reigning Meiji Emperor wrote the Charter Oath. A coalition of leaders (the Hanbatsu or southwestern domain clique) from southwestern Japan who overthrew the Tokugawa Shogunate drew up a modernization program and ruled the country into the twentieth century.

Asia Past and Present: A Brief History, First Edition. Peter P. Wan and Thomas D. Reins.
© 2021 John Wiley & Sons, Inc. Published 2021 by John Wiley & Sons, Inc.

continued to reign but not rule. Their declared goal was to rid Japan of the Western powers and eradicate Western influences. In fact, once they deposed the Tokugawa Shogunate, their goal became the creation of a "rich country, strong army." Their original declared goal being seen as unrealistic in the modern world, they revised their policy agenda to focus on a modernization program that could protect Japan in a predatory global environment. This the *Hanbatsu* achieved by embracing the time-honored convention of loyalty to the emperor. The Charter Oath–written by samurai from those southwestern domains–legitimized a modernization they had come to power vehemently opposing.

The Meiji leaders were a group of young, ambitious, and well-educated samurai, knowledgeable of both warfare and statecraft, and their ruthless push for Japan's modernization would produce amazing results. They built a centralized, modernized national government. The emperor was the face of it, and they were the power behind the throne. They kept all major decision-making powers to themselves, but always made sure to show the greatest ceremonial respect to the boy emperor. These *Hanbatsu*, also referred to as the "Meiji Oligarchs," had made promises for a permanent leg-islature in the new constitutional government structure, but delayed its implementation until 1889.

Their ambition for the transformation of Japan into a modern nation faced monumental chal-lenges. Japan had a long history of a feudal system wherein a person's station in life was determined by birth, not by merit. In order to create a social structure that resembled Western society, where equality of all was a fundamental tenet, the Meiji Oligarchs would have to dismantle Japan's rigidly stratified society. And so they set about to get rid of the local *daimyo* or lords' inherited domains, strip the samurai of their privileged status, and remove restrictions on the commoners.

They gave commoners the right to have surnames, and freed them from earlier occupational and residential restrictions, in 1870; organized the country into prefectures under national government jurisdiction and separated local lords from control of their domains in 1871, and later retired *daimyo* with generous pensions; and built a new conscript army, giving every man the right (indeed the duty) to join the army in 1872. At the same time, the government stripped the samurai of their privilege of being the exclusive class of warriors and put them on less generous stipends. Later, when the government reduced their stipends and forced them to accept government bonds in exchange, many quickly became impoverished.

The Meiji government continued the Tokugawa practice of relying on agricultural taxes as its main source of revenue, and collecting it from the owners of the land. But there was a significant difference. Back in Tokugawa times, absentee landowners held title to the land, while the villagers who cultivated the land paid the taxes; now the Meiji government introduced a new land system in which the villagers who actually cultivated the land received certificates of land ownership. The cultivator of the land and the owner of the land became the same person, and the absentee land-owners of the Tokugawa period were left with nothing.

Timeline for Japan's Rapid Modernization, 1868–1918	
1868–1912	Reign of Meiji Emperor (1852–1912)
1868	Southwestern domains (*Han*) overthrow Tokugawa Shogunate and restore Meiji Emperor with full imperial powers; leaders of southwest-ern domains (*Hanbatsu*) launch a modernization program and govern directly or indirectly into the early twentieth century
1868	Imperial Charter Oath legitimizes modernization

1871	Japan is politically reorganized into prefectures under the control of the central government; great lords (*daimyo*) lose control over their domains and are pensioned off; Ministry of Education established on the French model
1871–1873	Iwakura Mission visits Europe and the United States to get a firsthand grip on modernization and Western cultures
1872	Japan creates a modern conscript army, builds first railroad line, and constructs "demonstration" factories
1872–1876	Intellectual Fukuzawa Yukichi writes *An Encouragement of Learning* in 17 volumes
1873–1895	Crisis of 1873: Traditional-minded Meiji Oligarchs walk out of the cabinet, leaving reform-minded Meiji Oligarchs in control of the government for the next two decades
1874	Japan launches brief invasion of Qing China's Taiwan
1876	Japan forces Korea to sign the Ganghwa Treaty, which opens up treaty ports in Korea
1877	Satsuma Rebellion: The last and most violent rebellion by old-school samurai against the reform-minded Meiji Oligarchs; crushed by the conscript army of the national government
1877	Founding of Tokyo University
1880s	Emergence of the *Zaibatsu*, or economic conglomerates
1889–	Meiji Constitution establishes Japan as a constitutional monarchy headed by the emperor, who is "divine and inviolable"; constitution is amended in 1947 during the American occupation
1890	Imperial Rescript on Education: A basic statement on the purpose of education, focusing on skills and the Confucian values of loyalty to the throne and state; compulsory education is established
1890s	Intellectual Fukuzawa Yukichi shifts his emphasis on natural law as the foundational principle to one of Social Darwinism, suggesting global struggle and militaristic emphases
1891–1903	Russia builds Trans-Siberian Railroad to better compete in Asia
1894	Oligarchs allow the formation of political parties in the Diet
1894–1895	First Sino-Japanese War: Japan defeats Qing China, which gives up Taiwan and Liaodong Peninsula; Triple Intervention forces Japan to relinquish some of its Liaodong rights
1899	Diet sponsors program to establish agricultural cooperatives
1902	Anglo-Japanese Alliance: Formed to check Russian expansion in Asia
1904–1905	Russo-Japanese War: Japan defeats Russia and expands into Manchuria
1910–1945	Japan formally colonizes Korea
1914–1918	Japan joins Allied nations in World War I and expands its influence in East Asia and the Pacific
1918–1921	Japan sends 70,000 troops to Siberia, most likely to create a buffer state between the emerging Soviet Union and Japan

The Meiji government handled the question of church–state relations fairly successfully, at least in the short term. It proclaimed Shinto to be Japan's sole state religion in 1868, linking it with the imperial institution. In the longer term, that linkage contributed to the radicalization of Japanese politics in the 1930s and during World War II. Shinto as the state religion resulted in large numbers of Buddhists initially stubbornly protesting Buddhism's perceived downgrading. Meanwhile, the Western powers had exerted enough pressure to make the Meiji government lift the old ban on Christianity in 1873. Ultimately, Japan was left with three religions—Shinto, Buddhism, and Christianity—existing peacefully side-by-side as secular ideas and institutions began to take on greater prominence in Japanese society.

The wide-ranging reforms hurt an extensive swath of the population across the country, creating widespread discontent. Many peasants were unhappy with the compulsory military service and the new land and tax system. They rioted and staged uprisings in protest. Traditional merchants also expressed dissatisfaction because they found it more difficult to compete after losing many of the privileges they had enjoyed under the older Tokugawa system. Most problematic were the samurai. In Tokugawa times, they were the educated class with administrative experience. Now, although under the new regime many of them took on valuable roles as government administrators, military officers, businessmen, financiers, teachers, and colonists, nonetheless many former warriors found themselves unable to make successful transitions and chose to express their bitterness in violent ways.

The split stretched the ranks of the samurai from the top Meiji oligarchs to the grassroots. Reformers pushed for further Westernization, while conservatives favored restoring the traditional samurai class with its *bushido* values. The conservatives in government decided they wanted to make war on Korea with two chief objectives in mind. First, they wanted to force Korea to open up to Japanese trade, and second, they saw in this military operation a means to revive samurai vigor, values, and status. Overruled by the reformers, the more conservative element walked out of government. This "Crisis of 1873" left reform-minded oligarchs in control. But to mollify the samurai who had favored an invasion of Korea, the government launched a brief and successful invasion of China's Taiwan in 1874. However, the disaffected samurai refused to be appeased. Unemployed and impoverished, they donned their armor and took up their bows and arrows in a desperate rebellion. The "Satsuma Rebellion of 1877" was the last and the most violent samurai revolt against the approaching modern times, as best represented by Saigo Takamori. One of the leaders of the Tokugawa ouster and the Meiji Restoration, Saigo's "noble" but failed opposition to his former comrades in arms has led to his being designated "the last samurai." The Meiji Oligarchs crushed the rebellion in a textbook example of how a modern army, with its superior firepower, training, and strategy, can methodically wipe out an archaic army that is valiant but doomed.

The Meiji Restoration was revolutionary in many ways. It destroyed the feudal system of domain autonomy and established a centralized national government. It destroyed the feudal system and upheld the idea of equality of all men. And it opened up Japan to the world. This was a revolution from the top-down: A small, elite group of samurai successfully imposed fundamental reforms on an entire reluctant population. They made their difficult mission easier by shrewdly acting in the name of the emperor's long-established authority, and deftly using the national government bureaucracy of the Tokugawa Shogunate. They kept many old values, practices, and structures to promote their ultimate goal of Japan's modernization.

Following its tradition of "borrowing," Japan dispatched many delegations overseas on study tours, no longer to China but to Western countries. Most important among them was the Iwakura Mission of 1871–1873. It was the most significant of many similar missions in the Meiji period that brought back to the Japanese firsthand information about the outside world after centuries of "seclusion."

The **Iwakura Mission** (1871–1873) was a delegation the Japanese government sent to Europe and America. It consisted of high-ranking government officials and scholars, and took with it 60 students. Iwakura Tomomi (1825–1883) had the title of plenipotentiary ambassador, and he had three vice ambassadors who were ministers in the Japanese government. They had an official diarist who kept a detailed log of all their experiences. They met with heads of state, political leaders, big merchants and industrialists, and educators. They also visited government institutions, schools, factories, mines, and research facilities. Their mandate was twofold: one, to negotiate the repeal of the unequal treaties Japan had signed with Western powers; and, two, to study how the various aspects of modern Western society worked, and bring that information back to inform Japan's modernization drive. They failed totally on the first task, but were successful on the second, bringing back a wealth of information that Japan would use to modernize its government, economy, military, and education.

Emergence of Modern Japan

Reform-minded Meiji Oligarchs dominated the government for at least a quarter century after the Crisis of 1873. What they achieved in such a brief period was nothing less than phenomenal. They developed a constitutional monarchy, a modernizing economy, and an army and navy that demanded international respect. But it was a stormy course they sailed. While they pursued their goals, other groups had their own agendas. Conflicting interests would lead to frequent and violent outbursts. While the Charter Oath provided a provisional government structure and program, the Meiji Oligarchs needed to create a strong central government within a constitutional framework that would best sustain Japan's modernization efforts. Fukuzawa Yukichi's "Civilization and Enlightenment" movement provided a broad roadmap to modernization, be it in government, economic arrangements, or social issues. Nonetheless, specific policy recommendations tended to produce opposing camps.

Those opposing the Meiji Oligarchs preferred ideas and institutions demanded a national legislature that would balance the power of the oligarchs, and protect local interests and individuals' rights. They drew on Western political theory for support, and quoted the U.S. Bill of Rights. Consistent with their tradition of borrowing, Japan would pick a Western model for their constitution and government structure. Of the various European constitutions, Germany's was the most conservative, giving the emperor greater power than the others. The Meiji Oligarchs liked that, and made it their model. But they rejected the Western principle that the constitution and the legislature are the people's voice, and should serve as a check on government power to prevent anyone in high office from abusing the power entrusted to him. To the Meiji Oligarchs, the Japanese constitution and congress should not be the people's voice, but a vehicle for popular participation in the implementation of the emperor's will. They announced the Meiji Constitution (1890–1945) as the emperor's gift to his subjects. Without even the pretense of being an instrument developed by the people to curb the emperor's power, it proclaimed the emperor "divine," "sacred and inviolable," and supreme: Ultimate power rested with the emperor. The function of the Diet (the legislature) consisted of two houses. The House of Peers (upper house) was made up of old court nobles, ex-*daimyo*, and Meiji oligarchs; and the House of Representatives (lower house) was made up of men elected by their respective constituencies. The Cabinet was answerable only to the emperor, beyond Diet control. The emperor's power extended across the Privy Council, the Cabinet, the Diet, and the military general staff. The Constitution provided no mechanism for the critical function of coordination of these disparate branches of government. Instead, it was left to an informal practice of "private consultation." Those privileged to participate would be elder states-men of influence, notably the Meiji Oligarchs and court nobles. They would collectively decide on major issues, such as the selection of prime minister, who would be one of them. The Diet, how-ever, did have one critical power: control of the purse strings. It alone had the power to approve or veto government budgets. In this, it was similar to the U.S. House of Representatives. Theoretically, the emperor was above the fray of partisan politics. The popular right to vote was restricted to tax-paying property owners, who made up 1.1 percent of the total population.

The Meiji Oligarchs made nation building their central mission. They exercised immense power, saw themselves as the embodiment of the general good of the nation, and believed in a transcenden-tal cabinet (i.e., one that rose above personal ambition and partisan interests), in contrast to political parties who pursue the narrow preferences of interest groups. At the time the constitution was being developed, their power was like the sun at midday; no one questioned their leadership role in govern-ment. But their power was personal by nature, not defined by the constitution. Over time, political parties would rise to challenge their power, and the absence of formal constitutional backing for their privileged powers, such as the selection of the prime minister, would prove fatal to their power. Eventually, the Meiji samurai would fade into history while political parties would proliferate.

Ito Hirobumi (1841–1909). *Source:* Pictorial Press Ltd / Alamy Stock Photo.

Education

What the Iwakura Mission saw convinced them that the modern nations of the West functioned as an organic whole. The returning mission members concluded that the smooth operation of the government, the prosperous economy, and the powerful military were mutually dependent on one another. Education, increasingly public and widespread, played a pivotal role in that complex structure. Back in Japan, they emphasized the importance of education in preparing the next generation for Japan's modernization and competition on a global stage. They determined that Japan needed a workforce with basic skills in reading, writing, and mathematics to be factory workers, business clerks, and soldiers and sailors; it also needed men with higher levels of education to be managers and officers. To meet these two different levels of demand, Japan created a two-tier educational system: a general education for the masses, and an advanced education for the elite.

The Ministry of Education was established in 1871 on the French model, which was highly centralized through government regulation. National government policy determined not only the general direction of education but also the specific content, although schools were locally funded. The first "normal school" (teacher-training school) was established in 1872, and Tokyo University was established in 1877. Four-year and then six-year compulsory education was put in place over time. The 1890 Prescript on Education became the basic statement on the purpose of education. It focused on basic skills and the Confucian values of loyalty to the throne and state. Japanese schools became widely known for training in basic skills through rote learning and indoctrination with narrow nationalism and fanatical patriotism.

To jump-start its modern education, the government hired foreign experts to teach in Japan and sent numerous students to study abroad in Western countries. But this expensive policy lasted only as long as it was absolutely necessary. As soon as the Japanese had acquired enough expertise through such foreign contact, they replaced the foreign experts with Japanese personnel, and the preponderance of Japanese students would go to Japanese universities. Nonetheless, a small cadre of students continued to go abroad to gain expertise in the ways of the diverse foreign cultural practices.

The Economy

The government played a significant role in modernizing Japan's economy. Japan's initial capital and labor for industrialization could only come from the agricultural sector. The government helped boost agricultural production by encouraging the wide adoption of new technology, new strains of seed, new fertilizers, and new methods of cultivation, as well as the opening up of new lands to farming. Increased productivity also freed up agricultural labor that migrated to cities to fill the ranks of the new industrial workforce. When it became evident that a widening gap was separating urban and rural Japan, the Diet sponsored a program in 1899 to establish agricultural cooperatives in the hope of averting the kind of class conflict that plagued Western nations.

The government played an even greater role in modernizing Japan's industry. It completed Japan's first railroad line in 1872, and made Kyoto its first city to have trolley cars three years later. It built "demonstration factories," such as silk factories, textile mills, and cement plants, to show private investors that factories in light industry were technologically feasible and economically profitable. Private investors rushed in and carried on when they saw the successes of the demonstrations.

The government made large investments in strategic industries to develop Japan's military might, chiefly steel plants, shipyards, munitions factories, coal mines, and such. These state-run factories, like all state-run enterprises, fared poorly. So the government decided to sell off most of them at public auction in the late 1880s. Men with close ties to the government purchased them at bargain prices. This small handful of enterprises, often family-owned and closely associated with government, grew into huge monopolistic industrial and financial corporations that controlled the modern sector of the nation's economy. These conglomerates became known as *Zaibatsu*.

The modern sector of Japan's economy made moral claims that it was a service to the state and emperor to build a bank, a shipyard, a trading company, or a steel plant. This higher moral purpose gave them justification for receiving generous government assistance. It also gave the samurai class, who traditionally shunned money making, reason to enter the world of businesses. It wasn't long before the ex-samurai poured in to fill corporate positions as capable and dedicated executives. They translated the traditional Japanese values of group solidarity and mutual responsibility into corporate loyalty. It also justified a government policy of strong government support and guidance in a relatively free market environment. For example, the government made strenuous efforts to preserve Japan's economic independence by protecting its domestic market, conserving foreign currency, avoiding foreign loans, and holding down domestic consumption.

The Military

Meiji Oligarchs made the modernization of the Japanese military an essential component of their overall program of modernization. They rebuilt the armed forces on Western models, again taking an eclectic approach. They reorganized the army on the German model, establishing a general staff and creating a Staff College. They reorganized the navy on the British model. Although they purchased some of their guns and ships from Germany and England, they relied mostly on homemade equipment to arm and maintain their forces. Military modernization contributed to other aspects of Japan's modernization as well. It stimulated the growth of such industries as armaments, shipbuilding, mining, and even the making of shoes, uniforms, and tin cans. It also indoctrinated the large numbers of recruits from the backcountry with extreme nationalism and unquestioning loyalty to the emperor.

Yamagata Aritomo (1838–1922). *Source:* Library of Congress, Prints & Photographs Division, Reproduction number LC-USZ62-119071 (b&w film copy neg.).

Intellectual Trends

Japanese intellectuals started out embracing the heritage of the European Enlightenment, and then moved on in various directions. Fukazawa Yukichi (1835–1901) was one of the most influential thinkers of the Meiji period who forcefully promoted Westernization. He was an author, teacher, translator, entrepreneur, political theorist, and the founder of Keio University in 1858. He typified the intellectuals who first embraced the doctrine of natural law, which believes in the principle of "all men are created equal," but soon abandoned it to embrace Social Darwinism, which applies the basic tenets of Darwinism to explain conflict and progress in human society and the rise and fall of nations. In other words, he believed that the "jungle law" of competition, survival of the fittest, and progress applies not only to the natural world but also to human society. This harsh and "realistic" view of the human condition made it possible for him to condone the Japanese war of conquest of Korea and the First Sino-Japanese War.

On the War Path to Build an Empire

Korea, Taiwan, and Manchuria became Japan's stepping stones to empire. The Yi Dynasty in Korea had long been in serious decline by the 1800s. The peasantry suffered from having small landholdings, high taxes, and corrupt government. Rice riots, uprisings, and rebellions were frequent. Japan had long coveted a presence in Korea, but was less than successful. Now a modernizing Japan with ambitions to match its increasing strength was ready to make a move on Korea. But Korea had long been a tributary state to China, so Japan's ambitions put the two countries on a collision course. Japan succeeded in forcing the Ganghwa Treaty on Korea in 1876, which permitted it to establish diplomatic relations and open up three treaty ports. Rioting and rebellion broke out in Korea in 1893 and 1894, respectively, which gave both China and Japan an excuse to send in troops. The first Sino-Japanese War of 1894–1895 broke out, and the Japanese military quickly overpowered the Chinese Beiyang Army. Japanese troops marched victoriously northward through Korea, across the Yalu River into Manchuria, and captured China's port city Dalian on the tip of Liaodong Peninsula. The Imperial Japanese Navy also wiped out the Chinese Beiyang Fleet at sea. Japan had won its first major war on its path to building a colonial empire, and established itself as a dominant power in Asia.

In the Sino-Japanese Treaty of Shimonoseki that ended the war in 1895, China agreed to Korea's "independence"; heavy war reparations; the cession of Liaodong Peninsula, Taiwan, and the adjacent Penghu Islands; the opening of additional treaty ports; and the extension of "most-favored nation" status to Japan. For the next half century, Japan would rule Korea, eventually as a colony (1910–1945), and expand its occupation of Chinese territories. In emulation of Western powers, it had not only achieved a high degree of industrialization but also acquired colonies. As the only non-Western nation, it had joined the club of colonial powers as a junior member. But it was not a happy member of the imperial club. It felt discriminated against.

The Treaty of Shimonoseki had opened the way for Japan to reduce China's Liaodong Peninsula to a Japanese sphere of influence. But Japan was not the only foreign power staking out spheres of influence in China. Russia, Germany, and France saw the Japanese move as a threat to their interests, and joined forces to compel Japan to disgorge some of its war booty. Under pressure, Japan agreed to give up Liaodong Peninsula in exchange for more reparations in silver. The Triple Intervention in 1895 fanned the flames of strong anti-Western nationalist sentiment in Japan, and would contribute to the Russo-Japanese War a decade later.

Meiji Japan put a premium on national security, and their ambitions reached far beyond their own borders. They saw it as their duty to defend not only Japan's "line of sovereignty" but also its "line of interest." Both lines ran through Korea and into China. The navy was gratified by the acquisition of Taiwan in 1895, while the army was gratified by the formal acquisition of Korea in 1910. Nonetheless Japanese nationalists in general and its military in particular believed that Japan needed to dominate the surrounding seas as well. Both were unhappy at giving up the Liaodong Peninsula.

Japan was also very sensitive to the question of equality. Nationalist sentiment demanded the abolition of Western extraterritoriality and the restoration of tariff autonomy. Japan issued a new law code to demonstrate that it was equal to Western nations in terms of the rule of law. This put enough public pressure on Western powers to relinquish their extraterritoriality rights in Japan, which also opened additional treaty ports, thus incentivizing the Western powers to give up their control of Japan's tariff.

The Russo-Japanese War, 1904–1905

Czarist Russia was the most backward of Western powers, but it too wanted a piece of the China pie. It built the Trans-Siberian Railroad between 1891 and 1903 to connect European Russia to its territories in Northeast Asia. The Chinese Eastern Railway—a Russian-Chinese enterprise—and its southern branch ran through Manchuria to Dalian on the Liaodong Peninsula, giving St. Petersburg access to a much-needed warm-water port in East Asia. Russia's expansion threatened the interests of both Britain and Japan. As national interests shifted, so did military and diplomatic alliances. Britain and Japan, now faced with a common challenge, signed the Anglo-Japanese Treaty in 1902 that committed them to mutual support in the event of war. The alliance strengthened Japan's hand and enhanced its international standing.

The competition between Japan and Russia in China's Manchuria led to the outbreak of the Russo-Japanese War (1904–1905), just as the earlier competition between China and Japan over Korea had led to the First Sino-Japanese War (1894–1895). Japan launched a sneak attack on Russian troops in Dalian, defeating Russian forces on land and virtually wiping out its navy at sea. Japan followed up by extending its colonial control from Korea into Manchuria. Japan ruled Korea, Manchuria, and Taiwan in the same manner Western powers ruled their colonies—to extract the greatest benefit for themselves by whatever means it took.

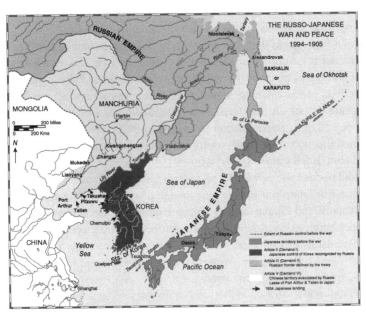

Map of Russo-Japanese War, 1904–1905. *Source:* Adapted from https://weaponsandwarfare.files.wordpress.com/2016/07/f-article-demandslg.jpg?w=768.

Japan's victory over Russia was the first time a non-Western nation defeated a Western nation. Prominent individuals in many—but especially in Asian—countries hailed Japan's victory. American President Theodore Roosevelt greeted it as the victory of a progressive Japan over a backward Russia. Chinese and Indian nationalists hailed it as proof that an Asian nation can defeat a Western power.

Japan's wars and spoils of war fueled its economic growth. Its steel, armaments, and shipbuilding industries grew rapidly. Japanese-built ships equaled any in the world in quality and quantity. Its light industry flourished. Its exports of silk outstripped China's. Its export of manufactured goods and import of raw materials indicated a change in the nature of its economy. By the end of the Meiji reign in 1912, its industrial sector accounted for 36 percent of its Gross National Product (GNP).

Its surge in economic growth brought the greatest benefits to the *Zaibatsu*, but the workers in those industries didn't share in those benefits. Conditions in industry continued to be harsh. Sixty percent of the workforce was female in the 1910s, but laws to protect women workers and child laborers were weak and slow in coming. A law limiting their working day to 11 hours didn't pass until 1916. Government response was blatant and ruthless. They worked in close collaboration with big business and passed laws that banned strikes (1900), employed troops against striking workers, and framed and executed leaders of radical anti-government groups. The unbearable conditions led to violent strikes. Copper miners went on strike in 1909, Tokyo streetcar workers went on strike in 1911, and rice riots broke out in 1918. As Kuwada Kumazo, a professor at Tokyo Imperial University and a member of the Diet's House of Peers, described the situation in the early twentieth century: "All sensible observers must admit that with rent and other necessary factors of living rising out of proportion to increases of wages and the unrelaxed severity of employers treating the employed, the voice of discontent against capitalists and employers is growing in volume and intensity."[2]

Japan and World War I, 1914–1918

World War I was mainly a struggle among Western nations, and the fighting took place mainly on European battlefields. Japan took advantage of the West's preoccupation with Europe to expand its influence in East Asia. It declared war on Germany in 1914 and seized German interests in and around China and the Pacific. It presented China with the Twenty-One Demands the following year in an attempt to take control of China. It joined Western powers in sending troops to Russia in a failed attempt to prop up the Russian Czarist government and bring down the Communist Soviet Union. Its expedition force in Russia was much greater than the combined forces of the United States, Britain, France, and Canada. By 1918, it had taken control of Eastern Siberia in addition to Manchuria and Korea. The West's desperate commitment to its war efforts in Europe prevented it from successfully competing economically with Japan in Asia, and created a demand for Japanese-manufactured goods, which stimulated rapid growth in Japan's production and export. Taking advantage of the West's weakness, Japan expanded economically, and jumped from being a debtor nation to being a creditor nation. Japan went to the Paris Peace Conference in 1919 as a member of the victorious Allied Nations, and was granted a permanent seat on the Council of the League of Nations. And the Treaty of Versailles officially transferred to Japan Germany's sphere of influence in China, and put under Japanese mandate Pacific islands that were formerly under German control.

---

2 As quoted in Michael L. Lewis, *Rioters and Citizens: Mass Protest in Imperial Japan* (Berkeley: University of California Press, 1990), p. 4.

Japan's limited role in WWI had paid off big-time. It was now a major player in the international arena and recognized as a major military and industrial power. But it did experience a humiliating setback when Tokyo proposed to add a "racial equality" clause to the Treaty of Versailles and was rebuffed by Western powers. Furthermore, after Japan became democratic in 1919, the Diet in a more open society now had to answer for its faulty domestic and humiliating foreign policy choices. In only a dozen years, those democratic choices in too many important cases would be seen by an expanding electorate as fundamentally flawed.

Suggested Readings and Viewings

Leo T. S. Ching, *Becoming Japanese: Colonial Taiwan and the Politics of Identity Formulation* (Berkeley: University of California Press, 2001).

Albert M. Craig, *Civilization and Enlightenment: The Early Thought of Fukuzawa Yukichi* (Cambridge, MA: Harvard University Press, 2009).

Peter Duus, *The Abacus and the Sword: The Japanese Penetration of Korea, 1895–1910* (Berkeley: University of California Press, 1998).

Takii Kazuhiro, *Ito Hirobumi: Japan's First Prime Minister and Father of the Meiji Constitution* (London: Routledge, 2014).

Donald Keene, *Emperor of Japan: Meiji and His World, 1852–1912* (New York: Columbia University Press, 2005).

Rotem Kowner, ed., *The Impact of the Russo-Japanese War* (London: Routledge, 2006).

Phillips O'Brien, *The Anglo-Japanese Alliance, 1902–1922* (London: Routledge, 2009).

Mark Ravina, *The Last Samurai: The Life and Battles of Saigo Takamori* (Boston: Wiley, 2005).

Sanshiro Sugata (1943), dir. by Akira Kurosawa.

19

Japan Goes from Liberalism to Militarism, 1918–1945

Truly, our seven hundred million brothers in China and India have no path to independence other than that offered by our guidance and protection.

—Kita Ikki[1]

Post–World War I Japan enjoyed unprecedented prosperity and international prestige. But signs of trouble abounded, for the emperor was weak, political parties were proliferating, and the military, ever growing in strength, became restive. For nearly half a century, Japan's relentless drive for modernization and several major war victories had given the nation a strong sense of national destiny, solidarity, and pride. Emperor Meiji had provided the nation with the symbol of national solidarity, and the Meiji Oligarchs had steered with a firm hand.

But now the situation had changed dramatically. The wars had been won, most of the Meiji Oligarchs were dead, Emperor Meiji had died (in 1912), and his successor Emperor Taisho (1879–1926, r. 1912–1926) was mentally ill. Consequently, leadership and common cause began to dissipate at the highest levels of power. Surviving Meiji Oligarchs, now joined by their protégés, continued to dominate political decision making, but their influence was dwindling. New men had been entering the bureaucracy through civil service examinations since 1885, and they were not beholden to the elder statesmen's patronage. The modern economy had produced a strong business class and middle class. The wars had strengthened the head of the military. The balance of power of Japan's body politic was shifting.

The Meiji Restoration had created the conditions for political parties to emerge and become active since the turn of the twentieth century. The Seiyukai, or Friends of Constitutional Government, Party became the most powerful political party in Japan from 1900 to 1921. Promoting big government and large-scale public spending, it was a pro-government alliance of bureaucrats, supported by landowners and the *Zaibatsu*. It often favored government control and opposed social reform. It was generally conservative despite its "liberal" label.

The economic slump of 1912 generated demands for cutbacks in government spending and ignited intense fighting among the various interest groups. While the Seiyukai continued to

---

1 As quoted in Kyusaku Tsunoda, William Theodore de Bary, and Donald Keene, eds., *Sources of Japanese Tradition*, vol. 2 (New York: Columbia University Press, 1958), p. 269. Kita's 1919 comment represented a moderate nationalist idea. Japan had long been a haven for nationalists from the rest of Asia, from Liang Qichao in China to Phan Boi Chau in Vietnam and later to Subhas Chandra Bose in India. The above quote heralds Japan's Greater East Asia Co-Prosperity Sphere.

Asia Past and Present: A Brief History, First Edition. Peter P. Wan and Thomas D. Reins.
© 2021 John Wiley & Sons, Inc. Published 2021 by John Wiley & Sons, Inc.

Timeline for Taisho Emperor, 1912–1926	
1912	Crown Prince Yoshihito (1879–1926) becomes Taisho Emperor
1912–1913	Taisho Political Crisis: In the economic slump of 1913, the military brings down the Seiyukai Party cabinet; "Movement to Protect Constitutional Government" demonstrates against military blackmail
1914–1918	World War I
1918	Post–World War I rice riots; demands for universal male suffrage; increased interest in Marxism and the Russian Communist Revolution
1918–1932	Beginning, decline, and demise of party government
1918	Hara Takashi/Hara Kei (1856–1921), a commoner and Seiyukai Party chief, forms the first party government selected by the Diet; advocates big government at home and conciliation with the West and China
1919	Versailles Peace Conference: Hara succeeds in having the German interests in China, including Qingdao, transferred to Japan, but fails to obtain a racial equality statement in the Treaty of Versailles
1921–1922	Hara's government attends Washington Conference, which limits the offensive military capabilities of the Western nations east of Singapore, but also transfers Qingdao back to China and assigns Great Britain and America larger battleship allocations than Japan in the disarmament agreement
1923	Tokyo Earthquake and outbreak of anarchism; government crackdown on anarchists, communists, and socialists
1924–1926	Count Kato Pataki becomes prime minister and continues Hara's foreign policy of conciliation; tries to play a balancing act between the political left and political right; gets General Election Law passed, giving all males over the age of 25 the right to vote; also gets Peace Preservation Act passed, which outlawed "dangerous thoughts"

insist on domestic spending, the Army was adamant about increased military spending. The odds favored the military in the final showdown, for the constitution stipulated that the chief of the general staff reported directly to the emperor, not to the cabinet, and an imperial ordinance in 1900 stipulated that only an active-duty officer could hold the office of Minister of the Army or Navy. So when the Army ordered the Minister of the Army to resign, the cabinet collapsed.

Politicians, journalists, and businessmen launched the "Movement to Protect Constitutional Government" in 1912–1913, holding massive demonstrations to protest against the military blackmail. Emperor Taisho called on Army general-turned-politician Katsura Taro to form a new cabinet. The Seiyukai refused to support him, and again the cabinet collapsed. For the first time in Japanese history, a political party, supported by public opinion and the media, had brought down a cabinet. Although Katsura eventually did manage to form a coalition that made him prime minister, his brief appointment was viewed as a plot by the "elder statesmen" to overthrow rule by the Constitution, and sparked widespread riots. This was the Taisho Political Crisis of 1912–1913. Three men followed as prime minister, and all three failed.

The Era of Party Government, 1918–1931

The post–World War I years are somewhat derisively called the Era of Taisho "Democracy." It can just as well be called the Era of Party Government. The period began with economic problems that produced social difficulties. Japan's economy enjoyed a brief period of prosperity after WWI, but it soon began to suffer prolonged inflation, driving up the prices of rice and most other consumer goods. The government aggravated the common people's plight by making large purchases of rice to support its expeditionary troops in Russia. The sharp rise in the price of rice and consumer goods hit both the rural and urban populations. Anti-government sentiment ran high, and led to the outbreak of a nationwide protest movement. It began with peaceful petitioning in rural villages, and quickly spread to towns and cities. Peaceful petitions soon escalated into peasants rioting, factory workers striking, mobs looting, and even fire-bombings of police stations and government offices. The violence of the rice riots in 1918 in scope, size, and degree was unparalleled in modern Japanese history. The government responded by arresting some 25,000 people and meting out penalties ranging from minor fines to death sentences.

Intellectual crosscurrents ran alongside Japan's economic and political developments. Before World War I, students of philosophy were long under the strong German influence of the Kantian and Hegelian schools. In the post-WWI years, their newly found interest was Marxism and the Russian Revolution. Japanese labor unions, inspired by this new revolutionary ideology, mounted large public demonstrations to demand universal male suffrage. In this crisis situation, the *genro* or "elder statesmen" selected Hara Takashi (also known as Hara Kei, 1856–1921) to be the next prime minister.

Hara's appointment in 1918 made him the "first" in many ways. He was the first party politician to be prime minister, since he was the president of the Constitutional Association or Seiyukai, which was the most powerful political party in the Lower House between 1900 and 1921. His government was the first "party government" in Japanese history, inaugurating the "Period of Party Government." As a commoner, his was the first cabinet to be headed by a commoner; his catch phrase as a politician was "commoner prime minister." He was also a baptized Catholic.

As prime minister, Hara promoted "big government," large-scale public spending, bureaucratic control, and militarism. Japanese politics was more complex and subtle than ever, now that elected party leaders were thrown into the political mix with elder statesmen, government bureaucrats, Army generals and Navy admirals, and representatives of business and the *Zaibatsu*. Government decision making became a high-wire balancing act among all these contending forces, and the outcome would be determined by their interplay. Hara realized that, among all these forces, only the government was elected, and he made strenuous efforts to weaken the power of the non-elected bureaucrats. But his refusal to use his majority in the Diet to ram through legislation for universal male suffrage without property requirements lost him support from the left, and he had never been a favorite of the right. In this political turmoil, he was assassinated by an ultraconservative railroad switchman, who was released only 13 years after he committed the crime.

Hara Takashi/Hara Kei (1856–1921) was first a journalist and then a diplomat before becoming a politician. He lived a relatively simple life all his life, and had few assets when he died. But among the possessions he left behind was his diary of several thousand pages. He left behind instructions that his diary was the most valuable of all his possessions, that it must be protected, and that it must be made public after some years. The "Hara Diary" has turned out to contain invaluable firsthand accounts of the political scene of his day. Most of the daily activities he chronicles are, moreover, accompanied with comments about political figures of his day, revealing previously unknown information and penetrating insight into people and events.

Rising popular discontent was stirring in the air. The Russian Communists had formed the Comintern to carry out its design of "world revolution," and it was working vigorously to organize the Chinese and Japanese Communist parties (founded in 1921 and 1922, respectively). In 1923, the Japanese Communist Party announced its goals: to end feudalism, abolish the monarchy, recognize the Soviet Union, and withdraw Japanese troops from Russia, China, Korea, and Taiwan. The Japanese government responded with a brutal suppression, and the radicals made an assassination attempt on Prince Regent Hirohito.

Japanese right-wing political forces were hard at work in parallel with the spread of left-wing radicalism. They were imbued with ultranationalism and militarism, and had formed ultranationalist societies that took an active part in domestic and foreign politics. They focused on fighting left-wing forces such as the socialists and communists after Japan's victories over China and Russia. The omnipresent Japanese police apparatus was more than willing to crush any radical movement. The Tokyo Earthquake of 1923 and the great fire that followed devastated the Tokyo–Yokohama region, killing around 100,000 people and unleashing anarchism. Rampaging mobs went on a spree of killing Koreans throughout the city. The police took advantage of breakdown of social order to round up socialists, communists, and anarchists.

Count Kato Pataki had to walk a tightrope as prime minister (1924–1926). He pushed two major pieces of legislation. One, the General Election Law, gave voting rights to all males 25 and over, which pleased the liberals. The second was the Peace Preservation Act, which attacked "dangerous thoughts" perpetrated by Japanese communists, and outlawed any advocacy of changing the political structure or abolishing private property, which appealed to the right-wing who worried about increasing left-wing influence, an expanded electorate, and the invasion of Western ideas. Kato also introduced moderate social reforms: legalizing labor unions, setting standards for factory conditions, establishing mediation procedures for labor disputes, and providing insurance for workers. Kato was a central figure in the Kenseikai Party, and a nobleman with close family ties to the Mitsubishi *Zaibatsu*. Highly skilled at playing the balancing act, his legacy represented the main accomplishments of the period of party government.

The next prime minister, Tanaka Giichi (1864–1929), was an Army general-turned-politician who was president of the Seiyukai Party. His career path was a telling indicator of the changing times: Military men traditionally despised politics, and for a general to accept the position of party leader highlighted the rising influence of parties. Also, the Seiyukai Party selecting a military man as party leader highlighted the continuing prestige of the military. Japanese politics was still a game reserved for the traditional elite.

Hamaguchi Osachi (1870–1931) was the president of the Minseito Party (Constitutional Democratic Party), and ran on a liberal platform committed to democratic politics, the parliamentary system, and world peace (1929). He won the election, but an assassination attempt by a right-wing fanatic left him fatefully wounded, and he died after only one month in office. His successor Wakatsuki Reijiro's government collapsed within a year (1931) when he lost control of the Japanese Army. His successor Inukai Tsuyoshi continued the effort to rein in the Japanese Army, and was assassinated (1932) while trying. His death marked the end of the Period of Party Government.

Japan did not have a tradition of party government. Its party politics was not based on mass political participation, and had little grassroots support. Therefore, it was inherently weak. Rather, its party politics was a game of shifting alliances among the elite groups: court nobles, military leaders, high-ranking bureaucrats, and major business leaders. Furthermore, political practices common in modern politics, such as conflicts among interest groups, appeals to self-interest, pork barrel politics, and ties with business, undermined voter support for them. By the late 1930s, when the Japanese military wielded unmistakable power over Japanese politics, the political parties voted to dissolve themselves into the Imperial Rule Assistance Association (1940–1945), which would be the single ruling party during the years of World War II. Party government had come to its official end.

Taisho Foreign Policy

Hara's foreign policy was to cooperate with Western powers and play by their rules. At the Paris Peace Conference in 1919, he successfully got the Western powers to legitimize Japan's seizure of the German spheres of influence in East Asia, including China's Liaodong Peninsula and some Pacific islands. But he failed to get them to make a declaration of racial equality. He signed the Washington Conference Treaties in the early 1920s, thereby accepting restrictions on the expansion of the Japanese Navy; agreed to withdraw Japanese troops from Russia's Siberia; adopted a more conciliatory policy toward China; and agreed to the U.S.-backed "open-door" policy in China. His China policy was designed to avoid costly Chinese boycotts: Japan's investments in China had accelerated after the outbreak of WWI, and now made up 80% of Japan's foreign investments, at a time when anti-Japanese sentiment in China was running high. Count Kato continued Hara's foreign policy of conciliation with the West and with China. Succeeding Count Kato, Tanaka abandoned Kato's foreign policy of conciliation. That was not surprising. He was a former general and not a professional politician, and he became prime minister when the Chinese Nationalist Party had launched the Northern Expedition (1927) and founded the Republic of China in Nanjing the next year (1928). Determining that the Chinese Nationalists threatened the Japanese sphere of influence in Manchuria, he sent troops to China's Liaodong Peninsula, which led to a clash between Japanese and Chinese troops.

Timeline for the Showa Emperor, 1926–1989	
1921–1926	Hirohito, later known as The Showa Emperor (1901–1989), serves as the ailing Taisho Emperor's regent
1926	Beginning of reign of the Showa Emperor, upon his father's death
1927–1928	In China, Jiang Jieshi's Northern Expedition threatens to destroy China's warlords and drive out the foreigners under a unified Republic of China in Nanjing
1928	Japanese Army officers assassinate Chinese Manchurian warlord Zhang Zuolin
1927–1929	General-turned-politician Tanaka Giichi serves as prime minister and abandons Kato's conciliatory policy toward China, but his cabinet collapses when he incurs the emperor's displeasure for failing to punish the Japanese Army officers who murdered Zhang Zuolin
1929–1939	The global Great Depression threatens political stability nearly everywhere and will have a major influence in Japan
1929	Hamaguchi Osachi (1870–1931) runs on a liberal platform for prime minister, is elected in 1929, and is assassinated in 1931
1930s	Kita Ikki (1883–1937), leading nationalist and populist intellectual, was executed by the government for questioning the role of the emperor
1931	The Shenyang/Mukden Incident leads to the Japanese Army seizing all of Manchuria
1932	The Shanghai Incident: Japanese Army attacks Shanghai

1932	The Period of Party Government ends and is replaced by "government by assassination"; the influence of the military steadily grows
1932–1945	Japan creates the puppet state of Manchukuo in the former State of Manchuria, with the last Chinese emperor Pu Yi serving as its titular leader
1932–1936	Emperor Pu Yi appoints prime ministers from the Navy, which is considered more moderate than the Army
1937–1945	The Lugouqiao or Marco Polo Bridge Incident outside of Beiping (renamed Northern Peace after Nanjing became China's capital) sets off the Second Sino-Japanese War
1937–1940	Japan's three military probes into Soviet Russia are turned back
1939	Japan's incursion into Soviet Russian–controlled Mongolia, the Nomonhan Incident, fails
1939–1940	Nazi–Soviet Pact sets off World War II in Europe
1940–1945	The Imperial Rule Assistance Association replaces all political parties for the duration of the war
1940	Japan joins Germany and Italy in Tripartite Pact
1941–1944	Prime Minister Tojo Hideki (1884–1948)
1941	Germany attacks Soviet Union; Japan attacks America at Pearl Harbor; Soviet Union is neutral in war against Japan
1945	The United States ends the war after atomic weapons are dropped on Hiroshima (August 6) and Nagasaki (August 9)
1945	August 8: Soviet Union joins war against Japan a week before it ends
1945	August 14: Japan surrenders to the Allied Powers

Meanwhile, a group of young Japanese officers in the Japanese Army in Manchuria engineered a plot in 1928 to assassinate local warlord Zhang Zuolin, who controlled much of Manchuria. The ultranationalist low-ranking Japanese officers had hoped to provoke war, which would have given them an excuse for war and the seizure of all of Manchuria. But that was not how things played out, for Zhang's son responded to his father's assassination by joining the Nanjing government and taking Manchuria with him. Tanaka's government collapsed when he incurred the displeasure of Emperor Showa (r. 1925–1989) for his failure to punish the murderers of Zhang Zuolin. This was a rare occasion when the emperor would directly intervene in a political decision. But more importantly, this event foreshadowed how the Army would take unilateral action in the future.

The Ascendance of Militarism in the 1930s

The party governments were an attempt to align Japan with the Western practices of liberal democracy and free trade, but an undercurrent of ultranationalism and militarism was surging against the political parties, even as they strived for a conciliatory and peaceful foreign policy.

Japan was experiencing the growing pains inherent in an economic transformation from a traditional agricultural society to a modern industrial society in the 1920s. The *Zaibatsu* were the big winners in Japan's modernization. Small businesses and small manufacturers were suffering.

Farmers' real income had declined by a third between 1925 and 1930. The poorest of them had to eat wild weeds, grass roots, and tree bark, and sell off their children to save the family. The transition was exacerbated by the return of competition from Western nations after WWI and the resurgence of nationalism in China.

Some political forces in Japan sympathized with the suffering in the countryside, and blamed modernity for Japan's woes. In their view, the culprits were the cities, the political parties, and the giant *Zaibatsu*. They advocated a return to the virtues of agrarianism and samurai values. Kita Ikki (1883–1937) was a leading theorist in this countercurrent in the 1930s before WWII. Enticed by the cause of the Chinese Revolution of 1911, he actually traveled to China to assist in the overthrow of the Qing Empire. But he returned to Japan in 1919 disillusioned by what he had seen in China, joined an ultranationalist organization with ties to the Japanese power establishment, and devoted his time to political writing and activism.

Kita Ikki called for egalitarianism at home and imperialist expansion overseas, to be realized through a kind of "socialism from above," imposed by a few dedicated men of ability in high places. His optimistic scenario was something like this: A military coup d'état ushers in a totalitarian regime under the direct rule of a strong leader, who suspends the constitution and reorganizes the Diet, which in turn nationalizes certain strategic industries, imposes limits on private wealth, and enacts a land reform to benefit the farmers. And all this would strengthen Japan to the point where it could liberate Asia from Western imperialism. His was a statist hodgepodge of ultranationalism and militarism, combined with Social Darwinism, socialism, agrarianism, and Fascism. From this position, he called for Japan to lead a war to free Asian nations from Western colonial control, and justified Japan's colonial conquests in Asia.

March 1st Movement, 1919.

He promoted "direct action," such as using intimidation, assassination, and unauthorized acts of war as means to achieving his goals. His call resonated in particular with young Army officers and small ultranationalist organizations. But his association with Army factions that failed in a 1936 coup attempt compromised him, and led to his imprisonment, secret trial in martial court, and execution.

The swing of the political pendulum from liberalism to the extreme right in Japan was a part of a global trend that took place during the global Great Depression. The Great Depression undermined many people's faith in democracy and capitalism. This was especially true in places where democratic values and practices were new and not firmly rooted. Individuals, tossed about by impersonal economic forces, felt totally vulnerable and helpless. They sought strength in large groups and charismatic leaders, and put their faith in violent action. The Russian Communist Party and its Revolution had set the gold standard for them: The Communist Party and the Soviet state became the great collective, Lenin and Stalin were its charismatic leaders, and they had achieved its goals by means of violence in war and peace. Many other nations would also resort to this black magic. Italian Fascism, German Nazism, and Japanese militarism were cases in point.

Japan's modernization had relied heavily on its exports to Western nations, especially to the U.S. market. When the Great Depression hit, the United States chose to look after its own interests first by raising its tariffs and shutting out imports. This protectionist policy dealt Japanese exports a heavy blow, aggravating the impact of the Great Depression. It also disillusioned them about the West, inducing them to believe that their efforts to emulate the Western model of free trade and liberal democracy were misguided. Both the military and the civil bureaucrats became convinced that Japan's only way of getting out of the Great Depression lay in a militarist government and overseas expansion—that an expanded Japanese empire would provide the much-needed raw materials, cheap labor, and markets. The Japanese Army saw itself as an independent agent of the emperor, saw party governments as usurpers of the emperor's prerogative, and hoped for a "Showa Restoration."

Japan already controlled Korea as a colony, and had a sphere of influence in adjacent China's Manchuria. It saw Manchuria as having great potential as an economic and military base for Japanese expansion, and envisioned turning it into a Japanese colony. Some low- and mid-level officers of the Japanese Imperial Guandong Army stationed in Manchuria, inspired by Kita's idea of direct action, created the Shenyang or Mukden Incident in September 1931: They provoked a military conflict, seized Manchuria, set up a puppet government (Manchukuo, or the State of Manchuria), and installed China's last emperor Pu Yi as its puppet emperor. When the League of Nations condemned its act of aggression, Japan haughtily walked out of that international body. Then the Japanese marines launched an attack in Shanghai (the Shanghai Incident, 1932). The party government in Tokyo was not in favor of these military actions, but neither did it firmly oppose them.

The domestic counterpart of the Shenyang and Shanghai Incidents was extremists taking "direct action" against party politics. Known as "politics by assassination," right-wing radicals in the Army attacked and killed prominent party, business, and liberal leaders. Coups and mutinies followed. Army assassins and mutineers were martyrs in the public's eye. But the emperor intervened by appointing prime ministers from the Navy, which was considered more enlightened and moderate than the Army. Cabinets headed by prime ministers from the Navy and including party men (1932–1936) cracked down and restored a semblance of order.

Tensions were high between the various centers of power, but the general trend was a power shift away from the political parties to the military and civil government bureaucrats. Together, they would be strong enough to change the course Japan would take.

Japan withdrew from the League of Nations, withdrew from the naval limitation agreements, and substantially increased its military budget. It beefed up its domestic repression, intensifying censorship, persecuting liberal authors, and banning their books. It stepped up domestic propaganda and indoctrination, filling the media with ultranationalist war hysteria.

Japan was plotting its expansion in Asia, as Nazi Germany expanded the war in Europe. The Japanese Army was eyeing Siberia and planning a "northward expansion" into the Soviet Union, while the Navy was salivating for the rich resources of Southeast Asia and planning a "southern expansion" into colonies of the West. The prospect of war with both Communist Russia and Western powers was enough incentive for Japan to enter an alliance with Germany in 1936, which was expanded in 1939 into the Tripartite Pact; Japan, Germany, and Italy were now allies and known as the "Axis Nations."

Japan in the Second Sino-Japanese War and World War II, 1937–1945

Japan's strategy for global conquest was divided into stages: It would start with the colonization of Korea, followed by the colonization of China's Manchuria, then all of China, and finally Southeast Asia and beyond. Its occupation of Korea and Manchuria did not threaten American interests seriously enough to make America give up the comfort of isolationism. But America was forced to act when Japan had occupied half of China and was marching its troops into Western powers' colonies in Southeast Asia.

The Outbreak of the Second Sino-Japanese War, 1937

Japanese encroachment on Chinese territory and sovereignty had been going on for decades, and intermittent fighting had been going on for just as long. But full-scale war did not break out until the Lugouqiao Incident (aka the Marco Polo Bridge Incident, outside Beijing, 1937). The Japanese Army provoked the conflict and prevailed in the ensuing fighting. But its hopes of a quick victory evaporated in the face of continued Chinese resistance. Japan also made three military probes into Russia in 1937–1940, which were beaten back.

Marco Polo Bridge. *Source:* Yves Hsu/Shutterstock.com.

But the Japanese government was encouraged by a string of battlefield victories in China. It raised its sights from a "quick war" of a partial conquest of China to a grandiose vision of a new order throughout East Asia. The new vision was named the Greater East Asian Co-prosperity Sphere, and Japan's role in it was the leader of Asian nations in a drive to free themselves from Western imperialism and Russian communism.

Japanese troops marched down the Chinese coast and captured China's capital Nanjing in 1937. What happened next was one of the most horrifying war atrocities in the annals of WWII—the Nanjing Massacre (aka the Rape of Nanking). The Nanjing Massacre, along with Japan's sneak attack on Pearl Harbor and the Bataan Death March, are among the most infamous of Japanese war crimes in WWII.

Japanese Army attacking Nanjing, 1937. *Source:* Keystone-France/Getty Images.

The Chinese Nationalist government evacuated its capital Nanjing in a rout, but managed to reestablish itself in its provisional capital in Chongqing, far up the Yangtze River, deep behind mountain ranges, and under year-round banks of thick clouds. It was digging in for a protracted war. Japanese troops continued their advance southward along the coast until they captured the southern port city Guangzhou (1938). Then Japan occupied French Indochina in 1940 under the Henri-Matsuoka Agreement. That move completely cut off China from the outside world. Japan was also poised to invade British Malaya, Hong Kong, Singapore, and the Dutch East Indies.

The United States, mired in its own problems, had earlier responded to Japanese aggression in China only by firing "paper bullets" (i.e., issuing diplomatic protests). But Japan's rapid advances in China and its threat to Western colonies farther south forced the United States to intervene with a much tougher posture: It demanded that Japan withdraw from both French Indochina and China (excluding Manchuria). When Japan refused to comply, the United States imposed an embargo of oil and scrap iron, and then froze Japanese assets in the United States (1940). These moves put a chokehold on Japan, since Japan produced no oil at home, and depended on imports of oil and iron to keep its economy and war machine running. Japan had to make a choice: Either yield to American demands, or fight back. To capitulate would mean giving up its vision of Japanese domination of East Asia, a goal it had worked toward for decades. It chose to move boldly forward. It was of particular importance to Japan to have access to the rubber and oil of the West's colonies in Southeast Asia. Battle-hardened Japanese troops swiftly marched into the British, French, Dutch, and Americans colonies, and drove them out.

Japan's Sneak Attack on Pearl Harbor and the Outbreak of World War II

While pushing ahead in China, Japan developed a grand strategy for war with America in the Pacific: It believed that it could deliver a staggering blow to the United States in the Pacific, and force a favorable redrawing of spheres of influence. Based on that conclusion, it took concrete steps to prepare Japan for war with America. Its National General Mobilization Law of 1938 placed the Japanese economy on a war basis, and increased the prime minister's powers at the expense of the Diet and civil liberties. The government forced education and the mass media to speak with one voice, whipping up nationalist and war hysteria; attacked and purged Western liberal ideas and popular tastes; organized urban residents into neighborhood units; and, to cap it all, merged all the various political parties into one single Imperial Rule Assistance Association (1940). Army General Tojo Hideki (1884–1948) became prime minister between 1941 and 1944.

America's disillusionment at the outcome of WWI had encouraged postwar isolationism, and the Great Depression had deepened it. President Franklin Roosevelt's internationalist position had little public support, and he had to make shamelessly devious maneuvers in order to prepare America for what he saw as its inevitable entry into a global conflict.

Japan launched a sneak attack on America at Pearl Harbor on December 7, 1941. The attack left 2400 Americans dead, and destroyed seven American battleships and 120 aircraft. Japan's attack freed Americans overnight from the embrace of isolationism. When President Roosevelt asked the Congress for a declaration of war on Japan, the entire nation stood behind him. When Congress declared war on Japan, the entire nation went to war as a united country. Nazi Germany and Fascist Italy declared war on America as Japan's allies through the Tripartite Pact. A full-fledged World War II was now underway. Japan, instead of forcing a favorable compromise from the United States, had engaged the world's most powerful nation in a life-and-death struggle.

Japanese attack on Pearl Harbor, December 7, 1941.

Japanese troops swiftly took control of Vietnam, Burma, Hong Kong, Malaya, the Philippines, and the Dutch East Indies (now Indonesia). In the American colony of the Philippines, the Japanese committed one of the worst war atrocities of WWII—the Bataan Death March (1942).

Japan's military operations were indisputably successful. But its military strategy was at odds with its economic policies and political propaganda. In rallying support for its Greater East Asian Co-prosperity Sphere, Japan set itself up as the leader of Asian nations in a war against Western colonialism. But its policies in the occupied countries were to stamp out any signs of resistance with extreme brutality, and to exploit the local economies to their last drop of blood. It didn't take long for the local peoples to see that Japan's claim to being the leader in an anticolonial war was nothing but propaganda, and that Japan was the new colonial power. They quickly turned against the Japanese conquerors.

In Korea, Japan imposed the harshest policies of colonization, but met with tenacious resistance. In China, the Nationalist government held out tenaciously in the mountainous regions of Southwest China, while the Communists expanded their presence in the countryside behind Japanese lines in North China. The vastness of China's population and territory limited Japanese occupation to major cities along the coast and transportation lines. The United States quickly recovered from the shock and loss of the Pearl Harbor attack, and threw into its war efforts the entire weight of its human and natural resources. Its awesome production capacity combined with China's rich human resources to produce a formidable force that mired the Japanese forces in China. The United States strengthened the Chinese government in Chongqing by pumping an endless flow of war supplies into China. And it began a steady advance across the Pacific toward Japan's home islands. Its victory at the Battle of Midway Island in 1942 checked Japan's advance in the Pacific, seized the war initiative, and marked the end of Japan's strategic expansion and the beginning of its strategic retreat. America's long-range bombers were soon launching bombing raids on Japan's home islands, bringing the war home to the Japanese. In one firebomb raid on Tokyo in one night in 1945, 100,000 inhabitants perished. Meanwhile, in Europe, Hitler's Germany surrendered in May 1945. The United States dropped an atom bomb on Hiroshima on August 6, leaving 200,000 dead or injured, and dropped a second one on Nagasaki on August 9. Soviet Russia declared war on Japan on August 8, and sent troops into China and Korea. The noose was tightening. Japan announced its surrender to the Allied Powers on August 14, 1945.

By dropping the atom bombs on Japan, the United States ended the war that Japan had started by making a sneak attack on Pearl Harbor. It also ushered in the "nuclear age" in human history. So far, Japan is the only nation in the world that has been the victim of nuclear weapons.

Hiroshima, August 1945. *Source:* Photo 12 / Alamy Stock Photo.

The Allied victory in World War II ended Japan's rise to dominance in Asia, and forced it to give up territories it had seized by waging one war after another for over half a century. Japanese troops and civilians were repatriated from all the territories it had once occupied. The Chinese regained control over China's territories. Taiwan was returned to China. Korea was freed from Japanese colonial rule. However, strong anti-Japanese sentiment continues there.

The end of WWII also marked the beginning of the end of five centuries of Western colonialism in this region. World Wars I and II had sapped them of their strength. Japan's victories had expelled the British, French, Dutch, and Americans from their colonies in Asia in the course of the war, and the colonial peoples resisted their return after the war. In 1946 the Philippines became independent, followed by India in 1947, and many others followed. And since modern nationalism in Asia was influenced by communism, the Chinese, North Korean, and North Vietnamese regimes that emerged after World War II were all communist. This made the region a major arena of struggle between the United States and the Soviet Union in the Cold War.

Suggested Readings and Viewings

Gordon Mark Berger, *Parties out of Power in Japan*, 1931–1941 (Princeton, NJ: Princeton University Press, 1977).

Herbert P. Bix, *Hirohito and the Making of Modern Japan* (New York: Harper Collins, 2016).

Peter Duus, *Party Rivalry and Political Change in Taisho Japan* (Cambridge, MA: Harvard University Press, 1968).

Grave of the Fireflies (1988), dir. by Isao Takahata.

Michael Lewis, *Rioters and Citizens: Mass Protest in Imperial Japan* (Berkeley: University of California Press, 1990).

Yoshihisa Tak Matsusaka, *The Making of Japanese Manchuria, 1904–1932* (Cambridge, MA: Harvard East Asian Monographs, 2001).

Rana Mitter, *Forgotten Ally: China's World War II, 1937–1945* (Boston: Houghton, Mifflin Harcourt, 2013).

Ramon H. Myers and Mark Peattie, eds., *Japanese Colonial Empire, 1895–1945* (Princeton, NJ: Princeton University Press, 1987).

Tetsuo Najita, *Hara Kei in the Politics of Compromise*, 1905–1915 (Cambridge, MA: Harvard University Press, 1967).

Shin'ichi Yamamuro, *Manchuria under Japanese Dominion*, trans. Joshua A Fogel (Philadelphia: University of Pennsylvania Press, 2006).

A. Morgan Young, *Japan under Taisho Tenno* (London: Routledge, 2010).

20

Japan since World War II

Hasn't the United States been irresolute and indecisive in her policy toward Japan? Was she ever quite sure of what she was doing? There is little doubt about America's good intentions, but on occasions when she should have taken a definite attitude, she tended to vacillate.[1]

When I became Foreign Minister in September 1945, I went to see Admiral Kantaro Suzuki who had been one of my mentors in the Peers' School, and asked him what policy I should pursue. The Admiral answered that it was important after a victorious war to wind everything up properly, but that, after losing a war, one had to know how to be a good loser.

—Yoshida Shigeru[2]

Japan's American Revolution, 1945–1952

Japan experienced its first-ever military occupation by a foreign power when it came under the American Occupation. It had gambled all and lost all. It had thrown itself into a war of global conquest with all its human and material resources; now defeated, it was left with nothing. The war had killed the cream of its population, destroyed its cities and economy, and even crushed its spirit and confidence. The Japanese expected a vindictive occupation, but America turned out to be a magnanimous occupation force. This made Japan more open to change and more willing to cooperate with American efforts to remake Japan in the American image.

The United States went into Japan with a set of Occupation policies. These policies were informed by American values and what America had learned from its Civil War, World War I, and the Great Depression. It had determined that it needed to "reconstruct" Japan's militarist tradition and feudalistic mindset. The question of whether to preserve or abolish the Japanese institution of the emperor was a topic of heated debate. Those in favor of its preservation had strong arguments on their side, for it was believed that the Japanese people would fight to the last person to defend their emperor, whereas they could be expected to cooperate if the institution was left in place. Later events proved this calculation was sound policy. Working with the emperor's support and through the Japanese bureaucracy, America was able to push their goal of reconstruction with minimal resistance. There were no assassinations, riots, or mutinies.

---

1 Quoted in David John Lu, *Sources of Japanese History*, vol. 2 (New York: McGraw-Hill, 1974), p. 228.
2 As quoted in John W. Dower, *Empire and Aftermath: Yoshida Shigeru and the Japanese Experience, 1878–1954* (Cambridge, MA: Harvard University Press, 1979), p. 312.

Asia Past and Present: A Brief History, First Edition. Peter P. Wan and Thomas D. Reins.
© 2021 John Wiley & Sons, Inc. Published 2021 by John Wiley & Sons, Inc.

General Douglas MacArthur and Emperor Hirohito. *Source:* World History Archive / Alamy Stock Photo.

General Douglas MacArthur (1880–1964) headed the American Occupation Authority and was responsible only to the U.S. government. He was known as the "blue-eyed shogun," and followed the shoguns' tradition in one important way: He would rule like a monarch, but show ceremonial deference to the emperor on all occasions. His policies were developed between him, his Occupation bureaucracy, and Washington, with additional input from Japanese participants. Policy implementation relied heavily on the Japanese government bureaucracy.

Timeline for Japan after 1945	
1945–1952	Japan's "American Revolution": America intends to demilitarize and democratize Japan. General Douglas MacArthur (1880–1964) heads the Occupation; known as the "blue-eyed Shogun," he rules like a monarch but shows respect to the Japanese emperor
1946–1948	International Military Tribunal for the Far East holds trials for war crimes by Japanese during World War II; Army General and wartime Prime Minister Tojo Hideki (1884–1948) is hanged for war crimes

1946–1954	Yoshida Shigeru serves as prime minister; he is staunchly pro-American in the Cold War and focuses narrowly on Japanese recovery and economic growth
1947–1991	America's Containment Policy
1947	Under U.S. Occupation, Japan adopts major postwar amendments to its constitution, creating a constitutional monarchy on the British model; the emperor renounces his divinity and becomes the human symbol of the nation; American Occupation Authority bans the general strike, presaging the "Reverse Course"
1947–1954	Reverse Course: U.S. policy in Japan shifts from reconstruction of Japan to revival of economic and military strength
1950	Japan develops "Self-Defense Forces" with American help
1950–1953	Korean War: American war procurements help Japan's economy
1951	U.S. signs a peace treaty with Japan, resulting in sovereignty with some restrictions
1952	U.S. and Japan sign Mutual Defense Treaty, which commits America to Japan's defense; this treaty is the cornerstone of Japan's minimalist defense policy into the twenty-first century; the rise of China and nuclear development in North Korea, combined with growing uncertainty of Washington's foreign policy, will likely produce an adjustment in Japan's military and diplomatic strategies
1954	Liberal Democratic Party comes to power; rules until the late 1980s
1955	Japan regains its pre-war production levels
1960	Tumultuous political confrontation between those for and against the first of many revisions of the Mutual Defense Treaty
1970s–1980s	Japan's single-minded drive for economic growth produces the "economic miracle" as the country becomes the second-largest global economy; attempts at denying Japan's acts of aggression and war crimes in World War II lead to "history textbook" controversies
1989	The essay "The Japan That Can Say No" reflects a newly acquired sense of national confidence and assertiveness; Emperor Hirohito dies
1960s–1990s	"Hollowing out" of Japan's economy occurs with the rise of the "little dragons (or tigers)": South Korea, Taiwan, Hong Kong, and Singapore
1990s–2010s	Japan's "Lost Decade" of economic stagnation begins and extends into the twenty-first century; Japan loses its second-place ranking in GDP to China
2000–2010s	The "graying of Japan" becomes an issue as the average family has fewer than two children
2012–	Abe Shinzo (1954–), grandson of Yoshida Shigeru, is elected prime minister to revive the nation's sluggish economy and to deal with the rise of China and the threat of North Korea

The Japanese economy was in a state of total ruin. The long and hard-fought war left it like a squeezed orange. Its roads and railroads, factories, and cities were all bombed out. Its farms were short on manpower and fertilizer. Its currency, bonds, and investments were worthless. Its financial institutions were in shambles. The best and the brightest of the next generation of young men and women had died in war. This sorry state of affairs was made worse by the addition of millions of demobilized troops and repatriated civilians. Famine was eminent, and it was at the very top of a long list of priorities. The American Occupation Authority acted promptly. It mobilized its unmatched transportation capabilities to bring in food and medical supplies. The worst of a potential famine was averted.

The basic long-term original policy of the American Occupation Authority was Japan's demilitarization and democratization. The individuals responsible for Japan's role in World War II had to be removed. The military, political, and economic institutions deemed responsible for the war had to be dismantled. An international war crimes tribunal (1946–1948) was set up. It tried 28 military and civilian Japanese leaders for war crimes, and sentenced seven of them to death. Army General and wartime Prime Minister Tojo Hideki (1884–1948) was hanged. In the end, roughly 200,000 military officers, civil officials, businessmen, and teachers were purged; about half of them were in the military. However, most of them were reinstated later, and some of them came to hold important positions in politics, government, and business. This and the decision to keep the emperor and the government bureaucracy in place resulted in a large degree of continuity in Japan's power structure.

Although the American authorities had decided to preserve the institution of the emperor, they had no intention of leaving it intact. Washington through MacArthur would "demystify" the emperor by shattering the myth that he was "divine" and "inviolable," as proclaimed in the 1889 Meiji Constitution. The emperor openly denied his "divinity" in a 1946 public address, and became the human symbol of the nation under a restructured Constitution in 1947.

General MacArthur, acting like Japan's new shogun, ordered his headquarters to draw up a new constitution for Japan to revise the Meiji Constitution. When completed, the Japanese people were told it was created by the Japanese themselves. Dutifully, the emperor accepted it and the Diet passed it in 1947. It established a British-style parliamentary government, where the leader of the majority party became prime minister and formed the cabinet. It ensured the freedom of the press and assembly, renounced war as a sovereign right (the no-war clause), and committed Japan to never maintaining armed forces. Japanese politics would never be the same again. Legal changes in the revised Constitution encouraged social change. In education, the American authorities abolished old ethics courses, and purged textbooks of militarism and ultranationalism. The Constitution ensured women's right to vote and equality in marriage. Changes in values would take more time.

The American authorities' land reform policy was the most successful. It believed that economic reconstruction was the foundation of social and political reform, and the system of land ownership was of vital importance in a country that still had a large agricultural population. It banned absentee landlordism, and set a cap on how much land a person could own: Excess land must be sold to the government, who would resell it to former tenants. This policy created an agricultural sector entirely made up of small farmers, completely wiping out Japan's complicated traditional system of land ownership, land tax, and land cultivation. It also led the agricultural sector to be the first to recover.

Japan's political system underwent some major changes during the occupation. The parties were reinvigorated under American Occupation. They harked back to the political parties and party governments of the pre-militarist decade. The pre-war conservative parties reemerged as the Liberal Party and the Democratic Party. The pre-war Socialist Mass Party became the Japanese Socialist Party. The Japanese Communist Party, now legitimate, regrouped. A free press, labor unions, and women became significant voices in the Japanese political arena. Yoshida Shigeru became the principal Japanese official to represent his country's side of politics to General MacArthur, who was the supreme commander of the Allied Powers. MacArthur served as de facto chief executive of Japan from war's end to 1951, and Yoshida became de facto prime minister, serving as such from 1946 to 1954.

The American Occupation Authority increasingly viewed economic development as a major goal. It initially viewed Japan's *Zaibatsu* as a major source of Japanese militarism and thus initially uninterested in reviving Japan's industry. So it set about to decentralize the economy, breaking up old holding companies, and banning *Zaibatsu* families from holding leadership positions in the economy. But by 1947, Washington became convinced that economic success—that is, a vibrant industrial and commercial environment—would go a long way to insure greater social and political harmony. Accordingly, the American Occupation Authority adopted the New Deal policies the United States had developed to address the Great Depression and its likely causes.

Labeled "Reverse Course," the policy included a provision to strengthen the Japanese labor movement, giving it the right to organize its own labor unions and engage in collective bargaining. When Radical Socialist and Communist parties planned a general strike for 1947, the cultivation of a more moderate labor movement proved to be more difficult for the occupation establishment to monitor. Whereas most of American labor focused on economic goals, Japanese labor had a strong radical political orientation. Nonetheless, the New Deal occupation model continued, firm in the belief that by dealing with economic problems, governments would minimize the likelihood of rampant radicalism. The "belly theory" of radicalism now shifted away from chiefly fascism before the war to the emerging Cold War environment after 1945. Thus began the Reverse Course between 1947 and 1952, which sought to make Japan the model of economic success in Asia now that China appeared likely to become a member of the communist world.

Japan's Transformation during the Cold War, 1952–1989

The Cold War was solidly underway by 1947. Tensions were high between the United States and the Soviet Union. In Asia, Mao Zedong was defeating America's wartime ally Jiang Jieshi on the battlefields of the Chinese civil war, and would soon establish a communist regime, the People's Republic of China, in 1949. And the following year, the United States found itself fighting a shooting war with Communist China in Korea. The Cold War was changing everything. For the next four decades, everything would be examined in the context of the Cold War between America and Russia, between the "Free World" and the "Communist Bloc."

The United States reexamined its earlier Japan policies in light of the Cold War, and found many lacking. The goal of the "reconstruction" of Japan was to create a peaceful or even docile Japan. But Cold War considerations now dictated America's agenda. And in the context of the Cold War, a weak Japan would invite communist subversion, and also deprive America of a strong ally. Now Washington needed a strong Japan and was ready to steer a "reverse course" in its "reconstruction" of Japan. It drew up plans to "revive" Japan economically and militarily. It suspended measures to break up the *Zaibatsu*, assisted in rebuilding their industries, made generous loans to them, opened up American markets to Japanese exports, purged Communists, and allowed those who were earlier purged for war-related activities to return to public life. It was prevented from openly re-arming Japan because of the "no-war clause" in Japan's Constitution, but it managed to find enough wiggle room to help Japan establish the Self-Defense Forces in 1950. That year, the outbreak of the Korean War (1950–1953) put this Reverse Course into full swing.

In 1951, Washington signed a peace treaty with Japan, officially ending its military occupation but maintaining some U.S. military bases on Japanese territories. Japan had regained its sovereignty with some restrictions. A U.S.-Japan Mutual Security Treaty followed in 1952, committing (in Article 5) America to Japan's defense, and becoming the cornerstone of Japan's minimalist defense policy into the twenty-first century. Japan and the Soviet Union never did sign a peace treaty because of disagreements over the status of four disputed small islands.

Yoshida Shigeru (1878–1967), head of the conservative Liberal Party, became Japan's first postwar prime minister between 1946 and 1954. He was anti-communist, pro-business, and anti-union.

His main goal was Japan's economic recovery and growth. In foreign policy, he resolutely sided with America in the Cold War in exchange for the security and economic benefits America offered. He refused to allow Japan to be drawn into burdensome military spending. With the Security Treaty, such spending became unnecessary, though he did build up a skeleton military force and stubbornly kept his military budget under 1 percent. His goals paralleled those of the United States in general. The conservative Liberal and Democratic parties merged to form the Liberal Democratic Party (LDP) in 1955, which was an amalgam of many factions, each with its own leader and membership. It continued the Yoshida policies, building strong ties with business and the government bureaucracy, and working closely with the United States.

The opposition was made up of a range of fragmented small parties. The three leftist parties constituted the opposition: the Socialist Party, the Democratic Socialist Party, and the Communist Party. They opposed the government's pro-American foreign policy and protested against America for maintaining military bases and reportedly storing nuclear weapons on Japanese territory. They also opposed the re-creation of a military establishment and worked to delay the expansion of the Self-Defense Forces as best they could.

Yoshida Shigeru (1878–1967). *Source:* Everett Collection Historical/Alamy Stock Photo.

The 1960s was characterized by political confrontation that peaked over the issue of renewing the U.S.-Japanese Security Treaty. Many felt that the treaty threatened to involve Japan in America's wars. The specter of nuclear war was particularly terrifying to the only people in the world who had experienced the horrors of a nuclear disaster. But Prime Minister Nobusuke Kishi rammed the treaty through the Diet in a highhanded way. The fact that Kishi had served in the Tojo cabinet hinted at a revival of the old establishment. Nonetheless, by the 1970s and 1980s, rapid economic growth strengthened the Liberal Democratic Party's political standing while the opposition parties struggled on the sidelines.

Japan managed to achieve spectacular growth because of favorable domestic and international conditions. It had taken full advantage of the favorable international environment created by the Cold War to advance its own goals of security and economic growth. Thus American war procurements during the Korea War and the Vietnam War (ca. 1950–1975) gave Japanese manufacturing a shot in the arm. "Made in Japan" had earlier signified inferior products, but by the 1970s quality control transformed the image of Japan's electronic equipment and automobiles into excellent merchandise. The global oil crisis of 1973 and thereafter made more fuel-efficient Japanese cars seem a better buy than America's gas guzzlers. Japanese production in 1947 was only 37 percent of its pre-war level, but by 1955 it had regained pre-war levels. By the late 1980s many observers of Japan were speaking of Tokyo replacing Washington as the world's largest economy by 2000.

Indeed, by the 1980s, Japan had surged ahead to be the world's second-largest economic power, trailing only America. Japan's postwar single-minded drive for economic growth had produced an economic miracle. Industries leading the way were shipbuilding, steel, heavy chemicals, automobiles, machine tools, consumer electronics, and optics. By the 1970s, names like Sony, Toyota, and Canon became household names across the world. In 1955, when Japan had just regained its pre-war level of production, it had a Gross Domestic Product (GDP) of $24 billion and a per-capita GDP of $268. By 1989 the figures were $2830 billion and $23,000, roughly a hundredfold increase in just over three decades.

Domestically, Japan had a cheap, well-educated, highly skilled, and highly disciplined workforce. It expanded and improved the quality of its education to cover the population in general. By the early 1980s, Japanese universities were turning out more engineers than the United States. It revived its manufacturing, marketing, and banking systems that were developed during the pre-war years. Labor unions were weak. Oil was cheap, at least until 1973. And under a system of state-protected free enterprise, the government continued to provide aid and guidance to help businesses grow and compete overseas. America gave it easy access to sources of raw materials and markets in American and American-dominated parts of the world. It also sponsored Japan's entry into international trade and financial organizations. And America's "security umbrella" enabled Japan to maintain a smaller military budget than any other developed nation. This in turn helped keep taxes low and keep the economy racing ahead at full steam.

Western nations began accusing Japan of unfair competition because the Japanese government provided its businesses with subsidies and protective tariffs, a harbinger of future issues between a rising China and the West. Some Americans and Europeans called on their own governments to intervene in similar ways; others suggested that they should study and emulate the Japanese model (the Beijing Consensus, or the Chinese model in the twenty-first century). People in Detroit smashed Japanese cars in public protest. Some people began calling the Japanese "economic animals."

But a slowdown in the pace of economic growth is inevitable as any economy matures, and in Japan, a double-digit growth rate was replaced by a 4 percent growth rate in 1973. Forces unfavorable to Japan's economic growth were beginning to take shape. Labor became more expensive because of rising living standards. Oil became more expensive because of the Arab oil monopoly. Government expenditures increased as new welfare and environmental policies were put in place. Competition began to come from the "Four Little Tigers," which now had the advantages that used to belong to Japan. Much of Japan's lower-tech manufacturing migrated overseas, causing Japan to complain of a "hollowing out" of its economy for the remainder of the twentieth century.

To adjust to these new realities, Japan shifted the composition of its economy to products and services that required much greater investment in capital, research, and technology. Its exports continued to thrive because of product quality and government protectionist trade policies. Its trade enjoyed a huge surplus with the United States. Japanese living standards rose to European levels. The Tokyo Dow and real estate had almost tripled in four years by 1989. A Japanese politician wrote an essay (later a book) titled "The Japan That Can Say No," reflecting a newly acquired sense of confidence and assertiveness. A new surge of nationalism was taking place alongside a sense of resentment at being the United States' junior partner.

As Japan's economy changed, so did its social structure. At the end of World War II, nearly half the Japanese population lived in the countryside. By 1989, most Japanese resided in cities, received a high school education, and worked in modern industries. Consumerism was the norm. Moderate affluence was taken for granted. Better educated, better paid, and better housed, Japanese had become urban middle class. Japan had reason to be confident about its approach to a modernization that included politics as well as economics. In this more self-assured setting, an expanded popular culture, like its automobiles and electronic devices, took Japan and often the world by storm. *Manga* and *anime* represent two such success stories. Generally speaking, *manga* are comic books or cartoons while *anime* are animated films. Although foreign ideas have influenced popular cultural stylists in the Japanese creative world, imaginative creators clearly draw most of their artistic inspiration from the Japanese setting. Often what begins as *manga* gets transformed into *anime*, the best example being *Akira*.

People tended to be meticulously dressed. The high cost of land and rent made housing expensive and cramped. But the neat little apartments were full of electronic gadgets: television and stereo sets, rice cookers, washers and dryers, and computers. Streets and parking lots were chock-full of small cars. Vacations and traveling became affordable and popular. Groups of Japanese tourists with cameras became a common sight in all parts of the world. Family size shrank to the nuclear family. The average family had less than two children in 2000.

The status of women improved. They had gained the right to vote and to receive an education at the best universities. Most of them would work for a time after graduation, get married, and become a full-time wife and mother. The sexes mixed more freely, love marriages became the norm, and arranged marriages the exception. Divorces, which were unthinkable in traditional Japan, were on the rise. But the feminist movement was weak. A very small number of women were found in high places in politics, industry, and business. Minority groups were ignored and suffered varying degrees of discrimination. Most of the indigenous Ainu people lived on reservations on the northernmost island of Hokkaido. Koreans, most of them born and educated in Japan, were another case in point.

In summary, the U.S. occupation of Japan was successful in achieving Washington's objectives. This success must first be attributed to shared interests and goals. America must also be given credit for its ability to work with trends and traditions that were already in place in pre-war Japan. Japan in the course of its modernization (late nineteenth and early twentieth centuries) had strong popular demands for reform in the system of land ownership, voting rights, labor rights, and women's rights. There was also opposition to militarism and authoritarianism. American-supported democratic reforms resonated with these demands, enjoyed popular support, and succeeded. The Reverse Course cut short many of the democratic reforms. America's new approach to Japan was reshaped by the Cold War, and resonated with a different set of Japanese traditions.

It revived the pre-war *Zaibatsu*, allowed the old bureaucracy to remain entrenched, reinforced ties between government and business, and allowed ultranationalism and militarist tendencies to regain strength.

Japan's Asian neighbors watched Japan's awesome economic growth with mixed feelings of admiration and fear. Some looked to Japan for a model of successful economic modernization. Scholars began speaking of the "Japanese model of development." It included a market economy combined with strong government involvement, authoritarian politics rather than liberal democracy, and an emphasis on education and group-oriented moral values. However, other people who still had vivid memories of Japanese atrocities in WWII were alarmed by the specter of an emerging economic and military giant that could try to revive a Japanese Empire.

Japan in Recent Years

Japan has remained strong and stable in the last few decades, but it has continued to face serious challenges. Its economy suffered a decade-long recession beginning in 1989. Land prices fell, corporate shares plummeted, banks became laden with bad loans, companies went bankrupt, and unemployment rose. All this was exacerbated by a pan-Asian recession that began in 1997. The government spent lavishly on public works projects in an attempt to stimulate the economy, but to little avail. Before it could get out of the so-called Lost Decade, Japan was hit again by the global downturn that began with America's Great Recession in 2008. It lost its second-place ranking in world GDP to China in 2010. No solution appears in sight, and widespread pessimism continues.

The inability of the Liberal Democratic Party to cure the recession undermined its popular support in the 1990s. Instead of being the sole ruling party, it has had to govern as the dominant party in a coalition since the mid-1990s. Left-wing politicians and political parties have fared no better. Diet seats held by left-wingers declined sharply. Japanese voters, who had witnessed Mao's "Cultural Revolution" and the disintegration of the Soviet Union, had lost faith in radical politics.

The aging of the population, or the "graying of Japan," represents Japan's most serious social problem. In 1980, every retired person was supported by five workers. By 2008, every retired person was supported by four workers. The projected figure for 2050 is every retired person will be supported by two workers. Other industrial countries with similar difficulties have tried the importation of immigrants, but Japan has long been accustomed to ethnic homogeneity and has shied away from the idea of introducing immigrant workers. Nonetheless, legal and illegal foreign labor has made its way to Japan. In a way, since the late nineteenth century many Asians have continued to "look east," arriving in Japan for various reasons. Still, foreign workers in Japan feel intense discrimination. The urban population is largely made up of recent migrants from the countryside. They were uprooted by rapid industrialization, and they miss a sense of belonging in the more impersonal urban setting. Some of them are attracted to cults and "new religions," and have taken irrational actions. The cult members that released nerve gas in the Tokyo subway station in 1995 were one case in point. That year the city of Kobe experienced a massive (Great Hansin) 7.3 earthquake, which killed more than 5000 people in the region and injured at least 14,000, in addition to the destruction of more than 100,000 structures.

1995 Kobe earthquake. *Source:* Kyodo News/Getty Images.

Japan's long-touted educational system has come under scrutiny. Critics are questioning whether a system known for its rote learning, stiff discipline, harsh competition, and indoctrination can turn out students with the creativity required in a global information age. The rise in teenage crime has raised the question of moral education in schools, which has been banned since the American Occupation. As in business and industry, Japanese education will likely adjust to a more competitive global setting.

But Japan has much strength. The basic foundation of its economic and social structures is healthy and strong. It has a well-educated, highly disciplined, and hard-working population. It still has a respectable per-capita GDP (world ranking in 2015: United States #5, Japan #24, and China #74). It leads the world in such important industries as steel, automobiles, and electronics. It enjoys a huge surplus in trade with the United States. Its government and private companies have made heavy investments in future industries. It is a top creditor nation. Its system of "lifetime employment," dented but still strong, provides a solid foundation for social stability. Such stability can be best illustrated by the orderly and peaceful response of the people in northeastern Japan after the massive tsunami and the following Fukushima nuclear disaster of March 11, 2011. The institution of family and marriage is relatively secure. Its living standards and life expectancy are among the world's highest. Cities are safe, the crime rate is low, and drug use is uncommon.

Scholars are divided on Japan's political future. The American Occupation Authority determined that the Japanese were given to militarism and imposed vigorous reforms, but the Reverse Course cut short those efforts. Japanese liberals often contend that notions of freedom, equality, and human rights have not taken firm root in Japan, and those forces closely allied to wartime militarism continue to be strong today. They fear that representative government may not be firmly rooted, and the potential for a revival of militarism is real. Others have confidence that liberal democracy will continue to prevail into the future. Both are based on historical precedence.

Fukushima Daiichi Nuclear Power Plant, March 11, 2011. *Source:* YOMIURI/Reuters/Newscom.

Those fearful of a militarist revival point to its samurai tradition (*bushido*). They believe that the militarist tradition not only dominates Japan's military, but also permeates the civil bureaucracy as the samurai morphed into bureaucrats during the Tokugawa Era. They also point out that, on the eve of World War II, the samurai in the military and their counterparts in civil government joined forces to launch Japan on a course of global militarist conquest. Those who are optimistic about a democratic future for Japan point to the two and a half centuries of peaceful development during Tokugawa rule, the two decades of party government before World War II, and the seven decades of "no war" since World War II. They believe that present-day Japan is different from pre-war Japan. A large, well-educated, and politically mature middle class has taken shape. This bulwark against militarism, reinforced by a long tradition of peace and democratic government, should be enough to ensure a liberal-democratic future for Japan.

But it is worth bearing in mind that America's "reconstruction" of Japan was cut short by the Cold War and the Reverse Course. Japan never went through the entire course of reflecting on its militarist past as did Germany, and it never firmly established the exact extent of the culpability of many of its wartime leaders for their wartime atrocities.

And there exists a small but muscular group of people in Japan today who have not given up on militarism. For example, men in high places in Japan have made statements of apology, mourning, and condolence with regard to World War II's atrocities, and expressed the hope that such atrocities would never be repeated. But they always stop short of explicitly taking responsibility or showing remorse for the atrocities that Japan committed. Iris Chang, author of *The Rape of Nanking* (both book and documentary), and others can make a case that the people of China "don't believe that an unequivocal and sincere apology has ever been made by Japan to China."

Other discordant voices keep coming out of Japan. Many Japanese prime ministers and political leaders continue to make pilgrimages to the Yasukuni Shrine, which is dedicated to the Japanese war dead, including some war criminals of World War II. The "history textbook" controversies continue. For example, the Japanese Ministry of Education in 1982 demanded that textbooks that stated the Japanese Army "invaded" Northern China be rewritten to read "advanced into" Northern China. And in addressing the "comfort women controversy," former Education Minister Nariaki Nakayama went as far as to declare in 2007 that he agreed with an email saying the "victimized women in Asia should be proud of being comfort women." Clearly, the military future of Japan could go either way. Concern for the possible revival of Japanese militarism is valid.

Japan also faces a host of contemporary domestic issues, many of them at least as consequential as the future role of the military. The economy remains mired in lethargy, and its future betterment will require substantial rethinking (as in China today) of the kind of mercantilist policies that worked in an earlier stage of economic development and in a different type of global competitive order. Can Japan (and China) open its (their) markets to the outside world? The country's social order will continue to confront a demographic downturn, and a low birth rate affects both family and community values and practices. Japan needs to replicate its population or look to immigration as an answer to its declining population. Such a decline also bodes ill for the economy, for even in a highly developed knowledge-based global order, the nation needs people to keep business, industry, and international trade competitive. Japan's leaders cannot count on technology replacing people faster than the population declines. Moreover, being a modern country with limited natural resources, access to those necessary resources via domestic technology, such as from nuclear power instead of coal or oil, creates other possible dangers. This is best exemplified by the March 2011 9.0 earthquake off the coast of northeastern Japan, a massive tsunami that flooded parts of Fukushima and Miyagi, and the resulting Fukushima nuclear power plant explosion that destroyed the facility. More than 15,000 people were killed, thousands more were missing, and countless others were exposed to radiation.

Japan's foreign policies during the Cold War, though sometimes challenging, largely followed the contours of America's priorities. Japan's foreign policy responsibilities are much more complex and uncertain than in Cold War days. Back then Japan's only credible threat was the Soviet Union, but the American Security Treaty provided Tokyo protection, a "nuclear umbrella." As the third decade of the twenty-first century begins, nuclear China and likely nuclear North Korea now present believable existential threats to Tokyo, while Washington's sometimes ambiguous foreign policy priorities call into question Japan's confidence in the long-term durability of the Security Treaty. That in turn raises the question of whether Japan will one day create an offensive, perhaps even nuclear, military capability. Imagine the cascading military consequences of Japan's rearmament, especially if it goes nuclear: China bulks up its nuclear arsenal; India panics and does the same; Pakistan follows the others.

On the other hand, Japan could submit to a possible Asian geopolitical future where China becomes the regional hegemon as America gradually withdraws, while Japan and the other Asian nations become Beijing's tributary states. In the meantime, Japan is forming agreements in Asia, particularly with India, to hedge against the near-certainty of a stronger China and the possibility of a less dominant America in the Indo-Pacific. And for the first time, Japan is seriously debating its military's upcoming role. The ongoing skirmish between Japan and China over the Senkaku Islands has the nation on constant alert, as evidenced by Japanese Air Force jets repeatedly scrambling to take off from Naha, Okinawa, to intercept a potential enemy in the East China Sea region. And for the first time since World War II, Japanese fighter jets are now on an aircraft carrier. Japan regularly discusses whether to create a military with offensive capability, possibly nuclear capability as well. But in the twenty-first-century setting, the roles seem to be reversed—China the likely aggressor, Japan the potential prey. There remains a border dispute between Tokyo and Moscow over the South Kuril Islands northeast of Japan. As the twenty-first century unfolds, Japan faces a complex array of questions about the future of the nation—economically, militarily, diplomatically, politically, and demographically—which if unanswered could produce an existential crisis. The September 2020 resignation of Prime Minister Shinzo Abe, whose strong ties to the United States and lengthy stable leadership at home provided numerous regional and global assurances, has produced a host of uncertainties about Japan's domestic and foreign policy future.

Suggested Readings and Viewings

John W. Dower, *Empire and Aftermath: Yoshida Shigeru and the Japanese Experience*, 1878–1954 (Cambridge, MA: Harvard University Press, 1979).

Thomas Fingar, ed., *Uneasy Partnerships: China's Engagement with Japan, the Koreas, and Russia in the Era of Reform* (Stanford, CA: Stanford University Press, 2017).

Joshua A. Fogel, ed., *The Nanjing Massacre in History and Historiography* (Berkeley: University of California Press, 2000).

Chalmers Johnson, *MITI and the Japanese Miracle: The Growth of Industrial Policy, 1925–1975* (Stanford, CA: Stanford University Press, 1982).

Richard Katz, *Japan, the System That Soured: The Rise and Fall of the Japanese Economic Miracle* (London: Routledge, 1998).

Michael Lewis, ed., *"History Wars" and Reconciliation in Japan and Korea: The Roles of Historians, Artists and Activists* (New York: Palgrave/Macmillan, 2016).

Michael Schaller, *The American Occupation of Japan: The Origins of the Cold War in Asia* (New York: Oxford University Press, 1987).

Daniel M. Smith, *Dynasties and Democracy: The Inherited Incumbency Advantage in Japan* (Stanford, CA: Stanford University Press, 2018).

Arthur Stockwin and Kweku Ampiah, *Rethinking Japan: The Politics of Contested Nationalism* (New York: Lexington Books, 2017).

Tokyo Story (1953), dir. by Yasujiro Ozu.

Yoshida Shigeru, *Yoshida Shigeru: Last Meiji Man*, ed. and trans. Hiroshi Nara (Boulder, CO: Rowman and Littlefield, 2007).

21

Korea in Modern Times

It is my greatest regret that among our people are some who believe that only a dictatorship can guide us through the troubles that beset our way. Still others shuddering at the destructive tactics of Communism, and fearing that the people have not within themselves the strength and wisdom to meet the needs of the time, have reluctantly come to believe that a dictatorship may be necessary for the immediate future at least. But we must not permit temporary doubts or uneasiness to prevent our laying the basis of fundamental principles that will stand the test of time. . ... Democracy is the only form of government under which the liberties of the people will be secure.

—Syngman Rhee[1]

Korea has been surrounded by foreign threats in premodern settings. Yet while chief threats China and Japan could invade and perhaps defeat Korea and possibly seize territory, its Confucian political and social order would only marginally be affected. After 1500, Western nations had made their way to the various Asian countries, including Korea, and gradually insinuated much of their commercial and religious culture into port regions across the continent. But until the nineteenth century, the West did not have the wealth and power to challenge the Confucian outlook in East Asia. By the mid-nineteenth century they did, as evidenced by China's defeat by Britain in the First Opium War. The brother of Jesus led the Taiping Rebellion that killed tens of millions in China shortly thereafter. And the Meiji Restoration in Japan put that country on a modernization program. In short, the twin threats of Western culture and military power as well as Japanese modernization led many of Korea's elite to consider the nation's response to such complications. Regent Heungseon, father of King Gojong (1852–1919), served as the de facto ruler of Korea in the mid-1800s. Alarmed at the ever-spreading Western presence in Korea, and the rapid disintegration of traditional Korean order and values, he decided to strengthen the authority of the central government, and tighten its long-standing policy of "exclusion."

Foreign Incursions

Western missionaries, usually in conjunction with Western governments, had achieved numerous successes in Asia. This typically produced Asian domestic efforts to contain or eliminate religious institutions whose ideas threatened traditional values. Korea had long had a ban on Catholic

---

1 From Syngman Rhee's August 15, 1948, inaugural presidential address on the formation of the Republic of (South) Korea, as quoted in Yong-ho Ch'oe, Peter H. Lee, and William Theodore de Bary, eds., *Sources of Korean Tradition*, vol. 2 (New York: Columbia University Press, 2001), p. 385.

Asia Past and Present: A Brief History, First Edition. Peter P. Wan and Thomas D. Reins.
© 2021 John Wiley & Sons, Inc. Published 2021 by John Wiley & Sons, Inc.

churches, but there were 12 French Jesuit priests living and preaching secretly in Korea who had won an estimated 17,000 Korean converts by 1858. When Russian ships arrived in Korea to demand trading and residency rights, the Korean Catholics proposed to the court that Korea ally itself with the French to fend off the Russians. The Regent appeared agreeable to the proposal and summoned the head of the Korean Catholic Church to the capital; but when he arrived, the Regent seized and executed him. A crackdown followed. The government massacred French missionaries and Korean converts alike in 1866. In retaliation, the French government dispatched a French Expeditionary Force to Korea. It seized Ganghwa Island at the mouth of the Han River, which led to the capital city of Seoul. Faced with stubborn resistance, the French decided to withdraw. But before leaving, they bombarded the government buildings, ransacked the storehouses, and looted the royal library on the island. These latter items would become the core of the "Korea Collection" in the National Library of France in Paris! Still, Korea succeeded in rebuffing France in its first armed encounter with a Western power and thus reinforced its commitment to isolationism for the next decade. Other foreign visitors would arrive.

Timeline for Modern Korea, 1860–1945	
1392–1897	Yi Joseon Dynasty
1860s	"Eastern Learning" movement led by Choi Je-u
1866	French military campaign against Korea
1871	U.S. military campaign against Korea
1876	Korea signs Ganghwa Treaty, Korea's first "unequal treaty," under Japan's threat of war; treaty ports opened
1884	Japan-backed progressive Gapsin Coup; put down by Qing China's General Yuan Shikai
1894	Donghak peasant rebellion
1894–1895	Japan-backed Gabo Reform; First Sino-Japanese War over control of Korea: Japan wins, Korea freed from Chinese suzerainty
1895	Korean Queen Min murdered by Japanese agents
1897–1910	Korean king establishes the Empire of Korea
1898	*Maeil Shinmun*, Korea's first newspaper, established
1900	Seoul-Inchon Railroad completed
1904–1905	Japan defeats Russia in the Russo-Japanese War
1905	Korea becomes Japan's protectorate after it signs Japan-Korea Treaty of 1905
1907	Korea loses its power to manage its internal affairs after signing Japan-Korea Treaty of 1907
1909	Korean independence activist An Jung-geun (1879–1910) assassinates Japan's resident-general of Korea and former four-time Japanese prime minister
1910	Korea becomes a Japanese colony after signing Japan-Korea Treaty of 1910
1910–1945	Japanese colonial rule of Korea
1919	Nonviolent March 1st Movement produces nationwide demonstrations, crushed by the Japanese military; Declaration of Korean Independence and the founding of the Provisional Government of the Republic of Korea in exile in Shanghai

1926	June 10th Independence Movement
1932	Korean independence activist Yung Bong-gil bombs Japanese military gathering in Shanghai, killing and wounding prominent Japanese military commanders and civil government officials
1937–1945	World War II
1945	The United States and the Soviet Union divide the Korean Peninsula at the 38th Parallel, the Soviets installing Kim Il-sung in the north and the Americans installing Syngman Rhee in the south

The United States' initial contact with Korea was amicable. American gunboat *USS South America* visited Korea in 1853, and it enjoyed friendly contact with local officials. In 1855 and 1865, several shipwrecked Americans received good treatment. But the "General Sherman Incident" of 1866 took a different course. The *SS General Sherman* was a British-owned, heavily armed merchant ship, and its explicit purpose of going to Korea was to open up Korea to trade. When it got stranded near Pyongyang, Korean officials met with them, agreed to provide them with food and provisions, but rejected all trade offers. The atmosphere turned ugly. The ship fired its cannons, kidnapped a Korean military officer, and engaged in sporadic fighting for four days. Eventually, Korean "fire ships" set fire to it. The American crew jumped into the river to escape the flames, only to be hacked to death in the water. The American government's demand for reparation was ignored. So the American minister to China went to Korea with an American expeditionary force to back up the American demands. But he couldn't make any progress with his demands either. When the American fleet sailed up the Han River to conduct surveys in defiance of the Koran ban, a Korean fortress opened fire, inflicting minimal damage. But in retaliation the American fleet demolished a total of five Korean fortresses.

Japan also wanted access to Korea. Tokyo dispatched a small warship to Korea in 1875 to survey the Korean coastal waters without Korean permission. When the warship arrived at Ganghwa Island and launched a small boat, a Korean fort opened fire. The Japanese warship returned fire, and left. They returned the following year with a whole fleet of warships, demanding an apology for the "Ganghwa Island Incident" and the signing of a commercial treaty. In the face of Japan's superior military might, the Korean government signed its first unequal treaty with a foreign power—the Ganghwa Treaty of 1876. It agreed to open up three ports to Japan, grant "extraterritorial rights" to Japanese subjects, and end Korea's tributary relationship with China. Japan had extracted concessions from Korea that were similar to those that U.S. Commodore Perry had extracted from Japan.

Korea's tributary status to China had been the major obstacle to foreign-power demands for trade. Now that those obstacles were gone, Western powers were quick to demand and receive similar privileges. Foreign troops, businessmen, diplomats, missionaries, and legations quickly showed up in Seoul. Western ideas and customs began spreading across the country. Foreign powers had successfully opened up Korea to the outside world by now. The days of the "Hermit Kingdom" and its "exclusion" policy were fading rapidly into distant memory.

The Protestant missionaries from the Presbyterian and Methodist churches, however, successfully made themselves welcome in Korea, and played an important role in helping Korea take its first steps toward modernization. Much credit goes to Presbyterian "doctor missionary" Horace Allan, who provided medical care to the Korean royal family. He later left the church to serve in the U.S. diplomatic corps, and eventually became a private businessman. He was instrumental in building Korea's trolley and railroad lines and waterworks, establishing telephone service, and helping America gain access to Korea's best gold mine. He illustrates how the missionaries combined spreading their faith and doing good works with serving the interests of the American government and private business.

Early Efforts at Modernization and Japanese Influence

In this context of foreigners and their ideas and institutions arriving in Korea, the Donghak Movement emerged in the early 1860s. *Donghak* means "Eastern Learning" in Korean, as opposed to "Western Learning." The movement's founder Choe Je-u (1824–1864) was an unsuccessful scholar who was alarmed at the spread of foreign influence in Korea and the incompetence of the Korean monarchy. He formulated an eclectic ideology that merged Confucianism, Buddhism, Daoism, and native shaman teachings, and included such modern Western ideas as nationalism, egalitarianism, and monotheism. It was both religious and sociopolitical, taking aim at foreign powers and the reigning monarchy. The government hounded him and eventually captured and executed him. Much of Choe's thinking would later inspire the Peasant Rebellion of 1894. There were striking similarities between the Donghak Movement and the Taiping Rebellion in China, especially as both challenged the existing regimes in Seoul and Beijing.

The Gaehwapa Party and the Gapsin Coup of 1884

A severe drought struck in 1882, and it was followed by famine. The government failed to pay its capital guard for months, causing the "Imo Mutiny of 1882." Mutinous troops looted rice granaries and attacked barracks and the royal palace. Mobs rioted in the streets, killing Japanese civilians and officers who were training Korean troops, and burned the Japanese legation. Both China and Japan responded by dispatching troops. General Yuan Shikai (1859–1916), commander of the Chinese troops, quashed the mutiny. This left the Chinese and the Japanese in a military standoff, but the two sides were able to defuse the situation by signing a treaty.

The *Gaehwapa* or Enlightenment Party represented a small group of young Korean reformers. Its founder Kim Ok-gyun (1851–1894) was a talented young man with an aristocratic background and an important position in the Korean government. He burned with a patriotic passion for Korea and a hatred of China's suzerainty, the Korean monarchy's corruption and ineptitude, and Japan's intrusion and oppression. But he soon was convinced that Korea could be saved only if it became modernized, and so reconciled himself with the goal of following Japan's Meiji model and obtaining Japan's assistance. He led a coup d'état, the Gapsin Coup of 1884, with the purpose of deposing the Korean monarchy and getting Korea out from under Chinese dominance. The Gaehwapa conspirators, backed by Japanese troops, seized the palace, took the king captive, and beheaded a handful of high officials. Unbeknownst to them, however, the Korean royal court had secretly requested Chinese military intervention. Chinese General Yuan Shikai, who was stationed in Seoul, launched a counter-coup, restoring the royal family and government.

Kim Ok-gyun (1851–1894) was a major player in Korea's drive for modernization. He was born into a poor Korean family, but adopted into the family of a powerful bureaucrat, which enabled him to get a good education and excel in the imperial civil service exams. On a visit to Japan (1881), he met with influential Japanese politicians who were eager to influence Korea's future, and he was sponsored by Fukuzawa Yukichi to study for a six-month stint at Keio University (1882). Back in Korea, he led a stormy political life that culminated in the failed Gapsin Coup (1884). As he spent the next decade in exile in Japan, he continued to plot the overthrow of the Korean monarchy. But he was pursued by Korean agents bent on assassinating him, and shunned by the Japanese government who saw him as a troublemaker and a diplomatic burden. Korean agents eventually murdered him when he was in China, where he had gone in hopes of enlisting China's help in attaining his goal in Korea.

Kim's body was shipped back to Korea, where the government declared him a traitor, subjected his body to the "punishment of a thousand cuts," and put his body on public display in a traditional form of humiliation for treason. Japan made an official protest to the Chinese government over the treatment of his remains. Fukuzawa Yukichi led a memorial service and erected a gravestone in his honor in Tokyo. Kim's assassination added fuel to the already tense relations between China and Japan.

During Yuan's suppression campaign, many Korean reformers and several Japanese legation personnel were killed, and the Japanese legation was burned. Kim Ok-gyun joined the Japanese ambassador and fled to Japan. The coup had lasted three days.

The Gapsin Coup of 1884 was known as a struggle between Korea's conservative royal court backed by China, and the Korean reformers backed by Japan. It lasted for only three days, but it left Qing China in direct control of Korea for the next decade. China and Japan avoided violent confrontation by signing another treaty, the Tianjin Convention, in which they agreed to pull their expeditionary forces out of Korea simultaneously, and give advance notice in the event of sending in troops again.

The Donghak Peasant Rebellion (1894) and the First Sino-Japanese War (1894–1895)

Earlier, a small group of Donghak members had organized the Donghak Peasant Guerrilla Army. Their message was: equality of all people before their god, land redistribution, tax reduction, and the expulsion of foreign powers. The message had a powerful resonance with the peasantry who rushed to join their ranks. As time passed, progressive-minded scholars, nationalists, and even *yangban* (aristocrats) joined. The peasant rebels, reinforced by the educated elite, were a formidable force. They attacked in 1894, and the rebellion spread across the country like wildfire. They were inspired by slogans like this:

"Protect peasant rights"
"Protect the peasants; protect their property."
"March to Seoul; purge the government"
"Expel the Japanese and Westerners; purify our sacred land"

Defeating government forces in war, they killed officials, landlords, merchants, and foreigners, and confiscated their land and wealth to distribute among the peasants. They eventually captured the capital Seoul and occupied the Royal Palace. A panicking Korean government asked the Chinese government to send troops to put down the rebellion. But even before the Chinese troops arrived, it had successfully negotiated a truce with the rebels.

Japan sent an even larger force to Korea, using China's dispatch of troops as an excuse, even though the Chinese government had duly notified the Japanese government as required by treaty.

They surrounded the Korean palace, confined the Korean king and queen, and began setting up a new government. The new pro-Japanese puppet government had Japanese Meiji oligarch Inoue Kaoru as its head, and included one of the Korean leaders of the Gapsin Coup of 1884, Park Yeong-hyo, who had been brought back from Japan.

The former Donghak rebels were alarmed at Japan's takeover of the Korean government, and once again took up arms in rebellion. But this time they faced the Japanese troops as well as the Korean government army. Their outdated bows and arrows, spears and swords, and flintlock muskets were no match for Japan's modern weaponry and well-trained troops. The peasant rebel army was wiped out, and its commander was captured and hanged.

Japan launched a surprise attack on the Chinese troops, swiftly defeating China on land and at sea, and then advanced into Chinese territory. Thus began the First Sino-Japanese War of 1894–1895. A defeated China signed the Treaty of Shimonoseki, in which it recognized the complete independence of Korea and ceded the Liaodong Peninsula and Taiwan to Japan. Tokyo had achieved its war goal of seizing control of Korea. It had also acquired China's Liaodong Peninsula, which it hoped to use to stop Russia's southward expansion into China Proper.

Japan's explosive expansion shocked some Western powers. Russia, as Japan's immediate rival, persuaded Germany and France to join it to put pressure on Japan to return the Liaodong Peninsula. Finding itself isolated and in a position of weakness, Japan backed down and returned it in exchange for more silver in reparation.

A new balance of power was shaping up in East Asia. China had lost its traditional status of hegemon. Korea's Yi Dynasty, viewed as both incompetent and ignorant, would soon collapse. Japan surged ahead despite its partial temporary setback in Liaodong. Russia, itself ruled by an oblivious monarchy and facing a chastened Japan, began a half-hearted modernization program to compete with the major imperial industrial nations in the region. Just how half-hearted would become painfully evident several years later when St. Petersburg found itself at war with Tokyo, which fielded a truly up-to-date military.

The Gabo Reform (1894–1896)

The new Japanese-backed Korean puppet government introduced ambitious reforms of sweeping magnitude. Known as the "Gabo Reform", the projected reform met the demands of the peasant rebellion and followed the general course of modernization that other nations of the time took. The restructurings had the strong backing of Japan and the sympathy of Germany and America. But the reformers were caught in a bind: The alterations had no roots in Korea, and by relying heavily on Japanese support the reformers risked letting the Japanese modernization program act as an instrument to colonize Korea. Worse yet, the Korean people might view the reformers as traitors.

Gabo Reform declared the following goals:
- To make Korea a sovereign nation (i.e., to end Korea's tributary status to China), and to recognize the king as the only ruler of Korea (i.e., not the Yangban elite)
- To abolish the class system and slavery
- To base admission to education on talent, base appointments to government posts on merit, and create a conscript army

Korea's Queen Min (1851–1895) was staunchly conservative and anti-Japanese. Seeing the rise of Russia's influence, she tried to strengthen Korea's position by playing Russia against Japan. The Japanese minister to Korea, eager to remove her influence, secretly organized a bunch of Japanese soldiers and thugs to depose her. They forced their way into the palace, killed Queen Min, and burned her body. King Gojong and his Crown Prince fled to the Russian legation for protection. There they stayed for about a year, while continuing to exercise influence on Korea's political developments.

But the assassination of Queen Min backfired. Rioting and uprisings broke out in protest to her murder, and Korean protestors attacked Japanese soldiers and residents. Japanese-backed Prime Minister Kim Honh-jip (1842–1896) was executed, and his assassins left his body in the street on display. King Gojong left the Russian legation where he had sought refuge, returned to his palace, and announced the founding of the Korean Empire (1897–1910).

Seo Jae-pil (1864–1951) was a Korean-American champion for Korea's independence. He was one of the organizers of the Gapsin Coup (1884), and when it failed, he fled to the United States, where he became a medical doctor and the first Korean to acquire U.S. citizenship. He was back in Korea from 1895 to 1898 as chief advisor to the Korean government, and again between 1945 and 1948 as chief advisor to the American occupation forces in South Korea.

He was a noted journalist and the founder of the first Korean newspaper in Hangul, the *Independent News.* When King Gojong was in the Russian legation, he generated public opinion to pressure him to leave the protection of the Russians and return to his palace.

The Gabo Reform—actually a series of reforms—occurred before and after the killing of Queen Min in 1895. It consisted of more than 200 reforms, including ending the class system, introducing a modern educational curriculum, creating a postal system, adopting the solar calendar, and ending the cutting of men's hair buns. The government's early steps toward modernization were certainly promoted by Japan, and many argue that the Gabo Reform measures largely benefitted the Japanese. It is certainly true that emerging modern economies typically rely heavily on the capital and technology of more developed economies, in Korea's case chiefly Japan. Such a relationship also enabled resource-poor Japan (but also other industrial countries) to thereby extract Korea's resources such as iron, coal, lumber, and so forth. Still, Korea's early modernizing experience eventually gave it the embryonic intellectual and organizational potential to become independent instead of languishing in "banana republic" status after colonial liberation.

Despite the short-term inability of the Gabo Reform measures to protect Korea from predatory nations, some Korean officials and intellectuals had a popular foundation upon which to base additional changes. The reform measures had awakened a sense of urgency for making significant changes to Korea's ancient culture. Reformers known as the "Progressives" fell into two groups. The more radical were those who had been active in the Gabo Reform, and they were pro-Japanese. The moderates would be active in the Gwangmu Reform during the period of the Korean Empire.

The Korean Empire (1897–1910) and the Gwangmu Reform

When King Gojong returned, he proclaimed the founding of the Empire of Korea (1897–1910), became Emperor Gwangmu, and launched the Gwangmu Modernization Reform. The government introduced change in attire early on. The emperor began to wear Prussian-style royal attire, diplomats donned Western suits, and soon all Korean soldiers and policemen were dressed in Western-style uniform. It encouraged industrialization and the building of modern urban infrastructure. The textile industry was in a boom, which created a demand for technological innovations, and the government responded by funding the establishment of technical and industrial schools. Korea began to locally manufacture machinery for spinning and weaving silk to replace expensive imported machinery. The emperor even authorized the creation of a Korea–America joint venture, the Seoul Electric Company, to operate a public electrical power network for urban lighting and streetcars, and sanctioned the first long-distance public telephone in 1902. He also launched an ambitious program to create a modern registry of land ownership to serve as the basis for a modern land tax system, but the outbreak of the Russo-Japanese War of 1904–1905 prevented it from being completed.

After that war, Korea's immediate history involved Japanese step-by-step activities in preparation of full colonization. With Russia on the sidelines regarding Korea, Tokyo forced the Japan-Korea (Eulsa) Treaty of 1905 onto an unwilling Korea, making it a protectorate. Essentially the country no longer had any diplomatic standing in the world. At home, domestic policy depended on the decisions of Resident-General Ito Hirobumi, a senior *genro* and former prime minister. Japan also began to push Russia out of adjacent Manchuria. Then Japan sought to minimize the influence of pro-Russian Koreans. In 1906, Yi Yong-ik, who had close ties to the emperor, was assassinated. The Japan-Korea Treaty of 1907 made it clear that the resident-general would now directly control Korea's domestic affairs. That year Tokyo also forced Emperor Gojong to abdicate in favor of his weak son, Sunjong. And the assassination of Resident-General Ito Hirobumi in October 1909 by Korean nationalist Lieutenant (Lt.) General An/Ahn Jung-geun set the stage for Japan's official colonization. This was accomplished by the Japan-Korea Treaty of 1910, the annexation treaty, which ceded Korea to Japan.

Japan's reasoning for seizing Korea can be surmised from the geopolitical context of the time. It wanted to protect its economic and political interests in adjacent Manchuria, then officially under the control of a weak Manchu Qing Dynasty (that would collapse the following year). Tokyo also sought to minimize or one day remove Tsarist Russia's political and economic interests there. Manchuria, through which a Russian-Chinese railroad operated, provided a valuable route into northern Korea, where the Russians sought the warm-water port of Wonson. Since the 1880s the Japanese government sought to prevent the Russian penetration of Korea, where at its southeastern-most point would leave St. Petersburg only several dozens of miles from the Japanese homeland. Since the early Meiji period, Tokyo concluded that Korea, either by itself or as China's protectorate, would be unable to defend itself. Japan's promotion of Korean modernizers seemed to be hopeless after more than a quarter century. This conclusion can best be seen in the thinking of Yamagata Yoritomo, Japan's then-paramount leader: "It goes without saying that Korean politics are corrupt and disorderly, and its people lack the ability or the spirit to make progress.... Hoping that Korea will institute sudden changes as our country did during the Restoration is like trying to catch fish in a tree."[2] Thus it did not require a great leap of reason for the aging Meiji oligarchs to conclude that Korea needed to be colonized by Japan to protect Japan.

Korea under Japanese Colonial Rule, 1910–1945

Japanese colonial policies and Korean resistance varied during the 35-year annexation. Japan's early policies, implemented only months after the assassination of Japan's de facto ruler of Korea, Ito Hirobumi, tended to be harsh. Governors-general replaced the resident-generals, and all

---

2 As quoted in Peter Duus, *The Abacus and the Sword: The Japanese Penetration of Korea, 1895–1910* (Berkeley: University of California Press, 1995), p. 197.

governors-general came from the military (by contrast, Japan's Taiwan colony was headed by a civilian governor-general). Under what amounted to martial law, Koreans could not publish any newspapers, form groups that contained the slightest hint of political activism, or remain on their land if the governor-general decided to relocate Japanese on it. Naturally these and other similar notorious practices created mounting Korean opposition to their foreign masters and a growing desire for independence. But the military arrested, jailed, and/or executed opposition activists. The Korean monarchy provided no real or symbolic institution around which Korean nationalists could rally. Many independence leaders found it necessary to leave Korea, usually ending up in Manchuria, other Chinese locations, or (strangely enough) Japan. It was there that a group of Korean students demonstrated for their country's independence on February 8, 1919, just three weeks before the much more famous "March 1st Movement."

On March 1, 1919, as talk of self-determination for nations could be heard across the globe and to memorialize the death of Gojong, Korean students in Seoul issued the Korean Declaration of Independence. The proclamation generated months of protests against Japanese rule, but the protestors were contained with brutal effectiveness. Nonetheless, the protests were sufficiently widespread and deep to alarm Japanese political leaders in Korea and at home. Thus slowly began a more tolerant administration. Then, on the occasion of Korean Emperor Gojong's death (1919), nationalists read a declaration of independence at a mass rally in Seoul. It set in motion the March 1st Movement that year.

Anti-Japanese rallies continued to break out, culminating in the nationwide Gwangju Student Uprising Movement of 1929. Japan's crackdown was swift and brutal; by one estimate, 7000 Koreans were killed in the next 12 months. That year some Korean nationalists in the safety of Shanghai founded the Provisional Government of the Republic of Korea in exile. That provisional government later declared war on Japan and Germany after Japan's attack on Pearl Harbor. After Japan's conquest of Shanghai in 1937, it relocated to Chongqing, then the provisional capital of Nationalist China. Military resistance to Japanese colonization was in general unrealistic because of the great imbalance of power. But the Koreans were determined to fight back. They crossed the border into China's Manchuria to carry on guerrilla warfare against the Japanese. When these bases became unfeasible, they joined the Chinese and Russian Communist forces.

Japan followed the general principle of colonial mercantilism in Korea. It systematically turned Korea into a source of raw materials, a market for its manufactured goods, and a military base for its expansionist adventures. It set out by building port facilities at Busan, connecting it to the capital Seoul by railroad, and extending the railroad to the Chinese border. Henceforth, Korean timber, rice, and fish, as well as its iron ore and coal, would flow steadily along this pipeline out of Korea and into Japan. And Japanese troops would also move along this pipeline to the Chinese border, where Japan would invade the territories of China and the Soviet Union. Japan tried to develop heavy industry in Korea. However, it could not sustain the flow of investments. And as the demands of World War II increased, instead of investing in Korea in order to extract more resources in the long run, Japan in its desperation began unlimited extraction with no thought of sustainability.

The Japanese government encouraged Japanese emigration to Korea. This was because it had inadequate farm land to sustain its large population, and because it would increase the size of the Japanese population in Korea, thereby bolstering its power in its colony. But this emigration program ran up against Korea's existing ban on ownership of land by foreigners. Therefore, Japan imposed a "land reform" policy on Korea that robbed poorer Korean landowners of their land, and sold it to Japanese settlers at discount prices. This created intense hatred among the peasantry for the Japanese.

The Japanese colonial government initially had a policy of "segregation," but when that failed they shifted to a policy of "assimilation." To achieve their goal of complete assimilation, they went to great lengths to wipe out any trace of Korean cultural identity. They sponsored Korean-language

March 1st Movement protest rally, 1919. *Source:* Archive PL / Alamy Stock Photo.

newspapers with a heavy pro-Japanese viewpoint, altered public monuments to remove their connection to their Korean roots, rewrote songs and poems originally dedicated to Korean emperors to instead sing the praise of Japanese emperors, and deleted ancient Korean texts that praised Korean military and cultural accomplishments. They also altered stone monuments with Chinese inscriptions to remove their association with China. A censorship agency confiscated and burned Korean history books.

Universal education became an important part of Japan's assimilation program. It built thousands of schools across Korea and opened them to the common people. The school system was based on the Japanese model: Its education was made an instrument to provide basic knowledge and practical skills, and to indoctrinate the students. Classes focused on the glorification of the Japanese Empire and its Imperial Household. Students had to worship at the school's Japanese Shinto shrine, and bow before the portrait of the Japanese emperor. Korean history was left out of the curriculum. The use of the Korean language was banned in all school and business activities. The Korean Crown Prince Yi Eun took a Japanese princess for his wife.

The Japanese effort to eliminate the Koreans' cultural identity backfired. A resurgence of Korean nationalism took place. Historians began to use ancient textual evidence to present Korean history from a Korean perspective. Revived interest in Korean history led to research in Hangul, the Korean alphabet, which in turn led to the establishment of a standardized Korean writing system in the 1930s. Nationalistic books were published underground. In 1932, Korean independence activist Yun Bong-gil bombed a Japanese military gathering in Shanghai, China. Among those killed were General Yoshinori Shirakawa, who had led the invasion of Shanghai in the previous months, and Kawabata Sadaji, government minister for Japanese residents in Shanghai.

Provisional Government of the Republic of Korea, doorplate. *Source:* Tada Images/Shutterstock.com.

The demands of war forced Japan to divert an increasingly larger portion of its workforce from productive jobs to military service. This created an acute labor shortage in Japan. Initially, the Japanese recruited Koreans to work in Japan. But as the shortage became ever more acute, the Japanese government stepped in and shifted the policy from "recruitment" to "conscription": It forcibly rounded up Korean labor conscripts and sent them to work in factories and mines in Korea, Japan, and Manchuria. The combined number of Korean immigrants and forced laborers in Japan exceeded 2 million at the end of the war. The estimated death toll of Korean laborers is 1.5 million out of a total of 5.4 million.

Japanese colonial rule was brutal. One of their common practices was "guilt by association" and "collective punishment." An entire Korean village could be subjected to looting, burning, raping, and slaughter when a single resistance fighter was found in the village. The victims of the notorious "Unit 731" were Korean as well as Chinese. Many of the sex slaves held in Japanese military brothels, euphemistically called "comfort women," were Korean. Among the atomic bomb victims in Japan included a total of 70,000 Koreans.

The Japanese military had separate Korean units. They were likely detailed to manage prisoner-of-war camps. They served as guards on the Bataan Death March, and in the construction of the Burma Railway. As guards, they were notorious for their brutal treatment of prisoners. They also specialized in counterinsurgency operations against Communist guerillas in China's Manchuria. As fighters, their courage and tenacity were known to be equal to that of the Japanese soldiers. A number of Koreans served in the Japanese government. The highest ranking of them was Lt. General Hong Sa-ik, who was in command of all the Japanese prisoner-of-war camps in the Philippines. Togo Shigenori (Park Shigenori) was Minister of Foreign Affairs and Minister of Greater East Asia. After World War II, a total of 148 Koreans was convicted war crimes, 23 of whom were sentenced to death.

The anti-Japanese provisional Korean government in exile brought together various Korean guerilla groups in China and Southeast Asia to form the Korean Liberation Army, and fought on the side of the Allies. Koreans organized the Korean Volunteer Army in Yanan, the area controlled by the Chinese Communist Party during World War II. That military unit eventually became the Korean People's Army of North Korea.

Korea after World War II

Korea was liberated from Japanese colonial rule with Japan's surrender to the Allies in 1945. U.S. and Soviet Russian troops entered southern and northern Korea, respectively. The postwar South Korean government had many high government officials who had served in the Japanese military. Best known among them were Park Chung Hee, who later became president of South Korea, and Chung Il-kwon, who became prime minister. The first ten Army chiefs of staff were all graduates of the Imperial Japanese Army Academy. Imperial Japan had left an unmistakable imprint on Korea. And anti-Japanese sentiment continues to be strong throughout Korea.

East Asia underwent profound transformation in the decades immediately after World War II. The European colonial powers were sapped of their vital energies by the two great wars, and their advances since the fifteenth century were now halted and turned back. Experiencing an awakening of modern nationalism, the colonial peoples were determined to prevent the return of their former colonial masters. India and Burma were the first to become independent in 1947. The People's Republic of China was founded in 1949. The Malayan Peninsula became independent in 1961. And Vietnam was free of foreign troops by 1975.

Modern Asian nationalism was often influenced by communism. The regimes of Mainland China, North Korea, and North Vietnam were all communist. This made the region a major battleground in the Cold War between the United States and the Soviet Union.

Two Koreas

Toward the end of World War II, American troops entered Korea from the south, and Soviet Russian troops entered from the north. This divided Korea into the American Occupation Zone and the Russian Occupation Zone. America and Russia agreed to a two-state solution after plans to reunite the country failed: a South Korea, officially known as the Republic of Korea, and a North Korea, officially known as the Democratic People's Republic of Korea. The two states were officially divided at the 38th Parallel. The South was anticommunist and pro-American, and the North was communist and pro–Soviet Russian. A divided Korea reflected the divide between the Free World led by the United States and the Communist Bloc led by the Soviet Union.

The two Koreas took different roads of development. South Korea developed a booming capitalist economy under a dictatorship with democratic window dressing, while North Korea struggled under a stifling communist dictatorship with a stagnant economy and an oversized military. When U.S. Secretary of State Dean Acheson left South Korea and Taiwan outside of America's defense perimeter in a well-known speech on January 12, 1950, Kim Il-sung got Soviet ally Josef Stalin to support a North Korean invasion of South Korea.

The Korean War, 1950–1953

North Korea invaded South Korea on June 25, 1950, with backing from Soviet Russia and the People's Republic of China, which had come to power in Beijing the previous October. The Pyongyang forces routed the poorly prepared South Korean military, pressing them into the southern tip of the Korean Peninsula. U.S. President Harry Truman made a resolute response to this blatant act of communist expansion. He got the United Nations to declare North Korea an aggressor state and sent UN troops to repel this act of aggression with military force. The UN armies were mainly made up of U.S. and South Korean troops and were commanded by U.S. General Douglas MacArthur of World War II repute. The Cold War had exploded into a hot war. But it was a war by proxy, for the two superpowers were not officially engaged in face-to-face fighting.

Timeline for Modern Korea, 1945–2019	
1945	Cold War (1945–1991) begins
1946	American and Soviet Joint Commission fails to form a unified Korean government
1948	August 15: Republic of Korea (South Korea) founded with Syngman Rhee (1875–1965) as president
	August 25: Democratic People's Republic of Korea (North Korea) founded with Kim Il-sung (1912–1994) as president
1950–1953	Korean War: North Korea invades South Korea; America intervenes and gains UN support for removing North Korean forces from the South; American and UN forces reach the Yalu River bordering China; China enters the war on the Northern side; a ceasefire and armistice are arranged, ending the fighting but not officially ending the war; Korea remains divided
1960	Student uprising launches the April Revolution, forcing Syngman Rhee to resign and go into exile
1972	First Red Cross North–South talks
1960s–1970s	South Korea's GDP increases by 500%
1980	Guangju Uprising: City of Guangju becomes a battleground between dissident students and the Korean military; nationwide martial law declared
1985	North Korea signs Nuclear Nonproliferation Treaty
1988	Twenty-Fourth Olympic Games held in Seoul, South Korea
1994	North Korean paramount leader Kim Il-sung dies and is succeeded by his son Kim Jong-il (1941–2011)
1998	South Korean President Kim Dae-jung implements Sunshine Policy, which involves North–South talks that can lead to policies in both Koreas that will lead to peaceful reunification
2000	First North–South summit between Kim Jong-il and Kim Dae-jung
2003	North Korea withdraws from Nonproliferation Treaty
2007	Second North–South summit between Kim Jong-il and Roh Moo-hyun
2009	North Korea conducts first nuclear test
2010	North Korea conducts second nuclear test
2011	Kim Jong-il dies and is succeeded by third son Kim Jong-un (1983–)
2013	Park Geun-hye (1952–), daughter of assassinated former South Korean President Park Chung-hee (1917–1979), is elected president of South Korea; she is impeached and removed from office on March 10, 2017
2013	Moon Jae-in (1953–)
2018	June 12: American President Donald Trump and North Korean Chairman Kim Jong-un meet in Singapore to bring about the "complete denuclearization of the Korean Peninsula" and other military and security issues

General MacArthur made a bold and brilliant strategic maneuver, landing his troops behind enemy lines at Inchon, and seizing the initiative of the war. He pressed forward, retook Seoul, and crossed the 38th parallel. He continued to press northward with President Truman's sanction, but when MacArthur's troops approached the border between North Korea and China, massive numbers of Chinese troops pushed UN forces south. The Chinese entrance into the war caught General Mac Arthur off-guard, and forced his troops into the southernmost part of the peninsula at Pusan/Busan. The situation was so desperate that MacArthur considered using atomic weapons on China.

Kim Il-sung. *Source:* AP Images/Peter Arnett.

Syngman Rhee. *Source:* Library of Congress Prints and Photographs Division [LC-DIG-hec-26756].

Keeping in mind that Cold War containment focused chiefly on American containment of the Russians in Europe, Truman believed that the war in Korea sapped Washington's military capabilities in Europe. When MacArthur's ground forces commander Lt. General Walton Walker was killed in a jeep accident, he was replaced in late December 1950 by Lt. General Matthew Ridgeway. Ridgeway eventually began to push the Chinese forces out of South Korea. By April 1951, Truman and MacArthur differed on how to proceed in Korea. On April 11, 1951, President Truman fired MacArthur for insubordination and put General Matthew Ridgway in command of all UN forces. Three days later, Ridgeway was replaced by Lt. General James Van Fleet. By this time Truman wanted to set up peace talks, and less aggressive UN actions northward seemed more likely to help the peace process. Ridgeway and Van Fleet better suited Truman's notion of how to handle the Korean conflict.

As the combat activities in Korea ground to a stalemate, the two sides eventually agreed to a ceasefire on July 27, 1953, after long and difficult negotiations. The fighting had ended almost exactly where it had begun. A Demilitarized Zone now separates the two sides, and it is one of the most heavily fortified places in the world. Since they never signed a peace treaty, the two sides are still in a state of war in a strictly legalistic sense. After the war, South Korea became firmly planted in the American Bloc in the Cold War, and North Korea continued as a member of the Communist Bloc.

North Korea's relationship with Communist China has been difficult ever since, Beijing fearing the possibility of the North Korean tail wagging the Communist Chinese dog. South Korea was in shambles after the war, for the war had destroyed a huge portion of its human and material wealth. In total, around 2.5 million of its people were killed, more than 80% of its infrastructure was destroyed, and one-half of its residential structures were leveled. The Korean Peninsula was reduced to an overall economic level comparable to that of the poorer countries of Africa.

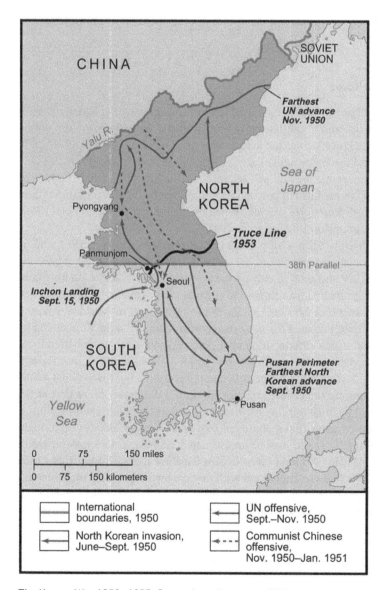

The Korean War, 1950–1953. *Source:* http://www.easy39th.com/korea/images/map.jpg.

Postwar Development: South Korea

But South Korean pulled off an economic miracle. It created a highly export-oriented economy that transformed the country into one of Asia's "Four Little Tigers," Its Gross Domestic Product (GDP) grew over 500% in the 1960s and 1970s. The share of manufacturing in its GDP rose from 9% to 27% from 1960 to 1975.

Its economic miracle was achieved under American tutorage and protection. It was also achieved under military dictatorships who worked hand-in-glove with big business. The Korean economy had at its core a uniquely Korean business organization—the "chaebol" ("business family" or "monopoly" in Korean). It is a business conglomerate of powerful multinational companies that enjoys government support. Best known among them are the "Big Four"—Samsung Electronics, Hyundai Group, LG Group, and KIA Group. It is the much-discussed "Asian model" of economic reform: economic development first, political reform (democracy) later.

Postwar Development: North Korea

While South Korea became prosperous and democratic, North Korea created the Kim dynasty. It produced mass starvation, gulags, and a totalitarian regime; it also eventually made the nation nuclear capable. Kim Il-sung (1912–1994) was the leader of North Korea from 1948 to his death in 1994, heading both the state and the Communist Party. His signature state ideology was the doctrine of "Juchea," meaning "independence and self-reliance" in Korean. He practiced one-man dictatorship and cultivated an extreme form of personality cult. When he died, 800 statues of him dotted the landscape across North Korea. He was succeeded by his son Kim Jong-il (1941–2011), who was then succeeded by his grandson Kim Jong-un (1983–).

Kim Il-sung was reportedly born to Protestant parents in Manchuria in China in 1913, and he joined an underground communist organization in his teens. He later joined a CCP-led guerrilla group in 1935, then joined the CCP and rose quickly up the army ranks. In 1940, he led his troops into the Soviet Union to avoid capture by Japanese troops, and was soon a captain in the Soviet Red Army. The Soviet occupation forces took him back to Korea toward the end of World War II, and installed him as the head of the newly created North Korean government. After the Korean War he adopted the Stalinist model of personal dictatorship and a state-controlled economy with a focus on heavy industry and arms production. He continued to follow a Stalinist hardline after the collapse of communism in Eastern Europe and the Soviet Union (1989–1991). But his Stalinist model of economic development worked no better in North Korean than it did in any other part of the world. Its economy was crippled by huge military expenditures and unprofitable state-run industries. Its agriculture was so unproductive that it could not feed itself. Years of floods and drought resulted in an intense famine that took the lives of an estimated 2.5 million to 3 million North Koreans (10% of the population). His rigid hold on a Stalinist hardline alienated him from China and Russia, and lost him favorable trade arrangements with them, which aggravated his problems.

In 1998, South Korean President Kim Dae-jung implemented the "Sunshine Policy" to improve North–South relations. The new policy allowed South Korean companies to start projects in the North. Kim Jong-il also showed signs of willingness to allow some degree of economic reform. He created the Kaesong Industrial Park just north of the Demilitarized Zone to import and develop new technologies. The plan was to have 250 South Korean companies participate and employ 100,000 North Koreans by 2007. However, by March 2007, it had only 21 companies, employing 12,000 North Korean workers.

Nuclear Crises

North Korea signed the Nuclear Nonproliferation Treaty (NPT) in 1985, went ahead to launch a nuclear program in 1994, withdrew from the NPT in 2003, conducted its first successful underground nuclear tests in 2006, and conducted second successful underground nuclear tests in 2009, followed by the successful launch of a short-range missile test later the same day. North Korea's possession of nuclear weapons has been a point of friction between North Korea and the United States for decades.

Many agreements were signed to defuse the nuclear tension but soon broken for lack of good faith on either side. The "Six-Party Talks" began in 2000, with participants from North Korea, the United States, China, South Korea, Russia, and Japan. The main goal was for North Korea and the United States to agree on an arrangement in which North Korea agrees to the suspension of its nuclear weapons program and the eventual elimination of its nuclear weapons, and in exchange the United States agrees to supply oil and nuclear energy generators to North Korea. North Korea has been consistently bellicose and irresponsible, making and breaking promises as it conducts nuclear and missile tests. China has shown a strong interest in the denuclearization of the Korean Peninsula in these talks. But the talks failed to produce any significant results through 2020. Whether the Singapore Summit of 2018 will amount to anything in the long term remains to be seen.

Third-generation Kim dynasty leader Kim Jong-un (1983–present) has displayed unusually brutal and erratic behavior, yet his impoverished regime does have ballistic missile and nuclear weapons capability. It therefore enjoys enormous importance to nations in the region. It also has the potential to implode, the prospect of which terrifies Beijing. The resulting chaos would not only send tens of thousands of North Koreans into China but also might result in the unification of the country under South Korean leadership. Such a Korea with American military on the Chinese border would very likely, furthermore, produce a Chinese intervention. But North Korea is one of the most secretive regimes in the world, and the outside world has great difficulty in ascertaining what is going on there currently, or what might happen next. Donald Trump's discussions with Kim Jong-un in Singapore on June 12, 2018, offered some hope of resolving the nuclear issue in the future. But the American

Chairman Kim Jung-un and President Donald J. Trump in Singapore. *Source:* Xinhua / Alamy Stock Photo.

president's decision to suspend wargames with South Korea after the discussion took much economic pressure off North Korea. Pyongyang's military always simultaneously countered Seoul's wargames with their own costly military exercises, a price that the northern regime could ill afford.

Stay tuned for the outcome, keeping in mind that Beijing will almost certainly have the deciding word on what kind of agreement North Korea can accept. Washington needs to be aware that not just Japan and South Korea have a stake in the Korean nuclear outcome. The rest of Asia views America as the only meaningful constraint on an expansionist China. Do the nations of Asia and globally maximize their perceived national interests in the context of an America determined to maintain the post–World War II commercial world order, or do they accept the likelihood of a Chinese mercantilist order displacing Washington's arrangements and thus try to make the best of it? That is to say, almost anything the future holds for North Korea could, for better or worse, at least fundamentally impact the region or even the global order. And so continues the "nuclear crisis," as well as the struggle between China and America over how nations will conduct themselves in the post–Cold War world.

Suggested Readings and Viewings

Richard C. *Allen, Korea's Syngman Rhee: An Unauthorized Portrait* (Tokyo: Tuttle, 2016).

Mark E. Caprio, *Japanese Assimilation Policies in Colonial Korea, 1910–1945* (Seattle: University of Washington Press, 2009).

Victor Cha, *The Impossible State: North Korea, Past and Future*, rev. ed. (New York: Ecco, 2013).

Mark W. Clark, *From the Danube to the Yalu* (New York: Harper, 1954).

Max Hastings, *The Korean War* (New York: Simon & Schuster, 1988).

Andrew C. Nahm, *Korea under Japanese Colonial Rule: Studies of the Policies and Techniques of Japanese Colonialism* (Kalamazoo: Center for Korean Studies, Western Michigan University, 1973).

Don Oberdorfer and Robert Carlin, *The Two Koreas: A Contemporary History*, rev. ed. (New York: Basic Books, 2013).

Robert Tarbell Oliver, with contribution by Syngman Rhee, *Korea: Forgotten Nation* (Washington, DC: Public Affairs Press, 1944).

Balazs Szalontai, *Kim Il Sung in the Khrushchev Era: Soviet and DPRK Relations and the Roots of North Korean Despotism, 1953–1984* (Stanford: Stanford University Press, 2006).

Tae Guk Gi: The Brotherhood of War (2005), dir. by Je-gyu Kang.

22

The European Struggle for India and the Emergence of Indian Resistance, 1707–1914

Man is born to conquer Nature, it is true, but the Occidental means by "Nature" only the physical or external Nature. It is true that external Nature is majestic, with its mountains, and oceans, and rivers, and with the infinite powers and varieties. Yet there is a more majestic internal Nature of man, higher than the sun, moon, and the stars, higher than this earth of ours, higher than the physical universe, transcending these little lives of ours, and it affords another field of study. There the Orientals excel, just as the Occidentals excel in the other.[1]

Introduction

By the turn of the twentieth century, only two Asian countries—Japan and Siam—could boast of native-controlled governments. All other nations existed under foreign rule: The Manchus controlled Qing China; the British governed India, Sri Lanka, Burma, Malaya, and Hong Kong and managed Afghanistan's foreign affairs; the French ruled Vietnam, Cambodia, and Laos; the Dutch ran the East Indies/Indonesia; the Spanish and then the Americans administered the Philippines; the Portuguese had holdings in Goa (India), Macao (China), and Timor (the East Indies); the Japanese annexed Taiwan and would soon absorb Korea (officially in 1910); Tsarist Russia occupied Central Asia and Siberia; and several imperial nations had numerous pieces (treaty ports, leaseholds, and/or spheres of influence) in China. As World War I approached, however, nationalism in the Asian dependencies emerged to challenge foreign domination and launch independence movements. This was no truer than in India.

As the Europeans arrived in Asia in the sixteenth century, much of their activities focused on India; at that time, the Mughal Empire had reached its highest level of political sophistication, religious forbearance, and cultural brilliance. By the onset of the nineteenth century, however, almost every aspect of Mughal imperial activity in India had suffered severe deterioration. This decline became most evident in the political realm. Even before the political fragmentation of India took place upon Mughal Emperor Aurangzeb's death in 1707, the Mughal rulers faced domestic opposition from the Sikh religion, chiefly in the Punjab, and from the non-Muslim Maratha Kingdom, located in much of central and northern India. At the same time, the Europeans gradually expanded their economic and political influence throughout the subcontinent. Thus native and foreign challenges to Muslim rule and Hindu opposition to Muslim and European

---

1 Swami Vivekananda (1863–1902), quoted in William Theodore de Bary, *Sources of Indian Tradition*, vol. 2 (New York: Columbia University Press, 1958), p. 99.

Asia Past and Present: A Brief History, First Edition. Peter P. Wan and Thomas D. Reins.
© 2021 John Wiley & Sons, Inc. Published 2021 by John Wiley & Sons, Inc.

interference with traditional cultural practices began a discussion of what it meant to be Indian. In Central Asia, much the same kind of conversation commenced as Russian political and cultural influences threatened customary Muslim practices there. This chapter will examine domestic discontent with Muslim and European activities, the development of British and Russian imperial enterprises in South and Central Asia, and the Asian responses to those expansionist undertakings.

Emergence and Dominance of the British in India	
1498	Portuguese arrive in India, conquer Goa in 1510
1600	Queen Elizabeth I charters English (later British) East India Company; trading post set up at Surat in 1608
1602	Dutch East India Company established
1620	Denmark sets up trading port in Tamil Nadu
1674	French create trading port at Pondicherry (now Puducherry)
1526–1707	Foreign Mughal Empire governs India
1707–1858	British govern much of India through the declining Mughal emperors
1498–1763	Europeans struggle for dominance in India; British defeat France in Seven Years' War/French and Indian War (1754–1763) for control of India, North America, and elsewhere
1757	Robert Clive defeats Nawab of Bengal
19th century–present	Hindu Renaissance launched by Ram Mohan Roy
1846	Treaty of Lahore ending the Anglo-Sikh War gives Jammu and Kashmir to British
1857–1858	Sepoy Mutiny put down, Mughal Empire formally dissolved, and British Parliament takes control of India away from the East India Company
1869	Mohandas Gandhi born
1876	Queen Victoria given title "Empress of India"
1885	Indian National Congress (later Congress Party) forms, beginning the movement toward self-rule and ultimately independence
1905	Partition of Bengal; reversed in 1911
1906	All India Muslim League created to promote Muslim interests

India under the Mughals contained numerous kingdoms, princely states, and lesser political and social entities, and their relationship to the Mughal monarchy depended upon many factors. Among these were local political issues, religious differences, and distance from the Mughal capital, all of which and more had always been problematic for foreigners attempting to rule India over the centuries, even in the best of circumstances. After Aurangzeb (1618–1707), the Mughal imperial nerve center and in particular its feeble monarchs began to lose control over the subcontinent. As some of Mughal political control fell into domestic hands at odds with the government—the Maratha Kingdom, the Sikh religious rebels, and other indigenous dissidents—the Europeans began to carve out spheres of economic influence. Moreover, invasions from Persia (1739) by Nadir Shah and from Afghanistan (1748–1767) by Ahmed Shah Abdali put much of what is today's Pakistan in foreign hands and resulted in several occupations of Delhi.

Meanwhile, European incursions beginning with the Portuguese in 1498—and, later, the Spanish, Dutch, Danes, French, and British—set up trading "factories" or enclaves along the Indian coastline. These enclaves included commercial centers and usually military fortifications to protect people, ships, and cargos from bandits on land and from pirates on the sea. Working with the Europeans were Indians of various backgrounds who served as laborers, artisans, guards, and most significantly intermediaries between the European nation and the local community. By the seventeenth century, the Dutch and the Danes had abandoned their factories and the Portuguese, though destined to remain in Goa until 1963, had little influence elsewhere in India. Thus the principal struggle for physical and intellectual control of India involved the Mughals, local or regional Indian elites, the French, and the English.

The British Conquest under the East India Company

The East India Company, also known as the English East India Company and later the British East India Company, began as a royally chartered joint stock company in 1600 and eventually received the monopolistic right to do business in Asia. It traded in silks and tea from China, spices from the East Indies, and opium from India, as well as other commodities from additional locations in Asia. In 1615 King James I sent Thomas Roe to negotiate with the Mughal Empire a commercial treaty that would give the East India Company the exclusive right to do business in Surat. Emperor Jahangir went so far as to open "all the kingdoms and ports of my dominions" to the English, thereby giving the company an enormous advantage in its dealings with local Indian elites and in its competition with other European East India Companies. By the mid-seventeenth century, the English East India Company had nearly two dozen factories, many of which had built forts. From these enclaves, the company negotiated commercial agreements with local elites, which eventually came to be commercial and political arrangements that ultimately gave the company actual control over vast amounts of Indian territory.

The French also made agreements with local Indian elites, who typically attempted to pit the European nations against one another. The French East Indies Company, established in 1664 to compete with other European nations for the Asian trade, succeeded in setting up a number of factories along the coast of India, and by the early eighteenth century constituted the only major competitor to the English. At that time, both English and French goals in India grew from mainly trade expansion to principally territorial expansion, as exemplified in the careers of Robert Clive and Joseph Dupleix, respectively. As these opponents struggled in India for their nations' supremacy there, events in Europe and North America soon pitted England against France in the first global conflict, the Seven Years' War (1756–1763). The war began in 1754 in North America, where it became known as the French and Indian War, but it soon spread to Europe and then to locations in Africa and Asia. In India, the British under Robert Clive defeated the French and its regional Indian ally (the Nawab of Bengal, Sirij-ud-daulah) at the Battle of Plassey in 1757, a campaign known as the Third Carnatic War (1757–1763). Thereafter French influence in India all but disappeared, and the British East India Company set up headquarters at Calcutta (now Kolkata) in 1772.

In that year the East India Company established its first official government in India. Warren Hastings became the company's initial governor-general, charged with overseeing and enlarging the company's territories and revenues. Territorial expansion came via wars, such as the Battle of Plassey, the Anglo-Maratha Wars, the Anglo-Mysore Wars, and the Anglo-Burmese Wars; via annexation due to company perception of Indian official corruption or poor governance, or lack of male heirs in princely states; or via economic techniques, as when in 1765 the company persuaded Mughal emperors to allow it to collect imperial taxes (the *diwani*) in additional parts of the empire. But London also instituted guidelines (the Regulating Act of 1773 and the India Act of 1784) that made the British government the ultimate authority as to British activities in India, guidelines that forbade the company from acting as a British political institution and that prohibited company interference in the governing of India. In theory, at least, the company acknowledged limits on its Indian activities. Practically speaking, however, the governor-general (and his council) enjoyed great latitude notwithstanding the impeachment of Warren Hastings by the House of Commons in 1787. Although the House of Lords acquitted Hastings in 1795 after a lengthy trial, Parliament had sent a message that it was watching over company actions in India. After a shaky start under Hastings, the company's governmental activities compared favorably to the court extravagance and corruption of the Mughals and local elites.

Between 1800, as the East India Company had firmly rooted itself in India's social setting, and 1857, when the Sepoy Mutiny broke out, Anglo-Indian cultural exchanges produced an array of emotional and intellectual consequences. On the one hand, these exchanges produced attitudes of sympathetic understanding and shared tolerance of each other's customary ways. On the other hand, such interactions also generated profound loathing and arrogant narrow-mindedness as well. A group of British officials and civilians serving in India referred to as "Orientalists" took up the study of India's recent and distant past, including its classical Sanskrit and current regional languages such as Bengali, Persian (then used at the Mughal court), as well as Arabic; investigated its rich religious traditions; launched archaeological excavations at ancient Indus Valley sites; and published the results of their studies. Chief among these scholars was Sir William "Oriental" Jones (1746–1796), who viewed India's past as rich and practical. British knowledge of Indian culture, he asserted, would be less "circumscribed and imperfect" and therefore aid British interests in India. Indians' greater familiarity with their history, Jones argued, represented the potential for a renaissance of the Hindu tradition, which had been eclipsed to a large extent by centuries of Muslim rule. Anglicists, best symbolized by Thomas Macaulay, wanted to educate Indians to serve the needs of Britain through the company. Macaulay believed the best way Indians could serve Britain's interests involved educating India's elite: "it is impossible for us, with our limited means, to attempt to educate the body of the people. We must at present do our best to form a class who may be interpreters between us and the millions whom we govern; a class of persons, Indian in blood and color, but English in taste, in opinions, in morals, and in intellect."[2]

Governors-General of the British East India Company, **1774–1858**

Name	Tenure of Office
Warren Hastings	1774–1785
Sir John Macpherson	1785–1786
Charles Cornwallis (Earl Cornwallis, then 1st Marquess Cornwallis)	1786–1793
Sir John Shore	1793–1798
Richard Wellesley (Earl of Mornington, then Marquess Wellesley)	1798–1805
Charles Cornwallis	1805–1805
Sir George Barlow	1805–1807
Gilbert Elliott-Murray-Kynynmound (Lord Minto, then 1st Earl of Minto)	1807–1813

---

2 Quoted in de Bary, *Sources of Indian Tradition*, p. 2:49.

Francis Rawdon-Hastings (Earl of Moira, then Marquess of Hastings)	1813–1823
John Adam	1823–1823
William Pitt Amherst (Lord Amherst, then Earl Amherst)	1823–1828
Lord William Bentinck	1828–1835
George Eden (Lord Auckland, then 1st Earl of Auckland)	1836–1842
Edward Law (Lord Ellenborough, then 1st Earl of Ellenborough)	1842–1844
William Wilberforce Bird	1844–1844
Henry Hardinge (Sir Hardinge, then Viscount Hardinge)	1844–1848
James Andrew Broun Ramsey (10th Earl of Dalhousie, then Marquess of Dalhousie)	1848–1856
Charles Canning (1st Earl Canning, then Viscount Canning)	1856–1858

Hindu Renaissance

Regardless of British educational emphasis, the education of Indians provoked a discussion among these "interpreters" about India's past, present, and future. This extended discussion, usually referred to as the Hindu Renaissance, is best exemplified in the thinking of Ram Mohan Roy (1772–1833) and Dayanand Saraswati (1824–1883). Roy founded the *Brahmo Samaj* or Divine Society in 1828 to improve Hinduism by eliminating many practices he considered harmful, such as *suttee/sati* (widow burning; literally, "true wife"), child marriage, caste, and idol worship. These practices, Roy argued, did not exist in Vedic times. For example, monotheism once existed in Hinduism, but centuries of unorthodox rituals and opinions produced idol worship. Rejecting the notion that the numerous images worshipped by the people are mere representations of God, Roy argued that "the truth is, the Hindoos of the present days have no such views of the subject, but firmly believe in the real existence of innumerable gods and goddesses, who possess, in their own departments, full and independent power; and to propitiate them, and not the true *God*, are Temples erected, and ceremonies performed."[3] Roy considered Hinduism to be fundamentally sound but in need of extensive reform, which his society could achieve via education.

Roy's close comrade Debendranath Tagore (1817–1905) kept the *Brahmo Samaj* alive upon Roy's death with financial aid and intellectual dialogue, likewise searching for the true spirit of Hinduism in the ancient Vedas. But clearly this search for religious truth resulted in large measure from an attempt to answer questions about Hinduism posed by Christians. As the *Brahmo Samaj* declined in influence by the end of the nineteenth century, a similar organization, the *Prarthana Samaj*, emerged to focus on many of the religious and social reforms of its predecessor. As well, Dayanand Saraswati founded the *Arya Samaj* or Society of *Aryas* or Noble Men to draw inspiration from the Vedas. But whereas Roy and Tagore wanted to establish Hinduism as equal to Christianity, Saraswati sought to declare Hinduism as the superior faith, the "*primeval eternal religion*," a religion "worthy of being believed by all men in all ages."[4]

Actually the sprouts of Indian nationalism got nourished by both Orientalists and Anglicists. Orientalists resuscitated an interest and pride in India's past, particularly among Hindus. The Anglicists provided a common language (English) and a cultural model—such as the newly emerging concept of nationalism in Europe—that combined to compose the "interpreters" who aided

---

3 de Bary, *Sources of Indian Tradition*, p. 2:22.
4 *Ibid.*, p. 2:83.

the British agenda in India. But modernization and its implied Westernization also gave birth to numerous indigenous opponents for various reasons. Religiously this produced several thinkers—especially Sri Ramakrishna (Sri Ramakrishna Paramahamsa, born Gadadhar Chattopadhyay, 1836–1886) and his student Swami Vivekananda (i.e., Narendranath Dutta, 1863–1902)—who reveled in the post-Vedic practices that Hinduism gradually embraced over the centuries. Far from attempting to do away with idol worship, caste, and such, they championed such practices.

For Ramakrishna, the devotion to God in the Bhakti tradition provided the path to salvation and it involved clearing one's mind of worldly distractions, but not material renunciation: "Verily I say unto you, you are living in the world, there is no harm in that; but you will have to fix your mind on God, otherwise you cannot realize Him." Those who seek to "modernize" Hinduism actually minimize it. "The difference between the modern Brahmanism [of the *Brahmo Samaj*] and Hinduism is like the difference between the single note of music and the whole music. The modern Brahmas are content with the single note of Brahman, while the Hindu religion is made up of several notes producing a sweet and melodious harmony."[5] Vivekananda, meanwhile, had no problem with "cleansing and repairing" Hinduism but feared reformers might demolish "the whole thing." He insisted that spiritual development involved serving the poor—a belief that strongly influenced Mohandas Gandhi—and created the Ramakrishna Mission to achieve that goal. Moreover, in one of the early "material West, spiritual East" declarations from Asia, Vivekananda explained that mastering the physical world without also mastering one's mind would not produce happiness.

> Man is born to conquer Nature, it is true, but the Occidental means by "Nature" only the physical or external Nature. It is true that external Nature is majestic, with its mountains, and oceans, and rivers, and with the infinite powers and varieties. Yet there is a more majestic internal Nature of Man, higher than the sun, moon, and the stars, higher than this earth of ours, higher than the physical universe, transcending these little lives of ours; and it affords another field of study. There the Orientals excel, just as the Occidentals excel in the other. Therefore it is fitting that, whenever there is a spiritual adjustment, it should come from the Orient. It is also fitting that when the Oriental wants to learn about machine-making, he should sit at the feet of the Occidental and learn from him. When the Occident wants to learn about the spirit, about God, about the soul, about the meaning and the mystery of this universe, he must sit at the feet of the Orient to learn.[6]

Indeed, all the armies and material techniques of the West cannot subdue spiritual India. Quite the contrary, claimed Vivekananda: "The only condition of national life, of awakened and vigorous national life, is the conquest of the world by Indian thought."[7]

The Sepoy Mutiny and the Emergence of Indian Nationalism

The Western authority of "Oriental" Jones and Thomas Macaulay and the Westernized responses of Roy, Tagore, and Saraswati not only generated religious opposition, as evidenced in the writings of Ramakrishna and Vivekananda. Such authority also met physical resistance, best exemplified in the

---

5 *Ibid.*, pp. 2:89, 2:93.
6 *Ibid.*, pp. 2:97, 2:99.
7 *Ibid.*, p. 2:100.

Sepoy Mutiny of 1857–1858. It has been commonly labeled the Indian First War of Independence, the Indian Rebellion of 1857, and the Great Rebellion, as well as other terms. The name Sepoy (*sepahi*), meaning soldier, describes the approximately 200,000 Hindu and Muslim Indians who served in the Indian army led by about 40,000 British officers and noncommissioned officers. The more immediate cause of the uprising had to do with the new rifles introduced into the army. The soldier had to "bite the pouch containing gunpowder before emptying the powder into the barrel. The pouch was coated with grease made from the fat of either pigs, anathema to the Muslims, or cows, sacred to the Hindus."[8] But longer-term reasons include the introduction of British ways, from the use of English as the official language of government to the increased activity of Christian missionaries to the elimination of *suttee*. But the company's goal of the eventual elimination of the more than 600 princely states most likely produced the elite reaction that made the rebellion possible. Under the British Doctrine of Lapse, only natural heirs (Hindu *maharajas* and Muslim *nawabs*) could inherit governmental authority in a princely state, thus enabling the East India Company to take control of those states with no natural heirs (i.e., where heredity lapsed).

Sepoy Mutiny/First War of Indian Independence, 1857–1858. *Source:* Felice Beato/Getty Images.

Officially beginning on May 10, 1857, the uprising resulted from the actions of one sepoy, Mangal Pandey, who in late March of that year rebelled against his British lieutenant, refusing to use the Enfield rifle and its cartridges coated with fat. He was arrested, court-martialed, and later hanged in April. Generalized unrest continued throughout the month, but not until May 10 at Meerut on the northern outskirts of New Delhi did the rebellion explode onto the scene. There sepoys also refused to use the new rifle, attacked the British troops in the garrison, and were able to spread to Delhi, where they "restored" the Mughal emperor, Bahadur Shah II, to power. Though significant

---

8 D. R. SarDesai, *India: The Definitive History* (Boulder, CO: Westview Press, 2008), p. 243.

parts of northern and central India came under Sepoy attack, most of the Indian army and the majority of the local Indian elite remained on the sidelines. The rebellion effectively came to an end in the spring of 1858, and while pockets of resistance continued to fight until 1859, the British regained control. The Mughal emperor was exiled to Burma, where he died in 1862. Most argue that the uprising took on such importance because the British commander at Meerut acted too slowly to quell the uprising. All agree that growing mutual animosities culminated in reciprocal atrocities. In any case, British India would never be the same as a result.

The outcome of the rebellion produced major changes for India. From the British side, the East India Company's rule came to an end in 1858, replaced by direct governing of India from London. Under the Government of India Act of 1858, *rajas* and *nawabs* made treaties with the British Crown giving them freedom from annexation; the Doctrine of Lapse ended. The act also allowed for traditional religious practices to continue without interference from the Crown. Henceforth the Crown ruled (Queen Victoria became empress of India in 1877) and the governor-general became the viceroy appointed by the Crown. The Viceroy's Council, created by the India Councils Act of 1861, now included Indians. The British preferred to work with the leaders of princely states and avoid Indian reformers and nationalists. The company's army was replaced by a military that favored the "martial races"—Sikhs, Rajputs, Jats, Pathans, and Gurkhas—thus slighting Hindu Brahmins and Muslims. From the Indian nationalist point of view, indigenous organizations capable of increasing Indian participation in government and promoting independence needed to be built. Until independence in 1947, the political battles waged took place among the British, the rulers of princely states, and Indian nationalists. The former two sought to maintain stability; the latter was divided over how best to promote the desired change.

Nationalism and the Formation of the Congress Party (1885) and the Muslim League (1906)

Nationalists formed two broad groups: those who resisted the Westernization Macaulay wanted, and those who protested the failure of the British to live up to many of the modern concepts they espoused at home but disregarded or even opposed in the colonies. Besides the rulers of princely states, only a small number of educated Indians shunned entirely modern ideas and techniques. Most of the rest of India's elite favored utilizing whatever the outside world offered if these offerings could force the British eventually to "quit," that is, leave India. Of those modernizers, some favored violence, others working within the system. Some argued for a single, all-inclusive organization such as the Indian National Congress (INC) or Congress Party to lead the united campaign against the British. Increasingly, since the British tended to favor the Hindus, Muslims came to believe that organizations dedicated to protecting religious, ethnic, or other interests needed to emerge to insure the protection of their concerns when an independent but overwhelmingly majority-Hindu India arrived.

In Mumbai in late December 1885, Allan Octavian Hume, Dadabhai Naoroji, Motilal Nehru, and Womesh Chandra Bannerjee along with 68 other delegates met to form the Indian National Congress (INC). The INC began as a moderate movement led by chiefly English-educated Indians drawing upon a range of ideas and emotions generated by the Hindu Renaissance. It was designed to promote Indian self-rule within the British imperial system, but increasingly complaints about British rule overshadowed the cooperation plan. Thus Naoroji, the first Indian member of the House of Commons, wrote *Poverty and Un-British Rule in India* in 1901, arguing that British governance created a "drain" on India economically. As he put it,

First All Indian National Congress in Bombay (Mumbai), 1885. *Source:* National Archives.

With material wealth go also the wisdom and experience of the country. Europeans occupy almost all the higher places in every department of Government directly or indirectly under its control. While in India, they acquire India's money, experience and wisdom; and when they go, they carry both away with them, leaving India so much poorer in material and moral wealth. Thus, India is left without, and cannot have those elders in wisdom and experience who in every country are the natural guides of the rising generations in their national and social conduct, and of the destinies of their country; and a sad, sad loss this is.[9]

By 1907, the INC had split into two factions, the Moderates and the Extremists.

Gopal Krishna Gokhale (1866–1915) best represented the INC's moderate faction, which focused on working within the British political framework. Gokhale and other moderates opposed British injustices and other deficiencies, believing that such shortcomings could be remedied by legal means such as education, debate, and greater Indian participation in the political and administrative processes. Thus he resisted taxation without representation, arguing that "in India the taxpayer has no constitutional voice in the shaping of these things [taxation]." To make matters worse, the taxes collected without Indian representation exceeded the amount needed to competently govern as they annually amounted to surpluses. The British claimed that their administration never saw a surplus. And while the British needed to reform its political system to allow for greater Indian participation, Gokhale also warned his fellow countrymen that Indians needed to reform its social system to allow for more equitable participation by those of lower caste. It was simply a question of "self-interest."

---

9 As quoted in SarDesai, *India*, p. 265.

How can we possibly realize our national aspirations, how can our country ever hope to take her place among the nations of the world, if we allow large numbers of our countrymen to remain sunk in ignorance, barbarism, and degradation? Unless these men are gradually raised to a higher level, morally and intellectually, how can they possibly understand our thoughts or share our hopes or cooperate with us in our efforts? Can you not realize that so far as the work of national elevation is concerned, the energy, which these classes might be expected to represent, is simply unavailable to us?[10]

Clearly a nationalist, Gokhale also recognized the importance of social unity and the power of mass involvement in the success of any nationalist movement, concepts Mohandas Gandhi later passionately embraced.

Bal Gangadhar Tilak (1856–1920) best characterized the extremist faction of the INC. He too recognized the significance of bringing the uneducated and low-caste members of society into the nationalist movement. Unlike Gokhale, however, Tilak took a much more militant position, going so far as to favor political assassination to achieve political ends. He sought to go beyond the Westernized Indians verbally sparring with the British overlords and bring the common people directly into the political fray. His chief instrument in mass mobilization was the boycott, a technique Mohandas Gandhi later used to great effect. As Tilak proclaimed, "The remedy is not petitioning but boycott. We say prepare your forces, organize your power, and then go to work so that they cannot refuse you what you demand." Boycott involved not only British goods but also nonparticipation in the British political authority in India. "At present, we are clerks and willing instruments of our own oppression in the hands of an alien government, and that government is ruling over us not by its innate strength but by keeping us in ignorance and blindness to the perception of this fact."[11] Tilak reasoned that he could draw on the common history and religion of the Hindus to win self-government. His perhaps exclusive Hindu (or possibly anti-Muslim) nationalism was sufficiently prevalent in early twentieth-century India, along with a British administration that dethroned Muslim rulers and favored Hindus, to lead Muslims to create the All India Muslim League.

Muslim Indians shared a Hindu desire to rid India of British rule, but Hindu and Muslim Indians shared increasingly different pasts, presents, and likely futures. Before the arrival of the Western nations, Hindus resisted Muslim rule culturally and politically. Muslim political hegemony did not indicate Hindu acceptance but merely practical recognition of Muslim power, and Hindus could take some comfort in the fact that the Persian model of monarchy under the Delhi sultans and Mughal emperors became increasingly an Indian model of kingship. In that setting, centralized government never fared well in India, as local rulers regularly resisted a national administration. Add to that the religious factor, by which Muslim rulers discriminated against non-Muslims, creating a wide gap between Muslim rulers and non-Muslim ruled that even Akbar's tolerant policies could not completely bridge.

Even in the political environment of anti-British feelings—across the Indian religious spectrum—it is clear that Hindus more readily utilized Western ideas and practices while Muslims more grudgingly accepted new ways of looking at the world. Syed Ahmad Khan, founder of the Muhammadan Anglo-Oriental College, reflected the willingness of some of the Muslim elite to acknowledge the value of new ideas. "The truth of Islam will shine the more brightly if its followers are well educated, familiar with the highest in the knowledge of the world; it will come under an eclipse if its followers are ignorant and backward."[12] Like many Muslims who saw the Indian National Congress as a vehicle for Hindu interests, he believed that Muslims needed to work with

---

10 de Bary, *Sources of Indian Tradition*, pp. 2:145, 2:149.
11 *Ibid.*, pp. 2:169–170.
12 *Ibid.*, p. 2:193.

Founding members at the formation of the All Indian Muslim League in Dhaka, 1906.

the British and shun the INC. As he argued, "the Congress cannot rationally prove its claim to represent the opinions, ideals, and aspirations of the Muslims."[13] The poet Muhammad Iqbal took things a step further, claiming faith comes before fatherland:

> Our Essence is not bound to any place;
> The vigor of our wine is not contained
> In any bowl; Chinese and India
> Alike the shard that constitutes our jar,
> Turkish and Syrian alike the clay
> Forming our body; neither is our heart
> Of India, or Syria, or Rum
> Nor any fatherland do we profess
> Except Islam.[14]

When the All India Muslim League formed in Dhaka (now in Bangladesh) in 1906, it did so in light of differing Hindu–Muslim goals. The organization wanted to protect Muslim interests, to counter INC policies harmful to Muslims, and to let the British know it would work within the system. In northern India, Hindi became an official language, marginalizing the Urdu of Muslims in the region. In 1905, Bengal was partitioned, diluting the political influence of a Muslim majority in northeastern India. As the British introduced political reforms allowing more Indian participation, increasingly the British became the only protector of minority Muslim rights in an administrative and legislative India increasingly in the hands of Hindus. The Muslims feared an independent India of majority Hindus and thus considered democratic government an instrument of Muslim marginalization given their much smaller population. They also feared a secular Indian government in the hands of a perpetual Hindu majority. And one of the first accomplishments of the Muslim League was getting the British to allow the creation of separate electorates under the British (and later under an independent, unified India). Nonetheless, as with the INC, the Muslim

---

13 *Ibid.*, p. 2:195
14 *Ibid.*, p. 2:204.

League became ever more at odds with British rule, and by World War I the two Indian organizations usually cooperated when working out policies with the British. Still, beneath the surface of cooperation lay the cultural foundations for two nations, the secular Socialist Republic of India and the religious Islamic Republic of Pakistan in 1947.

Britain's Response to Indian Nationalism

As Indian nationalism began to take root by 1900, George Curzon, the viceroy of India from 1898 to 1905, sought to reverse the momentum. His first assault on Indian nationalism came in 1901 with a plan to partition the province of Bengal, then including today's Bangladesh, West Bengal, Orissa, Assam, and Bihar. The partition involved combining what is today Bangladesh and Assam into East Bengal and the remainder into West Bengal, and it was made official in October 1905.

The result divided a highly nationalistic Bengali population into Hindu and Muslim communities. While Muslims appreciated the fact that they now had a majority in East Bengal, they and other Bengalis as well as non-Bengali Indians realized that the British had partitioned the province to weaken the nationalist movement by pitting Hindu against Muslim. As a consequence the All India Muslim League emerged, the INC became more radical, and mass-based Indian politics surfaced. Curzon then lost the confidence of Prime Minister Arthur Balfour, who forced him to resign his position. The partition caused such turmoil that it was repealed in 1911.

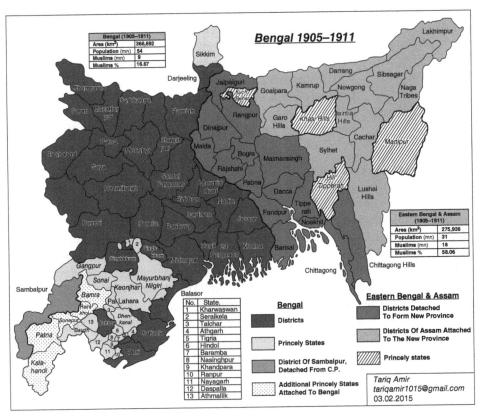

The partition of Bengal, 1905. *Source:* Tariq Amir, tariqamir1015@gmail.com, 03.02.2015.

Gilbert John Elliott-Murray-Kynynmound, the 4th Earl of Minto, succeeded Curzon as viceroy and served 1905–1910. He was appointed by a Conservative government in Britain that would soon be replaced by a Liberal one. Viceroy Minto reported to John Morley, chosen to be the Secretary of State for India by the new Liberal government. Together they produced the Morley-Minto Reforms (or Indian Councils Act) of 1909. The reforms extended the rights of Indian participation in the viceroy's Legislative Council and various provincial governors' councils, some of whose members were appointed and others elected. Both central and provincial bodies now included Indians whose property holdings or educational achievements made them eligible for membership. While this set of reforms did provide for greater Indian input into government policies, the British nonetheless retained control of these bodies, and in any case the viceroy could veto any legislative initiative. Moreover, for those elective seats, the Muslims were granted reserved seats and only Muslims could vote for those running for Muslim seats. This policy of separate electorates continued a policy of divide and rule seen in the earlier partition of Bengal. Although the Muslims welcomed certain political representation and the moderates of the INC viewed the reforms as a step toward self-rule, the Morley-Minto reforms upset most Hindus by making Muslim seats noncompetitive, while the extremists of the INC considered the Indian participation mere tokenism. But many Indians—both Hindus and Muslims—consider the reforms to be yet another step on the road to the partition of India in 1947.

As World War I approached, the stage was set for Mohandas Gandhi, who blended nationalist sentiment, the ideas of Gokhale and Tilak, the possibility of Hindu and Muslim unity, mass mobilization, and the demand for *swaraj* (literally *swa* or self-*raj* or rule) or independence to forge a movement that could dislodge the British Raj. All the more remarkable, Gandhi would hold together such diverse ideas, religions, castes, and regions while convincing his followers to remove the British peacefully.

Suggested Readings and Viewings

C. A. Bayly, *Indian Thought in the Age of Liberalism and Empire* (Cambridge: Cambridge University Press, 2012).

H. V. Bower, *The Business of Empire: The East India Company and Imperial Britain, 1756–1833* (Cambridge: Cambridge University Press, 2006).

Bernard S. Cohn, *The British in India* (Princeton, NJ: Princeton University Press, 1996).

William Dalrymple, *The Last Mughal: The Fall of a Dynasty, Delhi, 1857* (London: Bloomsbury, 2006).

Saul David, *The Indian Mutiny: 1857* (New York: Viking, 2002).

John Keay, *The Honourable Company: A History of English East India Company* (New York: Harper Collins, 1993).

David Kopf, *British Orientalism and the Bengal Renaissance, 1773–1835* (Berkeley: University of California Press, 1969).

Thomas R. Metcalf, *Imperial Connections: India in the Indian Ocean Arena, 1860–1920* (Berkeley: University of California Press, 2007).

Michael Wood, *The Story of India,* episode 6, "Freedom."

Stanley Wolpert, *Tilak and Gokhale: Revolution and Reform in the Making of Modern India* (Berkeley: University of California Press, 1962).

23

The Impact of World Wars, Revolution, and Nationalism in India and South Asia, 1914–1945

I worship God as Truth only. I have not yet found Him, but I am seeking after Him. I am prepared to sacrifice the things dearest to me in pursuit of this quest. Even if the sacrifice demanded be my very life, I hope I may be prepared to give it. But as long as I have not realized this Absolute Truth, so long must I hold by the relative truth as I have conceived it.

—Mohandas K. Gandhi[1]

World War I and Its Impact

Even though most people tend to think of World War I as a largely European affair, one that began with the assassination of an archduke of Austria-Hungary, the reach and effects of the Great War (as it was known before World War II) were truly global. One need only consider the number of countries involved in the conflict to appreciate this. Those who entered the war as combatants included nearly all of the nations of Europe, save those whose neutrality was honored: Switzerland, Sweden, Spain, Norway, Denmark, Greece, and Holland. Since all of the nations of Africa except for Ethiopia and Liberia had been colonized by European nations, most of them participated in the war, in most cases by sending needed laborers to work in the combatant nations. The nations of North America took part in the conflict as well, with Canada and the United States joining the fight and Mexico, with the Zimmermann Note, becoming indirectly involved. In Central America, the opening of the Panama Canal, a highly strategic passageway, focused attention on Panama and its neighboring nations, almost all of which eventually declared war on Germany, even if none of them committed troops to the fight. Many South American nations became involved directly—such as Brazil and the UK-administered Falkland Islands—as well as indirectly due to the sentiments and actions of ethnic inhabitants, many citizens of South American nations having migrated from European and Asian homelands that were belligerents in the conflict.[2]

As for the nations of Asia, they were very much involved in World War I. All of the European colonizers entered the war, meaning that their Asian colonies were drawn into the conflict by default, except for those of neutral Holland, meaning that Dutch Indonesia never joined the fight, nor did semi-colonial Afghanistan or Mongolia. But the remainder of colonized Asia did, usually by sending laborers to take part in support activities. On occasion, significant numbers of Asians took part

---

1 Mohandas K. Gandhi, *An Autobiography: The Story of My Experiments with Truth* (Boston: Beacon Press, 1957), p. xiv.
2 Ethnic Germans, Italians, Japanese, and Chinese made up significant parts of South American nations.

Asia Past and Present: A Brief History, First Edition. Peter P. Wan and Thomas D. Reins.
© 2021 John Wiley & Sons, Inc. Published 2021 by John Wiley & Sons, Inc.

in combat: Members of the Indian Army fought on the side of the Allies against the Central Powers in Europe on the Western front; in German East Africa; and in Mesopotamia and Gallipoli against the forces of Turkey, Germany's ally. Non-colonized Japan, China, and Siam also participated in the conflict, contributing different amounts of time, money, troops, and non-combatants.

The Great War resulted in a number of consequences for Asia, most of which weakened colonial regimes and strengthened nationalist movements. Only Japan and Russia of the imperial powers came out of the war stronger in Asia than when they entered. The war and its outcome forced most colonizers to reduce the size of their colonial administrations in order to meet the needs of wartime demands back home. This in turn gave indigenous nationalist movements greater maneuverability, given smaller numbers of imperial military and police to keep such groups in check. During the conflict, large numbers of colonized people—not just the elite but laborers and soldiers as well—spent time in Europe, where they achieved a better comprehension of their overlords' strengths and weaknesses. One clear insight gained was the enormous pessimism the war produced in the peoples of Europe, as evidenced in much of the postwar literature, such as Erich Remarque's *All Quiet on the Western Front* and George Orwell's *Burmese Days*. These and many other contemporary writings called into question the very worth of Western civilization and the morality of colonial rule.

Still, no European colony in Asia actually became independent after the conflict. Thus, to many in the colonial world, the highly touted promise of U.S. President Woodrow Wilson of self-determination for the subject nations in the wake of the "war to end all wars" rang hollow. By contrast, the Communist Revolution in Russia in 1917 had created a radical Bolshevik alternative to capitalism and democracy, both of which were increasingly associated with the causes of the war in much of the world. Moreover, Soviet Russia claimed to be anti-imperialist, an assertion that appeared genuine only if one ignored the "soviet republics" in Europe and Central Asia as well as the satellite status of Mongolia and other semi-colonial countries on the Soviet Russian frontier. Furthermore, after the war, Soviet aid to communist, nationalist, and/or independence movements in the emerging Third World[3] encouraged the indigenous leaders, even as it threatened the colonial regimes that still ruled them. Both communist and noncommunist leaders received Soviet money and training to help shed colonial rule. Finally, during World War II more than two million volunteer soldiers in the Indian Army fought the enemies of Britain, more than 200,000 in battle in various combat theaters. World War I helped bring into being fascist movements across the globe, a further indication that the capitalist-democratic model had lost much appeal.

The Treaty of Versailles (1919) and additional treaties concluding World War I sought to reconstitute a balance of power in Europe to minimize the likelihood of another ghastly conflict. The Congress of Vienna (1814–1815) had done that after Napoleon had run wild across Europe a century earlier, the result being a century of relative peace. This, however, proved only a whim, for the treaties the delegates drafted ended up being highly punitive to the defeated Germany, so much so that the balance of power in Europe was resigned to the past. Indeed, few nations—including the "Big Five" victorious nations of Great Britain, France, Japan, the United States, and Italy—came away from Versailles happy. France was disappointed in its wish to have Germany de-industrialized to prevent future German aggression. Italy wanted and believed it would get land along the Adriatic coast

---

3 After the Russian or Bolshevik Revolution in 1917, the nations of the world became increasingly viewed in the eyes of global leaders, intellectuals, and political activists of any persuasion as falling into one of three categories. The First World consisted of the industrial, developed capitalist and democratic world. The Second World, often termed the Soviet Bloc, comprised the socialist nations, which until after World War II included only the Soviet Union, and thereafter included Eastern European nations, China, Cuba, and Vietnam. The Third World included still colonized, newly independent, and underdeveloped nations.

Timeline for South Asia, 1914–1945	
1914–1918	World War I involved British colonies in South Asia
1915	Gandhi returns to India from South Africa
1916	Lucknow Pact brought together the moderate and extremist factions of the Indian National Congress and provided for set-aside seats for Muslims in provincial councils
1919	Amritsar (Jalianwala Bagh) Massacre
1919	Rowlatt Act provided for greater British power to control anti-British activities
1919	Government of India Act of 1919 provides non-sensitive government positions to Indians
1919	Treaty of Versailles, ending World War I, created by victorious Allies
1919–1924	Khilafat Movement by Indian Muslims to protect the Caliphate in Turkey from being destroyed by the victorious Allies
1920–1922	The Non-Cooperation Movement emerged as a result of the Amritsar Massacre, the developing Khilafat Movement, and Gandhi's ability to mobilize; it involved such actions as boycotting government schools and additional British government institutions and other such activities
1930	Gandhi's Civil Disobedience Movement begins
1930	Gandhi's Dandi Salt March to protest British salt tax seen as first action in the Civil Disobedience Movement
1939–1945	Good wartime relations between Sri Lankan leaders and the British
1940	Indian Muslim League demands (in the Lahore Resolution) the creation of a separate state of Pakistan
1942	August 8: Gandhi's speech telling the British to "Quit India"
1945	In the British General Election of July, Labour Party candidate Clement Attlee defeats Conservative Party leader and wartime government Prime Minister Winston Churchill, which sets the British political stage for Indian independence

(basically parts of what became Yugoslavia); it too was denied. In the wake of the negotiations, the U.S. Senate refused to ratify the Treaty of Versailles, meaning that America did not, as President Wilson vehemently wanted, join the postwar peace organization known as the League of Nations, a creation of the treaty. Japan wanted but did not get a racial equality stipulation in the treaty, and had to struggle to be able to keep the German leasehold of Qingdao in China's Shandong Province. Japan did, however, get the German Pacific islands north of the equator (the Marianas, the Marshalls, and the Carolines). Much of the British delegation, including economist John Maynard Keynes, argued that treating Germany too harshly—which most contemporary analysts of Versailles believe occurred in several treaty sections—would ensure a future Germany that would be bitter and hostile.

The non-Western world came away from the war typically disappointed and angry. Arabs who had been promised freedom from Germany's Turkish ally felt betrayed, as did European Jews who had been promised in the British Balfour Declaration (1917) a homeland in Palestine. Colonies in Asia and Africa witnessed none of the promised self-determination as a result of the Versailles Treaty. And in China, an explosion occurred in the May Fourth Movement of 1919, when Chinese became aware that the treaty awarded Qingdao (which ally Japan had taken from the Germans) to Japan, had not eliminated foreign rights in China, and did nothing to abolish the Twenty-One Demands (discussed below) Japan had made on China in 1915. Since Russia left the war in 1917 after the Communist Revolution, it did not participate in the making of the Versailles Treaty and was not bound by its terms. As many even at the time had feared, Germany found the treaty an appalling and humiliating document, one that would indeed generate popular resentment, much of which would aid the rise of the Nazi movement and Adolph Hitler. In brief, few nations or peoples viewed the treaty in positive terms, and fewer still felt strongly enough about it to defend it at all costs.

Nationalist Movements in South Asia, 1914–1945

Nationalism after World War I resulted from the global growing demand by ethnicities to break away from imperial overlords. In South Asia, this clearly meant nationalist movements organizing to oust the British overlords in India, Sri Lanka, and the Himalayan nations. But it also meant a struggle to determine which ethnic group in each nation would dominate when independence arrived. After World War I, nationalism trumped ethnicity and religion in South Asia. After World War II, when it became clear that Britain would depart, ethnicity and religion came to dominate the discussions of "who rules."

As World War I began, India already had two substantial organizations dedicated to the pursuit of greater Indian political participation in British India and ultimately devoted to the fulfillment of independence: the Indian National Congress (INC, later the Congress Party) and the Indian Muslim League (IML). The war now directly added tens of thousands of Indian soldiers, who fought in Europe on the Western front, in German East Africa, and in Turkish-controlled Iraq. Most Indian nationalists, including Mohandas Gandhi, supported the war, trusting that the participation of Indian soldiers would earn them the goodwill and respect of Western powers, especially Britain, and lead to greater Indian participation in government at home. As it turned out, it was not so much Indian participation in the war effort, but rather the pressure that Indian nationalist organizations put on the British during and after the war, which accounted for London's willingness to grant a larger role for Indians in the governing of India at war's end. The Lucknow Pact of 1916 between the INC and the IML provides the best evidence of Indian nationalism trumping ethnic advantage—at least in the short run. The INC met at Lucknow and worked out a reconciliation between the party's moderate and extremist factions, resulting in a more formidable organization in its negotiations with London. The pact also insured set-aside seats for Muslims in provincial councils in those parts of India where their numbers would not be sufficient to assure the election of Muslims. Thus the INC pact forged a united front better able to apply political pressure on the British.

The IML also contributed to the growing Indian nationalist crusade. The Khilafat/Caliphate Movement among Muslims in India emerged just before the outbreak of World War I in support of the sultan of Turkey, the Caliph or protector of Muslims across the globe. The IML and most Muslims believed that the European Balkan War of 1912–1913 and World War I constituted a Christian threat against the Turks and thus the Caliph. As the British stood on the opposite side of the Turks in both conflicts, Muslims in India resented the British even more (it was the British who had deposed the Muslim Mughal Empire), especially after Turkey ended up on the losing side of the war and saw its empire carved up in the peace settlement.[4] Thus the Khilafat Movement in conjunction with the Lucknow Pact forged a unification of the larger part of the Indian elite. As World War I ended, the IML and the INC seemed to speak as one in its dealings with the British.

---

4 The Ottoman Turkish Empire controlled Mecca, where Islam's most holy shrine, the Kaaba, was located. Kamal Mustafa, or Atatürk, created the secular Republic of Turkey and abolished the Caliphate on March 3, 1924.

At this point, a charismatic nationalist leader—Mohandas Gandhi—arose to provide the means most likely to result in the achievement of the short-term goal of greater Indian participation in British administration and eventually in bringing about a complete end to British rule.

The shift by Indian nationalists from a position of cooperation with the British to one of non-cooperation through active resistance played out, chiefly, in three important events: the passage of the Government of India Act of 1919 (i.e., the Montague Chelmsford reforms), the passage of the Rowlatt Acts in March 1919, and the Jalianwala Bagh (Amritsar) Massacre of April 13, 1919.

The Government of India Act of 1919, passed in December 1919, provided for the transfer of executive control in the provinces to Indian officials of such divisions as health, education, and public works (the "transferred lists"), yet the retention of British control in the more crucial areas of government, such as defense, foreign relations, and communications (the "reserved lists"). It also enlarged the Imperial Legislative Council, a majority of whose membership in both the upper and lower houses was elected. However, many of those elected came from the Princely States, which typically cooperated with the British, thus preserving a British-friendly majority. For its part, the INC denounced this British-Indian sharing of executive and legislative functions—known as diarchy—as tokenism, not as a meaningful shift toward Indian self-rule.

The Rowlatt Act of March 1919 also stirred Indian nationalist sentiments by making permanent the Defense of India Regulations Act of 1915, a (supposedly) temporary wartime measure taken in response to anti-British actions by Indians. These actions included a number of violent uprisings: the Ghadar Conspiracy, the Lahore Conspiracy, the Hindu-German Conspiracy, and the Singapore Mutiny of 1915, each of which also entailed British wartime enemies—the Germans, the Turks, and Irish Republicans—working with Indian nationalist movements to weaken the British war effort by instigating violence, particularly within the Indian Army. Indian nationalists had created the *Ghadar* (meaning mutiny or rebellion) Party in the United States with the support of German, Turkish, and Irish nationalists. The so-called Ghadar Conspiracy sought to overthrow the British government in India by inciting rebellion among Indians, especially those in the Indian Army. The movement included the Germans, who supported it through their consulate in San Francisco. It also somewhat involved British ally Japan, as Indian Nobel Laureate Rabindranath Tagore sought Japanese aid for the Ghadar Party. The Lahore Conspiracy also constituted an organized rebellion against the British throne in northwestern India, mainly in the Punjab, and included terrorist activities such as amassing stores of weaponry, destroying bridges and trains, robbing banks for funds, and killing police officers. In the wake of the actions of the Lahore Conspiracy, dozens of conspirators were captured and put on trial; 24 persons were executed, while the others received long prison sentences. The Hindu-German Conspiracy linked the German government and Indian nationalists in a broad range of anti-British activities throughout the war. Finally, the Singapore Mutiny of February 1915 occurred when rumors circulated that Indian military units in Singapore and Malaya would be shipped to fight fellow Muslims in Turkey. The mutiny lasted only a few days, but it involved roughly a thousand soldiers—mainly Muslims—who were defeated and tried, resulting in executions, life sentences, and lesser prison terms.

So, in the aftermath of the events that had unfolded in India and elsewhere during World War I, the British government made a set of seemingly contradictory moves in 1919 with the passage of the Government of India Act and the implementation of the Rowlatt Act, as the first tried to win back Indian cooperation even as the other sought to reassert British control. Instead of improving mutual understanding between the British on the one hand and Indian nationalists and the common people on the other hand, relations became even more antagonistic, probably beyond repair. When Gandhi denounced the Rowlatt Act and called for the people of India to protest, he generated a multitude of mass demonstrations across northern India. He believed that the use of *Satyagraha* or truth force by the people—manifested in individual fasting, marches, *hartals* or strikes, and other acts of civil disobedience—would finally erode Britain's ability to govern.

On April 13, 1919, in the Punjab, in the city of Amritsar, a series of demonstrations occurred that culminated in the shooting and killing and wounding of hundreds of Indians. The day began with pilgrims arriving in Amritsar, the Sikh religious center, and then proceeding to what is now called Jalianwala Bagh, today a memorial public garden but then a public square. Many in the crowd had come to celebrate the Sikh spring religious festival of Baisakhi, but given the unhappiness with the recent approval by the British of the Government of India Act and the Rowlatt Act, many of those entering both the city and Jalianwala Bagh had also come to protest. Brigadier General Reginald Dyer dispatched some 200 troops (mainly Indians and Gurkhas) to Amritsar in anticipation of INC-supported protests against the recently passed laws. Dyer feared the possible beginnings of another 1857-type rebellion, yet apparently gave no orders to the crowd of some 20,000 to disperse. As speakers were condemning the laws from a podium, it seems, Dyer suddenly gave the orders to fire into the protestors, many say because he wanted to intimidate people in the Punjab by making an example of the protestors and thus to deter future potential demonstrators. This "example" ended up killing approximately 450 people and wounding another 1500.

Jalianwala Bagh (Amritsar) Massacre Memorial. *Source:* saiko3p/123RF.

A Commission of Enquiry headed by Lord Hunter found General Dyer at fault and demoted him, while in the House of Commons on July 8, 1920, Winston Churchill denounced the killings as a "monstrous event." At the same time much of Great Britain viewed Dyer's actions as necessary, with many Britons contributing to a large defense fund for him. However one views what transpired at Amritsar, the incident clearly marked a major shift in Indian opinion regarding British rule, one perhaps more important than that triggered by the Sepoy Rebellion of 1857. As the *Times of India* commented when noting the death in 2009 of the last survivor of the Amritsar Massacre, the memorial created at Jalianwala Bagh highlights "the sacrifice of hundreds of unknown for India's freedom struggle."[5]

---

5 "Last Survivor of Jallianwala Bagh Massacre Dies," *Times of India*, June 29, 2009.

Gandhi and the Struggle for Indian Independence, 1920–1945

Thus began a decided shift in the Indian struggle, no longer chiefly for greater participation in the British administrative structure but principally for independence (*swaraj*) and by 1930 for complete independence (*purna swaraj*) from Britain. Amritsar and other events that stirred nationalist emotions in 1919 also marked the emergence of Gandhi as the leader of the independence movement. While his achievement was remarkable by any measure, his ultimate success in driving out the British resulted from his calm and measured approach to confrontation with the British—nonviolent (*ahimsa*) but active resistance (*satyagraha* or truth force, soul force) and mass mobilization—as well as from his genius in orchestrating the particular campaigns he launched in that decades-long confrontation. The central campaigns involved the Non-Cooperation Movement of the 1920s, the Civil Disobedience Movement in the 1930s, and the Quit India Movement of the 1940s.

The Non-Cooperation Movement officially began in 1920 based on resolutions passed at meetings of the INC that year. Although many in the INC feared non-cooperation would produce more Amritsar-like bloodbaths, the majority argued that only by placing great pressure on the British in the form of boycotting elections, withdrawing from government schools, refusing to serve in the military, and engaging in mass protests would they convince the British to rethink their position in India. Most particularly, non-cooperation became associated with the *Khadi* movement, the boycotting of British textiles and replacing them with homespun Indian clothing. Gandhi called off non-cooperation activities in February 1922 after Indian protestors killed more than a dozen police officers in Chauri Chaura (in the United Provinces). As others continued non-cooperation actions, Gandhi was arrested for his circulation of nationalist publications, and while in jail rethought how to better employ active resistance. Civil disobedience became the new approach.

Mohandas Gandhi leading joint Non-Cooperation and Khilafat Movements.

A good example of civil disobedience can be seen in the Salt Satyagraha or Dandi Salt March demonstrations, which Gandhi launched in March 1930. It involved the making of salt from seawater, an act that violated British Salt Laws. Salt had been taxed by Indian governments going back to at least the Mauryan Empire. It represented a typical tax imposed by many governments historically, China being a classic example. Since everyone needed salt for survival, the tax, as Gandhi noted, reached "even the starving millions, the sick, the maimed and the utterly helpless."[6] And though the tax had continued and fluctuated under the British and though it commonly accounted for less than 5 percent of British India's budget, it nonetheless represented a significant source of income. However, the salt tax suddenly doubled in 1923, consequently immediately upsetting those who had to pay it. Gandhi used this issue to launch his Salt Satyagraha and linked it to the call for complete independence from Britain.

Mohandas Karamchand Gandhi, who also came to be known as the Mahatma or Great Soul, successfully led the movement for Indian independence from Great Britain by drawing on an eclectic array of traditional and modern thought and organizational techniques. His application of nonviolence, "passive" resistance, and mass mobilization to the struggle against a more powerful, entrenched adversary gradually won the deep support of the Indian population and ultimately the grudging respect of the British government. Born of a merchant family, educated in the law in London, and shaped by colonial injustices, Gandhi emerged as an adult in the late nineteenth century when India's leading nationalist organization, the Indian National Congress, was divided into two camps: One was a group of moderates with secular liberal leanings who favored advancing toward independence largely by working within the colonial system to secure incremental British political reforms; the other faction, known as the extremists, was guided by religious teachings, supported the mobilization of the people, and endorsed the use of violence. Gandhi emerged to lead the independence movement after World War I by blending the most practical elements of the two factions. He enthusiastically embraced religious tradition and the mobilization of the masses to better put pressure on the British while shunning the use of violence. The issue of religion, however, led to two Indian traumas: the creation in 1947 of the separate Islamic state of Pakistan demanded by most of India's Muslims, and the assassination of Gandhi by a Hindu fanatic in January 1948.

The Dandi Salt March became the most celebrated incident in Gandhi's campaign for independence. It began when the Mahatma left his ashram in Sabermanti with his followers and picked up tens of thousands along the 240-mile route to his ultimate destination, Dandi, a city along the coast of the Arabian Sea. There he and his supporters took saltwater and allowed the water to evaporate on the beach, thus producing salt free of taxation. There he and 60,000 of his partners-in-crime were arrested for violating the salt laws, which permitted only the British to produce and sell salt. This and other salt marches brought out masses of protestors; led to abundant arrests, trials, and jailings; and put tremendous economic and political strains on the British administrative system. Gandhi's salt and other civil disobedience movements no doubt contributed to a new set of British political reforms contained in the Government of India Act of 1935.

---

6 As quoted in John Keay, *India: A History* (New York: Grove Press, 2000), p. 486.

Dandi Salt March, 1930. *Source:* Sueddeutsche Zeitung Photo / Alamy Stock Photo.

Before and after the salt march, Gandhi's principal efforts centered on independence, but many of the possible efforts had the potential to divide the independence movement. One campaign for more Indian participation in the British-run government had to do with elections. Thus, when the (Sir John) Simon Commission was created in 1927 to assess political developments under the Government of India Act of 1919, the commission included no Indians. The INC wanted Indian input into any such findings, but the IML—fearful of electoral reforms that would keep Muslims in perpetual minority status—demanded that the number of seats in any elected legislature be equal to the proportion of Muslims in the electoral district, regardless of the electoral outcome.

Memorial to the Dandi Salt Marchers. *Source:* naveen0301/Getty Images.

In 1928 the Indian All Parties Conference created the Motilal Nehru Committee to propose its plan for future governmental arrangements, which included set-aside seats for Muslims in both Central and Provincial legislatures. Later that year Mohammad Ali Jinnah of the IML issued his Fourteen Points, which demanded a federal system of government allowing what amounted to autonomy for those Muslim-majority regions, such as Bengal, Punjab, Sind, and Northwest Frontier. When the British government leadership changed parties from Conservative to Labour in 1929, Prime Minister Ramsey MacDonald proposed a new round of talks to be headed by Lord Irwin,[7] three Round Table Conferences (1931–1933) that now included Indian political leaders. However, once Muslim delegates to the talks demanded special treatment, other minority groups— Sikhs, Depressed Classes (members of low castes or *Harijans*), Anglo-Indians, 562 Princely States, and others—demanded the same.

In an attempt to satisfy the many different parties involved, the 1935 Government of India Act digested the political input of numerous interests and their proposals and produced a document that moved India closer to self-government and dominion status (promised by Lord Irwin in 1929) in the British Commonwealth. The 1935 Act provided for a federal central government but also allowed for provincial autonomy. While the document stipulated that once half of the states and provinces agreed to join the proposed federation, it could come into existence, the Princely States kept that from happening. The princes considered their interests best served under continued British direction, however much weakened London's control was becoming. The question of "Who governs?" became still more complicated after the 1937 provincial elections, in which the INC won sweeping victories in the provinces (though not a majority of the legislative seats) and the Muslims failed to win a majority vote in any province, even where there were Muslim majorities. This heightened the Muslim anxiety, already high among the Muslim elite, over the prospect of a federated political arrangement in which their interests might not be well served. Thus India entered World War II in September 1939 politically fragmented: The INC won the most votes but not a majority of those cast; the IML won control of some provincial governments, but nowhere succeeded in obtaining a majority vote; a majority of the provinces and states officially refused to join the federation in June 1939; and, in 1940, the IML demanded the creation of a separate state of Pakistan.

The Quit India Movement began formally in the middle of World War II, on August 9, 1942, when the INC passed a resolution calling for Britain to leave India. The INC stated goal of *swaraj* or self-rule had become increasingly clear and its actions increasingly militant since 1920. The history of Indian resistance to British rule was a long one: non-cooperation, civil disobedience, and non-participation in or opposition to British-sponsored political conferences or laws. This culminated before the war with nationalist leader Jawaharlal Nehru's 1938 statement to the British: Indian cooperation in any future conflict against the Nazis and Fascists depended on India being granted its independence. And when Britain declared war against the Axis without consulting Indian leaders, the INC passed a resolution of protest two weeks after the beginning of hostilities. Once independent, the INC promised, India would happily join the Allies in the "struggle for freedom" against the Axis powers. Otherwise, India would be forced to focus on its primary struggle for freedom against British imperial rule.

The British responded in August 1940 by asking for wartime cooperation by promising dominion status but also by stating that London would not hand over power to any government "whose authority is directly denied by large and powerful elements in India's national life."[8] This virtually guaranteed IML cooperation during the war. Britain's last attempt to obtain the cooperation of

---

7 Edward F. L. Wood had several titles: First Earl of Halifax, Lord Irwin, and Viscount Halifax, among others. He was Viceroy of India, 1926–1931.
8 As quoted in D. R. SarDesai, *India: The Definitive History* (Boulder, CO: Westview Press, 2008), pp. 301–302.

nationalist leadership in the INC before it issued the Quit India demand came in the form of the Cripps Mission. Sir Stafford Cripps (1889–1952), the Labour Party leader in Winston Churchill's War Cabinet (1940–1945), promised India dominion status at war's end, with the caveat that any province was allowed to decline to join the newly independent India. Since this wording ensured the creation of an independent Pakistan as well, Gandhi turned it down, rejecting the idea of an independent India partitioned into numerous independent states.

More direct Indian resistance to British rule in India occurred under the leadership of Subhash Chandra Bose (1897–1945), a onetime INC president who broke with Gandhi and organized his Forward Bloc and its Indian National Army for military struggle. He reportedly declared: "Give me blood and I will give you freedom." Bose's forces included the Indian National Army or Free India Army, composed mainly of expatriate Indians in Southeast Asia as well as some 40,000 troops from the British Indian Army in Singapore who had surrendered to the Japanese when they captured the island. Bose set up his own Free India government in exile on the Andaman and Nicobar Islands, which the Japanese had occupied in 1943. That same year a revolt in the British Indian Navy occurred in Bombay. Although the Japanese made raids on Madras and a few other East Indian locations, and though the British realized it could no longer depend on much Indian cooperation during or after the war, the Japanese and their Indian collaborators stood little chance of overrunning India. At war's end, Bose reportedly died in a plane crash in Taiwan. His fellow defectors were put on trial (the Red Fort trials) by the British in 1945–1946. The accused could count on popular support, typically hailed as heroes by Indian nationalists as well as by a mutiny in the Royal Indian Navy and Army as the trials proceeded. India's future first prime minister, Jawaharlal Nehru, and other members of the INC defended the accused, who were found guilty of greater or lesser crimes and given various sentences. Practically speaking, the leaders as well as the rank-and-file of Bose's Forward Bloc did not end up in jail. Some argue that the trials, the popular protests, and military mutinies as much as the INC and Gandhi convinced the British to "quit India."

10th Indian Division in Italy, July 22, 1944. *Source:* Imperial War Museums.

British Prime Minister Winston Churchill faced mounting troubles as World War II expanded. When Japan attacked Pearl Harbor in December 1941, bringing the United States in the conflict, Japan also invaded British colonial holdings in Asia. And while Japan had just provided Britain with its most important partner in the war, it was a mixed blessing. The American ally proved to be a two-edged sword, the new partner a massive source of manpower and war material but also one bent on ending colonization. Churchill boldly asserted that he had no intention of "presiding over the liquidation of the British Empire." And even though President Franklin Roosevelt nudged Churchill in the direction of decolonization throughout the conflict, conducting a war on two fronts took priority over issues of decolonization in both America and Britain. Nonetheless the obvious Indian hostility to the continued British presence led London to prepare, at least secretly, for a transfer of power even before the conclusion of the war. By June 1945, all Indian central government positions were given over to Indians save the military commander and the viceroy. Less than a month thereafter, the British Parliamentary elections of July 5, 1945, produced a large Labour Party majority under Clement Attlee and a readiness to begin a process of colonial divestiture. Gandhi, on the verge of getting the British to "quit India," now had the more formidable task of getting the Muslims to not quit India.

Sri Lanka

Several cultures influenced the development of civilization on Sri Lanka (known until 1972 as Ceylon), the large island located off the southeast corner of the Indian subcontinent: Indian, Portuguese, Dutch, and British. The early Sri Lankans came from India, and by the fifth century BCE people described as Sinhalese and Tamils accounted for the preponderance of the island's population. The Sinhalese spoke Indo-European languages and by the third century BCE embraced Buddhism. The Tamils, who spoke Dravidian languages, practiced Hinduism. Indian influence continually made its way into Sri Lanka over the centuries, through such means as military invasions from south Indian kingdoms and the acceptance of the caste system, which the islanders modified to suit their needs. From the third century BCE, Sinhalese and Tamil kingdoms regularly competed for supremacy, and religious competition between Buddhists and Hindus represented a large part of the antagonisms.

When the Portuguese began trading in Sri Lanka in the early sixteenth century, it was divided among two Sinhalese kingdoms—Kotte and Kandy—and a Tamil realm, Jaffna, but none was strong enough to unify the island. The Portuguese took advantage of rivalries among kingdoms and within royal families to take political control and introduce Catholicism. As the Dutch arrived in Asia, they too took advantage of competition among Sri Lankans and the Portuguese. Joining with the kingdom of Kandy, the Dutch by the early seventeenth century forced out the Portuguese and eventually conquered Kandy, soon becoming the island's supreme ruler and introducing Protestantism. However, when the Dutch supported France during America's Revolutionary War, the British—having taken control of India away from both the Mughal Empire and various European East India companies—entered Sri Lanka with the support of the Kandyan king, who had grown angry with the Dutch, who were ousted in 1796.

As with the earlier experiences of the Portuguese and Dutch, the British took advantage of Sri Lankan problems to consolidate their hold on the island. Not long after the Dutch departed, the Kandyan king became upset with the British, who sided with local Sinhalese elites offended by the king. When the British sent a military expedition to Kandy, the king escaped, whereupon the

British signed the Kandyan Convention in 1815 with the local elites. This agreement gave the British concrete control over the island with a "resident" rule through an impotent monarchy, the same approach London took in governing India and other of its colonies. In 1829 London established the Colebrooke-Cameron Commission to evaluate conditions on the island, particularly the British administrative system. Historically Sri Lanka was divided politically and culturally by kingdoms, ethnicities, and castes. The commission's findings in the *Colebrooke Report* of 1831–1832 called for an end to historical administrative divisions and the creation of Executive, Judicial, and Legislative Councils, the last of which contained a minority of Sri Lankan members. The commission also set up an educational system, with English as the language of instruction. Britain's civil service in Sri Lanka drew heavily from those having received British schooling, who along with an expanding mercantile class joined the traditional local elites, aristocrats, and monarchies to form the new Sri Lankan leadership. British administration and education provided the foundation for a Sri Lankan nationalist movement, which began with World War I.

As the war unfolded, Sri Lankans built on the existing nationalist foundation. They heard the allied powers speak of freedom and self-determination, and began to discuss the path toward their own independence. Moreover the nationalist movements in neighboring India provided a model of unity, this as the Indian National Congress and the Muslim League patched up their differences during the war. If communal disagreements in India could be overcome, Sri Lankan nationalists figured that the same could occur in Sri Lanka. Indeed, as communal upheavals erupted on the island in 1915, and as the British crushed them with excessive force, nationalist leaders such as the Sinhalese D. S. Denanayake took the opportunity to push even more vociferously for unity and self-government.

In 1919 Sinhalese and Tamils resolved many of their political differences sufficiently to form the Ceylon National Congress (CNC). After the war the CNC pushed for greater Sri Lankan participation in the island's governing and obtained British approval to draft a constitution in 1920, which when amended in 1924 provided only for minimal Sri Lankan sharing in the political process. In 1927 the (Earl of) Donoughmore Commission drew up policies to further the movement of Sri Lanka toward eventual independence by providing for universal suffrage and the formation of a State Council to create and implement political policy, headed by a Sri Lankan. But as in other colonies, once real political power became available, there was a scramble to grab as much of the power as possible for one's communal group.

Ten years later, the Sri Lankans would begin to form councils of their own. In 1937 the Sinhalese formed the Great Council of the Sinhalese or *Sinhala Maha Sabha,* with many of its members calling for the preeminence of Buddhism as the island's religion. In 1944 the Tamils established the All Ceylon Tamil Congress, even as other narrow interest groups based on communal loyalties developed before the end of World War II. While it is true that some political organizations formed with a unified Sri Lankan agenda, most such factions were leftist or communist parties that had only marginal support.

As it turned out, World War II set the stage for Sri Lankan independence. The strategic location of the island, from where hostile military forces could endanger the flow of Persian Gulf oil to the allies in Europe, Africa, or Asia, gave the Sri Lankans great leverage over the British, though Sri Lankan nationalists never threatened non-cooperation or resistance. Instead cordial relations prevailed between the British and the Sri Lankan elite during the entirety of the conflict, the British promising the Sri Lankans self-government after the war in return for their continued support. As well, since the Southeast Asian Command was headquartered there, the war generated hefty economic benefits for the people of the island. Thousands of military personnel spent money, while roads, public health services, and agricultural facilities were introduced or upgraded to augment the war effort.

In 1944 Lord Soulbury (Herwald Ramsbotham, 1st Viscount Soulbury) headed a commission to propose a new constitution for Sri Lanka to make the transition to self-government as smooth as possible. As with Muslims in India, the prospect of independence in Sri Lanka also meant minority status for many in a future government. The All Ceylon Tamil Congress (ACTC), created in 1944, proposed that Sinhalese have 50 percent representation in a future parliament, while the remaining 50 percent of the seats would be set aside for Tamils and other minorities to divvy up. The British rejected this arrangement, and the ACTC's leader G. G. Ponnambalam accepted Sinhalese control of an independent Sri Lanka led by D. S. Senanayake and called for all Ceylonese to cooperate with the duly elected leadership. British Crown Colony Sri Lanka became independent in 1948.

Himalayan Nations

Before 1945 Britain managed, not always successfully, relationships among the strategically located Himalayan nations—Sikkim, Nepal, and Bhutan. Most of the major rivers in water-scarce Asia originate there or in Tibet. Border disputes between British India and Manchu Qing China affected the Himalayan nations, which served as buffers between India and China. Culturally these buffer states reflected millennia of Indian influence, but Chinese influence has been significant since at least the early Qing Dynasty, when Beijing's political administration of Tibet took root. Tibet has possessed strong and lengthy cultural ties with India, while Russia has long had interests in Tibet and the Himalayan region—which, along with Persia, Afghanistan, and Central Asia, constituted the larger neighborhood in which the "Great Game" between Britain and Russia was played.

Until 1975, Sikkim remained an independent Buddhist monarchy influenced culturally over the centuries by India (60% of the population is Hindu), Nepal, Bhutan, Tibet, and Britain. Legend has it that an exiled Tibetan prince, Guru Tashi, organized tribes in today's Sikkim region. Its first established monarchy emerged in the mid-seventeenth century but proved to be incapable of preventing invasions from both Bhutan and Nepal. By the late eighteenth century, Sikkim found itself ruled, practically speaking, by Nepal. "Great Game" politics rescued Sikkim from the Nepalese, but Britain took control of the region as a stepping stone to Tibet. London feared the expansion of Russia into adjacent Tibet, and the occupation of Sikkim resulted in the kingdom becoming a puppet state of British India by the mid-nineteenth century. After World War I, Sikkim controlled its domestic affairs but its foreign relations were handled by the British. When India became independent in 1947, Sikkim voted not to become part of the Indian union, and its protectorate status as a kingdom remained the same as under the British, with India taking on Sikkim's foreign relations duties.

Bhutan emerged in the same cultural, political, and international environments as did Sikkim. By the seventeenth century, a unified monarchy emerged in the Buddhist kingdom when Tibetan monk Ngawang Namgyal (1594–1651) migrated to Bhutan. He set up an administration in which the king (*dharma raja*) served as a religious and temporal leader who oversaw a bureaucracy of religious and civil officials. He and his successors turned back several Tibetan and Mongol incursions into the eighteenth century. By then the British became the most likely threat to Bhutan, and sporadic conflicts between the East India Company and the Bhutanese monarchy eventually produced the concluding Duar War (1864–1865), won by the British. Again, "Great Game" politics likely dictated that London would do what was necessary to keep imperial Russia out the Himalayas and Tibet. This British goal was achieved with the help of Ugyen Wangchuck (1862–1926), the son of a provincial official who eventually became king (r. 1907–1926). Wangchuck defeated political rivals, brought about domestic stability, and cooperated with the British to enable London the gain the foreign advantage in Tibet through the Younghusband Expedition of 1903–1904, which produced the Anglo-Tibetan Convention (Treaty of Lhasa) of 1904. The essence of that document, accepted by the Manchu Chinese government in the Convention between Great Britain and China Respecting Tibet in 1906, stipulates that Britain will not annex Tibet if China does not "permit any other foreign State to interfere with the territory or internal administration of Tibet."

The Wangchuck Dynasty (1907–present) substantially weakened the *dharma raja* theocracy by creating a hereditary absolutist secular monarchy, the *raja* part; the *dharma* part is overseen by the *Je Khenpo*, the person responsible for Buddhist rituals, doctrines, and monasteries. The more modern monarchs have succeeded in maintaining domestic order and in protecting Bhutan against foreign threats by closely aligning itself with the British. In 1910 Bhutan signed the Treaty of Punakha with London, in which the British promised to protect the nation's independence, administer its foreign relations, and provide a stipend to the government. After World War II, the government of newly independent India continued the governmental activities and close interactions that British India had created with Bhutan.

Nepal also came under the cultural influence of its neighbors, largely Indian. It eventually embraced both Hinduism and the caste system. Authority in pre-modern Nepali society usually resided in the hands of kings, nobles, and clergy, each with limited powers. Over the centuries, Nepali kings had to pay certain kinds of tribute—sometimes symbolic, sometimes real—to India, and after 1206 to the Muslim monarchs who governed India. By the seventeenth century, Nepal also sent tribute to Manchu Qing China, which began to dominate neighboring Tibet. And in the eighteenth century, British East India began to exercise influence in Nepal. At the time Prithvi Narayan Shah (1723–1775) emerged to found the Gorkha or Shah Dynasty (1768–2008), the first modern Nepali monarchy. His death produced no strong successor, and for the next century or so foreign policy troubles with China and Britain led to unsuccessful wars and in bad treaties ending them. In 1846 court intrigue resulted in the Kot Massacre, the outcome of which resulted in the destruction of the old aristocracy and the emergence of military leader Jang Bahadur Rana (1816–1877). He took control of the government by making himself prime minister and by selecting the king for the powerless monarchy. He and his descendants ruled Nepal until 1951.

Opposition to the Rana "dynasty" had always existed at the Shah court, but World War I exposed Nepalese soldiers to the outside world, while Gandhi's nationalist activities in neighboring India provided a model for mass political organization. The creation of newspapers and political parties between the wars and the likely departure of the British, who had supported the Ranas, after World War II all worked to erode Rana rule. By then agitation against the government resulted in the resignation of the prime minister and forced the promise of reform by Rana leaders. A number of political parties and nationalist organizations formed the Nepali National Congress in 1947; its chief agenda item was the removal of the Rana regime, which occurred in 1951 along with the restoration of the monarchical power.

Conclusions

World War I, revolution, and a rising tide of nationalism in Asia, and in South Asia in particular, set the stage for the demise of colonial rule by the industrial nations. Britain's hold on India and Sri Lanka and influence in the Himalayas weakened, in part because of the economic and psychological costs of war to the mother country. Colonial subjects, quick to sense the weakness, seized the moment to forge independence movements that would one day become capable of forcing the British to "quit" their overseas possessions. World War II hastened that day.

In the immediate aftermath of World War II, three South Asian nations became independent: India and Pakistan in 1947, and Sri Lanka/Ceylon in 1948. Three others—Sikkim, Bhutan, and Nepal—got out from under British influence, though outside influence would continue as New Delhi replaced London in the Himalayas. These newly independent nations themselves generated further issues: (1) the secession of East Pakistan from Pakistan and the formation of Bangladesh in 1971; (2) the dispute between India and Pakistan over what had been part of British northern India, the territory of Jammu and Kashmir, a dispute still active; and (3) the civil war in Sri Lanka between the majority Sinhalese and the minority Tamils, a conflict that ended in 2010 with the victory of the Sinhalese. In 1945, though, only two British colonial administrative entities existed in South Asia: India and Ceylon. And in those colonies, maturing independence movements put constant pressure on the British to "quit" India and Ceylon. In the Himalayas, a smaller regional part of the Great Game playing field, Russia, China, and India jockey for advantage there along with the United States. In 1975, however, Sikkim opted to join the Indian union.

Suggested Readings and Viewings

Gandhi, dir. by Richard Attenborough. Columbia Pictures, 1982.

Mohandas Gandhi, *Autobiography: The Story of My Experiments with Truth* (New York: Dover Publications, 1983).

Nicholas Lloyd, *The Amritsar Massacre: The Untold Story of One Fateful Day* (London: I. B. Tauris, 2011).

Jawaharlal Nehru, *The Discovery of India* (New York: John Day, 1960).

Srinath Raghavan, *India's War: World War II and the Making of Modern South Asia* (New York: Basic Books, 2016).

The Story of India, Episode 6, "Freedom."

Nira Wickramasinghe, *Sri Lanka in the Modern Age: A History* (New York: Oxford University Press, 2015).

Water (2005), dir. by Deepa Mehta.

Stanley Wolpert, *Gandhi's Passion: The Life and Legacy of Mahatma Gandhi* (New York: Oxford University Press, 2002).

Stanley Wolpert, *Jinnah of Pakistan* (New York: Oxford University Press, 2005).

David Zurick and P. P. Karan, *Himalaya: Life on the Edge of the World* (Baltimore, MD: Johns Hopkins University Press, 1999).

24

India since 1945

From the ramparts of the Red Fort [residence of Mughal emperors], I would like to call people of the world to "come, make in India."[1]

India: Securing Indian Independence and Developing Political and Economic Institutions

The July 1945 elections in Britain settled the question of whether India would become independent, as the Labour Party that came to power set forth a policy of imperial divestiture. The remaining questions, therefore, became when independence would occur under what circumstances. The when turned out to be August 15, 1947, and the circumstances involved the partition of India into the nation-states of India and Pakistan, as well as the unresolved issue of Kashmir territory. Once the division of British India occurred, the next question had to do with what kinds of countries India and Pakistan would become. Setting up national political and economic institutions for a newly independent country always presents enormous challenges. India had been governed by foreigners since 1206: Delhi sultans, Mughal emperors, and the British. Moreover, the French, Portuguese, Dutch, and other Westerners had left some cultural imprints on India. Looking at religion alone, Islam and Christianity reshaped the political and cultural landscape. Persian and British imperial administrations reshaped the organizational and linguistic settings. Western science, technology, and industry had the potential to further transform traditional Indian ideas and institutions. How would a newly independent and largely Hindu India absorb or discard those outside influences?

The India that emerged in 1947 under the leadership of its first prime minister, Jawaharlal Nehru, began its "tryst with destiny" as a chiefly secular, socialist, and democratic nation. It was guided from the top down on the model of the then-current British welfare state, as outlined in the 1942 (William) Beveridge Report. After more than four decades of the "Nehru Dynasty"—Jawaharlal Nehru, his daughter Indira Gandhi, and her son Rajiv Gandhi—this command economy model looked less and less commanding to Indians. In the wake of the collapse of communism, India's lagging economic growth, and the rise of the little dragons and even the big dragon in China, New Delhi governments have made economic course corrections and switched to a more

---

1 Prime Minister Narendra Modi, speaking on Independence Day 2014, as quoted in the *Times of India*, August 15, 2014. From independence to the late 1980s, Indian governments were reluctant to welcome foreign businesses, but they reluctantly and slowly changed given China's rapid rise based on foreign capital, technology, and business. Modi seems to be speeding up the process.

Asia Past and Present: A Brief History, First Edition. Peter P. Wan and Thomas D. Reins.
© 2021 John Wiley & Sons, Inc. Published 2021 by John Wiley & Sons, Inc.

market-oriented economy, one more foreign investment friendly and more technology transfer welcome. While additional domestic problems remain—health, education, pollution, and other issues—India's vigorous economy in the early twenty-first century can now allow New Delhi, provincial, and local governments to address better those ongoing domestic concerns.

Timeline for India, 1945–Present	
1945	World War II ends; British election brings Labour Party to power and begins the process of decolonization
1947	India becomes independent as the Dominion of India; Jawaharlal Nehru become first prime minister; First Indo-Pakistani War erupts over Kashmir
1948	Hindu fanatic assassinates Mohandas Gandhi
1950	Dominion of India becomes the Socialist Republic of India under new constitution
1951	Congress Party wins first constitutional election
1962	Sino-Indian border war
1964	Prime Minister Nehru dies
1965	Second Indo-Pakistani War, also fought over Kashmir
1966	Nehru's daughter, Indira Gandhi, becomes prime minister
1971	Third Indo-Pakistani War begins over the independence of East Pakistan, now Bangladesh; Sino-Indian Friendship and Cooperation Treaty signed
1972	Simla Agreement ends the Third Indo-Pakistani War
1974	India explodes its first nuclear device
1975	Indira Gandhi issues state of emergency in wake of disputed election
1977	Birth control program causes political resistance; Congress Party loses election
1980	Indira Gandhi becomes prime minister again
1984	Sikh militants demand self-rule; Indian Army invades Sikh Golden Temple; Indira Gandhi assassinated by Sikh bodyguards; Rajiv Gandhi, her son, becomes prime minister (1984–1989); Bhopal chemical plant has gas leak, thousands die
1987	India sends peacekeeping troops to Sri Lanka, where a civil war (June 1983–May 2009) pits ethnic Tamils (Tamil Tigers) against the established ethnic Sinhalese government; Indian troops withdraw in 1990
1991	Rajiv Gandhi killed by supporters of Tamil Tigers; economic reforms begin
1992	Hindu fundamentalists destroy mosque built on former Hindu sacred site in Ayodhya
1996	The Hindu nationalist Bharatiya Janata Party (BJP) defeats Congress Party
1998	India and Pakistan have dueling nuclear tests
1999	Fourth Indo-Pakistani War (Kargil Conflict) fought in Kargil district of Kashmir
2000	U.S. President Bill Clinton visits India
2001	Terrorists attack Indian Parliament in December
2003	India and Pakistan announce a ceasefire in Kashmir
2006	U.S. President George W. Bush visits India, and the two countries sign a nuclear agreement providing India access to civilian nuclear expertise
2008	Pakistani terrorists attack numerous locations in Mumbai (Bombay) in late November, resulting in nearly 200 deaths

2009	Congress Party wins national election
2010	Hindu–Muslim violence continues; Maoist (Naxalite) insurgency continues; several separatist movements persist
2011	Three bombings in Mumbai kill 21 and injure hundreds more
2012	Woman raped on bus by six men dies and is followed by a spate of rapes
2014	Narendra Modi of BJP elected prime minister
2015	Prime Minister Modi suggests the establishment of an International Yoga Day in a 2014 speech at the United Nations; the United Nations adopts the suggestion, the first one being June 21, 2015

Indian Independence, Partition, and Setting Paths to the Future, 1945–1950

A number of important factors convinced the British to quit India, which they did less than two years after the end of World War II. One certainly was Mohandas Gandhi's ability to organize the common people of India to resist British rule. Another had to do with the costs of empire, and two wars in one generation. As well, during World War II, Chandra Bose (1897–1945), a former Indian National Congress member, collaborated with Japan. With Tokyo's help he formed the Indian National Army to drive the British out of India. It was composed of anti-British Indian nationalists in Southeast Asia and Indians in the British Army that surrendered Singapore to the Japanese in 1942. Although not successful in a military sense, politically it indicated growing popular discontent with British rule. Bose, a rival of Nehru and Gandhi, had argued for an independent India that should blaze a new trail to the future, one that had totalitarian overtones. If Bose had his way, it would not be Nehru's social democratic or Gandhi's more traditional India. Instead, independent India would be governed by some species of authoritarian rule.

But Bose died just as the war concluded, and India's future would be formed by an amalgam of British, Hindu, and Muslim ideas and institutions. The British election in July 1945 made Labour Party leader Clement Attlee the new British prime minister, and his government worked to insure the suitable timetable for a withdrawal of the British from India. To make that withdrawal most peaceful, London had to convince Muslims in general as well as numerous (562) Princely States to join the new, independent India. The closest the Congress Party, the Muslim League, and the British could come to keeping India intact occurred in 1946 with the "Cabinet Mission." Also known as the (Sir Stafford) Cripps Plan, it involved creating a weak central government with what are today Muslim-majority Pakistan and Bangladesh retaining autonomy. When Congress Party leader Jawaharlal Nehru rejected the plan, Prime Minister Attlee stated that the British would accept the idea of India's partition. Of course, the partition devil would be found in the political details. And in working out the details, the Hindus likely possessed the most leverage since the British wanted out and the Muslims had a numbers deficit.

The last viceroy of India, Lord Louis Mountbatten, took office in February 1947 and began setting the groundwork for that partition. He formed the Punjab Commission and Bengal Commission in June 1947 to draw lines separating India from West Pakistan (today's Pakistan) and East Pakistan (today's Bangladesh). The two commissions, which were headed by Sir Cyril Radcliffe, included a Congress Party and a Muslim League representative, effectively giving Radcliffe the power to make the ultimate decision as to where the lines of division in Punjab and Bengal would be drawn. On July 18, 1947, Parliament passed the India Independence Act, and shortly thereafter, on August 15, 1947, India became independent.

Although most people in northern India had a loose idea of where the lines of division fell, not until August 17 did the Radcliffe Line or Radcliffe Award partitioning India get made public. Partition also involved followers of the Sikh religion, a large majority of whom lived in Punjab where the religion's most sacred shrine was located, in the city of Amritsar. Partition furthermore implicated Kashmir, a Muslim-majority princely state headed by a non-Muslim, Maharaja Hari Singh. After much political maneuvering, Singh opted[2] to join India, a clash between India and Pakistan ensued, and eventually a line of division in Kashmir gave India about 60% of the land and 75% of the population, with the remainder, in the west, occupied by Pakistan. Typically Hindus and Sikhs left West Pakistan for India, while many Muslims left India for East or West Pakistan.

Partition produced numerous consequences, most negative and some which still bedevil India, Pakistan, and Bangladesh domestically and diplomatically. By the spring of 1948, close to a million people of what had been India perished in the migration of humanity to or from India or Pakistan. Many perished as a result of the journey itself, while the greatest number died from violence along the flight. Most knowledgeable observers claim that the British departure occurred too rapidly for any orderly and peaceful transition of power to take place. Many Indians refer to Britain's early exodus as a "shameful flight."

The new government of the Union of India, as the country was known until 1950, needed to establish order, staff positions once held by the British, and chart a course of political and economic development. Much of that involved implementing ideas and creating institutions that Mohandas Gandhi, India's independence leader for three decades, would not warmly endorse. As it turned out, less than six months after independence, a Hindu fanatic angered at Gandhi's tolerant attitude toward Muslims assassinated the *Mahatma* or great soul.

Although both Gandhi and Nehru embraced socialism as the proper economic and political paths for independent India to follow, their application of socialist thought differed substantially. Whereas Gandhi sought the decentralized economic development of his country from the bottom up—individual, village, province, and nation—Nehru favored top-down central government planning. While Gandhi viewed dispersed rural industry as the way to prevent the concentration of economic power and to encourage local self-sufficiency, Nehru believed large-scale, necessarily urban industry to be the better route to economic development. Likewise, politically Gandhi wanted to keep the power of government dispersed both to encourage greater political participation by the people and to prevent central government bureaucracy from dominating the political process while overlooking the needs of the average citizen. Nehru preferred to rely on far-seeing educated elite to dictate the nation's agenda. Gandhi sought to distance his country and people from Western civilization:[3] a sort of socialism with Indian characteristics, and a return to rural and less materialistic values, a big part of which would involve religion. Nehru, on the other hand, assumed that political and economic progress depended on more secular and urban ethical arrangements. Gandhi labeled his thinking *Sarvodaya*, a way of life that promoted the interests of all. One of Gandhi's protégés, Vinoba Bose, took the idea to mean communism without the violence. As Bose put it, "So far as the Communists' objective is concerned, I regard it as a good thing. The main point is how that objective is to be achieved."[4] Regardless of differences between Gandhi

---

2 The options for the Princely States were to (1) join India, (2) join Pakistan, or (3) become independent.

3 It should be pointed out that Gandhi drew quite a bit of his thinking from the West. He admired Jesus, John Ruskin, Leo Tolstoy, and Henry David Thoreau, as well as other Western thinkers, and of course socialism also came from the West.

4 William Theodore de Bary, *Sources of Indian Tradition*, vol. 2 (New York: Columbia University Press, 1958), p. 374.

and most of those who ruled India for the remainder of the twentieth century, Gandhi remained a great soul, the *bapu* or father of the nation. His thinking usually received serious respect when policy was discussed.

Nehru believed that large-scale industrialization provided the key to India's two principal items on the nation's agenda: social welfare and national defense. In a speech on Independence Day in 1947, the new prime minister declared "we also have to promote industrialization on a large and balanced scale so as to add to the wealth of the country and thus to the national dividend which can be equitably distributed." In short, Nehru wanted a welfare state or as he put it "democratically planned collectivism." The 1950 Constitution went so far as to say, in Article 38, "The State shall strive to promote the welfare of the people by securing and protecting, as effectively as it may, a social order in which justice, social, economic, and political, shall inform all the institutions of national life." From a national security point of view, Nehru added, "Defence consists today in a country being industrially prepared for producing the goods and equipment of defence."[5] For a country that had been under foreign rule since the thirteenth century, faced a hostile Pakistan next door, and confronted a unified Chinese dragon over the Himalayas, necessary military preparedness meant vigorous industrial development. At the outset, the central government would create and manage crucial industries, for example weapons, atomic energy, and the railway system. It also needed to create new or expand current strategic production industries, such as mining, steel, aircraft, maritime, and communications. Although this represented a large government involvement in the economy, it did not indicate full-blown socialism. Existing private industry remained free of government control (though not regulation), as did most newly emerging enterprises.

Defense, in Nehru's thinking, also meant protection against the pitfalls of foreign capital and technology in India's development. Technology resulted in labor-saving devices, which would lead to rural unemployment, as more efficient urban industries would undermine rural industry. The import of technology would also increase India's balance-of-payments deficit, thereby reducing the amount of Indian capital for development. Consequently India would remain dependent on the outside world. As well, Nehru argued, much of the fruits of foreign capital are returned to foreign lands in the form of profits and dividends. Similarly, dependence on the outside for capital and technology produces the risk of India—if not becoming recolonized in a fashion—falling too far under the influence of a foreign nation.

During Nehru's tenure as prime minister (1947–1964), this meant chiefly the United States or the Soviet Union. At that time, Dependency Theory became popular among academics and influenced many leaders in the developing world. It held that reliance on the industrial nations for capital and technology would prevent or severely retard the economic growth of developing nations, since the industrial world would extract the surplus capital necessary for domestic development. Consequently, government had to take the lead by using reason and science, applying scientific socialism, and banishing religion and superstition. Rational, efficient government would identify the nature of India's social problems and devise sensible and timely solutions. This meant rapid industrialization as occurred in Bismarck's Germany, Meiji Japan, and Stalin's Soviet Union—in all three cases, in little more than a generation. Of course, in all three examples authoritarian or totalitarian government took the lead. Would this be possible in a democratic India?

---

5 Quoted in Om Prakash Misra, *The Economic Thought of Gandhi and Nehru: An Analysis* (New Delhi: M D Publications, 1995), p. 85.

Socialist Republic of India, 1950–1991

The Nehru Dynasty and the Congress Party, with a few brief exceptions, ruled India in tandem from independence until Nehru's grandson Rajiv Gandhi was assassinated in 1991. It can be argued that a near monopoly of central government control for four decades by one party and one family almost certainly insured a number of harmful consequences. Although elections in theory provide a check on government behavior, long-term control of the central government by one party tends to result in greater nepotism, corruption, intellectual stagnation, and other assorted inefficiencies. All of these shortcomings and more characterized Nehru family–led governments. By contrast, more transparent and candid government typically exists when vigorous party competition occurs, usually forcing a ruling elite to be more responsive to citizen requests and complaints, and insuring a government leadership that is more likely to question the quality of its policies and performance.

On the other hand, the Nehru family provided four decades of relative government stability in those uncertain times after independence. As well, Nehru and his successors drew upon fairly solid institutions, Indian and British, to launch the new ship of state. At the time of independence, national, provincial, and local governments; a dependable civil service; a disciplined military; and an electorate and electoral processes were in place. Nongovernmental institutions relating to caste, religion, local political parties, and women's organizations also existed when the British exited. Liberal institutions such as a free press, an independent court system, and a public educational system also provided additional support for the newly independent India. An entrepreneurial class, good transportation and postal systems, and an established structure of markets set a foundation for economic development. Nehru and the political leaders who followed could thus count on an abundance of institutions, practices, and experienced people to build a better future. Indeed, much of what Indian nationalists claim as their tradition in reality was a fusion of Islamic, Western, and Indian traditions by the end of World War II.

Political and Economic Developments, 1950–1991

Whatever the "tradition" India's rulers inherited at the time of independence, the country faced political problems, economic difficulties, and foreign policy challenges that required the new government to draw from that "tradition" to cope with those responsibilities. The most important task was the creation of a constitution. The Constituent Assembly[6] wrote a lengthy constitution of 395 articles (more than 100,000 words) and approved the final version on November 26, 1949. When it went into effect on January 26, 1950, the Constitution created a "sovereign, socialist, democratic republic" headed by a prime minister. Theoretically appointed by the president but in fact chosen by the ruling party in the upper (*Rajya Sabha* or Council of States) and lower (*Lok Sabha* or the House of the People) houses of Parliament, the prime minister selects his or her ministers of government. The state legislatures elect members of *Rajya Sabha* for six-year terms, and the people elect members of the *Lok Sabha* for five-year terms. The duties of prime minister reflect the political thinking of Nehru, who wanted and got a constitution providing for a strong central government directed by a strong leader.

---

6 The Constituent Assembly consisted of 217 people elected by provincial legislatures in 1946 to draft a constitution. It served as the interim government of India from independence until the drafting and ratification of the Indian Constitution in 1949.

Nehru served as prime minister until his death on May 27, 1964, and during his tenure he did not have *carte blanche* to dictate policy. Although he continued to retain ongoing respect as a founding father, and though the Constitution gave him substantial authority, he encountered obstruction from opposition parties as well as resistance within his Congress Party. One source of disagreement had to do with Nehru's call for a speedy drive toward a socialist society, which even a good segment of the Congress Party attacked. Language represented another point of difference between Nehru and local and regional leaders. Nehru wanted a true union of India and believed that a uniform language—Hindi—would promote unity and minimize a sense of separatism. A majority of India, however, did not want an alien language—Hindi—imposed on them at the expense of their local native tongues. People across India wanted to retain their native languages—often regional languages spoken by tens of millions—such as Punjabi and Bengali in the north and various Dravidian languages in the south. Thus in the southern states a *Dravida* movement arose to promote regional languages such as Tamil, Telugu, and Malayalam. And regional activists north and south succeeded in gaining official recognition for their native languages, which numbered more than two dozen by 1991.

Moreover, much of the customs and leadership in provincial and local settings that had remained largely intact under Muslim and British rule now became threatened by the new Indian central government. Nehru sought to impose its uniform national agenda on an often unwilling local citizenry. As well, Nehru's religious agenda met with some opposition. He was an agnostic, though not hostile to religion, and wanted all religions to be treated equally. In that sense, Muslims (and others who practiced minority faiths) who remained in India after partition hailed Nehru's ecumenical outlook. But Nehru also wanted the people's nationalism to override the prejudices of religion or communalism, basically separate communities usually based on religious affiliation. And he wanted government policy to be formulated by the best and the brightest, which is to say, by secular people like Nehru.

In that version, though, Hindu fundamentalists particularly—what Nehru called "Hindu right-wing communalism"—as well as the Hindu communities generally believed that the government in New Delhi slighted their deeply held traditional religious ideas and practices. At the same time, members of non-Hindu religious communities did not want to abandon the communal organizations, beliefs, and (to some extent) protection religion provided. In other words, Nehru's political battles came down to a struggle between the secular intellectual community in New Delhi and the people in the hinterland—elites and masses alike—with religious, linguistic, and communal outlooks often at variance with the central government. This serious antagonism between the capital and the countryside continued through the remainder of the Nehru Dynasty and into the twenty-first century.

Nehru's successors inherited a political establishment that continued to assume the need for a tightly orchestrated agenda of nation building. Gulzarilal Nanda briefly served as acting prime minister after the death of Nehru, succeeded by Congress Party choice Lal Bahadur Shastri (1904–1966). Shastri's tenure proved brief (June 1964–January 1966) and was dominated by the Second Indo-Pakistani War.[7] This war began as a result of Muslim uprisings in India-controlled Kashmir, instigated as India viewed it by Pakistan. The Soviet Union brought the two warring nations together at Tashkent (then part of Soviet Russia but today in Uzbekistan), where Shastri died of a heart attack after signing a mutual agreement (with Pakistan's President General Muhammad Ayub Khan) that pledged neither nation would interfere in the other's internal poli-

---

7 The First Indo-Pakistani War occurred in 1947 over control of Kashmir.

tics. Indira Gandhi[8] (1917–1984)—Nehru's daughter, anticolonial activist, and a cabinet official under Shastri—was chosen by her party to replace Shastri, and was confirmed in that position when the ruling Congress Party won the February 1967 national election, though with a narrow majority.

Mrs. Gandhi's tenures as prime minister tested whether democracy and rigid central planning could peacefully coexist. Her first term (1966–1977) produced a number of highly significant developments. She launched a land reform program, put a limit on individual and corporate income, and nationalized banks, which resulted in splitting the Congress Party leadership. The year 1971 proved to be especially successful for the prime minister. In the March national election, her Congress faction won a decisive victory, which strengthened her political position. In December she led India to an equally decisive victory in the Third Indo-Pakistan War, which resulted in the creation of Bangladesh out of what was once East Pakistan. And she signed an important Treaty of Friendship with the Soviet Union. Three years later, India became a nuclear power. Yet at the height of her power and with a number of successful accomplishments, she felt it necessary to declare a state of Emergency, which gave her nearly dictatorial powers.

Several developing problems resulted in the Emergency, which lasted from June 25, 1975, to January 18, 1977, and several serious results followed the declaration of Emergency. The causes include the costs of war (the fighting and the refugees from Bangladesh), bad harvests, the spike in oil prices after the Yom Kippur (Arab–Israeli) War in 1973, a series of strikes, civil disobedience activities by political dissidents in and out of the Congress Party, and a court decision nullifying her 1971 election (for her supposed violation of election laws). The consequences of the Emergency limited people's freedoms, including the jailing of dissidents and the outlawing of organizations. During the Emergency, Mrs. Gandhi's son Sanjay (1946–1980) headed a population control movement that resulted in forced vasectomies and sterilizations. Sanjay became powerful enough that administration officials felt compelled to exceed the government's birth control targets, ends becoming more important than the means to achieve them. Sanjay also pushed a beautification program that resulted in the eviction of people in slums, frequently resulting in the killing of hundreds who resisted removal. The vast majority of the victims of Sanjay's projects were poor. The "reign of terror," as people often referred to it, ended because of mass popular protest and foreign governments' appeals.

Two months later a national election took place, and Mrs. Gandhi's chief opponents before and during the Emergency—Jaiprakash (J. P.) Narayan and Morarji Desai—joined with other anti-Emergency activists to form the Janata Party. It defeated Indira Gandhi and brought to office Mr. Desai, who served as prime minister from 1977 through 1979. Although this was the first peaceful transfer of power from one party to another, the Janata Party soon split into numerous factions, Desai resigned in July 1979, and he was replaced for a brief period by Charan Singh. A January 1980 national election returned Indira Gandhi's faction of the Congress Party [Congress (I), the "I" for Indira] and Mrs. Gandhi to power. Thus began meaningful party opposition to the Congress, to be followed by Congress beginning to reassess its policies, concluding (in 2014) with the emergence of an opposition party (the BJP) governing without the benefit of coalition parties.

---

8 Indira Gandhi married a Zoroastrian Parsi named Feroze Gandhi who was no relation to Mohandas Gandhi. Parsi refers to the language of Persia, Farsi, and to the people who came to India from Persia after the seventh century. Most of the Parsis practiced the Zoroastrian faith, and they became increasingly fearful of practicing their faith in Persia as it became predominantly Islamic.

> When I was growing up in India in the late 1960s and 1970s, [liberal institutions and traditions were] still strong but fraying. The Congress Party had morphed from a vibrant grass roots organization into a fawning, imperial court, appointed by and adoring of its popular leader, Indira Gandhi. Mrs. Gandhi pursued populist policies that were often unconstitutional and certainly illiberal.
> —Fareed Zakaria[9]

Perhaps what troubled much of the Indian elite was not so much the examples of illiberalism as the need for the political elite to compete for the hearts and minds of the people. The growing political participation of the non-elite and the emergence of new political parties to reflect the wants and needs of the average citizenry—instead of the top-down desires of the old, "far-seeing" elite—produced a messy, competitive, free-for-all political environment. In any event, one-party government had come to an end in India.

Mrs. Gandhi's second term as prime minister began in 1980 and ended with her assassination on October 31, 1984. Her son Sanjay, who had been elected to the Lok Sabha, had died in an airplane accident in June 1980. As her new administration had begun with the loss of Sanjay, her closest advisor, she brought in her older son Rajiv (coincidentally an airline pilot) to take his brother's place. The New Delhi government faced one overriding domestic problem during the late 1970s and much of the 1980s: ethnic and religious separatism. In northeastern India, numerous states were composed of many tribes whose inhabitants spoke local languages and called for the expulsion of "foreign"—that is, Indian—"invaders." In northwestern India, foreign and domestic threats created a sense of danger to the nation. The New Delhi government feared the consequences of the Soviet Russian invasion of Afghanistan in 1979. Afghanistan had historically been a launching pad for invaders of India, and it could possibly serve that role again, this time for the Soviets. Equally threatening was Pakistan's move toward pan-Islamic policies (and nuclear weapons) as fundamentalist Ayatollah Khomeini came to power in neighboring Iran in 1979. But the most immediate threat came from Sikh separatists in India's Punjab region. There, in the city of Amritsar, the Sikh Golden Temple had become the headquarters for Sikh fundamentalists who demanded a "Sikhistan" or "Khalistan"—that is, a separate Sikh nation. Mrs. Gandhi sent in the army (Operation Bluestar) to clear out what most Indians considered to be terrorists. Several thousand Sikhs died during the first week of June 1984. By the end of October that year, Mrs. Gandhi had been assassinated by two of her Sikh bodyguards. In response, Hindus killed thousands more Sikhs in the following weeks.

Rajiv Gandhi (1944–1991) succeeded his mother as prime minister at the request of India's president and immediately called for elections, which took place on December 24, 1984. Congress Party and Gandhi won a huge victory at the polls, largely on the basis of sympathy. His initial popularity enabled him to begin to break away from traditional Congress policies and practices to set the stage for India's dramatic economic reforms launched in 1991. Politically he focused on curbing corruption and cutting bureaucratic red tape (generally referred to as the License Raj) to make both government and the economy more efficient. Economically he reduced taxes and tariffs to increase incentive for more private investment—domestic and foreign—in an ailing economy that had been

---

9 Fareed Zakaria, *The Future of Freedom: Illiberal Democracy at Home and Abroad* (New York: Norton, 2003), pp. 107–108.

considerably government coordinated. Rajiv Gandhi also worked out hopeful agreements with leaders in provinces where religious, ethnic, linguistic, or other separatist movements had threatened the nation's unity and public safety. In foreign affairs, he drew closer to the United States, addressing a joint session of the U.S. Congress in June 1985, while remaining on good terms with the Soviet Union and its new leader, Mikhail Gorbachev. Gandhi also involved India in numerous regional undertakings, such as participating in the South Asian Association for Regional Cooperation, sending troops to help end Sri Lanka's ongoing civil war; into India's West Bengal, where local Gurkhas in the north wanted to separate and become part of Nepal; and in November 1998 to the Republic of Maldives, where a political coup involving one side in the Sri Lankan civil war (the Liberation Tigers of Tamil Elam) attempted to oust a government friendly to India.

But by 1989 a promising Gandhi administration faced numerous setbacks, leading to Rajiv Gandhi's removal as prime minister on a no-confidence vote in Parliament on December 2. In the northeast, a flood of refugees from Bangladesh enraged non-Bengali minorities residing there, leading to ceaseless fighting. Bangladesh, which had been East Pakistan, became independent from Pakistan in 1971. The separation produced a gush of refugees escaping the violence, but Bangladesh's enduring dire poverty continued to generate refugees through the 1980s, and India could not stem the flow. In the northwest, organized Sikh militants, many using violence, persistently demanded an independent Khalistan, thus resulting in a permanent crisis situation in Punjab.

But corruption probably most undermined Gandhi's administration. V. P. Singh, the finance minister in Gandhi's government, discovered that numerous individuals and businesses had evaded taxes. When Gandhi transferred Singh to become defense minister in early 1987, Singh uncovered what became known as the Bofors scandal. It involved the Swedish defense company Bofors, which reportedly paid some of Gandhi's friends to get some of India's defense contracts. The 1987 midterm elections resulted in the Congress Party losing seats, and two years later V. P. Singh left the Congress Party, formed a coalition opposition National Front (Janata Dal) Party, and ousted the Congress from leadership in the 1989 election. Singh's tenure proved short and chaotic, ending in November 1990. Singh was replaced as prime minister by Chandra Shekhar, who had formed yet another coalition group to produce electoral victory that lasted little more than half a year, until June 1991. A month earlier, Rajiv Gandhi was assassinated by members of the Liberation Tigers of Tamil Elam while campaigning for a Congress Party candidate running for Parliament.

Political and Economic Course Corrections, 1991–

The Nehru Dynasty had come to an end politically—at least temporarily—with Rajiv Gandhi's death, but India's original developmental model also concluded economically with the recognition that the economic policies of Mohandas Gandhi, Jawaharlal Nehru, and Indira Gandhi had failed. Surveying the records of Asian developing nations in 1991, Japan, the little dragons, and even Communist China, Communist Vietnam, and the former Soviet Union had substantially abandoned government-orchestrated development and largely embraced market economics. And their economies soared. By that time two major opposition parties had emerged in India to challenge the Congress Party: the Bharatiya Janata Party (BJP), whose economic principles called for more entrepreneurship and less government, and the Janata Dal, formed from factions of the Janata Party and the Bharatiya Lok Dal. Returning to power as the leading party in a coalition government in 1991, the Congress Party also began the move to a more open economy in the face of an ominous economic situation.

According to one 1992 Indian assessment, "A growing and vibrant economy for India requires a radical reorientation of policy away from controls imposed by a heavily interventionist state. Four decades of state-guided development have given India slow growth, rising unemployment and growing dependence on imported capital goods and technology."[10] P. V. Rao succeeded Rajiv Gandhi as Congress Party leader and became prime minister as a result of the national elections of May–June 1991, which gave the Congress Party the greatest number of seats (but not a majority) in the Parliament. Significantly, Rao appointed Manmohan Singh as finance minister in 1991, and with great gusto Singh launched the economic reforms that began to advance the Indian economy. Singh, a future prime minister, was even more direct. In an interview with America's Public Broadcasting System in Boston in 2001, he explained that India

> had an unsustainable fiscal deficit. Our central government fiscal deficit was as high as 8.5 percent of GDP. India had an unsustainable balance-of-payments deficit. The current account deficit was close to 3.5 percent of GDP, and there were no foreign leaders who were willing to finance that deficit. Our foreign exchange reserves had literally disappeared, so we were on the verge of bankruptcy, and the nation faced an acute collapse of its economy.[11]

Although the economic policies of post-independence central governments constituted the principal cause of economic crisis, a number of other factors also contributed to the decision to reform. The Gulf War of 1991 caused a spike in oil prices, Indians working in the Gulf States temporarily lost their incomes, and population increases absorbed what little growth the economy produced. Thus when Manmohan Singh took control of the Finance Ministry, he modified or removed many programs that had hindered economic growth. He began by opening India to foreign investment and technology, weakening the License Raj by cutting the red tape necessary for domestic and foreign businesses to begin operations, shrinking the size of the government budget and its workforce, and devaluing the Indian currency, the rupee. While such programs did produce some unemployment, inflation, and political opposition from the left-wing parties, these new programs represented the core of the Congress Party and its chief opposition, the BJP. That is to say, the two largest parties in India had together promoted a market-oriented economic agenda.

If something of an economic consensus had emerged after 1991, no national political leadership settlement appeared. When the Congress Party under Prime Minister Rao suffered defeat at the polls in 1996, the BJP under Atal Bihari Vajpayee formed a government that lasted 13 days. Thereafter no party would be capable of gathering a majority in parliament until 2014. All central governments between 1996 and 2012 were alliances—often unstable—of several parties. But three major parties—Congress, BJP, and Janata Dal—controlled the alliances. From June 1996 to March 1998, the Janata Dal governed under two prime ministers, H.D. Gowda and Inder Kumar Gujral; from March 1998 to May 2004, the BJP headed the central government, again under Atal Bihari Vajpayee; and from May 2004 until 2012, Congress returned to power selecting Manmohan Singh as prime minister. To that point no party has had the power to stray too far in one political, economic, or social direction or the other. As one study of India concludes,

---

10 Ramesh Thakur, "India after Nonalignment," *Foreign Affairs* (Spring 1992): https://www.foreignaffairs.com/articles/asia/1992 - 03-01/india-after-nonalignment.

11 Interview with Indian Prime Minister Manmohan Singh, *Commanding Heights*, February 6, 2001, WGBH Public Broadcasting System, Boston, www.pbs.org/wgbh/commandingheights/shared/minitextlo/int_manmohansingh.html#4.

While the constant shifts in coalitions and interest groups may be perceived as unstable, the diversity in Indian politics actually serves as glue that holds the political system together. Cross-cutting interdependencies between the multitude of interests force compromise, stability and centrism within Congress and the BJP. Caste conflicts override religious and ethnic divisions, while regional solidarity undercuts intra-regional divides. Although the diversity in Indian politics may inspire stability, it also creates barriers to reform.[12]

According to a 2011 *Economist* investigation, the biggest barrier is the government. "What happens in India is not because of the government but in spite of the government."[13] The election of Narendra Modi of the Bharatiya Janata Party and his reelection in 2019 seems to indicate that some global political leadership in the 2010s sought to change the direction of established ways of governing. Xi Jinping's emergence in 2012 as Chinese leader and Donald Trump's election in 2016 as America's president–leaders in three different political settings–suggest a serious search is underway for more responsive government to more daunting problems in a more competitive world.

Social Developments

Social problems related to caste, language, religion, and ethnic separatism, while remaining troublesome since independence, have been confronted by government, nongovernmental organizations, and individuals. The 1950 Indian Constitution outlaws any discrimination against "Scheduled Castes" or Dalits, often referred to as Sudras (laborers or people in many service industries) and Untouchables (for example, those dealing with dead bodies). The Dalits constitute roughly 15% of the Indian population, and affirmative action–like laws have set aside a certain percentage of jobs in the economy for them, while Dalit intermarriage with upper-caste people is increasing. Kocheril Raman Narayanan (1920–2005), India's president from 1997 to 2002, was a Dalit. Though discrimination against Dalits remains, the end of official caste distinction has enabled individuals more easily to make choices about such things as marriage and politics on their own. In terms of national government-approved languages, the 1950 Constitution stipulated Hindi and English to be official, with English to be phased out by 1965 unless it created an undue burden on people. This meant that non-Hindi-speaking people would have to learn Hindi, and that added to the ongoing furor over local languages being ignored by New Delhi. Thus the Official Languages Act in 1963 extended the use of English, and gradually 26 other languages have been deemed official in various provinces and union territories. Eventually standard spoken Hindi will likely take root in all of India given the power of television and other national media.

Religious and ethnic tensions remain more stubborn problems across India, where more than 80% of the population is Hindu. Religion accounted for the creation of Pakistan. And while most Indian Muslims did not want to remain a part of independent India, by 2011 about 13% of India's population was Muslim. They represent the descendants of people who, for a variety of reasons, did not or could not migrate to Pakistan. Christians, Sikhs, Buddhists, Jains, and other religious denominations make up the remainder of the population. Not surprisingly, religious fundamentalism has produced clashes between chiefly Hindus and Muslims. Islam in Pakistan, India, and Bangladesh turned more radical after the success of Ayatollah Khomeini's 1979 revolution in Iran.

---

12 Charles Wheelan, Sandeep Ahuja, Jaime Allentuck, et al., *Economic Reform in India: Task Force Report* (Chicago: The Harris School, The University of Chicago, 2006), p. 5.

13 "The Half-Finished Revolution," *Economist,* July 21, 2011, http://www.economist.com/node/18986387.

A more radical form of Hinduism arose during Rajiv Gandhi's administration with Hindutva, founded in the 1920s by Vinayak D. Savarkar.

Hindutva, which means Hinduness or a Hindu way of looking at the world, nonetheless claims that the essence of India can be found in its culture, which is basically Hindu but also includes the various religions practiced in India. Outwardly, it is an anti-secular movement to preserve traditional practices endangered by modernization. Inwardly, it utilizes a very secular and modern institution, the nation-state, to promote its cultural nationalism. Thus the term "Hindu" can be applied to all who claim India—not a religion, language, caste, or other distinction—to be their emotional homeland. You may be a hyphenated Indian—Muslim-Indian, Christian-Indian, Bengali-Indian—but you are primarily an Indian. Some three dozen Hindutva organizations belong to the Sangh Parivar, meaning Family of Associations. These groups include political parties (most notably the BJP), labor movements, artists' associations, lawyers' groups, charity societies, and so forth; membership is in the tens of millions. Generally these associations are hospitable to business but also wary of globalism, which they claim harms local industry and village agriculture. They are also friendly to Dalits but hostile to caste, which they assert divides India. In foreign policy, they tend to support Israel. And even the most radical of these associations, the Shiv Sena, has worked with Muslim organizations for common political ends, though few Muslims in India view Shiv Sena positively.

The most prominent ongoing issue dividing Hindus and Muslims has to do with the 1992 destruction of the Babri Mosque in Ayodhya by 150,000 Hindus. Built in 1527 to honor the first Mughal emperor, Babur, Hindus have considered the site holy as the god Rama (Ram Lalla) had been born there. Rumors over the centuries claimed that a Hindu temple had been torn down in order to build the mosque, and evidence from the 1992 mosque debris confirmed such a temple. A temporary temple was built on the remains of the mosque, provoking Muslim protests and a lawsuit. In 2010 an Indian court divided the site into three parts: one going to Muslims, one to the Hindu sect Nirmohi Akhara, and one to those Hindus claiming the land for Ram Lalla. Highly symbolic, the struggle in Ayodhya represents only a tiny fragment of Hindu–Muslim battles across India, much of them quite bloody. A brittle relationship also continues to play out between India and those wishing to separate from it. This is true of India-controlled Kashmir, where the vast majority of the inhabitants are Muslim. Many Sikhs in Punjab continue to push for an independent Khalistan. And in northeastern India, what had been Assam until independence began to be divided along ethnic lines into several provinces, what are now commonly referred to as the Seven Sister States (Arunachal Pradesh, Assam, Manipur, Meghalaya, Mizoram, Nagaland, and Tripura). Substantial numbers of people in those provinces do not view themselves as Indians, and numerous liberation-type movements are attempting to bring about separation from India.

Foreign Policy and Terrorism Issues since 1991

Clearly 1991 represented a turning point for India at home and abroad. As noted, domestic economic reform took off while overseas the Soviet Union, one of India's important allies, collapsed. As well, by 1991 neighboring China's economic reforms, begun in 1978, had thrust the Middle Kingdom far ahead of India in terms of wealth and power. India's border war with China in 1962 did not end well, continuing border issues between the two nuclear powers still have hazardous potential, and Tibet's Dalai Lama resides in India, thus providing another source of antagonism between the two competing nations. Perhaps to check the rise of China, the United States and India worked out a Civil Nuclear Agreement in 2005 whereby the United States would cooperate with India on the development of peaceful uses of atomic energy. The U.S. Congress and the Indian Parliament approved the agreement in 2008. The following year the two countries established a Strategic Dialogue, an annual meeting to assess common problems and to plan long-term cooperative programs to deal with those problems. Still, India remains cautious about its long-term relationship with Washington. In 2012 a study supported by India's National Defence College as well as the Centre for Policy Research produced *NonAlignment 2.0: A Foreign and Strategic Policy for India in the Twenty First Century.* One of its numerous conclusions underscores New Delhi's caution: "Given that India has more interests in 'direct' competition with China, and less with the U.S., it may be tempting to conclude that the U.S. is a likely alliance partner. But this conclusion would be premature."[14] Moreover, since China views India "not as a threat in itself, but as a 'swing' state whose association with potential adversaries could constrain China," therefore India's "posture towards China must be carefully nuanced and constantly calibrated in response to changing global and regional developments."[15]

Nonetheless, India's most pressing foreign policy challenge has remained Pakistan ever since its inception in 1947. India has fought four Indo-Pakistani wars since then: 1947, 1965, 1971, and 1999. Three have started over Kashmir, and the 1971 conflict began as East Pakistan seceded from Pakistan and became Bangladesh. India aided Bangladesh, which had been East Bengal Province in India before independence. Meanwhile Pakistan obtained nuclear capability in May 1998 and likely possesses at least 100 nuclear weapons. The two countries have experienced not only wars but numerous border skirmishes that could have led to more serious conflicts. Additionally, India views the relationship between the two countries as especially menacing because Pakistan has close relationships with terrorist groups and their leaders, some residing in Pakistan, one being Osama bin Laden who was killed in Abbottabad in May 2011.

India's terrorist problems are both foreign and domestic. According to the South Asian Terrorism Portal, India is the target for nearly 200 terrorist, separatist, insurgent, or extremist groups. Many are headquartered and/or funded from abroad, such as Mutahida Jehad Council and numerous organizations working for the freeing of Kashmir from India, often based in Pakistan. Frequent attacks from Pakistan have occurred, the most notable being the 2008 attack on Mumbai that killed 172 people, likely led by Hafiz Saeed, head of the Jama'at-ud-Da'wah, a supposed charity but in fact an arm of the terrorist organization Lashkar-e-Taiba (LeT). In April 2012, the United States put a bounty of $10 million for the arrest and conviction of Saeed for terrorist activities. The Bombay bombing represented only one of at least nine recent deadly incidents in that city. Terrorist bombings there in 2006 at a railway station killed 206 people, and in 2011 a series of bombings attributed to Indian Mujahideen killed 26. Numerous other major Indian cities have experienced terrorist attacks, several instigated by foreign groups, many by domestic ones. In February 2012, an Israeli diplomatic vehicle was bombed in New Delhi, reportedly by agents of Iran, possibly by the terrorist group Hezbollah. But most terrorist attacks are committed by groups native to India. One example is the Khalistan Zindabad Force, a Sikh organization, which wants an independent Khalistan carved out of Punjab; another is the National Socialist Council of Nagaland-Isak-Muivah, which demands an independent Nagaland be carved out of northeastern India. Several other such groups use violence to achieve freedom from Indian control.

---

14 Sunil Khilnani et al., eds., *NonAlignment 2.0: A Foreign and Strategic Policy for India in the Twenty First Century* (New Delhi: National Defence College and Centre for Policy Research, 2012), p. 32.
15 Khilnani, *NonAlignment 2.0*, p. 14.

Conclusion

India experienced a number of serious bumps on the road to independent governance, but it steadily constructed a fairly stable democratic political structure, a promising economic foundation, imperfect but tolerable compromises regarding social issues, as well as a reasonably successful relationship with most of the rest of the world. Politically, one-party rule gave way to political competition and the peaceful transfer of power from the three-decade governing of the Congress Party to an opposition party. The Emergency and its potential for dictatorship, the assassinations of Indira Gandhi and her son Rajiv, chronic government corruption and inefficiency, plus prolonged economic troubles shook, but did not undermine, the basic democratic institutions that independent India inherited and developed. The transition to more market-based arrangements has enabled India to create a much more efficient economy. While a modernized economy has produced global competition, environmental degradation, and assorted other problems, it has also lifted tens of millions of citizens out of poverty. Socially the central government also compromised on issues of local languages, ethnicity, and religion to reduce the tensions among people of diverse backgrounds. Nonetheless popular discontent due to numerous unresolved difficulties remains an ongoing source of potential political trouble. Success breeds growing expectations.

Suggested Readings and Viewings

Bandit Queen (1984), dir. by Shekhar Kapur.

Bidyut Chakrabarty, *Indian Politics and Society since Independence: Events, Processes and Ideology* (London: Routledge, 2008).

Earth (1998), dir. by Deepa Mehta.

Rob Jenkins, *Democratic Politics and Economic Reform in India* (Cambridge: Cambridge University Press, 1999).

Ananth Krishna, *India since Independence: Making Sense of Indian Politics* (New York: Pearson, 2011).

Zareer Masani, *Indira Gandhi: A Biography* (New York: Crowell, 1976).

Leonard Mosley, *The Last Days of the British Raj* (London: Weidenfield and Nicholson, 1961).

B. A. Prakash, *The Indian Economy since 1991: Economic Reforms and Performance*, 2nd ed. (New York: Pearson, 2011).

Lance Price, *The Modi Effect: Inside Narendra Modi's Campaign to Transform India* (New York: Quercus, 2015).

D. R. SarDesai and Raju G. C. Thomas, eds., *Nuclear India in the Twenty-First Century* (New York: Palgrave, 2002).

Mark Tully and Satish Jacob, *Amritsar: Mrs. Gandhi's Last Battle* (London: Cape, 1985).

Stanley Wolpert, ed., *Encyclopedia of India, 4 vols.* (New York: Charles Scribner's, 2006).

Stanley Wolpert, *Nehru: A Tryst with Destiny* (New York: Oxford University Press, 1996).

25

In India's Orbit: South Asian Nations in the Cold War Setting and the Rise of China

He was not just head of state and father of the nation but its constitutional caliph.[1]

Introduction to South Asia since 1945

Once it became apparent that Britain would "quit India," the next question facing India's leaders then became: Would India remain unified (a unitary India) or become divided (the two-nation solution)? When partition in 1947 divided India and gave birth to Pakistan, the new nation encountered great difficulties. The country began geographically fragmented: West Pakistan in the northwestern part of colonial India, and East Pakistan (now Bangladesh; essentially eastern Bengal) in colonial India's northeast. As well, it had just been separated from two significant influences. Pakistan had been intimately connected by culture to India but was now disconnected politically. Pakistan also had been linked to the British—its government, ideas, and institutions—but was now fundamentally if not completely detached by independence. Religion complicated matters as well. Although the founders of Pakistan claimed to be creating a secular nation, the principal reason for partition and the creation of a Pakistan was religion, in this case Islam. Into this muddled context, Pakistan's leaders had to deal with nation-building issues such as the appropriate power of the central government, the proper approach to economic development, the official national language, and the role of traditional thought and behavior. Almost immediately, the tensions among regional and linguistic groups in Pakistan suggested considerable future troubles.

Pakistan and later Bangladesh experienced not only domestic disarray, as might be expected in newly independent nations. They also had to juggle those internal problems along with troubles from the outside world, one part of which was India. Partition had created a smaller India and a geographically divided Pakistan, one part in the west and another in the east separated by a thousand miles of India. Partition immediately caused roughly one million deaths, as millions of Hindus, Muslims, Sikhs, and others were killed as they attempted to migrate to more ethnically safe locations. Four Indo-Pakistani wars also became a regular strain on nation building. Pakistan and India took different sides in the Cold War, India working closely with the Soviet Union while Pakistan sided with the United States and the People's Republic of China. After the Soviet invasion of Afghanistan in 1979,

---

1 The historical assessment, likely quite accurate, of John Keay, *India: A History* (New York: Grove Press, 2000), pp. 502–503.

Asia Past and Present: A Brief History, First Edition. Peter P. Wan and Thomas D. Reins.
© 2021 John Wiley & Sons, Inc. Published 2021 by John Wiley & Sons, Inc.

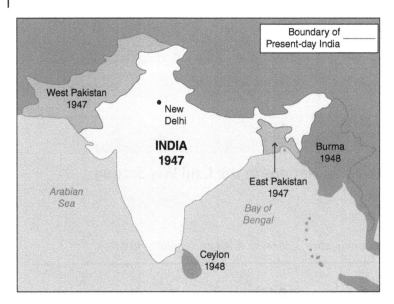

India and neighboring states, and the years each achieved independence. *Source:* https://thebritishraj. weebly.com/uploads/2/7/4/7/27471501/4978109_orig.png.

Pakistan worked closely with anti-Soviet forces in Afghanistan and placed more emphasis on the Islamic nature of the country after the revolution succeeded in Iran that same year.

When the Taliban emerged in Afghanistan after the Soviet departure in 1989, Pakistan remained supportive of its activities and thus became tied to terrorist activities in South Asia that continue to the present. The arrival of al Qaeda in Afghanistan and its attack on the United States on September 11, 2001, have resulted in Pakistan walking a tightrope between working with Washington while supporting terrorists in Afghanistan and Pakistan. Although the United States and NATO have neutralized al Qaeda in Afghanistan, it moved next door to Pakistan, where al Qaeda leader Osama bin Laden was killed by U.S. Navy SEALs in May 2011. However, the successful emergence of ISIS (Islamic State in Iraq and Syria; sometimes ISIL, Islamic State in Iraq and the Levant) in the Middle East has begun to impact South Asia and, as in the Middle East, supplant al Qaeda. Since its inception Bangladesh has worked closely with India but has attempted to remain truly non-aligned with the rest of the outside world and as it dealt with pro-Maoist and pro-Soviet domestic radical groups during the Cold War and terrorist groups after the Cold War.

Beyond the former Indian territories, the Himalayan nations—in 1945 Sikkim, Bhutan, and Nepal—found themselves dealing with new governments in both India and China, between which they are located. Added to that geopolitically frightening reality, they also had to forge meaningful nation-building programs in light of chiefly linguistic and ethnic differences. Off the South Asian subcontinent, Sri Lanka and Maldives have faced the same kinds of problems that other nations in the region have experienced. Sri Lanka has had to overcome religious (mainly majority Sinhalese Buddhists versus Hindu Tamils), ethnic, linguistic, and even caste differences that had been kept largely in check by the British but that emerged and regularly produced riots after independence in 1948. Instability and violence generated a massive and lengthy civil war (1983–2009), and while the government formed a reconciliation commission in 2010 to produce "lessons learned" from that tragedy, it was immediately attacked as biased by minorities in Sri Lanka and later by the United Nations. By September 2015 pressure from the outside world forced a newly elected government to form a new reconciliation commission that included a "Compassionate Council" composed of Sri Lankan religious officials. Tensions remain high. On the Maldives island chain southwest of India, a century or more of political turmoil has kept this Sunni Muslim community of a half-million people unstable. The instability scares off the chief source of income, tourism. Moreover the rise of China and Beijing's ability to project naval power into the Indian Ocean region makes India, the chief economic and political influence on the islands, quite anxious.

Islamic Republic of Pakistan

Although Pakistan came out of the same British imperial institutional framework as India, it began with several serious handicaps that India escaped. Tragically Muhammad Ali Jinnah, Muslim League leader and father of the country, died on September 11, 1948, just 13 months after assuming political control. Jinnah had supported a more secular approach to politics, one that called on citizens to rally around the nation instead of language, tribe, region, or religion. Rather quickly the military, whose attitude toward participatory government was tepid at best, began to fill the political leadership vacuum. Geographically, the original composition of territorial Pakistan (an acronym formed from **P** for Punjab, **A** for Afghania [the northwest frontier], **K** for Kashmir, **S** for Sind,

Mohammad Ali Jinnah. *Source:* World History Archive / Alamy Stock Photo.

and **Istan** for Baluchistan) included two regions separated by a thousand miles of northern India. West Pakistan, as it was termed, included the provinces listed above in Pakistan's name. The nation's designation failed to include any reference to the part of Bengal that became East Pakistan.

From the onset, Bengalis never believed they enjoyed an equal standing with the western side of the new Pakistan nation. Furthermore, the two distant segments of Pakistan had evolved two conspicuously different cultures within the broader Indian tradition. Language represented one of those significant differences. Urdu, an Indo-European language based on Hindi incorporating local Pakistani terms, is written in Persian script. Bengali, another Indo-European language, is written in a design that evolved from Brahmi script, used as early as the reign of Ashoka. Since West Pakistan controlled the government of Pakistan, and because that early government insisted upon Urdu as the official language, East Pakistan realized that its interests and needs counted for little. Additionally, the imposition of Urdu on those provinces in West Pakistan whose people spoke other languages also produced resistance to the new central government. At the top of West Pakistan's agenda was the incorporation of the former princely state of Kashmir into Pakistan, while people in East Pakistan (the majority of the nation's population) had little interest in Kashmir. Pakistan thus confronted more than its share of serious problems that a newly independent nation commonly inherits.

In March 1940 the Muslim League passed the Lahore Resolution that called, at the very least, for regional autonomy under the British and later under an independent India. However, most people familiar with Indian politics interpreted the resolution as a call for a distinct Muslim nation once the British departed India. Still, not all Muslims in British India sought a separate Muslim state. Nobel Prize nominee Allama Mashriqi (1888–1963), for instance, first fought for independence from Britain and then to preserve India's unity, for which Muslim extremists accused him of treason and attacked him. Writer and mathematician Abul Kalam Azad (1888–1958) also resisted British rule and pressed for a unified India. Indeed, he proclaimed that the very idea of Pakistan "goes against my grain." His approach—and that of most Muslims opposing partition—called for a confederation-like nation that allowed for a great deal of regional, ethnic, linguistic, and religious freedom under a weak central government. He became India's first education minister. Khan Abdul Ghaffar Khan (1890–1988) was a Pashtun supporter of Mahatma Gandhi before independence and an opponent of partition. After independence this "frontier Gandhi" criticized Gandhi's acceptance of partition, reportedly telling him "you have thrown us to the wolves." Most Muslim opponents of partition believed that common culture could overcome religious differences, that foreigners would take advantage of both nations given their mutual hatred, and that such hatred would mutually harm both countries. And since the Muslim League called for a secular and democratic nation, many Muslims opposed the creation of a Pakistan that was bound to turn its back on religious tradition. Moreover, partition would not result in most Muslims moving to Pakistan, as indeed they did not, and those who did migrate would suffer much death and misery. And obviously the geographical separation of Pakistan would create colossal governing problems.

Of course there existed another possibility, neither a unified India nor the two-nation alternative. Most Muslims in Bengal who favored partition sought two separate Muslim political entities, one in what is today Pakistan plus the other in Bengal. The Tiger of Bengal, Abul Kasem Fazlul Huq, sought that second Muslim territory. He likely did not get it because Muslims feared the British would reject the idea of more than one Muslim state. It might lead to other groups demanding special status, autonomy, or even independence from India, making it more difficult for the British to leave in an orderly and timely fashion. Consequently when it became apparent the

British did intend to quit India, the desire for at least one Muslim state overrode the Bengali dream for its own nation—at least until 1971.

Dominion of Pakistan, 1947–1956

Once the time for partition arrived, *Quaid-e-Azam* or Great Leader Muhammad Ali Jinnah served as governor general for the British monarch. He and his successors represented King George VI and later Queen Elizabeth II in the Dominion of Pakistan, part of the British Commonwealth of Nations. Practically speaking, though, Jinnah governed Pakistan, and as de facto chief executive he presented his assessment of Pakistan's problems and prospects. Speaking to the Constituent Assembly[2] of Pakistan, which had just elected him to the presidency of that body only days before independence, Jinnah set forth the chief difficulties the new nation faced: bribery, public and private corruption, black marketeering, and nepotism. Pakistan, Jinnah asserted, needed a government that focused on the people's welfare primarily without regard to "colour, caste or creed." When he became governor general of the Dominion of Pakistan after independence, Jinnah served not only as the British government's chief officer in Pakistan but also as the founding father of his nation.

Jinnah inherited a new country with little industry, whose chief source of income came from farming, and where most of the farmland was held by a small number of landlords. Although the East Pakistan population was fairly homogeneous culturally, West Pakistan consisted of numerous rival regional and ethnic groups, princely states, unwelcome Urdu-speaking migrants from India, as well as a Pashtun population in the northwest that likely did not consider itself Pakistani first and foremost. Pashtuns were the descendants of people whose land had been Afghan before the territory got annexed by Britain in 1893 and attached to British India. In short, Pakistan began its independence with an array of domestic problems as well as the battle between India and Pakistan over Kashmir. And once Jinnah died, so steadily did the idea of a secular, democratic Pakistan. His political successor, the first Prime Minister of Pakistan Liaquat Ali Khan, was considered a founding father of his nation as well as a secular democrat. But before Liaquat Ali Khan's assassination in 1951, most of the foundation for an Islamic Pakistan had surely been established issues in order to establish Pakistan.

Pakistan's First Constituent Assembly commenced in 1947 to create a constitution and to serve as a national legislature until the constitution became adopted. Jinnah was still alive and could say, as he did to the Assembly, "You may belong to any religion or caste or creed—that has nothing to do with the business of the State." By 1949 the Assembly passed the Objectives Resolution, which declared Pakistan would be a democratic country where Allah is sovereign and government programs would be created and administered "as enunciated by Islam." Martial law ended the First Constituent Assembly in 1954, and when the Second Constituent Assembly convened in May 1955 it produced the nation's Constitution, which duly ended the Dominion of Pakistan and ushered in the Islamic Republic of Pakistan on March 23, 1956. The new Constitution provided for a structure of government and a list of rights, which on paper looked to be a progressive document but in practice failed to provide political stability. By 1958, however, General Ayub Khan proclaimed martial law, establishing the military as the preeminent force in Pakistani politics into the twenty-first century.

---

2 Pakistan's Constituent Assembly was formed to create a constitution for the new nation and to serve as a parliament until that constitution became operative. It existed between August 11, 1947, and October 24, 1954, when it was temporarily dissolved. The Second Constituent Assembly operated from May 28, 1955, until March 23, 1956, when the Constitution it wrote came into operation and the nation became the Islamic Republic of Pakistan. That first constitution was eliminated on October 7, 1958, when the government declared martial law.

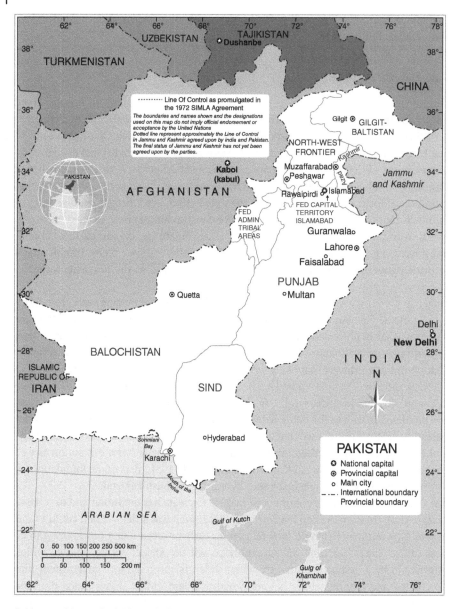

Pakistan with provincial boundaries.

Islamic Republic of Pakistan, 1956–2018: Political and Economic Developments

Political instability has distressed Pakistan from its inception. The country has fluctuated between civilian and military rule, produced three constitutions between 1956 and 1973, lost half of its territory and population when East Pakistan seceded in 1971, experienced ongoing regional and ethnic outbreaks of violence, somewhat coped with the domestic repercussions of neighboring Iran's Islamic upheaval in 1979 and the Soviet Union's invasion of Afghanistan that same year, and finally attempted to juggle the internal costs of America's war against al Qaeda and the Taliban in

Afghanistan after 2001. However, these do not include the stresses brought on by the several Indo-Pakistani wars as well as the Cold War. Nor does it include the original problem of attempting to create a nation on a broadly religious basis. By 2008, Pakistan found itself on the verge of becoming a failed military state.

For half a century (1958–2008), Pakistan lived under perpetual political instability, which included several declarations of martial law or emergencies, coups and attempted coups, at least three constitutions and numerous amendments to those documents, as well as assassinations, attempted assassinations, and executions of presidents and former presidents. Those 50 years also witnessed the jailing and forced exile of high-level political participants as well as accidental deaths. In short, politics in Pakistan during that period came under military control, sometimes with civilian leadership façades but usually through in-your-face military rule. Typically the immediate justification for military intervention was some kind of disorder—riots, economic troubles, conflicts with India, or the felt need to make an example of some senior civilian government official attempting to promote policies abhorrent to the military. Temporary emergency military rule usually became more lengthy military administration. After the 2008 elections and the impeachment of the president, however, the balance of political power in Pakistan has tended to shift toward civilian. Nonetheless the military retains the preponderance of government power, even if it needs to be more cautious in the use of its abundant muscle.

How the Pakistani Military Ruled, 1958–2008

The army chiefs take six important steps. They co-opt the bureaucracy; use accountability against politicians; entrench the army in civilian and political affairs; create a new breed of politicians subservient to them under the guise of local government reform; hold elections to create some sort of democratic legitimacy; and finally move to co-opt the judiciary.

Source: Jayshree Bajoria, "Pakistan's Constitution," Council on Foreign Relations.

General Pervez Musharraf (1943–) illustrates the military's domination of Pakistani politics into the twenty-first century. He came to power in 1999 in a coup against civilian Prime Minister Nawaz Sharif (1949–), who had been active in electoral politics for nearly two decades. Sharif was immediately placed under house arrest and Musharraf proceeded to consolidate political control, in 2001 appointing himself president. The terrorist attacks on the United States that September made Pakistan an essential ally in the war on terror and gave Musharraf American political support as well as much economic backing. Nonetheless, during Musharraf's authoritarian rule several positive changes began to emerge. He provided amnesty to numerous political activists jailed for assorted "crimes." Women's rights laws were passed by the legislature and signed by Musharraf, but he took criticism from opponents of the law and from women's organizations for not enforcing the laws. A liberalization of the media also took place, a move that would come back to haunt Musharraf in 2008 when its influence helped to force him to resign. And the massive presence of America in Pakistan for the war against the Taliban in Afghanistan most likely provided something of a check on the military.

Musharraf's fall from power in 2008 resulted from a number of factors that together created a perfect political storm. The more open media created an ongoing drumbeat of criticism, women's organizations increased the popular disapproval, charges of corruption added to the growing discontent, while the civilian side of the government, particularly the National Assembly and courts, began to challenge the president on a number of fronts. The 2007 presidential election increased the political tensions, especially after former Prime Minister Benazir Bhutto returned from exile to contest the parliamentary election of 2008. Musharraf won the October presidential bid as most political parties boycotted the election. In November he declared a state of emergency, and the following month Benazir Bhutto, leader of the opposition Pakistan People's Party (PPP) likely to win the January 2008 parliamentary elections, was assassinated. Her death put off the election for a month, but did not change the expected result. When the liberal to socialist PPP took control of the National Assembly, it began to institute measures to drive the president from power. When the United States added to the call for Musharraf to step down, he chose resignation to resistance. In August 2008 the National Assembly impeached him, and a week later he resigned. The Electoral College then selected Asif Ali Zardari (1955–), Benazir Bhutto's widower, as president.

Pakistani political activities since 2008 indicate less military involvement in the political process, though its influence remains enormous. The 2008 elections—for the National Assembly and for the presidency to replace Musharraf—appeared comparatively free of violence and electoral corruption. After Musharraf's resignation, the National Assembly reestablished the 1973 Constitution, which placed the Parliament over the president. The Parliament chose Yousaf Gillani (1952–) to be prime minister. As a result of the 2013 election the PPP, which had won the 2008 election, allowed the peaceful transfer of power from a liberal civilian government to a conservative one. Nawaz Sharif of the right-of-center Pakistan Muslim League returned to be prime minister for a third term, while his fellow party member Mamnoon Hussain (1940–) was elected president. The Pakistani Supreme Court disqualified Sharif from the July 2018 election for corruption, but his brother Shehbaz Sharif represented the Muslim League on voting day. Polls suggested that Sharif and the Muslim League would emerge victorious, but in fact Imran Khan and his PTI Party (Pakistan Tehreek-i-Insaf), while perhaps not the military's "favorite son" as some have suggested, won the election. Khan, the former cricket star, is seen as charismatic, mercurial, very pro-China, very anti-Trump, and cozy toward Iran. He once remarked that he wanted Pakistan to be more "like Iran." Though the army remains in the political background, most Pakistanis—including Khan—are aware this could rapidly change. Although a peaceful election and transfer of power occurred, Pakistan's numerous other festering problems remain. Not likely to change is the rampant corruption across the political spectrum.

Pakistan's economic growth mirrored its early political development, experiencing both notable advances and appalling stagnation since independence in 1947. Generally, the industrial and technological sectors did well, while most of the population—farmers and tribes people—continued to experience a woeful standard of living. Although the nation's gross domestic product increased during this time, widespread corruption, an underground economy, careless fiscal policies, inadequate infrastructure, poor education, ethnic hostilities, religious fundamentalism, political instability, geographical division, and military clashes with India all worked to undermine a more steady and balanced growth. Nonetheless, Pakistan's economic structure had changed substantially as the twenty-first century approached. Agriculture had constituted a bit more than half of the economy in 1947 but made up only roughly one-fourth by the 1990s; industry moved from 8 percent to more than one-fifth of the economy; the service industry—such sectors as transportation, communications, construction, and customer activities—made less dramatic but still important growth during this period. As well, much of the economic development can be attributed to foreign aid, most of which America provided to its Cold War ally after the two countries signed the 1954 Mutual Defense Assistance Agreement.

Pakistan's economic program, as in the case of India, operated on the assumption of top-down central government planning. Like Nehru, Jinnah absorbed the basics of the 1942 Beveridge

Report, which outlined the government's approach to economic development. It was seen as the model of development that would most likely and quickly alleviate poverty. By 1950 the Colombo Plan, another British initiative, originally brought together Commonwealth nations in South and Southeast Asia to promote economic and social development.[3] In Pakistan the central government established a Planning Board in 1953 to establish a national economic plan. Beginning in 1955 a series of Five-Year Plans was launched, and today they still serve as the guide to Pakistan's economic development. At best, these plans had lofty goals but produced scanty results. According to one Pakistani writer, "Almost all five-year plans prepared during political or military regimes were shelved in the country's history after regime change and none of them succeeded in getting the desired results."[4] Perhaps that is another way of saying economic development in Pakistan occurred, as in India, "in spite of the government."

Several factors account for Pakistan's economic undertakings in a chaotic political and international setting. As in India, Pakistan inherited a British infrastructure that provided something of a foundation for development. Pakistan also benefitted from the technical and economic assistance in the Colombo Plan, the Asian Development Bank, the World Bank, the International Monetary Fund, as well as American military and economic aid. Pakistani governments began developmental plans with the assumption that the central government needed to dominate, if not monopolize, economic planning and direct the carrying out of those plans. By the 1980s, however, Pakistani rulers shifted to more market-oriented economic arrangements. Perhaps this was due, as some argue, to the influence of the Ronald Reagan administration; perhaps it reflected an awareness that top-down planning had serious economic shortcomings, as evinced in not only Pakistan but also India, China, the Soviet Union, and other such development models; or perhaps the economic success of the "little dragons" convinced Pakistan's leaders. Nonetheless, while the average Pakistani may not have climbed out of or far from grinding poverty, the nation could boast of a growing modern economic and technological sector capable of producing nuclear weapons. By the turn of the twenty-first century, it seems, Pakistan had a fairly good idea of what not to do economically. The big question became what to do politically.

Foreign affairs remains intimately tied to domestic policy. During the Cold War, America supported Pakistan to counter the Soviet Union's support for India. Things became much more complicated when the 1979 Revolution in Iran began to spread its radical Islamic message, and that same year the Soviet Union invaded Afghanistan to support an unpopular Marxist government there under attack from the Mujahedeen. America supported the Mujahedeen, funneling military and other aid through Pakistan to the rebels, who fought the 100,000 Soviets to a standstill. When the Soviets withdrew in 1989, the Mujahedeen became entangled in a domestic conflict with the Taliban, a Mujahedeen splinter group that governed Afghanistan from 1996 to 2001. During the Taliban tenure, Osama bin Laden created a radical Islamic base in Afghanistan from which the 9/11 attacks on America were organized. In May 2011 American forces killed bin Laden in Abbottabad under the blind watchful eye of the Pakistani military and government. Although the Taliban was quickly dispatched after the 9/11 attacks and bin Laden was killed, America has maintained a useful relationship with Pakistan, in part because it provides the easiest access to and from Afghanistan for American troops and war material, in part to prevent Islamabad from becoming completely dependent on Beijing, and in part to have long-term access to an Afghanistan with a highly uncertain future.

---

3 The Colombo Plan for Cooperative Economic and Social Development in Asia and the Pacific was the product of the Commonwealth Conference of Foreign Ministers in Colombo, Sri Lanka (then Ceylon), in January 1950. The Colombo Plan membership later came to include non-Commonwealth countries as well.
4 Mehtab Haider, "All Five-Year Plans Were Failures," *The News*, January 20, 2011, http://www.thenews.com.pk/TodaysPrintDetail.aspx?ID=28401 & Cat=2.

As America has reduced its combat operations in Afghanistan, the Taliban reemerged, and as of 2020 it constitutes a significant political variable in Afghanistan and the region.

Osama bin Laden's compound in Abbottabad, Pakistan. *Source:* UPI/Alamy Stock Photo.

During the past quarter century, Pakistan was significantly impacted with refugees, a greater American presence, and the prospect of India trading places with America as the major power in Afghanistan. Pakistan wants "depth" in Afghanistan, meaning that Islamabad needs to work with and develop a friendly relationship with the Afghan Taliban (even as it attempts to crush the Pakistan Taliban). Islamabad also needs to concern itself with its neighbor Iran, with greater Russian involvement in Central Asia, and about Washington's role in the region.[5] Pakistan suffers from political corruption, voter fraud, inflation in double digits, unemployment that has skyrocketed to 15% since 2008, and poverty. The UN Human Development Index listed Pakistan near the bottom of the index at number 145 out of 187 nations. Given that both democratic and autocratic governments have failed to address most of Pakistan's domestic and foreign problems, and given that foreign relations in the region are at best ambiguous, there is little reason to be optimistic about its future.

People's Republic of Bangladesh

What constitutes today's Bangladesh is a part of the larger cultural region of Bengal, located in the northeastern part of historical India before 1947. The partition of India that year created the nation of Pakistan, which was separated into western and eastern parts separated by northern India. The

---

5 Of course, China has remained a player in the region, but Beijing and Islamabad have had a relatively good relationship during the Cold War and the Sino-Soviet hostilities, when the Soviet Union supported India and China supported Pakistan.

division of India also separated the province of Bengal. East Bengal, which was majority Muslim, became East Pakistan and West Bengal, which was majority Hindu, remained a part of India. East Pakistan differed from West Pakistan in several ways. Linguistically people in the east spoke Bengali while those in the west spoke Urdu, Balochi, Sindhi, Pashto, and Punjabi (nearly 50% for the latter). Demographically the east made up slightly more than half of Pakistan's population, and over 90% of the people are Bengalis. Politically, the west dominated the political system, which meant the nation's economic policies tended to favor the west. From Pakistan's inception, political differences between West and East Pakistan dominated government policy. Ultimately, the two "wings" of Pakistan could not resolve what turned out to be conflicting visions of each wing's path to the future. Islam, what Jinnah and other leaders claimed to be the justification for the partition of India, proved not to be sufficient to hold the country together.

Political and Economic Developments, 1947–1971

When Pakistan became independent, Bengalis in East Pakistan assumed they would enjoy a great deal of autonomy from the central government. Aside from such things as foreign relations, defense, and common currency and weights and measures, Bengalis would be free to govern themselves. Several early clashes over national language and political representation in the government can be seen in the creation of the All-Pakistan Awami League in 1949. It stood up for Bengali interests but had little support beyond East Pakistan. The following year, Prime Minister Liaquat Ali Khan declared in a speech in East Pakistan that "as long as I am alive no other political party [than the Muslim League] will be allowed to work here."[6] This skirmish reached a climax in 1954 when provincial assembly elections led to the colossal defeat of the Muslim League by two East Pakistan political parties. The Awami League (People's League) and the Krishak Sramik Party (Peasants and Workers Socialist Party) formed a United Front to challenge the Muslim League, seen by most in East Pakistan as an instrument of the elite in West Pakistan. The coalition put forth a twenty-one-point platform, often called the Charter of Freedom, which rallied East Pakistanis and earned the Muslim League a paltry nine of 237 seats contested in East Pakistan.

To defuse the potentially explosive political differences, politicians on both sides compromised to produce two significant reforms. One was the consolidation of the several ethnic and princely states of West Pakistan into what became known as "One Unit." It became one province, West Pakistan, while East Pakistan, already one ethnic (Bengali) unit, became the other province. Though this gave less populated West Pakistan equality, East Pakistan most likely viewed parity as a political victory. The second reform was contained in the 1956 Constitution. It established that each province be given equal representation in the national legislature, which would be located in Dacca (Dhaka), East Pakistan, while the administrative capital would be located in the West (first Karachi, then Rawalpindi, and finally Islamabad). But constitutional government lasted less than two years, and in 1958 Ayub Khan established martial law, thus returning to West Pakistan the control of the national government. The new 1962 Constitution continued to concentrate political power in the west, as the president now had the power to appoint ministers of state without legislative approval. The following year Sheikh Mujibur Rahman (or Mujib, 1920–1975), long a proponent of Bengali freedom, became head of the Awami League and made East Pakistan autonomy his party's central objective.

---

6 As quoted in M. Rashiduzzaman, "The Awami League and the Political Development of Pakistan," *Asian Survey* 10, no. 7 (July 1970): 575.

When the Awami League met at Lahore in 1966, Rahman issued a six-point program that amounted to East Pakistan becoming a separate state. The program demanded reforms that institute a weak federal parliamentary government elected by universal suffrage, and the legislature's membership would be apportioned on the basis of population. Moreover, each province would be allowed to create its own currency, budget, taxes, and militia. Two years later, as protests, riots, and strikes destabilized the country, Ayub Khan arrested Rahman, but this action merely made "Mujib" a popular symbol of Bengali self-determination. And in March 1969 Ayub Khan stepped down as ruler, replaced by another general, Yahya Khan, who proceeded to place the country under martial law. But Yahya Khan also began to move the country toward more civilian leadership and called for elections to be held in December 1970. Before the election, Yahya ended the One Unit policy of equal political representation for West and East Pakistan, the latter now receiving 162 of 300 seats in the national legislature based on its larger population. When the election took place on December 7, the Awami won 160 of East Pakistan's 162 seats, while in the West Ali Bhutto's Pakistan People's Party won only 81 of the 138 seats, the other seats going to a number of smaller parties. The Awami League should have formed the new government—almost certainly under Mujib's leadership—given its control of more than half of the seats in the National Assembly. Instead Yahya did not allow the Assembly to convene as scheduled on March 3, 1971, whereupon strikes and riots broke out in the east. Yahya ultimately deployed 90,000 troops to quell the uprising. Bengalis resisted, chiefly through the Mukti Bahini or Liberation Force, and formally declared independence on April 17. By the end of 1971, the Indian Army entered the conflict and defeated the Pakistan military. Bangladesh's continuing independence was protected by geography and India.

Independence, Political Developments, and Economic Plans, 1971–2018

The new nation faced enormous problems in its first decades. Perhaps one million Bengalis died in the war of independence, another eight to 10 million refugees escaped to India, in addition to the quarter-million deaths that had resulted from a cyclone in November 1970. The physical destruction and economic costs produced further problems for Bangladesh. Moreover, the political groundwork for the country was in disarray. General Ziaur Rahman ("Major Zia," 1936–1981), who had declared Bangladesh's independence, also appointed himself president. Meanwhile, Mujibur (Mujib) Rahman, in prison in West Pakistan since 1968, returned to Bangladesh in January 1972. He took control of the government, which was headquartered in the nation's capital, Dhaka. Mujib put together the country's Constitution, based on "Mujibism," which promoted nationalism, socialism, secularism, and democracy. Until his assassination on August 15, 1975, the *bangabandhu* (Love Bengal), as Mujib was called, presided over steady political and economic deterioration. The first national election in 1973 gave Mujib's Awami League a massive victory at the polls, but by 1975 Mujib had outlawed political parties (including the Awami League, now called the Bangladesh Peasants, Workers' and People's League). As well, Mujib had the Constitution revised to allow him to serve as a virtual dictator. Not only was the *bangabandhu* becoming more authoritarian, he tolerated massive corruption, and he failed to make a dent in the colossal poverty of his citizens. Moreover, many in the military disliked Mujib's pro-Indian and pro-Soviet foreign policies.

Just a few years into independence, it was possible to foresee the most likely future of Bangladeshi politics. The military played the preeminent role, with elections or promised elections serving as a façade for legitimacy at home and abroad. As in Pakistan, the political process in Bangladesh typically involved military intervention, violence, political arrests and jailing, coups, and assassinations mixed with halting attempts at democratic government. Numerous parties took part in various elections and referenda, usually in a context of protests, strikes, boycotts, and assorted

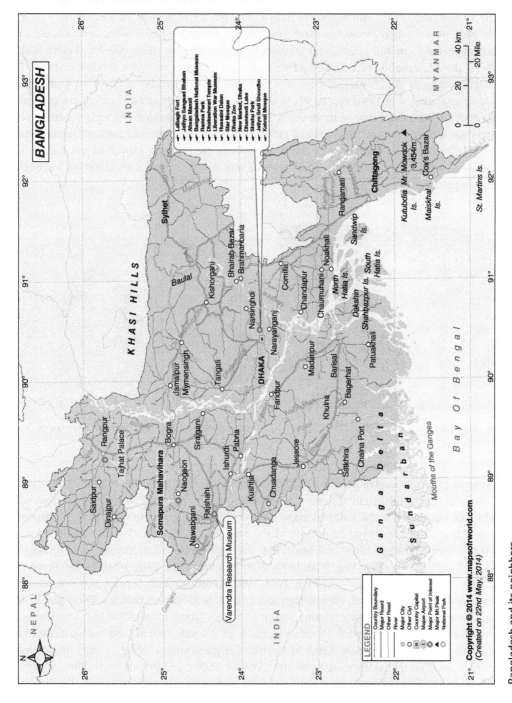

Bangladesh and its neighbors.

social and economic turmoil. Between 1975 and 1991, military and civilian political leaders varied as to the degree Islam should be a factor in the new nation's agenda; they had contrasting visions of economic development; and there were contested views of foreign policy, especially with respect to Indian and Russian relations.

By 1991, politics in Bangladesh had somewhat settled down. While numerous political parties continued to contest elections, two parties emerged as the most likely winners: the center-left and secular Awami League (AL) and the center-right and religious Bangladesh Nationalist Party (BNP). At the same time, though numerous candidates for the nation's highest office campaigned, two women appeared to be the most likely winners in presidential contests: Sheikh Hasina Wajed (1947–) of the AL, daughter of a founding father and former prime minister, assassinated in 1975; and Begum Khaleda Zia (1945–), widow of a founding father, founder of the BNP, and former president, assassinated in 1981. From 1991 to the present, one of those two leaders has governed Bangladesh with the exception of three years. And though assassination attempts occurred, corruption persisted, and natural disasters and military intervention remained constant hazards, and while fierce individual and party rivalry persisted, government ultimately involved political parties and their candidates, elections, and parliaments, as well as a decreased direct intervention of the military in politics.

Sheikh Hasina Wajed. *Source:* UPI/Alamy Stock Photo.

Begum Khaleda Zia. *Source:* SK Hasan Ali/Alamy Stock Photo.

A number of factors contributed to Bangladesh's sluggish economic growth after its separation from Pakistan. As East Pakistan, it seldom received priority in national Five-Year plans, especially in industrial expansion. It also suffered major setbacks resulting from the 1971 war for independence, which probably destroyed 20 percent of the economy. In the decades after independence, Bangladesh created a Planning Commission that oversaw a series of multiyear plans before the end of the Cold War: First Five-Year Plan, 1973–1978; Two-Year Plan, 1978–1980; Second Five-Year Plan, 1981–1985; and Third Five-Year Plan, 1985–1990. Assistance from foreign governments and internationals organizations helped to design and finance development policies. These plans generally suffered from excessive government planning and regulation, exemplified in the nationalization of industry, which retarded the development of human capital and nongovernmental organizations needed to increase national wealth. The government relied on bureaucrats who typically focused on managing existing wealth. As well, public and private corruption, marginal infrastructural and educational investment, misdirected foreign capital, and minimal technology input all contributed to disappointing economic growth. Consequently, the majority of the population did not experience much economic improvement. From independence until 1990, economic growth in real Gross Domestic Product per person tended to be negative or at best negligible. Nonetheless one major improvement occurred as a result of government policies and their implementation: the reduction in the rate of population increase, whose growth in the past had neutralized feeble economic growth.

Economic activities have experienced significant, generally positive changes since 1991. Government still constitutes the largest influence on economic development, as evidenced by the continuation of Five-Year plans. In part, this is because most government officials have little regard for private enterprise, but also because various national and international aid organizations and funds typically operate through government organizations. And since corruption in government is widespread, much of the incoming funds never arrive at their targeted destinations. Moreover, state-owned industries typically operated at an annual loss of roughly 2 percent since independence. When the BNP took control of the government in 1991, it took steps toward selling off state-owned enterprises, reducing corruption and burdensome regulations, and attracting private foreign capital. But workers affected by such privatization protested, generating much political pressure, and when the Awami League came to power in 1996 it put such programs on hiatus. Since then, the two parties have alternated in control of the government and have fought to guide Bangladesh to the future with their rather different political agendas.

Yet Bangladesh has made some economic improvements. Since roughly 2000, the per capita income has more than doubled while those classified as living in dreadful poverty has declined by more than half, to 9 percent. The Grameen Bank, a microcredit organization created by economics professor Dr. Muhammad Yunus in 1983, provides the best example of effective private entrepreneurship. Yunus, who won the Nobel Peace Prize in 2006 for his and the bank's "efforts to create economic and social development from below," sought to create "capitalism with a human face." The bank makes loans to the very poorest in Bangladesh, with no collateral requirement, and usually to women. Unfortunately the government has attempted to politicize the bank, thereby reducing its effectiveness. Adding to the country's woes, in the December 2018 national election Sheikh Hasina was returned as prime minister, though many argue through massive corruption. The vote produced a colossally one-sided victory to Hasina, who continues to govern in 2020. Many agree with one foreign observer that the country was taking a "precipitous slide toward authoritarianism."[7]

As well, religious and ethnic rebellious movements arose or arrived to challenge the Dhaka government by the 1990s. The Rohingya, who seek to establish a Muslim state in western Burma, have fled that country and settled in eastern Bangladesh. More than a quarter million of these Muslim ethnic refugees place a burden on already-overwhelmed government efforts to deal with rural poverty and threaten to destabilize relations between the two neighbors. Radical Islamic groups engaging in terrorist bombings also threaten to undermine the struggle to create stable civilian government. Jamaat-ul-Mujahideen Bangladesh (JMB) is linked to Pakistan's Lashkar-e-Taiba (LeT) and Britain's al-Muhajiroun, as well as to oil money in Saudi Arabia and Kuwait. Many moderate Muslim Bangladeshis fear that given the country's fragile institutions, foreign militant Muslims will descend on Bangladesh—as Osama bin Laden and al Qaeda did in Afghanistan during and after the Soviet invasion—and, in conjunction with local militants, end the nation's wobbly secular, democratic institutions. This "Talibanization" of Bangladesh has been suggested by a number of authors, most recently in Hiranmay Karlekar's *Bangladesh: The Next Afghanistan?*

---

7 "Bangladesh's Farcical Vote," *New York Times*, January 16, 2019, p. A-24.

The Himalayan Nations

Before 1945, Britain managed, with varying degrees of success, relationships among the Himalayan nations—Sikkim, Bhutan, and Nepal. In the wake of decolonization, however, those nations found themselves caught between independent India and Communist China, rivals in the ongoing Cold War setting. With the collapse of the Soviet Union and the rise of China and India, the Himalayan mountain region became home to several sometimes antagonistic nuclear powers. As well, the major rivers in water-scarce Asia originate there. Border disputes in the region continue, most importantly between India and China and India and Pakistan. The Himalayan nations have served as a buffer between China and India, and thus have strategic importance to the surrounding major powers. Tibetan refugees headquarter themselves in India, thereby straining relations between Beijing and New Delhi.

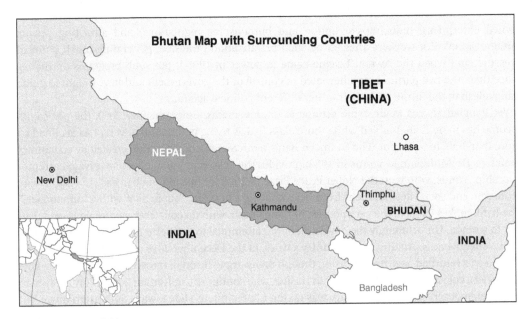

Bhutan and its neighbors.

Sikkim

Until 1975, Sikkim remained an independent kingdom influenced culturally over the centuries by India, Nepal, Bhutan, Tibet, and Britain. By the mid-nineteenth century, "Great Game" politics drew Russia into the foreign relations of the territories surrounding India. Britain feared the expansion of Russia into Tibet (a British territorial goal) through adjacent Sikkim, and this produced London's occupation of Sikkim, which led to the kingdom becoming a puppet state of British India. After World War I Sikkim retained control of its domestic affairs, but its foreign relations were handled by the British. When India became independent in 1947 and Sikkim voted not to become a part of India, its status remained the same as it had been under the British, with New Delhi instead of London guiding Sikkim's foreign affairs. In the wake of the Sino-Indian border war of 1962, India sought the incorporation of Sikkim (located on China's border) into India. In 1975 Sikkim held a vote as to whether the kingdom should remain independent or join the Indian union. On April 14 that year, the people of Sikkim opted to become the 22nd state of India.

Bhutan

Historically, Buddhist Bhutan has been connected by culture and politics to neighboring giant empires and tiny kingdoms. A politically unified monarchy emerged in the seventeenth century under a Tibetan monk who migrated to Bhutan in 1616. By the eighteenth century the British East India Company's century-old uneven relationship with Bhutan led to the Duar War (1864–1865), which produced a British victory. Britain wanted to position itself in Bhutan, again with Great Game geopolitics in mind, to keep Russia from expanding into Tibet through Bhutan. By the late nineteenth century, the rise of political leader Ugyen Wangchuck (1862–1926; r. 1907–1926) led to close cooperation between Britain and Bhutan. When Wangchuck became king in 1907, he convinced the religious, economic, and political elites to create a more reformist absolutist monarchy, and in the Treaty of Punakha (1910) allowed Britain to take control of the nation's foreign affairs. This served London's interests and gave the tiny nation British protection from both Russia and China, at least until the end of World War II.

Bhutan, then as now, had to deal with radically different power relationships in Asia. With the departure of Britain from India in 1947, Bhutan had the option of joining India or becoming independent, and it chose the latter, but with the same relationship it had with the British. Specifically, it gave Bhutan complete freedom in domestic affairs but New Delhi assumed control of the kingdom's foreign affairs. Yet India did not possess the same protective capacity that Britain had given the much stronger and Communist governments in Russia and China. Still, Indo-Russian relations were strong during most of the Cold War and thus afforded Bhutan some protection against China. This Indo-Bhutanese foreign policy relationship lasted until 2007, when the India-Bhutan Friendship Treaty returned foreign policy control to the kingdom but concurrently called for the two states to "cooperate closely with each other" on foreign policy issues.

At home, a spate of domestic reforms produced a more open society but also greater domestic clashes. These post–World War II changes included the elimination of slavery and serfdom, the creation of a national assembly, and land reform. The National Assembly achieved the right to appoint the Cabinet after 1998, and in 2006 the king abdicated, preparing the way for constitutional government, which occurred as a result of the 2008 election.

Ethnic, language, and gender problems seem to dominate the political debate in Bhutan. The Nepalese minority and language problems in Bhutan continue to divide the country, while the position of women remains remarkably pitiable. According to one Bhutanese opinion poll, "nearly 70% of **women** believed they deserved a beating if they argued with their partner, refused sex or neglected their children."[8] The government seeks to assess its success at nation building with a Gross National Happiness index. On such an index, it would appear that the Nepalese minority is somewhat unhappy, while one can incongruously conclude that Bhutanese women are relatively happy. Clearly this happiness project is a work in progress.

Nepal

Like all of the early Himalayan kingdoms, Nepal came under the influence of Indian culture, especially its religions. While Bhutan became preponderantly Buddhist, Nepal eventually embraced Hinduism and the caste system. Authority in pre-modern Nepali society usually resided in the

---

8 Mark Magnier, "Bhutan King Marries Commoner," *Los Angeles Times*, October 13, 2011, http://www.latimes. com/news/nationworld/world/la - fg-bhutan-royal-wedding-20111014. My emphasis.

hands of kings, nobles, and the clergy, each with limited power. As well, Nepali kings had to pay some form of tribute to Hindu and Muslim rulers of India, often to China, and to the British East India Company by the eighteenth century. By that time the first modern monarchy emerged, the Gorkha or Shah Dynasty (1768–2008), which came under the control of a military leader and his descendants (the so-called Rana Dynasty). The emergence of Gandhi in India after World War I influenced Nepal, where mass political organizations and opposition publications applied political pressure on the Rana administration. World War II and London's departure from South Asia further undermined military rule, which ended in 1951, thus resulting in the restoration of the monarch's powers.

Nepali politics since the return of the monarchy have proven to be tumultuous. The country has lived under six constitutions, the power of the king under these constitutions typically remained unclear, while ethnic, linguistic, and caste divisions constantly destabilized the country. These and other problems led to a decade-long civil war beginning in 1996, during which time the Crown Prince assassinated much of the royal family in 2001. Although King Gyanendra Shah (1947–) ended the civil war in 2006, the monarchy collapsed in 2008 due to popular opposition across the political spectrum. The emergence of the Republic of Nepal that year did not end political volatility, as evidenced by the governmental musical chairs of constantly changing parties of varying but usually radical political persuasions. Domestic politics has been further complicated by increasing Chinese economic and political involvement in Nepali society. The Chinese presence resulted in large part from Nepal's fear of being too dependent on India; this was solved by using China as a counterbalance. In that thorny political context, President Ram Baran Yadav (1948–) introduced the sixth constitution in September 2015. It made Nepal a secular republic, thereby alienating much of the majority-Hindu community. All of this took place in the wake of the April 2015 Nepali earthquake, which killed thousands and left tens of thousands injured and/or homeless. Bidhya Devi Bhandari (1961–) of the Communist Party of Nepal (Unified Marxist-Leninist) was chosen president indirectly by the Electoral College in 2015, and she was reelected in 2018. Bhandari's Prime Minister Khadga Prasad Sharma Oli (or KP Oli, 1952–) and a majority of the Cabinet are also members of her party. The once-dominant India-sympathetic Nepal Congress Party now fights for political significance, as does India in Nepal. Lots of vital challenges remain on the nation's agenda.

Sri Lanka

Known as Ceylon until 1972, Sri Lanka peacefully achieved its independence from Great Britain in 1948. The island nation, which had been ruled by a series of European nations since the sixteenth century, came under British control in 1796. Administratively, it remained a colony separate from British India administratively. The population was composed of migrants from India and the Arab world, and the people divided chiefly along ethnic and religious lines. The majority of the inhabitants arrived from India, but others originated in Malaya, Indonesia, and the Arab world: The earliest came from the north as early as the third century BCE and tended to be Buddhists; the second wave from the mainland reached Sri Lanka in the nineteenth century CE and tended to be Hindu; and Muslims in Sri Lanka began arriving in the seventh century, largely from the Arabian Peninsula and later from South India. While numerous ethnic, religious, caste, and other differences exist, the chief struggle historically has been between the majority Sinhalese Buddhists and the Tamil Hindus, both under the British and during independence.

Colonial Ceylon, 1802–1948

British rule kept most of the fissures on the island in check, in part because of administrative expertise and in part due to the lack of a unified opposition—at least before World War I. Gandhi and the Indian National Congress became an inspiration for the Ceylonese National Congress, formed in 1919. But as the British opened access to its colonial organizations for Ceylonese, and as it became more evident that independence was a genuine possibility, the big struggle—as in India—became who would rule a democratic Ceylon once the British were gone. As World War II concluded and decolonization commenced, both Sinhalese and Tamils united to launch the new nation. Tamil leader G.G. Ponnambalam (1901–1977) of the All Ceylon Tamil Congress (ACTC) called for his followers to cooperate with Ceylon's first prime minister, Don Stephen (D.S.) Senanayake (1883–1952) of the United National Party (UNP). Two clear examples of national unity among early independence leaders were the promotion of both Tamil and Sinhala as official languages and religious toleration for all, particularly for Buddhists and Hindus.

Independent Ceylon/Sri Lanka, 1948–1983

Politics in the post-independent Dominion of Ceylon quickly began to fragment into smaller partisan organizations across the ethnic spectrum. In less than a year the Ceylon Tamil Congress split, thereby weakening the already minority position of the Tamils in the political process. Under Ponnambalam the ACTC promoted Ceylonese unity, but increasingly ethnic Tamil nationalism became the trademark of Ceylonese Tamils. The UNP leadership also began to quarrel, and the death of UNP leader Senanayake in 1952, arguably the indispensable cohesive political national glue, split the UNP into factions. By the 1956 elections, a country that began independence with two major parties supporting Ceylonese unity found itself with the more radical wings of those parties forming their own political organizations, which divided along ethnic lines. S.W.R.D. Bandaranaike (1899–1959) created the Sri Lanka Freedom Party, which focused on making the Sinhalese language the only national language, replacing English, and promoting Buddhism as the nation's dominant faith. The Tamils now depended on the new Federal Party to champion their causes since ACTC from which it emerged had lost the confidence of most Tamils. Nonetheless the once-discredited UNP made a comeback in the 1965 elections, but economic troubles and the (largely Sinhalese) party reaching out to Tamils again divided the party and brought about its downfall in the 1970 election.

A coalition of political parties led by the (largely Sinhalese) Freedom Party won the 1970 election, promising in the campaign to make the country a republic. By the time Ceylon became the Republic of Sri Lanka in 1972, cooperation among the two major ethnic groups became increasingly rare, while social unrest across the political and ethnic spectra produced protests, strikes, attempted coups, and insurrections for the following decade. Domestic politics became ever more radical, perhaps reflecting the general global extremism of the time. The Maoist Janatha Vimukthi Peramuna (JVP) or People's Liberation Front launched an insurrection. As it was generally an ethnic Sinhalese movement, the Sinhalese government of Sri Lanka had to not only worry about its internal security but, more importantly, be concerned that India might very well intervene to protect the Hindu Tamil minority (which it did between 1987 and 1990). The elections of 1977 brought the UNP back to power with the support of many Tamils, and it appeared that a new cooperation between Sinhalese and Tamils was within reach. But the emergence of a radical separatist Tamil movement, the Liberation Tigers of Tamil Elam (LTTE), ultimately undermined what little remained of national cohesion. Although the UNP attempted to integrate the Tamil population after its victory in the 1978 election by producing a new constitution in 1978, the Tamil Tigers and a large part of the Sinhalese community became fervently irreconcilable. The Prevention of Terrorism Act of 1979, moreover, seemed to be directed toward only one side of the political divide—the Tamils. The nation moved relentlessly toward civil war.

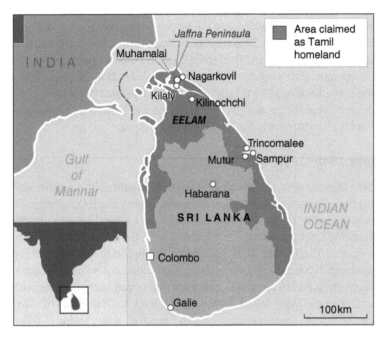

Sri Lanka.

Sri Lanka, Civil War, and Reconciliation, 1983–present

The Tamil Tigers/LTTE, as they came to be known, represented a much larger and more dangerous insurrectionary movement than the JVP. Numerous Tamil nationalist organizations had emerged in the twentieth century to promote Tamil interests, and by 1972 these movements—including the LTTE, which had formed that year—joined the Tamil United Front (TUF), which later became the Tamil United Liberation Front (TULF). Its immediate goal was the creation of an independent Tamil region in eastern and northern Sri Lanka, and it generally hoped to do so within the electoral system. The Tamil Tigers broke from the TULF in 1976 to challenge what they considered to be the TULF's hopelessly nonviolent Gandhian approach. Instead, Vellupillai Prabhakaran (1954–2009), founder of the LTTE, explicitly and primarily utilized violence to achieve independence. He embraced the ideas of Indian radical nationalist Subhash Chandra Bose, who had joined with Japan in World War II to fight the British. A brilliant military leader, Prabhakaran effectively combined guerrilla warfare, terrorism, extortion (the "Tiger Tax"), and peace talks to keep the Sri Lankan forces at bay for a quarter century. He perished in battle on May 18, 2009, the same day the Sri Lankan government proclaimed victory in the civil war. More than 25,000 Tamil Tigers died during the conflict, along with roughly 20,000 government troops, plus another 75,000 or more civilians—Sinhalese and Tamil—as well as some 1500 Indian forces.

Since 2009 a painful process of national reconstruction has begun. When the LTTE insurgency ended, President Mahinda Rajapaksa (1945–) called for the creation of the Lessons Learned and Reconciliation Commission to investigate the causes of the conflict, specify the atrocities committed, and search for the best approaches to reconciliation. The 2011 commission report findings have been labeled dubious by numerous organizations—such as Amnesty International and Human Rights Watch—claiming that the government whitewashed its often ghastly behavior. The United Nations concluded that both sides committed butcheries. The 2010 election, tarnished by bombings and killings, has been contested by the losing candidate and conqueror of the LTTE, General Sarath Fonseka (1950–). He has been harassed, court-martialed, and jailed—and eventually released—by the winner, President Rajapaksa. Although the Rajapaksa administration has been seen as mired in corruption, nepotism, and other crooked practices, he seemed a likely winner of the January 2015 presidential election. This appeared more probable after Pope Francis, on his visit to Sri Lanka prior to the vote, was seen blessing the incumbent. Instead, reformer Maithripala Sirisena (1951–) eked out a victory, followed by an August 2015 parliamentary election triumph.

A pro-Western nation at the time of independence, Sri Lanka never really veered toward attachment to any single power and tended to maintain a policy of nonalignment. It remained a member of the British Commonwealth and by the 1980s improved relations with the United States, mainly for economic reasons. Even before the rise of China, Sri Lankan foreign policy sought to minimize dependence on India and avoid antagonizing New Delhi by not forming close alliances with the outside world. The "rise of the dragon" with its ability to influence smaller nations—especially in Asia—with investment and technology began to affect Sri Lanka and its relationship with India. Beijing sent not only money, expertise, and equipment to Sri Lanka but also elements of its navy. For more than a decade, Prime Minister and then President Mahinda Rajapaksa drew closer to China, to the point of creating great anxiety in India. This, in addition to Rajapaksa's nepotism, corruption, and authoritarian tendencies, led Sri Lankans to prevent the president's attempt at a third term in the January 2015 presidential election and the following August parliamentary election. The presidential winner, Maithripala Sirisena, promised a reform program and a more traditional foreign policy of avoiding attachments that will provoke New Delhi.

Maldives

Located to the southwest of India, the Sunni Muslim nation of Maldives consists of numerous atolls totaling some 1200 islands with a population of roughly 400,000. Its people came from a number of foreign locations. The earliest significant population with a cultural impact came from Dravidian-speaking people in southern India in the late first millennium BCE; later, Sinhalese migrants from Ceylon and Arab merchants from the Middle East arrived. From 1153 when the last Buddhist king embraced Islam until the arrival of the Portuguese in the sixteenth century, the Sultanate of Maldives remained independent. Although the Portuguese briefly established a formal government from 1558 to 1573 and the Dutch exerted much influence in the islands thereafter, the Maldives operated free from direct foreign control until 1887. In December that year, the sultan signed an agreement with the British that made the Maldives a British protectorate, administered from Ceylon. In 1953 the Sultanate, governed by the Huraa Dynasty since 1757, was temporarily ended and replaced by a republic whose president, Muhammad Didi (1910–1954), instituted a range of reforms, notably in education and women's rights. He was overthrown and the Sultanate reestablished before the end of the year. Maldives achieved independence on July 26, 1965; joined the United Nations that year; established republicanism in 1968; and became a member of the British Commonwealth in 1972.

Growing political ferment on the islands became evident in the 1930s and has continued into the twenty-first century, along with widespread lawlessness. The country has operated under at least a dozen constitutions, the original one designed to limit the absolute power of the hereditary sultans. Since the creation of the Second Republic in 1968, seven presidents have assumed office, several under questionable electoral circumstances; one was arrested while in office, and another forced to resign; riots and attempted coups have surrounded electoral politics; and one president, Maumoon Abd al-Gayoom (1937–), was elected six times by the Parliament, serving from 1978 to 2008. The first democratic election for chief executive occurred in 2008, and while multiple parties and numerous candidates have participated since then, corruption has been the hallmark of the process. Thus in 2014 the nation's Supreme Court arrested and jailed the Electoral Commission members involved in the 2013 presidential election. They were accused of not following the rules for runoff elections. In March 2015, a former president was given a 13-year prison term for alleged terrorism, a sentence that was reduced to house arrest. Nonetheless, that 2013 election eventually produced a presidential winner, Abdulla Yameen (1959–), but he has since been targeted for assassination by ISIS.

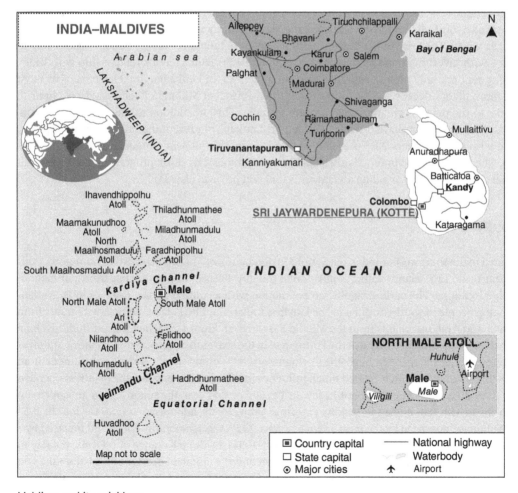

Maldives and its neighbors.

A September 2018 election ousted pro-Chinese Yameen and installed Ibrahim Mohamed Solih as the new president. Solih likely garnered 58% of the vote largely by raising the specter of a dangerous China, which resonated with the electorate. His pitch to voters was simple: too much Chinese money borrowed for infrastructure, too much corruption involved in the borrowing, too much national debt ("debt-trap diplomacy"), and too much Chinese influence on Yameen. For the immediate future, pro-India Solih will guide the small but strategically important nation. The country has historically been connected to India both culturally as well as economically, and since the British departed most of the Maldives infrastructure has been financed, created, and maintained by India. The island country depends on tourism for much of its income, and political turmoil and lawlessness have reduced the number of visitors to the country, thus creating an economic crunch. Thus terrorism, lawlessness, and corruption remain Maldives' chief domestic concerns, affecting as they do social stability, reliable and trustworthy government, and the ability of the country to continue to attract travelers from abroad. Most vacationers seek serenity and security where relaxation and comfort can be anticipated.

But with the rise of China, new foreign policy issues have also arisen in the region. As with Sri Lanka, China approaches the Maldives as an economic and technological suitor and potentially a military guest. From Beijing's outlook, both Sri Lanka and Maldives provide China leverage in its relationship with India. The two island nations offer maritime linkages connecting China to its interests in the Middle East (oil) and Africa (oil and other raw materials). These are troublesome possibilities from Indian security and American strategic perspectives.

The domestic and foreign challenges of small South Asian nations continue.

Suggested Readings and Viewings

Stephen P. Cohen, *The Idea of Pakistan* (Washington, DC: Brookings Institution, 2004).

Earth (1998), dir. by Deepa Mehta.

Jeffrey Clifford Holt, *Sri Lanka: History, Culture, and Politics* (Durham, NC: Duke University Press, 2011).

Owen Bennett Jones, *Pakistan: Eye of the Storm* (New Haven, CT: Yale University Press, 2003).

Robert D. Kaplan, *Monsoon: The Indian Ocean and the Future of American Power* (New York: Random House, 2011).

Hiranmay Karlekar, *Bangladesh: The Next Afghanistan?* (New Delhi: Sage Publications, 2005).

Kashmir: Valley of Despair (1998), dir. by Marion Mayer-Hohdahl.

Mahandra Lawoti, *Contentious Politics and Democratization in Nepal* (Thousand Oaks, CA: Sage, 2007).

No Fire Zone: The Killing Fields of Sri Lanka (2013), dir. by Callum Macrae.

Partition of India: Legacy of Blood (1998), dir. by Christopher Mitchell.

Ahmed Rashid, *Descent into Chaos: The United States and the Failure of Nation Building in Pakistan, Afghanistan, and Central Asia* (New York: Penguin, 2008).

Leo Rose, *The Politics of Bhutan* (Ithaca, NY: Cornell University Press, 1977).

Willem Van Schendel, *A History of Bangladesh* (Cambridge: Cambridge University Press, 2009).

Rajesh Venugopal, *Nationalism, Development and National Conflict in Sri Lanka* (Cambridge: Cambridge University Press, 2018).

John Whelpton, *A History of Nepal* (Cambridge: Cambridge University Press, 2005).

Stanley Wolpert, *India and Pakistan: Continued Conflict or Cooperation?* (Berkeley: University of California Press, 2010).

26

Mainland Southeast Asia since 1945

I learned to ignore criticism and advice from experts and quasi-experts, especially academics in the social and political sciences. They have their pet theories on how a society should develop to approximate their ideal, especially how poverty should be reduced and welfare extended. I tried to be correct, not politically correct.[1]

—Lee Kuan Yew

Southeast Asia since 1945

World War II, for both winners and losers, vastly accelerated the demise of the industrial nations' formal colonial or client state arrangements across most of the globe. This was particularly true in Asia, where nationalist movements had begun to mature by the time war began in July 1937 in China. With the Japanese attack on Pearl Harbor, all Southeast Asian nations were eventually occupied. In those countries, pro- and anti-Japanese individuals and groups emerged. Yet it should be noted that for national populations as a whole, none trusted (much less liked) Japan. It also needs to be pointed out that decades or centuries of colonial rule did not make Western overlords popular. These feelings about the industrial nations resulted in some nationalist movements supporting Japan, in part because of their anti-Western message, in part from the belief that Japan would likely win the conflict. Other nationalist organizations joined the anti-Japanese effort of the Allies, thinking the West would prevail or that its ideals were more attractive. Still other nationalist groups worked with both sides, hoping to emerge the principal nationalist movement at war's end. In any case, by the summer of 1945, Southeast Asia could boast of dozens of organized, armed, and nationalist movements that sought—peacefully or violently—to replace colonial regimes.

When the Japanese departed Southeast Asia, political power vacuums temporarily appeared. As the Western armies took surrender of the Japanese military, clashes between those armies and some nationalist movements occurred. Even in British and American colonies, where the people had been informed that independence would take place, struggles among competing nationalist movements broke out. The British took surrender of Japanese forces in Indonesia, and the British and Nationalist Chinese did the same in Indochina. Keeping the Dutch and the French out of the surrender process, it was hoped, would minimize conflict with local nationalist movements. This turned out to be wishful thinking. The emerging Cold War complicated already messy situations

---

1 Lee Kuan Yew, *From Third World to First: The Singapore Story, 1965–2000* (New York: HarperCollins, 2000), p. 688.

Asia Past and Present: A Brief History, First Edition. Peter P. Wan and Thomas D. Reins.
© 2021 John Wiley & Sons, Inc. Published 2021 by John Wiley & Sons, Inc.

across Southeast Asia. Many of the nationalist movements had communist connections, leanings, and/or leadership. Thus what began as chiefly internal differences among nationalists often involved international participants, as the communists supported their surrogates and the West assisted theirs. By the 1950s most Southeast Asian nations had attained independence.

At that point, the foremost issue became which model of modernization—Soviet, Western, or some combination of domestic and foreign strategies—represented the best path to the future. In South Asia, places like India, Pakistan, or Bangladesh might disagree about the details of modernization, but some form of socialism seemed the preferred economic framework within which change would occur. In East and Southeast Asia, by contrast, market-based economics competed with socialist or communist approaches. As well, while there were disagreements about political arrangements across Asia, each nation appeared to prefer some kind of strong central government, whether democratic, authoritarian, or totalitarian. That usually meant, as well, opposition to any kind of meaningful federalism that might give local tribal, ethnic, or religious groups some kind of excuse for separatist action. It also typically led to the imposition of an official national language. And most nationalist leaders sought, at least initially, a secular society. Even though Hindu, Buddhist, and Islamic organizations had formed much of the foundation for nationalist movements in most of Asia, newly independent nations and their leaders tended to worry that religious (or other) loyalties might trump national loyalty. Moreover, nationalist leaders often viewed religion as a drag on modernization and thus frequently manipulated or marginalized religious institutions.

Lee Kuan Yew (1923–2015). *Source:* Michael Stroud/Getty Images.

Into the 1960s, the competition between command-style economies and political systems on the one hand and market-oriented economies and democratic or authoritarian political systems on the other looked to be close. Indeed, talk in America often indicated the West was losing the competition. Novels such as *Quiet American* and *Ugly American* questioned America's standing in the eyes of the Third World, while studies such as Walt Rostow's *Stages of Economic Growth* offered a "Non-Communist Manifesto" that could win over the people of Asia, Africa, and Latin America. Yet by the time the Vietnam War ended in 1975—even as three dominos fell (Laos, Cambodia, and Vietnam) to communism, even as the Soviet Union had caught up with the United States militarily, and even as the American economy was staggering from high oil prices and stagflation—Asian "little dragons" or "little tigers" exploded onto the economic scene. Of the original four dragons—Hong Kong, Taiwan, South Korea, and Singapore—only the latter came from Southeast Asia. But before the end of the Cold War, Thailand and Malaysia joined their ranks and Indonesia's economy began to take off. Significantly, Vietnam also shifted to a market economy after *Doi Moi* reforms in 1986. The collapse of communism may not have signaled the "End of History," but it did indicate a victory for market economics. Even the laggards in Southeast Asia—Myanmar, Laos, Cambodia, and the Philippines—showed signs of economic improvement. The political arrangements there remain to be settled, as do the social and cultural consequences of economic development. Southeast Asia will need to address the rise of China and India, America's future role in the region, the impact of terrorism, and the anxieties of global economic and cultural interaction. But on balance, the region has made remarkable progress on many fronts since independence and seems likely to address—perhaps not always smoothly at first—the challenges of successful growth.

Timeline for Mainland Southeast Asia, 1945–2019	
1945	August 15: World War II ends
	September 2: Ho Chi Minh proclaims Vietnamese independence
1946–1954	First Vietnam War; French defeated at Battle of Dienbienphu in 1954; Geneva Conference divides Vietnam into Communist North and non-Communist South
1947	Burmese nationalist leader Aung San assassinated
1948	Burma becomes independent from Britain
1947–1973	Military rule in Thailand, with king as symbol of national cohesion
1948–1960	The Emergency in Malaya pitted the victorious British and ethnic Malays against native ethnic Chinese Communist insurgents
1949	October 1: Mao Zedong's Communists proclaim the People's Republic of China
1953	Cambodia becomes independent from France
1953–1970	As prince or king, Norodom Sihanouk governs Cambodia; Lon Nol overthrows Sihanouk in 1970; Lon Nol ousted by the Khmer Rouge in 1975
1954	Laos becomes independent from France
1957	Malaya becomes independent from Britain
1961–1975	U.S. air bases established in Thailand for operations in Laos and Vietnam
1962–2011	Burmese military rules
1963	Malaysia formed by the addition of Singapore, Sabah, and Sarawak to Malaya
1965	Singapore secedes from Malaysia and becomes independent
1955–1963	Ngo Dinh Diem rules South Vietnam; assassinated in November 1963
1965–1973	Political chaos after Diem's killing brings in American combat units to aid South Vietnam, launching Second Vietnam War

1975	North Vietnam defeats South Vietnam, reunifies country
1975	Communist Pathet Lao takes control of Laos
1975–1979	Khmer Rouge takes control of Cambodia and produces the Killing Fields
1975–1989	Vietnamese Army occupies Cambodia, defeating Khmer Rouge
1985–2019	Cambodia's Hun Sen moves toward authoritarian rule
1986	Vietnam adopts Doi Moi reforms
1989–2019	Myanmar's democracy leader Aung San Suu Kyi challenges military rule and also is called into question over her unwillingness to deal with the Rohingya crisis
1995	United States establishes diplomatic relations with Vietnam
2001–2019	Battle between elected Prime Minister Thaksin Shinawatra and his sister Yingluck Shinawatra, also elected prime minister, on the one hand, and the military who ousted them on the other
2015	Lee Kuan Yew, Singapore's founder and de facto leader, dies
2011–2019	Burmese military begins to liberalize, though slowly

Colonial Burma to the Republic of the Union of Myanmar

Burma has experienced a host of problems, most of them self-inflicted, since the end of World War II. Aung San (1915–1947), the country's popular leader, seemed to be the person who could unite the multiethnic Burmese nation and lead it to independence. His Anti-Fascist People's Freedom League (AFPFL) began to move away from its leftist political stances in 1946, as evidenced by removing communists from leadership positions to appease the British. A more moderate nationalist movement, it was believed, would smooth the transition to independence. This produced a nationalist leadership battle. Both Aung San and U Saw (1900–1948) went to London to negotiate the terms of an agreement that set the details for independence. Aung San signed the agreement, but Saw ultimately repudiated the terms, claiming that Aung San made too many concessions to the British. In April the AFPFL won the vast majority of seats for the Constituent Assembly, a victory that supported the Burmese agreement with Britain. The Constituent Assembly drafted the national constitution, but in July 1947 Aung San was assassinated by an accomplice of a political rival, likely U Saw. U Nu, AFPFL's second in command, succeeded Aung San as Burma's nationalist face. He had the tasks of dealing with the communists and ethnic minorities at home and transitioning to independence from Great Britain. Independence occurred on January 4, 1948.

U Nu maintained civilian political leadership of the central government until the military (*Tatmadaw*) took control in a 1962 coup. The power vacuum produced by Aung San's death accelerated political and ethnic fighting that was complicated by corruption and stagnant economic circumstances. Consequently the military played an increasingly important role in domestic governmental activities. In foreign policy the nation took a non-aligned position, keeping on good terms with both sides of the emerging Cold War. At home the Nu administration put forth an economic initiative known as the *Pyidawtha Plan*. Launched in 1952, it sought to balance tradition and modernization while pursuing national development and international involvement. It was a model for the "small is beautiful" concept popularized outside of Burma as Buddhist economics. Nonetheless it tended to be state-directed economics whose benefits would be seen in social welfare programs.

But by 1956 Nu's lethargic economic program combined with ongoing insurgencies brought the military under General Ne Win (1911–2002) closer to power, and in 1962 what had been informal military direction had become actual military government. The coup that ousted U Nu initially had supporters and opponents across the political spectrum. But gradually many of the supporters turned against the government. The program, labeled "The Burmese Way to Socialism," was launched in April 1962 and managed by the military's Burmese Socialist Programme Party (BSPP). This "Burmese Way" would approximate Buddhist socialism with modern secular characteristics, not all that different in concept from U Nu's policies. But it imposed more extensive restrictions on people's behavior.

By 1987 economic conditions had so deteriorated that the government launched a new economic policy with some market features. By then Ne Win had remained in power in various capacities until August 8, 1988, when popular protests known as the 8888 Uprisings forced him out. The 8888 Uprisings, or People Power Uprising, jolted the military leadership, which scrambled to hold on to power. Still directing the affairs of state from behind the scenes, Ne Win designed a new organization with new leadership and policies to deal with new domestic circumstances. The generals henceforth discarded former isolationist policies, shed numerous socialist programs, held elections, but attempted to maintain the military's political domination. This amounted to a political high-wire balancing act, but given major global political upheavals in the 1980s—in the Philippines and Vietnam in 1986, South Korea and Taiwan in 1987, Burma itself in 1988, China and Eastern Europe in 1989, as well as India, Russia, Mongolia, and Central Asia in 1991—ongoing but very plodding reform seemed to be the only alternative to the complete loss of power by the *Tatmadaw*.

The BSPP had failed not only in the eyes of the people but as well in the thinking of the military leadership. The military created the State Law and Order Restoration Council (SLORC) and later the State Peace and Development Council (SPDC). The SLORC, designed as an organization to restore order, existed from September 1988 to November 1997. The temporary SPDC consisted of several senior generals, most of them a better-educated generation of leaders who wanted to formulate better measures to contain popular discontent and new economic and political policies that would minimize many of the causes of political discontent. In September 1988 the generals promptly legalized political parties (more than 200) and promised early elections, which took place in May 1990. In July 1989 the SPDC approved the change of name for the country from Burma to Myanmar, a tip of the hat to the dozens of non-Burman minorities inhabiting the country.

A guarded optimism suggested that the popular vote would advance the nation's interests by removing the military government. By the time of the election, nearly 100 political parties had fielded candidates, but Aung San Suu Kyi and what became the National League for Democracy (NLD) won the hearts of Myanmar's people, capturing 392 of the 479 seats in Parliament. In July the government declared martial law, thus negating both the constitution and election results, and soon placing Aung San Suu Kyi under house arrest. SLORC went out of business in 1997, replaced by the SPDC, composed of newly minted senior generals in the *Tatmadaw*. Nonetheless, owing to growing unpopularity of de facto military rule and economic stagnation as evidenced by protests and uprisings, military rule (in theory) came to an end in March 2011. By then elections put NLD people in Parliament, and in 2012 Aung San Suu Kyi won a seat in a by-election. By March 2018, with the resignation of President Htin Kyaw, Aung San Suu Kyi had become the de facto ruler of Myanmar.

Suu Kyi inherited a nation attempting to transition from misguided and brutal military regimes to parliamentary democracy, from ill-advised social and economic isolation to more active participation in the global economy, and from multiethnic tribalism to more tolerant ethnic and religious social relations. Today, the military grip on politics is receding and an evolving civilian rule appears to be authentic. Myanmar's entrance into the globalized world also looks to be progressing well, though a modernizing economy does create some domestic disturbance. The country's chief challenges will be foreign culture and international politics, encounters that post-independence

Aung San Suu Kyi (1945–). *Source:* Drn/Getty Images.

Myanmar largely avoided by its isolationist agenda. Suu Kyi and parliamentary government are in the midst of a massive ethnic disaster in the case of the Rohingya Muslims. Suu Kyi's father seemed to have the leadership qualities in colonialism's final days to bring about ethnic harmony. Will his daughter?

British Malaya to the Federation of Malaysia

Malaysia's journey from colony to nation encountered numerous obstacles, including ethnic animosity, a serious (chiefly ethnic Chinese) rebellion of more than a decade, political struggles based largely on ethnicity, economic development issues with ethnic overtones, and the advent of terrorism affecting internal and foreign affairs. Ethnic strains existed in Malaya before, during, and after British rule. The most evident and important of these tensions have occurred between the majority-Muslim Malays (more than 50% of today's population, often referred to as *bumiputera* or sons of the soil, as are indigenous peoples) and the largely Buddhist or Confucian Chinese (roughly 25%). Other groups that tend not to be Muslim and that have issues with majority Malays are Hindu Indian (7%), and indigenous peoples who belong to Christian and other religions (about 15%).

Racial and cultural issues have divided the inhabitants of today's Malaysia, just as they did during British colonial rule. These divisions led to a very rocky nation-building start for postwar Malaya. Soon civil war (the Emergency, 1948–1960), a secession of Singapore from Malaysia (1965), and race riots (1969) threatened to tear the country apart. By 1970 Malays, largely through United Malays National Organization (UMNO), took control of an increasingly strong central government and created institutions that favored ethnic Malays. UMNO also presided over strong economic development under Mahathir Mohamad during the last two decades of the twentieth century. Tensions remain among the various ethnicities, so much so that the country's political, economic, and social concerns are still considered primarily in terms of race and ethnicity. Nonetheless, typically differences now get resolved within an accepted political process, a successful if often flawed process that has allowed the country to devote more attention to economic and social development. Ethnic relations have improved; a stronger national identity has advanced among most of the citizenry; successful economic development has brought the country greater prosperity; political conduct, while not without venality, has allowed capable leadership to emerge; and terrorism, though present in domestic and international organizations, has been largely kept in check. As a result, Malaysia has entered the second decade of the twenty-first century a plausible if still shaky Asian success story.

Decolonization, the Emergency, Independence, and State Formation, 1945–1970

When World War II ended, a weakened Britain had decided progressively to divest itself of an empire it could no longer afford or administer. The war also intensified strains between Malays who had cooperated with the Japanese during the occupation and the ethnic Chinese who had resisted the Japanese military. When London attempted to consolidate the various parts of British Malaya into the British-administered Malayan Union on April 1, 1946, the Malays resisted. They opposed the Union partly because the powers of the several sultans in the numerous Malay states had been substantially removed, and partly since the Union provided for a liberal citizenship requirement, making it easy for ethnic Chinese and Indians to gain citizenship, which conceivably meant a Malay-minority Union. The immediate result was the establishment of UMNO, which was formed a month before the Union came into being. Most Chinese liked the Union arrangements, particularly the Chinese Communist Party of Malaya. That put Britain in an awkward position of being supported by communists in the early Cold War years, and London began to consider other political arrangements for its colony. Thus emerged the Federation of Malaya on February 1, 1948. The Federation gave the states making up the Union greater controls over its inhabitants. This the Chinese and Indians did not like as it would more likely place most of them under Malay local government control.

Four months later civil war broke out—the Emergency, which produced more than 10,000 deaths—between the British and the Communist Party of Malaya plus its military unit, the Malayan Races Liberation Army (MRLA). Although London experienced several setbacks early on, by 1950 British forces and the Malay people began to check the insurgency. Part of the counterinsurgency's success was due to the lack of support for the communists, including minimal ethnic Chinese backing. The insurgents obtained little material aid from beyond Malaya, while the British had the help of the Royal Australian Air Force. The British also successfully isolated the insurgents from indigenous popular or material aid, while they inflicted slight casualties on the local population by minimizing the use of artillery and aerial bombing. Moreover, the British had promised independence in the immediate future, further winning "the hearts and minds" of the people. At the same time, on the political front the UMNO formed what has been termed the Alliance (*Perikantan*), a coalition including the Malayan Chinese Association and the Malayan Indian Congress. The Alliance worked out a consensus on a constitution under which independent Malaya would operate.

With the Emergency successfully winding down, independence officially became a reality on August 31, 1957. The new country—still called the Federation of Malaya—became a constitutional monarchy that contained 11 Malay states, all on the Malay Peninsula. The ceremonial king

(*Yang ti-Pertuan Agong*) was chosen by (and from) the nine hereditary sultans of the peninsular Malay states, while the prime minister, elected by the lower house of Parliament, served as the head of government. The constitution made Islam the state religion but allowed for freedom of religion, favored Malays over other ethnicities, and specified Malay and English as the official languages. Singapore did not get included because of its large ethnic Chinese population (which concerned the Malays), its reputation for radical politics (which concerned both Malays and the British), and the possibility that the port of Singapore would fall to communism if the insurgency succeeded (which concerned the British and the West). However by the early 1960s Malaya began to consider adding new territories, all former or current British territories, to form the nation of Malaysia. These included Singapore, Brunei, Sabah (British North Borneo), and Sarawak, the latter three on the island of Borneo as Malaya called it, Kalimantan as Indonesia referred to it. Indeed a struggle between those two nations, known as the Confrontation or *Konfrontasi*, hastened the creation of Malaysia, though without the addition of oil-rich Brunei, which remained a British protectorate until 1984. Singapore opted out of the Malaysian Federation and became an independent state on August 9, 1965.

Even without the large ethnic Chinese population of Singapore, Malaysia continued to experience cultural clashes. And these clashes always developed into political struggles, between the Chinese and Malays to be sure, but also between rival Malays. In the May 1969 elections, the Alliance coalition won but with a declining portion of the vote. Its chief rival, the largely Chinese Democratic Action Party (DAP), had made a strong showing calling for an end to the special constitutional position of the Malays. As DAP supporters demonstrated in Kuala Lumpur, fighting erupted between the demonstrators and Malays. The street battles lasted until late July; several hundred to perhaps 2000 people (mainly Chinese and Indians) were killed, with hundreds more injured; and the government declared a state of emergency that lasted until November 2011. But the Kuala Lumpur riots also exposed a rift between Malays, particularly Tunku Abdul Rahman (1903–1990), a founding member of UMNO and independent Malaya's first prime minister, and Mahathir Mohamad (1925–present), a challenger who would later serve as Malaysia's prime minister from 1981 to 2003. Tunku (a princely title generally used in reference to Abdul Rahman) desired to integrate ethnic Chinese into Malay society, while Mahathir sought to promote ethnic Malay interests. Although Mahathir was ejected from UMNO, in the long run he emerged triumphant. Tunku resigned his premiership while Mahathir's amended New Economic Policy, designed to mollify and favor Malays, progressively became the nation's path to the future. Challenges to Malay-first or any other government policy became cause for arrest, and such measures applied to members of Parliament as well.

UMNO, the New Economic Policy, and Mahathir Mohamad, 1970–2003

Mahathir Mohamad has dominated or substantially influenced Malaysian politics for the past four decades. Mahathir had become a seasoned politician before he became prime minister in 1981. As a student he wrote articles dealing with current events for school publications as well as for the *Straits Times*, was a member of the Muslim Society, and in 1946 joined UMNO. After obtaining his medical degree in 1953, he served as a physician initially for the government and later in private practice. Mahathir was elected to Parliament in 1964, lost his bid for reelection in 1969, and soon after was expelled from UMNO for labeling Prime Minister Tunku Abdul Rahman soft on the Chinese and indifferent to the plight of the Malays. In the wake of the 1969 Kuala Lumpur race riots, Mahathir took this argument and expanded it to explain the Malay race's lack of success in its homeland compared to Chinese and Indians in *The Malay Dilemma* (1970). The dilemma involved choosing either to promote Malaysia's quickest path to economic growth via ethnic Chinese and Indian entrepreneurship at the expense of the Malay population, or to forego maximum economic development in exchange for bringing the Malays up to rough parity with the Chinese and Indians. The book put forth a new program, a revised and upgraded New Economic Policy. This involved affirmative action—which by 1971 would require that 30% of all hires in new businesses be *bumiputera*—that would bring Malays into near equivalence with non-Malays, at which point racial antagonisms would wane. He remained in political exile only briefly, rejoining UMNO in 1972, winning reelection to Parliament in 1974, becoming a vice president of UMNO in 1975, and serving as deputy prime minister from 1978 to 1981. During his tenure as prime minister (1981–2003), he provided political stability at the top and transformed Malaysia's economy and society, but he also engaged in reprehensible political activities at home and stirred up a hornet's nest of controversy with his racist and outlandish rhetoric regarding Chinese, Indians, and Jews.

Mahathir Mohamad after his 2018 election victory. *Source:* MANAN VATSYAYANA/Getty Images.

Mahathir began his tenure as prime minister with an agenda to transform Malaysia politically, economically, and socially. This meant reducing the political power of both the sultans in their states as well as the *Yang ti-Pertuan Agong*, the sultan serving as head of state who had the power to declare (or not) a state of emergency. This Mahathir did by constitutional amendment, which now gave emergency declaration powers to the prime minister. Economically, he promoted the modernization of Malaysia by "looking east," that is, favoring Asian models of development based on "Asian values." This particularly meant the Japanese model, which by the 1980s had apparently put Japan on the road to becoming the strongest economy in the world. This model called for close cooperation between business and government. It also resulted in the privatizing of many government enterprises and the creation of value-added service and manufacturing industries—banking, electronics, chemical, textile, and machinery—to produce new products for export. Income from these products would be supplemented by the export of more traditional items such as natural resources and agricultural products. This called for the expansion of educational facilities and the upgrading of communication and transportation systems. But the process of modernization substantially meant the social mobility and economic betterment of the majority Malays through affirmative action. The *bumiputera* received special consideration for government jobs, housing, and educational positions; many government enterprises were privatized in a way that gave *bumiputera* and UMNO cronies priority in ownership and staffing; and government public works projects tended to favor ethnic Malays.

By the mid-1980s, however, considerable political opposition from both old challengers beyond UMNO and new rivals within the party began to question the substance and style of the perplexing prime minister's policies and oratory. Tengku Razaleigh Hamzah challenged and nearly deposed Mahathir as UMNO party leader in 1987. The next year Mahathir engineered the dismissal of the president of the Supreme Court for an unfavorable court decision regarding UMNO political infighting; and in 1996 another member of that judicial body was sacked for investigating political cronyism in UMNO. In 1998 Dr. M, as Mahathir was often called, then turned on his likely heir apparent, Deputy Prime Minister Anwar Ibrahim (1947–present). Anwar was charged—most believe falsely—with corruption and sodomy, convicted, and ended up in prison; his sentence for corruption ended in 2004, and that year a court overturned his sodomy conviction; he was again arrested in 2008—while running for a seat in Parliament, which he won—on new sodomy charges and acquitted in 2012, when he was again arrested, this time for illegal assembly. Anwar presented a challenge to Mahathir. He was popular, had been labeled "Asian of the Year" by *Newsweek*, and came to oppose affirmative action and other aspects of Mahathir's economic program. Mahathir also cracked down on the media and opposition parties and groups. He often utilized the Internal Security Act of 1960 and the Police Act of 1967, which allow for preventive detention and other measures those in power deem necessary to maintain harmony (that is, typically to silence or bully critics of the government).

While serving as prime minister and after his official retirement, Mahathir also became associated with numerous boondoggles, gaffes, as well as purposeful offensive comments. He promoted speculations by the nation's central bank (Bank Negara Malaysia) in the early 1990s that lost more than US$6 billion; backed his nation's (abortive) attempt to corner the market on tin in the early 1980s; sponsored the Perwaja Steel Company, which failed; and supported the Bakun Dam project, which also failed. Mahathir moreover attacked nearly anything or anyone he disliked. Malays as a people did not live up to his competitive standards, and his two successors as prime minister have occasionally been on the receiving side of Mahathir's criticisms. He criticized India for retarding its economic growth by being democratic instead of autocratic. Western values and institutions, especially the International Monetary Fund, received Dr. M's censure. Jews came in for his most frenzied bitterness, accusing them and Israel of numerous high crimes (manipulating global politics and finance) and misdemeanors (hooked noses), with financier George Soros singled out as the chief culprit.

Nonetheless, Mahathir survived the challenges of domestic politics (without launching purge trials, gulags, or extermination campaigns) and generally worked well with the outside world. He overcame political rivals, ongoing heart problems, his bad policy choices, and the Asian economic downturn of 1997. Abroad he condemned al Qaeda's attack on the United States (though he criticized the American war on terror), cooperated with Washington in counterterrorism efforts, kept radical Islam in check at home, and managed a fruitful modernization program within a Muslim society. Indeed, he is typically referred to as the father of the country's transformation. At the same time as he launched secular modernization goals, Mahathir established Islam as the state religion of Malaysia in 2001. That is to say, he successfully balanced hazardous domestic and foreign issues without notably compromising his goals for the nation.

Malaysia since Mahathir's Departure and His Return, 2003–2019

Politically, post–World War II Malaysia has been dominated by the UMNO, usually in coalition with other parties. Between 1951 and 1973, The Alliance was the name of that coalition; after 1973 it has been the National Front or *Barisan Nasional*. Until 2003, two individuals dominated the Malaysian political scene by heading the coalitions and developing the nation's agenda: Tunku Abdul Rahman and Mahathir Mohamad. Since then political leadership has become less reliant on a charismatic personality, which is to say leadership decisions are becoming group decisions instead of individual ones. The struggle for political leadership has also become more competitive among the coalitions, as new parties, alliances, and nongovernmental organizations emerge to challenge the ruling party.

Deputy Prime Minister Abdullah Ahmad Badawi (1939–2010), an Islamic scholar, succeeded Mahathir as prime minister in October 2003 with Dr. M's blessings. Elections early the following year produced a major victory for the National Front, but numerous problems faced the Abdullah government. The 2004 tsunami killed dozens and damaged coastal housing and port facilities, while large-scale flooding hit the country in 2006 and 2007. The global economic downturn of 2008–2009 produced a decline in the export sector, but the strong domestic financial and commercial sectors kept the nation from experiencing major recession. An ongoing illegal immigration (mainly Indonesians) issue has produced political opposition to what is considered lax enforcement of laws. The illegals are viewed as possible terrorists, common criminals, or potential job takers, and the government has regularly instituted apparent deportation campaigns. Anwar Ibrahim did not go away. When he was let out of jail in 2004, it was viewed as an indication of political liberalization. Since then Anwar has been organizing to challenge the National Front with his People's Alliance (*Pakatan Rakyat*, or PR), but his re-arrest in 2008 for sodomy has revived charges of political corruption at the highest levels. Economically Abdullah cut back on programs Mahathir had promoted while focusing more of the government's economic attention to agriculture and the environment, especially the rainforests of Borneo, while steering the nation through the global economic slump. Abdullah remained prime minister after UMNO's March 2008 election victory, even though the National Front lost its two-thirds majority in Parliament, largely as a result of the electoral victories of Anwar Ibrahim and his People's Alliance. Nonetheless he resigned his position in April 2009, by which time Mahathir, UMNO leadership, and a good part of the population had called for him to step down.

Mohd Najib bin Abdul Razak (1953–present), the son of Malaysia's second Prime Minister Abdul Razak Hussein, followed Abdullah as prime minister. Najib, who was first elected to Parliament in 1976, has served in many government ministries since the 1970s. When he came to office in 2009, Najib indicated that he wanted to bring the country together. He began by freeing several people jailed under the Internal Security Act, lifting the prohibition on some newspapers, and promoting the 1Malaysia movement designed to put Malaysia ahead of ethnic and religious divisions. Economically Najib replaced the New Economic Policy by launching the New Economic Model for Malaysia in March 2010.[2] It is part of a larger, more comprehensive Economic Transformation Programme that involves (1) People First, Performance Now—a 1Malaysia focus on national unity, economic growth for all, and an efficient, results-oriented government; (2) Government

---

2 In 1991 Prime Minister Mahathir Mohamad launched Vision 2020, designed to elevate Malaysia to little dragon or tiger developmental status. It involved the main points of the New Economic Policy and the New Economic Model, with focus on creating high-value-added goods and services.

Transformation Program—designed to create a more efficient government, as well as less crime and corruption and better education and infrastructure in both countryside and city; (3) the New Economic Model; and (4) the Tenth Malaysia Plan—which prioritizes key result areas of the economy. The New Economic Model aims to improve the living standards of Malaysians by 2020 through more privatization, less emphasis on affirmative action, and greater stress on wealth creation policies. The government maintains that Malaysia is living in a global economy and needs to remain an open and friendly environment for business to remain competitive. The country needs to create more high-skill jobs, which require high-talent citizens and will create high-salary employees. The gap between rich and poor can best be narrowed not by government boondoggles or affirmative action but through the above-mentioned wealth creation reforms.[3] Critics complain that ethnic Malays and poorer people will suffer, Anwar Ibrahim argues that the program is all style and no substance, while others contend that it merely represents Najib's version of the New Economic Policy with a different label.

While Malaysia continues to make robust progress on the economic front, its political process and ethnic advancements remain less energetic. The National Front is losing popularity as is UMNO, and though not in much danger of losing the election that was originally scheduled for 2012 and postponed until May 2013, the chances of regaining the two-thirds majority the National Front lost in 2008 were slim. Rallies in the spring of 2012 by *Bersih* ("clean") organizations promoting cleaner government, especially a fairer electoral system, have produced large demonstrations and in response large government attempts—beatings and jailing—to prevent such rallies. Meanwhile Anwar Ibrahim prepared for the election that he hoped would make him the next prime minister. At the same time, ethnic Chinese support for the National Front seems to be ebbing, which promises trouble for the ruling government on at least two counts. First, fewer Chinese will vote for Najib and the National Front. Second and less obvious but in the long run more significant, ethnic Chinese are leaving Malaysia for greener pastures. The affirmative action policies—even though somewhat diluted—favoring Malays in conjunction with cronyism and corruption make neighboring Singapore and other locations look increasingly attractive. Such a brain drain would severely weaken Malaysia's ability to achieve its economic development plans. Nonetheless, Malaysia has the luxury—or at least a medium-sized bonus—of a relatively peaceful international environment, enabling it to focus more on domestic issues.

The 2013 general elections returned Prime Minister Najib Razak to office, dashing again the hopes of Ibrahim. Nonetheless, ongoing corruption in the Razak administration brought former Prime Minister Mahathir Mohamad out of retirement. The 2018 general election put 92-year-old Mahathir Mohamad back in control of the country, with the suggestion that he would step down before the next election in favor of Anwar Ibrahim, his one-time ally, one-time enemy, and now evidently heir apparent.

Colonial Singapore to Republic of Singapore

The defeat of Japan returned Singapore to British control. During the following two decades before the creation of the Republic of Singapore in 1965, Singapore underwent several political changes. It had been a part of the Straits Settlements since 1826, then the Straits Settlements Crown Colony

---

3 The entire New Economic Model for Malaysia can be view online at the *Business Times* website: http://www. btimes.com.my/Current_News/BTIMES/Econ2007_pdf/New%20Economic%20Model.

since 1867; was a Singapore Crown Colony since 1946; by 1959 became a self-governing Crown Colony; in 1963 was a part of the newly created Malaysia; and emerged in 1965 as the Republic of Singapore. Since then the island nation (one main island and about 50 smaller islands) of five million people has been governed only by the People's Action Party, formed in 1954 by British-educated Lee Kuan Yew (1923–2015), who became the country's first prime minister. Singapore's government is headed by the prime minister, elected by a unicameral Parliament historically composed of fewer than six opposition party members in a body that has contained 79–87 seats. Since its creation the city-state/nation-state has arisen to be one of Asia's successful little tigers, and most claim this is due to Lee Kuan Yew's wise economic policies, which drew on a Singapore variation of market economics and the "Asian values" of its citizens. This success occurred in no small part, it is also claimed, because of Lee's "soft authoritarian" political guidance, roughly the same modernization model that accounted for South Korea's and Taiwan's earlier economic take-offs. Upon Lee's retirement from official leadership in 1990, he has remained behind the scenes, turning formal power over to his protégés, Goh Chok Tong and then his eldest son, Lee Hsien Loong. Singapore remains the most successful of the Southeast Asian nations economically, but by 2012 it has yet to experience a real transfer of political power. Stay tuned.

Lee Kuan Yew and the Rise of Independent Singapore, 1945–1965

When World War II ended, Singapore had experienced not only death and destruction, but also the presence of armed indigenous organizations that had been supported by either the Allies or the Japanese. In September 1945 the British Military Administration, under Lord Louis Mountbatten, became the interim government of Malaya until the formation of the Malay Union in April 1946. At that time the Singapore Crown Colony was also formed, creating a colonial bureaucracy administered by the British and by 1948 providing some local participation in government affairs. The appointed governor and an Executive Council clearly represented London's interests, while local interests got a hearing through the Legislative Council. It consisted of 22 members, only six of which were elected. Moreover, the governor could veto much of what the Legislative Council did or proposed. Postwar Asian revolutionary movements, including the Emergency in Malaya, frightened colonial and newly independent national governments attempting to reestablish order. While radical organizations persisted on the Malay Peninsula, the British fairly successfully neutralized such movements in Singapore. The colonial authorities applied the State of Emergency to Singapore, where the Malayan Communist Party represented the only significant threat to British control. But that threat receded by the late 1950s, as the British came closer to approving self-government in the colony and as the communist insurgency in neighboring Malaya collapsed.

During the decade and a half after the war, local individuals and organizations dedicated to bringing about Singapore's independence appeared and typically worked within British political limitations. Lee Kuan Yew (1923–2015) emerged as the leading political actor, while the two most important institutions were the Progressive Party and the People's Action Party (PAP). The moderate Progressive Party, created in 1947, did well during the late 1940s and early 1950s, handily winning the 1948 and 1951 elections. It was well organized and favored the British position of gradual change at a time when the insurgents put forth a basically revolutionary alternative. As Chinese demands for a greater voice in the governing of the island developed, the British created the (Sir George William) Rendel Constitutional Commission in November 1953 to consider how best to afford a larger role for the local population. The Rendel Constitution, which became operational in 1955, provided for a Legislative Council of 32 seats, 25 of which were chosen by vote.

Thus began the ascendancy of the more radical but not revolutionary PAP, created in 1954 and headed by lawyer Lee Kuan Yew, then known as Harry Lee. Singapore voters liked the more aggressive positions of PAP, particularly the demand for timely independence. Although the PAP won only three seats in 1955, it would take control of the government four years later. PAP had pushed hard for Singapore self-government and the British responded with the State of Singapore Act in 1958, allowing for self-government in 1959. The elections that year gave PAP an overwhelming victory and made Lee Kuan Yew the prime minister. The PAP set up the conditions that would enable Singapore to join what would soon become the nation of Malaysia. Thus Malay became the official language, while radicals and communists in the PAP were purged. In 1963 Singapore joined Malaysia as an autonomous state but problems with the union soon developed. The most important source of Singapore's discontent was the affirmative action policies of Malaysia, which favored ethnic Malays and put Chinese at a disadvantage for jobs and education. Ultimately Malaysia's Tunku Abdul Rahman and his UMNO expelled Singapore, while Singapore's Lee Kuan Yew and his PAP withdrew from Malaysia. The divorce occurred on August 9, 1965, when the Republic of Singapore was born.

Lee Kuan Yew, Cosmopolitanism, and the Soft Authoritarian Model of Development, 1965–1990

Singapore's secession from Malaysia did immediately produce a unified nation. Roughly 15% of the population was Malay while another 10% was Indian. Though the Chinese accounted for nearly 75% of the island's citizens, divisions had long existed within that majority community. One faction favored creating a Chinese state free from its colonial past. Thus Chinese needed to become the dominant language of government and education, and the creation of Chinese-language Nanyang University in 1955 was meant to serve that end. Prime Minister Lee Kuan Yew and other leaders took a more inclusive approach, fearing the same kind of ethnic violence that had disrupted Malaysia over the decades would plague Singapore if ethnic Malays and Indians resisted Sinification. Moreover, by the government adopting English as the chief language, Singaporeans would possess a significant advantage in the global economy where English remains the primary language of international discourse. Lee's position won the day, as exemplified by the incorporation of Nanyang University into the English-language National University of Singapore. Singapore became a founding member of the Association of Southeast Asian Nations (ASEAN) in 1967.[4] It belongs to the United Nations as well as numerous regional and international organizations, and has set up diplomatic missions around the world. Its military, created and trained by the Israel Defense Force, is one of the best in Southeast Asia. In brief, Lee's vision of Singapore has sought to promote a more cosmopolitan society at home and a security-conscious people whose nation is afloat in regionally and globally troubled waters.

Singapore began its nation building in a Cold War climate where the best protection against the threats to its security tended to be intelligent and stable government. Consistent political management facilitated the formation of a credible national defense, a sensible foreign policy, and a practical economic development program. In Lee Kuan Yew's mind, intelligent and stable government meant that he and his PAP would oversee the nation's development. The PAP

---

4 It was formed to promote cohesion among nations in the region against the threat of communist insurrections, but has since the end of the Vietnam War become an organization to promote the economic interests and international safety of its 10 member states.

has ruled Singapore since 1959; no opposition candidate to Parliament won a seat until 1981, and he was eventually fined and jailed for a minor (and possibly nonexistent) campaign irregularity. A few other opposition candidates have won seats since then, but Singapore remains a one-party state. Under PAP leadership, the government also has controlled much of the economic and social life of the people. Welfare, housing, education, and organized labor are all controlled by the government. The government also attempts to regulate the people's ethics by promoting values that emerge from a patriarchal family, hard work, and respect for education—basically Confucian values. These and other "soft authoritarian" practices, Lee argued, enabled Singapore to become one of the world's leaders in per capita income when his term as prime minister ended in 1990. Yet with all this government intervention in people's lives, Singapore has regularly been rated as one of the freest environments in which to operate economically.

Singapore's rapid economic development has followed a familiar path to prosperity since World War II. Japan, South Korea, Taiwan, and Hong Kong all launched their economic "miracles" in a politically authoritarian environment a decade or so before Singapore. Until 1952, Japan lived under American occupation in which the government guided policies, South Korea and Taiwan began under dictatorships that eventually gave way to democracies in 1987, and the British oversaw colonial Hong Kong until 1997. Each culture reflected centuries of Confucian thinking and behavior that stressed the family unit, hard work, and education. And each developed to the maximum its human capital—its citizens—since each physical environment provided few natural advantages. Several freedoms accounted for Singapore's (and other nations') economic growth. Freedom from foreign invasion increased as Singapore developed its military capabilities, which was fortified with certain or implicit American military protection of the island (significant after the British military departed Singapore in 1971). And the sea lanes of Asia, on which Singapore depended for its economic health, remained open to commerce because of the American Navy, which has sea and air port rights in the island nation. Singapore allowed foreign investment, which is usually accompanied by the transfer of cutting-edge technology. Free trade in one of the world's largest ports also encouraged economic development, as did law and order, a highly educated citizenry, a relatively corruption-free business atmosphere, and an increasingly clean and attractive physical environment. And, as with the other "little dragons," Singapore became a model for nations beginning or revising their modernization programs, with China, Indonesia, Vietnam, and Cambodia being prime Asian examples. While Lee does not maintain that the Confucian model of development will remain a successful approach in the future, he does have confidence that what he calls the cultural basics will enable Singapore to adjust.

Singapore in Transition, 1990–2019

Lee Kuan Yew also successfully prepared for the inevitable transition of power as he approached his 70s. He wanted to insure that Singapore remained a society committed to observing Confucian values, the essential resources needed to prevent reverting to careless or corrupt thinking and behavior. In a 1994 interview with Fareed Zakaria, Lee summed up his thinking about the part government plays and the role of traditional values in modern Singapore. "In the West, especially after World War II, the government came to be seen as so successful that it could fulfill all the obligations that in less modern societies are fulfilled by the family." But when government displaces the family, the social fabric will begin to suffer as the nurturing family gives way to an impersonal bureaucracy and individual irresponsibility.

The government can create a setting in which people can live happily and succeed and express themselves, but finally it is what people do with their lives that determines economic success or failure. Again, we were fortunate we had this [Confucian] cultural backdrop, the belief in thrift, hard work, filial piety and loyalty in the extended family, and, most of all, the respect for scholarship and learning.[5]

He chose two protégés who embraced a modern Confucian attitude. Goh Chok Tong (1941–present) served as prime minister from 1990 to 2004. Goh has been viewed as a leadership bridge between Lee the father and his son, Lee Hsien Loong (1952–present). Lee the younger has governed as prime minister since 2004. Both successors shared the elder Lee's political and social agenda, both had received British and American educations, and both apprenticed in government ministries and in party and electoral politics. Still, the elder Lee remained in the background as "Senior Minister" and later as "Mentor Minister" until his definite (?) retirement in 2011 at age 88. He died in 2015. Politically the PAP reigns practically unchallenged, while economically Singapore weathered the 1997 Asian Contagion as well as the 2009 global downturn and remains a model of prosperity. If one ignores government infringement of individual rights, Singapore has created an impressive record. Lee Hsien Loong remains Singapore's leader in 2020, but the likelihood of an ongoing Lee dynasty seems unlikely, as major rifts exist within the founder's family.

Singapore skyline. *Source:* Iryna Rasko/Shutterstock.com.

---

5 Fareed Zakaria and Lee Kuan Yew, "Culture Is Destiny: A Conversation with Lee Kuan Yew," *Foreign Affairs* 73, no. 2(March–April 1994), pp. 113–114.

People's rights represent the one area where Singapore's image seems to suffer. Lee believes that a harmonious society needs to be created and maintained, and too much freedom threatens the social order. Thus excessive political freedom—that is, a meaningful political opposition—will likely hinder or undermine progress on the proper path to PAP's development program. Consequently opposition politicians have to consider the real possibility of going to jail, being sued, or both before they take a position contrary to the government's. Former Member of Parliament and Socialist Front Party member Chia Thye Poh spent more than two decades in jail without trial. He was arrested in 1966 for his involvement in demonstrations. J. B. Jeyaretnam of the Workers' Party won a seat in Parliament in 1981 and 1984, but was arrested and convicted in 1986 for election irregularities, a verdict that was finally overturned. Nonetheless he was sued by Lee Kuan Yew for libel and lost the suit. Chee Soon Juan, head of the Singapore Democratic Party, has been jailed for protesting and sued for defaming Lee Kuan Yew. Chee lost the suit and went bankrupt, unable to pay the fine. His bankruptcy has disqualified him from running for office. Chee has since gotten the money to pay his fines and will be eligible to run in future elections

Other politicians and media outlets unfriendly to the government often find themselves in civil court, while academics with undesirable points of view can kiss their tenure chances goodbye. In the view of Singapore's government, irresponsible commentary—that is, freedom of the press—needs to be restricted. Thus magazines such as the *Far Eastern Economic Review* have been banned, and newspapers like the *International Herald Tribune* have been sued, first in 1995 and later in 2010, for writing inflammatory articles about prominent politicians (that is, the Lee family). In 2007 the *Financial Times* apologized for writing a similar critical article dealing with "prominent politicians." Other media such as podcasts, video casts, websites, and blogs and motion pictures operate under strict government guidelines. Janet Jackson's song "Would You Mind" had to be "revised" before it could be sold in Singapore. An episode of the television show *Ally McBeal* was banned due to two women kissing. Such alternate lifestyles include homosexual acts, which are illegal, though the government seems to be "evolving" (Lee Kuan Yew's 1994 word) toward more openness on issues of sexual orientation. In the world of education, the case of Dr. Cherian George, an associate professor at Nanyang Technological University, has again raised the question of academic freedom in Singapore. He was denied tenure in 2013, ostensibly because of insufficient scholarly output but many argue due to George's writings and commentaries on provocative political issues in various media. Indeed, one of the external evaluators on George's tenure committee—in addition to hundreds of students who signed a petition objecting to the tenure denial and speaking of the teacher's sterling qualities—called George a "superstar." Will such controversies involving freedom of thought add to the country's "brain drain"?

Then there are social issues the rulers of Singapore promote and attack. Traditional family patterns get government reinforcement, while alternate family lifestyles—especially single-mother families—Lee Kuan Yew (and, for that matter, much of Singapore and East Asia) believes to be dysfunctional and best discouraged by positive government policies. Lee considers that education will enable women to understand the centrality of the traditional family. As well, education will enable women to be economically independent should it become necessary. Negative government policies, such as denying women pursuing unacceptable family lifestyles access to government housing and other benefits, are also available to discourage dysfunctional social lifestyles. Certain alternate religious beliefs, as well, will bring government suppression, as in the case of Jehovah's Witnesses—outlawed since 1972—which has produced jail time for some of their believers. Individual freedom requires individual responsibility, and Lee does not trust that such responsibility will occur in sufficient amounts—without government nudging—to keep society in a healthy condition.

Lee Kuan Yew and his successors have effectively guided Singapore through the complex network of international politics. Once the Cold War ended, the rise of China and the advent of terrorism presented a different set of problems for Singapore (and the rest of Asia). China's growing economic and military power by the end of the twentieth century has created fear of eventual Chinese supremacy in Asia. This has resulted in Singapore and most other Asian nations searching for countervailing forces, including nations as well as international and regional organizations. One such approach has been the development of closer relationships with each other (ASEAN, for example), and another is a warmer attitude toward Washington. America has been termed the most distant, most dominant, and yet least dangerous of Asian Pacific nations.

Terrorism presents another problem requiring international cooperation. Although not exclusively Islamic, terrorism has been associated with Muslim countries as well as nations with significant Muslim populations, which is to say most Asian nations. Muslim-majority Malaysia and Indonesia tend to be moderate, and they fear the rise of terrorist organizations in their midst. They are inclined to cooperate with global and regional anti-terrorist organizations and sympathetic neighboring nations, which harbor the same fears of death, disruption, and destruction commonly occurring in Afghanistan and much of the Middle East. Singapore's Muslim Malay population also reflects a more moderate approach to religious issues, but just to be sure, the government has taken a guiding, paternalistic approach—as it does in most other areas of Singapore's life. Thus the government stresses the importance of education in upgrading the Muslim community's quality of life, but the *madrassas* and their curricula and texts are overseen to minimize the kind of radical results evident in places like Pakistan.

Colonial Vietnam to Socialist Republic of Vietnam

As Japan realized that the war in the Pacific was a lost cause, it began to position itself for postwar Asia. Part of that positioning involved getting rid of Western colonial rule. In Vietnam this took the form of terminating the Matsuoka-Henri Agreement of August 1940 with the Vichy French government. Tokyo then granted Vietnam token independence from France on March 9, 1945, and appointed Bao Dai the nominal head of state. Japan proceeded to round up French troops and jail them. At the same time, those individuals and institutions that France had controlled in Vietnam now came under Japanese control, including Emperor Bao Dai. Meanwhile, the Viet Minh, which had organized during the war to resist both Japan and France, found itself in a position to claim legitimacy by the summer of 1945. When the Viet Minh occupied Saigon that August, it declared itself the provisional government of Vietnam. On August 28, Emperor Bao Dai turned over official power to the provisional government created by the Viet Minh. The very day Japan officially surrendered, September 2, Ho Chi Minh declared independence for the Democratic Republic of Vietnam in Hanoi.

The Cold War and the First Vietnam War, 1945–1954

When World War II ended, the Viet Minh and the French attempted to work out some agreement to make the transition to independence. Neither side likely agreed on what independence would involve. As it turned out, Vietnam and France soon realized that the future of Vietnam and the rest of French Indochina substantially rested in the hands of several other countries. The emerging Cold War and the onset of decolonization in Asia raised the important question of which way newly independent states would lean, toward America and its allies or to the Soviet Union and by

1949 Communist China and its supporters. In addition to anticolonial wars and their uncertain outcomes, the Cold War's Korean War (1950–1953) deepened anxieties in both the West and the Soviet Bloc about their future interests in Asia.

Increasingly the fighting that broke out by the end of 1946 between the French and the Viet Minh—the First Vietnam War—concerned the Cold War adversaries. Accordingly, the Soviets and later the Chinese supported the Viet Minh effort to oust the French, while America and its allies assisted the French. Cold War priorities slowly changed Franklin Roosevelt's and Harry Truman's anticolonial stance, and ultimately Washington felt obliged to support the French military effort until it collapsed at the Battle of Dien Bien Phu in the spring of 1954. That May the Geneva Conference divided Vietnam between Communist North Vietnam and non-Communist South Vietnam, the French began to depart, and the United States inaugurated what would become a two-decade effort to contain the spread of communism in Vietnam.

Divided Independent Vietnam, 1954–1975

To fill the power vacuum created by France's departure and hopefully to contain the Viet Minh expansion into the south, Washington hurried to find and support a suitable leader that could win the backing of the Vietnamese people. A few months after Geneva, America also formed the Southeast Asia Treaty Organization (SEATO), a military alliance composed of Asian and non-Asian nations allied to stop the spread of communism in Southeast Asia. China, in addition to having fallen under communist rule, was also viewed by America as the guiding force of Vietnamese communism. Should the Viet Minh conquer the south, it would only be a matter of time before the rest of Southeast Asia would fall to communist aggression, essentially under Beijing's dominance. From the Truman administration onward, this idea became known as the Domino Theory—one domino (i.e., nation) after another domino. Thus the American sense of urgency to find a non-communist Vietnamese nationalist who could—with Washington's military and economic aid and advice (the Truman Doctrine concept)—keep Ho Chi Minh's Viet Minh at bay. The person ultimately selected was Ngo Dinh Diem (1901–1963), a Catholic born in what was then North Vietnam.

Ho Chi Minh. *Source:* Hulton Archive/Getty Images.

Diem consolidated his power in his Republic of Vietnam with the help of Edward Lansdale, a CIA agent and American Air Force general. Lansdale had successfully directed a counterinsurgency effort in the Philippines against the Huks. He worked with Philippine politician Ramon Magsaysay, who became president and began to institute reform programs to win "the hearts and minds" of the people. Lansdale sought to repeat his Philippine success in Vietnam, working with Diem to overcome not just the communist Viet Minh but also gangsters and non-communist political rivals. Diem unexpectedly consolidated power through determination and by depending markedly on his family and on a million Catholic refugees who resettled in South Vietnam. In the short run, Diem became "Asia's Miracle Man" and gained greater support from American Presidents Dwight Eisenhower and John Kennedy.

Several factors brought about the downfall of Diem in 1963 and the introduction of American combat troops in 1965. The Viet Minh reorganized as the National Liberation Front (NLF) in 1960, designed to focus on the military liberation of the south from Diem and his American supporters. As well, growing discontent with Diem appeared from much of the South Vietnamese population. The non-communist southern elite had been shunted aside for government positions by northern Catholic refugees. Buddhists, who made up the vast majority of the population, increasingly viewed the Diem government as anti-Buddhism, leading to public protest demonstrations and self-immolations. The Strategic Hamlet Program was calculated to transfer peasants into hamlets where they and their crops would be protected from the Vietnamese Communists (Viet Cong, or VC) and their supporters. With mounting discontent, the Kennedy administration concluded that Diem and his family had to go. That intention was transmitted to the leadership of the South Vietnamese Army, which assassinated Diem three weeks before Kennedy was assassinated.

Diem's exit created a power vacuum in South Vietnam, while Kennedy's killing required America's new president, Lyndon Johnson, to deal with the political chaos in Saigon. As the power vacuum negatively affected the war effort against communists, Johnson decided to "go big," that is, to use American military superiority to rescue the ever-changing and shaky Saigon government. While Washington had deployed advisors who often engaged the communists, all presidents and most military leaders had opposed the commitment of combat forces; once Johnson made the decision, though, the military got on board. However, the military was divided about how to conduct the war so as not to draw in Beijing and Moscow, Hanoi's benefactors. As the war dragged on without significant progress, protests and an upcoming presidential election in America began Washington's drawdown, known as Vietnamization.

Increasingly the war would be fought by the South Vietnamese military, assisted by America. This policy originated with President Truman's containment policy, an essential part of which Johnson abandoned and presidential candidate Richard Nixon made central to his promise to end the Vietnam War. The Vietnamization program after 1968 worked well enough, with an improved South Vietnamese military performance and with nearly no American combat troops in Vietnam on the eve of Nixon's bid for reelection in 1972. Likely insuring Nixon's November victory at the polls was the signing of a temporary cease fire, which became the basis for the Paris Peace Accords, signed in January 1973. America withdrew with the promise to continue to provide material support for South Vietnam. However, the Watergate scandal eventually forced Nixon to resign and Congress to reduce to nearly nothing said material support. In April 1975, after the "decent interval" Nixon and his advisors hoped would elapse between America's withdrawal and Saigon's collapse, Hanoi entered Saigon and overthrew the remnants of the South Vietnam government. The country became geographically united.

Vietnam under Communism, 1975–2019

Hardliner Le Duan (1907–1986), de facto leader of North Vietnam after Ho Chi Minh's death in 1969, led Hanoi's unified government. After a brief political transition from wartime operations, the Socialist Republic of Vietnam emerged in July 1976. By that time numerous southerners were executed, jailed, reeducated, or sent to labor camps. Hundreds of thousands of others escaped, becoming "boat people" in search of a better life elsewhere. Reconstruction after decades of destruction became one of the chief aims of the new government. All of this required money and talent, and the bulk of the funds were designed to come from five-year plans, centrally directed economic activity that focused on agriculture. Much of the talent had fled, or remained but were deemed untrustworthy. The Second Five-Year Plan (1976–1980) centered on the collectivization of agriculture, but it and a subsequent plan proved woefully underachieving. By 1986 Le Duan had died and much of the revolutionary leadership passed from the scene, while a new generation of nation builders emerged to change the economic course of Vietnam.

Known as *Doi Moi*, it is sometimes referred to as "Socialism with Vietnamese Characteristics," a euphemism acknowledging a departure from socialism—though not from dictatorship. Indeed, the 1978 reforms in China under Deng Xiaoping and the 1985 *perestroika* and *glasnost* restructurings in the Soviet Union under Mikhail Gorbachev helped Vietnam make the transition. So too did the even earlier reforms that produced dynamic economies in the little dragons of South Korea, Taiwan, Hong Kong, and Singapore. Since Doi Moi was launched, Vietnam's economy has grown rapidly and improved the financial well-being of its people. The World Bank estimates that per capita income in Vietnam has increased from $100 annually in 1993 to $1130 by 2010, while the percentage of those in poverty has decreased from 58% in 1993 to 14.5% in 2008.

The more open attitude in Hanoi helped lead to the establishment of diplomatic relations with the United States in 1995, but this was no doubt also a result of the collapse of the Soviet Union, Hanoi's chief source of economic aid, and a consequence of China's rise. Since 2016 if not earlier, it seems, the party has been abandoning the idea of collective leadership and embracing China's Xi Jinping's consolidation of political power in the hands of one leader, in Vietnam's case Nguyen Phu Trong. He came to power in October 2018 with the death of President Tran Dai Quang. Trong now holds two crucial political posts, those being president as well as Communist Party general secretary. No political leader since Ho Chi Minh has held both positions at the same time.

Protectorate of Cambodia to Kingdom of Cambodia

In March 1945, just before Japan's surrender in September, Tokyo deposed what remained of the French colonial administrative system across Indochina, including Cambodia. King Norodom Sihanouk (1922–2012) declared Cambodian independence. That same March, Son Ngoc Thanh (1908–1977), an anti-French nationalist leader who joined with Japan, declared himself prime minister of Cambodia. When the French returned before year's end, they sought to root out as many nationalist individuals and organizations as possible. This included neutralizing Thanh, an opponent of Sihanouk, whom the French believed to be a more pliable nationalist. In the French Union, colonies and protectorates achieved some trappings of independence but not full freedom. By 1953, when Cambodia achieved its complete independence, the country had developed or expanded organizations designed to oust the French and build their nation. Thanh had created the anti-communist Khmer Serei or Free Khmer, while the Khmer Issarak or Independent Khmers pursued an anti-French leftist agenda. But all political activity occurred under the charismatic leadership of the monarchy under Sihanouk until his removal in 1970.

When American combat units entered the Vietnam conflict in 1965, Washington looked at Cambodia as a country supposedly neutral but actually unwilling and/or unable to dislodge the VC, who used Cambodia as a sanctuary. That year Sihanouk broke diplomatic relations with the United States, allowed the North Vietnamese to use a Cambodian port, and provided a de facto military sanctuary for the North Vietnamese on the South Vietnamese border. By 1969, America decided to turn combat operations in South Vietnam over to the Saigon military. Since the North Vietnamese and VC forces in Cambodia constituted an existential threat to the newly restructured Saigon Army, American forces attacked Communist Vietnamese forces in Cambodia in order to degrade their military capabilities. The following year Lon Nol (1913–1985), a military officer under the French and later the Cambodian Army's chief of staff, staged a coup against Sihanouk. At the time, Sihanouk was close to Beijing and aligned with his former enemy, the Communist Khmer Rouge headed by Saloth Sar, aka Pol Pot (1925–1998). Lon Nol reestablished diplomatic relations with the United States and turned the Cambodian army against both the North Vietnamese and the Khmer Rouge. But as Washington withdrew from Vietnam, and as the American Congress began cutting money and weaponry for military operations in Southeast Asia, Lon Nol's military campaigns faltered and ultimately failed. The Khmer Rouge entered Phnom Penh in April 1975.

Khmer Rouge Communism, the Killing Fields, and a New Beginning, 1975–2018

The Khmer Rouge emerged in the early 1960s as a radical insurgency with the idealistic goal of an agrarian utopia. While espousing socialist themes, it kept its communist platform and foreign connections secret until after coming to power. The Khmer Rouge traded on the notion that its agenda was native Khmer in origin, and that the purity of the Khmer people would ultimately overcome any obstacle. Upon taking Phnom Penh, the Khmer Rouge immediately began to depopulate the cities and send their inhabitants into the countryside to engage in agricultural labor. April 1975 began the year zero, a French Revolution concept when the Reign of Terror established the year 1, a removal of all oppressive ideas and institutions of the past. Anything feudal (traditional), foreign (e.g., western medicine), or religious (such as Buddhism) was removed from daily life. This allowed the government (in this case, the Khmer Rouge in 1975) to start from scratch, a blank slate on which the Khmer Rouge could establish a model, classless society. Pol Pot and his associates swept across the countryside, coming to and clearing cities, and establishing an unsustainable agrarian economy. Most of the million or more people who died by 1979 in the "Killing Fields" were executed, worked to death, or perished of malnutrition. Sadly, even the utopian ideal may have been simply a deceptive means by which Pol Pot could best consolidate political power.

As in the French Revolution, popular discontent with the regime in what was called Democratic Kampuchea weakened the regime, as did gross economic inefficiency as well as growing fractures in the Khmer Rouge leadership. Moreover by 1976 Cambodia became a battleground not only between the Khmer Rouge and the Cambodian people but also as another chapter in the ongoing Sino-Soviet dispute. The Khmer Rouge and its Chinese supporters formed one side of that dispute, while the Vietnamese army and its Soviet Russian backers shaped the other. After three years of growing tensions between the Khmer Rouge and Vietnam, Hanoi launched a full-scale attack on the Khmer Rouge in December 1978. Well over 100,000 Vietnamese soldiers soon routed the Khmer Rouge and quickly established the People's Republic of Kampuchea (PRK, later the State of Cambodia), a communist regime friendly to Vietnam. Under Hanoi's guidance, the PRK attempted to reestablish some kind of normalcy to Cambodia.

Skulls recovered from the Killing Fields. *Source:* Shaun Higson / Alamy Stock Photo.

The Vietnamese occupation and supervision of Cambodian affairs lasted until the final withdrawal of Hanoi's soldiers in 1989. The Khmer Rouge had not been exterminated, and an ongoing campaign continued. Tens of thousands of people attempted to return to their homes and search for loved ones. Several hundred thousand refugees made their way to Thailand to escape the horror and hunger in their homeland. Ongoing ineffective economic policies that Hanoi directed at home were also deployed in Cambodia and contributed to the country's sufferings. And the collapse of the Soviet Union, Vietnam's economic and technological benefactor, removed the funding for Vietnam's occupation as well as the financing and expertise for economic development in Vietnam and Cambodia. Into this improved but still fragile and dreadful setting came agreements from various domestic and foreign contending forces to allow the United Nations to oversee the Cambodian creation of governmental and social institutions as the first step in rebuilding a devastated nation.

A number of events in the 1990s put Cambodia on a path to peace and then, if not prosperity, at least improved economic circumstances. The UN Transitional Authority in Cambodia arrived in early 1992 with a mandate to deal with human rights issues, elections, governmental administration, law and order, refugees, and the nation's infrastructure. In 1993 an election involving several political parties resulted in the creation of a constituent assembly to draft a new constitution that year. The new document allows for the restoration of the monarchy under Norodom Sihanouk, though the king's powers are minimal. Nonetheless a royal party of sorts has become one of the two most important contenders for political power, Prince Norodom Rannaridh's FUNCINPAK. The other is the Cambodian People's Party under Hun Sen (1952–present), a former Khmer Rouge official who defected to the Vietnamese and served in Hanoi's State of Cambodia government. He has been prime minister of Cambodia from 1985 to 2020, under both the Vietnamese and the nation's new constitution. During his rule the Khmer Rouge were effectively eliminated, and most of its top leaders were put on trial; Pol Pot died in 1998 without coming to trial. Nation building has proceeded, and the country is now more stable than it has been in a half century. Nonetheless, serious problems remain: AIDS and other sexually transmitted diseases are prevalent, Phnom Penh has become a pedophile's destination, corruption is rampant, a major deficiency of electrical power weakens industrial and agricultural potential, and relations with Thailand remain tense.

Protectorate of Laos to Lao People's Democratic Republic

Historically what became a unified Laos in the twentieth century had been a territory whose frontiers changed and whose leaders came from the royalty of three kingdoms. These kingdoms often paid tribute to Vietnam or Siam, but when French annexation occurred in 1893, Paris created a unified administration whereby a French "resident" guided the policies of the remaining (after 1904) monarchy in Luang Prabang. France also set the Laotian frontiers with Siam, Cambodia, and Vietnam. At the conclusion of World War II, French rule returned to Laos, as with its other imperial holdings, with the intention of keeping those possessions.

Nationalist Developments, the Cold War, and Independence, 1945–1961

In March 1945 when Japan removed the façade of French rule, Crown Prince Sisavang Vatthana (1907–1978) and King Sisavang Vong (1885–1959), under pressure, declared independence. But by August the monarchy retracted the declaration; it wanted to resume its protectorate status with Paris's promise of freedom in the French Union. At the same time the nationalist movement *Lao Issara* or Free Lao declared independence and set up a government in Vientiane, minus the monarchy, with the support of the Viet Minh. By year's end, French troops had returned and with royal backing drove the *Lao Issara* out of Laos. Shortly thereafter Paris declared Laos a constitutional monarchy. Nonetheless until 1975, political battles in Laos would be fought between supporters of monarchy and opponents. And the Cold War divisions in the wider world also made their way into Laos, with the monarchy generally preferring a pro-Western or neutralist stance and the opponents pursuing a neutralist or pro-communist agenda. But members of the royal family could be found on both sides, given the numerous wives of the king and their male offspring half-brothers of the Crown Prince.

When Laos achieved its full independence in 1953, the political lines had been drawn fairly well. Out of the *Lao Issara*, which had disbanded in 1949, came the Pathet Lao, an armed insurgency in league with the Viet Minh and devoted to the ouster of the Royal Lao government. The principal royal participants were three princes: Prince Souvanna Phouma (1901–1984), a pro-Western, later neutralist supporter of the king; Prince Souphanouvong (1909–1995), a pro-communist leader of the Pathet Lao; and Prince Boun Oum (1912–1980), a staunchly pro-Western backer of the monarchy. As the war in Vietnam increasingly became an international affair, the North Vietnamese occupied more parts of Laos adjacent to Vietnam, creating the "Ho Chi Minh Trail" leading to South Vietnam. Russia and China on the one hand came to provide aid to the Pathet Lao, while America and its allies attempted to assist non-communist forces in Laos from neighboring Thailand.

Coalition Governments and the Second Vietnam War, 1962–1975

Already unstable political conditions began to deteriorate markedly and rapidly by 1961. The North Vietnamese, who had been in Laos militarily since the end of World War II, began to accelerate the arming and training of the Pathet Lao. In 1959 Hanoi created Group 959 especially to supply the Pathet Lao (just as they had created Group 559 to supply the Viet Cong/National Liberation Front in South Vietnam). That is, Hanoi formed these groups to launch armed conflict that would result in the overthrow of the Royal Lao government in Vientiane and the South Vietnamese government in Saigon. Even greater turmoil ensued when an American-trained

Laotian army officer and heretofore supporter of the Royal Lao government, Kong Le (1934–2014), staged a coup d'état in August 1960 against the monarchy, charging it with being too pro-Western and consequently insufficiently nationalist. By that December Kong Le had been ousted by General Phoumi Nosavan (1920–1985), and the general favored Sisavang Vatthana, since 1959 the king. The Russians now supported Kong Le, the CIA could not control Phoumi Nosavan, and the Pathet Lao remained America's chief concern, while the war on the ground became increasingly unfavorable to Washington.

By this time the American commitment to Laos substantially increased, both materially and symbolically. From Udorn in northern Thailand, the CIA through its airline Air America supplied materials to Phoumi to defeat both Kong Le and the Pathet Lao. In early 1961 elements of two U.S. Air Force squadrons arrived in Vientiane and Udorn, then set up a communications link between the Laotian and Thai capitals; by the spring of that year, a U.S. Marine combat brigade from Okinawa landed in Udorn. Meanwhile symbolically Washington organized a SEATO military exercise in Thailand, Operation Air Bull, to demonstrate U.S. determination to prevail in the Laotian international conflict. As well, in May much of the Udorn military personnel were sent to Nong Khai, on the Thai side of the Mekong River across from Laos, ostensibly to display America's pride in John Glenn's recent space flight (in Washington's space race with the Soviet Union). Actually Washington sought to underscore its resolve to check the spread of communism, possibly with direct American military intervention in Laos.

Laotian Prince Souvanna Phouma and President John Kennedy. *Source:* Abbie Rowe. White House Photographs. John F. Kennedy Presidential Library and Museum, Boston.

Nonetheless by June 1961 it appears that the new John Kennedy administration had decided not to make Laos a key to containment. The Royal Lao government was wobbly at best, and during his early months in office Kennedy had to cope with larger issues: the Bay of Pigs, a Vienna summit with Soviet leader Khrushchev, and the erection of the Berlin Wall. In that setting, Washington began to work out a negotiated settlement with the Soviets, signed at Geneva in July 1962, that led to a declaration of neutrality for Laos. The country then formed a sham coalition government composed of the three princes but in fact dominated by communists in conjunction with neutralists. Promptly the civil war resumed, but without direct American, Russian, or Chinese participation. For the remainder of the Vietnam War, North Vietnam occupied much of Laos, America military personnel working with Hmong Laotians occupied (the "secret war") some of the hill country, and Moscow and Beijing supplied the Pathet Lao. When the Vietnam War concluded in 1975, the charade that was coalition government in Vientiane also concluded with the advent of a communist government.

Laos under Communist Rule, 1975–2020

Once the Paris Peace Accords set the stage for America's withdrawal from Vietnam in early 1973, a similar drawing down of American military activities in Laos got underway. The Vientiane Agreement of February 1973 brought about an official cease fire among Laotian factions, and that September a settlement was reached whereby all foreign forces would be withdrawn by the end of the year. While Hanoi did disband Group 959, it did not remove its more than 35,000 troops, just as it kept Vietnamese military personnel in Laos after the 1954 and 1962 Geneva Agreements. Moreover the loss of American air support both enabled a more efficient supplying of the Pathet Lao by Hanoi and an easier campaign against the Royal Lao government and the Hmong hill people. The communists defeated the Royal Lao government and abolished the monarchy.

Essentially Hanoi replaced France in the administration of Indochina, occupying Cambodia and overseeing the activities of the Lao People's Revolutionary Party (LPPR), the regime that possesses the monopoly of political power. As in Vietnam, there ensued a major exodus of people likely to be imprisoned or killed by the government. Reeducation camps ("seminar camps") appeared to insure that the people of questionable loyalty would reassess their views about the new government; many of these "students" either perished in what were labor camps or were deemed unsalvageable and killed. The Buddhist religious leadership came under intense surveillance or was confined to their monasteries. Initially centrally directed Five-Year Plans emerged to get the war-torn country economically healthy, but by 1986 (as in Vietnam) the government switched to a market-based economy. While economic growth has been positive since the reforms, the country still finds it difficult to get sufficient foreign investment, in part because of low basic skills among the people that modern enterprises require. More than 70% of the population is employed in the agricultural sector, which tends to produce low-paying jobs. Nonetheless the poverty rate has dropped, the global economic situation has improved since the downturn in 2008, greater foreign investment is arriving (especially in the creation of hydroelectric power), and by 2015 Laos could boast a stock market. The LPPR will hold its next national congress in early 2021.

Independent Thailand: Civilian and Military Governments, the Cold War, and the First Vietnam War, 1945–1973

Since it became a constitutional monarchy in 1932, Thailand has experienced 20 coups d'état (the most recent in 2014) and lived under 20 constitutions (a 2014 draft constitution was repealed in 2017). It is fair to conclude that the country's political system has typically been less than stable.

From World War II until his death in 2016, King Bhumibol Adulyadej (1927–2016; r. 1946–2016) reigned as a popular symbol of the nation. For almost all of that time the military has ruled, with brief intervals of civilian governments being constantly manipulated or overthrown by one general or another. During the Cold War, governments in Bangkok worked very closely with the United States until the end of the Vietnam War and thereafter somewhat cautiously. As with the rest of Southeast Asia, there is much anxiety over the rise of China and the enduring influence of Washington. The transition from the aging and ill monarch to his unpopular son, King Maha Vajiralongkorn (1952–), will likely test the viability of the current political system.

Less than a year after Japan's surrender in 1945, young Thai King Ananda Mahidol (1925–1946, r. 1935–1946) died, likely murdered, and his younger brother Bhumibol Adulyadej ascended the throne. The king had been abroad during World War II, when Thailand declared war on the United States, and the military—with Japanese oversight—governed the country. The Thai military lost some credibility having been associated with the losing Japanese militarists, and civilian government briefly took over in 1944. By 1947 the ousted wartime Prime Minister Plaek Phibunsongkhram (or Phibun, a field marshal; 1897–1964) returned to power via a coup and remained in power until 1957. A brief three-month civilian government was followed by a succession of general officers, Sarit Thanarat (1908–1963) and Thanom Kittikachorn (1911–2004), who ruled until December 1972. Washington recognized military rule in Thailand as a necessary part of the global effort to contain the spread of communism, just as the United States earlier supported Soviet Russia and other communist movements, the Mafia, as well as other unsavory allies in the greater battle against Nazi Germany and militarist Japan. In 1954 Thailand joined SEATO and by the early 1960s approved the building of major air bases for American use in operations in Vietnam and Laos. Meanwhile a communist insurrectionary movement in Thailand cemented Thai–U.S. relations, as both sides sought to defeat yet another guerrilla movement in Asia.

The communist subversive campaign in Thailand is a longstanding one but first became significant in 1961, when Pathet Lao's territorial gains in Laos opened the way for the communists to establish guerrilla bases in the northeast. Small communist groups entered Thailand, concentrating on organizing party cells and indoctrinating villagers. They played on local grievances, particularly government neglect in the fields of health and education and promised remedial action. The youth were recruited, sent to Laos or Communist China for indoctrination and paramilitary training, and returned to the northeast.

Source: Central Intelligence Agency, *Communist Insurgency in Thailand,* National Intelligence Estimate no. 52166, July (Washington, DC: CIA, 1966), p. 5.

Nonetheless as operations in Indochina wound down and Americans departed Thailand, economic troubles mounted, and dissatisfaction with military rule produced both a change in government and the emergence of a more effective domestic political opposition.

Civilian and Military Governments, 1973–2000

Thailand in 1973 faced numerous and serious domestic and foreign challenges that shook the country to the core. At home the National Student Center of Thailand (NSCT), a collection of numerous university student organizations born in the globally tumultuous 1960s, led a series of demonstrations that year. In October NSCT, supported by other elements in Thailand, staged massive marches protesting the military dictatorship (martial law since 1958), Japanese imports, the arrests and jailing of many student demonstrators, and assorted other grievances. Many of those grievances had economic grounds, chiefly university graduates unable to find jobs commensurate with their education. As well, the skyrocketing prices of oil that year, inflation, and the departure of the American military and its massive spending all conspired to increase the cost of living and weaken the economy. In any case, as activists neared the king's residence in one of the marches, an explosion produced a pitched battle between the students and the military, a clash resulting in more than 75 deaths and several hundred wounded.

In the short term, protestors achieved a major victory by the removal of General Thanom Kittikachorn, who had run the government as prime minister since 1963. In the longer term as well, the protests indicated that students and their supporters now had to be considered in the political deliberations by the ruling elite. For the remainder of the twentieth century, political parties and civilian prime ministers officially represented a rising national political leadership in Thailand. But behind the scenes, the military let it be known there were political red lines the civilians could not cross, though sometimes lines were blurred or clearly crossed. Still, from late 1977 until early 1991, the military directly ruled.

Thailand's 1992 political crisis illustrates the changing nature of Thai politics. When protests against military rule emerged in 1991, a civilian bureaucrat became the generals' choice for prime minister. The military hierarchy believed Anand Panyarachu (1932–present) could be manipulated, but in office Anand issued a number of reforms and butted heads with the military, especially over its draft constitution and its ongoing control of the media. Though Anand lasted only three months, the remainder of the century produced civilian rule in Bangkok for all but one year.

These realities set the stage for the twenty-first century's ongoing political standoff: the military, the monarchy, and their chief clients—bureaucrats, business interests, and ethnic Chinese—versus a rising urban middle class and growing student population, newer industries, and a declining but still significant farming population. Aside from the 1997 "Asian Contagion" economic downturn, Thailand's economy in the last quarter of the twentieth century displayed clear signs of growth. As the problems associated with becoming modern are steadily overcome, the problems associated with being modern need to be identified and addressed. Since the turn of the twenty-first century, defining the chief problems and crafting the acceptable solutions have divided Thai society, but the role of the monarchy adds a new dynamic to the political struggles.

Red Shirts, Yellow Shirts, and the Future of Thailand, 2001–2018

While Thailand's new century continued to indicate the growing viability of civilian government, and as civilian rule increasingly became the promotion of populist policies, many of the country's traditional symbols of authority and admiration came under greater scrutiny. The military's prestige as national protector remains intact given the disputes Bangkok has with all of its immediate neighbors, but its intervention in national politics has long been viewed by the populace with increasing discontent. At the same time, the role or even the existence of the monarchy has become a topic of impassioned debate. The American-born, Swiss-educated King Bhumibol Adulyadej had been viewed as a national unifying force in Thai politics, particularly when the country experienced major constitutional crises in 1973 and 1992. However, the aging and ailing monarch has expired, and the highly unpopular Crown Prince (now King) Vajiralongkorn did not inherit the admiration his father could draw upon. In that context, Thai politics began with a January 2001 national election won by the Thai Rak Thai (Thais love Thais) Party led by former policeman and billionaire entrepreneur Thaksin Shinawatra (1949–present). Thaksin's party garnered 40 percent of the vote as a peaceful transfer from one civilian party and government to another took place. His reelection in 2005 and the party's winning an absolute majority in the Parliament suggested that substantive as well as procedural democratic politics had taken root in Thailand. Political power was shifting from Bangkok and the south to northern agricultural areas. As the military, the monarchy, and urban Thailand faltered in terms of image and power, the Constitutional Court of Thailand has stepped in to curtail the growing populist clout, outlawing political parties and removing government officials. Thaksin and his wife were accused of corruption, the prime minister removed from office by military coup, and both tried and convicted in court. The Constitutional Court abolished Thaksin's Thai Rak Thai Party, whose members then proceeded to join the People's Power Party, which was abolished by the same court in 2008.

Supporters hold banner of former Thai Prime Ministers Thaksin Shinawatra and his sister Yingluck Shinawatra. *Source:* Bloomberg/Getty Images.

Thaksin's removal as prime minister brought a year of military rule, but then democratic government appeared to return in 2008. However, political clashes between traditionalists and populists also returned—between the "Yellows" (People's Alliance for Democracy, or PAD) who rallied for monarch, military, and the nation's south, and the "Reds" (United Front for Democracy against Dictatorship, or UDD) who championed the interests of the north, the rural poor, plus much of the nation's youth and growing middle class. In the 2011 national election, Thaksin's followers got behind the candidacy of his younger sister Yingluck Shinawatra (1967–present) and her Pheu Thai Party. Her resounding victory again looked to be an encouraging step toward civilian government and populist programs. But less than two years into her term, the Constitutional Court ejected her from the prime minister position for alleged corruption, at which point another general, Prayut Chan-o-cha (1954–present), took control of the government. The 2014 military coup, the twelfth since 1932, gave the generals the task of drafting yet another constitution, the twentieth since 1932.

Several drafts emerged before the final constitutional document finally was presented for a referendum vote by the people. The first iteration of the new constitution was about to be submitted for the people's vote in 2015, but then removed; the generals were apparently afraid it would be voted down. The second iteration was submitted to the people in August 2016, but to insure its passage the military did not allow any campaigning. It passed, but complications followed with the death of the beloved long-reigning King Bhumibol Adulyadej on October 13 that year. His successor, son Maha Vajiralongkorn (Rama X of the Chakri Dynasty), wanted to make further changes to the already-ratified constitution, modifications that gave more power to the military and the monarchy. The changes also included new methods of voting that were likely to reduce the ability of a populist party or popular leaders, such as the previous two duly elected prime ministers, to muster large majorities in the Parliament. One of the changes included adding further powers to the Constitutional Court that had just ousted Yingluck Shinawatra a few years earlier. Confusing the political setting even more, a terrorist bombing in August 2015 at the Erawan Hindu Shrine and an ongoing Islamic insurgency in southern Thailand heightened anxiety in a population already stressed by political and economic uncertainty. A highly criticized March 2019 highly restricted election keeps the military in power, but ongoing popular protests calling for a reform of both government and monarchy continue.

Conclusions

Mainland Southeast Asia's transition to independence and modernization varied by native culture, foreign colonizer, and Cold War patron. Clearly the kind of independence leader a country produced—Ho Chi Minh or Lee Kuan Yew, for example—influenced the transition to nation building. Typically former British colonies fared better than those under French, Dutch, or American rule. The consequences of changeover were also influenced by the emerging Cold War and which model of development, broadly speaking, the new nations chose to emulate. All countries began with soft authoritarian governments, but those disposed to more market-oriented economics tended to do better economically. As well, those nations more inclined to be open to foreign capital and technology imports as opposed to some form of self-sufficiency likewise normally prospered. By the end of the Cold War, market economics became the preferred model, as even communist countries abandoned central planning across the economies. Moreover, while modernization progressed, it produced numerous problems that remain to be resolved: environmental issues, the drug and sex trade, border disputes, and terrorism, to name the most obvious. The rise of China and the uncertain role of the United States in Asia require each nation to rethink how its best interests can be realized.

Suggested Readings and Viewings

Chris Baker and Pasuk Phongpaichit, *A History of Thailand*, 2nd ed. (Cambridge: Cambridge University Press, 2009).

David Chandler, *A History of Cambodia*, 3rd ed. (Boulder, CO: Westview Press, 2000).

Leon Comber, *Singapore Correspondent* (Singapore: Marshall Cavendish, 2012).

Duong Van Mai Elliott, *The Sacred Willow: Four Generations of a Vietnamese Family* (New York: Oxford University Press, 1999).

Enemies of the People (2009), dir. by Rob Lemkin and Thet Sambath. A documentary on the Khmer Rouge regime in Cambodia.

Tsuyoshi Hasegawa, *The Cold War in East Asia, 1945–1991* (Stanford, CA: Stanford University Press, 2011).

R. W. Komer, *The Malayan Emergency in Retrospect: Organization of a Successful Counterinsurgency Effort* (Santa Monica, CA: Rand Corporation, 1972).

Lee Kuan Yew, *From Third World to First: The Singapore Story, 1965–2000* (New York: Harper Collins, 2000).

R. S. Milne and Diane K. Mauzy, *Malaysian Politics under Mahathir* (London: Routledge, 1999).

Norman G. Owen, *The Emergence of Modern Southeast Asia: A New History* (Honolulu: University of Hawaii Press, 2005).

Puruambo (2005), dir. by Pavol Barabas. A documentary on New Guinea, focusing on the island's population and environment.

Josef Silverstein, ed. *The Political Legacy of Aung San, rev. ed.* (Ithaca, NY: Cornell University Press, 1972, 1993).

Lewis Sorley, *A Better War: The Unexamined Victories and Final Tragedy of America's Last Years in Vietnam* (New York: Harcourt, Inc., 1999). Compare to Gregory Daddis, *Westmoreland's War: Reassessing American Strategy in Vietnam* (Oxford: Oxford University Press, 2014) and his *Withdrawal: Reassessing America's Final Years in Vietnam* (Oxford: Oxford University Press, 2017).

David I. Steinberg, *Burma/Myanmar: What Everybody Needs to Know* (New York: Oxford University Press, 2010).

Martin Stuart-Fox, *A History of Laos* (Cambridge: Cambridge University Press, 1997).

Nicholas Tarling, ed., *From World War II to the Present, vol. 2, part 2 of Cambridge History of Southeast Asia* (Cambridge: Cambridge University Press, 1999).

We Were Soldiers (2002), dir. by Randall Wallace. A motion picture about America's early combat role in Vietnam. Compare to *Platoon* (1987), dir. by Oliver Stone.

Shelton Woods, *The Story of Vietnam: From Prehistory to the Present* (Ann Arbor, MI: Association for Asian Studies, 2013).

27

Insular Southeast Asia since 1945

"As a boy, Narendra Modi helped his father sell tea to support their family. Today he's the leader of the world's largest democracy, and his life story—from poverty to prime minister—reflects the dynamism and potential of India's rise."[1]

Not long after President Sukarno uttered those words in a 1965 speech, a coalition of Muslim generals staged a successful coup that removed from power the man who had brought independence to Indonesia 16 years earlier. Southeast Asia's largest nation and the world's largest Muslim country, Indonesia experienced what other newly independent modernizing countries typically bumped into, a major course correction. The thrill of freedom from direct foreign rule gave way to reassessment of the assumptions about what kinds of political, economic, social, and global arrangements and leaders would guide the nation to a more prosperous future. Across the island nations of Southeast Asia, domestic, regional, and international struggles –often occurring simultaneously– served to make a transition to prosperous independent nations a continuous challenge.

Netherlands East Indies to the Republic of Indonesia

The end of World War II began the closing struggle to win Indonesian independence, which occurred in 1949 with the defeat of the Dutch who had sought to reestablish colonial rule once Japan departed. Achmed Sukarno emerged as the charismatic leader who hoped to create an imperial Greater Indonesia (*Indonesia Raya*). It would include all of the Netherlands Indies, Malays and non-Malays in British-colonized Malaya and northern Borneo, as well as Portuguese-controlled East Timor. Sukarno had to devise the means to bring together numerous religions plus more than 300 ethnicities and 700 linguistic groups across approximately 15,000 islands. Sukarno's immense early popularity soon began to fade as both nationalist leaders and the general population increasingly viewed their leader as politically corrupt and dictatorial as well as economically inept and impractical. The nation's enormous oil reserves and other natural resources, substantial foreign financial and technological assistance, and a program for political unification and economic development had been squandered by his bad policies and lavish living.

---

1 Siddhartha Deb, "Unmasking Modi," New Republic, May 3, 2016.

Asia Past and Present: A Brief History, First Edition. Peter P. Wan and Thomas D. Reins.
© 2021 John Wiley & Sons, Inc. Published 2021 by John Wiley & Sons, Inc.

Timeline for Insular Southeast Asia, 1945–2019	
1945	August 15: World War II ends
	Japan surrenders Spratley and Paracel Islands (and, in the 1952 San Francisco Treaty, renounces claims) to China
1946	July: The Philippines becomes independent from the United States
1949	Indonesia becomes independent from Holland
	October 1: Mao Zedong's Communists proclaim the People's Republic of China
1960s–present	Numerous Southeast Asian nations and China lay claims of sovereignty and/or natural resource rights to the South China Sea region's land, sea, and subterranean locations
1963–1966	The creation of Malaysia—part of which is located on the island of Borneo in Malaysia (referred to as Kalimantan in Indonesia)—produces tense situations and minor combat operations between the two countries, known as the *Konfrontasi*
1964, 1969, 2013	Race riots in Singapore, the first two between ethnic Chinese and Muslim Malays, and the 2013 riots between ethnic Chinese and ethnic Indians
1965	October 1: Muslim generals oust President Sukarno, resulting in hundreds of thousands of leftists, communists, and ethnic Chinese being killed
1965	General Muhammad Suharto becomes leader of Indonesia
1969	Race riots in Malaysia between ethnic Chinese and Malays cause the declaration of a national emergency
1972	Ferdinand Marcos declares martial law
1975	September: Papua New Guinea becomes independent from Australia
	November: Revolutionary group Fretilin declares East Timor independence
	December: Indonesia invades East Timor and occupies it until 1999
1981	Marcos ends martial law
1983	Opposition leader Benigno Aquino killed on his return to Manila
1984	Brunei becomes independent from Britain
1986	Marcos ousted; Cory Aquino brings People Power
1998	President Suharto's 33-year rule of Indonesia ends; democracy begins
2001–2018	Battle between elected Prime Minister Thaksin Shinawatra and his sister Yingluck Shinawatra (also elected prime minister) on the one hand, and the military who ousted them on the other
2002	May: East Timor becomes fully independent Timor Leste
2004	December 26: Indian Ocean tsunami kills a quarter-million people, chiefly in Indonesia, Thailand, and Sri Lanka

2016	Rodrigo Duterte elected Philippine president, launches anti-drug campaign that has killed perhaps 20,000 people, and embraces China's Xi Jinping
2017	February: Election for governor of Jakarta pitted incumbent ethnic Chinese and Christian Basuki "Ahok" Purnama Tjahaja, who was favored to win until accused of blaspheming Islam, lost the race, and was imprisoned for blasphemy; Indonesia's Supreme Court upheld his conviction in March 2018
2018–2020	Malaysian voters elect 92-year-old Dr. Mahathir Mohamad, the nation's former ruler and standard bearer of the Pakatan Harapan coalition of parties, by defeating his former protégé Prime Minister Najib Razak of the Barisan Nasional coalition, Mahathir's earlier political home; he resigned in March 2020

By 1965 Sukarno's public support tumbled as demands for concrete reform trumped bombastic nationalistic rhetoric. Muslim, military, and economic leaders began to abandon Sukarno as the economy deteriorated; Sukarno's secularism upset traditional religious and social practices; and authoritarian rule threatened local, regional, and national political interests. Perhaps most frightening was the growing strength of the two-million-member Communist Party of Indonesia (PKI), with its ties to Moscow, Beijing, and Sukarno himself. A September–October 1965 coup headed by a group of Muslim generals, with Washington's encouragement, removed Sukarno and replaced him with anti-communist General Mohammad Suharto, who would rule the nation until his removal in 1998. Since then Indonesia has lived under democratic institutions, elected political leaders, and had civilian control of the military. While experiencing numerous bumps in the road to the future—separatist movements, terrorist troubles, environmental challenges, corruption difficulties, infrastructure weaknesses, natural disasters, and economic downturns, to list only the most obvious—the government has typically managed to address, if not fully resolve, the problems within a constitutional framework.

Winning Independence, 1945–1949

As the Japanese Empire crumbled in 1945, nationalist movements in colonial Asia sensed that ideal conditions for an earlier-than-anticipated independence had arrived. In the case of the Netherlands Indies, nationalist leaders Achmed Sukarno and Mohamad Hatta realized that somewhere between the eventual expulsion of Japan and the attempted return of the Dutch, the foundation for independence needed to be established. In June Sukarno announced the *Pancasila*, the five principles designed to bind the new nation together. These included the belief in one God; justice and humanity; the unity of Indonesia or nationalism; republican government that would produce political consensus; and social justice, likely some point between the welfare state and state socialism. National unity also required a national language. It became Bahasa, a widely spoken Malay-derived language that would subordinate regional languages to the new national tongue. Legal and illegal nationalist organizations that had emerged under the Dutch and Japanese—including military units, which had been formed by Tokyo to facilitate governing the islands—sprang into action. A leading movement among these organizations was the *Pemuda*, radical youth and student groups whose history involved the kidnapping of Sukarno and Hatta (just before the Declaration of Independence for the Republic of Indonesia on August 17 and the promulgation of the constitution on August 18), participation in the ouster of Sukarno in 1965, as well as the removal of Suharto in 1998. As the Japanese departed, disorder broke out in numerous locations involving political and criminal organizations and individuals. By the time the British military arrived in September, clashes between Indonesian groups and the British forces began and continued throughout the year. Meanwhile, the Dutch began returning.

Although factionalism weakened the Indonesian nationalist movement (now largely the leadership of the Republic of Indonesia), and while the war in Europe had exhausted the Dutch, Indonesians still occupied the stronger political and probably military positions. This became clear once the allied forces departed Indonesia and chronic fighting between Dutch and Republican forces erupted in the waning months of 1945. Accordingly, the Dutch eventually worked out the Linggadjati (or Cheribon) Agreement with Republican forces in November 1946. It acknowledged the legitimacy of the Republic on the major islands of Java and Sumatra, the remainder of the islands remaining under Dutch control until such a time when all of the islands would join together to form the United States of Indonesia. At that point the Dutch monarch would serve as head of state in what would become the Netherlands-Indonesian Union. By July the following year, the Dutch renounced the agreement and military conflict between the two erupted again. In January 1948 another cease fire was arranged (the Renville Agreement) by the United Nations' Good Offices Committee, composed of Belgian, Australian, and American delegates. The committee continued Dutch sovereignty in Indonesia but also provided for elections in the Dutch-controlled parts of Java and Sumatra. Up to this point, the United States had to deal with conflicting interests. On the one hand, Presidents Franklin Roosevelt and Harry Truman had supported an anticolonial stance, which would presumably give American government and business organizations direct access to an independent and hopefully friendly Indonesia (as well as other former colonial territories). On the other hand, once the Cold War began, the interests of Holland (and other European colonizers) became crucial in building a coalition of anti-communist nations. American interests in Europe trumped its Asian interests. Moreover, the likelihood of a friendly Indonesia seemed questionable given the Republican leadership's cozy relationship with the PKI. Washington's attitude would change by the end of the year.

Indonesian independence likely arrived early due to a shift in outlook among Republican leaders and a communist rebellion against the Republic in Madiun in east Java. Under the Dutch and the Japanese, the Communist Party had been deemed illegal, but once the war ended the new republic restored its legality. However, a dissident faction of the PKI rebelled against the government in Madiun in September 1948. The rebels justified their action because the Republican government had signed the Renville Agreement, and the balance of the PKI leadership (perhaps reluctantly) supported the rebellion. By this time Mohammad Hatta had become prime minister (and simultaneously vice president) of what was becoming a more moderate Republican government, and by year's end the government had put down the insurgency. Thus sensing that a government hostile to communism would likely come to power once independence happened, Washington put pressure on the Dutch to negotiate a timely process of decolonization with the Indonesian leadership (or face the loss of Marshall Plan[2] money). Mohammad Roem representing Indonesia and Jan Herman van Roijen for Holland worked out an agreement whereby both sides would honor a cease fire, the Indonesian leadership would join the Round Table Conference (which they did between August and November), and the Dutch would accept unconditional independence of Indonesia (except for West New Guinea). The conference also called for the election of a Constituent Assembly. Independence officially occurred on December 27, 1949.

The Sukarno Years, 1950–1965

Politically, diplomatically, and economically, Indonesia's elite failed to create consensus or at least a preliminary arrangement about how the country should operate during its early independence years. Between 1945 and 1950, Indonesia operated under three constitutions: the 1945 document, which provided for a strong president; the 1949 Federal Constitution, which became the nation's basic law upon achieving independence that year; and the Provisional Constitution of 1950, which downplayed the federal (Dutch-created) arrangements with states from the 1949 document and moderated the power of the presidency from the 1945 edition. In 1959, Sukarno reinstituted the 1945 Constitution, though it represented only a fig leaf for his evolving dictatorship. For the duration of Sukarno's rule, he fought to increase his power as president against increasing numbers of those who came to believe that their founding father sought to become a despot.

Politically speaking, Sukarno had little faith in elections, political parties, or power sharing, evidenced by his proclamation of martial law in 1957. His "Guided Democracy" launched a year earlier was muscular on Sukarno's guidance and scrawny on participatory democracy. In foreign affairs, too, his apparent non-aligned policy launched in the 1955 Bandung Conference gave way to confrontations with the Dutch in Western New Guinea, with Malaysia and its incorporation of the northern parts of Borneo, with the British because it supported Malaysia, with the United Nations because it recognized Malaysia, and especially with the United States because Washington worked to undermine Sukarno's increasingly leftist government. The Indonesian leader clearly moved away from non-alignment as he developed a decided preference for Soviet Russian and Communist Chinese mentors.

Economically as well, Sukarno proved to be unequal to the task of developing a solid modernization program for either the people or the nation. He alienated property owners, domestic or foreign, and frightened away the sources of capital and technology that the country needed for development. He did so in the name of self-reliance, something China, India, and other developing nations also attempted to one extent or another, ultimately unsuccessfully. The early post–World War II economic successes in Asia—Japan, South Korea, Taiwan, Hong Kong, and Singapore—were those that carefully utilized outside capital and technology and were able to do so because they provided a fairly safe and friendly environment for investment. The essential issue surrounding national self-reliance was how best to get there, and some countries found the route earlier than others. Indonesia under Sukarno was not one of those countries. While no newly independent nation can presume a trouble-free transition to freedom, some basic policy agreements about the nation's future—among both the elite and the populace—should be expected.

---

2 The American Marshall Plan, named after Secretary of State George C. Marshall, sought to rebuild Europe economically to contain Soviet activities on the continent.

Achmed Sukarno and Fidel Castro. *Source:* UtCon Collection/Alamy Stock Photo.

Sukarno did not provide the essential leadership or effective plan to achieve the progress he promised, and a September 1965 military coup effectively ended his rule. As Sukarno's rule became less popular during his last decade in power, he attempted to rally the population with popular nationalist, anti-Western, and even religious messages. Labeled *nasakom*, it included the key constituencies Sukarno needed to produce political procedures in a nondemocratic political setting. The term *nasakom* was an acronym derived from the words for nationalism, religion, and communism, and it required a difficult balancing of these three crucial sectors by Sukarno. Most army and religious leaders detested the communists, the chief reason they supported the creation of *Golkar* by Sukarno in 1959.

Add to this the Indonesian people's dislike of ethnic Chinese, who made up a large part of the PKI and the majority of the business community, and that left little room for presidential miscalculation. At first Sukarno succeeded. He portrayed Indonesia as the leader of the emerging world, which he hosted at the Bandung Conference in 1955, but by 1965 he withdrew Indonesia from the United Nations. Like China, India, and Pakistan, he launched a nuclear weapons program that would further heighten the nation's prominence once the bomb was successfully tested, an event that never occurred. He openly turned to Moscow and Beijing for technical expertise and economic aid, but much of Beijing's aid ended up in the hands of the PKI in the form of weapons. Furthermore, hyperinflation and a rapidly growing population crippled an already feeble economy and severely reduced the president's popularity among the common people, the chief victims of economic stagnation.

The country seemed prepared for "the year of living dangerously," a phrase used by Sukarno in 1964 to promote PKI ideas and programs, one of which was the so-called fifth force. It involved a peasants' and workers' militia to join with the regular military units. Coming on the heels of the end of martial law, this was viewed by the military as an attempt to weaken its leading role in politics and as yet another move by Sukarno to marginalize the army. Thus, by the autumn of 1965, domestic issues—a failing economy, the army's fear of increasing marginalization, and fear by the military leadership and most Muslims of the growing power of the PKI—all conspired to produce the removal of Sukarno. So did foreign issues, particularly America's concern about Sukarno's connection to China and much of the rest of Southeast Asia, which feared an aggressive, revolution-exporting Indonesia under communism. Since the Strait of Malacca represented a major strategic location as a major choke point, both Beijing and Washington realized that in the long run, the Strait of Malacca in unfriendly hands represented a security threat in the Cold War. What has come to be known as the "Malacca Dilemma," which refers to both the Malacca Strait and the Lombok/Makassar Strait, made the question of who ruled Indonesia crucial to a number of nations and their leaders. Certainly from President Sukarno's point of view, 1965 undoubtedly had become quite dangerous.

The transfer of political power in Indonesia started on September 30, and by the spring of 1966 President Sukarno's political power had vanished as Major General Muhammad Suharto (1921–2008) emerged as the nation's leader. The transfer began with an attempted coup by a leftist faction in the army loyal to Sukarno and tied to the PKI. It was assumed as well by diplomatic personnel and the Indonesian army leadership that the People's Republic of China had likely aided the coup leaders in some fashion and perhaps was supporting Sukarno in his attempt to develop nuclear weapons. The coup was meant to strengthen Sukarno's position by eliminating factions in the army—initially headed by the Army Chief of Staff General Abdul Haris Nasution (1918–2000)—who wanted Sukarno, the PKI, and leftism in general neutralized. The attempted coup—labeled the *Gestapu* by Suharto—was crushed by another army faction headed by Nasution and Suharto. They and others in both the military and clergy were fearful that the involvement of the PKI would produce communist control of the government should the coup succeed. The countercoup leadership guided an outburst of ferocity that moved far beyond a clash of military factions—from village to town to city. For six months or more, several hundred thousand (perhaps as many as a million) people died, largely PKI members and ethnic Chinese.

Muhammad Suharto and the New Order, 1965–1998

President Sukarno physically survived the September–October upheaval, but his political power vanished as quickly as General Suharto's control grew. In 1966 Sukarno issued (likely under great pressure) the *Supersemar* document, which gave Suharto the equivalent of martial law powers; by 1967 Suharto became acting president, and in 1968 he officially became president. Meanwhile Sukarno ended up in forced retirement, where he died in 1970. The New Order under Suharto contained several of the Sukarno-era ideas and institutions, though they characteristically were transformed to serve Suharto's very different agenda than his predecessor's. Authoritarian government with significant military influence continued; *Pancasila*, the five principles of Sukarno, remained the nation's official ideology, though with Suharto interpretations; and political parties continued to be marginalized, with military-controlled *Golkar* (the "functional groups") becoming the government's "political party" throughout Suharto's rule. But major changes in direction began almost immediately under Suharto as well. In foreign policy, Suharto's government quickly rejoined the United Nations, unofficially joined with the United States in the Cold War struggle with the Soviet Union while officially proclaiming neutrality, and typically became a friendlier and more cooperative neighbor with other Southeast Asian nations. Indonesia's invasion of East Timor in 1975 (see below) became an obvious exception. At home, the New Order's domestic agenda gave priority to reestablishing social order after the 1965 upheaval, firming up Suharto's political position, and reversing the nation's distressing economic plight.

Economic revitalization actually became one of the easier agenda items to accomplish. Suharto quickly opened the country to foreign investment and technology, which in turn helped to build both new industries as well as a native technocratic elite. Together with oil income, which substantially increased after the Arab oil embargo in 1973, the government could now invest in infrastructure—transportation, education, health care facilities, and so forth—which contributed to the increased standard of living as well as the life expectancy for the average citizen. When Suharto came to power, half of the nation's population lived in poverty; by the early 1990s, that number had declined to less than 15 percent. Yet many of the sources of economic success set the stage for domestic discontent, which, in conjunction with the Asian Financial Crisis of 1997, brought about the downfall of Suharto's more than three-decade rule in 1998.

Suharto's politics created the conditions that provided for a reasonably stable social order and a fairly unified group of economic planners. This has been far from unusual in successful modernizing nations, at least economically speaking. One-party government existed in Meiji Japan, Bismarck's Germany, Mahathir Mohammad's Malaysia, Lee Kuan Yew's Singapore, and Chiang Kai-shek's Taiwan, and during authoritarian rule in South Korea. But Suharto's politics also generated political opposition for several reasons. Part of his politics meant family, friends, and the military flourished because of corruption and nepotism, while the average entrepreneur suffered. Meanwhile the unpopular ethnic Chinese also prospered disproportionately to the general population. Large-scale foreign investment generated popular fear of foreign domination, a common fear in the developing world at least since the American Revolution when Britain invested heavily in the United States. The amalgamation of nongovernmental organizations into *Golkar* made political and social organizations little more than instruments of the government. And though Suharto put on the face of a religious Muslim by going to Mecca in 1991, he did so given the growing power, influence, and opposition of Muslim intellectuals, who had been effectively isolated from political leadership.

Separatism, demonstrations, and other forms of hostility to the government had been effectively kept in check for three decades. But the "Asian Contagion" economic downturn of 1997, in conjunction with the accumulation of grievances over the decades against the Suharto government, began the undoing of his authoritarian rule. Widespread street demonstrations provided the knockout blow, and he resigned on May 21, 1998. But as in the earlier political transition from Sukarno to Suharto, political mayhem in the transfer of leadership from Suharto to reform governments accompanied the transfer of power. Riots broke out during the spring and summer of 1998, and perhaps 1000 to 5000 people were killed, several thousand wounded, while numerous women were raped and businesses looted and/or destroyed. The majority of the victims came from the ethnic Chinese population across the country, and it is estimated that 1–2 percent of that community left Indonesia.

Reformasi: Democracy, 1998–Present

Thus Indonesia began its experiment in democracy after nearly a half-century of autocratic rule under Sukarno and Suharto. Indonesians typically refer to this new political stage of their history as *Reformasi*, or Reform. The principal reform involved the redirection of political power chiefly from the central government largely to regional and local areas. Accordingly, free elections in 1999 and thereafter dispersed much more power to the people than had existed before democratic rule. Other reforms included freedom of the press, independent political parties and other nongovernmental institutions such as unions, and the freeing of political prisoners. While corruption remained an important problem and though the army continued to wield substantial though decreasing influence, the political system seemed to be moving in directions that most people appreciated. Still, these greater freedoms sometimes produced disorder. Activities restrained under authoritarian rule—terrorism, separatism, along with regional, religious, and ethnic violence—reappeared to challenge the new, less dominant central government. Nonetheless, this democracy with Indonesian characteristics mostly has contained, if not completely overcome, these challenges.

The term *Reformasi* can contain numerous types of reform, but it predominantly has indicated political transformation to democratic government. The first and most important step toward reform included the removal of Suharto and his advisors. He was replaced as president by Bacharuddin Jusuf "B. J." Habibie (1936–present), who had been appointed vice president by Suharto just two months before. Although an old friend of the resigned president, Habibie launched a series of actions that put the nation on the path to a more open political system. Most significantly, he reshuffled the Cabinet and set dates for parliamentary and presidential elections. The first free direct election to Parliament[3] since 1955 took place in 1999, with numerous political parties competing for seats in Parliament. Initially, the president was selected by the People's Consultative Assembly, which appointed Abdurrahman Wahid (1940–2009) in 1999; removed him on July 23, 2001; and selected Wahid's vice president, Megawati Sukarnoputri (1947–present), in his place. In the first direct election for president in 2004, Susilo Bambang Yudhoyono (1949–present) defeated several candidates to win the five-year term and was reelected in 2009. Notwithstanding corruption, nepotism, and other ills often associated with the early years of a nation's participatory politics, the electoral process has continued without coups or revolutions.

The 2014 general election brought Jokowi or Joko Widodo (1961–) to the presidency. This former governor of Jakarta, Widodo defeated former Lt. General Prabowo Subianto, a businessman and former husband of the late president Muhammad Suharto's daughter. He did not come from the Indonesian military and political elite. His administration has focused on building infrastructure, expanding education, improving public health, and instituting a land reform program. Although Widodo retained enough popular support to win reelection in 2019, even his supporters admit that his administration's progress is far from robust and that corruption is rife. His rival in the 2019 election provided a rematch of the 2014 presidential contest, in which Prabowo ran on a law-and-order platform and promised to clean up the rampant corruption in and out of government.

Religion and terrorism remain important political topics as well. Basuki Tjahaja Purnama became governor of Jakarta when Joko Widodo left that post to become president. As an ethnic Chinese and as a Christian, he began to run afoul of religious fundamentalists in his attempt to win election to that position. This seasoned and once-popular politician, affectionately known as Ahok, was defeated for election to the governorship in 2017; most believe this was because fundamentalists stirred up opposition based on his ethnicity and religion. Support for that theory can be seen in the arrest, conviction, and jailing for two years of Purnama on charges of blasphemy for allegedly insulting Islam. Although Sharia law is only practiced in one Indonesian province, Aceh, other provinces are considering adopting it. ISIS-inspired attacks in 2018, including suicide bombings, have produced dozens of deaths and more injuries. While Indonesia remains a relatively moderate Muslim-majority country, religion and terrorism are essential concerns in an evolving democratic society.

---

3 The Parliament in Indonesia is referred to as the People's Consultative Assembly or *Majelis Permusyawaratan Rakyak* (MPR). It was created in 1971, but not until the 1999 elections did its membership get chosen in an honest setting.

Joko Widodo, President of the Republic of Indonesia, 2014–. *Source:* The Asahi Shimbun/Getty Images.

In that sense, all *Reformasi* presidents have made lasting contributions thus far to the success of participatory government in Indonesia. Accordingly, President Habibie not only put in place an electoral process but also peacefully withdrew from the 1999 race for the presidency when the *Majelis Permusyawaratan Rakyak* (MPR) issued a vote of no confidence in him. President Wahid, known popularly as Gus Dur, contributed to a more civil political environment by rejecting the idea of Indonesia becoming an Islamic state, lest it slight the numerous non-Muslim citizens. Long an opponent of anti-Chinese thinking and behavior, this Muslim cleric and former head of the Nahdlatul Ulama (NU)—Indonesia's largest Muslim organization—proposed allowing the ethnic Chinese to take part openly (that is, legally) in many of their cultural traditions heretofore prohibited. He also attempted—mostly unsuccessfully—to bring the military under his control.

The presidency of his successor, Megawati Sukarnoputri, was characterized by efforts to maintain the nation's unity in the wake of the Bali terrorist bombings in 2002 and yet another separatist insurgency in the province of Aceh (in northern Sumatra). And though Megawati's sour grapes behavior in her defeat in the first popular election for president in 2004 left much to be desired, she nevertheless calmly accepted the judgment of the electoral system and the people. Retired General Susilo Yudhoyono, the victor in that presidential contest, distributed various Cabinet positions to members (including four women) of the numerous political parties that made up the coalition that enabled him to win. Yudhoyono appointed a United Indonesia Cabinet from eight different parties, reflecting the realization that the nation's leadership needed a substantial amount of political harmony in order to govern effectively. His reelection in 2009, in the midst of the economic crisis and other problems, suggested that the political process has achieved a fair amount of legitimacy in the eyes of the people.

Peaceful transfers of power from one candidate or party to another cannot be taken for granted. Indeed, the first three of the four presidents serving during the *Reformasi* did not get reelected. Although the power of incumbency could be used to stay in power, Habibie, Wahid, and Sukarnoputri accepted the process. The first two also took courageous and unpopular stands, aware that such positions could hurt them politically. Habibie called for a popular vote on independence by the people of East Timor, who chose independence. Wahid certainly angered much of the population with his attempts to improve conditions for ethnic Chinese, and few likely applauded his calling for the opening of relations with Israel. But their inability to get reelected likely resulted from the central government's loss of control over the provinces, which to be fair had much to do with the process of political decentralization associated with the *Reformasi* policies. Also, none of the first three presidents had a reputation as hands-on administrators. As well, terrorism, corruption, unemployment, inflation, declining foreign investment, and human rights issues continued to be festering problems. Though those problems continued under the Yudhoyono administration, he has projected an image of managerial competence.

Reformasi economics have produced mixed but generally positive results. During the first decade of reform, the nation experienced the consequences of two major economic downturns: the 1997 Asian Contagion and the 2007–2009 global recessions. In the context of simultaneous major political changes, Indonesia has suffered economic setbacks, but by 2013 it has laid the foundation for steady economic growth. Thus the nation's Gross Domestic Product (GDP) grew 8% in 1996, 4.7% in 1997, then, at the height of the contagion, declined 13.6%; and roughly a decade later, the GDP was 4.6% in 2009 and remained above 6% through 2013. Since 2004 President Yudhoyono has promoted his "pro-growth, pro-poor, pro-employment" stimulus program. It focuses on opening up the economy by reducing regulations, encouraging foreign investment, confronting corruption, and reducing or removing government subsidies on a number of items, most notably on oil. The above reforms, it is argued, will improve the economy by encouraging investment, which tends to decline with too much regulation and too much crony capitalism. A friendlier and more transparent economy will generate jobs, thereby reducing unemployment (in the 6–7% range since 2009) and improving the people's standard of living. While corruption and inflation remain important lingering problems, the poverty rate in Indonesia has declined since 2004, when it was estimated to be 16.7%, falling to 9.8% in 2018 according to the World Bank.[4]

Indonesia's foreign affairs have seriously influenced not only economic activities but an array of other domestic issues as well. Thus China has invested heavily in the country, which has likely enhanced the economy but at the price of increasing popular displeasure. First of all, it represents money that is Chinese in a country where Chinese-Indonesians already control a disproportionate amount of economic activity. And with the money is the fear that Beijing might influence other segments of Indonesian society, particularly anxiety that China's authoritarian political outlook that might seep into the country. America is viewed as the better source of capital and technology transfer, but that might not always be available in the amount or kind that Indonesia deems most desirable. Jakarta's relations with its immediate neighbors also present ongoing challenges. For example, Indonesia invaded and occupied what had been Portuguese Timor in 1975, and such action not only stirred hatred in the hearts of the Catholic Timorese but also raised fears in other nations in Southeast Asia, where numerous border disputes continue unresolved. President Habibie's call for a Timorese plebiscite on independence in 1998 helped to ease fears of a "greater Indonesia" revival. Environmental issues also present enduring challenges in the region. While the issue of global warming is regularly discussed, since melting glaciers affect the coastlines of some 15,000 islands, legal and illegal logging provides more immediate complications. Indonesia's

---

4 World Bank, "Indonesia," https://data.worldbank.org/country/indonesia.

logging as well as expanding farming result in runaway deforestation, which has the potential for long-term domestic disaster. But they more directly cause choking smog, as loggers and farmers burn the residue from their logging and land-clearing activities, with the thick smoke affecting both Indonesians and those nearby in Malaysia, Singapore, and Brunei.

Indonesia Enters the Twenty-First Century

Indonesia has experienced a great deal of turmoil in its quest to throw off the yoke of colonial rule, establish stable political foundations, and create a modern economy in the globalized world. The formation of balanced political ideas and institutions and effective economic strategies occurred during the Cold War, when young independence leaders and later their disciples had to choose, broadly speaking, between authoritarian government and Marxist economics on the one hand, and democracy and capitalism on the other. While the government side of things remains unresolved, the economic side has fairly well been decided in terms of market economics. In both politics and economics, Indonesia has taken steps toward democracy and the market. The young electoral process, imperfect as it is, has overcome two economic crises, which proved fatal to both Japan and Germany during the depression. The people's standard of living has moved forward; radical Islam is in check for the moment; anti-Chinese sentiment, though still pervasive, seems to be declining; and decentralized government since 1998 has allowed different ethnicities and regions greater decision-making power. In other areas, old and new challenges remain. Women have much greater freedoms as they have greater access to education and employment, yet in some regions *Sharia* law has reemerged to encourage polygamy. Those favoring multiple wives argue that the more spouses, the less prostitution and adultery, while rich men can spread their wealth to more women. Trafficking in women and children has yet to be successfully checked. And while the government and businesses talk the talk of good environmental behavior and of an end to corruption, very little walking the walk has taken place. All in all, though, Indonesia has made important course corrections in its march toward a better future.

Indonesia is closely tied to the nearby emerging nations of Timor Leste, Papua New Guinea, and Brunei. Brunei shares the island of Borneo/Kalimantan with Malaysia and Indonesia, and contains enormous oil wealth. Catholic Timor Leste shares the island of Timor with Muslim Indonesia. Christian Papua New Guinea shares the island of New Guinea with Muslim Indonesia. Religion, ethnicity, wealth, and national rivalry are and will likely remain issues that make the region subject to regional skirmishes, while competition for supremacy in the western Pacific between the United States and China and access to raw materials in the region can yield an international conflict.

Portuguese Timor to East Timor to Timor Leste

By the seventeenth century, Portugal took control of the eastern half of Timor Island (East Timor or Portuguese Timor), and the Dutch occupied the western half of the island (West Timor or Dutch Timor). By World War I, the Portuguese and Dutch had settled on a line of division of the island. When Indonesia became independent from Holland in 1949, it took control of most of what had been the Dutch East Indies, including Dutch Timor. The Portuguese continued to rule East Timor until August 1975, when its colonial rule came to an end. By that time, three Timorese political factions had emerged, and a brief civil war ensued. Indonesia temporarily resolved the question of who governs by invading East Timor and occupying it until 1999. That year, with Indonesian President Habibie's approval and under UN monitoring, the people of East Timor voted on whether to join Indonesia or become independent. The people chose independence, and East Timor officially became Timor Leste on May 20, 2002.

Portuguese Rule, 1945–1975

Although Portugal had been neutral in World War II, the conflict nonetheless impacted East Timor. The Japanese invaded the island, and the Dutch and Australians rallied much of the local population to resist Japan, resulting in at least 50,000 Timorese deaths. After the war, Portugal returned to govern, which it did in conjunction with the Catholic Church and the Portuguese-educated Timorese elite. By the 1960s, the UN General Assembly and its Committee for Decolonization got involved in Portugal's administration of East Timor, declaring it to be a non-self-governing territory. While the United Nations recognized Portugal as the legitimate administrator of East Timor, the United Nations was also directing Portugal to prepare the East Timorese for independence and self-government. The collapse of Antonio Salazar's fascist government in 1974 set in motion Portugal's speedy process of decolonization.

Nonetheless, Portugal's departure by December 1975 did not result in Timorese rule as various political factions fought among themselves for control of the country. Fretilin, a socialist independence movement created to oust Portugal, claimed to be the legitimate government of East Timor. At the same time, the Timor Democratic Union sought to retain a connection with Portugal, while the Popular Democratic Association of Timor wanted East Timor to become a part of Indonesia. President Suharto settled East Timor domestic disputes. The Indonesian military invaded on December 7, 1975, just several days after Fretilin declared East Timor's independence. The United Nations passed a resolution (No. 384 in 1975) condemning Indonesia for the invasion and Portugal for not discharging its responsibilities as the administering agency of East Timor. In any case, Indonesia occupied East Timor for the next 24 years. That occupation resulted in perhaps as many as 200,000[5] Timorese deaths and the forced relocation of as many as a quarter-million in a country of approximately one million people.

Indonesian Occupation, 1975–1999

Several reasons account for Indonesia's decision to invade East Timor. The western part of Timor was already a part of Indonesia, and with the power vacuum created by the Portuguese departure, it seemed only natural to incorporate the eastern part that Portuguese colonialism had wrongfully appropriated. More significant, though, was the Cold War setting. Vietnam, Cambodia, and Laos had just months before fallen under communist control, and the Timorese organization likely to grasp power—Fretilin—looked to be a leftist regime that would align itself with communism. The United States, in particular, feared that yet another domino would fall. Many argue that President Gerald Ford gave President Suharto the go-ahead for the invasion. Neighboring Australia dreaded the prospect of a pro-communist foe on its doorstep, as did most Southeast Asian nations that were not under communist control. The Suharto government in Indonesia had come to power a decade earlier due to the threat of communism and had no intention of allowing a potential communist foothold to take root nearby. Moreover, an independent East Timor might serve as a rallying point for other regions in Indonesia that wished to break away from Jakarta's control. In 1976 Indonesia made East Timor its 27th province.

Indonesia's occupation produced ongoing domestic misery and increasing foreign condemnation, but not until the Cold War ended did the likelihood of independence appear more promising. From the outset Fretilin launched an insurgency that did battle with the Indonesian army,

---

5 According to the findings of East Timor's 2006 Commission for Reception, Truth and Reconciliation (*Commisao de Acolhimento, Verdade e Reconciliacao*, or CAVR), at least 102,000 and as many as 183,000 people perished due to the Indonesian occupation. See http://www.cavr - timorleste.org for more data and methods. The U.S. State Department estimated the number to be somewhere between 100,000 and 250,000.

resulting in much death and destruction. However, in addition to combat casualties were killings, rapes, and torture by the Indonesian soldiers and the various militias they supported on the civilian population. Other human rights abuses included the mandatory relocation of Timorese, involuntary sterilizations, and imprisonment without trial. Thousands of Timorese were relocated to the Indonesian part of Timor, and more than 100,000 Indonesians got resettled in East Timor to reduce the intensity of solidarity against the occupation (shades of Stalin's ethnic relocations in Central Asia). By the 1980s, though, both domestic and international efforts began to indicate signs of hope in the struggle against Indonesia.

At home, the formation of several solidarity organizations began to take place. The National Pact for East Timor (a coalition of parties), the East Timor Action Network (an alliance of nongovernmental organizations), and the National Council for Maubere Resistance (Maubere being Timor's largest ethnic group) laid the foundation for more structured opposition. Much of that resistance can also be seen in the people's remarkable embrace of the Catholic Church during the occupation. When the Indonesian invasion began, only 20% of the population considered themselves practicing Catholics; by 1999, that number had grown to roughly 95%. Abroad, the United Nations began issuing resolutions against Indonesia's abuses during the occupation. In 1989 Pope John Paul II visited East Timor, highlighting the plight of the people under the occupation. The Santa Cruz Massacre on the outskirts of Dili, the capital, on November 12, 1991, set the stage for the imposition of increasingly successful pressure on the Suharto government to end human rights abuses. Both the U.S. Congress and Presidents George H. W. Bush and Bill Clinton agreed to impose bans on the training and sale of some military weapons to Indonesia, though such efforts came at the initiative of Congress and with foot-dragging by the presidents. In 1996 Bishop Carlos Belo (1948–present) and Jose Ramos-Horta (1949–present) received the Nobel Peace Prize for their efforts on behalf of the East Timorese people and their desire for self-determination. This honor further reminded and made more visible the horrors of the occupation. Thus, on the eve of President Suharto's departure, significant domestic and foreign resistance to his occupation had emerged.

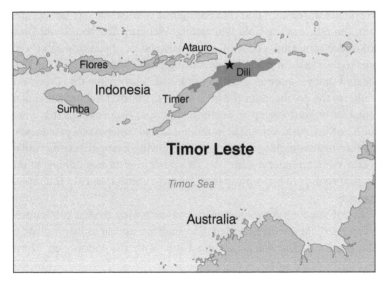

Timor Leste.

Indonesia's departure from East Timor and the arrival of an independent Timor Leste resulted from a number of immediate causes. The most important were the Asian Contagion of 1997, which helped to undermine Suharto's rule and set the stage for his removal in May 1998; and Indonesia's *Reformasi* spirit, in the context of growing international pressure, soon led President Habibie to propose some form of autonomy for East Timor. When that was rejected Habibie offered a referendum, which occurred under UN sponsorship on August 31, 1999. In a nearly 100% turnout, 78% of the voters chose independence over autonomy within Indonesia. In the wake of the referendum, the Indonesian military and their Timorese militia[6] went on a two-month campaign of demolition—killing, looting, and generally destroying infrastructure. The United Nations dispatched a peacekeeping force to restore order and to assist the East Timorese in their transition to independence in 2002. When Indonesia freed nationalist leader Xanana Gusmao (1946–present) and the last of its soldiers left East Timor on October 30, the occupation came to an end.

Timor Leste, 1999–Present

The people of East Timor had roughly 30 months after Indonesia's departure to establish the political arrangements for their nation. Domestic difficulties complicated the process. The economic sector had been devastated, the relative Timorese unity began to fray with the withdrawal of the Indonesian enemy, and tens of thousands of refugees began returning home. On the positive side, Australian and UN peacekeeping troops provided a stabilizing presence, even though the foreign military presence on Indonesia's border hurt Jakarta's feelings. In addition to foreign troops, outside developmental organizations and specialists arrived to help East Timor establish a foundation for the future. Chief among these was the UN Transitional Administration for East Timor. It managed numerous functions normally done by government until East Timor's official independence on May 20, 2002. During the UN administration, Timorese people formed a National Council to provide input to UN officials, the collaboration resulting in the creation of a cabinet, a military force, a foreign ministry, and so forth. Most important, the election of a Constituent Assembly (which became the unicameral National Parliament the following January) took place on August 30, 2001, when 16 parties fielded candidates for the 88 seats. Fretilin won 55 of the seats and thus pretty much wrote the constitution, which went into effect on Independence Day. As well, the United States provided economic aid to help rebuild much of the infrastructure destroyed during and in the aftermath of the occupation. Thus, by Independence Day, East Timor possessed much of the physical essentials to launch the new nation.

When the United Nations turned over responsibility for administration to the East Timorese elected and appointed officials the following May 20, the country could count on a fair amount of political unity as well as popular leadership. Three presidential elections have produced three different presidents: Xanana Gusmao (2002–2007), Jose Ramos-Horta (2007–2012), and Taur Matan Ruak (1956–present) (2012–present). The president serves as chief of state, appoints the prime minister, and is commander of the army. In 2008 President Ramos-Horta endured assassination attempts and wounds from those attempts, and acting presidents took over the duties of that office for brief periods. Three parliamentary elections resulted in three different governing parties (Fretilin, CNRT or National Congress for Timorese Reconstruction, and Independent) as well as four prime ministers: Mari Alkatiri (1949–present) (2002–2006), Jose Ramos-Horta (2005–2007),

---

6 Governing and occupying elites have historically utilized Timorese militia to gain intelligence and terrorize opponents. This occurred under the Portuguese, the Japanese, as well as the Indonesians.

briefly Estanislau da Silva (1952–present) from May to August 2007, and Xanana Gusmao (2007–present). Although elections and transfers of power have been generally accepted, major civil unrest[7] occurred in 2006 after the election. East Timor/Timor Leste has experienced chronic disorder and violence, so much so that the U.S. State Department advised visitors to the island to exercise extreme caution.

Timor Leste has good relations with the outside world, a fact that helps the domestic economy. Its major source of revenue comes from oil and natural gas, the major market for which is neighboring Australia. This allows for the continued upgrading of infrastructure, which improves economic development. Strained relations between those two countries over their maritime boundary in the Timor Sea, which is over who controls how much of the oil and gas rights there, were resolved in September 2017. Democracy continues to operate, though no single party seems capable of gaining a majority in the Parliament while political corruption is rampant, making effective government difficult at best.

Nonetheless the unemployment rate approaches 20% and people living below the poverty line exceed 40%, chiefly because less than 5 percent of the nation's GDP comes from agriculture while nearly two-thirds of the population (just under a million and a half people) is engaged in agricultural labor. Chronic disorder scares away foreign investment, minimizing the likelihood that the surplus of rural labor can turn to urban employment. The good news involves Timor Leste's friendly (or at least not hostile) neighbors and the international community generally. Significantly, President Megawati Sukarno of Indonesia and Xanana Gusmao for Timor Leste exchanged diplomatic relations shortly after official independence. Catholic Philippines and Portuguese-speaking Brazil have close political and economic ties with the new nation. By 2013 Timor Leste had high hopes of being accepted into the Association of Southeast Asian Nations (ASEAN), a sure sign of political arrival. Since then Timor Leste has had observer status in ASEAN, which denied it membership in 2018, largely for domestic reasons.

Territory of Papua and New Guinea to Papua New Guinea

Papua New Guinea is a preponderantly Christian country that belongs to a group of western Pacific islands known collectively as Melanesia. It occupies the eastern half of the island of New Guinea, the western half being a part of Indonesia and before 1949 a part of the Netherlands East Indies. Its people are largely of Austronesian background and their livelihood has derived chiefly from agriculture and fishing, though today logging also has become a major source of income. In the early sixteenth century, the Spanish and Portuguese came into contact with the inhabitants of the island. At that time Spaniard Don Jorge de Meneses allegedly used the Malay term *Papua*, meaning "frizzled," in reference to the people's hair, and it became a conventional term for the island and its people; two decades later, Spaniard Inigo Ortiz de Retez visited the island and named it New Guinea because its people looked to him much the same as the inhabitants of African Guinea. That name has also become a customary term for the island and often its people.

By the late nineteenth century, the entire island of New Guinea had fallen under European control. The Dutch ruled the western half of the island, which became known as Netherlands New

---

7 The three major causes for the spring 2006 unrest came first from a clash between recently fired soldiers and the national army that fired them; second from gangs of thugs that ran rampant until Australia, New Zealand, and Malaysia sent peacekeeping forces to restore a fragile order; and third from a clash between the president and the prime minister.

Guinea or Dutch New Guinea. In 1884 Britain and Germany divided the eastern part of the island, referred to as British Papua in the southeastern portion of the island and German New Guinea in the northeastern segment. The British assigned administration of British Papua to Australia, which also took administrative control over German New Guinea with the outbreak of World War I in 1914. The League of Nations in 1920 gave Britain mandate to rule the eastern part of New Guinea Island, which was referred to as the Territory of New Guinea. With the Japanese attack on British and American locations in Asia, Japanese and American military forces occupied various parts of the island at different times until the end of the war. The United Nations oversaw Australia's administration of the territory until it achieved independence in 1975. The British monarch serves as the chief of state in Papua New Guinea, and a British governor general represents the crown there.

Since the end of World War II, the government and people of Papua New Guinea have experienced numerous domestic and foreign challenges. At home, political unsteadiness has resulted from several major causes. The Parliament, which elects the prime minister, is composed of numerous political parties. This has resulted in the inability of a single party to form a stable government in the Parliament for any length of time. Although the country has had more than a dozen prime ministers since independence, the turnover of leadership before independence was even more noticeable, and so political steadiness has become marginally upgraded. Parliament has recently had an ongoing battle with the Supreme Court. In August 2011 Parliament removed Prime Minister Sir Michael Somare and appointed Peter O'Neill as prime minister. The Supreme Court ruled that the removal of Somare was illegal, thus prompting Somare's supporters to launch a mutiny. The mutiny was short-lived. The following year O'Neill defeated Somare in a parliamentary election, the results of which both contestants accepted. But the opening of an Australian-run asylum center in New Guinea in 2013 produced more and continuing political instability. O'Neill's victory in a 2017 election continued him in office as prime minister, and he remained the nation's leader through 2019, when he was succeeded by James Marape.

Today the country has numerous pressing domestic problems. Poor infrastructure, inadequate educational facilities, and appalling lack of political integrity all combine to reduce the government's image in the eyes of the people. As well, a separatist movement threatens an already wobbly central government, which is located in Port Moresby on the main island of New Guinea. The island of Bougainville has had a three-decade political and military battle with the national government over control and use of the wealth from its natural resources. Bougainville has worked out a deal with the national government, receiving a great deal of autonomy and much of the island's riches in return for cessation of hostilities.

Abroad, Papua New Guinea is a member of the British Commonwealth, has had a checkered but normally good relationship with neighboring Australia, and is working to join ASEAN. ASEAN represents a large economic bloc with much influence, but as with Laos, Cambodia, and Burma—which were initially seen as political, economic, or cultural riff-raff but later invited to join the organization—Papua New Guinea seems so far to be getting the cold shoulder from ASEAN. Nonetheless, the 21-nation Asia-Pacific Economic Cooperation Forum met in November 2018 in the nation's capital Port Moresby, with American Vice President Michael Pence attending, suggesting that the young nation's status is climbing. The country's relationship with Indonesia, with which it has a border on the island of New Guinea, has been historically troubled. The western part of the island is viewed by many in Papua New Guinea as culturally theirs, and the Free Papua Movement (*Organisasi Papua Merdeka*) formed in the late 1960s to unite the two parts of the island. The close Cold War relationship between the United States and Indonesia after 1965 likely spelled the doom of such unification in the near future. China's interest in the country's natural resources, particularly natural gas, has led Beijing to extend loans ("debt book diplomacy") to New Guinea and to build an industrial complex there.

2018 Asia-Pacific Economic Cooperation Forum. *Source:* ITAR-TASS News Agency / Alamy Stock Photo.

A more common problem in the 2010s has become refugees, largely Muslims fleeing suffering in their countries of birth. Australia is a highly desired destination of most of these migrants, but Canberra has worked out an economically attractive arrangement for the government of Papua New Guinea. The refugees will be processed in New Guinea (on Manus Island) and then resettled in various parts of New Guinea for Australian financial aid. The local populations there, as in Australia and in much of the rest of the world, appear to be in a less welcoming mood than at the turn of the twenty-first century. Washington has become more involved there, as classic migration, environmental, economic, and military interests in America and Asia search for help for a variety of problems facing New Guinea particularly and the region more generally.

Sultanate of Brunei to Brunei Darussalam

Located on the island of Borneo (Malaysia)/Kalimantan (Indonesia), Brunei appears historically in the seventh century. Two centuries later it became a tributary state of the Srivijaya, a Hindu kingdom on the neighboring Indonesian island of Sumatra. Later Brunei fell under the temporary control of the Majapahit Empire (1293–1527) on the adjacent island of Java, where Buddhism and Hinduism flourished. But Brunei threw off Majapahit vassalage and came to control the island of Borneo and parts of what are today the Philippine Islands. Brunei converted to Islam as Indian influence there came to reflect Islamic rule under the Muslim Delhi sultans, then governing India. When Awang Alak Betatar, the ruler of Brunei from 1363 to 1402, embraced Islam he became known as Sultan Muhammad Shah. With the arrival of the Europeans, Brunei's territory gradually contracted, and in the nineteenth century the British gained control of northern Borneo. By 1889 Brunei was reduced to a small Sultanate that had become a British protectorate. World War II brought Japanese occupation, after which Brunei returned to British rule.

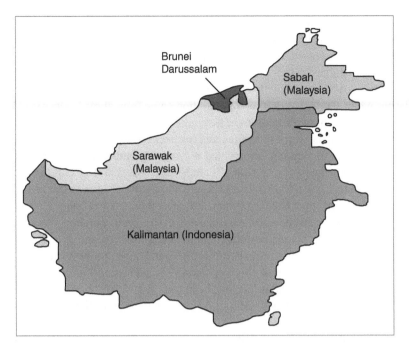

Brunei, on the Island of Kalimantan (Indonesia) / Borneo (Malaysia). *Source:* © John Wiley & Sons, Inc.

Postwar Brunei progressively moved toward self-government and independence. In 1950 this oil-rich sultanate came under the control of Omar Ali Saifuddin III (1914–1986), and during his rule Brunei inaugurated a constitution in 1959, creating a constitutional monarchy. In the early 1960s, as Sarawak, Sabah, and Brunei considered joining Malaysia, a revolt broke out in Brunei. The Brunei People's Party won the September 1962 election, wanted to end the sultan's powers, and sought to form a new nation composed of Brunei, Sabah, and Sarawak. The party was tied to the Sukarno Indonesian government (which controlled three-quarters of Kalimantan/Borneo), to the Philippines, and to several leftist organizations. This prompted the sultan of Brunei to invalidate the election, ban the People's Party, and declare martial law. In December that year, the Brunei Revolt broke out, launched by Brunei leftists and supported by Indonesia, which wanted a friendly government in Brunei. The British sent troops to quell the revolt, which it quickly did, but Indonesia launched their *Konfrontasi* to prevent the creation of Malaysia. In that conflict, the British helped Malaysia while Brunei got involved by allowing the British to deploy troops from its territory against Indonesia. Ultimately Brunei opted to remain a British protectorate and not to join Malaysia, largely because it feared its oil wealth would be siphoned off by Kuala Lumpur. Relations between the two nations have been rather cool since.

By the mid-1960s, British pressure for Brunei to become more democratic led to Sultan Omar's abdication in 1967 but did not lead to democracy. The new sultan, Hassanal Bolkiah (1946–present), officially became ruler in 1968 and remains in power to this day. His authority is based on the concept known as *Melayu Islam Beraja* or Malay Muslim Monarchy, basically a divine-right absolutist monarchy. Brunei remained a British protectorate until 1971, but until its independence in 1984 London took responsibility for the sultanate's foreign affairs and defense. The government remains in the hands of the sultan and many royal family members, while the Legislative Council, various political parties, and the sultan's subjects in general operate within the constraints imposed by the government. About two-thirds of the subjects are of Malay background, perhaps 15 percent are ethnic Chinese, while the remainder is imported foreign labor. Most the Chinese and all of the foreigners lack citizenship, a policy designed to assure a Malay-Muslim majority culturally.

Brunei's wealth has diminished domestic discontent, but it has also raised several issues. Can the Sultanate continue to count on wealth based chiefly on oil and gas? Is a country of 400,000 in danger of major culture clashes when 100,000 of that total population come from abroad? Does such an abundance of wealth create corruption difficulties? The country is attempting to diversify its economy, to limit the time foreigners may work in Brunei, and to check corruption—even when it occurs in the royal family. Prince Jefri Bolkiah has created an ongoing embarrassment for his brother, the sultan of Brunei. The prince—whose family includes four wives and 17 children as well as a harem—has hotels, a mansion on Long Island in New York, a ranch in Las Vegas, along with several hundred other properties, more than 2000 cars, and several planes and boats. He has been in and out of the news because of his playboy activities and extravagant spending—by one estimate, $50 million a month. As well, his sexual interests—involving women, art, and names (one boat is named "tits" while its two dinghies are called "nipple 1" and "nipple 2")—insure that he will remain in the news. Moreover, his legal troubles across the globe continue to attract unwanted media attention. Word has it that the prince has been put on a $50,000 per month stipend and had many of his trinkets confiscated by the sultan. Such behavior by a royal family member could trigger political trouble down the road.

Brunei will likely remain a wealthy nation and continue to avoid many of the regional problems its neighbors face. At home the government has preserved a peaceful environment in a land of plenty. Abroad, it can confidently look to protection from Britain and the United States should troubles from any of its neighbors arise. The country also maintains a good relationship with Singapore. Of course, a perfect political storm—falling oil prices, corruption, royal extravagance, irate immigrants, South China Sea troubles, local and exiled democracy advocates, and religious issues—could conspire to topple the monarchy in the near future. The gradual introduction of Sharia law, launched in three stages beginning in May 2014, created much apprehension in Brunei and from abroad. Will strict laws, strictly applied, with strict punishments including execution (in the third stage) be carried out? Given that Brunei's oil and natural gas resources will run out in the next quarter century or so, given that foreign investment can help compensate for that eventual loss of oil income, and given that foreign investment will be less likely in a strict Sharia law environment, a religious reign of terror seems less probable. As of 2019, there were no executions to report.

Commonwealth of the Philippines to Republic of the Philippines

The end of World War II produced both sighs of relief and agendas for recovery. What were the priorities for the Philippines? For most Filipinos, psychological recovery and physical reconstruction from the wartime damage led the list of "to do" items. This was particularly true in urban areas where living conditions were most life-threatening given the destruction of housing, public health facilities, and basic infrastructure. At the same time, dealing with those who collaborated with the Japanese and preparing for independence also required prompt and focused attention. All of these serious issues had to be addressed in a Cold War environment, a setting made all the more serious with the onset of the communist Huk insurgency. The Huks remained a dangerous threat to the new republic into the mid-1950s. As the Philippines sided with the West in the Cold War, and since much of the American anticommunist efforts in Asia relied on U.S. bases in the Philippines, the Cold War impact on the Philippines played a major role in the nation's politics. At the national level, at least, no president won reelection from 1946 to 1969, in part due to two untimely deaths, partly to domestic political and economic issues, but also because of Cold War domestic disputes, particularly those involving American bases. As America became more involved in the Vietnam War by 1965, the war added to existing socioeconomic problems and created a more impassioned political environment.

Philippine politics after 1965 has revolved around the presidency and later the martial law administration of Ferdinand Marcos (1917–1989). Essentially the question to be answered was: Would the Philippines be governed and modernized by an authoritarian regime as in South Korea, Taiwan, Singapore, and other newly independent and economically successful nations? Or would the democratic process, with all of its checks on government, provide the best means of guiding the country on the road to orderly—if bumpy—progress? The authoritarian path Marcos chose in 1972 had failed to lift the country after a decade of martial law, and dissidents began to multiply and organize. Senator Benigno S. Aquino, Jr. (1932–1983), emerged as the chief opposition to Marcos, and his murder in 1983 set the stage for the downfall of Marcos in 1986.

But the ouster of Marcos did not resolve the question of what kind of government the nation should adopt, nor did it resolve many of the problems the country has experienced since independence. The attempted military coup in 1987 against President Corazon Aquino (1933–2009) certainly does not represent democratic sentiment. As well, Ferdinand Marcos's widow Imelda Marcos emerged as a rallying point for those who supported her husband's approach to politics, running for and losing the race for president twice and winning a congressional seat. Her son and daughter have also won elective office in the twenty-first century. And while the economy has improved since the turn of the century, poverty remains painfully high. The Huk insurgency has subsided but its New People's Army remains a thorn in the government's side, while terrorist groups, particularly the Abu Sayed, continue to threaten the nation's stability. The American bases issue seemingly got resolved in 1991, when the United States and the Philippines could not agree on future arrangements for America's continued presence. But the rise of China and ongoing terrorist threats produced several agreements (one as recently as 2012) between the two countries for the return in a limited way of American forces. Lawlessness and corruption remain rampant, as in much of the rest of Asia, but dreadful social conditions could easily provide the inspiration for radical alternatives to the existing political thought and institutions.

Independence, the Onset of the Cold War, and Social Concerns, 1945–1965

The first two decades of Philippine independence produced an array of challenges for the new republic. As physical recovery from the war proceeded, the government had to deal with the emotional issue of collaboration. This largely involved those from the *ilustrados* or educated and landed elite, who disproportionately worked in some fashion for the Japanese. That presented several problems. Since World War I, the *ilustrados* have controlled—and still greatly influence—Philippine politics. The United States had governed with the cooperation of the *ilustrados* before the war against Japan and had attempted to insure that the same elite would launch Philippine independence. But both Washington's elite (among whom disagreements about America's Philippine policy flourished) and the vast majority of the Philippine people (including a majority of the *ilustrados*) wanted collaborators punished. Thus the Filipino People's Court, whose members were appointed by President Sergio Osmena (1878–1961), convened in September 1945. Headed by Harvard Law–trained Lorenzo Tanada, the court was underfunded and understaffed. Moreover, likely wartime collaborator Manual Roxas (1892–1948) got the political seal of approval from General Douglas MacArthur, the man who promised to, and indeed did, "return" to liberate the Philippines. The Court charged another collaborator, Japanese puppet President Jose Laurel (1891–1959), with 130 counts of treason. But by 1947, the People's Court had become if not quite a sad joke then an institutional disappointment. Before the April 1946 election, People's Court member Elpidio Quirino (1890–1956) resigned to defend Roxas. Roxas then made Quirino his vice presidential running mate. Roxas defeated Osmena and proclaimed a general amnesty in 1948 just before his death, thus making Quirino the new Philippine president. Quirino defeated Laurel in the 1949 election, but by then the stigma attached to collaboration had considerably subsided.

While the Philippines were beginning to repair wartime destruction and mishandling the collaboration matter, the people prepared for the transition to independence on July 4, 1946.[8] That transition involved the future relationship between the United States and the Philippines. The chief details of that relationship were contained in treaties and agreements made during the first decade of independence. The most vital include the 1946 Treaty of Manila, the Bell Trade Act/Philippine Trade Act of 1946, the 1947 Military Bases Agreement, and the 1952 Mutual Defense Treaty. The Manila Treaty, which granted the Philippines independence, was signed on Philippine Independence Day in 1946. That year the Bell Trade Act established economic relations between the two nations. It called for free trade of sorts until 1954, allowing America to export freely to the Philippines and the Philippines to export to America without tariffs, though not without quotas. Thereafter the United States could then begin to impose tariffs on Philippine products. Other aspects of the Bell Trade Act allowed for preferred American economic influence, such as allowing Americans equal access to natural resources and investment opportunities as Filipinos. The Philippine Rehabilitation Act of 1946 provided American funds to help rebuild the war-torn economy.

At the same time, the Cold War and the process of decolonization in Asia generated insurgency movements and thus possibly Philippine and American interests. Accordingly, America attempted to prepare for hostile activities in the Philippines and the rest of Asia. The Military Bases Agreement of 1947 gave America ongoing control of 23 bases, the most significant being Clark Air Base and the Subic Bay naval facility. In 1956, the United States began the process of revising the agreement, which had generated a great deal of popular opposition in the Philippines. Washington gave up most of the bases and acknowledged that the Philippines retained sovereignty over the bases the Americans would continue to utilize. And a U.S. Military Advisory group was established to train and equip the Philippine armed forces. In 1951, as the Cold War raged across the globe—and "hot wars," most notably in Korea and Vietnam—Washington and Quezon City[9] agreed to a Mutual Defense Treaty. It called for each signatory to come to the aid of the other if under attack. The message was quite clear: An attack on the Philippines would be considered an attack on the United States. As well, Washington rallied numerous nations with interests in Southeast Asia to form an alliance in 1954. Known as the Southeast Asia Treaty Organization (SEATO), it was formed to contain the spread of communism in the region. But its membership consisted chiefly of countries beyond Southeast Asia. Only the Philippines and Thailand became SEATO members; the others claimed to be non-aligned or—in the case of Vietnam (North and South), Cambodia, and Laos—were forbidden by the Geneva Conference of 1954 from joining. The Huk insurgency, supported by

---

8 In August 1964, President Diosdado Macapagal changed the nation's Independence Day to June 12, designating that day in 1898 when Emilio Aguinaldo declared Philippine independence from Spain as the official Philippine Independence Day. July 4 is now known as Philippine-American Friendship Day.

9 Quezon City, in the greater Manila area, was the Philippine capital from 1948 to 1976; since then, Manila has served as the capital city.

the Communist Party of the Philippines, created a sense of urgency in Washington and among the leaders of the Philippine government.

The Huk[10] movement appeared in the early years of World War II and remained a major political player in Philippine politics in the decade after that war for the same reason: because of the Philippine elite. The bulk of the *Ilustrados* and landlords collaborated with the Japanese during the war. When the same *Ilustrados* and landlords reemerged to govern an independent Philippines after the war, the people faced government corruption, nepotism, and inefficiency in conjunction with a major land tenure problem. These produced a crisis of legitimacy for the national and local governments. Subsequently discontented peasants—particularly those in Pampanga Province on Luzon Island—joined the Huk movement in droves. Led by Luis Taruc (1913–2005), the Huks arose initially to provide leadership for land reform in the 1930s and for resistance to the Japanese during World War II. When the war ended, the Huks offered a revolutionary alternative to the existing postwar Philippine government. During the 1930s Taruc left his business, turned his attention to the land tenure problems facing the Philippine peasants, and joined the Socialist Party, which was then the legal arm of the Communist Party of the Philippines. With the Japanese invasion, Taruc became the leader of Philippine Huk guerrillas who gained a wartime reputation as patriots and reformers. After the war, Taruc ran for a seat in the Philippine House of Representatives, was elected, but then was not permitted to take his seat. The official reason was election fraud, but actually it was due to his leadership of a leftist organization. Thus began the Huk insurgency.

The Huk–Philippine government struggle, which raged until 1954, involved three principal participants: Luis Taruc, Ramon Magsaysay, and Edward Lansdale. Taruc cobbled together a combat force of some 50,000 insurgents for a number of reasons. Chief among them was a gradual breakdown in the relationship between the landed elite and the poor tenant farmers. Historically this patron–client bond involved the patron/landlord providing protection or some other kind of assistance, for instance loans, to the clients/tenants. The worsening relationship began to come apart just as the 1929 global depression got underway. Deteriorating land tenure issues during the depression, such as the higher cost of rents that found the peasants keeping less than half of what they produced, also contributed to rural discontent. Traditionally peasants had been guaranteed enough of the harvest to support their families at a subsistence level. When that guarantee began to disappear, the peasants believed that the landlord had failed to uphold his side of the relationship and many felt justified in rebelling against the now-flawed system. The hostility between landlord and peasant intensified when Japan occupied the Philippines, and the landlords typically collaborated with the invaders while the peasants, under Huk leadership, fought them.

At war's end, the newly independent Philippine government policies and practices soon produced a Huk resistance. Government corruption and the military's indiscriminate killing and destruction in pursuit of the Huks also helped to swell the ranks of the rebels. Nonetheless, the government began to turn the tide against the insurgents, the bulk of whose leadership had been captured in 1950. Moreover, the Huks had no meaningful outside material support, since the insurgency had no friendly adjacent source of weaponry or sanctuary. As well, the United States began vigorously supporting the elected government with weapons and a counterinsurgency specialist, Air Force officer and CIA agent Edward Lansdale (1908–1987). Lansdale worked closely with Ramon Magsaysay (1907–1958), a Liberal Party congressman who was picked by President Quirino to become Secretary of National Defense. Both men recognized the chief causes of the

---

10 Huk is the common name given to the organization known as *Hukbong Bayan Laban sa Hapon* or *Hukbalahap*, headed by Luis Taruc between 1942 and 1954.

insurrection and came up with a program to remove those causes. To reverse the peasants' negative view of the military, the dynamic duo used the army to help the rural population. Feeling that President Quirino resisted his suggestions for further agrarian reform, Magsaysay resigned from the Liberal Party and ran for president in 1953 on the Nacionalista Party ticket. He defeated Quirino handily, likely with much CIA money and other assistance. President Magsaysay launched a program to resettle both tenant and landless farmers on surplus government land, set up rural credit agencies, and made available a host of other organizations designed to help the struggling farmer. By 1954, the Huk movement had indeed subsided as Magsaysay's programs began to take hold. Unfortunately, his death in a 1957 plane crash removed the reformist vigor and began a return of the old elite.

Magsaysay's immediate successors as president laid the groundwork for the rule of Ferdinand Marcos by not successfully dealing with crime, corruption, and feeble economic growth. Vice President Carlos Garcia (1896–1971) assumed the presidency on the death of Magsaysay and then won election to the office. His administration is best known for its anticommunism and Filipino nationalism. Garcia supported America's foreign policy in Asia, but his Filipino First Policy criticized foreign economic influence. This criticism was largely directed at American investments in the Philippines, and Garcia reduced foreign imports to encourage Filipino businesses. The Filipino First program likewise attacked the economic power of Filipinos of ethnic Chinese background. Moreover, Garcia's nationalist program resulted in a change in America's use of military bases. In 1959 Washington and Quezon City entered into the Bohlen-Serrano Agreement, which reduced the 1947 military bases lease agreement with America from 99 years to 44 years. Vice President Diosdado Macapagal (1910–1997) overcame Garcia in the 1961 presidential election. Many believe that the CIA financed Macapagal's campaign. This likely occurred as a result of Garcia's ardent but, as Washington viewed it, misdirected nationalism. When Macapagal assumed the presidency, he reversed Garcia's policy of reducing foreign imports, claiming this had less to do with foreign imports and more to do with Garcia's corrupt crony capitalism that favored Garcia's business friends. Macapagal usually worked to promote more open and competitive markets, but an ongoing anemic economy, widespread corruption, and rampant lawlessness prevented Macapagal from winning reelection.

Democracy and Its Discontents: Marcos, Martial Law, and People Power, 1965–1986

In the presidential election of 1965, candidate Ferdinand Marcos presented an image of wartime guerrilla leader, accomplished legislator, and dazzling lawyer. His Nacionalista Party platform of reform called for rural development, infrastructure expansion, economic growth, and "the genuine rule of law." His victory over Macapagal suggested that Marcos had opened the door to a popular feeling of hope. But as his administration got underway, only the public works programs could be considered successful. Quite early it became apparent that no meaningful land reform would be possible given the interests of the landed elite, a failure that plagued all pre- and post-independence administrations. Corruption and lawlessness plus Muslim and communist insurgencies seemed beyond the president's ability to handle without extraconstitutional powers. As the 1969 election approached, Marcos began using the military—as Magsaysay had done earlier—largely to carry out infrastructure projects. Marcos continued to expand the military role in typically civilian government functions after his impressive and corrupt victorious campaign against Sergio Osmena, Jr. He became the first Philippine president to achieve a second term.

Marcos began his second term facing angry demonstrations and ended it (or perhaps extended it) prematurely with a declaration of martial law. Three antigovernment forces illustrate the growing discontent with the newly inaugurated president. One—tied to ongoing Muslim–Christian relations and referred to as the Corregidor Incident or the Jabidah Massacre of March 18, 1968— resulted from the killings of at least two dozen Moro Muslim soldiers in the Philippine Army. These soldiers were to be given special training for a possible campaign in Sabah, a British colony that became independent and joined the newly created nation of Malaysia. In 1967 the sultan of Sulu had ceded Sabah to the Philippines, Marcos then claimed Sabah, and the Muslim soldiers on Corregidor revolted at the prospect of fighting fellow Muslims. As news of the deaths of the soldiers got out, Benigno Aquino and the Liberal Party used the incident in the 1968 election. As well, ongoing Muslim protests and animosity continued into Marcos's second term, with the activists now organized into the Moro National Liberation Front. The second hostile force that Marcos faced was the newly reconstituted Communist Party and its military arm, the New People's Army. And more broadly, the third opposition group likely involved a large cross section of the people who believed that Marcos had stolen the 1969 election. In January 1970 numerous protests took place, ending in the "Battle of Mendiola" late that month. Marcos had just opened Congress and barely escaped 10,000 angry protestors, four of whom died in the ensuing clash with police. Increasingly, Aquino emerged as the leader of the loyal opposition.

As Marcos's second term proceeded, growing fears emerged that the president would attempt to evade the two-term limit on presidents. Since the Congress had passed a resolution in 1967 calling for a constitutional convention to replace the 1935 American-sponsored document, people wondered if the new constitution would keep the two-term limit. Meanwhile, chronic bombings of suspicious but uncertain origins destroyed property and eventually killed people, including several opposition Liberal Party candidates in the 1971 midterm elections. At the same time, the constitutional convention in June 1971 established a two-term limit, but Marcos got it invalidated, by bribery according to his critics. He answered his critics by calling for a "New Society," a society that strict democratic principles would thwart. Marcos noticed that the emerging "tigers" or "dragons" in East Asia had one thing in common: authoritarian government. A strong ruler with a sturdy state structure would launch the new order. Standing in Marcos's way and threatening Philippine stood several antagonists. He reasonably feared the Muslim and communist insurgencies as well as corrupt bureaucrats and media critics. Marcos most likely dreaded even more the ever-increasing popularity of his chief political rival, Benigno "Ninoy" Aquino. In this setting of uprisings, lawlessness, and heated political competition, Marcos proclaimed martial law on September 23, 1972.

Martial law lasted nearly a decade after his reelection, ending in 1981. Martial law as promoted aimed to create the order necessary for New Society reforms. While halting efforts were made in land reform and superficial attempts to curtail corruption were advertised, Marcos helped his friends and family (Imelda Marcos reportedly owned more than 1000 pairs of shoes and in other ways plundered the nation's treasury) and punished his enemies economically. Politically many of his enemies, such as Benigno Aquino, ended up in jail. Just as dreadfully, he turned the military into an organization whose commanders got rewarded on the basis of political reliability instead of talent. When he left office, the nation was in deep debt. Still, some of Marcos's programs could be considered genuine accomplishments. His relationship with the United States, for example, produced two significant outcomes. He successfully renegotiated a military bases deal in 1979 that established Philippine sovereignty over those bases, and the following year, with Washington's urging, Benigno Aquino was released from prison and allowed to go to America for medical treatment. Three years later, when Aquino returned to the Philippines, he was killed at the airport. Few doubted then or now that Marcos had him assassinated, and eventually President Ronald Reagan

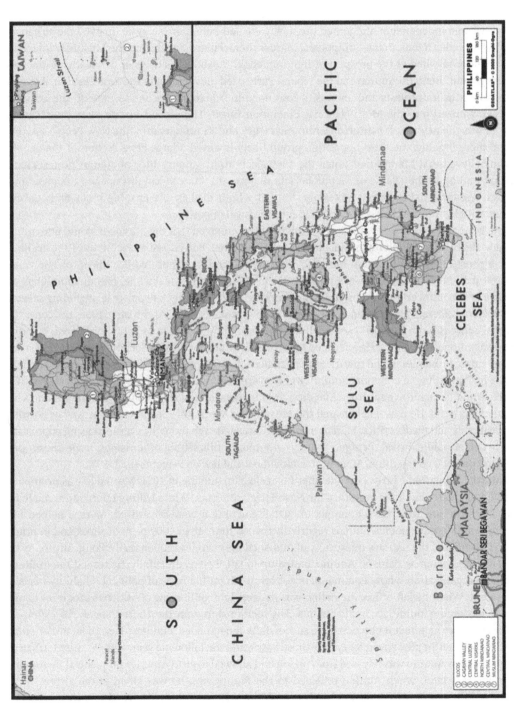

Republic of the Philippines. *Source:* © John Wiley & Sons, Inc.

pulled the plug on the Philippine ruler. By that time the Catholic Church and much of the military had deserted Marcos, who went into exile in Hawaii in 1986 and died there in 1989.

Return to Democracy, 1986–Present

Aquino's death and Marcos's departure ushered in the People Power Revolution headed by Corazon "Cory" Aquino (1933–2009), widow of the slain politician. Cory Aquino's movement had mass support, so in December 1985 Marcos called a "snap" election (an earlier-than-required election) for February 1986 to head off growing anti-Marcos demonstrations. The "Marcos" results of that election made him the winner, but few believed the numbers, and even greater protests erupted. In that context, the Philippine elite along with Washington sided with Mrs. Aquino, and she was declared the election winner and sworn in as Philippine president. Thus began the effort to restore democratic government, a part of which included the writing of a new constitution. Cory Aquino traveled to Washington to cement her country's relationship with America and spoke before a joint session of the U.S. Congress. Mrs. Aquino also fended off seven attempted coups during her tenure, which ended in 1992.

> Three years ago, I left America in grief to bury my husband, Ninoy Aquino. I thought I had left it also to lay to rest his restless dream of Philippine freedom. Today, I have returned as the president of a free people. In burying Ninoy, a whole nation honored him. By that brave and selfless act of giving honor, a nation in shame recovered its own. A country that had lost faith in its future found it in a faithless and brazen act of murder. So in giving, we receive, in losing we find, and out of defeat, we snatched our victory.
>
> *Source:* Speech of Her Excellency Corazon C. Aquino, President of the Philippines, delivered during the Joint Session of the United States Congress, Washington, DC, September 18, 1986.

While a symbol of courage and determination, she achieved mixed results in a number of important areas. In 1991 Aquino attempted but failed to extend the military bases agreement, when the "Magnificent Twelve" Philippine senators defeated the treaty, temporarily ending American military presence in the Philippines the following year. Nor could she erode the crony capitalism and assorted other corrupt practices that were hallmarks of the Marcos years. Additionally her attempts to tackle the nation's poverty, especially the plight of the farmer, met with few accomplishments. But Mrs. Aquino did preside over a peaceful transfer of office to her successor, Fidel Ramos (1928–present). Ramos is typically credited with starting to get the country out of the financial mess left by Marcos, in part by making his country friendly to foreign investment and encouraging private enterprise free of crony capitalism, though the Asian financial crisis of 1997 temporarily slowed economic growth. He also attempted to work out relationships with insurrectionary movements, such as the Communist Party, the Moro National Liberation Front (MNLF), and the Moro Islamic Liberation Front (MILF). Presidents Aquino and Ramos steered the political and economic turnarounds in the Philippines as the twenty-first century approached.

Corruption, attempted coups, and insurrections continued to plague Philippine politics in the new century, but greater government stability and economic growth have emerged to become the new national expectations. But it is also true that the old elite endure, two of the three twenty-first-century presidents being the children of former presidents. However, Joseph Estrada (1937–present), successor to Fidel Ramos, did not come from Philippine high society. Estrada, born Jose Ejercito, grew up in a middle-class family, became a movie star, and had lengthy political experience, serving as a mayor, senator, and vice president before being elected president. He oversaw the making of the Visiting Forces Agreement with America in 1998, largely a result of Muslim insurrectionary activities in the southern Philippines and their possible connection to Middle Eastern terrorists. His six-year term was cut short in 2000 when the House of Representatives impeached Estrada for corruption and perjury. But before the Senate trial concluded in 2007, street protests drove the president from office in 2001. So while corruption will never likely be completely eliminated in the Philippines, Estrada's removal became a cautionary tale for future politicians.

Vice President Gloria Macapagal-Arroyo (1947–present) served out the remainder of Estrada's term and was elected president in her own right in 2004. She also inherited the "tradition" of attempted coups, one in 2007 resulting in her issuing a state of emergency. Efforts by the Philippine House to impeach her for corruption failed, but charges of election irregularities and the illegal use of state lottery funds finally caught up with her. After her presidency ended, and her election and reelection to the Philippine House, she was arrested for those latter charges. She remains under home or hospital arrest, depending on the status of her numerous health problems.

After a brief career in business, Benigno "Noynoy" Aquino III (1960–present) joined the "family business" of politics. His grandfather became the Speaker of the House under the Japanese, his father was a senator and activist likely assassinated by Marcos supporters, and his mother was the central figure in the People Power movement that ousted Marcos and later became president. Teetotaler Noynoy served in the Philippine House and Senate, ran for the presidency in the 2010 election in the wake of his mother's recent death, and promised to strengthen the nation's defenses, a Social Contract to empower the people, and a campaign against corruption. The emphasis on defense is partly a reaction to the ongoing insurrections but largely now over the presence of China—especially its island building—in the South China Sea. The empowerment effort promised to improve the balance of power between the poor and the wealthy, but the economy—even with its 5 percent growth since the turn of the twenty-first century—has not been so generous with the agricultural sector, where most people work and where wages are lowest. Articles of impeachment have also been introduced in the House, alleging that the president has violated constitutional strictures.

The 2016 presidential election produced a populist president, Rodrigo Duterte (1945–present), who promised to shake up the political system. While Duterte will deal with substantially the same problems the country has faced since independence, his prime objectives focus on rooting out drugs and corruption. The longtime mayor of Davao in Mindanao, Duterte as president has gone after drug dealers with a vengeance, leading some to claim he is even sanctioning the formation of extralegal vigilante death squads to eliminate the traffickers and other criminals as well.

Foreign relations will likely gain greater interest in voters' minds, as China edges ever closer to Philippine territory and Washington sends uncertain signals as to its future role in Asia. But it remains unclear if President Obama's America was making a significant "pivot" to Asia (from the Middle East) and if President Trump's America (especially after America withdrew from the Trans-Pacific Partnership) more likely reflects America's future role in Asia. Washington has a 1951 Mutual Defense Treaty and a 2014 Enhanced Defense Cooperation Agreement with the Philippines. American military personnel have been operating in the Philippines, largely dealing with anti-terrorist activities on the southern island of Mindanao. Duterte ran for president opposing the establishment of American military bases in the Philippines. He also has moved away from Washington and drawn his country closer to Xi Jinping and China, even though Beijing and Manila have conflicting claims in the South China Sea.

Suggested Readings and Viewings

Anders Carr, *Great Powers, Great Strategies: The New Game in the South China Sea* (Annapolis, MD: Naval Institute Press, 2018).

Helen-Louise Hunter, *Sukarno and the Indonesian Coup: The Untold Story* (Westport, CT: Praeger, 2007).

Benedict J. Kirkvliet, *The Huk Rebellion: A Study of Peasant Revolt in the Philippines*, 2nd ed. (Lanham, MD: Rowman & Littlefield, 2002).

Andrea Molnar, *Timor Leste: Politics, History, and Culture* (Oxford: Routledge, 2011).

Puruambo (2005), dir. by Pavol Barabas. A documentary on New Guinea, focusing on the island's population and environment.

Graham Saunders, *A History of Brunei*, 2nd ed. (Oxford: Routledge, 2002).

David Joel Steinberg, *The Philippines: A Singular and a Plural Place*, 4th ed. (Boulder, CO: Westview Press, 2000).

Nicholas Tarling, ed., *From World War II to the Presen, vol. 2, part 2 of Cambridge History of Southeast Asia* (Cambridge: Cambridge University Press, 1999).

Adrian Vickers, *A History of Modern Indonesia* (Cambridge: Cambridge University Press, 2005).

John Walco, *A Short History of Papua New Guinea*, 2nd ed. (Oxford: Oxford University Press, 2014).

Lynn T. White III, *Philippine Politics: Possibilities and Problems in a Localist Democracy* (Oxford: Routledge, 2014).

Year of Living Dangerously (1982), dir. by Peter Weir. An Australian motion picture about events surrounding the 1965 overthrow of Achmed Sukarno in Indonesia.

28

Colonialism, Independence, and Nation Building on the Northern Frontiers of India and China, 1850–2019: Afghanistan, Central and Inner Asia, and the Russian Far East

For Muslims everywhere Saudi support for the Taliban is deeply embarrassing, because the Taliban's interpretation of Islam is so negative and destructive.[1]

Introduction

To the north of India and China, ongoing battles among empires intensified in the nineteenth century—between Tsarist Russia and Britain above India in Afghanistan and Central Asia, as well as among expansive Russia and Britain and declining Manchu Qing China in Tibet and Mongolia. The jockeying for power and position across the Eurasian steppe between Russia and Britain has been labeled the "Great Game." While some of the contestants in that struggle have been added or subtracted over the decades, and though the positions of those participants have changed, a "great game" continues in the region into the twenty-first century. British India is replaced by independent India; Tsarist Russia became the Soviet Union and eventually the Russian Federation; Manchu Qing China departed, replaced by Republican China and now the People's Republic of China; colonized Central Asia under Tsarist rule gave way to Soviet colonization under the Communists and now consists of five independent nations; Mongolia left the Qing Dynasty orbit and fell under Soviet direction, and eventually became truly independent with the collapse of the Soviet Union in 1991.

As India and China reemerge as the principal national influences in Asia, what happens on their frontiers takes on growing importance. Russia and the United States remain the premier global nuclear powers, but since both have extensive interests in Asia, the rise of nuclear China and nuclear India presents new challenges as well as older problems. Smaller nations on these frontiers often present difficulties that have the potential of drawing in nuclear powers. Since World War II numerous flashpoints have emerged on these frontiers: between the United States/United Nations and China and Russia in Korea; between India and Pakistan; between India and China; between Russia and Afghanistan; between the United States/NATO and the Taliban in Afghanistan; and between China and the Soviet Union, to name just the most dangerous. Other flashpoints—for example, between North Korea and South Korea, North Korea and Japan, locations and nations with interests in the South China Sea or the Indian Ocean, and other locations—have made military conflict among the great powers a real possibility.

---

1 Ahmed Rashid, *Taliban: Militant Islam, Oil and Fundamentalism in Central Asia*, 2nd ed. (New Haven, CT: Yale University Press, 2000), p. 211.

Asia Past and Present: A Brief History, First Edition. Peter P. Wan and Thomas D. Reins.
© 2021 John Wiley & Sons, Inc. Published 2021 by John Wiley & Sons, Inc.

During the Cold War, relationships between the two principal competitors, though typically tense, were nonetheless controlled. Cold War conflicts tended to occur between American allies—such as South Korea or Pakistan—and Soviet allies, for example North Korea or India. As the Cold War and its priorities passed into history, modernizing nations in Asia developed or acquired nuclear weapons—China, India, Pakistan, and perhaps North Korea—making their actions more difficult to control, coordinate, or influence. The best check on nearly any nation's rash behavior is the likelihood that war could truly destroy successful economic development. Of course, failing states such as Pakistan or North Korea have less to lose, making their actions more difficult to predict or contain. Moreover, should the United States show signs of reducing its Asian presence, it would shake up the balance of forces in that region of the world. For example, should Japan conclude it could not count on the protection of America's nuclear umbrella, it would almost certainly rearm and likely develop its own nuclear arsenal. Such a turn of events would begin an Asian arms race, as China would feel threatened; as China upped its military development, India would take notice; that would alarm Sunni Pakistan, as would Shi'a Iran as it moves toward nuclear status; Indonesia would probably join the arms race; and so on. Managing developments in an increasingly wealthy and powerful Asia will require a great deal of skill and a fair amount of luck.

Afghanistan

By the nineteenth century, the "Great Game" began as Russia's control in Central Asia and improved relations with Persia threatened Afghanistan, a customary base from which foreigners invaded India. Thus anxious British India officials wanted to drive the Russians out of Central Asia, which is what the Russians accused London of attempting as it moved north into Punjab and Kashmir, closer to Central Asia. Britain also moved into Afghanistan to check Russia's advances in the region, but this provoked opposition from the Afghans. The ensuing three Anglo-Afghan wars fought between 1838 and 1919 were designed not only to keep the Russians out but also to insure that the Afghan monarchy would be under British direction. Once in substantial control, the British took the opportunity to establish a line of demarcation between what then was western India (today's Pakistan) and Afghanistan. The Durand Line, named after Sir Henry Mortimer Durand, drew a new frontier between British India and Afghanistan. It severed much of eastern Afghanistan and a large part of the ethnic Pashtuns therein, and put the land and its people under British control in 1893.

Timeline for Afghanistan, 1850–2019	
1838–1919	British engage in three Anglo-Afghan wars to keep Russia out of Afghanistan, the gateway to India that the British controlled
1893	Durand Line set, annexing parts of ethnic Pashtun territory for British India
1919	Afghanistan declares independence from Britain
1953–1978	Mohammad Daoud becomes prime minister (1953), resigns that office (1963), and stages coup ending Afghan monarchy and establishes a republic (1973); assassinated by pro-Soviet elements he once courted (1978)
1979–1989	Soviet Union invades to support its side in the Afghan civil war

1979–1996	Mujahedeen, with American and Pakistani aid, defeat the Soviets but fail to establish a viable government
1996–2001	The Taliban, an offshoot of the Mujahedeen, establish the Islamic Emirate of Afghanistan
2001	al Qaeda, headquartered in Afghanistan, launches a terrorist attack on the United States (9/11); by that December, the Taliban are driven from its capital in Kabul
2001–2015	American and NATO forces attempt to crush Taliban and create a stable central government; their combat forces depart, and the fate of the central government and the Taliban remain undecided
2019	The United States conducts talks with the Taliban to work out terms for American withdrawal of all or most of its forces

The Durand Line created problems then and continues to generate misfortunes today. Before the turn of the twentieth century, the Pashtuns launched a jihad against the British, and the people began to switch from a more moderate Sufi Islam to a more fundamentalist outlook. Now a part of northwestern Pakistan, the region has become the nerve center of terrorist groups, such as the Afghan Taliban and the Haqqani Network. Until India achieved independence in 1947, though, Britain kept Russia (Tsarist and Soviet) out of Afghanistan.

British influence in Afghanistan began to wane with the advent of nationalism in the nineteenth century. The thought and behavior of Mahmud Beg Tarzi (1865–1933) best illustrate a nascent Afghan move from tribal and religious priorities to more national concerns. He was a modernizer with secular leanings who opposed religious fundamentalism, and whose newspaper *Serej-al-Akhbar* became the nucleus for those Afghans desiring social change and genuine freedom from foreign meddling. World War I weakened colonial administrations across the world as most powers focused on the conflict in Europe, thereby allowing anticolonial organizations to emerge. In the case of Afghanistan, the emergent monarchy sought to create a stronger central government administration to more effectively deal with tribes scattered across the mountainous nation. Centralization reached its height between 1919 and 1929 during the reign of Amanullah Khan (1892–1960). At home he inherited a fledgling bureaucracy and a national army of sorts, which he strengthened and used against the British in the Third Anglo-Afghan War (1919). The Rawalpindi Agreement ended the fighting and set the stage for the 1921 Anglo-Afghan Treaty. That document officially ended the war and gave the country complete independence from Britain, but it also secured the Afghan acceptance of the Durand Line. The Afghans do regard the treaty valid regarding the Durand Line.

While Amanullah's centralizing agenda provided short-term successes, those very successes provoked tribal and ethnic resistance, especially of Tajiks. Amanullah was ousted in 1929, and four years of brief monarchies followed, ending with the accession of Afghanistan's last monarch, Mohammed Zahir Shah (1914–2007). His four-decade reign (1933–1973) survived the turbulent 1930s, World War II, and most of the Cold War, and actually began to develop something of a modern infrastructure. As it turned out, most of his earliest modernizers came from Axis countries, whose aid the Afghans ditched by proclaiming neutrality (under pressure from the British and the Soviets) in World War II. By then the nation henceforth had to be especially cautious about which nations could provide the foreign support necessary for any national development.

At the conclusion of World War II, the Afghan monarchy faced numerous difficulties. Domestically it had to deal with modernization matters, which involved the liberalization of society, including a more open press and the creation of a National Assembly. The age-old problems of tribal and ethnic divisions also continued to trouble the monarchy, which particularly needed to counteract the Pashtun demand for a separate homeland. The Pashtun issue also complicated foreign affairs, as a good part of the Pashtun population lived in the northern and western parts of what was about to become Pakistan. As well, the king's cousin Muhammad Daoud (1919–1978) became prime minister in 1953, continuing most modernizing programs, but his foreign policies produced diplomatic turmoil. He pushed the issue of a Pashtunistan, thereby producing strained relations with Pakistan where a large segment of the Pashtun population lived as a result of the Durand Line. The other involved the Soviet Union, with which Daoud wanted to improve relations. By 1963 Daoud resigned, but reforms at home continued in 1964 with a new constitution. The document limited the power of the king but also allowed much more legislative and judicial freedom, resulting in a great deal of ethnic and religious dissention among the Afghan political elite. The National Assembly involved elections to that body, thereby creating a vibrant and contentious electoral process. As the monarchy failed to handle satisfactorily basic domestic and diplomatic affairs, and as growing public opinion turned against the king, Daoud and the military took the opportunity to overthrow the monarchy in 1973, creating a republic.

Post-Monarchy Afghanistan, 1973–2019

Daoud enlisted the support of secular leftists at home and the Soviet Union from abroad. The leftists, typically the urban Marxist faction of the People's Democratic Party of Afghanistan (PDPA), sought to construct a socialist Afghanistan. The more radical tribal and chiefly rural division of that party received support from the Soviet Union. As it called for the immediate creation of a communist state, Daoud gradually removed leftists. He steadily drifted away from dependence on the Soviets, formed his own National Revolutionary Party in 1976, and promulgated a new constitution in 1977. By 1978 Daoud's near-dictatorial power given by the new constitution, his alienation of Islamists, the declining influence of PDPA, and Afghanistan's likely move toward the United States produced a coup d'état on April 27, 1978. Daoud and his family were killed, and the Saur (April) Revolution was underway.

Into this tumultuous context came the Soviet Union, supporting PDPA leader Babrak Karmal (1929–1996), who headed the Afghan central government until 1986. Soon they instituted a radical agenda designed to demote tradition and Islam while promoting atheism and socialism. The agenda soon caused friction within the party and growing opposition among the people. As the government rapidly neared collapse, along with the emergence of the *Mujahedeen* (struggle), and with the growing support of the United States on the side of the *Mujahedeen*, the Soviet Union decided to intervene formally on Christmas Eve 1979. The invasion represented yet another illustration of the Brezhnev Doctrine, the right of the Soviet Union to aid a friendly socialist government in danger of being overthrown.

The Soviet occupation between 1978 and 1989 brought the United States into the region with its support for the *Mujahedeen*, while the Islamic revolution in Iran made that nation a major political actor in the area as well. Complicating matters was the arrival of foreign al Qaeda fighters doing battle against the Soviet Union. After the Soviet withdrawal in February 1989, the Mujahedeen defeated the remaining Soviet-backed Afghan government. At the same time, though, the Afghan Taliban (Pashto for student), a Mujahedeen splinter group, grew in power and by the mid-1990s effectively displaced the Mujahedeen, creating the Islamic Emirate of Afghanistan. Before being deposed in 2001, the Taliban destroyed the magnificent Silk Road Bamiyan Buddhist statues in Afghanistan. When Osama bin Laden's al Qaeda (the base) launched its attack on the United States on September 11, 2001, the United States and NATO deployed forces to Afghanistan to destroy al Qaeda. However, Washington soon realized that al Qaeda had moved its operations to Pakistan. Most of the American fighting took place with the Afghan Taliban, which had ruled the country from Kabul. It was expelled in 2001 with the help of the Afghan Northern Alliance, a coalition of northern Afghan ethnic groups opposed to the largely Pashtun Taliban.

While the Taliban never disappeared, post-9/11 Afghanistan witnesses a constant state of violence, destruction, and instability. The United States has attempted principally to create a successful counterterrorism effort and to build a central government capable of obtaining a maximum of popular support and stability, and secondarily to launch social reforms. This effort soon took second place to the destruction of Saddam Hussein's regime in Iraq after 2003, and by 2009 the new American president Barack Obama decided to end Washington's combat operations in both locations. As with the Iraq drawdown, the American departure from Afghanistan has seen resurgence of insurgencies. Donald Trump ran for president in part on a foreign policy platform of fewer overseas combat operations, and in early 2019 President Trump's administration is negotiating with the Taliban to bring most or even all of American forces home from Afghanistan. At the same time, it remains to be seen if the central government in Kabul can survive the American withdrawal.

The armed campaigns against the Taliban and al Qaeda have produced mixed results. On the positive side, the United States has kept the Taliban at bay and driven al Qaeda into Pakistan, where bin Laden was killed in 2011. The Afghan government—for all its shortcomings—has begun to develop and strengthen its institutions, including an "evolving" electoral process. The building of roads, bridges, schools, and medical facilities through the Afghanistan Infrastructure and Rehabilitation Program provides jobs and desirable modern facilities. Women certainly have benefited from post-911 political, social, and economic life without the Taliban. Most recent reforms improve the likelihood that the people will cooperate in military operations against the Taliban.

America's focus on improving Afghan society, though subordinate to advances in military and government structure, may have the best chance of enduring without outside support. Focus on education, women's rights, the idea of public health, and elections will not likely be completely reversed, regardless of which political entity emerges victorious. The circumstances in a post-American Islamic Republic of Afghanistan will continue to reflect an ongoing debate within Afghanistan about what kind of society the people want and can reasonably expect to begin building. The outcome of the civil war will determine—at least in the short run—what direction the nation will take. On the negative ledger, the central government has only minimal support in the countryside, where the civil war is likely to be won. Corruption remains rampant. Social practices such as *bacha bazi*, which allow Afghan officers to kidnap and rape young boys; early and forced marriages; *baad*, or giving away girls to settle disputes; as well as numerous other social practices will not likely disappear soon, but embryonic alternatives to such traditions will likely be remembered regardless of future regimes. But the nation's future will also be influenced by America's involvement. Donald Trump's 2016 election as president occurred in part because of his emphasis on America reducing its military commitments overseas. Will Washington negotiate with the Taliban and pull the plug in Afghanistan? All of Afghanistan, all of Asia—indeed, all of the world—waits to discover America's future global role. Regardless, Afghanistan remains a failed state whose improved immediate future is in grave doubt.

Central Asia

To the north of India and China, rivals Britain and Russia became the principal contenders for influence or control in Afghanistan, Central Asia, Tibet, Mongolia, and Siberia. For centuries the Russians had been expanding east of the Ural Mountains, and by the sixteenth century had begun military campaigns into Muslim Central Asia that led to commerce and colonization. Under Catherine the Great in the eighteenth century, Russia strengthened its position there somewhat by pursuing a policy of religious toleration (as conquest proceeded). When the Russian military in 1865 captured Tashkent (capital of today's Uzbekistan), the preponderance of Central Asia became Russian Turkestan, officially in 1867 with the appointment of Governor General Konstantin Petrovich von Kaufman. To the south, another Turkestan existed in the northern part of Afghanistan, and to the east yet another, Chinese Turkestan (today's Xinjiang Province). The border between Russian and Chinese Turkestan became a point of potential conflict by the mid-nineteenth century in the strategically significant Ili Prefecture of Xinjiang Province. As Russia pushed eastward across Eurasia, it came to desire commercial access to the resource-rich Ili territory, where a mountain pass also controlled access to the rest of Xinjiang Province. The 1851 Treaty of Ili gave Russia commercial and diplomatic (consulates) rights in Ili that rapidly produced brisk business activities. Very soon thereafter, however, rebellions broke out across China—Taiping, Nian, and a Muslim one in Gansu and Shaanxi Provinces—at the same time the Second Opium War got underway. Yakub Beg, a Muslim rebel from Kokand in today's Tashkent, took advantage of China's weakness to invade Ili and establish Kashgaria. Because it cut off Russian trade, since the Russians suspected the British of supporting Yakub Beg's activities (because it diverted him away from India), and as the Chinese faced bigger problems elsewhere, the Russians occupied Ili in 1871. Although the Russians claimed no territorial aspirations, they nonetheless actually worked with Yakub Beg (as did the British) to continue their occupation.

Faced with rebel and Russian problems on the land frontier while confronting European and Japanese challenges on the maritime frontier, Qing officials—Manchu and Han Chinese—debated which frontier posed the bigger threat to China and thus deserved more attention. Manchu Prince Gong and Chinese modernizer Li Hongzhang favored strengthening the coastal defenses and developing a modern navy, and argued that a campaign in Xinjiang would be expensive and the outcome uncertain. In any case, Xinjiang was far removed from Beijing and therefore less crucial than the heart of China along the coast. The advocates of land frontier defense, such as Zuo Zongtang, viewed Russia as expansionist and not likely to stop with the territory around Ili. Russia demanded not just commercial concessions, which typified European demands along the Chinese coast, but wanted to expand into Xinjiang and threaten the Chinese position in Mongolia. Moreover, Russia remained permanently located north of China and would remain a perpetual concern, whereas foreigners along the China coast, except for Japan, resided far away. The Court sided with Zuo and the frontier defenders and supported a continuing campaign against all troublemakers in Xinjiang. Thus in 1875, after Zuo Zongtang had crushed the Nian and Muslim rebellions, Zuo was appointed to defeat Yakub Beg, which was accomplished by 1877, symbolically with the suicide of the Muslim leader. Turning to the Russian presence in Ili, the Chinese government negotiated a bad Treaty of Lavidia in 1879, which returned Ili to China but also gave up much surrounding territories, including two essential mountain passes, to the Russians. China got back most of those territories in the Treaty of St. Petersburg in 1881, owing mainly to Russia's domestic and diplomatic problems.

Central Asia, 1850–1945

What is today identified as Central Asia in the past was referred to as Russian Turkestan or Western Turkestan, to distinguish it from Eastern or Chinese Turkestan. Under Tsarist Russian colonization, the government attempted to rule these largely Muslim territories and their numerous ethnicities through local elites. Usually Tsarist officials permitted local customs, but when native intellectuals, merchants, and pan-Islamists organized movements that challenged Russian control, the government fairly successfully overwhelmed them. Territories in Central Asia where Tsarist Russian had established a strong sphere of influence quickly became absorbed by the Soviet Union. Initially the organizational subdivisions of Central Asia were termed "autonomous" or "people's" Soviet Socialist Republics. During the 1920s, under Soviet leader Vladimir Lenin's Commissar of Nationalities, Josef Stalin, the autonomous or people's part of each republic's name disappeared and the "Soviet Republics" of Tajikistan, Kyrgyzstan, Kazakhstan, Turkmenistan, and Uzbekistan came under Moscow's direct control. When Stalin became the Soviet leader shortly after Lenin's death in 1924, he began massive public works projects in Central Asia that depended on a system of forced labor, which existed across the Soviet Union. Many of these projects tied the various and disparate parts of the Soviet Union together, as did the promotion of the Russian language.

Timeline for Central Asia, 1850–2019	
1850–1917	Tsarist Russian expansion absorbs what are today the territories in Central Asia making up the nations of Turkmenistan, Tajikistan, Uzbekistan, Kazakhstan, and Kyrgyzstan
1917–1921	Central Asians attempt to break away from Russia during the revolution but are defeated by the Red Army
1917–1930	The Communist Revolution in Russia creates the Soviet Union, which incorporates most of the territories that Tsarist Russia held; Central Asian territories become Soviet Socialist Republics in the Soviet Union
1920s–1930s	Collectivization in the Soviet Union under Josef Stalin produces massive misery; Moscow's anti-Islamic policies produce discontent
1941–1945	While Siberia was the central gulag, Central Asia could be considered a close second for the dishonor; it also becomes a dumping ground for prisoners of war and a location to which Moscow could retreat if needed
1991	All Central Asian Soviet Socialist Republics secede from the Soviet Union but join the Commonwealth of Independent States linked to Russia
1991–2015	Central Asian nations remain relatively secular, attempting to keep radical Islam in check
1991–2019	Political turnovers occur more often with the deaths of leaders than their being voted out

During the 1930s and 1940s, Central Asia remained under Moscow's effective control due to a broad array of Soviet policies. Traditional ethnic homelands had much of their populations dispersed throughout Central Asia, thereby diluting the possibility of ethnic solidarity and strengthening the likelihood of ethnic hostilities among Central Asians. The traumas of Stalin's collectivization produced economic dislocation, and famine produced Central Asia's "harvests of sorrow," but it also established Moscow's authority. Fortifying that authority were the purge trials of the mid-1930s, which in Central Asia as in other parts of the Soviet Union eliminated Stalin's rivals. Thus Central Asia's educated elite disappeared, leaving the region and its ethnic groups practically speaking leaderless. By this time the Latin script and ultimately the Cyrillic script had replaced the Arabic script, further disconnecting Central Asian Muslims from their past. During World War II, hundreds of thousands of Central Asians ended up in Europe fighting the Germans, while tens of thousands of German prisoners of war and assorted European POWs and political prisoners ended up in Central Asia. Overall, by the end of World War II, the Soviets had succeeded in minimizing Central Asian resistance to its rule.

Central Asia, 1945–2019

Central Asia has undergone three clearly defined—and often interrelated—experiences since the end of World War II: Soviet anti-Islamic rule, independence, and religious fundamentalism. From that time until the collapse of the Soviet Union in 1991, the peoples of Central Asia lived in Soviet Republics inhabited by numerous ethnic groups that had been scattered about the region by Josef Stalin in order to minimize ethnic solidarity against Soviet rule. Nonetheless some organized resistance to Soviet rule had existed in Central Asia through Islam since the 1917 Communist Revolution succeeded. Even Mikhail Gorbachev s liberalization program generated Islamic resistance. According to one Central Asian observer, *perestroika* portrayed Islam as

> the enemy of modernization and a rallying point for anti-Russian feelings amongst Central Asia's ethnic groups. Gorbachev's own anti-Muslim views were reinforced by the Central Asian leaders, who feared that any Islamic revival amongst the population would lead to demands for greater democracy and freedom, posing a threat to their grip on power.[2]

As events of the twentieth century clearly illustrate, the collapse of imperial governments that once held people of different ethnic, religious, or linguistic backgrounds together typically produces domestic, regional, and even global tragedy. The nations of Central Asia certainly provide evidence to support that assertion.

After October 1991 Turkmenistan, Uzbekistan, Tajikistan, Kyrgyzstan, and Kazakhstan all broke away from what had been the Soviet Union and became independent states. Nonetheless after several centuries of Tsarist and Soviet Russian control in Central Asia, many cultural and economic ties to Russia understandably continue. And today all newly independent Central Asian nations became associated with the Commonwealth of Independent States (CIS), a Russian-dominated organization made up of former "socialist republics" in Asia and Europe. But anxiety about the former Russian overlord and neighbor is never far from people's thinking. Meanwhile, those same nations also had to deal with the turmoil in nearby Afghanistan that continued after the Soviet withdrawal. Most of the chaos resulted from Islamic fundamentalism generated by domestic religious movements as well as by Afghan Taliban and its unofficial but genuine sponsor, Pakistan. Dictatorial governments also produced opposition movements whose demonstrations and violence are often blamed on religious fundamentalists. And after 9/11, America's involvement in that war also generated a large American presence in Central Asian nations in the form of

---

2 Ahmed Rashid, *Jihad: The Rise of Militant Islam in Central Asia* (New Haven, CT: Yale University Press, 2002), pp. 39–40.

military bases, antidrug cooperation, and border security. Such a presence naturally worried adjacent Iran, Russia, and China.

But even if religious fundamentalism and its consequences in nations adjoining Central Asia are excluded, those emerging self-governing nations would face the thorny problem of reconciling church and state issues. As in much of the rest of Asia, Central Asian nation building is going to be a secular, ethnic, and religious process. Will those elements combine to produce a volatile explosion of clannish violence or a healthy mixture of national cooperation? Tossed into any assessment of Central Asia and its some 90 million people's future are the likely consequences of the region's enormous supply of natural resources and the changes the resulting influx of foreign money and technicians will bring. The outcomes will largely be determined by the nations and their citizens, but also by events in adjacent countries as well as by the major powers—Russia, China, India, and the United States.

Mongolia

The Mongols had reverted to nomadic lifestyle and tribal fragmentation by the late fifteenth century after the imperial glory days of Chinggis Khan and Kublai Khan. Mongols residing in Central Asian territories above India converted to Islam, and many played a role in the forming of the Mughal Empire in India. Mongols in the Mongolian heartland above China embraced Tibetan Buddhism (Lamaism) and became caught between an expanding Russia and a China always attentive to its inner-Asian frontier. When the Manchu Qing Dynasty came to power in China in 1644, it had already absorbed Mongols in Inner (southern) Mongolia. The Manchus got the people in Outer (northern) Mongolia to accept Manchu supremacy in return for their help in fighting the Dzungars in western Mongolia and Chinese Turkestan (Xinjiang). The Dzungars fell to the Manchus by the mid-eighteenth century, China thereby securing its northern and western frontiers. Earlier, the Treaty of Kyakhta/Kiakhta in 1727 had given the Manchus rule over most of Mongolia, thus keeping most Mongols beyond Russian control, but it also gave Russia trade and religious privileges in Beijing, and the Qing government did not list Russia as a tributary state.

Timeline for Mongolia, 1850–2019	
1636–1911	Inner (southern) Mongolia under Manchu Qing Chinese rule
1691–1911	Outer (northern) Mongols submit to Manchu Qing rule
1911	Qing Dynasty collapses and Outer Mongolia declares independence; Chinese army invades Outer Mongolia in an attempt to retain all of Mongolia; China fails, and eventually Outer Mongolia effectively becomes today's Mongolia
1911	Inner Mongolia remains a part of the new Republic of China
1920	Mongol leftists join forces with Communists (Reds or Bolsheviks) in Russia, who defeat Whites (anti-Communists) in Siberia and then drive the Chinese out of Mongolia
1920s–1940s	Mongolia falls into the orbit of the Soviet Union
1939	Mongol and Soviet troops turn back Japanese invasion of Mongolia
1949–1991	Mongolia remains a Soviet ally in the Sino-Soviet split

1986	Mikhail Gorbachev withdraws Soviet troops from Mongolia
1992–2015	Mongolia issues new constitution and electoral politics slowly becomes competitive
1992–2019	Resource-rich Mongolia produces customers and riches as well as the need to not become dependent on anyone, particularly Russia or China

As the Manchu government in China experienced both foreign assaults and domestic uprisings in the nineteenth century, Outer Mongolia began to slip beyond Beijing's control. The Chinese Republican Revolution of October 1911 overthrew Manchu rule and the Chinese imperial dynastic system, further weakening China's administrative system and accelerating Outer Mongolia's movement against Chinese control. Several issues drove the Mongol opposition to Chinese rule. One was the creation of an Outer Mongolian militia to use against possible Russian incursions, with the militia funding coming not from China but falling on Mongol shoulders. Outer Mongolia's financial system, however, was controlled by Chinese merchants to whom many Mongols became indebted. In Inner Mongolia during the last decades of Manchu rule, ethnic Han Chinese migration had been allowed by Beijing, resulting in Mongol pasture land being converted to agricultural land by Han Chinese.

In December 1911 Outer Mongolia, with Russian and Japanese support, declared its independence from China, claiming that its relationship with China had been through the Manchus, now toppled. Nonetheless Mongolia's status remained uncertain as Asian and global crises temporarily prevented the emergence of a guarantor of Mongolia's independence. As the Japanese worked to gain influence in Mongolia to counter China and Russia, World War I broke out in 1914, temporarily reducing Russian activity there. Nonetheless in a 1913 agreement between Russia and China, both had concurred that Mongolia would remain under Chinese suzerainty while allowing for Mongol autonomy. Practically speaking, the effect produced Russian control in Outer Mongolia and Chinese control in Inner Mongolia. At the same time the Chinese Republic under Yuan Shikai, already shaky, disintegrated into warlordism by 1916. When Yuan died in 1916, Tsarist Russia—notwithstanding its imminent demise due to war, corruption, and the Communists—had expanded Russian influence in Asia yet again. And when the Bolshevik Communist Revolution succeeded in Russia a year later, the now Bolshevik Russia returned as a major force in Mongolia. In February and March 1919, it sponsored a conference of Mongols in Soviet Siberia, where the formal proclamation of independence occurred. Until the collapse of the Soviet Union in 1991, Mongolia remained a client state of Moscow. Meanwhile, Inner Mongolia remained under Chinese control, and the territory was divided into several Chinese provinces.

Mongolia, 1911–1945

Political developments in Mongolia between the wars represented a decisive victory for Moscow. The Chinese Revolution of 1911 allowed the Mongols to break away from Beijing's control, and they established a theocratic government headed by the Bogdo Khan or holy ruler. Tsarist Russia took advantage of China's disorder to succeed China as Mongolia's de facto overseer, but then World War I focused Russia's attention on Europe and a Chinese warlord took control of the Mongol capital, whereupon the Bogdo Khan acknowledged Chinese sovereignty. When the Bolsheviks succeeded in defeating their civil war rivals in 1921, the Soviet Union re-established significant control of Mongolia's internal affairs.

In March 1921 the Mongolian People's Party (after 1924 the Mongolian People's Revolutionary Party, or MPRP) held its First Party Congress in Siberia and proclaimed the Mongolian People's Provisional Government. By July that year, the Bogdo Khan government officially became a limited monarchy in the new People's Government of Mongolia; in September Mongolia proclaimed its formal independence; by October the National Provisional Little Hural or legislature came into being; and in November an Agreement on Mutual Recognition and Friendly Relations was signed with Moscow. When opponents of the new government and its Soviet protector appeared, they were arrested and executed. By the end of 1923, Mongolia had become a satellite of the Soviet Union, and in November 1924 the Mongolian People's Republic was proclaimed after the last Bogdo Khan died. By the time Stalin came to power in the Soviet Union in 1927, the Mongolian nobility and the clergy had lost their traditional privileges, the government directed the nation's economy, and Mongolia's foreign policy reflected Soviet viewpoints. Mongolia was the only other communist country to emerge globally before World War II.

Developments in Mongolia through World War II largely mirrored Stalin's policies in the Soviet Union. Khorloogiin Choibalsan (sometimes Choybalsan; 1895–1952), supported by the Soviets, began the Stalinization of Mongolia. He purged his "rightist" rivals in the ruling MPRP, confiscated the private property of the nobles and the Buddhist clergy, ejected monks from monasteries, and executed much of the Buddhist leadership. As well, he launched a Soviet-style five-year plan in a nomadic society. This involved the elimination of remaining private property, which included the herds (primarily horses, camels, sheep, goats, cattle, and yaks) of the nomads who represented the preponderance of the population. It also produced a number of consequences, including popular resistance, which resulted in the killing or jailing of dissidents in and out of the MPRP. Most particularly, it reduced but far from eliminated the impact of the Buddhist church, as one scholar notes:

> The elimination of the lamas as a political institution, by destroying its economic base, still did not mean final victory over the old regime. The cultural influence of the lamas remained strong. Even in 1932 the Comintern agents had to admit that the 'the lamas remained the cultural leaders of the Mongolian population: as teachers, the only doctors and craftsmen.' In addition to the church lamas, there were the so-called 'black' lamas who lived among the people in camps and settlements.[3]

Further undermining economic health was the expulsion of Mongolia's ethnic Chinese, who formed the heart of the nation's mercantile activities.

Popular rebellion and foreign threats forced the Soviets to rethink its restructuring of Mongolian society. Widespread opposition to the economic policies that were destroying traditions and producing famine threatened to make the Mongolian regime and its Soviet patron unpopular enough to enable an aggressive Japan to appear as a potential liberator to the people. The possibility of a Japanese invasion of Mongolia (keeping in mind Japan's invasion of neighboring Manchuria in September 1931) led Stalin through the Comintern to scale back collectivist programs in what became known as the New Turn Policy. This represented a more measured path to socialist development that continued until the end of World War II. Although political struggles continued throughout the interwar years, Soviet policy after 1931 chiefly centered on the development of infrastructure that would aid in the defense of Mongolia (and thus the Soviet Union).

---

3 Irina Y. Morozova, *The Comintern and Revolution in Mongolia* (Cambridge: Mongolia and Inner Asia Studies Unit, University of Cambridge, 2002), p. 37.

Mongolia, 1945–2020

From the end of World War II to the end of the Soviet Union, Mongolia underwent evolutionary domestic changes, while in foreign affairs it established its current frontiers that became accepted, most importantly by its neighbors but as well by the global diplomatic community. Economically, the nation began to accelerate modernization by making the pastoral and agricultural sectors more efficient and by expanding the industrial sector. A series of Five-Year Plans, beginning in 1948, set the economic priorities and established the means by which the blueprints would be implemented. Until the Soviet collapse, Mongolia worked within Moscow's foreign policy framework. Part of that framework focused on (Nationalist) China. The Sino-Soviet Treaty of Friendship and Alliance, signed August 14, 1945, established the Chinese-Mongolian frontier. In the treaty China gave up any claims to "Outer Mongolia," which is today's Mongolia; Mongolia (through the Soviet Union) gave up any claims to "Inner Mongolia," which is what in 1947 was restructured into the Chinese provinces of Suiyuan, Chahar, Rehe, Liaobei, and Xing'an, plus parts of Gansu and Ningxia Provinces. Later, under the Communists, Inner Mongolia was reorganized into the Inner Mongolia Autonomous Region.

As the Communists were about to come to power and create the People's Republic of China, Chinese leader Mao Zedong sent Liu Shaoqi to Moscow, where in the summer of 1949 he negotiated with Josef Stalin another Sino-Soviet treaty. But by the late 1950s a split between the two Communist giants had begun, producing border clashes in the 1960s, which in turn produced the presence of a large Soviet army in Mongolia. When the 1949 treaty expired in 1979, China invaded Vietnam—a Soviet ally—over Hanoi's invasion of Cambodia, a Chinese ally. The Soviet Union, about to invade Afghanistan, did nothing. Eventually relations between the two countries began to improve, as evidenced by Soviet leader Gorbachev's arrival in China to meet with China's leader Deng Xiaoping in 1989, as it turns out, on the eve of the Tiananmen Square bloodbath. By then, the Soviets had withdrawn from Afghanistan and had promised the Mongolian government it would remove all its troops by 1992. Into the twenty-first century, China has become a rising power while Russia, in Asia at least, has become a demographic and economic dwarf.

Events in the Soviet Union, Eastern Europe, and China in 1989 greatly influenced political actions in Mongolia. Massive demonstrations in China during the spring, mass migration of East Europeans to Hungary and then to Austria during the summer, and the tearing down of the Berlin Wall in November helped Mongolians decide to challenge the existing Communist monopoly in politics. The Soviet military did nothing to confront the protestors, though next door in China the military did put down protestors. Still, the Soviet military, not the Chinese, was stationed in Mongolia. By December the people took to the streets, generating massive demonstrations against the government and producing an opposition organization, the Mongolian Democratic Union (MDU). Demands from the MDU included the legalization of opposition parties, the termination of the (Communist) MPRP's "leading role" in politics, and elections to the Great People's Hural (GPH), the national legislature. Though the MPRP dragged its feet, by May 1992 the constitution was amended to allow elections and opposition parties. The July election gave the MPRP 60% of the vote and 86% of the seats in the Great Hural, while the opposition candidates drew 40% of the vote and 14% of the seats. And though the MPRP initially dominated the political scene, it often had to form coalition governments in order to govern, and it has regularly lost elections. As well, the offices of president and prime minister have alternated between the MRPR and the Democratic Party, a more right-of-center party composed of earlier opposition parties. Tsakhiagiin Elbegdorj (1963–present), Mongolia's president elected in 2009, received his education in the Soviet Union and in the United States at the University of Colorado and Harvard University. The 2020 Mongolian legislative election gave the Mongolian People's Party control of 62 of the 76 seats in parliament, quite an accomplishment given it garnered just under 45 percent of the vote in the multiparty system.

Mongolia's economy has had ups and downs since 1990. The collapse of the Soviet Union disconnected Mongolia from Russia's market system and ended subsidies from Moscow. Bad weather between 2000 and 2002 also nearly halted economic growth during that time. Gradually, though, it connected with global institutions—the Asian Development Bank, the World Bank, and the World Trade Organization—that assisted Mongolia with modernizing the economy. Given Mongolia's vast supply of natural resources and given rising China's great demand for such resources, a strong two-way trade has been established between the two neighbors. Mongolia has also steadily privatized the once state-run economy. This has become more evident since the election of President Elbegdorj, known to have libertarian economic leanings. Although Mongolia seems to be moving in generally positive political and economic directions, it does face several problems: double-digit inflation, corruption, and substantial dependence on Russia for energy and on China for exports (roughly 90%). Given the rough political region, Mongolia has maintained relatively good relations with its neighbors. Over the longer term, Mongolia's biggest challenges will be dealing with its larger neighbors, managing its growing economy, and coming to terms with the social changes a globalized economy produces.

Siberia and the Russian Far East

Although Russia and China had been neighbors of sorts, no serious territorial troubles occurred until the seventeenth century along what is today the border between northeast China (Manchuria) and the Siberian frontier. Much of the terrain that is today the maritime provinces of Russian Siberia had been geography lightly controlled by Russia or China before the seventeenth century, important but not vital geography so distant from Beijing and St. Petersburg. By the mid-seventeenth century, Russia had reached the Sea of Okhotsk and began moving south toward the Amur River basin, but the Treaty of Nerchinsk (1689), negotiated with a muscular China, stopped the Russian advance. More important were Russia's wars with its northern European neighbors at the time. As well, the Manchus did not focus on settling the Amur area, concentrating instead on consolidating their hold on China proper.

Timeline for Russian Far East, 1850–2020	
1850–1917	Ethnic Russian migration into the Asian parts of Russia
1891	Trans-Siberian railroad connects Russia, beginning in Moscow, with the Pacific Ocean at Vladivostok and other locations in Asia
1917–1921	Russian civil war between the Reds and Whites brings greater Russian control into Asian Russia
1921–1945	Communist victory in the civil war makes Russian Siberia a stepping stone to anticolonial Asian activists
1945–1991	During the Cold War, the Russian Far East became a key region for Russian military—for Soviet offensive and defensive war plans, and for the Korean War and assorted Asian insurgencies
1991–2015	Fall of the Soviet Union places Russian Far East low on the list of the nation's priorities
2015–2019	Debate continues among China and Russian specialists as to whether the post–Cold War relationship between the world's two largest countries is a ""marriage of convenience" or a "strategic alliance"

By the mid-nineteenth century, when Chinese weakness became apparent, Russians had begun aggressively settling along the Amur under the leadership of Nikolai Muraviev, governor-general of Eastern Siberia. The domestic Taiping and other rebellions as well as the foreign Second Opium War (1856–1860) kept China occupied with more vital crises than the Amur territories on the frontier. Although Chinese officials protested the Russian presence, Beijing's domestic and other foreign troubles resulted in the signing of an unfavorable agreement regarding the Amur River region. The Treaty of Aigun (1858) called for Russia to get territory north of the Amur River and specified that both countries would jointly occupy the land east of the Ussuri River. China initially refused to ratify the treaty, but later did so (in the Convention of Peking in 1860, which also gave Russia sole occupation of the region east of the Ussuri), fearing Russia would join Britain and France in the Second Opium War. With the freeing of the serfs in 1861, even more Russians migrated east, and by the turn of the twentieth century the Trans-Siberian Railroad further solidified Russia's hold on eastern Siberia.

By the late nineteenth century, Russian expansionist objectives in Asia had yet to be fully realized. Although the port of Vladivostok (meaning "Ruler of the East") could be classified a warm-water port, it was nonetheless frozen over for a third of each year. Thus Russia looked south, into Korea and Manchuria, for more economically functional and strategically valuable ports, not to mention access to additional raw materials. And of course movement into those and other new areas continued the political chess game with Britain and launched a new one with emerging Japan. Already in an 1876 treaty Russia and Japan established a line of demarcation off of mainland Asia when both countries agreed that Sakhalin Island would be Russia's while Japan got the Kuril Islands. But two decades later, in the wake of China's defeat in the First Sino-Japanese War (1894–1895), Japan's attempts of occupy southern Manchuria met with the Triple Intervention of Russia, France, and Germany. Not coincidently, Russia particularly wanted to keep Japan off the Liaodong Peninsula (today's Liaoning Province), where the ice-free ports of Lushunkou/Port Arthur and Dalian/Dairen/Dalny were located.

Manchu Qing China worked out a secret agreement in 1896 allowing for Russian penetration of Manchuria, above all for the creation of the Russian-controlled Chinese Eastern Railway, in return for a promise of Russian aid in the event of future Japanese incursions into China or Korea. In 1898 Russia got the two Liaodong ports and the surrounding territories at the southern end of the Liaodong Peninsula, and it became known as Kwantung/Guandong, meaning "east of the pass" (at the eastern terminus of the Great Wall).[4] Britain countered by leasing the territory of Weihaiwei, a port on the Shandong Peninsula, across from Liaodong Peninsula. When the Boxer Rebellion broke out and the rebels seized the foreign legations in Beijing, eight nations sent armies to break the siege, including Russia. All kept military detachments, allowed by the Boxer Protocol of 1901, but the Russian Army never departed China, and ended up occupying parts of Manchuria. Both Britain and Japan feared Russia's presence in Manchuria and formed the Anglo-Japanese Alliance of 1902. Negotiations between Russia and Japan over Russian troops in Manchuria failed, and Japan attacked Russia commencing the Russo-Japanese War. The Treaty of Portsmouth of 1905 not only gave Japan Kwantung but also the southern half of Sakhalin Island as well as railroad rights in southern Manchuria. Russia retained railroad rights in northern Manchuria until the Russian Revolution of 1917, when those rights reverted to the Chinese.

---

4 Kwantung in Japanese is *Kanto*, the plain on which Tokyo is located; it is also the name of a Japanese army (the Kanto Army) that devastated parts of China during World War II. Japan took Kwantung from Russia after the latter's defeat in the Russo-Japanese War of 1904–1905, and kept it until 1945.

By World War I, then, the imperial powers had carved out colonies, spheres of influence, leaseholds, and treaty ports across the frontiers north of India and China. Nor was it clear that these possessions would permanently remain in the hands of the current overlords, as the powers jockeyed and fought for advantage. But by this time nationalist movements had emerged to begin the process of removing foreign overlords and achieving independence. World War I, the surfacing of communist and fascist movements, the depression, and World War II provided new opportunities for nationalist movements in Asia to thrive.

The Soviet Union in Central and Inner Asia

Russian interest in Central and Inner Asia and Siberia predates the Communists coming to power in Russia in 1917. Those territories had been areas that expanding empires—Russian, British, Chinese, and Japanese—sought to annex or control for economic and geopolitical reasons. Before World War I those regions contained (and still do possess) raw materials in great abundance. Control of those lands also checked the expansion of rival empires. By World War I, the Chinese Revolution of 1911 had ousted the foreign Manchu Qing Dynasty and ended the old imperial system of government; the Russian Revolution had created the Soviet Union; and the global conflict had brought into play the Anglo-Japanese Alliance of 1902. By war's end, China had fragmented into numerous warlord domains, the Soviet Union became mired in a civil war against anticommunist forces; and the alliance between Britain and Japan began to deteriorate.

Consequently, between the end of World War I and the conclusion of World War II, the balance of power in Asia shifted appreciably. China took steps toward national unification under Chiang Kai-shek's/Jiang Jieshi's Nationalist Party, and World War II generated peasant nationalism, which Mao Zedong's Communist Party promoted. The Soviet Union also became a more considerable force, as it prevailed in its civil war by 1921, consolidated its power at home, and began to project its influence beyond Russia through the Communist International (Comintern). Japan during that time became the dominant force in Asia until the waning years of World War II. Tokyo found itself increasingly at odds with Britain, America, China, and the Soviet Union as it moved to create its Greater East Asia Co-Prosperity Sphere. Japan's defeat in World War II and Britain's loss of empire after that conflict created a power vacuum. This enabled the Soviet Union, China (under the Communists after 1949), and the United States to become the principal political leaders in Asia.

The Soviet Union/Siberia/Russian Far East

World War I resulted in the collapse of Tsarist Russia, the emergence of Soviet Russia, and significant changes in Russia's geopolitical role in Asia. From 1917 to 1921 a civil war raged between the Communist Reds and the anti-Communist Whites, and the Reds' (or Bolsheviks'/Communists'/Soviets') final victory over the Whites occurred in the Russian Far East. From the beginning, the Soviet government presented itself to the colonial world as an opponent of imperialist privileges. Playing on that theme, Moscow utilized locations in the Soviet Union, particularly in the Siberian Far East, to launch anticolonial, nationalist, and/or Communist movements to strengthen its position in Asia and to undercut its Western and Japanese rivals there.

Soviet leaders viewed Siberia in several ways: as a location to which the government could relocate in the face of German or Japanese attack, always a real possibility between the wars; as an agricultural and industrial frontier that required conscript/convict/political prisoner labor to realize economic development; and as a base from which to launch political and economic operations throughout Asia. Economically the raw materials of Siberia provided many of the materials needed for modernization efforts, while forced labor supplied inexpensive workers to carry out the several Five-Year Plans that Stalin devised. Moscow planned to focus most development along the Trans-Siberian Railroad line, which connected the Soviet capital with the Russian Far East and points in between. In the process, a number of gulags—basically penal communities of involuntary laborers—emerged to supply a reliable and cheap source of workers. Few of these workers ever returned to their homes, and as they died new political prisoners or prisoners of war took their places.

The Soviet Union also continued to pursue many Tsarist foreign policies in Siberia, which enhanced the interests of chiefly the Soviet nation and secondarily its new Communist ideology. That is to say, the interests of the Soviet state typically trumped Communist ideological purity when the two came into conflict. Indeed, one of the chief Marxist-Leninist principles—internationalism, as opposed to "petty bourgeois nationalism"—was promoted to rally a broad coalition of nations behind Moscow's self-interested priorities instead of allowing individual national Communist parties to pursue largely national priorities. And even when critics or rivals attacked Soviet Russian policies as hypocritical, Moscow could respond by arguing that the interests of the Soviet state had to take precedence. Without the leadership of the only Communist government in the world, the timely defeat of global capitalism would be seriously compromised.

To promote Russian interests in Asia, Lenin created the Communist International[5] or Comintern in 1919. At the Second Congress of the Comintern held the following year, Lenin presented his "Theses on the National and Colonial Questions," which placed emphasis on class struggle in Asia as a major battleground in the struggle against global capitalism. That same year, Soviet Comintern agents began to make their way to various parts of Asia to found Communist parties: Indonesia in 1920, China in 1921, Japan in 1922, and most everywhere else in Asia as a global depression unfolded during the 1930s. Moscow set up training schools and organized conferences in the Soviet Union and at various locations in Asia for those Asians leading anticolonial, nationalist, or communist movements. One such conference was the First Congress of the Toilers of the Far East, held in Petrograd (originally St. Petersburg, later Leningrad, and again St. Petersburg) and Moscow in January and February 1922. Revolutionaries from Asia met chiefly to counter the ongoing Washington Conference (1921–1922). Gregory Zinoviev of the Soviet Union gave the opening address, in which he rallied the Asian delegates with a call for global, not just European, revolution. The Soviet Union sought influence across Asia, which the Comintern labored to create from its Far Eastern Bureau headquarters in Shanghai.

Naturally much of the Comintern's efforts in Asia focused on China itself. In 1922 Comintern agent Adolph Joffe arrived in China, giving lectures at Peking (Beijing) University and meeting with Sun Yat-sen to set the groundwork for a movement—a united front composed of China's Nationalist and Communist parties—to oust the nation's warlords and unify the country. To further a sense of solidarity with nations experiencing colonization or imperial occupation, Moscow in a 1924 treaty with China gave up its extraterritorial rights there. Moscow attempted to manipulate the course of Chinese Communist Party (CCP) developments through its control of "returned students," that is, though CCP members who were trained in the Soviet Union and returned to China to lead the revolution there. Such Comintern agents as Otto Braun (1900–1974), a German national working for the Comintern in China between 1932 and 1939, also helped to guide Moscow policy in China. He summarizes his duties: "After graduating from the Frunze Military Academy in Moscow in spring 1932 I was assigned to China by the ECCI (Executive Committee of the

5 The creation of the Comintern in 1919 actually established the Third International, which lasted until 1943. The First International or the International Workingmen's Association operated from 1864 to 1876. The Second International lasted from 1889 to 1916. Each of the Internationals produced several Congresses or meetings. The Comintern reappeared as the Cominform or Communist Information Bureau from 1947 to 1956.

Communist International). Roughly speaking, it was my job to act as a military advisor to the Chinese Communist Party in its two-sided fight against Japanese imperialist aggression and the reactionary regime of Chiang Kai-shek."[6]

In Japan and Vietnam, the Comintern also scored significant achievements, but in India Communism experienced much less success. Richard Sorge, another German national who served as an agent for the Comintern (and later for the Soviet army) in China, had cover as a "journalist." Sorge recruited Japanese China specialist and intellectual Ozaki Hotsumi, and when both were living in Japan Sorge penetrated the German embassy in Tokyo while Ozaki had access to high-level officials in the Japanese government. Among other things, they were able to discover Germany's plan of an impending invasion of the Soviet Union in 1941 as well as Japan's intention not to invade the Soviet Union that same year. In Vietnam between the wars, one scholar concludes that the "Vietnamese communist movement operated under the strategic direction of the Comintern in Moscow."[7]

Between the wars, the development of communism in India suffered from three principal difficulties. One involved a competition for party leadership between the British Communist Party and the Indian Communist Party. Another had to do with the suitability of communism for India. If communism were to take root in India, many on the left believed, it needed to serve Indian interests and not be simply some Bolshevik model designed with Russian interests and conditions in mind. Finally, Indian Communist Party leader M. N. Roy, in his *The Future of Indian Politics*, feared that reliance on the middle class to secure independence would produce a leadership that would tend to protect its interests while neglecting the sufferings of the poor. And without addressing the needs of the poor, middle-class leaders would not be capable of forcing the British to "quit India."

Comintern exploits in Asia produced mixed results. Thus, although activities in China fostered anticolonial and communist organizational developments that could successfully mobilize large numbers of people, such activities also produced Moscow-trained anti-cmmunists. In China, for instance, Chiang Kai-shek (Jiang Jieshi) used the Nationalist Party to nearly destroy the Communist Party in the 1920s and 1930s. And the CCP ousted Braun in 1939, illustrating an emerging nationalist sentiment under the new party leadership of Mao Zedong. In Indonesia, even the Indonesian Communist Party regularly refused to follow Comintern directives between the world wars. In Vietnam, the Vietnamese Communist Party, which was formed in 1930, only grudgingly accepted the Comintern directive to recognize the Indochinese Communist Party as the leading anticolonial organization, so as to include Laos and Cambodia in the struggle against France. And five years later, the same Comintern at its Seventh World Congress stipulated that anticolonial activities be dropped and cooperation with the French be launched in order to form a Popular Front against global fascism. Elsewhere in Southeast Asia, ethnic, geographic, and political differences made it difficult to forge unified communist or anticolonial movements. In Malaya, ethnic Chinese and Malays could not find common ground, and by 1930 the Malayan Communist Party (MCP)—which was overseen by the Comintern—was given the task of supervising the developments of communist parties in Burma, Siam, and the Dutch East Indies, where Comintern and MCP manipulations aggravated existing internal disagreements.

---

6 Otto Braun, *A Comintern Agent in China, 1932–1939*, translated from the German by Jeanne Moore with an introduction by Dick Wilson (Stanford, CA: Stanford University Press, 1982), p. 1.
7 William J. Dukier, *The Comintern and Vietnamese Communism*, Papers in International Studies, Southeast Asia Series no. 37 (Athens: Ohio University Center for International Studies, 1975), pp. 40–41.

Still, by 1934, according to an analysis by British police in Malaya, "the reorganization of the Comintern Apparatus in Shanghai has taken place and a regular subsidy has been received" by the Malayan Communist Party, which has "considerably altered the rather gloomy picture of the M.C.P."[8] And from the formal establishment of the Communist Party of India in 1924, questions about how to win over the people to communism called into question the usefulness of any kind of one-size-fits-all Moscow model of revolutionary actions. Moreover, the Nazi-Soviet Pact of 1939 obliged nationalist, communist, and anticolonial leaders in Asia to question the supposed Comintern desire to fight fascism, at least until Nazis invaded the Soviet Union in 1941. The Comintern's official death in 1943 occurred as World War II made individual or national salvation more essential than some theoretical international solidarity.

Nonetheless, all things considered, Moscow and the Comintern largely succeeded in promoting the interests of the Soviet Union in Asia. Perhaps the most significant success was the Sorge spy ring in Japan, which alerted Moscow to the fact that Japan would not be attacking the Soviet Union, thereby allowing Stalin to move his Asian troops to the European front against the Germans. Moreover, while many Soviet policies toward Asia rubbed Asian nationalists and communists the wrong way, and though Moscow could never force its clients to adhere strictly to Comintern guidelines, both Moscow and those receiving its money, materials, and training concluded that their ultimate goals outweighed their differences. The Comintern had created or substantially aided in the creation of Asian organizations that stimulated anti-Western and anti-Japanese activities in Asia. That would become apparent after World War II, when Comintern-supported political parties came to power in North Korea, China, and northern (and eventually all of) Vietnam; when anti-Western or neutralist governments emerged in such places as India, Indonesia, Burma, Cambodia, and Laos; and even when communist insurgencies in the Philippines (the Huks) and Malaya (the Emergency) made strong but ultimately unsuccessful bids for power.

The Soviet Far East became a crucial region during the Cold War era. A divided Korea directly involved Moscow during the Korean War (1950–1953), and North Korea remained a client state of the Soviets until the end of the Cold War. It remained a point of possible direct conflict between the United States and the Soviet Union. Japan fell under America's nuclear umbrella at least since the creation of the 1951 Security Treaty, its 1960 Treaty of revised Mutual Cooperation and Security, as well as later updates. Mongolia was another client state that, along with North Korea, served as a buffer against China once the Sino-Soviet split got underway in the late 1950s. During the Vietnam War, most of the Soviet and Eastern European weaponry arrived in North Vietnam via the Soviet Far East. And when that war ended, the Soviet Union became the chief benefactor to the Communist government in Vietnam. The Soviet Navy ended up in Vietnam's chief port, Cam Ranh Bay, thus militarily both north and south of Communist rival China. During those post–World War II years, the Soviet Far East was connected economically nearly completely to its European western half and to Eastern Europe. It conducted very little trade with northeast Asia. The Soviet Far East existed as a military-industrial complex whose purpose and identity began to change as both China and the Soviet Union launched reform programs. The end of the Cold War generated massive dislocations in the region.

The region that became the Russian Far East after 1991 suffered more than a name change. Financial backing from Moscow all but disappeared, while unsubsidized transportation costs between the European and Asian parts of Russia further damaged Far Eastern economic development. Naturally the Far East region wanted to pivot its developmental attention to its neighbors,

---

8 As quoted in Cheah Boon Kheng, *From PKI to the Comintern, 1924–1941: The Apprenticeship of the Malayan Communist Party* (Ithaca, NY: Cornell University Southeast Asia Program, 1992), p. 71.

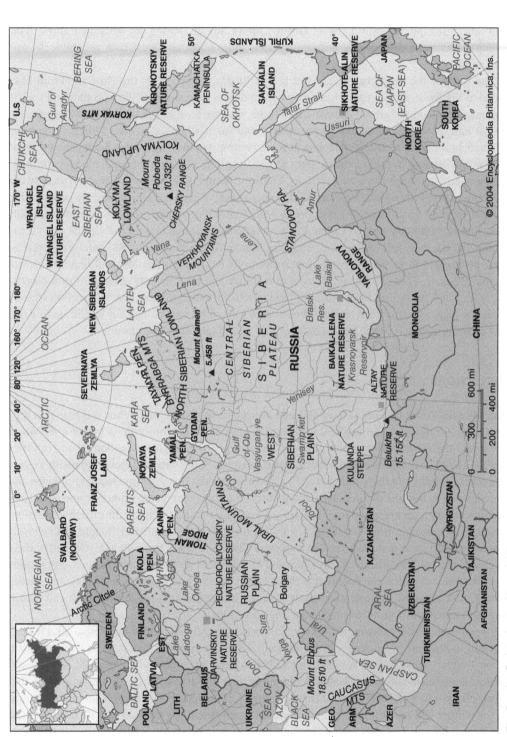

The Russian Federation and its neighbors.

particularly Japan, China, and South Korea. But Moscow for the most part has created barriers to such neighborly economic exchanges. One reason for the barriers is the Russian fear that Russia might simply become a "banana republic," providing natural resources to the more vibrant economies of East Asia. Moreover, both China and Japan have the potential to dominate not only economically but diplomatically as well. Given China's already strong presence in Central Asia, Beijing seems to be strategically positioning itself to its north and west both geopolitically and economically.

Then there is the demographic disaster that is Russia, especially in the Far East. From Lake Baikal to Vladivostok, the region has a population of less than seven million people (and declining), many of them not ethnic Russians, and those who are have issues with Moscow's neglect of the Far East. Moreover, as China's investment in the Far East grows, so does Chinese migration, which includes farmers, laborers, technicians, and entrepreneurs. Even those foreigners willing to consider investment in the region are put off by corruption, bureaucratic regulations, poor infrastructure, and the soaring cost of electricity. Vladimir Putin (1952–present), who has ruled Russia as President and Prime Minister since 2000, wants to keep Russia a major power. He believes that to do so requires a marriage of convenience with China. Fully aware that this could eventually make Russia a tributary state of China, Putin nonetheless is trading oil for cash in the short term, hoping that the cash will help revive a stagnant Russia. At the same time, Russian leaders realize that a permanent Russian command of activities in its Far Eastern territory will require a demographic presence. That will oblige Moscow to mobilize and relocate part of its European population to the Far East. Putin has also reconfigured much of Russia's nuclear arsenal to reflect China's rise in the region. Moscow has brought the Far East a bit closer chronologically by eliminating two time zones, reducing the time between the capital and Vladivostok to six hours.

Conclusions

Since 1945, all Asian nations have established new political institutions. While it is true that they reflect many traditional and colonial aspects, the Asian leaders who came to power after World War II had their own notions about the kind of ideas and the sort of institutions their countries needed. All too often, theories did not conform to realities. Some nations adjusted to reality sooner than others, while still others remain lost in a fog of war or the prison of intellectual fundamentalism. But even in the best of circumstances, political instability produced economic and social dislocations at home, an invitation for domestic or foreign extremists to exploit the unstable situation. Nonetheless some countries are making the transition from more traditional thought and behavior to more modern ideas and practices. On India and China's frontier, these include, with all of their ongoing problems: Kazakhstan, Kyrgyzstan, and Mongolia. More problematic nations with serious problems but still with some potential include Tajikistan, Turkmenistan, Uzbekistan, and Russia (in its Far East region). Though these modern urban/industrial ways produced wealth and power, they also caused political, social, and economic dislocations.

The more successful modernizers owe their success typically to durable and resourceful leadership and to resilient private and public traditional and colonial institutions. The less successful nation builders lacked such resources or failed to take advantage of them. Afghanistan and Pakistan are realistically failed states. Afghanistan remains at war, and only the winner of that largely civil conflict will begin to launch a program of unity and development. There is no guarantee the winner will adopt a practical program of improvement. As for Pakistan, its northwestern frontier is inhabited by tribes with little or no sense of being Pakistani. They are Pashtuns whose land belonged to Afghanistan before 1893. Much of the rest of the country is divided by language and ethnicity, while terrorists from home and far and wide consider the territory to be a launching pad for their particular causes. In that region, the course of events in Iran and the sources and availability of energy will likely determine the future of religious fundamentalism both in Asia and across the globe.

Suggested Readings and Viewings

Thomas Jefferson Barfield, *Afghanistan: A Cultural and Political History* (Princeton, NJ: Princeton University Press, 2010).

Anthony Best, *British Intelligence and the Japanese Challenge in Asia, 1914–1941* (New York: Palgrave Macmillan, 2002).

O. Edmund Clubb, *China and Russia: The "Great Game"* (New York: Columbia University Press, 1971).

Robert D. Crews, *For Prophet and Tsar: Islam and Empire in Russia and Central Asia*
(Cambridge, MA: Harvard University Press, 2006).

Peter Duus, Ramon H. Myers, and Mark R. Peattie, eds., *The Japanese Informal Empire, 1895–1937* (Princeton, NJ: Princeton University Press, 1989).

Martin Ewans, ed., *Britain and Russia in Central Asia, 1880–1907* (London: Routledge, 2007).

Arne Haugen, *The Establishment of Soviet National Republics in Soviet Central Asia* (New York: Palgrave, 2003).

Dirk Hoerder, *Cultures in Contact: World Migrations in the Second Millennium* (Durham, NC: Duke University Press, 2002).

Peter Hopkirk, *The Great Game: The Struggle for Empire in Central Asia* (New York: Kondansha International, 1992).

Peter Hopkirk, *Trespassers on the Roof of the World: The Race for Lhasa* (Oxford: Oxford University Press, 1983).

Chalmers Johnson, *Instance of Treason: Ozaki Hotsumi and the Sorge Spy Ring* (Stanford, CA: Stanford University Press, 1964).

Robert Johnson, *Spying for Empire: The Great Game in Central and South Asia, 1757–1947* (London: Greenhill Books, 2006).

Shoshana Keller, *To Moscow, Not Mecca: The Soviet Campaign against Islam in Central Asia, 1917–1941* (Westport, CT: Praeger, 2001).

The Kite Runner (2008), dir. by Marc Forster.

Liu Xiaoyuan, *Reins of Liberation: An Entangled History of Mongolian Independence, Chinese Territoriality, and Great Power Hegemony, 1911–1950* (Stanford, CA: Stanford University Press, 2006).

Kiran Maitra, *Roy, Comintern and Marxism in India* (Calcutta: Darbar Prokashan, 1991).

Sergey Radchenko, *Half a Leap across an Abyss: How Russia Lost Asia, and the Cold War* (New York: Oxford University Press, 2013).

Rory Stewart, *Afghanistan: The Great Game—A Personal View* (BBC, 2012).

Judith Thornton and Charles E. Ziegler, *Russia's Far East: A Region at Risk* (Seattle: University of Washington Press, 2002).

29

Asia in the Twenty-First Century: The Problems of Progress

Contrary to expectation, it has turned out that the growth of our knowledge about nature has not made it any easier to reach rational decisions regarding man's fate. Instead, whereas the technological consequences of scientific progress have rendered the making of such decisions ever-more pressing and their effects ever-more grave, the intellectual consequences of scientific progress have made us aware of the difficulty, if not impossibility, of seeing the long-range results of our actions, while at the same time destroying the foundations for our judgment of their value.[1]

It is fair to say that every Asian nation has sought, among other things, to create wealth for the betterment of its people and power to protect that public. Understandably the modernization programs that nations employed to achieve wealth and power varied, and fluctuating aspects of tradition were also utilized to achieve desired progress. Since all Asian nations justifiably exhibited a sense of urgency in the struggles for speedy independence and effective nation building, it nonetheless ideally required nations, groups, and individuals to question the promises of progress, whether in the realms of science, politics, economic development, or other realms of humankind's undertakings.

It also dictated that people—particularly those with disproportional wealth, education, influence, or other advantages—to exhibit some measure of prudence when promising that the means a nation will use to create chosen ends can actually be achieved within acceptable guidelines. Looking back over the last three-quarters of a century or more of history in the region, some nations and leaders were more successful and efficient than others in achieving growing stages of modernization. Such will likely be the case as nations attempt to deal with the consequences of being modern.

Nation building in Asia has not proved equally fruitful among the countries of the continent, but most nations there have realized varying levels of economic attainment and social and political adjustment. Typically political and social progress has proved to be more challenging as many old problems continue to fester. Achieving independence, choosing political and economic paths to modernization, and implementing the chosen policies to bring about improvements for nation and citizen have proved to be formidable tasks. Making domestic course corrections in the process often took time and produced political and other clashes. The Cold War complicated the process, as nations characteristically had to consider the impact of their modernization agendas in light of American and Soviet interests. When communism collapsed in 1991, terrorism—decades old but

---

1 Gunther S. Stent, Paradoxes of Progress (San Francisco: W. H. Freeman, 1978), p. 1.

Asia Past and Present: A Brief History, First Edition. Peter P. Wan and Thomas D. Reins.
© 2021 John Wiley & Sons, Inc. Published 2021 by John Wiley & Sons, Inc.

Timeline: Asia in the Twenty-First Century	
2001	April 1: American spy plane hit by Chinese fighter; lands on Hainan Island
	September 11: Osama bin Laden's al Qaeda in Afghanistan attacks the United States, which sends forces to eliminate bin Laden's organization as well as the Afghan Taliban government that gave bin Laden sanctuary
2004	December 26: Indian Ocean tsunami kills nearly 300,000 people
2006	September 19: Thai military coup ousts Prime Minister Thaksin Shinawatra
2008	May: Magnitude 7.9 earthquake hits Sichuan Province in China, killing nearly 90,000 people
	August: Summer Olympic games held in Beijing, China
	November 26: Islamic terrorist organization based in Pakistan launches four-day attack on Mumbai, killing 164 people
2011	March 11: Magnitude 9.0 earthquake produces a massive tsunami that destroys Japan's Fukushima nuclear power plant, which releases radioactive materials into the environment and kills at least 15,000 people
	May 2: Osama bin Laden killed in Abbottabad, Pakistan, by American SEAL Team Six
2013	May: Rohingya crisis in Myanmar's Rakhine State begins
	September 7: China's President Xi Jinping introduces the One Belt, One Road policy (also called the Chinese Marshall Plan) to link China economically by land and sea to Eurasia and East Africa, much like the historical land and maritime Silk Roads of the country's past
2014	May 7: Thai Constitutional Court ousts Prime Minister Yingluck Shinawatra; military rules
2015	February 5: Founding Prime Minister of Singapore Lee Kuan Yew dies
2016	May 20: Democratic Progressive Party candidate Tsai Ing-wen inaugurated president in Taiwan
	July 25: Philippine President Rodrigo Duterte launches his war on drugs during State of the Nation speech
2017	January 23: The United States withdraws from the Trans-Pacific Partnership
2017	September 14: North Korea fires intermediate-range ballistic missile over Japan and continues to pursue nuclear weapon capability
2018	February: Winter Olympic games held in Pyeongchang, South Korea
2018	June 12: President Donald J. Trump and Chairman Kim Jong-un meet in Singapore

largely in the political shadows—emerged to muddle domestic and international affairs. Moreover, as the modernization programs began to succeed across most of Asia, those very successes frequently produced new problems. Thus, Asia began the twenty-first century with circumstances of continuing and fresh problems.

Political Conditions

Politically, nearly every Asian nation has a problem of instability, questionable legitimacy, administrative inefficiency, and ingrained corruption, or all four. Only a few nations have experienced sustained governmental institutional steadiness since World War II ended. Japan, Taiwan, Singapore, and India—though feeling occasional bumps on the political road—all can claim to possess political legitimacy. Japan accepted the American Occupation, embraced much of the American reform program and the Liberal Democratic Party's rewarding economic agenda, and rallied around Prime Minister Shinzo Abe's attempts to deal with the palpable threat of North Korea. Taiwan transitioned from dictatorship to democracy, from one-party to multiparty government, and from representing China in the United Nations to near-diplomatic quarantine, yet continues to exhibit a stable though vigorous political life. In practice a one-party state, Singapore under the leadership of Lee Kuan Yew and son (there was a brief dynastic break between the two Lees) rose from the turmoil produced by World War II, the Malayan Emergency, the bad marriage with Malaysia, and the 1964 Malay-Chinese race riot. Today Singapore boasts stable government, clean streets, a Racial Harmony Day that is genuine, and a booming economy. India has faced leadership assassinations and religious, ethnic, linguistic, terrorist, and separatist challenges. As well, bureaucratic inefficiency and enduring corruption have weakened the government's ability to address those challenges. Nonetheless, the nation's institutions and leaders have so far met the challenges.

The remaining Asian nations have to varying degrees more serious, even existential problems. Afghanistan has experienced chronic civil and international wars since 1973. In South Asia, Pakistan is on the cusp of failed statehood. The Himalayan states are caught in the middle of an ongoing struggle between India and China, best evidenced by the 2017 election in Nepal that many observers believe will determine which of the two Asian giants will dominate the region, at least in the immediate future. Sri Lanka experienced a lengthy ethnic-based civil war from which it is attempting to recover; and Maldives politics have been regularly marred by violence. The Central Asian states continue to deal with the inherited problems of Russian colonization and Islamic fundamentalism.

In Southeast Asia, Burma is attempting to recuperate from decades of military rule and contemporary ethnic violence between Buddhists and Muslims. Thailand suffers through continuing military intervention in civilian government. A long list of human rights abuses remain to distress Malaysia, where strained relations between ethnic Chinese and Malays persist to provide the chief causes of political unsteadiness. Indonesia has recovered from the gross maladministration of Achmed Sukarno and the lengthy military rule of Mohammad Suharto; democracy arrived on the eve of the twenty-first century, only to see the reemergence of religious intolerance, as seen in the gubernatorial election of the governor of Jakarta in 2017. The Philippines has swung between corrupt democracy and even more corrupt rule by Ferdinand Marcos, followed by more dishonest government, as well as an ongoing nearly half-millennium war between the nation's Christian majority and a Muslim insurrectionary movement in the south. The Sultan of Brunei possesses great oil wealth but also faces a majority population of temporary immigrants providing services. East Timor became Timor Leste after a quarter century of (undesired) Indonesian occupation and has transitioned to democracy under (desired) UN occupation, a democracy nonetheless tainted by ongoing political violence. Papua New Guinea remains a nation evolving from colonial rule and tribal identity to independence and the need to maximize its natural resource wealth in a context of massive government corruption. Cambodia and Laos, the two dominos that fell at the end of the Vietnam War, have struggled under the consequences of war, dictatorship, and corruption. Fortunately, Vietnam has begun to liberate itself from revolutionary rhetoric and economic stagnation since its *Doi Moi* reforms in 1986, though the country remains saddled with one-party dictatorship, a gulag, and entrenched corruption.

In East Asia, China suffered civil war in the wake of World War II and then endured more than a quarter century of Mao Zedong's megalomaniacal mismanagement, economically reformed by Deng Xiaoping in 1978 but politically still a one-party state whose people continue to search for new governmental arrangements. South Korea has survived the Korean War and an authoritarian government that ultimately became democratic, created an economy that made it one of the little dragons, and hosted the Summer Olympics in 1988 and the Winter Olympics in 2018. North Korea, one of the few remaining Stalinist states, created an economy that has generated several million deaths due to starvation and malnutrition but has nonetheless produced intercontinental ballistic missiles (ICBMs) and is on the verge of achieving nuclear weapons.

The good political news can be seen in the movement from autocratic to more democratic governmental institutions and practices in South Korea, Taiwan, and perhaps Bangladesh. Vietnam and China have transitioned from harsh totalitarian rule to more moderate autocratic governing, though since 2017 Xi Jinping has shown strong signs of moving back to more government and party control from Beijing. Singapore's de facto one-party state seems likely to remain a "soft authoritarian" regime. In Vietnam, China, and Singapore, robust economies appear to trump the demand for greater political and other freedoms.

Economic Developments

Given the Asian political environment, it appears that nearly every nation possesses the necessary governmental strength to put forth economic development blueprints for wealth creation. While some such designs may be constrained by flawed thinking, bureaucratic inefficiencies, or other difficulties, quantifiable economic progress can be anticipated. For example, the International Monetary Fund indicates that as a region, Asian economies in aggregate grew from 5.3 percent in 2016 to 5.5 percent in 2017. Healthy global economic activity only strengthens Asia's economic outlook, since the region depends on the outside world for demands for its goods and services. In any case, Asian optimism appears to offset the risks, chiefly the possibility of economic downturns in China and/or the West.

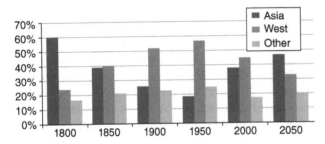

Share of global economic output, 1800–2050.

Economic successes in turn make social problems easier to address. Moreover, as countries transition from rural agricultural to urban industrial societies, the problems associated with becoming modern take on less importance as the problems accompanying being modern become more conspicuous. Governments and societies will need to work out arrangements regarding the environment, housing, jobs, wages, working conditions, and other such topics—issues that had been worked out over the millennia of rural life and labor—and require new arrangements to be fashioned for what will be largely urban environments. Asian cultures will also need to come to something of a consensus on new—or at least open—social activities that challenge inherited social practices regarding family, demographics, gender, ethnicity, and sexual orientation. Each of those topics will involve both individuals and interest groups that each government and society needs to harmonize.

Asia is the chief source of the world's pollution, with China and India producing the lion's share of the contamination. Environmental degradation is something every nation, community, or individual experiences in rapid economic development settings. Natural resource extraction sites and factories produce waste that needs to be eliminated. This can be done in a safe manner, but such a careful approach has economic costs for businesses or governments. To cut costs, private companies and public administrations often disregard measures designed to minimize ecological harm. All too often the result is the disposal of unwanted byproducts in careless, typically dangerous ways that turn out to be more cost-effective techniques. Since most of Asia is facing a shortage of water, it is all the more necessary that existing water resources be treated with reverence.

The more common outcomes include factories dumping toxic waste—pesticides, lead, coal dust, dioxins, carbon monoxide, sulfur dioxide, arsenic, and other dangerous effluents—into bodies of water (where food sources dwell) or into the ground, producing fouled rivers and lakes or water tables. Aside from the usual suspects in the damaging of the environment, the individuals contribute to the fouling of communities. A shortage of toilets in Asia usually results in tens of millions of people relieving themselves in nearby bodies of water or on the ground, further impairing the medical well-being of the general population—with shorter life expectancy, lung cancer, lead poisoning, and a host of other maladies—particularly children and the elderly. In India and likely elsewhere, public defecation puts women at risk of being raped. These examples hardly exhaust the sources of environmental squalor.

E-waste provides yet another significant source of pollution. Discarded electronic materials from across the globe get dumped in Asia—things such as old computers, computer monitors and televisions, cell phones, and so forth. About 70 percent of these kinds of waste end up in China, particularly Guiyu in Guangdong Province, although additional Asian dumping grounds exist. E-waste products are stripped for parts, and much of what remains (much of it toxic) pollutes the dumping sites and nearby localities, affecting the health of the inhabitants. Air pollution comes not only from factory chimneys, where smoke and other contaminants end up in the atmosphere, but also from logging, produced when the leftover materials from logging are burned, generating thick smoke that wafts chiefly across much of Southeast Asia but is an unwelcome fact of life in numerous other Asian regions. The potential for better public health increases with wealth, science, and technology—with access to education, toilets, clinics, hospitals, and medical professionals—but it takes time for public opinion, wealth, know-how, and political commitment to get translated into improved disease prevention and treatment.

Social Issues

Social practices in Asia are also starting to be debated. Something of a consensus on new—or at least open—social practices that challenge inherited social customs regarding religion, ethnicity, family, demographics, gender, ethnicity, and sexual orientation need to be arrived at. Many of these matters were addressed over the centuries in much of the first industrializers in the Western world and Japan, yet only within the past century are such human behavior topics being publicly questioned in most of the continent. Unresolved social issues stir the emotions of both national leaders and the citizenry in general, and always present the possibility of producing domestic violence, political instability, and even the involvement of regional or international organizations.

Prime time
Most Asian countries will be in a "second wave" of aging societies
that follows the aging of industrial countries, including Japan.

(old-age dependency rate)[1]

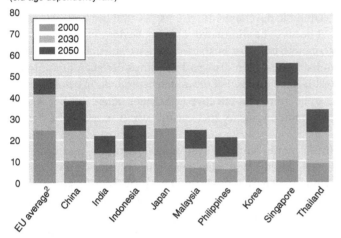

Old age dependency rate in Asia, 2000–2050. *Source:* Population Division of the Department of Economic
and Social Affairs of the United Nations Secretariat, *World Population Prospects: The 2004 Revision* and *World
Urbanization Prospects: The 2003 Revision.*
[1] Data refer to projected shares of the population aged 65 and above relative to the population aged
15–64 under the assumption of medium levels of fertility rates.
[2] "EU average" refers to the simple average of data for the following six countries: Belgium, France,
Germany, Italy, the Netherlands, and the United Kingdom

Religious and ethnic antagonisms produce various levels of antagonism in every nation, and in
Asia they are numerous and usually quite serious. South and Central Asian antipathies abound.
The meaning of Islam is at the core of political instability in Afghanistan and will likely remain so
into the future. In Central Asia, religion had been largely kept in check under Soviet rule, but since
the 1990s a battle—of varying intensities—between each state and Islamic fundamentalism has
emerged and will remain a source of political instability. And while the civil war in Sri Lanka has
concluded, the ethnic and religious tensions between Buddhists and Hindus continue, and similar,
if less severe, religious clashes between those two religions endure in the Himalayan states. In
Sunni Muslim Pakistan, the struggles are largely between the nominally democratic state and
Islamic fundamentalists of various sorts. But Shia Muslims and Christians often suffer deadly
attacks from religious militants. These fights constantly threaten an overt military intervention in
government operations. And the government in Bangladesh has zealously fought to keep domestic
and foreign religious radicals at bay. In India, historical religious divisions as well as contemporary
Islamic and Hindu fundamentalist organizations continue to give all levels of government chronic
difficulties. Sadly, religious tensions in South and Central Asia are likely to remain long beyond the
current generation of political, ethnic, and religious leadership.

Southeast Asian nations face many of the same, though typically less menacing, ethnic and religious divides that distress the more western parts of Asia. Neighboring Myanmar, a multiethnic
(135 groups according to the Myanmar government) and multilinguistic nation, continues to deal
with those differences that stretch back to pre-colonial times. One of those ethnic/religious conflicts involves the Rohingya ethnicity, not recognized as legitimate by the government.

Rohingya are Muslims who reside in the Myanmar state of Rakhine and who practice a mixture of Sufi and Sunni Islam. They originally migrated from Bangladesh (formerly East Pakistan before its independence from West Pakistan in 1971, or referred to as the eastern region of Bengal in British India before 1947). They claim their ancestors came to Burma (Myanmar after 1989) as early as the fifteenth century. Most Rohingya came to Burma in the nineteenth and twentieth centuries, when the country was governed as a part of British India until 1937. The word Rohingya likely derives from the word Arakan, the name of a previous state in Myanmar that roughly reflects the territory of the current Myanmar state of Rakhine. The Rohingya, who constitute about one-third of the Rakhine population, are both religiously and linguistically different from the rest of the multi-ethnic Rakhine Buddhist population. When Burma became independent in 1948, the Rohingya were denied citizenship but since the 1990s can gain temporary residency. Major ethnic violence erupted in 2017, resulting in the migration of hundreds of thousands of Rohingya, chiefly to Bangladesh, Malaysia, and Indonesia.

A similar Muslim–Buddhist divide exists in the southern parts of Buddhist Thailand near the northern border with Muslim Malaysia, a divide that often flares into violence. A more harmonious relationship can be seen among Singapore's ethnic Chinese majority and the Hindu and Muslim minorities. The growing appearance of religious censors and the mounting popular demands for strict application of Sharia law in Malaysia, Indonesia, and Brunei foretell escalating religious strains in the foreseeable future. Civil and Sharia courts exist in Malaysia, and specific things such as marriage, divorce, and inheritance as well as more general issues of morality end up in the Sharia system. So does conversion by a Muslim to another faith, which requires the approval of a Sharia court. Much the same applies in Indonesia (and numerous other majority-Muslim countries or regions of a nation), where local governments and Sharia courts create stern religious laws and interpret them rigorously. Given that political parties and leading politicians in both Malaysia and Indonesia depend on the support of Muslim clerics and the voting public, it seems highly unlikely that politicians will stray too far from popular sentiment. Brunei is a sultanate where great oil wealth keeps the citizens contented enough, but the royal family also resists wandering into dangerous religious territory. To maintain or enhance the monarchy's acceptance, in 2014 Sultan Hassanal Bolikah introduced Sharia law, which, if fully enforced, allows for penalties ranging from fines and jail time to amputations, stoning, and execution for a long list of religious crimes.

Tensions have existed between Christian and Muslim Filipinos for centuries, largely on the southern Philippine island of Mindanao. Nonetheless stories of cooperation and compassion are becoming more common. In 2017 a Muslim community in Zamboanga, the island's capital, extended the hand of friendship to Christians there by helping to rebuild a Catholic chapel. At the same time, Christian leaders banded together to help rebuild Marawi, a Muslim-majority city in Mindanao where a destructive clash between the Philippine military and Muslim militants took place. These are not isolated examples of Muslim–Christian kindheartedness in the southern Philippines and provide some optimism that a better relationship can be worked out between the two communities. In short, practitioners of minority religions in Southeast Asian nations remain keenly aware that one's religion can still lead to serious trouble, even death, even if the adherent is simply a follower. Governments are also acutely mindful that they walk political tightropes between the desires and demands of secular modernization and the yearnings and burdens of inherited traditions.

Religion and custom come to the fore when challenged by modern social practices, particularly as they relate to the family and community. Freedom of marriage defies arranged marriages most common in agricultural societies. The role of women undergoes significant transformation as females in urban settings and gradually in rural ones have access to education, a typical route to success in the city. Education delays marriage, reduces (along with birth control) the number of children one produces, and offers job opportunities that generate greater economic independence. In the city, women's organizations emerge to provide a voice and a growing range of services when it comes to handling issues of violence, equality of opportunity, child care, and so forth. Sexual orientation also emerges as a heated topic in modernizing societies. In urban locations homosexuality, cross dressing, and other practices shunned in traditional times have become more commonly accepted and openly practiced in most of Asia. People in rural settings remain largely intolerant of sexual and other objectionable practices of the city. Villagers will likely need to head to nearby towns and cities to participate in alternative lifestyles.

The traditional family was buffeted not only by traditional ideas and institutions but by modern concepts and organizations as well. Many modern governments have the capability to impose policies on a country that the people oppose and that, worse yet, don't work. A good example would be China's population policies between 1949 and 1978, which allowed for birth control but also did not discourage population growth. Even considering the tens of millions of deaths from starvation resulting after the Great Leap Forward in the late 1950s and the million people who perished as a result of the Cultural Revolution from 1966 to 1976, China's population became a major project when Deng Xiaoping took control of the country in 1978. His "One-Child Policy" limited families to one child in the urban areas and two in the countryside. While it slowed the nation's population rate of growth, it also transformed the Chinese family to a unit with no brothers and sisters, no aunts and uncles, and an out-of-balance sex ratio. Since only one child was allowed, tradition demanded that the child be a boy, and so modern medicine via ultrasound would identify female fetuses to be eliminated in the hopes that the next pregnancy would produce a male fetus.

Increasingly, daily life requires individuals to adjust to greater freedoms available, particularly in the cities of Asia. One often no longer needs to be a farmer, marry a partner chosen by others, or reside with or near the parents. In that context of greater choice and likely greater economic independence, a person could choose to marry or not; have many, few, or no children; and pursue a career of one's choice and a lifestyle of one's desire. Some of those choices will likely clash with family customs. In developed economies such as Japan, South Korea, Taiwan, Hong Kong, and Singapore, urbanites will probably pursue a college education, enter the professions, marry later, and have fewer children. Such behavior by the majority of the youthful population runs the risk of demographic disaster.

By the mid-twentieth century, developing nations had concluded that successful economic expansion policies could only occur in a context of much-reduced population growth. Combining government birth control policies—voluntary or mandatory—along with greater individual choice easily ran the risk of the population pendulum swinging too far to the other side, resulting in a birth dearth. In Japan, where life expectancy is 83, the percentage of the population over 65 has risen from 9 percent in 1980 to 27 percent in 2017 and is expected to reach 40 percent in 2060. The country's total population has been in steady decline since 2010, and the fear is there will be a shortage of native-born people to finance the country's pension obligations, care for the aging pensioners, and maintain a cutting-edge economy. Then again, the modern world makes it possible for a good part of a population to make bad choices regarding eating, smoking, and exercise. Diabetes, lung cancer and emphysema, and cardiovascular problems will certainly help to reduce the life expectancy and thus some pension commitments. The Singapore government has been subsidizing (chiefly ethnic Chinese) professionals to have additional children. South Korea, Taiwan, and Hong Kong face similar circumstances.

Complicating the Asian demographic world, in India and China (and elsewhere) the long arm of tradition—the desire for a male child—in conjunction with modern medicine has produced a sex ratio imbalance. Ultrasound technology and abortion make it possible to determine the sex of a fetus and abort the unwanted female. In China, the sex ratio is roughly 1.15 (perhaps as much as 1.20 since 2004) male to female at birth, and in India 1.12 at birth. The ratio does not favor the female in either country until after 65 years. At the very least, men face some difficulty finding a marriage partner. Further confounding modern family life is China's attempt to control population growth by the late 1970s with a one-child policy. It has led not only to forced sterilization of females and increased abortion to insure a male offspring; it will also soon reconfigure the Chinese family, eliminating brothers and sisters as well as aunts and uncles, and will shortly produce a society where fewer working-age people will be found to pay for pensions and to care for increasing numbers of seniors whose later mortality adds to the problem. Although many of China's one-child practices have been curbed, it now turns out that many urbanites nonetheless seem to prefer having only one child.

Trafficking, Gangs, and Corruption

Growing Asian wealth and swelling global demand for raw materials and value-added goods and services also create significant challenges for the continent. One of the leading difficulties involves trafficking in those items, difficulties compounded by widespread government and private corruption. In terms of quantity, lumber is the principle product illegally cut, shipped, imported, or purchased. There also exists a large black market in endangered species, either animal or plant: ivory, tiger penis, rosewood, and other products. Many of the species are said to enhance sexual performance and can now be purchased by growing numbers of more affluent Asians. Overfishing the seas for the voracious Asian appetite also plays a large part in illicit undertakings. Trafficking in drugs—the old standby opium and its derivatives, as well as synthetic concoctions—can be obtained in every nation. The North Korean government actually sells such products to obtain foreign currency. Both the environment and the populace are degraded by these illicit activities.

Human trafficking likewise produces ongoing sources of misfortune. While Asian nations annually allow millions of their citizens to work abroad voluntarily, millions also are sent unwillingly to work in conditions of what amounts to indentured servitude. As with other trafficking activities, organized crime gangs transport and place individuals within a person's country or across frontiers into a foreign location. In impoverished rural areas or small towns, normally facilitators make financial arrangements whereby the parents are paid for the future services of their children. Sometimes the lack of opportunity at home and the lure of the city result in the voluntary migration of the young into urban locations, where organized crime will typically recruit and place them. There are several markets for human beings. Usually businesses want cheap docile labor for otherwise legitimate industries. Quite often young women will be dragooned int the sex industry. In China, where the one-child policy has led to a shortage of women, young females are procured and offered as brides in cities. Regardless of occupation or legal status, migrant workers usually find themselves unpopular with local residents and subject to chronic exploitation.

Asia's Tinder Boxes

Asia is brimming with hotspots just one spark short of a prairie fire that could produce major regional or international conflict. In conjunction with preexisting troubles brought on by modernization, nations also face a host of threatening old and new challenges. Even a brief catalog of these underlying difficulties will plainly illustrate the fragile nature of Asia's existing geopolitical, ethnic, and internal national arrangements.

Border disputes that stretch back decades or even centuries exist nearly everywhere on the continent. The more obvious disagreements illustrate the potential for catastrophe. The question regarding the control over Kashmir divides India and Pakistan even as China claims a portion of that troubled land, called Aksai Chin and occupied by Beijing. There is also a dispute over Doklam, a territory between China and Bhutan and occupied by forces of both India and China. India and Pakistan have fought several wars since the end of World War II; India and China did battle in 1962 and 2020; India and China also differ on issues surrounding Tibet. The Dalai Lama has a Tibet-in-exile headquarters in northern India, which calls into question China's sovereignty over Tibet. Thus three nuclear powers have an array of frontier issues that will keep Asia and the world on edge in the foreseeable future.

Almost all of the frontiers in Southeast Asia were drawn by colonial overlords, and before the European arrival in the 1500s there existed elastic borders drawn by the expanding and contracting frontiers set by Burmese, Thai, Khmer, Cham, and Indonesian kingdoms and empires, which always created disgruntled ethnic groups ruled by others. The frontier between Thailand and Malaysia regularly produces clashes between Buddhist Thais and Muslim Malays; in 2016 both countries agreed to consider a border wall to minimize conflict. Thailand and Cambodia, both Buddhist, nonetheless dispute the border separating the two nations, as do Cambodia and Laos.

The potential for serious trouble relating to contested control of islands, reefs, and other maritime territories in Asia remains quite high. Differences between Japan and Russia involve five of the 56 islands in the Kuril Island chain, through which the Russian Navy accesses the Pacific Ocean. Any conflict between the two will likely involve the United States because of its Security Treaty with Japan. The 81,000-square-mile East China Sea houses eight islands with contested sovereignty, including the Senkaku/Diaoyu Islands that Japan has held since 1895; the American Security Treaty with Japan also applies to those islands. The South China Sea, through which more than $5 trillion of commerce flows annually, presents an even greater likelihood of unfriendly encounters occurring. Several Asian countries have claimed sovereignty over various land forms there, including China, Taiwan, Vietnam, Malaysia, Indonesia, and the Philippines.

All of the disputed islands in the East and South China Seas involve economic, geostrategic, and natural resource potential, including chiefly fish, oil, and natural gas. The Council on Foreign Relations estimates that the South China Sea alone holds 11 billion barrels of oil and 120 trillion cubic feet of natural gas. All of them also either already possess or offer the potential for military bases, largely naval and air force capabilities, in the region. Since 2013 China has been enlarging reefs in the Paracel and Spratley chains, building facilities from which it can project military power. Practically, this will enable Beijing to hit targets more than 1000 miles away from those upgraded reefs or to challenge more effectively U.S. naval and land-based forces in most of East Asia. Ultimately, China hopes to replace America as the arbiter of how business is conducted in Asia, reviving Beijing's old tribute system. Thus all of the disputed islands provide likely triggers for conflict in the area that could involve outside forces.

Separatist movements within numerous countries add to Asian anxiety about yet one more cata-lyst for conflict. The case of Taiwan is the best example of separatism. When the province of Taiwan was ceded to Japan in the Treaty of Shimonoseki in 1895, it remained under Tokyo's control until 1945. Japan returned the island to the Republic of China, then governed by Chiang Kai-shek's Nationalist government. But the ethnic Chinese (at least 90% of the island's population) resented their treatment by Chiang's officials. A February 1947 uprising by the Taiwanese was crushed, but resentment continued to grow. At the time, Chiang's Nationalist Party government in Nanjing was locked in mortal combat with Mao Zedong's Communist Party, a struggle that the Communists won, creating the People's Republic of China in 1949. However, the Cold War salvaged the Nationalist government, which now controlled only Taiwan province. America supported Chiang as the nation's legitimate government while the Soviet Union backed Mao. Both Nationalist and Communist governments have agreed that Taiwan was a part of China; the ongoing civil war in China differed over which government was the legitimate one. When Washington officially recog-nized the Beijing government in 1979, America's Taiwan Relations Act promised defensive aid to Taiwan and suggested that America would intervene in any conflict in which Beijing attacked Taiwan. Meanwhile, the vast majority of the island's population has wanted de facto independence for Taiwan, a move that surely would result in a Beijing attack. After the emergence of democracy in Taiwan in 1987, the pro-independence Democratic Progressive Party (DPP) has fielded candi-dates for various government positions, winning many central government offices, including the presidency in 2000, 2004, 2016 and 2020. Although desiring de facto independence, no DPP gov-ernment has taken the disastrous step of declaring official independence. Washington's "strategic ambiguity" regarding its likely response to a mainland invasion likely means that a vanity declaration of independence by a Taiwan government would not result in America's intervention, while an unjustified invasion of Taiwan by Beijing would involve the United States militarily. Nonetheless Taiwan presents a continuing flashpoint that would likely involve the United States.

Other Asian separatist movements will most likely not produce the kind of repercussions a war in Taiwan would entail. China also faces major separatist movements on the mainland, with the Muslim Uighurs in Xinjiang Province and the Tibetans in Xizang (Tibet) Province, and there have even been calls for an independent Hong Kong. Indonesia's persistent separatists include the prov-ince of Aceh, once the Sultanate of Aceh that wants to be the Republic of Aceh. On the island of New Guinea, the western part now under the control of the Jakarta government yearns to become a separate Republic of West Papua. India has several separatist movements. The Muslim majority in Kashmir desires independence, the ethnic Nagas are striving to create an independent People's Republic of Nagaland, and the ethnic Assamese want their own independent state. Several ethnic groups in Myanmar also seek to secure independence, among them the Chin, the Kachin, the Karen, the Shan, the Wa, and the Mons. On the Malaysian portion of Borneo, several organizations are working for the independence of Sarawak, under the British the former Sultanate of Sarawak. Muslims on the southern Philippine island of Mindanao have been in a half-millennium conflict with the largely Christian Philippine government, first under the Spanish, then the Americans, and now an independent Philippine administration. These examples represent the major self-rule movements in Asia but do not exhaust the numerous other, though smaller, indicators of internal instability across the continent.

While local separatist movements have engaged in terrorist activities, there is always the possi-bility of outside terrorist support for separatists could result in other anti-terrorist outside partici-pation to defeat the separatists. Abu Sayyaf and the Moro Islamic Liberation Front are only the most notable groups in the southern Philippines engaging in protracted terrorist activities, aided by outside terrorist groups such as Indonesia's Jemaah Islamiyah and even al Qaeda. The local terrorist groups regularly engage the Philippine military, which is now being assisted by U.S. military personnel. The 2008 terrorist attack on Mumbai was only the most prominent of continual Islamic fundamentalist assaults on the city and numerous other locations in India. The 2008 violence against India and several others originated in Pakistan, though some have turned out to be home-grown, including Hindu fundamentalist attacks on Indian Muslims. The 2002 Bali bombing in that Indonesian tourist locale was traced to Jemaah Islamiyah; Afghanistan and Pakistan suffer daily violence by the Taliban, the Haqqani network, and other extremist organizations. Actually, no Asian country has avoided terrorist outbursts by various assortments of extremist groups in the twenty-first century, and many of the attacks have had or will have the potential to be the event that destabilizes a government, provokes a civil war, leads to war between rival nations, or brings in extra-regional nations that take sides in the conflict.

An array of other potentially destabilizing events will continue to produce anxiety across Asia. National, ethnic, and religious differences within and between nations—the Rohingya in Myanmar, the Muslims in Sri Lanka, and the overseas Chinese in Malaysia and Indonesia, to cite just a few present and past examples—could ignite confrontations that could escalate to war capable of disrupting the entire region's economic livelihood. North Korea's growing nuclear capabilities—and the possibility of their export to states and terrorist groups—threaten to undermine and antagonize already tense relations with Japan, terrorize South Korea, and present Beijing with a problem child that even tough love may not be able to restrain. Competition for scarce water resources will likely soon become a source of trouble. An Asia Society Leadership Group study notes that while Asia possesses more than half of the global population, it possesses less drinkable water per capita than any other continent save Antarctica. Not all freshwater remains fresh, as populations and industries pollute waterways. More people and more industries consume greater amounts of water and pollute much of it, thus diminishing the amount of water available for human consumption and agriculture. Industries and farmers needing water will produce less food and manufacture fewer goods, likely reducing the demand for labor. Untreated water also becomes a transmitter of diseases. In short, less access to water can quickly become a national security issue.

Since the mountains in China and India are the origins of most of Asia's water supply, and since the rise of those two countries is occurring at a time of declining access to water necessary to sustain the rise, expect the likelihood of domestic and foreign troubles across Asia for the remainder of the century. India and China—the cultural models for the rest of Asia before the domination of the industrial West—seek to reestablish lost prominence. While the role of the United States and Russia in Asia will decline in the twenty-first century, their economic, cultural, and military influence will continue to be significant, if for no other reason than as buffers against Chinese and Indian overbearing conduct.

The rest of Asia will remain highly suspicious of the two Asian giants' intentions. They expect, among other things, political bullying and economic intimidation of neighbors and perhaps military expansion as well. They expect the balance of power and likely the economic rules of commercial activity to shift slowly away from Washington and toward New Delhi and Beijing. We will likely encounter a "Back to the Future" in Asia with China and India both reclaiming their heritages of greatness but on a continent of smaller (and often wealthier) nations considerably more capable of defending themselves against the rising colossuses.

Meanwhile, the patterns of daily Asian life will gradually alter to meet the needs of people in increasingly modern settings with their associated problems. But some things will remain unchanged. Ever-present nature will remind everyone that several kinds of disasters of the past will be repeated. In the Pacific Ocean's "Ring of Fire," earthquakes are regular facts of life:

Tangshan in 1976, Kobe in 1995, Fukushima in 2011, and the Indian Ocean tsunami in 2004 set off by an earthquake. Volcanos have also wreaked devastation and will continue to do so: Japan's Mount Kusatsu-Shirane in 2018 was a small reminder; the ash from the Mount Pinatubo eruption in the Philippines in 1991 cooled the earth; Bali's Mount Agung in 2017. Regular cyclones hit Bangladesh and kill at least hundreds, often thousands, sometimes tens of thousands, and in 1970 at least a half-million people.

Some disasters prove to be manmade. The Tangshan earthquake killed several hundred thousand Chinese; most resulted from collapsed buildings that were poorly built. The Fukushima nuclear power plant was inundated by a tsunami due to its proximity to the ocean where the earthquake occurred. Tens of millions of deaths resulted from Mao Zedong's Great Leap Forward in the 1950s, while several million deaths occurred in North Korea in the 1990s resulting from capitally deficient political priorities and grossly distorted economic policies. Deaths from fires in textile factories, collapses in coal mines, exposure to environmental pollution, experiencing economic and social inequality, as well as numerous other causes are never completely avoidable but are usually mostly preventable. As a citizenry increasingly perceives government and private corruption to be the cause of one disaster after another, the more likely growing citizen anger toward "the system" will lead to social instability. Nearly every political entity in Asia is walking a tightrope, attempting to balance tradition and modernization at home while dealing with regional and global threats, real or imagined, and without a safety net in most cases. Good government can maintain the social balance, but one misstep and the exact consequences are uncertain but not good.

Assessing Asia

As always, the histories that get written reflect to some extent the concerns of time and culture. Historians who do original research frequently choose topics that are sometimes timely (war in wartime), now and then trendy (overweening emphasis on theory), and occasionally just plain ideological (Marxist or religious paradigms). The results of such research will form monographs from which scholars—with the same limits researchers face—writing general synthetic histories draw much of their materials. The general histories will inform the general public, whose ideas of the "other" will likely reflect the biases created by the original researchers and textbook writers. "Much of what attracted me to the Chinese revolution was a fantasy—more accurately a series of overlapping fantasies, some promulgated in China, others held by progressive political activists abroad. The Chinese revolution ran a complex course that had little to do with its status as an object of desire or a political inspiration."[2]

Newer generations of historians usually have the advantages of additional evidence, critiques of those earlier writings, the passing of many earlier trends, and earlier writers reevaluating their work in the context of greater experience and more objectivity. In the twenty-first century, Mao Zedong is no longer a flawless revolutionary and Chiang Kai-shek just a diehard reactionary. Both turn out to be, among other things, blemished nationalists in today's historical community. What is true of two of China's most important twentieth-century political leaders applies as well to other individuals, ideas, and institutions in revolutionary China, in Asia, and globally. Research and its synthesis can provide context, perspective, and better insight. Some will deliver an improved understanding of Asia in a globalized world; some will not.

---

2 Gail Hershatter, "Disquiet in the House of Gender," *Journal of Asian Studies* 71, no. 4 (November 2012): 873.

Suggested Readings and Viewings

Graham Allison and Robert D. Blackwill, eds., *The Grand Master's Insights on China, the United States, and the World* (Cambridge, MA: MIT Press, 2013).

Asia's Underworld (2012–2014), dir. by Oman Dhas; 2 seasons, 14 episodes.

John J. Cogan, Paul Morris, and Murray Print, eds., *Civic Education in the Asia-Pacific Region: Case Studies in Six Societies* (London: RoutledgeFalmer, 2001).

James David Fann, *A Land on Fire: Environmental Consequences of the Southeast Asian Boom* (New York: Basic Books, 2008).

Develeena Ghosh, *Shadowlines: Women and Borders in Contemporary Asia* (Cambridge: Cambridge Scholars Publishing, 2012).

Philip Hirsch, ed., *Routledge Handbook of the Environment in Southeast Asia* (London: Routledge, 2016).

Robert B. Marks, *China: An Environmental History*, 2nd ed. (Boulder, CO: Rowman and Littlefield, 2017).

Rhacel Parrenas, *Illicit Flirtations: Labor, Migration, and Sex Trafficking in Tokyo* (Stanford, CA: Stanford University Press, 2011).

Morris Rossabi, ed., *Governing China's Multiethnic Frontiers* (Seattle: University of Washington Press, 2004).

Jeff M. Smith, *Cold Peace: China-India Rivalry in the Twenty-First Century* (Lanham, MD: Lexington Books, 2015).

Meera Subramanian, *A River Runs Again: India's Natural World in Crisis, from the Barren Cliffs of Rajasthan to the Farmlands of Karnataka* (New York: Public Affairs, 2015).

Frank B. Tipton, *The Rise of Asia: Economics, Society, and Politics in Contemporary Asia* (Honolulu: University of Hawaii Press, 1998).

Index

Please note that page references to photographs or maps will be followed by the letter 'f'. Names of Chinese, Japanese, Korean and Vietnamese individuals begin with the surname. But in Vietnam, individuals are usually known by last name: thus Ngo Dinh Diem is referred to as Diem, though there are some exceptions, such as Ho Chi Minh, who is best known by his surname.

Asia Past and Present: A Brief History, First Edition. Peter P. Wan and Thomas D. Reins.
© 2021 John Wiley & Sons, Inc. Published 2021 by John Wiley & Sons, Inc.